THE **PRINCETON** REVIEW

THE
STUDENT ACCESS
GUIDE TO
THE BEST
COLLEGES

1992 EDITION

Other books in The Princeton Review Series

THE PRINCETON REVIEW

THE
STUDENT ACCESS
GUIDE TO
THE BEST
COLLEGES

1992 EDITION

BY TOM MELTZER,
ZACH KNOWER, AND
JOHN KATZMAN

VILLARD BOOKS ▼ NEW YORK 1992

Library of Congress Cataloging-in-Publication Data
Meltzer, Tom.
   The student access guide to the best colleges/by Tom Meltzer, Zachary Knower, and John Katzman.
      p.   cm.
   At head of title: The Princeton Review.
   ISBN 0-679-73866-5
   1. College, Choice of.   2. Universities and colleges—Admission.
I. Meltzer, Tom.   II. Princeton Review (Firm)   III. Title.   IV. Title: Princeton Review student access guide to the best colleges.
LB2350.5.K6   1992
378.1'056'0973—dc20   92–19452

Manufactured in the United States of America on paper using partially recycled fibers

9 8 7 6 5 4 3 2

First Edition

FOREWORD

Every year, over two million high school graduates go to college. To make sure they end up at the *right* school, they spend several hundred million dollars on the admissions process. This money pays for countless admissions officers and counselors, a bunch of standardized tests (and preparation for them), and many books like—but not as good as—this one.

It's so expensive because everyone in the admissions world likes it this way. As a group, colleges resist almost every attempt to systematize or simplify the process. Admissions officers want to believe that nothing they do could be done better by a computer. So they make the process a lot more mysterious than it needs to be.

Even the most straightforward colleges hide the information you would want to know about the way they'll evaluate your application: What grades and SATs are they looking for? Do their reported SAT averages include minority students, athletes, and legacies (kids whose parents went to their school)? Exactly how much do extracurricular activities count? What percentage of the aid they give out is work-study (at minimum wage) and what percentage is in grants?

We couldn't get answers to these questions from many colleges. In fact, we couldn't get answers to *any* questions from some schools (we've excluded these schools since they have bad attitudes, and you probably wouldn't want to go there).

Colleges seem to have the time and money to create beautiful brochures (which generally show that all college classes are held under a tree on a beautiful day); they should just tell you what sort of students they're looking for, and what factors they'll use to consider your application.

Until then, this book is your best bet. It's not a phone book containing every fact about every college in the country. And it's not a memoir written by a few graduates in which they describe their favorite dining halls or professors. We've given you the facts you'll need to apply to the few hundred best schools in the country. And enough information about them—which we gathered from hundreds of counselors and admissions officers, and tens of thousands of students to let you make a smart decision about going there.

One note: we don't talk a lot about majors. This is because most high school students really don't know what they want to major in—and the ones who do almost always change their minds by the beginning of junior year. Choosing a school by the reputation of a single department is often a terrible idea.

As complicated and difficult as the admissions process is, we think you'll love college itself—especially at the schools listed in this book.

Good luck in your search.

— John Katzman
June 1992

ACKNOWLEDGMENTS

This book absolutely, positively would not have been possible if the following people had not made exceptional contributions: Andrea Paykin, who designed and then pagemade most of the book; Julian Ham, whose pagemaking work was also invaluable; Faye Dunkley and Niki Gondola, who together processed the seemingly endless torrent of surveys; Kirsten Stadheim, Andrea Nagy, and Shannon Hudnall, who, with remarkably cheerful dispositions, coordinated survey distribution for huge portions of the country; and Val Vigoda, who surveyed countless schools in Virginia, D.C., upstate New York, and New England, and then, when we hit the wall and it seemed like we couldn't finish the book on time, came through again by writing a bunch of student life boxes. Friends, your lives now officially belong to you again.

The following people were also instrumental in the completion of this book. They coordinated the surveys in their cities and provided us with invaluable information about the quality of area schools; they essentially served as associate editors. These folks are: Andy Barr, George Cigale, Carl and Chase Emmons , Pam Hirsch , David Kwok, Bill Lindsley, Paul Maniscalco, Wade McKinney, Eric Moore, Linda Nessim, Jerry Pederson, Steve Quattrociocchi, Joel Rubin, Jeri Samson, Michael Ueland, Jim Weinberg, Mark Wolfe, and Clare Zagrecki. Thanks also to Alicia Ernst, Amy Harrington, Jon Hein, Mark Novitz, and Rob Zopf at our New York offices, and to all the folks at Villard, particularly our editor, Stephanie Long. And, thanks to our parents, families, friends, and Zach's fiancee, Jody, who understood when we sometimes didn't return their calls.

Thanks are also due to the following folks who went out and distributed the surveys and who otherwise contributed to the success of this book: Matt Abramson, Cindy Allison, Sarah Andre, Gil Aronow, Naneen Baden, Jin Hi Bae, Kip Baggett, Michael Barker, Siddique Bello, Dan Brown, Brad Brubaker, Robert Bryant, Jessica Buchen, Victoria Burke, Sarita Cargas, Dennis Chester, David Chin, Robert Cohen, Roberto Colon, Theresa Connely, Mark Cosover,

Greg Couls, Tom Craig, Kevin Crossman, Chad Daybell, Brett Deutsh, Mike Dix, Sabine Dobler, Leigh Anne Duck, Paul Edelblut, Karl Engkvist, Scott Erikson, Jay Exum, Pat Farrell, Jon Feldman, Renah Feldman, Paul Foglino, Rachel Forsyth, Jennifer Frank, Shea Friedland, Paula Gardner, Pete Garner, Dawn Gifford, Jay Glick, Deb Golder, Lauren Graham, Jim Gray, Robert Scott Greacen, Nancy Green, Adam Gross, Brian Harward, Chris Hoiles, Andy Hunn, Becky Hutcheson, Duncan Ireland, Eric Jackson, Lynn Kaufer, Spencer Kayden, Scott Kelley, John Kenyon, Joe Kissell, Marc Kossover, Patty Krebs, Jane Lacher, Harold Lee, Eric Letsinger, Erica-lee Lewis, Laura Light, Bill Lindsley, Andrew Lutz, Gary Marcus, Chris Marks, Kerry Marr, Sunshine Mathon, Lisa McDaniel, Alan McIvor, John McWeeny, Stan Meriken, Mark Metz, Erin Moody, Eric Moore, Molly Moore, Mike Mussina, Trudy Ohnsorg, Dan Osborn, Gina Ottoboni, Glen Pannell, Gillian Perrone, Dori Pietrowicz, Lynn Pinckney, Karen Powers, Jim Reichen, Matt Renie, Ted Resnick, Ken Riley, Joel Risberg, Jenny Robbins, Joel Robinson, Jessica Russell, Jeri Samson, Drew Schafer, Scott Schaefle, Art Scherson, Steve Schortgen, Steven Schwartz, Roland Schwarz, Tom Servo, Brook Sibel, Keely Sikes, Darryl Siry, Andrew Solomon, Daneet Steffens, Paul Stouber, Elizabeth Taggart, Rachel Teisch, Duke Tufty, Mike Ueland, Jason Van Driesche, Fleurette Vincent, Harvey Weinstein, Lisa Whitaker, Doug Wick, Kit Wilson, Susan Yerger, and Brooke Zibel.

Some of the quantitative data in this book is courtesy of College Counsel; our thanks to Wayne Griffith and Bill Coolbaugh. Their service, The College Advisor, uses a detailed questionnaire to create an excellent 50-page report listing of the schools you should explore. For more information about The College Advisor, call 800-248-5299.

CONTENTS

PART ONE

INTRODUCTION

How to Use
This Book

There was a void in the college guide market and we have filled it with this book. No other book provides in-depth descriptions of schools AND in-depth statistics about admissions, financial aid, and student body demographics. And, more important, no other college guide is based on the input of so many students.

More than 28,000 students at the 245 colleges included in this book participated in the survey. Except at some extremely small schools (undergraduate enrollment below 1,000), we heard from at least 100 students on every one of the campuses described between these covers.

On our survey, we asked students to answer 67 multiple-choice questions on subjects ranging from the school's administration to their social lives, and from the quality of food to the quality of teaching. We asked them to tell us what other schools they had applied to. Finally, we asked students for their comments.

The combination of the ratings and comments form the substance of our articles about the schools. We wanted you to hear from as many of your (potential) future classmates as possible, to get a real sense of how happy they are: when they're in their classrooms and in their campus organizations; at their fraternity parties and at their demonstrations; on their way to get extra help from a professor or on their way into town to blow off some steam; getting food from their meal plans and getting the financial aid packages that determine whether they'll return for the following semester. The idea is, if you know about their responses in advance, you can figure out if you'd be happy at a school before you go there.

We also received completed surveys from over 40 independent college counselors. We asked them to recommend schools in their regions for inclusion in this book, and we used their recommendations to formulate our list of the nation's best schools. We also asked for comments on these schools' academic departments, admissions and financial aid policies, and hospitality toward groups that fall into the "high risk" category regarding marginalization—that is, minorities, and those with physical and learning disabilities. The counselors' comments on these subjects are incorporated into the text of this book.

How did we get it done? The Princeton Review has offices in over 50 American cities. Every year over 30,000 students enroll in our SAT and graduate test preparation courses; those students are either on their way to college or have just graduated. Some of our teachers attend the schools featured in this book; others have recently graduated and still live in the area; we even teach our courses on some of these campuses. Because of this, we already had in place the kind of army necessary to get a project this massive accomplished: all we had to do was mobilize it. Although some campuses didn't exactly welcome us with open arms, very few ultimately refused us access to their students. Those schools—Centre, Macalester, Purdue, University of Delaware, and University of Redlands—are not included in this edition of *The Student Access Guide to the Best Colleges,* but we hope to include them in future editions. The students themselves were great, even at those schools where we showed up during finals week. Their insightful comments are what's most valuable about this book.

This book also contains several indexes. The first one, a compilation of entertaining quotations from students across the country, is one we just couldn't resist including. The second lists the top and bottom schools in various categories, based on the results of our student surveys. When you look at the bottom schools in a category, please remember that EVERY school in this book is an excellent institution—that's why it's in a guide to the best colleges. A third index lists the names and business addresses of the independent college counselors who contributed in the creation of this book.

■   ■   ■

How This Book Is Organized

Each of the colleges and universities listed in this book has its own two-page spread. To make it easier to find information about the schools of your choice, we've used the same format for every school. Look at the sample pages below:

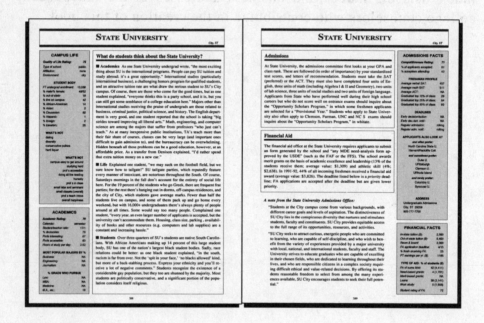

Each spread has eight components, four "sidebars" (the narrow columns on the outside of each page, which contain mostly statistics) and four "boxes" (the big boxes in the middle that contain text). Here's what's in each:

The Sidebars

The sidebars contain various statistics which were culled either from our own surveys, from questionnaires sent to the schools, or from College Counsel, an independent educational consulting group.

Here are brief descriptions of each heading:

■ Quality of Life Rating

How happy students are with their lives outside the classroom. This rating is given on a scale of 60 to 100—kind of like your school grades, with 60 being the lowest passing grade. This rating was determined using the results from our surveys. We weighed several factors, including students' overall happiness, the beauty, safety, and location of the campus, comfort of dorms, food quality, and ease in dealing with the administration. Note that even if a school's rating is in the low 60s, it does not mean that the quality of life is horrible—there are no "failing" schools in this book. A low ranking just means that the school placed low compared with others in this book.

■ Type of school

Whether the school is public or private.

■ Affiliation

Any religion with which the school is affiliated.

■ Environment

Whether the campus is located in an urban, suburban, or rural area.

■ FT undergrad enrollment

The number of undergraduates who attended the school full time.

■ All headings from % male/% female through % transfers

The demographic breakdown of the full-time undergraduate student body.

■ What's Hot/What's Not

Summarizes the results of our survey. The lists show what students felt unusually strongly about, both positively and negatively, at their schools (see the end of the introduction for a more detailed explanation of items on the list).

■ Academic Rating

On a scale of 60 to 100, how hard students work at the school and how much they get back for their efforts. The number was determined based on results from our surveys to students and administrators.

Factors weighed included how many hours students studied, how vigorously they did assigned readings and attended all classes, and the quality of students the school attracts; we also considered the student/teacher ratio, the students' assessments of their professors' abilities and helpfulness, and the students' assessment of the school's administration (in those areas where administrators directly affect the quality of education).

■ *Calendar*

The school's schedule of academic terms. A "semester" schedule has two long terms, usually starting in September and January. A "trimester" schedule has three terms, usually with one before Christmas and two after. A "quarterly" schedule has four terms which go by very quickly: the entire term, including exams, usually lasts only nine or ten weeks. A "4–1–4" schedule is like a semester schedule, but with a month-long term wedged between the fall and spring semesters.

■ *Student/teacher ratio*

The ratio of full-time faculty members to undergraduates.

■ *% Doctorates*

Percentage of teachers who have a Ph.D. or higher degree in their primary field of instruction.

■ *Profs interesting*

The average answer given in our survey in answer to the question, "In general, how good are your instructors as teachers?"

■ *Profs accessible*

The average answer given in our survey in answer to the question, "In general, how accessible are your instructors outside the classroom?"

■ *Hours of study per day*

The average number of hours studied per day reported by students in our survey.

■ *Most popular majors by %*

The three most popular majors at the school, as reported either by the admissions office or by College Counsel.

■ *% Grads Who Pursue*

The percentage of graduates who continue their education in law, business, medicine, or other graduate studies, within a year of receiving their bachelor's degrees.

■ *Competitiveness Rating*

How competitive admissions are at the school, on a scale of 60 to 100. This number was determined by several factors, including the class rank of entering freshmen, test scores, and percentage of applicants accepted. By incorporating all these factors, our competitiveness rating adjusts for "self-selecting" applicant pools. Caltech, for example, has a competitiveness rating of 100, even though it admits a surprisingly high percentage of applicants (43%). Caltech's applicant pool is "self-selecting"; that is, nearly all the school's applicants are exceptional students.

■ *% Of applicants accepted*

The percentage of applicants to which the school offered admission.

■ *% Acceptees attending*

The percentage of those who were accepted who eventually enrolled.

■ *Average verbal SAT, Average math SAT, Average ACT*

The average test scores for entering freshmen. When specific averages were not available, we approximated scores using ranges provided by the school (these scores are denoted with an asterisk *). Please note that these numbers are averages; so about half of the students accepted at the school scored below the number in each category. Don't be discouraged from applying to the school of your choice even if your combined SAT scores are 80 or even 120 points below that average, because you still have a chance of getting in. Remember that many schools rely on other factors of your application (such as your grades) more heavily than test scores.

■ *Graduated top 10%, top 20%, top 50% of class*

The percentage of entering freshman who ranked in the respective percentiles of their high school classes.

■ *Early decision/action deadline*

The deadline for submission of application materials under the Early Decision or Early Action plan. Early Decision is generally for students for whom the school is a first choice. The applicant commits to attending the school if admitted; in return, the school renders an early decision, usually in December or January. If accepted, the applicant doesn't have to spend the time and money to apply to other schools. Students may apply Early Decision to only one school. Early Action is similar to Early Decision, but less binding; applicants need not commit to attending the school, and in some cases, may apply Early Action to more than one school. The school, in turn, may not render a decision, choosing to defer the applicant to the regular admissions pool. Each school's guidelines are a little different; it's a good idea to call and get full details if you plan to pursue one of these options.

■ *Early decision/action notification*
The date by which you can expect a decision on your application under the Early Decision or Early Action plan.

■ *Regular admission deadline*
The date by which all materials must be postmarked (or, in rare cases, "In-office") to be considered for regular admission for the fall term.

■ *Regular admission notification*
The date by which you can expect a decision on your application under the regular admission plan.

■ *Applicants Also Look At*
These lists were formulated with data from our on-campus surveys. We asked students to list all the schools they had applied and those at which they were accepted. Schools they named most often appear in these three lists. When students usually rejected a school in favor of the current school, that school appears under "and rarely prefer"; schools that split applicants evenly with the current school appear under "and sometimes prefer"; and schools that students usually chose over the current school appear under "and often prefer." For example, students in our survey who were accepted at both Princeton and the University of Pennsylvania generally chose Princeton. Therefore, on Princeton's feature page, U. Penn appears in the "and rarely prefer" category (because students rarely preferred U. Penn to Princeton), and on U. Penn's feature page, Princeton appears in the "and often prefer" category (because students often preferred Princeton to U. Penn).

■ *Address*
The address and phone number of the undergraduate admissions office.

■ *In-state tuition*
The tuition at the school for a resident of the school's state. Usually much lower than out-of-state tuition for state-supported public schools.

■ *Out-of-state tuition*
The tuition at the school for a resident of the school's state.

■ *Room & board*
Estimated room and board costs.

■ *FA application deadline*
The date by which materials must be received by the financial aid office to be considered for financial aid. For some schools, it's a "postmarked by" date, and for some schools, there is no official deadline, but there is a date for priority consideration.

■ *% Frosh receiving FA*
The percentage of entering freshman who receive some form of financial aid.

■ *PT earnings/year ($)*
The average amount of money a student makes annually by working part-time.

■ *FA of some kind*
The percentage of full-time undergraduates who received any financial aid, and the average amount of the award (includes loans, grants, scholarships, work study, etc.)

■ *Need-based grants*
The percentage of full-time undergraduates who received need-based grants or scholarships, and the average grant or scholarship value.

■ *Merit-based grants*
The percentage of full-time undergraduates who received merit-based grants or scholarships, and the average grant or scholarship value.

■ *Loans*
The percentage of full-time undergraduates who took out loans, and the average loan value.

■ *Work study*
The percentage of full-time undergraduates who received work study awards, and the average award value.

■ *Student rating of FA*
A curved number ranking of students' satisfaction with their financial aid packages, based on their answers to our survey.

■   ■   ■

The Boxes

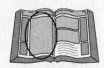

What do students think about...

This box summarizes the results of the surveys we distributed to students at the school. It also includes information from the surveys completed by independent college counselors, and incorporates statistics provided by the schools themselves and the College Counsel. It is divided into three subheadings: Academics, Life, and Students. The "academics" section reports how hard students work and how satisfied they are with the education they are getting, and also tells you which academic departments our respondents rated favorably. The "life" section describes life outside the classroom and addresses questions ranging from "How nice is the campus?" and "How comfortable are the dorms?" to "How popular are fraternities and sororities?" and "How easily and frequently do students of different ethnic origin interact?" The "students" section tells you about what type of student the school traditionally attracts.

Admissions

This box tells you what aspects of your application are most important to the school's admissions officers. It also lists the high school curricular prerequisites for applicants and which standardized tests (if any) are required. Finally, it lists other schools to which applicants apply, according to the admissions office. (To find out what students told us on the same subject, check out the admissions sidebar.) We used the admissions office's responses to our questionnaire to write these boxes; when the office did not respond, we gathered the information from the school's undergraduate catalog.

Financial Aid

This box summarizes the financial aid process at the school: what forms you need and what types of aid are available. Again, we used the financial aid office's responses to our questionnaire; when the office did not respond, we gathered the information from the school's undergraduate catalog.

Note from Admissions

This box contains text written by the school's admissions officers in response to our invitation "to write anything you wish, but you might wish to use this space to let prospective students know what makes your school special, or to tell them what you look for in your typical admittee that other schools may not look for in theirs." When a school failed to provide us with an answer to this question, we excerpted an appropriate passage from the school's catalogue.

What Did We Learn from the Survey?

As well as providing us with invaluable information about specific undergraduate programs, our questionnaires, when viewed collectively, also provided some interesting information about the nation's elite college population. While it is impossible to say anything universally true about all 30,000 of our respondents (except that they're all college students), the following generalizations accurately represent what the vast majority of them told us. If what you read on these next few pages challenges some of your preconceptions about what college life is like, it will have served its purpose: to help you more wisely select the undergraduate program that will make you happiest.

Academics

By far the most important factor influencing students' satisfaction with their academic programs is the quality of their professors. By quality we mean not only academic qualifications (degrees earned, major articles published, major awards won), but also the professors' abilities to serve as teachers. Year after year, students at the nation's most famous research-oriented universities learn that academic prestige and the ability/desire to teach undergraduates do not go hand in hand. At such schools, professors are often preoccupied with their graduate students (those studying for master's and doctoral degrees) or their own research. They are also often under tremendous pressure from their university to publish frequently, thereby further distracting them from their undergraduate students. Remember also that most of what you learn in college, while difficult, is pretty basic material to scholars. You do not need the world's foremost expert on particle physics to teach you any college physics course; what you need is someone who knows how to make that material intelligible to undergraduates. Those students most satisfied with their academic programs are generally those at small, undergraduate-oriented schools where professors' attentions are turned entirely to teaching and helping students. This can't be stressed enough: if you go to Harvard or Caltech expecting to get the best education in the nation, and if you assume that as part of that education your professors will shower you with attention and interest, you are probably in for a big letdown.

Students also told us about "political correctness," a hot issue on college campuses today. The term p.c., as it is often abbreviated, indicates an attitude of concern for the ways in which structures (or "signifiers") in society—at colleges, some of the hot "structures" are the curriculum and the English language—reinforce societal prejudices based on gender, ethnicity, and class. College curricula, for example, contain books by white, upper-class males in great disproportion to their numbers in society. A p.c. critique would point this out, would probably also point out that these books were ordained "classics" by other white, upper-class males, and might finally suggest that students' overwhelming exposure to these books (without equal time granted to books by women, the poor, blacks, etc.) serves to reinforce one point of view while effectively shutting out others. Other p.c. concerns include the impact of terminology: p.c. thinkers argue that terms like "handicapped" and "disabled" are demeaning to those confined to wheelchairs. "Physically challenged" is the p.c. option.

The whole p.c. issue is very heady and very political. It has even become a hot topic in the national press—*Time, U.S. News & World Report,* and *Harper's* all did major articles on it last year, and there are two guide books by conservative organizations telling you how to avoid a p.c. education—for two reasons: 1) some claim that p.c. itself stifles academic freedom with its unyielding attitude toward all non-p.c. opinions, and 2) it is a sore spot with political conservatives who entirely disagree with its beliefs. What we learned from students, however, is that p.c. is not nearly so big a deal on campus as it is to politicians and pundits off-campus. While you are likely to encounter more than a few p.c. professors during college, most students remain basically nonpolitical regardless of their professors' ideologies. Where "p.c." is of the greatest annoyance is among the student body, where some students grab hold of it and become dogmatic language- and thought-police. These students stage and attend protests frequently, criticize friends self-righteously, and rarely display any trace of a sense of humor. P.C. students are no more of a nuisance than campus right-wingers; it's just that in most places there are more of the former. Our advice is, as you read the school profiles, keep an eye out for those campuses at which students are particularly politicized. Political issues will dominate social life here, and you should consider this when you choose where to spend your next four years.

Life

When it comes to location, respondents to our survey overwhelmingly preferred cities to suburbs, towns, and rural sites. All the schools that ranked in the top 20 for student satisfaction with location are in major cities (except University of Colorado, Boulder, which, according to students, is practically a ski resort). Six are in New York City, giving it the title of America's unofficial best college town. Chicago, Washington, D.C., and Boston all placed more than one school in the top 20. On the bottom of the pile are decaying industrial cities (Bethlehem, PA; Worcester, MA), quiet towns well removed from major metropolitan areas (Middletown, CT; Crawfordsville, IN; Riverside, CA); and isolated rural areas (Storrs, CT). A few low-rated schools are in larger, more dangerous cities (Newark, NJ). In addition, most of the low-ranking school locations are cursed with bad weather for much of the year. The importance of a school's location is often undervalued by those shopping for colleges; while it shouldn't be your prime concern, remember that you will be living in the city/town you choose for the next four years. School can be a very stressful experience, and other factors that can increase or relieve that stress—such as location and how well you fit in with your fellow students—cannot be dismissed.

Another thing we learned: small schools inhibit what is generally considered a "normal" social scene. At schools with fewer than 1,500 students, we were told, students rarely date in the traditional sense; they either "settle down" with someone for four years, or they "hook up" once and then spend the next few weeks trying to avoid the person they hooked up with. Or, they have no romantic experiences at all. The reason is that, at these schools, the community is too small: everybody knows and cares about everyone else's business, making it hard to go out on a casual date without becoming the talk of the campus. Schools of this size are often also those at which the Greeks dominate social life, although the Greeks can be dominant at larger schools as well. Keep your eyes open for such schools: there is a definite type of person who fits into a Greek-dominated scene, and a type who does not. Those who fit in tend to be from white upper-middle-class backgrounds and hold conventionally conservative political and social attitudes. Those who don't fit this mold often find life at Greek-dominated schools depressingly stifling. If you're unsure how you'll fit in at such a school, go visit one for a few days.

We'd like to add an editorial comment based on numerous essays from angry students: campus-wide drinking prohibitions don't work!!! Such regulations douse school spirit (few students are interested in any campus-sponsored activity if they know security guards will be actively enforcing no-drinking rules) and provoke the students (who resent what they consider the school's intrusion into their personal lives). On top of it all, "dry campus" policies don't prevent students from drinking: in some cases, students actually reported that such policies encouraged their drinking because it provided both the challenge and the enjoyment inherent in disobeying a dumb rule. At a few "dry" schools we found that, ironically, the policy had served to increase the popularity of illegal narcotics (which are easier to conceal). On most campuses, by the way, drinking remains much more popular than drug use. Drugs are not entirely ubiquitous, but, except at a few women's schools and at Brigham Young, drinking is a substantial fact of life on every college campus in the country. If you're looking to avoid a drinking- and drug-based social scene in college, your best bet is probably at a large school, where the sheer number of students allows social communities of all types to flourish. Don't get us wrong: there's plenty of drinking going on at big schools, but there are also more alternatives.

Students

It has come to be an accepted truism that college students get more conservative with each passing year. This may in fact be true—this was our first survey, so we cannot yet track trends—but we were surprised to find that the national student population is not as conservative as we had been led to believe. Our survey showed us that American college students as a whole still fall slightly to the left of "middle-of-the-road," or centrist, politics. Of the 244 student bodies we surveyed, 135 are, on the whole, left of center, while only 66 are to the right of center; the rest occupy the center. As a rule, the farther a student body leans to the left, the more pervasive the influence of political correctness. The farther a student body leans to the right, the more likely it is that alternative lifestyles and ideologies, such as homosexuality or feminism, will meet with overt hostility.

Minority representation at many top schools remains distressingly low. The most prestigious, high-profile schools (the Ivies, for example) have little trouble attracting qualified minority students. The next tier of schools, however—those that are excellent but are less well known or are located in more remote areas—lack either the ability or desire to attract minority students of similar quality. To make matters worse, the few minority students who attend such schools are often made uncomfortable by the lack of a substantial peer group. The inability of these schools to help their few minority students fit in dissuades other minorities from attending these schools, thereby perpetuating the problem. While ethnically oriented and single-sex schools offer an excellent alternative for those uncomfortable at predominantly white, upper-class schools, they don't address the larger problem of how to create an undergraduate atmosphere in which students of all backgrounds can study together and reap the benefits of their diversity of experiences. We offer no solutions—we'll leave that debate to the nation's educators, sociologists, and politicians—but as you read this book, look at the descriptions of the student body and the student body demographic breakdowns, and think about how comfortable you'll be among your peers at the schools described.

The most important thing we learned from our survey is that there is a tremendous diversity of educational opportunities available in the United States. Look through this book and you will surely find at least one school that is just right for you (whether you get accepted there is another question). We also found that motivated, thoughtful, and intelligent people—30,000 of whom took the time to fill out our survey—are out there taking advantage of those opportunities. Good luck to you in your quest to join them.

■   ■   ■

What's Hot/What's Not

Our "What's Hot/What's Not" lists, located in the "Student Life" sidebar on each school's two-page spread, are based entirely on the results of our on-campus surveys. In other words, the appearance on these lists of such categories as "financial aid," "ethnic diversity," and "library" are based on the opinions of students at those schools (NOT on any numerical analysis of library size, endowment, etc.) Some of the terms that appear in these lists are not entirely self-explanatory; these terms are defined below:

bursar: The office at which you pay your bills. At some schools, trips to the bursar are frequently long, unnecessary, and frustrating. At such schools, this category shows up in the "What's Not" list.

catalog: When you pick up most schools' catalogs, you'll probably be impressed by the amazing breadth of courses offered. At some schools, however, many listed courses are offered infrequently. We've found that this happens often enough and is annoying enough to students that we asked them how well their catalogs reflected the courses actually being offered; their answers are reflected by this category.

diversity: We asked students whether their student body was made up of diverse social and ethnic groups. This category reflects their answers to this question. Note that this category is not limited to *ethnic diversity* (which you can figure out by looking at the student body demographics). Even at an ethnically diverse school, for example, this category can appear on the "What's Not" list if students all come from the same social background, share similar goals and political views, etc.

honest students: We asked students how prevalent cheating was at their school.

interaction: We asked students whether students from different class and ethnic backgrounds interacted frequently and easily.

profs outside class: We asked students how easy it is to get extra help from their professors.

profs in class: We asked students how interesting their professors were in class.

profs teach intros *or* TAs teach intros: At some schools, teaching assistants (usually graduate students) teach nearly all introductory-level courses. At others, professors teach these courses. As a rule, it's better to be taught by a professor. This category appears in the "What's Not" list.

profs teach upper-level courses *or* TAs teach upper-level courses: At some large universities, you'll continue to be taught by teaching assistants even in your upper-level courses. At schools where this is the case, this category appears in the "What's Not" list.

small classes (overall): We asked students how many of their classes had fewer than 20 students in them. Their answer to that question is reflected by this category. Students generally prefer smaller classes because they offer more student-to-student and student-to-professor interaction.

studying hard: We asked students how many hours a day they studied (excluding time spent in class).

suitcase syndrome: At a "suitcase" school, students go back home nearly every weekend. This category reflects whether the school is a "suitcase" school.

town-gown relations: We asked students whether they got along with local residents; their answer to that question is reflected by this category.

■   ■   ■

Glossary

Achievement Tests: Subject-specific exams administered by the Educational Testing Service (the SAT people). These tests are required by some, but not all, admissions offices. English Composition and Math Level I or II are the tests most frequently required.

ACT: The American College Test. Like the SAT but less tricky. Many schools accept either SAT or ACT scores; if you consistently get blown away by the SAT, you might want to consider taking the ACT instead.

distribution requirements: Students at schools with distribution requirements must take a number of courses in various subject areas, such as foreign language, humanities, natural science, and social science. Distribution requirements do not specify which courses you must take, only which types of courses.

FAF and FFS: The Financial Aid Form and the Family Financial Statement. Most schools require that applicants complete either one or the other to be considered for financial aid.

4-1-4: A type of academic schedule. Its like a semester schedule, but with a short semester (usually one month long) jammed between the two semesters. Most schools offer internship programs or nontraditional studies during the short semester.

Greek system: Fraternities and sororities.

humanities: These include such disciplines as art history, communication, drama, English, foreign languages, music, philosophy, and religion.

merit-based grant: A scholarship (not necessary full) given to students because of some special talent or attribute. Artists, athletes, community leaders, and geniuses are typical recipients.

natural sciences: These include such disciplines as astronomy, biology, chemistry, genetics, geology, mathematics, physics, and zoology.

need-based grant: A scholarship (not necessary full) given to students because they would otherwise be unable to afford college. Student need is determined on the basis of the FAF or FFS.

p.c.: Politically correct. A genuine buzz-word on campuses today. It signifies either 1) an enlightened awareness of how society rewards certain members and punishes other solely on the basis of class, ethnicity, and gender; or

2) an unrelenting, humorless hypersensitivity on all issues even remotely related to class, ethnicity, and gender.

RA: Residence assistant (or residential advisor). Someone, usually an upperclassman or graduate student, who supervises a floor or section of a dorm, usually in return for free room and board. RAs are responsible for enforcing the drinking and noise rules.

SAT: Scholastic Aptitude Test. A college entrance exam required by many schools; some schools will accept either the ACT or the SAT.

social sciences: These include such disciplines as anthropology, economics, geography, history, international studies, political science, psychology, and sociology.

TA: Teaching assistant. Most often a graduate student, a TA will often teach discussion sections of large lectures. At some schools, TAs and graduate students teach a large number of introductory-level and even some upper-level courses. At smaller schools full professors generally do all the teaching.

work-study: A government-funded financial aid program that provides assistance to financial aid recipients in return for work in the school's library, labs, etc.

■   ■   ■

Schools Ranked by Category

About the Indexes That Follow

One of the great things about a multiple-choice survey is that the results give you lots of numbers. We wanted to present those numbers to you in a fun and informative way; hence, the following rankings of schools in 64 categories. As you read through these, please remember that every one of the schools profiled in this book is excellent; even those ranked at the bottom of categories are still among the nation's best. Focus on those categories that are important to you: do you want to go to a school where discussion takes up most of the class time? Would you prefer to be lectured to only? Do you care? Do you want to go to a school where partying is prevalent? Or would you rather go somewhere with a subdued social scene? By looking through these lists, you should be able to get a good idea of what are and are not important considerations in choosing your college. And besides, as we said before, lists are fun.

We've broken the rankings down into nine categories: Academics; Administration; Quality of Life; Politics; Demographics; Social Life; Extracurriculars; Parties; and Schools By Archetype. For this final set of rankings, we combined student responses to several questions to determine whether a school was a "jock" school, a "hippie" school, etc. Within each category the schools are listed in descending order of "hippieness," "jockness," etc.

■ *The best academics:*

California Institute of Technology
Princeton University
Yale University
Harvard College
Massachusetts Institute of Technology
Stanford University
Amherst College
Wellesley College
Columbia University
Haverford College

Williams College
Rice University
Northwestern University
Bowdoin College
Davidson College
Colgate University
University of Pennsylania
Smith College
Deep Springs College
Claremont College–Harvey Mudd

■ *The toughest to get into:*

California Institute of Technology
Harvard College
Princeton University
Stanford University
Yale University
Massachusetts Institute of Technology
Amherst College
Rice University
Duke University
Swarthmore College

Claremont College–Harvey Mudd
Brown University
Williams College
Cornell University
Columbia University
University of California–Berkeley
University of Pennsylania
Haverford College
Dartmouth College
Northwestern University

■ *Students hit their books:*

California Institute of Technology
Massachusetts Institute of Technology
Reed College
Rose-Hulman Institute of Technology
Swarthmore College
University of Missouri–Rolla
Bryn Mawr College
Rhode Island School of Design
Claremont College–Harvey Mudd
Smith College

College of Holy Cross
Illinois Institute of Technology
Bucknell University
Oberlin College
Wabash College
Davidson College
Carnegie Mellon University
Cornell University
Mount Holyoke College
Saint John's College

■ *Students hate their books:*

George Washington University
Seton Hall University
Florida State University
Penn State University
University of Florida
Saint Mary's College of Maryland
University of South Carolina
Emerson College
SUNY Binghamton
Manhattanville College

Clemson University
Baylor University
Hofstra University
Temple University
Millsaps College
SUNY Albany
University of California–Irvine
University of Oklahoma
Oglethorpe University
George Mason University

■ *Most interesting teachers:*

Sweet Briar College
Marlboro College
Hampden-Sydney College
University of the South (Sewanee)
Austin College
Agnes Scott College
Mount Holyoke College
Deep Springs College
Wabash College
Goddard College

Smith College
Eugene Lang College
Hendrix College
Washington and Lee University
College of the Atlantic
University of Dallas
Simon's Rock of Bard College
Wellesley College
Amherst College
Williams College

■ *Bring NōDōz and Jolt:*

Georgia Institute of Technology
SUNY Stonybrook
California Institute of Technology
Case Western Reserve University
Stevens Institute of Technology
Temple University
Rensselaer Institute of Technology
New Jersey Institute of Technology
Hofstra University
Iowa State University

University of Arizona
Auburn University
West Virginia University
New York University
Rutgers University/Rutgers College
University of South Carolina
University of Maryland–College Park
Ohio State University
Clemson University
University of California–Santa Barbara

■ *You'll know your professors:*

Sweet Briar College
College of the Atlantic
Agnes Scott College
Saint John's College
University of the South (Sewanee)
Marlboro College
Mount Holyoke College
Wabash College
Rhodes College
Goucher College

DePauw University
Washington and Lee University
Swarthmore College
Davidson College
Colby College
Haverford College
Goddard College
Bryn Mawr College
Grinnell College
University of Richmond

■ *Teach and run professors:*

CUNY
New Jersey Institute of Technology
Georgia Institute of Technology
University of Minnesota
University of South Carolina
West Virginia University
Iowa State University
Parsons School of Design
Temple University
University of Arizona

Massachusetts Institute of Technology
Auburn University
Rutgers University/Rutgers College
University of Kansas
University of California–Irvine
University of Oklahoma
SUNY Albany
Penn State University
University of Pittsburgh
University of Wisconsin

■ *Class discussions encouraged:*

Saint John's College
Goddard College
Simon's Rock of Bard College
Sarah Lawrence College
Bennington College
Reed College
Marlboro College
Hampshire College
CUNY–Hunter College
College of the Atlantic

Guilford College
Knox College
Parsons School of Design
Babson College
Princeton University
Bard College
Deep Springs College
Juilliard School
New College–University of South Florida
Colorado College

■ *Class discussions rare:*

California Institute of Technology
Georgia Institute of Technology
Massachusetts Institute of Technology
University of Minnesota
Case Western Reserve University
Johns Hopkins University
Rensselaer Institute of Technology
Florida State University
Colorado School of Mines
University of Missouri–Rolla

Vanderbilt University
University of Rochester
University of Florida
SUNY Buffalo
University of North Dakota
Northwestern University
Creighton University
Worcester Polytechnic Institute
West Virginia University
Pennsylvania State University

■ *Great libraries:*

Princeton University
Harvard/Radcliffe College
Wesleyan University
Dartmouth College
Oberlin College
Washington and Lee University
University of Virginia
Lehigh University
Cornell University
Trinity University

Colby College
University of Rochester
Bucknell University
Haverford College
Mount Holyoke College
University of North Carolina–Chapel Hill
Swarthmore College
Smith College
Northwestern University
Saint Lawrence University

■ *BYOB (bring your own books):*

Spelman College
Morehouse College
Tufts University
Bard College
Hollins College
Bennington College
Seton Hall University
Illinois Wesleyan University
Stevens Institute of Technology
George Washington University

Catholic University of America
Deep Springs College
University of Rhode Island
Golden Gate College
Duquesne University
Hiram College
American University
DePaul University
Fairfield University
James Madison University

■ *Students happy with financial aid:*

Deep Springs College
Cooper Union
Marlboro College
Sweet Briar College
Wabash College
Oglethorpe University
Rhodes College
Mount Holyoke College
Hampden-Sydney College
Knox College

Beloit College
University of Dallas
Bennington College
Lake Forest College
College of the Atlantic
California Institute of Technology
Haverford College
University of the South (Sewanee)
Agnes Scott College
Claremont Colleges

■ *Students dissatisfied with financial aid:*

CUNY–Hunter College
SUNY Binghamton
Rhode Island School of Design
SUNY Albany
Spelman College
Howard University
Temple University
Syracuse University
University of Massachusetts–Amherst
University of Maryland–College Park

West Virginia University
Hofstra University
University of California–Los Angeles
College of Holy Cross
SUNY Stonybrook
University of Wisconsin–Madison
Drexel University
James Madison University
Juilliard School
Seton Hall University

■ *Things run smoothly:*

Williams College
Bucknell University
Rose-Hulman Institute of Technology
Washington and Lee University
Sweet Briar College
Hampden-Sydney College
Davidson College
Wellesley College
Princeton University
University of the South (Sewanee)

Swarthmore College
Amherst College
Grinnell College
Haverford College
Baylor University
University of Richmond
Hendrix College
Bryn Mawr College
Claremont–Claremont McKenna
Mount Holyoke College

■ *Long lines and red tape:*

Rutgers University/Rutgers College
Stevens Institute of Technology
Temple University
University of Maryland–College Park
University of Minnesota
SUNY Albany
University of Massachusetts–Amherst
New College–University of South Florida
University of California–Irvine
University of Rhode Island

Parsons School of Design
Columbia University
University of California–Berkeley
University of Pittsburgh–Pittsburgh Campus
University of Vermont
CUNY–Queens College
Emerson College
Bennington College
University of Dallas
Howard University

■ *Happy students:*

Duke University
Sweet Briar College
Colby College
University of the South (Sewanee)
Hampden-Sydney College
Northwestern University
College of the Atlantic
Dartmouth College
Brown University
Stanford University

University of Dayton
Rhodes College
Washington and Lee University
California Polytechnic State University
Deep Springs College
Swarthmore College
Marlboro College
Bucknell University
Saint Mary's College of California
Colorado College

■ *Unhappy students:*

Illinois Institute of Technology
Temple University
Adelphi University
New Jersey Institute of Technology
CUNY–Hunter College
California Institute of Technology
Stevens Institute of Technology
Johns Hopkins University
Drexel University
Claremont College–Harvey Mudd

University of Chicago
University of Maryland–College Park
Northeastern University
University of Minnesota
Case Western Reserve University
Colorado School of Mines
SUNY Stonybrook
Golden Gate College
University of Missouri–Rolla
Massachusetts Institute of Technology

■ *Campus like Eden:*

College of the Atlantic
Rhodes College
Sweet Briar College
Wellesley College
University of Richmond
Furman University
University of the South (Sewanee)
Colby College
University of California–Santa Cruz
Mount Holyoke College

Princeton University
Swarthmore College
Colgate University
Agnes Scott College
Washington and Lee University
Dartmouth College
Saint Mary's College of California
Stanford University
Pepperdine University
Williams College

■ *Campus like Cleveland*:*

Cooper Union
Parsons School of Design
Illinois Institute of Technology
CUNY–Hunter College
New Jersey Institute of Technology
SUNY Albany
New York University
Temple University
Massachusetts Institute of Technology
Golden Gate College

Drexel University
Boston University
Claremont College–Pitzer College
Case Western Reserve University
University of Dallas
Claremont College–Harvey Mudd
University of Pittsburgh–Pittsburgh Campus
Eugene Lang College
Rutgers University/Rutgers College
Rochester Institute of Technology

*We're just kidding about Cleveland. Please don't call or write us. It's actually very nice there. They have a great art museum.

■ *Great food:*

Sweet Briar College
College of the Atlantic
Bowdoin College
Deep Springs College
Cornell University
Dartmouth College
Goddard College
Marlboro College
James Madison University
Gettysburg College

Smith College
Miami University
Davidson College
DePauw University
Bryn Mawr College
Trinity University
Grinnell College
Emory University
Hobart/William Smith College
Brigham Young University

■ *Bring a bag lunch:*

SUNY Albany
Stevens Institute of Technology
Eckerd College
New Jersey Institute of Technology
New College–University of South Florida
Worcester Polytechnic Institute
Reed College
Vassar College
Spelman College
Saint Bonaventure University

Lake Forest College
Simon's Rock of Bard College
Rice University
Fisk University
Saint Mary's College of Maryland
Saint John's College
University of Wisconsin–Madison
Clemson University
University of Massachusetts–Amherst
Oglethorpe University

■ *Dorms like palaces:*

Sweet Briar College
Smith College
Skidmore College
Bryn Mawr College
Agnes Scott College
New College–University of South Florida
Mount Holyoke College
Hampden-Sydney College
Trinity University
Wellesley College

Cornell University
Bowdoin College
College of the Atlantic
Bucknell University
Marlboro College
DePauw University
Dartmouth College
Rhodes College
Deep Springs College
University of Richmond

■ *Dorms like prisons:*

Arizona State University
Illinois Institute of Technology
Florida State University
California Polytechnic State University
Fisk University
SUNY Stonybrook
Morehouse College
SUNY Albany
Lake Forest College
Clemson University

Howard University
Temple University
West Virginia University
Emerson College
Parsons School of Design
University of Oregon
University of Arizona
Simon's Rock of Bard College
Illinois State University
University of Southern California

■ *The best quality of life:*

Sweet Briar College
College of the Atlantic
Deep Springs College
Rhodes College
Hampden-Sydney Collge
Dartmouth College
Colby College
Marlboro College
Mount Holyoke College
University of the South (Sewanee)

Washington and Lee University
Swarthmore College
Bowdoin College
Brigham Young University
University of Richmond
Williams College
Smith College
Vanderbilt University
Grinnell College
Furman University

■ *Most conservative students:*

Hampden-Sydney College
Brigham Young University
Baylor University
Bucknell University
Rose-Hulman Institute of Technology
Babson College
Creighton University
Saint Joseph's University
Sweet Briar College
Wabash College

Vanderbilt University
Miami University
University of Dayton
California Polytechnic State University
Clemson University
University of North Dakota
Fordham University
Washington and Lee University
Furman University
University of Illinois–Urbana

■ *Most liberal students:*

Eugene Lang College
Goddard College
Hampshire College
Reed College
Sarah Lawrence College
Grinnell College
Bard College
College of the Atlantic
Wesleyan University
Bennington College

Simon's Rock of Bard College
New College–University of South Florida
University of California–Santa Cruz
Swarthmore College
Guilford College
Lewis and Clark College
Claremont College–Pomona College
Saint John's College
Bryn Mawr College
Spelman College

■ *Most politically active:*

Rutgers University/Rutgers College
Eugene Lang College
Goddard College
Sarah Lawrence College
University of Colorado–Boulder
College of the Atlantic
Hampden-Sydney College
Wesleyan University
Hampshire College
Georgetown University

Rhodes College
Carleton College
Wheaton College
Bard College
New College–University of South Florida
Beloit College
Reed College
SUNY Binghamton
Swarthmore College
Guilford College

■ *What election?*

Iowa State University
California Institute of Technology
Saint Bonaventure University
Alfred University
CUNY–Hunter College
University of Rhode Island
Villanova University
Rhode Island School of Design
Clarkson University
Rochester Institute of Technology

SUNY Buffalo
Penn State University
Saint Joseph's University
Marquette University
University of Kentucky
Illinois Institute of Technology
Massachusetts Institute of Technology
University of Arizona
Bentley College
Worcester Polytechnic Institute

■ Diverse student body:

Harvard/Radcliffe College
Brown University
University of California–Berkeley
Stanford University
Rutgers University/Rutgers College
George Mason University
Massachusetts Institute of Technology
Mount Holyoke College
Wesleyan University
Columbia University

Bryn Mawr College
Juilliard School
Wellesley College
CUNY–Queens College
SUNY Buffalo
Case Western Reserve University
Oberlin College
Parsons School of Design
Boston University
Manhattanville College

■ Homogeneous student body:

University of Richmond
Bucknell University
Villanova University
Providence College
Fairfield University
Washington and Lee University
University of New Hampshire
Hollins College
Reed College
Fisk University

California Polytechnic State University
Gustavus Adolphus College
Saint Lawrence University
Gettysburg College
Morehouse College
University of Vermont
Miami University
Hampden-Sydney College
Kenyon College
Furman University

■ Races and classes get along:

Deep Springs College
Bryn Mawr College
Parsons School of Design
Bennington College
Goddard College
Saint John's College
Marlboro College
Simon's Rock of Bard College
New College–University of South Florida
Stanford University

Mount Holyoke College
University of Dallas
Rhode Island School of Design
California Institute of Technology
Juilliard School
Bucknell University
Grinnell College
Eugene Lang College
New Jersey Institute of Technology
Cooper Union

■ Race and class relations strained:

University of Richmond
Fairfield University
Baylor University
Miami University
Hobart/William Smith College
Vanderbilt University
Villanova University
Morehouse College
Hollins College
Duke University

University of Notre Dame
Texas Christian University
Lafayette College
Saint Lawrence University
Auburn University
Denison University
University of New Hampshire
Furman University
California Polytechnic State University
University of Vermont

■ *Gays out of closet:*

Bryn Mawr College
Grinnell College
Simon's Rock of Bard College
Rhode Island School of Design
Goddard College
Bard College
Reed College
Hampshire College
Sarah Lawrence College
Bennington College

New College–University of South Florida
Wesleyan University
Vassar College
Juilliard School
Oberlin College
Beloit College
Tufts University
Smith College
Parsons School of Design
Carleton College

■ *Gays still in closet:*

Lafayette College
Washington and Lee University
Rose-Hulman Institute of Technology
Randolph-Macon College
Rhodes College
College of Holy Cross
Villanova University
Brigham Young University
Wofford College
Clarkson University

Muhlenberg College
University of Dayton
Baylor University
Colorado School of Mines
Seton Hall University
Wittenberg University
Franklin and Marshall College
DePauw University
Claremont–Claremont McKenna
Manhattanville College

■ *Gay community accepted:*

Deep Springs College
Bennington College
New College–University of South Florida
Eugene Lang College
Reed College
Simon's Rock of Bard College
Marlboro College
Bryn Mawr College
Goddard College
College of the Atlantic

Hampshire College
Bard College
Rhode Island School of Design
Parsons School of Design
Sarah Lawrence College
Grinnell College
Smith College
Vassar College
Oberlin College
Juilliard School

■ *Homophobic:*

Lafayette College
Baylor University
Rose-Hulman Institute of Technology
Washington and Lee University
Brigham Young University
Randolph-Macon College
Bucknell University
Morehouse College
Hampden-Sydney College
Furman University

Clemson University
Fairfield University
Villanova University
Providence College
Colorado School of Mines
University of North Dakota
Wofford College
College of Holy Cross
University of Notre Dame
Clarkson University

■ *Bible is required reading:*

Brigham Young University
University of Notre Dame
University of Dallas
Baylor University
Furman University
College of Holy Cross
Pepperdine University
Creighton University
Saint Olaf College
Providence College

Brandeis University
Villanova University
Fisk University
Fairfield University
University of Dayton
Morehouse College
Wake Forest University
Catholic University of America
University of the South (Sewanee)
Fordham University

■ *Pagans:*

Eugene Lang College
Reed College
Bennington College
Hampshire College
Sarah Lawrence College
Simon's Rock of Bard College
Bard College
Bucknell University
College of the Atlantic
Vassar College

Rhode Island School of Design
New College–University of South Florida
Hobart/William Smith College
Marlboro College
Colorado College
Carleton College
Wesleyan University
Claremont College–Pitzer College
Grinnell College
Haverford College

■ Old-fashioned dating:

Brigham Young University
Spelman College
University of Florida
Sweet Briar College
Morehouse College
Howard University
Florida State University
Agnes Scott College
University of Kansas
Fisk University

University of South Carolina
Hollins College
Arizona State University
University of Rhode Island
University of Oklahoma
North Carolina State University
University of Arizona
University of Tennessee–Knoxville
University of North Carolina–Chapel Hill
University of Kentucky

■ Travel in packs:

Deep Springs College
Williams College
College of Holy Cross
Duke University
Middlebury College
Stanford University
Gustavus Adolphus College
Santa Clara University
Claremont College–Harvey Mudd
Princeton University

Bowdoin College
California Institute of Technology
Georgetown University
Bryn Mawr College
Trinity University
Wesleyan University
Cooper Union
Providence College
Northwestern University
Vassar College

■ Students turn each others' heads:

Denison University
University of Richmond
Miami University
Texas Christian University
Southern Methodist University
Vanderbilt University
Howard University
Saint Lawrence University
Bucknell University
Washington and Lee University

Villanova University
Middlebury College
Clemson University
Brigham Young University
University of Colorado–Boulder
Skidmore College
Trinity College
University of California–Santa Barbara
Gettysburg College
Baylor University

■ Students turn each others' stomachs:

Johns Hopkins University
Stevens Institute of Technology
Massachusetts Institute of Technology
Claremont College–Harvey Mudd
Case Western Reserve University
California Institute of Technology
Colorado School of Mines
University of Chicago
Rensselaer Institute of Technology
Brandeis University

New Jersey Institute of Technology
Illinois Institute of Technology
Cooper Union
Rose-Hulman Institute of Technology
Worcester Polytechnic Institute
Carnegie Mellon University
Georgia Institute of Technology
Washington University
University of Missouri–Rolla
Clarkson University

■ *Great college towns:*

Oglethorpe University
Columbia University
DePaul University
American University
Simmons College
Juilliard School
Parsons School of Design
Barnard College
Southern Methodist University
Tulane University

Emerson College
University of Colorado–Boulder
Catholic University of America
Boston University
Emory University
Harvard/Radcliffe College
Cooper Union
Massachusetts Institute of Technology
Georgetown University
Agnes Scott College

■ *Trapped on campus:*

Vassar College
New Jersey Institute of Technology
Wabash College
Wheaton College
Wesleyan University
Lehigh University
Union College
Saint Mary's College of Maryland
Lafayette College
Bard College

Clark University
Connecticut College
Wittenberg University
Brandeis University
Bennington College
University of Notre Dame
Bates College
Sarah Lawrence College
Hiram College
Simon's Rock of Bard College

■ *Town-gown relations are good:*

Rhodes College
Davidson College
Brigham Young University
Furman University
Marlboro College
Hampden-Sydney College
University of Dallas
Southern Methodist University
University of the South (Sewanee)
University of North Dakota

Colorado School of Mines
Wofford College
Agnes Scott College
University of Richmond
Wake Forest University
Guilford College
Eugene Lang College
Texas Christian University
Creighton University
University of Dayton

■ *Town-gown relations are bad:*

Sarah Lawrence College
Hobart/William Smith College
Providence College
Illinois Institute of Technology
Bennington College
University of Southern California
Lehigh University
Wittenberg University
Trinity College
Lafayette College

Vassar College
Union College
Temple University
Villanova University
University of Pennsylvania
DePauw University
SUNY Albany
Clark University
University of Maryland–College Park
Simon's Rock of Bard College

■ *Students pack the stadiums:*

Williams College
University of North Carolina–Chapel Hill
Duke University
University of Kentucky
University of Notre Dame
Clemson University
Villanova University
Providence College
Penn State University
University of Florida

University of Tennessee–Knoxville
Seton Hall University
Brigham Young University
Syracuse University
University of Connecticut–Main Campus
Indiana University
North Carolina State University
University of Southern California
University of Iowa
Ohio State University

■ *Do we have a stadium?*

Goddard College
College of the Atlantic
Eugene Lang College
New College–University of South Florida
Parsons School of Design
Bennington College
Deep Springs College
Sarah Lawrence College
Golden Gate College
Saint John's College

Reed College
Hampshire College
Juilliard School
Rhode Island School of Design
Cooper Union
Emerson College
Marlboro College
Bard College
Simon's Rock of Bard College
University of Chicago

■ *Everyone plays intramural sports:*

Providence College
University of Notre Dame
Baylor University
Rice University
Carleton College
Wabash College
Trinity University
Oglethorpe University
University of Richmond
University of California–San Diego

Massachusetts Institute of Technology
Williams College
Clemson University
Hendrix College
Gustavus Adolphus College
Hiram College
Colorado College
Furman University
University of Dayton
Saint John's College

■ *Nobody plays intramural sports:*

Eugene Lang College
Parsons School of Design
Golden Gate College
Goddard College
Juilliard School
Bennington College
Sarah Lawrence College
Rhode Island School of Design
Emerson College
Hollins College

Spelman College
New College–University of South Florida
College of the Atlantic
Simmons College
Reed College
Fisk University
Bryn Mawr College
Simon's Rock of Bard College
Barnard College
Hampshire College

■ Great college radio station:

Goddard College
Emerson College
Saint Bonaventure University
Seton Hall University
Illinois Wesleyan University
Reed College
Franklin and Marshall College
Denison University
CUNY–Hunter College
Guilford College

DePauw University
Beloit College
Hendrix College
Bates College
Howard University
Skidmore College
Grinnell College
Carleton College
Union College
University of the South (Sewanee)

■ College newspaper gets read:

Howard University
University of Pennsylvania
Goddard College
University of Florida
University of Wisconsin–Madison
University of Maryland–College Park
University of California–Los Angeles
University of Virginia
University of Connecticut–Main Campus
Cornell University

West Virginia University
Penn State University
Rutgers University/Rutgers College
University of New Hampshire
Northwestern University
Tufts University
Syracuse University
University of Iowa
University of Notre Dame
Emory University

■ College theater is big:

Juilliard School
Yale University
Skidmore College
Bennington College
Emerson College
Vassar College
Goddard College
Marlboro College
Drew University
Northwestern University

Simon's Rock of Bard College
Eugene Lang College
Bryn Mawr College
Harvard/Radcliffe College
Wesleyan University
University of Pennsylvania
Sweet Briar College
Goucher College
Hendrix College
Carleton College

■ *Lots of beer:*

Colgate University
Williams College
Bucknell University
University of the South (Sewanee)
Lafayette College
University of Dayton
Lehigh University
Dartmouth College
Saint Mary's College of Maryland
Randolph-Macon College

Providence College
Claremont–Claremont McKenna
Wake Forest University
Denison University
University of California–Santa Barbara
University of Virginia
Duke University
Connecticut College
University of Florida
University of Vermont

■ *Lots of hard liquor:*

Bucknell University
Washington and Lee University
Colgate University
University of the South (Sewanee)
University of Virginia
Millsaps College
Hendrix College
Bennington College
Lafayette College
University of Florida

Tulane University
Florida State University
University of Vermont
Vanderbilt University
Emory University
Saint Mary's College of Maryland
Randolph-Macon College
University of Maryland–College Park
Austin College
Denison University

■ *Lots of soft drinks:*

Brigham Young University
Golden Gate College
CUNY
New Jersey Institute of Technology
Cooper Union
Illinois Institute of Technology
Goddard College
Parsons School of Design
Wellesley College
Bryn Mawr College

Pepperdine University
Eugene Lang College
California Institute of Technology
Mount Holyoke College
Oberlin College
College of the Atlantic
Case Western Reserve University
Spelman College
Morehouse College
Simon's Rock of Bard College

■ Reefer madness:

New College–University of South Florida
Sarah Lawrence College
Simon's Rock of Bard College
Reed College
Claremont College–Pitzer College
Bennington College
Bard College
University of Vermont
Rhode Island School of Design
Hampshire College

Hobart/William Smith College
University of California–Santa Barbara
SUNY Albany
College of the Atlantic
University of Colorado–Boulder
University of California–Santa Cruz
Skidmore College
Lewis and Clark College
Emerson College
Vassar College

■ Don't inhale:

Deep Springs College
Brigham Young University
Rose-Hulman Institute of Technology
Golden Gate College
California Institute of Technology
Agnes Scott College
New Jersey Institute of Technology
Case Western Reserve University
Wellesley College
Illinois Institute of Technology

Sweet Briar College
Colorado School of Mines
Bryn Mawr College
Simmons College
Harvard/Radcliffe College
Stanford University
Georgetown University
Furman University
Mount Holyoke College
University of Notre Dame

■ Go Greek:

Washington and Lee University
DePauw University
Lehigh University
Lafayette College
University of Richmond
Millsaps College
Wabash College
Southern Methodist University
Union College
Randolph-Macon College

Denison University
Iowa State University
Baylor University
Dartmouth College
Saint Lawrence University
Spelman College
University of Southern California
Wofford College
Texas Christian University
University of Virginia

■ 99% frat-free:

Rice University
Carleton College
Haverford College
College of the Atlantic
Bennington College
Goddard College
Sarah Lawrence College
Skidmore College
Williams College
Grinnell College

Oberlin College
Saint John's College
Connecticut College
Claremont–Claremont McKenna
Goucher College
Vassar College
Marlboro College
Hampshire College
Simon's Rock of Bard College
Rhode Island School of Design

■ *Party schools:*

Tulane University
Bennington College
University of California–Santa Cruz
Florida State University
SUNY Albany
Union College
West Virginia University
University of Vermont
Denison University
Lafayette College

Hobart/William Smith College
Clemson University
Penn State University
University of Wisconsin–Madison
University of South Carolina
University of Texas–Austin
University of Californa–Los Angeles
Syracuse University
University of Dallas
Lehigh University

■ *Serious schools:*

Deep Springs College
Golden Gate College
Brigham Young University
California Institute of Technology
New Jersey Institute of Technology
Wellesley College
Bryn Mawr College
Mount Holyoke College
Illinois Institute of Technology
CUNY

Smith College
Cooper Union
Simmons College
Parsons School of Design
Sweet Briar College
Furman University
Agnes Scott College
Goddard College
Case Western Reserve University
Auburn University

■ *Jock schools:*

Clemson University
Wabash College
University of Richmond
University of Virginia
Florida State University
Union College
Colgate University
Ohio State University
North Carolina State University
Wake Forest University

Indiana University
University of Tennessee–Knoxville
Dartmouth College
Penn State University
Villanova University
Seton Hall University
Duke University
University of Illinois–Urbana
Baylor University
University of North Carolina–Chapel Hill

■ *Girlie man schools (i.e. no jocks):*

Golden Gate College
Parsons School of Design
Goddard College
Eugene Lang College
Juilliard School
Deep Springs College
College of the Atlantic
Bennington College
Sarah Lawrence College
New College–University of South Florida

Rhode Island School of Design
Bryn Mawr College
Hampshire College
Reed College
Simmons College
Simon's Rock of Bard College
Emerson College
Cooper Union
California Institute of Technology
Marlboro College

■ *Schools stuck in the 60's:*

Hampshire College	Bard College
Reed College	Lewis and Clark College
Goddard College	Simon's Rock of Bard College
University of Chicago	Wesleyan University
College of the Atlantic	University of Oregon
New College–University of South Florida	Eugene Lang College
Claremont College–Pitzer College	University of California–Irvine
University of Connecticut–Main Campus	George Washington University
Guilford College	Hobart/William Smith College
Colorado College	American University

■ *Schools stuck in the 80's:*

Rose-Hulman Institute of Technology	California Institute of Technology
Brigham Young University	Wabash College
Furman University	Case Western Reserve University
Colorado School of Mines	Howard University
Baylor University	Austin College
Morehouse College	New Jersey Institute of Technology
Fisk University	Saint Joseph's University
Spelman College	Babson College
University of North Dakota	Sweet Briar College
Golden Gate College	Hampden-Sydney College

■ *Lots of sex (might be lying):*

Bennington College	Kenyon College
University of California–Santa Cruz	Union College
Denison University	Saint Lawrence University
Manhattanville College	Tulane University
West Virginia University	University of Vermont
Simon's Rock of Bard College	University of Rhode Island
SUNY Albany	Saint Bonaventure University
Rhode Island School of Design	Syracuse University
Sarah Lawrence College	Lehigh University
Bard College	SUNY Binghamton

■ *Saving it for marriage (might be lying):*

Brigham Young University	Auburn University
California Institute of Technology	Princeton University
University of Notre Dame	Pepperdine University
Deep Springs College	Harvard/Radcliffe College
Furman University	Case Western Reserve University
New Jersey Institute of Technology	University of Dayton
Golden Gate College	Wellesley College
Mount Holyoke College	Bryn Mawr College
Claremont College–Harvey Mudd	Cooper Union
Stanford University	Northeastern University

■ Nerd-vana:

California Institute of Technology
Claremont College–Harvey Mudd
Johns Hopkins University
Massachusetts Institute of Technology
Stevens Institute of Technology
Colorado School of Mines
Cooper Union
Rose-Hulman Institute of Technology
Rensselaer Institute of Technology
Oberlin College

New Jersey Institute of Technology
University of Chicago
Haverford College
Case Western Reserve University
Illinois Institute of Technology
University of Missouri–Rolla
Carleton College
Worcester Polytechnic Institute
Carnegie Mellon University
Wabash College

PART TWO

THE BEST
COLLEGES

What do students think about Adelphi University?

■ **Academics** Adelphi University is not for everybody, as some of our respondents found out too late. Students who come without a specific agenda are often disappointed; as these students rightly point out, they could get pretty much the same education from one of New York's fine state schools for a third to half the cost. However, for those serious about pursuing pre-professional studies—such as business administration and health sciences—Adelphi may be worth the extra money ("excellent career programs" said one area college counselor). Students looking for individual attention will certainly get more of it here than they would at a SUNY: "Small informal classes are the reason to come here, if you can afford it," said one undergrad. The university's program for the learning disabled was praised by all area counselors and has a well-deserved national reputation. Also notable is the school's core curriculum, which requires all students to take approximately one year's work of courses that take a comprehensive approach to the arts and sciences. The university is currently actively recruiting students from areas other than Long Island, an effort that may well bring Adelphi's reputation more in line with the hype on its t-shirt: "Adelphi, the Harvard of New York." Most student complaints concerned the library, the administration ("an out-of-touch pack of paper hounds"), and the cost. In general, students are satisfied with the level of instruction, which they find challenging but not overly demanding. Those students who achieve superior grades in their majors are encouraged to enroll in more difficult, graduate-level courses.

■ **Life** Adelphi is still a commuter school—most of its students grew up on Long Island and continue to live at home through school. Campus life gets pretty dead on weekends, and although New York City is only 40 minutes away by Long Island Railroad, not that many students take advantage of the Big Apple's proximity. Those who live on campus inhabit dorms and eat food that students graded "below average." Garden City "is quiet, safe, and provides a pleasant atmosphere for academics. Lots of good shopping," said one student. There are lots of bars nearby, but not within walking distance. The campus is dry, which "increases the number of drunk drivers on the road," according to one student, although drinking is not a big-time activity here anyway.

■ **Students** Although Adelphi has recently begun to pull in students from outside the New York/Long Island area, the student body still has a decidedly Long Island feel to it. Minority students are fairly well represented here: 10 percent of the students are black, another 5 percent are Hispanic. Students reported that campus race relations were "pretty good." Asked how happy they were, students gave themselves a "C+," well below the national average of "B."

ADELPHI UNIVERSITY

Admissions

The admissions department reports, "A composite score of 950 on the SAT, a 'B' cumulative grade point average, and rank in the top third of the graduating high school class are preferred. However, variances exist for special programs. The Admissions Committee carefully reviews and evaluates each application based on the abilities, purposes, and interests of the applicant." Essays, extracurricular activities, a personal interview, letters of recommendation, and "a record of leadership, personal, in tangible record form," are also considered. Adelphi is well known for its excellent programs for those with learning disabilities; in 1991, approximately seven percent of the entering class had some such disabilities. Students who apply to Adelphi most often also apply to Hofstra, St. John's University, NYU, and SUNY Stonybrook.

Financial Aid

The financial aid office at Adelphi University requires applicants to submit the FAF. The school's most recent catalog notes, "Adelphi offers a full range of scholarships. Scholarships are generally awarded to students which high academic records or expertise in a particular area." New York State residents are also eligible for a wide range of state-sponsored merit- and need-based grants. Eligible students are encouraged to apply for loans from the Stafford, Perkins, PLUS, and SLS loan programs. Part-time employment is available through the Financial Aid and Career Services offices.

A note from the Adelphi Admissions Office:

"Experience the life of Adelphi University—in the classroom, in faculty offices, in the library, in the dormitories, and on continuum. Features that make Adelphi an outstanding university include: an original curriculum enhanced by a core of liberal arts and science courses; a unique selection of distinctive academic and co-curricular programs tailored to meet individual needs and interests; a distinguished faculty who are not only involved in ongoing research and publishing, but who are dedicated to teaching and noted for establishing caring relationships with students; a diverse student body composed of more than 3000 undergraduates who represent approximately 30 states and 55 foreign countries; a campus located in a beautiful suburban town that is easily accessible to New York City— a metropolis rich in cultural and educational opportunities. Campus life will provide students with the opportunity to put ideas into practice. Experience Adelphi!"

ADMISSIONS FACTS

Competitiveness Rating:	**68**
% of applicants accepted:	67
% acceptees attending:	45

FRESHMAN PROFILE

Average verbal SAT:	490
Average math SAT:	540
Average ACT:	NA
Graduated top 10% of class:	8
Graduated top 25% of class:	41
Graduated top 50% of class:	89

DEADLINES

Early decision/action:	NA
Early dec./act. notif.:	NA
Regular admission:	rolling
Regular adm. notif.:	rolling

APPLICANTS ALSO LOOK AT

and often prefer:
CUNY–Queens College
NYU
Boston U.
SUNY Albany
SUNY Stonybrook
Columbia U.

and sometimes prefer:
St. John's U.
Hofstra U.

and rarely prefer:
Seton Hall U.

ADDRESS

Undergraduate Admissions
South Avenue
Garden City, NY 11530
516-877-3050

FINANCIAL FACTS

In-state tuition ($):	8,800
Out-of-state tuition ($):	8,800
Room & board ($):	4,920
FA application deadline:	5/1
% frosh receiving FA:	69
PT earnings per yr. ($):	1,500

TYPE OF AID: % of students ($)

FA of some kind:	63 (NA)
Need-based grants:	NA
Merit-based grants:	NA
Loans:	NA
Work study:	NA
Student rating of FA:	67

AGNES SCOTT COLLEGE

CAMPUS LIFE

Quality of Life Rating:	**89**
Type of school:	private
Affiliation:	Presbyterian
Environment:	suburban

STUDENT BODY

FT undergrad enrollment:	518
% male/% female:	0/100
% out-of-state:	47
% live on campus:	97
% African-American:	10
% Asian:	1
% Caucasian:	85
% Hispanic:	2
% foreign:	4
% transfers:	7

WHAT'S HOT

dorm comfort
financial aid
small classes (overall)
location
dating
gay community visible
profs outside class
profs in class
town-gown relations
gay community accepted
campus appearance

WHAT'S NOT

marijuana
intramural sports
library

ACADEMICS

Academic Rating:	**89**
Calendar:	semester
Student/teacher ratio:	8/1
% doctorates:	92
Profs interesting:	97
Profs accessible:	97
Hours of study per day:	3.61

MOST POPULAR MAJORS BY %

English:	18
Psychology:	18
International Relations:	11

% GRADS WHO PURSUE

Law:	5
MBA:	3
Medicine:	3
M.A., etc.:	22

What do students think about Agnes Scott College?

■ **Academics** Most really small schools are hamstrung in their efforts to offer students a full complement of studies. Tiny Agnes Scott, an all-women's school in Atlanta, however, allows students to cross-register at 18 other area colleges and universities. The result is that Scott students get "the best of both worlds: the friendly comforts of a small college and the opportunities of a larger school." Most students take the vast majority of their classes at Scott, where they enjoy a capable, energetic faculty. Explained one student, "The faculty is the highlight of the school. They are very interested in our education and enjoy building relationships with the students." Students here work hard and told us that "the class work isn't out of reach but it is very demanding." Warned one, "Scott is the paper-writing capital of the South. When you get here, be prepared to write." Despite the intense (and sometimes stressful) academic atmosphere, "competition among students is minimal. Instead, you are constantly pushed to improve your own performance regardless of your ranking in the class." Curricular highlights include the Global Awareness Program, which sends almost half of the undergraduates overseas for the "pleasantly unsettling experience" of discovering "that [their] view of the world is not universally shared." Students pursue traditional liberal arts and social science majors and live under an honor code that allows them to leave dorm doors unlocked and take tests unproctored. Summed up one student: "as a senior I can honestly say that I have learned far more about myself as an individual than I would have at a large co-educational institution. This school is dedicated to getting rid of the girl and educating women."

■ **Life** Agnes Scott is surrounded by so many large co-ed schools that its single-sex student body does not seem to negatively impact social life (as it often does at single-sex schools). Although one student reported that "developing a romantic relationship can prove difficult if you do not have the time or motivation to get involved with the Georgia Tech or Emory frat scene," most student responses emphasized students' access to "the opportunities of a big city with many area colleges: social events (frat parties), sporting events (football, basketball, baseball) and friendships." Scott's campus is among the nation's most beautiful. On-campus life centers around study and clubs ("we have many great leadership opportunities on campus," reported one student).

■ **Students** In their descriptions of each other, Scott students stress the air of camaraderie that permeates the campus. Wrote one, "Agnes Scott is great if you want to graduate having made a lot of friends that seem almost like family; the bonds formed here are unique." Black students (who are moderately well-represented in the student body) told us that "It's difficult being black on this campus. All activities are either geared toward the majority (white heterosexuals) or call for a lot of interaction with Emory or Tech." Students are relatively liberal, especially for Southerners.

AGNES SCOTT COLLEGE

Decatur, GA

Admissions

The admissions office reports "We consider every student on an individual basis and look for evidence of solid academic preparation, ability, motivation, maturity, and integrity. Every completed application—with its accompanying school transcript(s), recommendations, and standardized test results—will be read carefully." High school performance and standardized test scores are most important to admissions officers here; letters of recommendation, essays, and extracurricular activities are also considered. Agnes Scott does not require any specific high school courses but does recommend a rigorous college prep curriculum. The office also notes that "successful candidates for admission normally have graduated in the top quarter of their high school class." Applicants must provide scores for either the SAT or ACT. Applicants to Agnes Scott are often also applicants to University of Georgia, Emory, Georgia Tech, Vanderbilt, Rhodes, and Furman.

Financial Aid

Agnes Scott requires submission of a FAF and a copy of the most recent tax return. The school provides merit-based grants for academics and leadership to about one fifth of the student body, and half of all undergrads receive need-based grants. Loans recommended include Stafford (50% of all undergrads, an average value of $2750), SLS, Institutional, Agnes Scott Parent Loan Plan and PLUS. The financial aid office notes "Agnes Scott attempts to meet 100% of demonstrated need for all students who apply for aid by the stated deadlines. A new Middle Income Assistance Program offers grants to students based on academic achievement, activities and family resources for families with gross incomes from $40,000 to $80,000."

A note from the Agnes Scott Admissions Office:

"Agnes Scott's tradition of academic excellence continues today with a student body academically representative of the top women students in the nation. Agnes Scott has everything you need to get the most out of college. Personal attention from quality faculty—a faculty/student ratio of 8 to 1. Diversity—students come from 27 states and 17 foreign countries. Global Awareness programs offer Agnes Scott students international educational experiences. An honor code, governed by students, allows self-scheduled exams. State-of-the-art facilities and renovated dormitories. Atlanta—home of the 1996 Olympics."

ADMISSIONS FACTS

Competitiveness Rating:	**77**
% of applicants accepted:	81
% acceptees attending:	37

FRESHMAN PROFILE

Average verbal SAT:	523*
Average math SAT:	563*
Average ACT:	NA
Graduated top 10% of class:	47
Graduated top 25% of class:	72
Graduated top 50% of class:	93

DEADLINES

Early decision/action:	NA
Early dec./act. notif.:	NA
Regular admission:	3/1
Regular adm. notif.:	rolling

APPLICANTS ALSO LOOK AT

and often prefer:
North Carolina State U.
U. Tennessee–Knoxville

and sometimes prefer:
Creighton U.
Auburn U.
Florida State U.
Rhodes College
Furman U.
Sweet Briar College

and rarely prefer:
Hollins College

ADDRESS

Undergraduate Admissions
141 East College Avenue
Decatur, GA 30030-4298
800-235-6602

FINANCIAL FACTS

In-state tuition ($):	10,945
Out-of-state tuition ($):	10,945
Room & board ($):	4,515
FA application deadline:	5/1
% frosh receiving FA:	70
PT earnings per yr. ($):	1,200

TYPE OF AID: % of students ($):

FA of some kind:	70 (11,150)
Need-based grants:	55 (6,100)
Merit-based grants:	22 (4,300)
Loans:	57 (4,300)
Work study:	48 (1,175)
Student rating of FA:	95

CAMPUS LIFE

Quality of Life Rating: **76**

Type of school:	private/public
Affiliation:	none
Environment:	suburban

STUDENT BODY

FT undergrad enrollment:	1,845
% male/% female:	56/44
% out-of-state:	25
% live on campus:	85
% African-American:	4
% Asian:	1
% Caucasian:	93
% Hispanic:	1
% foreign:	3
% transfers:	6

WHAT'S HOT

gay community visible
cost of living
living on campus
marijuana
attending all classes
hard liquor
beer

WHAT'S NOT

college newspaper
caring about politics
religious clubs
location

ACADEMICS

Academic Rating: **89**

Calendar:	semester
Student/teacher ratio:	11/1
% doctorates:	82
Profs interesting:	84
Profs accessible:	82
Hours of study per day:	3.05

MOST POPULAR MAJORS BY %

Art:	20
Ceramic Engineering:	15
Business:	12

% GRADS WHO PURSUE

Law:	NA
MBA:	NA
Medicine:	NA
M.A., etc.:	27

What do students think about Alfred University?

■ **Academics** Alfred University is justifiably famous for its studies in ceramics and glassworks. How many schools offer even one major in these fields? AU offers three: ceramic art and design, engineering, and science. Furthermore, the ceramics program is publicly funded, and its students pay about one third the tuition those enrolled in the school's private divisions pay. Twelve percent of the students major in the visual and performing arts, but AU is not simply an art school. In fact, almost one fourth of the students are engineers, and there are large business and pre-med populations. Said one student, "it's amazing that such a fantastic education can be found in Grizzly Adams country." A demanding core curriculum requires that all students pursue a substantial liberal arts program in addition to the rigors of their majors. Students reported that classes are small, the administration is helpful, and professors are accessible and talented teachers. Reported one student (who seems destined for a career in public relations), "Take big school education and mix it comfortably with small school personal attention. Throw in a little small town security and you have the recipe for Alfred University. If you miss a lot of classes, you can expect to be contacted by your professor to find out why."

■ **Life** AU students probably wish the school were somewhere else. It's a testimony to the school's other fine qualities that its students scored well in our overall happiness category despite giving the surrounding area very low grades. Alfred and the nearby mountains are great for those who love outdoor activities, but with Rochester and Buffalo each almost two hours away (and with roadways icy much of the school year), urban distractions are hard to come by. Reported one student, "Alfred is a great small university. But if you want to have a wild time while in school, this is not the place." Students get bored in their spare time, as evidenced by the high popularity levels of beer, alcohol, and marijuana. Bring your Scrabble board.

■ **Students** Remote Alfred attracts few minority students: well over nine in ten students are white. The male to female ratio is 56 to 44, and boys who don't find girlfriends at Alfred will be hard-pressed to find them anywhere else in the area. Students reported that there is a noticeable gay community but that it is not well integrated into the mainstream of the Alfred student body. In fact, some would argue that there is no mainstream of the student body: reported one student, "Due to the small size of the university, there are many tight cliques and sometimes discriminatory groups. Students here are not altogether independent." Not everyone would agree, however, and quite a few respondents voiced more encouraging opinions. One such student wrote that "everyone is friendly and very accepting of the diverse group of people who are here."

ALFRED UNIVERSITY

Admissions

The admissions department reports that "Alfred University considers applications on an individual basis and pays particular attention to the unique qualities each applicant possesses...Candidates are encouraged to select challenging courses throughout their high school career." After high school curriculum, Alfred considers your grades and letters of recommendation as most important; test scores are reportedly relatively unimportant. Applicants must complete four years of English, three years of math, two years of science, and two years of social studies/history. Art and design applicants must also submit portfolios, which are reviewed and graded by a faculty committee. Alfred's 80 percent acceptance rate is deceptive: most students admitted here did very well in high school and on standardized tests. The reason so many get in is that only better students have heard of this place.

Financial Aid

The financial aid office at Alfred University requires applicants to submit the FAF and a form generated by the school. The school awards merit scholarships on the basis of academic excellence and/or artistic ability. Alfred students borrow money on the following plans: Perkins, Stafford, SLS, and EXCEL. Many columns in the FA sidebar contain double figures; the figure on the left pertains to the public New York State College of Ceramics, the figure on the right to the privately funded colleges.

A note from the Alfred Admissions Office:

"Alfred is a unique blend of both public and privately funded units. The Colleges of Business, Liberal Arts and Sciences, and Engineering and Professional Studies are private. The New York State College of Ceramics is composed of the School of Ceramic Engineering and the School of Art and Design. This blend of public and private provides Alfred students with access to the resources of New York's best public educational system, while maintaining the quality and close personal attention found only at private institutions."

ADMISSIONS FACTS

Competitiveness Rating:	**81**
% of applicants accepted:	68
% acceptees attending:	26

FRESHMAN PROFILE

Average verbal SAT:	539
Average math SAT:	602
Average ACT:	26
Graduated top 10% of class:	42
Graduated top 25% of class:	77
Graduated top 50% of class:	99

DEADLINES

Early decision/action:	12/1
Early dec/act. notif.:	12/15
Regular admission:	2/1
Regular adm. notif.:	3/1

APPLICANTS ALSO LOOK AT

and sometimes prefer:
SUNY Buffalo
SUNY Albany

and rarely prefer:
Clarkson U.
RIT
U. Mass–Amherst

ADDRESS

Undergraduate Admissions
Box 765
Alfred, NY 14802
607-871-2115

FINANCIAL FACTS

In-state tuition ($):	13,960
Out-of-state tuition ($):	13,960
Room & board ($):	4,470
FA application deadline:	5/1
% frosh receiving FA:	65
PT earnings per yr. ($):	800

TYPE OF AID: % of students ($):

FA of some kind:	65 (8,400)
Need-based grants:	NA
Merit-based grants:	NA
Loans:	NA
Work study:	NA
Student rating of FA:	84

AMERICAN UNIVERSITY

Washington, D.C.

CAMPUS LIFE

Quality of Life Rating:	**78**
Type of school:	private
Affiliation:	Methodist
Environment:	city

STUDENT BODY

FT undergrad enrollment:	5,874
% male/% female:	40/60
% out-of-state:	78
% live on campus:	60
% African-American:	6
% Asian:	3
% Caucasian:	75
% Hispanic:	4
% foreign:	12
% transfers:	5

WHAT'S HOT

location
caring about politics
diversity
dating
marriage
marijuana
Grateful Dead

WHAT'S NOT

cost of living
library
requirements are easy
overall happiness
campus appearance

ACADEMICS

Academic Rating:	**80**
Calendar:	semester
Student/teacher ratio:	14/1
% doctorates:	91
Profs interesting:	80
Profs accessible:	82
Hours of study per day:	3.2

MOST POPULAR MAJORS BY %

Social Sciences:	20
Communications:	10
Marketing & Distribution:	7

% GRADS WHO PURSUE

Law:	NA
MBA:	NA
Medicine:	NA
M.A., etc.:	33

What do students think about American University?

■ **Academics** For a long time location was considered the only major drawing card of AU, but the school's academic reputation and, accordingly, its applicant pool have recently been on the rise. Many students noted that although the school once had a reputation as a party school, that characterization no longer holds true. One student's response was typical: "This school has made a successful transition from a 'party school' into a fine academic institution. I find the classes challenging, stimulating, and interesting. Unfortunately, this trade-off has resulted in a striking and pervasive stagnation of the social scene." American's strongest programs are those related to government: professors and guest lecturers here are frequently government bigwigs or ex-bigwigs. Also notable is American's Cooperative Education Program, which serves about 500 students (in all majors, not just in business and technical fields) annually. The co-op program allows students to work at government offices, political think-tanks, broadcast networks, and arts agencies, and thereby gain valuable work experience while earning college credit.

■ **Life** Washington, D.C., is the magnet that draws many students to American University. Those who choose the school for this reason clearly aren't disappointed: American students were among the nation's happiest with their school's location. Said one student, "Washington, D.C., is a great place with a lot of action. At night you can go to one of dozens of bars and clubs rather than to some mandatory rush party." Others noted that D.C. affords students many opportunities for government-related jobs and internships. As is often the case at urban schools, school spirit is low, as is interest in intercollegiate sports. Washington certainly competes with AU for students' attention. But school spirit is probably also affected by the absence of "school spirits": AU's campus is dry. One effect of this policy has been, predictably, to drive the social scene off-campus and into frats and the city. Some students are fairly resentful of the situation. Students here smoke more pot than students elsewhere, perhaps because it's easier to smoke than to drink in dorms.

■ **Students** American students are particularly proud of the diverse make-up of their student body. Twelve percent of students here are foreign nationals. As one AU student put it, "American University is like a trip abroad—everyday we are in close contact with foreigners, especially those of us living in the international dorm. There's no way to escape the great diversity on campus, which makes up its own culture." Said another, "AU is the original melting pot, living and thriving in D.C." Still, a surprising number of respondents characterized their classmates as a homogeneous group of affluent white folks. More than a few complained that snobbery and ostentation are common here. The student body leans farther to the left than most, although the school is by no means a hotbed of radicalism.

AMERICAN UNIVERSITY

Admissions

American University's application notes that the academic credentials of entering students have consistently improved in recent years, and that as a result, academic achievement is the most important aspect of your application. But like many colleges in this book, American also looks beyond your numbers: "Motivation and seriousness of purpose are also factors in admission, and are often revealed in the level and rigor of courses you have taken, comments from your guidance counselor or teacher, and your commitment to other activities and accomplishments." American's admissions office ranked GPA (and academic record) as the most important part of the application, followed by standardized test scores, extracurriculars, letters of recommendation, interview, and essays. All applicants must submit SAT or ACT scores, and Achievements are recommended (the English Composition and Math II) for placement. American requires that your high school curriculum have included four units of English and three units of mathematics (including two in algebra). Also recommended are at least two units of lab science, three units of social studies, and two units of foreign language. Students who apply to American also often apply to George Washington, Georgetown, Boston U., and Syracuse.

Financial Aid

American University requires financial aid applicants to complete the FAF only. The school awards grants for academic and athletic merit (in '91–'92, 30% of all undergrads received such a grant; the average award was approximately $2,360). The school's financial aid office recommends loans to 35% of its students (breakdown not available). Among the scholarships available are Frederick Douglass Scholarships, which provide full or partial tuition to certain minority applicants (specifically defined by AU as "applicants who are of African-American, Hispanic, Asian, Alaskan Native, or Native American descent.") First preference on these scholarships is given to graduates of D.C. high schools, and then to graduates of high schools nationwide.

Excerpted from American University promotional materials:

"The American University is known as a truly international center of learning. Located in the most important and interesting capital in the world, we are respected for our approach to education—our faculty infuse classroom theory with professional experience, their research informs and inspires the world outside our gates, and our students test the abstract against reality through study abroad and Washington-area internships and cooperative education jobs. American is also noted as a place where differences in culture and in point of view are respected even while we celebrate the common experiences all members of the human family share."

ADMISSIONS FACTS

Competitiveness Rating:	**85**
% of applicants accepted:	23
% acceptees attending:	30

FRESHMAN PROFILE

Average verbal SAT:	548
Average math SAT:	587
Average ACT:	NA
Graduated top 10% of class:	35
Graduated top 25% of class:	77
Graduated top 50% of class:	95

DEADLINES

Early decision/action:	NA
Early dec./act. notif.:	NA
Regular admission:	2/1
Regular adm. notif.:	4/15

APPLICANTS ALSO LOOK AT

and often prefer:
U. NC–Chapel Hill
Northwestern U.
Emory U.

and sometimes prefer:
Catholic U. of America
Boston College
Goerge Washington U.
U. Maryland

and rarely prefer:
U. Delaware
Loyola Marymount U.

ADDRESS

Undergraduate Admissions
4400 Massachusetts Ave., NW
Washington, D.C. 20016-8001
202-885-6000

FINANCIAL FACTS

In-state tuition ($):	13,506
Out-of-state tuition ($):	13,506
Room & board ($):	5,972
FA application deadline:	3/1
% frosh receiving FA:	60
PT earnings per yr. ($):	1,200

TYPE OF AID: % of students ($):

FA of some kind:	60 (10,400)
Need-based grants:	30 (4,714)
Merit-based grants:	30 (2,360)
Loans:	35 (5,051)
Work study:	NA
Student rating of FA:	71

AMHERST COLLEGE

CAMPUS LIFE

Quality of Life Rating: **88**

Type of school:	private
Affiliation:	none
Environment:	small town

STUDENT BODY

FT undergrad enrollment:	1,561
% male/% female:	55/45
% out-of-state:	84
% live on campus:	97
% African-American:	6
% Asian:	8
% Caucasian:	76
% Hispanic:	6
% foreign:	3
% transfers:	1

WHAT'S HOT

deans
administration (overall)
honesty
requirements easy
profs in class
gay community accepted
dorm comfort
small classes (overall)
leftist politics
overall happiness

WHAT'S NOT

fraternities/sororities
catalog
dating
working a job

ACADEMICS

Academic Rating: **91**

Calendar:	semester
Student/teacher ratio:	9/1
% doctorates:	82
Profs interesting:	94
Profs accessible:	89
Hours of study per day:	3.46

MOST POPULAR MAJORS BY %

Social Sciences:	23
Letters/Literature:	21
Life Sciences:	12

% GRADS WHO PURSUE

Law:	9
MBA:	1
Medicine:	11
M.A., etc.:	30

What do students think about Amherst College?

■ **Academics** Professors are the heart and soul of the solid liberal arts education available at Amherst College. They garner rave reviews from students, who describe them as "outstanding," "concerned," and "friendly." Small classes, mostly taught by the professors themselves, maximize the learning experience and ensure the faculty's accessibility. Enthused one sophomore, "I spend about two hours a week talking with a chemistry professor whom I consider a very good friend. I don't think that happens very often at big schools." Students here work hard, but don't feel they are competing for grades; most truly consider learning to be its own reward. (Wrote one student, "There is pressure here but it comes from yourself. Students are stressed out, but it's because most are incredibly active.") "Incredibly active" indeed; Amherst students enjoy the many opportunities to get involved that the school's size affords them. Remarked one, "Amherst allows me to do so many things I could never do on a large campus: play two sports, or be student treasurer and editor of a magazine and also row crew." When students tire of their small college community, it is easy to take a class or audition for a play at one of the other four schools in the Five College Consortium (UMass-Amherst, Smith, Hampshire, and Mount Holyoke); the Five College system, according to students, "gives you all the opportunities of a large university, without any of the drawbacks."

■ **Life** Several years ago, fraternities and sororities were abolished at Amherst. This move by the administration has had a dampening effect on campus social life; one student described the current social scene as "nonexistent." The last few years have been trying ones, as "socially Amherst is still struggling to find its niche. Students turn to small private parties to make up for the lack of campus events." Weekend "tap" parties (usually beer-oriented and held in upperclass dorms) are "still well-attended (especially by Five College women)." Despite the voids in their social world, students are still committed to the Amherst tradition of playing hard, and report overall that they are extremely happy. With their own lovely campus, the small town of Amherst and the four other colleges at their doorsteps, students at Amherst will find plenty of diversions.

■ **Students** Amherst is definitely a culture mix, boasting a minority population that constitutes almost one quarter of the student body. Although most are proud of this surprisingly diverse populace, there are scattered complaints that most students are still from the upper- or upper-middle classes. ("Ethnic and social diversity are different. Amherst is ethnically diverse, but most come from the same socioeconomic levels," explained one student.) There is some truth to the reputation of Amherst students for looking like "J. Clones," but the efforts of the administration in this area are admirable indeed, especially in relation to those of some other colleges we have seen.

AMHERST COLLEGE

Admissions

From Amherst's undergraduate catalogue: "Although admission to Amherst College is highly competitive, there is no rigid formula for gaining admission. We are particularly interested in students with a strong intellectual perspective and curiosity about a broad range of knowledge. We seek applicants from a variety of races, classes, ethnic and economic groups, whose multiple perspectives will contribute significantly to a process of mutual education both in and outside the classroom." Strongly recommended in your high school curriculum: four years of English, mathematics through pre-calculus; three or four years of a single foreign language; two years of history and social science; and at least two years of natural science, including one year of a lab science. "We evaluate candidates in terms of both achievement and promise, emphasizing the extent to which the students has taken advantage of educational opportunities presented." Applicants are required to take three Achievement tests (one should be English Composition, with or without the essay), and either the SAT or ACT.

Financial Aid

Financial aid applicants to Amherst must complete the FAF and a form generated by Amherst's financial aid office, and submit copies of their parents' W-2 forms. All grants awarded by Amherst are need-based only. Over a third of the undergrads at Amherst receive scholarship grants, and about 40% receive loan and employment assistance. According to the undergraduate catalog, after allowances have been made for family and student contributions from savings and income, the "self-help" level which the student is expected to fulfill via college employment and long-term loans is roughly $3,800. In addition to Stafford and Perkins loans, Amherst offers its own institutional loan.

Excerpted from Amherst College promotional materials:

"Amherst College looks, above all, for men and women of intellectual promise who have demonstrated qualities of mind and character that will enable them to take full advantage of the College's curriculum.... Admission decisions aim to select from among the many qualified applicants those possessing the intellectual talent, mental discipline, and imagination that will allow them most fully to benefit from the curriculum and to contribute to the life of the College and of society. Whatever the form of academic experience—lecture course, seminar, conference, studio, laboratory, independent study at various levels—intellectual competence and awareness of problems and methods are the goals of the Amherst program, rather than the direct preparation for a profession."

ADMISSIONS FACTS

Competitiveness Rating:	**99**
% of applicants accepted:	20
% acceptees attending:	44

FRESHMAN PROFILE

Average verbal SAT:	642
Average math SAT:	678
Average ACT:	30
Graduated top 10% of class:	88
Graduated top 25% of class:	97
Graduated top 50% of class:	100

DEADLINES

Early decision/action:	11/5
Early dec./act. notif.:	NA
Regular admission:	1/1
Regular adm. notif.:	4/15

APPLICANTS ALSO LOOK AT

and often prefer:
Harvard/Radcliffe College
Yale U.
Princeton U.

and sometimes prefer:
Dartmouth College
U. Mass–Amherst
Brown U.

and rarely prefer:
U. Virginia
Vassar College
Tufts U.

ADDRESS

Undergraduate Admissions
Amherst, MA 01002
413-542-2328

FINANCIAL FACTS

In-state tuition ($):	15,515
Out-of-state tuition ($):	15,515
Room & board ($):	4,400
FA application deadline:	2/1
% frosh receiving FA:	40
PT earnings per yr. ($):	1,250

TYPE OF AID: % of students ($):

FA of some kind:	40 (NA)
Need-based grants:	43 (12,878)
Merit-based grants:	NA
Loans:	NA (2,162)
Work study:	NA
Student rating of FA:	92

UNIVERSITY OF ARIZONA

Tucson, AZ

CAMPUS LIFE

Quality of Life Rating:	**73**
Type of school:	public
Affiliation:	none
Environment:	city

STUDENT BODY

FT undergrad enrollment:	22,743
% male/% female:	52/48
% out-of-state:	30
% live on campus:	75
% African-American:	2
% Asian:	4
% Caucasian:	79
% Hispanic:	10
% foreign:	3
% transfers:	11

WHAT'S HOT

cost of living
dating
Top 40
intercollegiate sports
rap/hip-hop

WHAT'S NOT

TAs teach intros
TAs teach upper-levels
honest students
small classes (overall)
attending all classes
living on campus
small labs and seminars

ACADEMICS

Academic Rating:	**72**
Calendar:	semester
Student/teacher ratio:	17/1
% doctorates:	87
Profs interesting:	65
Profs accessible:	64
Hours of study per day:	2.73

MOST POPULAR MAJORS BY %

Business & Management:	26
Engineering:	11
Social Sciences:	10

% GRADS WHO PURSUE

Law:	NA
MBA:	NA
Medicine:	NA
M.A., etc.:	35

What do students think about the University of Arizona?

■ **Academics** Although the University of Arizona has a long-standing reputation as a party school, its academic strengths are many. Students here can obtain an excellent undergraduate education if they know where to look. The temptations to "slack off" here are many—a beautiful, palm-tree laden campus, gorgeous weather, and many classmates whose attitude towards academics is casual—and serious students must learn to resist these long enough to get their work done. If they do, the rewards can be great. The U of A boasts several outstanding offerings, including a very demanding engineering program, and renowned departments in astronomy, cell biology, chemistry, English, nursing, and most of the social sciences. One student wrote, "The U of A is a good school for students who know exactly what they want to major in, don't need career guidance, and are personally motivated. No spoon feeding here!" Self-discipline is especially key given that the average student here is not particularly studious. If you want to blow off work, no one will stop you. Other drawbacks: most classes are extremely large and are often taught by teaching assistants. Overall, students gave professors average marks for those at a public university. Many agree that if students take the initiative, faculty members are willing to help. One sophomore enthused, "The teachers are great and almost always available."

■ **Life** As one student put it, "On campus there is ALWAYS something to do." Outdoor activities abound in this resort-like environment. With approximately 300 days of sunshine per year (one student speculated that there were about 360), parties and concerts can be held outside in all seasons. Social life here is continuous and lively and the university's reputation for partying is well-deserved. Fraternities and sororities are popular, but certainly not the only options. Some students live on campus, but dorm rooms are small and hard to get. Most upperclassmen move to nearby apartments. A sort of "reverse commute" occurs at the U of A as off-campus students flock to the school on the weekends for social events, sometimes in greater numbers than during the week for classes. Sports are very big at the U of A, "particularly men's basketball and football," according to student fans. Most agree that a car is necessary for getting around, and for making road trips (skiing, surfing and drinking for those under 21 are all available only a few hours away in various directions). The city of Tucson did not garner positive reviews ("Tucson is a hole"), but that may be the only aspect of life that students do not enjoy. In general, the University of Arizona is a happy, fun-loving place to spend four years.

■ **Students** Most students here are from Arizona, but the out-of-state contingent is growing. U of A boasts a 21 percent minority population, about half of which is made up of Latino students.

UNIVERSITY OF ARIZONA

Admissions

The admissions office reports that "expectancy formulas and GPA and test score cut-offs are used," but did not provide those formulae to us. Based on UArizona's admissions rate and other data available to us, we estimate the SAT cut-off at 850 (combined score) and ACT at 19 (composite) for in-state applicants, 1000/23 for out-of-state residents. UArizona also considers essays, letters of recommendation, and extracurricular activities in the admissions process. Applicants must have completed four years of English, three years of math, and two years each of science and social studies. Admissions decisions are decided on a rolling basis. Applicants to UArizona most often also apply to UColorado–Boulder, UCLA, USC, and UC–San Diego.

Financial Aid

The financial aid office at the University of Arizona requires applicants to submit either the FAF, the FFS, or the USAF Singlefile Form. Merit-based grants are awarded in numerous categories, including academics (16% received such a grant; average value: $1,948) and athletics (1.5%; $10,460). The school's bulletin notes that "Departmental scholarships are often available, and [students] are encouraged to make direct contact with their academic departments for information." Students participate in a number of loan programs, including Stafford, PLUS, SLS, NSL, and HPSL. The deadline listed in the FA sidebar is a priority deadline.

A note from the University of Arizona Admissions Office:

"The University of Arizona has steadily grown to become the nation's fifteenth ranked public research university. A world leader in astronomy, space science, medicine, anthropology, classical archaeology, cognitive science, arid land management, systems engineering, and more, the University has vigorously turned its attention to the education of its undergraduates.

"To initiate better out-of-classroom contact with students, ten University faculty have established offices in residence halls. Students are encouraged to become involved with faculty by assisting them in research projects. Extensive internship and Cooperative Education programs are established to provide students with invaluable work-related experience. Socially and culturally, the University offers hundreds of activities, with something for every political, religious, and academic interest.

"The focus here is on you, and substantial programs are available to assist you: from adjusting to college life and studying; to academic advising; to interviewing for jobs in your senior year. Extensive support is available and is there for the asking."

ADMISSIONS FACTS

Competitiveness Rating:	**73**
% of applicants accepted:	71
% acceptees attending:	42

FRESHMAN PROFILE

Average verbal SAT:	480
Average math SAT:	533
Average ACT:	23
Graduated top 10% of class:	32
Graduated top 25% of class:	63
Graduated top 50% of class:	91

DEADLINES

Early decision/action:	NA
Early dec./act. notif.:	11/1, 12/1
Regular admission:	3/1
Regular adm. notif.:	rolling

APPLICANTS ALSO LOOK AT

and often prefer:
UC Irvine
U. Washington

and sometimes prefer:
U. Wisconsin
U. Ohio
U. Iowa

and rarely prefer:
Baylor U.
Arizona State U.

ADDRESS

Undergraduate Admissions
Tucson, AZ 85721
602-621-3237

FINANCIAL FACTS

In-state tuition ($):	1,528
Out-of-state tuition ($):	6,934
Room & board ($):	3,702
FA application deadline:	3/1
% frosh receiving FA:	37
PT earnings per yr. ($):	NA

TYPE OF AID: % of students ($)

FA of some kind:	33 (NA)
Need-based grants:	NA (1,820)
Merit-based grants:	NA
Loans:	37 (4,045)
Work study:	2 (1,000)
Student rating of FA:	72

ARIZONA STATE UNIVERSITY

Tempe, AZ

CAMPUS LIFE

Quality of Life Rating: **74**

Type of school:	public
Affiliation:	none
Environment:	city

STUDENT BODY

FT undergrad enrollment:	23,840
% male/% female:	52/48
% out-of-state:	27
% live on campus:	12
% African-American:	3
% Asian:	3
% Caucasian:	82
% Hispanic:	7
% foreign:	4
% transfers:	14

WHAT'S HOT

suitcase syndrome
working a job
dating
conservative politics
good looking students

WHAT'S NOT

TAs teach intros
living on campus
small labs and seminars
college theater groups
honesty
campus is easy to get around
catalog

ACADEMICS

Academic Rating: **67**

Calendar:	semester
Student/teacher ratio:	19/1
% doctorates:	68
Profs interesting:	69
Profs accessible:	71
Hours of study per day:	3.07

MOST POPULAR MAJORS BY %

Business & Management:	30
Social Sciences:	12
Public Affairs & Protective Svcs:	8

What do students think about Arizona State University?

■ **Academics** One student summed up the ASU experience this way: "There is an education for you here. The teaching is excellent and the facilities superior. Nothing, however, is handed to you; you must want an education and seek it out. With 45,000 students, the majority of the student body is focused on socializing rather than learning." That's ASU in a nutshell: a fine school with plenty of opportunities for a great education and even more opportunities to have a good time. One quarter of the students pursue business-related degrees in an excellent, well-funded program ("the school basically caters to business majors," complained an elementary education student). The engineering college, attended by 6% of undergrads, is also nationally renowned. For an institution with a "party school" reputation, students work pretty hard: they average over three hours of study a day, and indicated that they take class attendance and course reading seriously. Their complaints focused on the sometimes difficult-to-negotiate bureaucracy (wrote one respondent, "the red tape gets pretty tangled. It's the part of college life that causes a lot of stress—but, you'll get through"). As is often the case at large public universities, space in required courses is too frequently limited, causing a lot of frustration for upperclassmen. Said one, "it is much easier to get the schedule you want when you're a freshman or sophomore. One can come to a standstill in his education if classes are full. In my case, the registrar incorrectly processed my pre-registration, but I'm still the one who has to fight for my classes." Still, going to a large school also has its benefits, as one undergrad explained: "It's a pleasure to attend a school that offers so many services, such as Mac and IBM computers, the finest rec center in the country, a fantastic campus paper, and literally hundreds of clubs to be involved with."

■ **Life** Commenting on the quality of life, one student told us, "ASU is a country club; who wouldn't want to come here?" The school has excellent sports and recreation facilities, a "beautiful, nondepressing campus," and weather that is "warm and sunny 340 days of the year." No wonder most students told us that they're having a great time. Fraternities and sororities are active participants in the school's social life, but they are by no means the only game in town. Many students live off-campus (there's limited availability of dorms), and parties in their apartment complexes are plentiful; the city of Tempe also offers a wide choice of nightspots. Most students come here knowing that ASU is a party school, and, while they don't ignore their studies, they certainly find time to pursue an active social life of partying and dating.

■ **Students** With over 30,000 undergraduates, ASU has a student body that's not easy to categorize. Most of the students are Arizona natives and, like most Arizona residents, they are politically very conservative. The stereotypical Sun Devil is relatively affluent and deeply involved in the Greek system.

ARIZONA STATE UNIVERSITY

Admissions

"Admission standards are competitive and you are expected to have excellent academic records" according to Arizona State's brochure. Applicants to the university must have a cumulative high school GPA of at least 3.0, and should have graduated in the top 25% of their high school class. All students applying must submit SAT or ACT scores. The recommended high school curriculum includes four years of English, three years of mathematics, and two years each of social science and lab science. Applicants to the Liberal Arts and Science College should also have taken two years of a foreign language.

Financial Aid

Financial aid applicants to Arizona State University must complete the FAF, FFA or SingleFile (USAF), and submit a copy of their parents' most recent return. The school awards athletic scholarships (1% of all undergrads received one last year; the average value was $7,000) and academic scholarships (14% of all undergrads received one; average value $1,335). Among the other merit-based scholarship awards offered by the school are those for "general academics," leadership, music, debate, and dance (14% of all undergrads received one of these other awards; average value: $1,335). The loan office at ASU recommended Stafford loans to 45% of those applying for financial aid in '90–'91; they also recommend PLUS, SLS, Perkins, and TERI loans. The deadline for priority consideration is March 1.

A note from the Arizona State Admissions Office:

"Each semester more than 42,000 students from 120 countries and 50 states choose to study at ASU, the sixth largest university in the United States.

"We are proud to offer nationally recognized programs in Solid State Electronics, Geochemistry, Exercise Science, Preventive Psychology, Dance, Creative Writing, and many more. Our research facilities include the $13 million Engineering Research Center, one of only eight University Research Centers in the United States.

"We strive to ensure that each and every student receives a challenging and rewarding educational experience at ASU. By offering you a wide variety of academic programs, modern facilities, cultural experiences, student services and activities, we believe you will see *that there's a place for you at ASU.*"

ADMISSIONS FACTS

Competitiveness Rating:	**65**
% of applicants accepted:	77
% acceptees attending:	40

FRESHMAN PROFILE

Average verbal SAT:	448
Average math SAT:	512
Average ACT:	22
Graduated top 10% of class:	23
Graduated top 25% of class:	47
Graduated top 50% of class:	80

DEADLINES

Early decision/action:	NA
Early dec./act. notif.:	NA
Regular admission:	6/15
Regular adm. notif.:	rolling

APPLICANTS ALSO LOOK AT

and often prefer:
UCLA
U. Colorado

and sometimes prefer:
U. Minnesota
UC Irvine
U. Arizona

and rarely prefer:
San Diego State U.
Northern Arizona State U.
UC Davis

ADDRESS

Undergraduate Admissions
Tempe, AZ 85287-0112
602-965-7788

FINANCIAL FACTS

In-state tuition ($):	1,528
Out-of-state tuition ($):	6,934
Room & board ($):	3,638
FA application deadline:	3/1
% frosh receiving FA:	55
PT earnings per yr. ($):	1,543

TYPE OF AID: % of students ($):

FA of some kind:	60 (NA)
Need-based grants:	NA (8,200)
Merit-based grants:	NA
Loans:	44 (3,600)
Work study:	12 (2,280)
Student rating of FA:	75

COLLEGE OF THE ATLANTIC

Bar Harbor, ME

CAMPUS LIFE

Quality of Life Rating: **95**

Type of school:	private
Affiliation:	none
Environment:	island

STUDENT BODY

FT undergrad enrollment:	201
% male/% female:	44/56
% out-of-state:	80
% live on campus:	30
% African-American:	<1
% Asian:	1
% Caucasian:	98
% Hispanic:	1
% foreign:	3
% transfers:	10

WHAT'S HOT

gay community accepted
campus appearance
food
leftist politics
honesty
in-class discussion
Grateful Dead
small classes (overall)
marijuana
dorm comfort
profs outside class

WHAT'S NOT

fraternities/sororities
college radio station
intercollegiate sports

ACADEMICS

Academic Rating: **80**

Calendar:	other
Student/teacher ratio:	10/1
% doctorates:	62
Profs interesting:	94
Profs accessible:	97
Hours of study per day:	3.54

MOST POPULAR MAJOR BY %

Human Ecology:	100

% GRADS WHO PURSUE

Law:	NA
MBA:	NA
Medicine:	NA
M.A., etc.:	10

What do students think about College of the Atlantic?

■ **Academics** College of the Atlantic, a tiny college nestled in Maine's rocky coastline (on Mount Desert Island), offers its 200+ students degrees in a single major: Human Ecology. COA's alternative, interdisciplinary approach wins raves from most participants, who love the focus and "self-directed" nature of their education. Mainly, courses deal with the relationships of humans to marine and ecological issues; the handful of full-time professors are all experts in these and related topics. Because of its small size, COA boasts exceptional faculty-student relationships. Most students call instructors by their first names and feel like "equals in the classroom; we're not like sponges at the mercy of a professor." Within the broad range encompassed by Human Ecology, students are free to design their own programs of concentration. Remarked one glowingly, "if you want control of your education (instead of enrolling with a 10-page book of requirements) and are motivated enough to do what it takes, you can really get a lot out of this place." Dedication is key; grades are given only at the student's request, so students must be self-motivated to keep up with the workload here. Warned one, "If you're not a self-starter, don't come here."

■ **Life** Many COA students agree that their island is "the most beautiful place in the whole world." Students ranked it the nation's most beautiful campus, with every respondent giving it an "A" for beauty. The excellent dining hall (which serves the second best college food in the country, according to our surveys) offers a spectacular view of the island, attesting to the students' good taste in surroundings. Students here are in love with the outdoors, and spend as much time as possible there. It's not uncommon to see people biking to school or walking down by the ocean in 10-degree weather, and new arrivals are urged to "bring all their camping, hiking and canoeing equipment!" The closely knit "family atmosphere" of COA also allows students a "unique opportunity to explore democracy" through the college's "self-governance system, which is based on the New England town meeting." Only first-year students live in dorms, although more residential halls are under construction; most others live in nearby Bar Harbor. The social scene is soft-pedaled here, with a decided lack of mainstream college activities (no fraternities, sororities, beer bashes, etc.—although that ever-popular mainstay, pot-smoking, is alive and well). But the "self-starter" attitude carries over to social life, and people enjoy finding their own ways to have fun.

■ **Students** Students at COA tend to be white, politically left-leaning, accepting of the boisterous gay population, and generally happy with their choice of college. Bar Harbor in winter is quite an isolated, sheltered place, however, and some worry about the future: "Due to COA's size and uniform student population, it is easy to universalize problems and think of cute, idealistic solutions. I wonder if I will be adequately prepared for the real world after graduation."

COLLEGE OF THE ATLANTIC

Bar Harbor, ME

Admissions

College of Atlantic states that "Gaining admission to COA is a process of careful selection—both on the student's part and on the part of the College. COA is not for everyone, and for this reason we urge applicants to learn as much as they can about the College before applying. We're looking for imaginative, idealistic, intellectually curious, genuinely concerned young people—people who want their lives to make a difference in the world." At COA, the admissions committee first looks at your essays and high school transcript, as well as your interest in the COA program. These are followed by your interview and letters of recommendation. The interview is not required, but is strongly recommended. SAT or ACT scores are also not required, but are "helpful in assessing the academic ability of students from schools which do not give grades or have nontraditional programs."

Financial Aid

College of the Atlantic requires that you submit the FAF and copies of your and your parents' most recent tax returns. All grants are need-based only. The deadline of February 15 is not a hard deadline, but "a recommended deadline for priority consideration." A typical aid package from the school "might contain a combination of a COA grant, Stafford Student Loan, and a work study award." COA also offers a school-sponsored loan, available through the financial aid office. The deadline listed in the FA sidebar is a *priority* date.

A note from the College of the Atlantic Admissions Office:

"College of the Atlantic (Bar Harbor, ME) is a four-year liberal arts college, offering as its sole degree a Bachelor of Arts in Human Ecology. Located on Mount Desert Island and half a mile from Acadia National Park, students are encouraged to use the island as a classroom, while actively participating in their education. Programs in public policy, education, and marine biology offer the opportunity to study and work with the town community on both social and environmental issues."

ADMISSIONS FACTS

Competitiveness Rating:	**71**
% of applicants accepted:	70
% acceptees attending:	46

FRESHMAN PROFILE

Average verbal SAT:	541
Average math SAT:	547
Average ACT:	NA
Graduated top 10% of class:	33
Graduated top 25% of class:	48
Graduated top 50% of class:	85

DEADLINES

Early decision/action:	NA
Early dec./act. notif.:	NA
Regular admission:	3/1
Regular adm. notif.:	rolling

APPLICANTS ALSO LOOK AT

and often prefer:
Tufts U.
Bard College

and sometimes prefer:
Evergreen State College
Marlboro College
Hampshire College
Eckerd College

and rarely prefer:
U. New Hampshire
U. Maine
U. Rhode Island

ADDRESS

Undergraduate Admissions
105 Eden Street
Bar Harbor, ME 04609
207-288-5015

FINANCIAL FACTS

In-state tuition ($):	10,380
Out-of-state tuition ($):	10,380
Room & board ($):	3,200
FA application deadline:	2/15
% frosh receiving FA:	65
PT earnings per yr. ($):	1,200

TYPE OF AID: % of students ($):

FA of some kind:	65 (8,671)
Need-based grants:	68 (4,234)
Merit-based grants:	NA
Loans:	NA
Work study:	46(1,800)
Student rating of FA:	96

AUBURN UNIVERSITY

CAMPUS LIFE

Quality of Life Rating: **69**

Type of school:	public
Affiliation:	none
Environment:	suburban

STUDENT BODY

FT undergrad enrollment:	16,926
% male/% female:	55/45
% out-of-state:	40
% live on campus:	17
% African-American:	4
% Asian:	1
% Caucasian:	93
% Hispanic:	1
% foreign:	1
% transfers:	4

WHAT'S HOT
marriage
working a job
cost of living
prudes
religious clubs
intercollegiate sports

WHAT'S NOT
diversity
food

ACADEMICS

Academic Rating: **70**

Calendar:	quarterly
Student/teacher ratio:	17/1
% doctorates:	81
Profs interesting:	65
Profs accessible:	65
Hours of study per day:	2.92

MOST POPULAR MAJORS BY %

Business & Management:	27
Engineering:	20
Education:	12

% GRADS WHO PURSUE

Law:	3
MBA:	8
Medicine:	1
M.A., etc.:	15

What do students think about Auburn University?

■ **Academics** Auburn University, located in the heart of Alabama, is very much a product of its region. Tradition, conservatism, school spirit, and an academic philosophy that strongly emphasizes the pragmatic are the hallmarks both of the university and its students. Because it is a land-grant institution, Auburn focuses on, and excels in, agricultural studies: Agricultural engineering and veterinary medicine are both considered superior by students and independent counselors. Also highly regarded are the schools of architecture, pharmacy, nursing, and engineering; the business school is considered "up and coming." A very large university, Auburn is subdivided by field of specialization into 11 smaller schools; all students, however, must complete a core program that requires study in math, science, social science, the fine arts, literature, and writing. As at most large schools, students at Auburn complained that their teachers were both uninspiring in class and difficult to get extra help from outside of class—professors here ranked among the bottom 20 in both categories in our survey. On the positive side, students noted that the school is extremely affordable, especially for native Alabamans.

■ **Life** As a school of 20,000, Auburn is able to provide a vast array of activities to its students. Opportunities to participate in jazz bands, classical ensembles, choruses and choirs, theater and dance companies, and TV, radio, and newspaper production are there for anyone who is so inclined. The students' main rallying point, however, is the football team; the Tigers, who have produced such superstars as Bo Jackson, are immensely popular with the students. Other sporting events are also well attended as well; men's basketball, in particular, is a popular and well-supported program. Auburn's 31 fraternities and 18 sororities figure prominently in the school's social scene and also provide housing for many of the 80 percent of students who do not live on campus. Students gave the town of Auburn (pop. 30,000) below average grades, calling it "friendly but too quiet." Montgomery, a city of 200,000, is about an hour away by car. When students yearn for the "big city," they head for Atlanta, about two and a half hours away.

■ **Students** For a public university, Auburn does a good job of drawing out-of-state students; about one third of Auburn's undergrads come from outside Alabama (mostly from neighboring states). Auburn does a less admirable job of attracting minority students, however; despite the fact that 25 percent of Alabama's residents are black, African-Americans make up only 4 percent of the Auburn student body. Respondents reported that on-campus race relations—what few opportunities exist for them—are strained. Apparently, for better and worse, Auburn maintains the traditions of the South.

AUBURN UNIVERSITY

Admissions

According to Auburn's information brochure, "Entrance requirements are based primarily on a combination of high school records and college ability test scores from either the ACT or SAT. Special admission opportunities are available to applicants who do not meet regular entrance requirements. A preprinted application and notice of acceptance will be mailed to all prospective freshmen in Alabama who meet a required grade point average, have attained a minimum required SAT or ACT score, and have requested ACT or SAT to include Auburn as a score recipient." As of 1990, the high school curriculum requirements are four years of English, three years of mathematics (including Algebra I and II and either geometry, trigonometry, or calculus), two years of science (one year of biology and one year of physics), and three years of social studies. Recommended are an additional year each of science and social studies and a year of a foreign language. All applicants must submit SAT or ACT scores.

Financial Aid

Financial aid applicants to Auburn must complete the FFS and a form generated by Auburn's financial aid office. In '91–'92, 8% of all undergrads received an athletic scholarship; the average value was $1,081. Scholarships are also available for talent, residency, academic or leadership merit, and minorities. Auburn employs over 2,500 students on its campus. In addition to Stafford and Perkins loans, Auburn offers its own institutional loans, and recommends PLUS and SLS loans.

Excerpted from Auburn University promotional materials:

"Auburn University is a comprehensive land-grant university serving Alabama and the nation. The University is especially charged with the responsibility of enhancing the economic, social, and cultural development of the state through its instruction, research, and extension programs. In all of these programs the University is committed to the pursuit of excellence.

"The University assumes an obligation to provide an environment of learning in which the individual and society are enriched by the discovery, preservation, transmission, and application of knowledge; in which students grow intellectually as they study and do research under the guidance of a competent faculty; and in which the faculty develops professionally and contributes fully to the intellectual life of the institution, community, and state. This obligation unites Auburn University's continuing commitment to its land-grant traditions and the institution's role as a dynamic and complex comprehensive university."

ADMISSIONS FACTS

Competitiveness Rating:	**70**
% of applicants accepted:	79
% acceptees attending:	44

FRESHMAN PROFILE

Average verbal SAT:	509
Average math SAT:	579
Average ACT:	24
Graduated top 10% of class:	23
Graduated top 25% of class:	58
Graduated top 50% of class:	85

DEADLINES

Early decision/action:	12/1
Early dec./act. notif.:	NA
Regular admission:	9/1
Regular adm. notif.:	rolling

APPLICANTS ALSO LOOK AT

and often prefer:
North Carolina State U.
Clemson U.
Furman U.
Georgia Tech
Vanderbilt U.

and sometimes prefer:
U. Tennessee–Knoxville
Florida State U.

and rarely prefer:
U. Alabama

ADDRESS

Undergraduate Admissions
Auburn U., AL 36849-3501
205-844-4080

FINANCIAL FACTS

In-state tuition ($):	1,596
Out-of-state tuition ($):	4,788
Room & board ($):	3,167
FA application deadline:	3/15
% frosh receiving FA:	55
PT earnings per yr. ($):	2,000

TYPE OF AID: % of students ($):

FA of some kind:	45 (NA)
Need-based grants:	NA (1,659)
Merit-based grants:	NA
Loans:	34 (2,748)
Work study:	4 (1530)
Student rating of FA:	76

AUSTIN COLLEGE

Sherman, TX

CAMPUS LIFE

Quality of Life Rating: **80**

Type of school:	private
Affiliation:	Presbyterian
Environment:	city

STUDENT BODY

FT undergrad enrollment:	1,188
% male/% female:	51/49
% out-of-state:	10
% live on campus:	70
% African-American:	2
% Asian:	3
% Caucasian:	89
% Hispanic:	4
% foreign:	1
% transfers:	2

WHAT'S HOT

profs in class
attending all classes
doing all the reading
campus easy to get around
small lectures
profs outside class
interaction
hard liquor

WHAT'S NOT

college radio station
location
Grateful Dead
food
gay community visible
town-gown relations

ACADEMICS

Academic Rating: **80**

Calendar:	4-1-4
Student/teacher ratio:	14/1
% doctorates:	80
Profs interesting:	97
Profs accessible:	91
Hours of study per day:	3.55

MOST POPULAR MAJORS BY %

Business & Management:	25
Social Sciences:	22
Life Sciences:	12

% GRADS WHO PURSUE

Law:	6
MBA:	3
Medicine:	8
M.A., etc.:	23

What do students think about Austin College?

■ **Academics** Austin College (located in a suburb north of Dallas, NOT in Austin) is a small liberal arts school "big enough to have facilities that larger schools have but small enough that you can really get to know the faculty and other students." Students here are "highly competitive" and "definitely have academics as their first priority"; approximately 40 percent proceed to graduate school when they leave AC. Excellent student-faculty relations and small classes are AC's greatest attributes; professors are "very personable" and receive high grades for teaching and accessibility. One student wrote, "I am on a first-name basis with all of my teachers, and I feel that they are there for my benefit, not their own." The strongest departments at AC are reportedly political science/international relations, education, the natural sciences, and business and management. The three-course, interdisciplinary "Heritage of Western Culture" program is widely praised by students, one of whom described it as "what makes this school worthwhile." On the downside, many students complained that the administration is not terribly responsive to students. As one student put it, "It's very frustrating when the administration makes decisions which affect no one but the student body, and yet doesn't give us an appropriate vote on the issues." All in all, however, students are very satisfied with AC, which they characterize as challenging both academically and intellectually. Summed up one student: "Since the day I walked on this campus I've been bombarded with new ideas about politics, the traditional family, and religion. I've come to see the value of all three."

■ **Life** "One thing is for certain," explained one student, "this is definitely NOT Austin, Texas." Most agree that "AC isn't in a great location," and consider Sherman a bit too quiet (although a few look on the bright side— "Sherman is the ideal college town—no distractions!" wrote one). The social scene is also quiet: summed up one student, "Most of the students come here to get a good education, not to find a significant other." This emphasis on work before play leaves some students cold. One complained, "You have to wait four years for a date." Fraternity and sorority parties form the nucleus of AC's social world. Drinking, not surprisingly, is popular, and for some makes up for the "lack of an exciting social scene"; Beer and hard liquor are more popular here than at most colleges, although the town's "dry" regulations sometimes put a damper on things alcoholic. Most students live on campus in "comfortable dorms." Prospective students must prepare themselves for AC's strong work ethic and occasionally partyless weekends, but most will find plenty to do.

■ **Students** Austin College is predominantly white, Texan and conservative; some students "wish we had more diversity in the student body." There is no visible gay community on campus. For the motivated, pre-professional student who enjoys a close-knit, intense atmosphere, Austin College could be the perfect undergraduate destination.

AUSTIN COLLEGE

Admissions

According to Austin's undergraduate catalog, "The admissions committee weighs carefully all factors which bear upon an applicant's likelihood of success at Austin College... Applicants are judged by their academic records and by other indicators concerning their ability to live in and contribute positively to the Austin College community." Applicants are recommended to have taken four units of English, three units of math (including algebra and geometry), three units of science (including at least one lab science), two units of a single foreign language, two units of social studies and one unit of art/music/theatre. They should have also graduated in the top half of their high school classes, and must submit scores "at a level adequate for success at Austin" from the SAT or ACT.

Financial Aid

Financial aid applicants to Austin College must submit the FAF, a form generated by Austin's financial aid office, and a copy of their parents' tax return. Approximately one third of the aid at Austin is scholarships, with the remaining need met through loans and employment. Aid amounts range from $100 to full tuition and room/board. According to Austin's undergraduate catalog, "an *estimate* of a student's need can be obtained by sending the FAF to the director of financial planning prior to the January 1 [CSS] filing date. However, to receive the official aid award, the current FAF must be submitted after January 1 to the CSS." Among the merit awards at Austin are those for academic ability, leadership, religious affiliation, and county/state residence. Austin also offers its own institutional loans.

Excerpted from Austin College promotional materials:

"The first college in Texas to grant a graduate degree, Austin College has a heritage that is unsurpassed in Texas higher education. Dr. Daniel Baker, principal organizer of the College in 1849, was a Princeton-educated Presbyterian missionary. From its founding by Brazos Presbytery, Austin College has been related to the Presbyterian Church and that relationship has given distinctive flavor to its rich and influential history.

"Today, Austin College's 60-acre campus includes modern facilities such as the Abell Library Center, Arthur Hopkins Social Science Center, and Ida Green Communications Center which contains a 550-seat theatre, an art gallery, television studios and conference rooms. The campus provides a delightful mixture of architectural landmarks as well as ample modern facilities. The campus reflects the philosophy of Austin College. There is a mixture of old and new; there is tradition but no overdependence on traditional educational methods; there is pride in the past and excitement about the future."

ADMISSIONS FACTS

Competitiveness Rating:	**73**
% of applicants accepted:	86
% acceptees attending:	46

FRESHMAN PROFILE

Average verbal SAT:	510
Average math SAT:	561
Average ACT:	24
Graduated top 10% of class:	36
Graduated top 25% of class:	68
Graduated top 50% of class:	90

DEADLINES

Early decision/action:	11/15
Early dec./act. notif.:	NA
Regular admission:	7/1
Regular adm. notif.:	rolling

APPLICANTS ALSO LOOK AT

and often prefer:
Trinity College
U. Texas

and sometimes prefer:
Southwestern U.
Baylor U.
Texas A & M U.
Southern Methodist U.

ADDRESS

Undergraduate Admissions
900 North Grand Ave., Suite. 6N
Sherman, TX 75091
214-813-2387

FINANCIAL FACTS

In-state tuition ($):	9,465
Out-of-state tuition ($):	9,465
Room & board ($):	3,605
FA application deadline:	5/1
% frosh receiving FA:	75
PT earnings per yr. ($):	1,200

TYPE OF AID: % of students ($):

FA of some kind:	78 (NA)
Need-based grants:	NA
Merit-based grants:	NA
Loans:	NA
Work study:	NA
Student rating of FA:	86

BABSON COLLEGE

Wellesley, MA

CAMPUS LIFE

Quality of Life Rating: **84**

Type of school:	private
Affiliation:	none
Environment:	suburban

STUDENT BODY

FT undergrad enrollment:	1,584
% male/% female:	67/33
% out-of-state:	48
% live on campus:	80
% African-American:	1
% Asian:	1
% Caucasian:	81
% Hispanic:	2
% foreign:	9
% transfers:	3

WHAT'S HOT

profs encourage discussion
living on campus
small lectures
conservative politics
campus appearance
food

WHAT'S NOT

college radio station
religious clubs
classical music
alternative rock
gay community visible
requirements easy

ACADEMICS

Academic Rating: **82**

Calendar:	semester
Student/teacher ratio:	11/1
% doctorates:	90
Profs interesting:	87
Profs accessible:	89
Hours of study per day:	3.35

MOST POPULAR MAJORS BY %

Finance:	15
Marketing:	14
Accounting:	12

% GRADS WHO PURSUE

Law:	1
MBA:	3
Medicine:	NA
M.A., etc.:	NA

What do students think about Babson College?

■ **Academics** "Don't come here unless you want to know business!" emphatically wrote one junior on the back of her survey. It's pretty obvious advice: after all, Babson College is the school where *everybody* majors in some business field. Marketing, entrepreneurial studies, accounting, economics, finance, banking—all are popular and excellent majors at this challenging school for tomorrow's business leaders. Students gave their professors, most of whom are past (or current) successes in the business world, good marks: wrote one, "Professors are very accessible and willing to help." Professors generally encourage discussion and emphasize hands-on, pragmatic analysis: as one student explained, "most things done here (academically speaking) are done with jobs specifically in mind." Babson also provides students with their first taste of corporate competitiveness: as one student reported, "Competition is fierce. I've often found myself lying to my classmates about how much time I spend studying for exams, hoping it will influence them not to study as seriously. We'll do anything to get ahead." Grading is difficult, which serves to intensify the competition among classmates. Almost all our respondents expressed satisfaction with their academic programs, and one beamed that "every year this school gets a better reputation because its programs continue to diversify and the school continues to excel in business leadership."

■ **Life** Students gave Babson good grades in many "quality of life" categories. Their responses to our survey indicates that the food is good, the dorms safe and comfortable, and the campus is beautiful and easy to get around. Students complained, however, about the quality of their social lives. "The social life is there if you want it. You just have to be involved," offered one student optimistically, and clubs and events, especially those with business-related themes, are said to be popular; most students, however, wrote that the Babson social scene "stinks." A two-to-one male-female ratio goes a long way toward explaining their dissatisfaction, and the intense competitiveness among students can't help. Students told us that frats play at best a nominal role on campus, despite the fact that many go Greek. Of course, Boston is very close, so a good time is never more than a short train ride away.

■ **Students** It should come as no surprise that Babson's student body is among the most politically conservative in the country. After all, these aren't just college students, they're the future Chamber of Commerce. Wrote one student, "If you're not interested in business and bucks, don't come. If you like the sixties, don't come." One student assessed herself and her classmates this way: "Most students come from middle- to upper-class backgrounds. Many have family businesses or their own businesses. We are extremely driven and goal-oriented and we have high expectations of ourselves." Wrote another student, "Babson is a conservative, lily-white business school that fits the needs of its students like a glove." Minority representation is scant.

BABSON COLLEGE

Admissions

The admissions office of Babson College considers your GPA and the "rigor of your high school curriculum" to be the most important components of your application here, followed, in descending order of importance, by standardized test scores, essays, extracurricular activities, letters of recommendation, and interview. Babson requires its applicants to have completed three years of math at the level of Algebra I and above; and strongly recommends a complete college preparatory curriculum, including three years of science and two years of foreign language. Scores for either the SAT or the ACT, and for two Achievements, are required. Applicants to Babson most often also apply to Bentley, Boston College, and Bryant.

Financial Aid

The financial aid office at Babson requires applicants to submit the FAF and a form generated by the school. Merit-based grants are awarded on the basis of academic achievement, but most of the aid the school provides is to those who demonstrate need. Grants typically make up two thirds of a Babson aid package; loans and part-time employment make up the other third. Babson claims to meet 100 percent of the demonstrated need of all students it accepts.

A note from the Babson Admissions Office:

"Babson College is the premier college of business management in the country."

ADMISSIONS FACTS

Competitiveness Rating:	**74**
% of applicants accepted:	69
% acceptees attending:	42

FRESHMAN PROFILE

Average verbal SAT:	490*
Average math SAT:	560*
Average ACT:	NA
Graduated top 10% of class:	24
Graduated top 25% of class:	62
Graduated top 50% of class:	93

DEADLINES

Early decision/action:	12/1
Early dec./act. notif.:	NA
Regular admission:	2/1
Regular adm. notif.:	4/1

APPLICANTS ALSO LOOK AT

and often prefer:
U. Pennsylvania

and sometimes prefer:
Fairfield U.
Boston College

and rarely prefer:
Boston U.
Providence College
U. New Hampshire
U. Connecticut
U. Mass–Amherst
Bentley College

ADDRESS

Undergraduate Admissions
Babson Park
Wellesley, MA 02157-0901
617-239-5522

FINANCIAL FACTS

In-state tuition ($):	14,272
Out-of-state tuition ($):	14,272
Room & board ($):	6,150
FA application deadline:	2/1
% frosh receiving FA:	45
PT earnings per yr. ($):	1,200

TYPE OF AID: % of students ($):

FA of some kind:	42 (NA)
Need-based grants:	NA
Merit-based grants:	NA
Loans:	NA
Work study:	NA
Student rating of FA:	84

BARD COLLEGE

CAMPUS LIFE

Quality of Life Rating: **80**

Type of school:	private
Affiliation:	none
Environment:	rural

STUDENT BODY

FT undergrad enrollment:	1,023
% male/% female:	49/51
% out-of-state:	70
% live on campus:	94
% African-American:	7
% Asian:	1
% Caucasian:	73
% Hispanic:	4
% foreign:	10
% transfers:	1

WHAT'S HOT

gay community accepted
leftist politics
marijuana
financial aid
alternative rock
in-class discussion
small classes (overall)
doing all the reading
profs in class

WHAT'S NOT

fraternities/sororities
library
intercollegiate sports
location

ACADEMICS

Academic Rating:	**85**
Calendar:	4-1-4
Student/teacher ratio:	10/1
% doctorates:	90
Profs interesting:	92
Profs accessible:	87
Hours of study per day:	3.41

MOST POPULAR MAJORS BY %

Social Sciences:	36
Visual & Performing Arts:	29
Letters/Literature:	19

What do students think about Bard College?

■ **Academics** Bard College offers its 1000+ undergrads a "rich academic environment," "attentive and demanding" professors, and a "strong element of independence" in its curriculum. Described by its students as "a sink or swim college," Bard has many strengths, perhaps the most outstanding of which is the individual attention each student receives. Everyone is required to complete a Senior Project before graduation (a thesis-type paper or other original work), and many describe this experience as "absolutely the most valuable part of a Bard education." Another high-quality asset is the school's progressive Excellence and Equal Cost Program (EEC), which makes Bard available to top students at a state school price. One recipient gratefully acknowledged that "the EEC scholarship is the only way I could afford a private school"; another told us that "the EEC program makes Bard a place to think." Students emphasized that an independent streak is essential for successful Bard students; wrote one, "If you take the initiative and have interest, you get all the encouragement and opportunity you need." Students gave high marks to their professors for both in-class and out-of-class performance. Visual and performing arts students make up nearly one third of Bard's student body; liberal arts and social science majors are also popular and are reportedly excellent.

■ **Life** Bard's lovely campus is located in the relatively isolated small town of Annandale-on-Hudson, New York. Students agree that not much is happening in Annandale or in nearby Red Hook ("it's a ghost town, but very pretty"), and those without cars can feel "stranded on campus. A car is a must!" The seclusion of the college "bores many people into fleeing to New York City, but the others stay here and find interesting ways of entertaining themselves." Actually, the social life here can be lively; there are no fraternities or sororities ("not PC" says one student), but many think "some dorms have become like them." Theater is very popular on campus—not surprisingly, given the number of drama majors here. Living conditions overall are "not princely," although the nicest dorms are appealing. Some students gripe that "we have buildings from the time of Lincoln, and plumbing from the time of Plato."

■ **Students** Nearly one in 10 Bard students is a foreign national, lending a real international flavor to the campus. The typical Bard student is extremely liberal politically, so much so that the school has been described as a "left-wing free-for-all." Members of this politically correct vortex, according to one student, "work so hard to be nonconformist that everyone ends up with similar values, causing intolerance of differing (conservative) perspectives."

BARD COLLEGE

Admissions

According to Bard's undergraduate catalog, the admission committee "seeks evidence of academic preparedness and intellectual curiosity. The evaluation of an applicant includes an appraisal of the curriculum and rigor of the secondary school. The student's commitment of time and effort to scientific research, an art form, to social, political, or environmental issues, to volunteer work or employment or other extracurricular achievements is considered important in the Admission decision." Submission of standardized test scores is neither required nor recommended. Bard has an unusual alternative admission process called the Bard Immediate Decision Plan (IDP). The IDP is a one-day session "designed to provide students with a more informed opinion of the College and greater access to the admission process. The candidate participates with other candidates in a college-level seminar, and meets with an admission counselor. During the interview, the candidate is informed of the Admission Committee's decision." The candidate's application file must be complete for an immediate decision to be rendered.

Financial Aid

Financial aid applicants to Bard are required to complete the FAF (or FFS) and a form generated by Bard's financial aid office, and submit a copy of their parents' most recent tax return. In '91–'92, the average package was broken down as follows: 69% was met by a scholarship or grant; 23% was met by loan(s); and 9 percent was met with work study. In '90–'91, 19 percent of all undergrads received an academic scholarship, with an average value of $16,500. 65 percent of those receiving aid will get a scholarship of some kind, ranging from $500 to the full price of tuition.

Excerpted from Bard College promotional materials:

"The awakening of thought. Everything seems quite ordinary, at first: You are sitting in a class, reading at home, practicing, working, or making something in a studio. Your mind connects with an ongoing tradition of inquiry and study. And you become aware of a community of ideas as old as humankind, in which you, as a unique, thinking being, are compelled to participate.

"The world becomes more vivid and interesting after an authentic experience like that. The engagement required to follow through with your ideas becomes a priority, and the search for a college becomes, as it should be, the quest for a truly higher education.

"If you approach Bard in this spirit, you will find yourself in the company of young men and women who also are interested in college as a profound, life-changing experience. Like you, they have tasted the transformative power of great thoughts and ideals."

ADMISSIONS FACTS

Competitiveness Rating:	**79**
% of applicants accepted:	54
% acceptees attending:	37

FRESHMAN PROFILE

Average verbal SAT:	590*
Average math SAT:	637*
Average ACT:	NA
Graduated top 10% of class:	35
Graduated top 25% of class:	60
Graduated top 50% of class:	90

DEADLINES

Early decision/action:	12/1
Early dec./act. notif.:	1/1
Regular admission:	2/15
Regular adm. notif.:	early April

APPLICANTS ALSO LOOK AT

and often prefer:
Middlebury College
Colby College
Bowdoin College

and sometimes prefer:
Sarah Lawrence College.
Vassar College

and rarely prefer:
Hampshire College
Antioch College
Evergreen State College
Bennington College

ADDRESS

Undergraduate Admissions
Annandale-on-Hudson,
NY 12504
914-758-7472

FINANCIAL FACTS

In-state tuition ($):	16,650
Out-of-state tuition ($):	16,650
Room & board ($):	5,565
FA application deadline:	2/15
PT earnings per yr. ($):	1,500

TYPE OF AID: % of students ($):

FA of some kind:	52 (15,000)
Need-based grants:	45 (10,384)
Merit-based grants:	NA
Loans:	41 (3,000)
Work study:	NA (1,300)
Student rating of FA:	94

BARNARD COLLEGE

CAMPUS LIFE

Quality of Life Rating: **81**

Type of school:	private
Affiliation:	none
Environment:	city

STUDENT BODY

FT undergrad enrollment:	2,098
% male/% female:	0/100
% out-of-state:	60
% live on campus:	90
% African-American:	NA
% Asian:	19
% Caucasian:	69
% Hispanic:	4
% foreign:	3
% transfers:	6

WHAT'S HOT

location
gays accepted
religion
leftist politics
alternative rock
campus easy to get around
administration
diversity
deans

WHAT'S NOT

intramural sports
hard liquor
campus appearance

ACADEMICS

Academic Rating: **84**

Calendar:	semester
Student/teacher ratio:	8/1
% doctorates:	90
Profs interesting:	85
Profs accessible:	81
Hours of study per day:	3.4

MOST POPULAR MAJORS BY %

Social Sciences:	28
Letters/Literature:	23
Psychology:	10

% GRADS WHO PURSUE

Law:	7
MBA:	1
Medicine:	6
M.A., etc.:	9

What do students think about Barnard College?

■ **Academics** Women at Barnard College are in the unique position of having several educational environments at their disposal. First there is Barnard, considered "extremely empowering" for women; then there is Columbia University, renowned for its Ivy League academics; and finally, there's New York City, famous for just about everything. Classes at Barnard are small and taught by well-respected professors (never teaching assistants). Students gave high ratings to the faculty for being "accessible and willing to help" (one certain advantage Barnard has over Columbia University). English, foreign languages, political science and the natural sciences are reportedly the strongest departments here; pre-medical studies are particularly competitive. Arts students can combine their talents with a liberal arts education in an interdisciplinary option unique to Barnard. Barnard students may take courses at Columbia U., and nearly all do. Women here love the fact that they "have access to all of Columbia, but do not have to deal with its bureaucracy." Columbia-Barnard relations aren't entirely amicable, however. Some students feel that Barnard is neglected by the university because it refused to merge with Columbia U., choosing instead to remain a single-sex institution. Students in our surveys praised their deans, and have a warm relationship with the Barnard administration as a whole.

■ **Life** Barnard students describe themselves as "chic, sophisticated and very New York." They prize the varied experiences they have daily as residents of the Big Apple. One woman wrote, "it's great to learn about chemistry, other cultures and religions in the classroom, and self-defense in the subway." The "small-town school setting" of the Barnard campus within the decidedly big-city setting of New York creates a supportive, safe home base for students and allows them to absorb urban culture at the same time. The social scene is inextricably tied into that of Columbia, although Barnard's own extracurricular activities have been beefed up lately in an effort to increase unity. Athletic teams draw members from both sides of the street, as do some dorms and cafeterias (the only kosher one is at Barnard). Most students live on campus, partly due to the outrageous rents in the area. The dating scene is plagued by the competition between Barnard and Columbia women; between the two undergraduate populations, women outnumber men three to one.

■ **Students** Barnard students have long been known as feminists. Intense, liberal political commitment is common. There is a visible and very well-accepted gay community here. One student wrote, "if you come to Barnard, sit in the Macintosh smoking section and scope women, you will find you never want to leave this place." A 31 percent minority population creates a diverse atmosphere: with the campus, Columbia and New York City to choose from, students are hard pressed to run out of social, cultural and other options. For the "strong-minded, determined, intellectual woman," Barnard should not be overlooked.

BARNARD COLLEGE

Admissions

The admissions office reports that it "does not have test score cut-offs, nor do we have formulas. We consider and read *every* application with careful attention." Barnard considers high school curriculum and performance the most important factor in the admissions process. Essays are next-most important, followed, in order of importance, by letters of recommendation, extracurricular activities, standardized test scores, and an interview. Barnard recommends that applicants have completed four years of English, three years each of math and a foreign language, two years of lab science, and one year of history. Applicants must also provide scores for either the SAT or the ACT, and three achievements (of which English composition must be one). Barnard applicants most often also apply to Columbia, Wellesley, Smith, and NYU.

Financial Aid

The financial aid office at Barnard College requires applicants to submit the FAF, a form generated by the school, and their parents' tax return. Barnard participates in the following loan programs: Stafford, Perkins, PLUS/SLS, and SHARE. The school's most recent catalog states that "*insofar as possible*, Barnard assists qualified students who demonstrate financial need...The decision of the Committee on Admissions to admit a student is *not* affected by the fact that a student has applied for or demonstrated need for financial aid [emphasis added]."

A note from the Barnard College Admissions Office:

"Barnard College, a small distinguished liberal arts college for women, affiliated with Columbia University, is located in the heart of New York City. The College enrolls 2200 women from all over the United States, Puerto Rico, and the Caribbean. Sixty countries, including France, England Hong Kong and Greece are also represented in the student body. Students pursue their academic studies in over 35 majors, and are able to cross-register at Columbia University. The low faculty to student ratio, 1 to 8, allows for personal attention in small, stimulating classes.

"Barnard's Career Services Office offers over 1,000 internships a year to interested students. Recent sites have included the Metropolitan Museum of Art, CBS Sports, Cornell Medical Center, Legal Aid Society, MTV, New York Woman Magazine, Universal Pictures, Goldman Sachs, The Apollo Theatre, and many other locations."

ADMISSIONS FACTS

Competitiveness Rating:	85
% of applicants accepted:	57
% acceptees attending:	51

FRESHMAN PROFILE

Average verbal SAT:	600
Average math SAT:	620
Average ACT:	NA
Graduated top 10% of class:	56
Graduated top 25% of class:	86
Graduated top 50% of class:	91

DEADLINES

Early decision/action:	11/1
Early dec./act. notif.:	NA
Regular admission:	2/1
Regular adm. notif.:	4/1

APPLICANTS ALSO LOOK AT

and often prefer:
Yale U.
Columbia U.
Brown U.
Northwestern U.
Wellesley College
U. Chicago

and sometimes prefer:
Dartmouth College

and rarely prefer:
NYU
Brandeis U.

ADDRESS

Undergraduate Admissions
3009 Broadway
New York, NY 10027-6598
212-854-2014

FINANCIAL FACTS

In-state tuition ($):	15,874
Out-of-state tuition ($):	15,874
Room & board ($):	6,892
FA application deadline:	2/1
% frosh receiving FA:	55
PT earnings per yr. ($):	1,400

TYPE OF AID: % of students ($):	
FA of some kind:	55 (NA)
Need-based grants:	NA
Merit-based grants:	NA
Loans:	NA
Work study:	NA
Student rating of FA:	77

BATES COLLEGE

Lewiston, ME

What do students think about Bates College?

■ **Academics** The Puritan work ethic is alive at Bates College. Not only do students at this fine liberal arts school work hard, but they do so knowing that the rewards of their labor will be less than they desire: Bates professors are notoriously difficult graders. Wrote one student, "Classes are impossible, grading is difficult, but if one works four to five hours a day, B's are obtainable. A's are difficult if not impossible in most courses." Four hours a day for a B? Oddly, most students don't seem to mind. In fact, they seem to relish the challenge. It helps that students feel professors and administrators go out of their way to create an atmosphere conducive to learning. Professors teach all courses and provide "a lot of personal attention," particularly to students who fall behind their classes. More than a few go beyond the call of duty, helping students with personal as well as academic problems. Students appreciate the administration's liberal governance of the school. As one put it, "with few rules and regulations, students have to learn to be responsible for themselves, a skill they will need in the real world." Psychology, history, and biology are the most popular majors here, and the visual and performing arts programs are beginning to flourish.

■ **Life** Bates College has no fraternities or sororities, and most students are glad about it. Wrote one student, "the lack of fraternities and sororities creates a very friendly atmosphere within the school by eliminating exclusion and hierarchy." There is an active social scene because, as one student explained, "we are a very strong community. Participation in sports, clubs, and especially student organizations, is strongly encouraged within the school." As for parties, "During the week, the library is packed and students are hard at work. On the weekends, everyone unwinds and parties." Students drink a good deal to ward off the cold weather and the academic pressures. Wrote one student, "We love the school's alcohol policy: it has none. Kids are going to drink anyway, so why not let them use it, abuse it, and learn from it?" One frequently cited negative was that the small student body inhibits the dating scene (a common complaint at small schools). Students praised the food and the dormitories, and several mentioned that, for those who choose to live off-campus, huge Victorian houses are nearby and affordable.

■ **Students** Bates draws students from all over New England: only 12 percent of the students are natives of Maine. The school has a 12 percent minority population (not the *same* 12 percent). The student body is predominantly white and preppy. While most students are happy here, there is a significant minority for whom the atmosphere is too cloistered. "This place reeks of upper-class white self-absorption," wrote one such dissident. Still, many described their fellow students as "friendly, down-to-earth, and amiable." As a whole the students "are particularly interested in social and political issues, which makes class discussions energetic and interesting."

BATES COLLEGE

Admissions

Bates College reportedly uses "no cut-offs, no formulas" in evaluating its applicant pool. Standardized test scores are an *optional* part of the application here; if submitted, they are considered as part of the application, but applicants are not penalized if they withhold test scores. Essays and high school record are considered the most important components of the application; extracurricular activities, interviews, and standardized test scores (if submitted), are also important, but less so. Letters of recommendation are considered the least important aspect of the application. Applicants are required to have completed a "traditional college prep curriculum" to be considered for admittance. Students applying to Bates most often also apply to Bowdoin, Colby, Williams, and Middlebury.

Financial Aid

Bates requires the FAF, your most recent tax return, and a form generated by the FA office. The school awards no merit-based grants, but over one third of current undergrads received an award of nearly half of the school's combined tuition and room/board last year (see sidebar). The financial aid office writes "Although the vast majority of our admissions decisions are 'need blind,' our dean reserves the responsibility to make final admissions decision in keeping with available financial aid." This is the case at many colleges, but few are willing to admit it.

A note from the Bates Admissions Office:

"The people on the Bates admissions staff read your application carefully, several times. We get to know you from that reading; your high school record and quality of your writing are particularly important. We strongly encourage a personal interview, either on campus or with an alumni representative."

ADMISSIONS FACTS

Competitiveness Rating:	**88**
% of applicants accepted:	42
% acceptees attending:	33

FRESHMAN PROFILE

Average verbal SAT:	580
Average math SAT:	640
Average ACT:	NA
Graduated top 10% of class:	51
Graduated top 25% of class:	85
Graduated top 50% of class:	99

DEADLINES

Early decision/action:	12/1
Early dec./act. notif.:	12/20
Regular admission:	2/1
Regular adm. notif.:	4/4

APPLICANTS ALSO LOOK AT

and often prefer:
Amherst College
Wesleyan U.
Tufts U.
Williams College
Bowdoin College
Middlebury College

and sometimes prefer:
U. Vermont
Colby College
Colgate U.

ADDRESS

Undergraduate Admissions
Lewiston, ME 04240
207-786-6000

FINANCIAL FACTS

In-state tuition ($):	21,400
Out-of-state tuition ($):	21,400
Room & board ($):	incl. above
FA application deadline:	2/15
% frosh receiving FA:	60
PT earnings per yr. ($):	1,300

TYPE OF AID: % of students ($):

FA of some kind:	60 (13,500)
Need-based grants:	37 (10,000)
Merit-based grants:	NA
Loans:	40 (2,980)
Work study:	40 (1,300)
Student rating of FA:	78

BAYLOR UNIVERSITY

CAMPUS LIFE

Quality of Life Rating:	**81**
Type of school:	private
Affiliation:	Baptist
Environment:	city

STUDENT BODY

FT undergrad enrollment:	9,955
% male/% female:	45/55
% out-of-state:	22
% live on campus:	30
% African-American:	3
% Asian:	4
% Caucasian:	88
% Hispanic:	4
% foreign:	1
% transfers:	5

WHAT'S HOT
marriage
religion
intramural sports
religious clubs
conservative politics
administration (overall)
top 40
caring about politics
fraternities/sororities
intercollegiate sports

WHAT'S NOT
gay community visible
gay community accepted
interaction
diversity

ACADEMICS

Academic Rating:	**74**
Calendar:	semester
Student/teacher ratio:	19/1
% doctorates:	NA
Profs interesting:	84
Profs accessible:	80
Hours of study per day:	2.6

MOST POPULAR MAJORS BY %

Business & Management:	28
Education:	15
Social Sciences:	7

What do students think about Baylor University?

■ **Academics** Baylor University offers an inexpensive, top-quality education in a religious atmosphere. The Baptist church, with which the school is affiliated, exerts a strong influence on social and academic life. A strong core curriculum, including Bible study (of course), literature, math, and science ensures a well-rounded education for undergrads, one in four of whom pursue degrees in business and management. Pre-medical studies and education are other popular majors. Professors and administration received high marks from the student body, who particularly liked the fact that profs, not TAs, teach most introductory courses. One student reported that "Baylor has a very laid-back atmosphere," and academically, that's true; the average student puts in two and a half hours of study a day, well below the national average.

■ **Life** Freshmen arriving at Baylor should be prepared to cast aside their preconceptions of what college life is like, particularly if those preconceptions include images of heavy partying, licentiousness, and a generally liberal atmosphere. That's what life at the quintessential East Coast liberal arts school is like, but Baylor is...well, different. As one student told us, "the beauty of Baylor lies in its Christian values, its attractive campus, and the student and alumni pride. Baylor has the nation's largest homecoming parade. It is the most exciting weekend of the year!" Baylor prohibits drinking, dancing, cohabitation, and gambling, and means it! Football, church, and the Greek system take the place of those typical college activities and form the nucleus of Baylor's social universe (often referred to as "the Baylor bubble."). Explained one undergrad, "Baylor is essentially the buckle in the Bible belt. You just have to get used to the atmosphere and remember that you are in school for an education." Surprisingly, students reported drinking to be about as popular as it is at the average school, although, not surprisingly, drugs are unpopular. Students don't much like Waco; as one told us, "Many of the students here complain about the lack of things to do. When asked what there is to do on weekends, they will reply, 'Go to Dallas or Austin (both 100 miles away).' The truth is that there is quite a bit to do in Waco, a lot of great places to go. Also, the university sponsors a lot of activities, especially for freshmen."

■ **Students** Among students at competitive colleges, Baylor's are the nation's third most conservative. Only 18 percent of our respondents identified themselves as Democrats, compared to the 67 percent who identified themselves as Republicans. They are also the nation's fourth most religious student body. Over three quarters of the students are from Texas. The student body is overwhelmingly white: the 12 percent minority population is pretty evenly divided among Asians, blacks, and Hispanics, so that representation of each minority is scant.

BAYLOR UNIVERSITY

Admissions

Baylor's admissions catalog notes, "All students who enter Baylor University as freshmen enter the College of Arts and Sciences with the exception of those who plan to pursue a degree in music. During their second year, those students in the College of Arts and Sciences who choose one of the professional schools such as the School of Business, the School of Education or the School of Nursing may apply for admission to one of those schools. Those students admitted to the University who intend to major in music should also qualify for admission to that school at the time they enter the University in order to avoid undue delay in the completion of their degree program." Baylor prescribes four years of English, two years of mathematics (three years for students who plan to enter premedicine, predentistry or nursing), two years of lab science and two years of social sciences (one of which must be history). To be eligible for admission, applicants must also have graduated in the top half of their high school class, and have "acceptable" scores on the SAT or ACT. The catalog adds, "In connection with these admissions criteria, it should be noted that Baylor students as a group demonstrate well above average academic achievement and potential."

Financial Aid

Financial aid applicants to Baylor College must complete the FAF and a form generated by Baylor's financial aid office. Among the scholarships available: Ministerial (Southern Baptist undergrads who plan to enter the ministry); Valedictorian ($1,000 for freshman year only to valedictorians); Presidential (50 scholarships ranging from $6,000 to $10,000 over four years to freshmen who score over 32 on the ACT or 1250 on the SAT and rank in the top 10 percent of their high school class); National Merit, National Achievement and National Hispanic Finalists. Various minority, athletic, departmental and need-based scholarships are also available.

Excerpt from Baylor University's promotional materials:

"Baylor University is concerned with the spiritual, moral, and intellectual development of those who come within its sphere of influence. It is committed to a caring relationship among its students, faculties, administrators, and regents—a caring that is characterized by understanding, forgiveness, and respect for individuality. The University is proud of its Christian heritage, and it strives to be an institution stimulated both by the power of God and by the search for truth as it plays out its unique role in the educational community."

ADMISSIONS FACTS

Competitiveness Rating:	**65**
% of applicants accepted:	88
% acceptees attending:	56

FRESHMAN PROFILE

Average verbal SAT:	490*
Average math SAT:	550*
Average ACT:	23*
Graduated top 10% of class:	NA
Graduated top 25% of class:	70
Graduated top 50% of class:	95

DEADLINES

Early decision/action:	NA
Early dec./act. notif.:	NA
Regular admission:	rolling
Regular adm. notif.:	rolling

APPLICANTS ALSO LOOK AT

and often prefer:
Southern Methodist U.

and sometimes prefer:
U. Oklahoma
Tulane U.
Texas Christian U.

and rarely prefer:
Texas A & M U.
Austin College
Southwestern U.
U. Texas–Austin
Trinity U.

ADDRESS

Undergraduate Admissions
P.O. Box 97056
Waco, TX 76798-7056
817-755-3435

FINANCIAL FACTS

In-state tuition ($):	5,500
Out-of-state tuition ($):	5,500
Room & board ($):	3,658
FA application deadline:	5/1
% frosh receiving FA:	60
PT earnings per yr. ($):	NA

TYPE OF AID: % of students ($):

FA of some kind:	60 (NA)
Need-based grants:	NA
Merit-based grants:	NA
Loans:	NA
Work study:	NA
Student rating of FA:	76

BELOIT COLLEGE

Beloit, WI

CAMPUS LIFE

Quality of Life Rating: 82

Type of school:	private
Affiliation:	none
Environment:	city

STUDENT BODY

FT undergrad enrollment:	1,074
% male/% female:	44/56
% out-of-state:	78
% live on campus:	95
% African-American:	4
% Asian:	6
% Caucasian:	88
% Hispanic:	2
% foreign:	10
% transfers:	3

WHAT'S HOT

gay community accepted
college radio station
financial aid
small classes (overall)
cost of living
profs outside class
interaction
leftist politics
marijuana
caring about politics
administration (overall)
profs in class
profs teach intro courses

WHAT'S NOT

location

ACADEMICS

Academic Rating: 82

Calendar:	semester
Student/teacher ratio:	12/1
% doctorates:	86
Profs interesting:	91
Profs accessible:	93
Hours of study per day:	3.31

MOST POPULAR MAJORS BY %

Anthropology:	7
Economics & Management:	7
Literary Studies:	7

% GRADS WHO PURSUE

Law:	6
MBA:	10
Medicine:	4
M.A., etc.:	20

What do students think about Beloit College?

■ **Academics** Considered a "safety school" by many college applicants, Beloit College does an outstanding job of convincing its students that enrolling at Beloit was a fortuitous choice. Don't be fooled by the high admission rate: Beloit is an excellent liberal arts college, with stellar departments in anthropology, English and geology. In nearly all areas, academics are considered "very demanding," with an emphasis on student participation. Course-related trips, independent and foreign study, internships, and field work of all kinds are encouraged here—learning at Beloit "is not a passive experience." Students rated all aspects of their academic life very highly, praising the small class size ("the low teacher/student ratio makes learning easier and more enjoyable") and the exceptional faculty accessibility ("professors are incredibly supportive, inside and outside the classroom"). Even the administration got kudos: the deans, bursar, and other administrators were described as "very visible and approachable."

■ **Life** Some of the more carefree students at Beloit live by the motto, "you can always retake a class, but you can never relive a party." The social scene here is very lively, and most of it takes place on campus, where almost everyone resides. (Even seniors, who are the only ones allowed to move off campus, usually stay in dorms in order to be near the fun.) Drinking and pot-smoking are prevalent, according to our surveys, and Greek organizations are becoming more popular. There is rarely a shortage of things to do on campus, perhaps because "the town of Beloit is a dump; therefore, we have to create our own opportunities." Students tend to find fun on their own turf, but they also like the fact that "if a person wants to get away, cities like Madison, Chicago, Rockford, and Milwaukee are easy to visit." Extracurriculars are many and varied (thanks in part to the "significant activity fee," which prompted some complaints). Especially popular are the radio station and intramural sports of all types. As one student put it, "We're not a metropolis, but we sure keep busy!" All this activity concentrated among such a small student body apparently creates an intense but very positive atmosphere; as a result, students reported themselves happier with their overall college experience than most students elsewhere.

■ **Students** Known for being much less traditional than its midwestern neighbors, Beloit "is a comfortable place for liberals and individualists." As one student reported, "If you are into political correctness then you will be at home; if not, you will have many exciting debates." The undergraduate population is not incredibly diverse, by students' accounts, but there is a sizable number of foreign students. The overriding climate on campus is one of tolerance and acceptance of all kinds of students; those with different backgrounds and lifestyles are welcomed into the friendly Beloit community.

BELOIT COLLEGE

Admission

The admissions office reports that "we are looking for interesting, intelligent, curious, involved students who have a sense of humor and who want to take personal responsibility for their educations." High school curriculum and grades are the most important components of the application, followed by extracurricular activities, essays, letters of recommendation, interviews, and, finally, standardized test scores. The admissions office recommends that applicants have completed four years of English, three years of science, three years of math, three years of social studies, and two years of a foreign language. Students applying to Beloit most often also apply to Macalester, Grinnell, Earlham, Knox, Lawrence, UWisconsin–Madison, and UIllinois–Urbana–Champaign.

Financial Aid

Beloit requires a FAF, a Student Aid Report, your parents' most recent tax return and a form generated by the financial aid office. Academic scholarships are award to 6% of all undergrads, at an average value of $2,468. Loans recommended include Stafford (to 40% of undergrads, at an average of $2,628 each), Perkins (17%; $1,824), PLUS, SLS, and Beloit College Loans. According to the Beloit FA office, "Admission decisions are based on academic achievement and potential for growth, not on a family's ability to pay for college." All of last year's freshmen who applied for aid received some type of award.

A note from the Beloit College Admissions Office:

"Compared to the 'average' college student, Beloit students are more intellectually curious, adventurous, creative, and friendly. They are concerned with ideas, issues of public service, human understanding, and making the world a better place. They come from 45 states and 36 foreign countries. Beloit is one of a select group of truly diverse undergraduate communities where dialogues that begin in the classroom continue in the dining hall and on the playing fields. The focus at Beloit is great undergraduate teaching with a student/faculty ratio of 12:1. Beloit emphasizes learning, not grades. Beloit students learn how to think and write, not just pass tests. It is a powerful environment for an undergraduate, residential experience in the arts and sciences. Beloit students are being prepared to attend the best graduate and professional schools, to succeed in important diverse careers, and to serve the nation as constructive citizens."

ADMISSIONS FACTS

Competitiveness Rating:	**67**
% of applicants accepted:	83
% acceptees attending:	32

FRESHMAN PROFILE

Average verbal SAT:	507*
Average math SAT:	553*
Average ACT:	25*
Graduated top 10% of class:	25
Graduated top 25% of class:	47
Graduated top 50% of class:	81

DEADLINES

Early decision/action:	12/15
Early dec./act. notif.:	1/15
Regular admission:	3/15
Regular adm. notif.:	rolling

APPLICANTS ALSO LOOK AT

and often prefer:
Carleton College
U. Wisconsin–Madison

and sometimes prefer:
Lawrence U.
Grinnell College
Ohio Wesleyan U.
U. Illinois–Urbana
Knox College
Earlham College

ADDRESS

Undergraduate Admissions
700 College Ave.
Beloit, WI 53511
608-363-2500

FINANCIAL FACTS

In-state tuition ($):	12,900
Out-of-state tuition ($):	12,900
Room & board ($):	3,300
FA application deadline:	4/15
% frosh receiving FA:	73
PT earnings per yr. ($):	950

TYPE OF AID: % of students ($):

FA of some kind:	73 (9,977)
Need-based grants:	80 (6,943)
Merit-based grants:	6 (2,468)
Loans:	54 (3,017)
Work study:	63 (1,193)
Student rating of FA:	97

BENNINGTON COLLEGE

CAMPUS LIFE

Quality of Life Rating:	**82**
Type of school:	private
Affiliation:	none
Environment:	rural

STUDENT BODY

FT undergrad enrollment:	569
% male/% female:	41/59
% out-of-state:	96
% live on campus:	90
% African-American:	2
% Asian:	3
% Caucasian:	92
% Hispanic:	2
% foreign:	1
% transfers:	5

WHAT'S HOT

gay community accepted
in-class discussion
classical music
college theater
interaction
leftist politics
marijuana
small classes (overall)
food
rap/hip-hop
profs in class
profs outside class

WHAT'S NOT

location
interaction

ACADEMICS

Academic Rating:	**75**
Calendar:	semester
Student/teacher ratio:	8/1
% doctorates:	42
Profs interesting:	93
Profs accessible:	92
Hours of study per day:	3.44

MOST POPULAR MAJORS

Foreign Languages
Letters/Literature
Visual & Performing Arts

What do students think about Bennington College?

■ **Academics** Bennington College offers its students the rare chance to design their own academic programs of study, and then to follow through under close faculty supervision. The educational philosophy at this proudly nontraditional school is "centered around nurturing independence, creativity and self-determination." Grades are replaced by written evaluations, conventional classes by "seminars and tutorials," and exams by final papers and projects. Because of a tiny undergraduate population and the high price of tuition (Bennington is the most costly college in the country), the school is able to devote large amounts of money to each student. Thus, classes are small, facilities are excellent, and teachers are very accessible. The negative side is that departments are also small, limiting the variety of courses available. But most students felt that the dedication of professors more than makes up for this. One student explained: "So you want to study economics? There are only two econ courses offered each term. But don't despair: the profs are here to teach and be available. A dance major that has never balanced a checkbook should know that after intense, personalized classes here, s/he will be ready for business school." The strongest programs here are arts-related, and creativity of all kinds is emphasized. Interdisciplinary majors are encouraged: "I found my voice in oil paints, children's literature, and anthropological ethnographies," said one student. All in all, Bennington has a lot to offer the artistic, especially those with "that one overriding passion." As one student warned, "There is a great deal of academic freedom here, and it requires a disciplined student to get the most out of Bennington."

■ **Life** The nontraditional aspects of Bennington extend to its social atmosphere. There are "no frats or football games here," and "the 'date' is an outmoded concept." Partly because of the small number of people and the isolation of the rural Vermont campus, life can get "claustrophobic" at times. One student commented that it "is not for the socially squeamish." Sports are not popular here. The most widespread extracurricular activities, according to our surveys, are drinking and enjoying controlled substances (though there is little pressure to join in—people are "generally considerate toward those who choose not to.") Social freedoms are many; Bennington students may even select roommates of the opposite sex if they are so inclined. Artistic pursuits abound, and many believe the best thing about Bennington is that "all forms of expression are given space."

■ **Students** If you are looking for acceptance of alternative lifestyles or beliefs, Bennington may be the place for you. There are "so many nonconformists that it is actually the conservatives who don't conform." Many students are self-described "outcasts" or "misfits," perhaps because of their artistic leanings. Bennington College is "not for everyone," cautioned one student, but for those who like its emphasis on individual artistic development, it offers a rigorous and rewarding education.

BENNINGTON COLLEGE

Admissions

The admissions office reports that Bennington College "does not have a formula nor do we have a cut-off." "Quality of academic program" is the most important factor in admissions here, followed in descending order of importance by letters of recommendation, interview, essays, high school grades, extracurricular activities ("this could be higher if someone has a special talent in art, music, writing, etc.," noted the admissions office), and standardized test scores. Bennington requires no specific high school courses, but recommends a college preparatory curriculum including a foreign language, math, and science. Applicants to Bennington most often also apply to Sarah Lawrence, Bard, Smith, and Hampshire.

Financial Aid

Bennington requires financial aid applicants to complete the FAF and a financial aid form from its own office, and to submit a copy of their parents' most recent tax return. If applicable, a divorced/separated parent's statement must also be submitted. All financial aid awards are need-based only. In '91–'92, the average grant was $12,955, and the average loan was $2,900 (all of the loans recommended by the FA office were Stafford loans). Thirty percent of all undergrads participated in the work-study program.

A note from the Bennington Admissions Office:

"At Bennington students design their own academic program within the College's educational guidelines. Because students work at what they care about most within the classroom, much of their social activity is closely related to their coursework. The result is intense and varied creative activity (concerts, plays, reading and lectures) involving students, faculty and guest artists. One-on-one tutorials with faculty is the norm for upper-class students; with work at Bennington culminating in a Senior Project or Thesis in the fourth year."

ADMISSIONS FACTS

Competitiveness Rating:	**79**
% of applicants accepted:	70
% acceptees attending:	43

FRESHMAN PROFILE

Average verbal SAT:	NA
Average math SAT:	NA
Average ACT:	NA
Graduated top 10% of class:	18
Graduated top 25% of class:	45
Graduated top 50% of class:	77

DEADLINES

Early decision/action:	12/1
Early dec./act. notif.:	12/20
Regular admission:	3/1
Regular adm. notif.:	4/1

APPLICANTS ALSO LOOK AT

and often prefer:
Vassar College

and sometimes prefer:
U. Connecticut
Boston College
U. Vermont
Sarah Larwence College
Hampshire College

and rarely prefer:
U. New Hampshire

ADDRESS

Undergraduate Admissions
Bennington, VT 05201
802-442-6349

FINANCIAL FACTS

In-state tuition ($):	19,400
Out-of-state tuition ($):	19,400
Room & board ($):	3,800
FA application deadline:	3/1
% frosh receiving FA:	50
PT earnings per yr. ($):	925

TYPE OF AID: % of students ($):

FA of some kind:	51 (NA)
Need-based grants:	NA (12,955)
Merit-based grants:	NA
Loans:	NA (2,900)
Work study:	30 (NA)
Student rating of FA:	97

BENTLEY COLLEGE

CAMPUS LIFE

Quality of Life Rating: **83**

Type of school:	private
Affiliation:	none
Environment:	suburban

STUDENT BODY

FT undergrad enrollment:	3,797
% male/% female:	55/45
% out-of-state:	44
% live on campus:	78
% African-American:	2
% Asian:	3
% Caucasian:	85
% Hispanic:	3
% foreign:	6
% transfers:	3

WHAT'S HOT

Top 40
catalog
diversity
dating
administration (overall)

WHAT'S NOT

registration
classical music
studying hard
leftist politics
caring about politics
doing all the reading

ACADEMICS

Academic Rating: **73**

Calendar:	semester
Student/teacher ratio:	19/1
% doctorates:	82
Profs interesting:	82
Profs accessible:	84
Hours of study per day:	2.69

MOST POPULAR MAJORS BY %

Accounting:	28
Management:	17
Marketing:	14

% GRADS WHO PURSUE

Law:	1
MBA:	2
Medicine:	NA
M.A., etc.:	NA

What do students think about Bentley College?

■ **Academics** If you're interested in pursuing an undergraduate business degree, you really should check out Bentley College. Practically every student here is studying accounting, business administration, or marketing (those few who don't pursue business programs have to write their own curricula), so BC students definitely hobnob with some of the business leaders of tomorrow. Core curriculum requirements demand that students receive a good grounding in basic business theory and ethics and in computers regardless of major (liberal arts requirements, meant to ensure a well-rounded education, are less demanding and less successful). Bentley is particularly strong in the study of international business; its Center for International Business Education and Research, run in conjunction with Tufts University, allows students ample opportunities to study, pursue research projects, and travel. Students are enthusiastic about their professors, whom they repeatedly described as extra-helpful outside of class. And even though students don't work too hard here—about two and two-thirds hours a night—most agree that they are getting a top-notch education in an extremely pleasant environment. It's also a school whose star is on the rise, as one student noted: "Bentley is a conservative business school that is moving in the direction of being more well-rounded in academics, political views, and social aspects of what college is all about." Note: students must have their own personal computers (which can be bought or rented through the school).

■ **Life** Bentley is located in Waltham, a Boston suburb that is 15 minutes from Harvard Square by shuttle bus. Said one student, "the location is amazing; secluded, safe, yet with easy access to Boston." Students here definitely find time to party: weekends start on Thursday nights and run through Sunday, during which bar- and club-hopping are popular. When the weather allows, students will spend nights hanging out around the beautiful campus or going to frat parties. Boston's proximity notwithstanding, frats and sororities play a big role in Bentley social life. "The Greeks add a huge number of activities to Bentley and the community," reported one student; said another, "Bentley College would be nothing without Greek life." School spirit is strong, although some students yearn for a more serious athletic program. One student's remarks typified the prevalent attitude here: "Your college years are the best years of your life and Bentley College allows you to enjoy them as well as get an excellent education that will provide the world with great business leaders in the very near future."

■ **Students** Students here are very conservative, although many just plain don't care about politics. "Preppy" is a word that classmates frequently use to describe each other. Foreign nationals make up a good portion of the minority population here, and separate groups mostly stay separate.

BENTLEY COLLEGE

Admissions

The admissions office reports, "We do not use any 'cut-offs.'" High school GPA and curriculum are the most important parts of your application here. Standardized test scores are considered next, then essays, extracurricular activities, and letters of recommendation are reviewed. An interview, while recommended, is the least important component. Applicants are required to have completed four years of English, four years of math (algebra I, II, and geometry all count), two years of social studies, one lab science, two years of a foreign language, plus three more courses in speech, advance accounting, or any of the previously listed fields. It should be obvious, but we'll say it anyway: the student who has shown some prior interest in the business world has a better chance of gaining admittance to Bentley. Bentley applicants most often also apply to Boston College, Babson, UMass-Amherst, and Bryant.

Financial Aid

Bentley requires financial aid applicants to complete the FAF and to submit a copy of their parents' most recent tax return. Last year, the average need-based grant at Bentley was $4,837, and the average loan was $2,722 (primarily Stafford Loans). Some Bentley undergrads also received athletic scholarships (1%; average value $17,690) and academic grants (5%; average value $7,189). Minority scholarships are also available. Eighteen percent of all undergrads participated in the work-study program.

A note from the Bentley Admissions Office:

"If you are interested in studying business and want to be in the Boston area, you should consider Bentley College. Founded in 1917, Bentley is a four-year accredited, coeducational institution recognized for excellence in accounting, business, and financial management education. Located in Waltham, Massachusetts, it is the eighth largest of 87 independent institutions of higher education in the commonwealth. The 110-acre campus is located on the crest of Cedar Hill in Waltham, nine miles west of Boston. Most of the College's 44 buildings were constructed since moving to this campus in 1968.

"Bentley offers eight bachelor of science degrees in business-related fields as well as a bachelor of arts program where a student may design his or her own field of concentration. The college also awards master's degrees in six business concentrations."

ADMISSIONS FACTS

Competitiveness Rating:	**67**
% of applicants accepted:	79
% acceptees attending:	36

FRESHMAN PROFILE

Average verbal SAT:	457*
Average math SAT:	520*
Average ACT:	NA
Graduated top 10% of class:	20
Graduated top 25% of class:	49
Graduated top 50% of class:	88

DEADLINES

Early decision/action:	12/1
Early dec./act. notif.:	12/20
Regular admission:	3/10
Regular adm. notif.:	4/1

APPLICANTS ALSO LOOK AT

and often prefer:
Fairfield U.
Babson College
Boston College

and sometimes prefer:
U. Connecticut
Northeastern U.
U. Mass–Amherst
U. New Hampshire
Boston U.

ADDRESS

Undergraduate Admissions
175 Forest Street
Waltham, MA 02154-4705
617-891-2244

FINANCIAL FACTS

In-state tuition ($):	11,340
Out-of-state tuition ($):	11,340
Room & board ($):	4,768
FA application deadline:	2/1
% frosh receiving FA:	59
PT earnings per yr. ($):	1,100

TYPE OF AID: % of students ($):

FA of some kind:	55 (NA)
Need-based grants:	NA (4,837)
Merit-based grants:	NA
Loans:	NA (2,722)
Work study:	18 (NA)
Student rating of FA:	71

BOSTON COLLEGE

CAMPUS LIFE

Quality of Life Rating: 75

Type of school:	private
Affiliation:	Roman Catholic
Environment:	suburban

STUDENT BODY

FT undergrad enrollment:	8,355
% male/% female:	45/55
% out-of-state:	62
% live on campus:	67
% African-American:	3
% Asian:	6
% Caucasian:	82
% Hispanic:	5
% foreign:	2
% transfers:	4

WHAT'S HOT
requirements easy
location
in-class discussion

WHAT'S NOT
fraternities/sororities
TAs teach upper levels
attending all classes
campus easy to get around

ACADEMICS

Academic Rating: 82

Calendar:	semester
Student/teacher ratio:	14/1
% doctorates:	90
Profs interesting:	72
Profs accessible:	73
Hours of study per day:	3.42

MOST POPULAR MAJORS BY %

Business & Management:	25
Social Sciences:	24
Letters/Literature:	13

% GRADS WHO PURSUE

Law:	9
MBA:	3
Medicine:	2
M.A., etc.:	8

What do students think about Boston College?

■ **Academics** To those unacquainted with the school, the name "Boston College" evokes the image of a tiny liberal arts school tucked away in Cambridge. This image couldn't be more inaccurate: Boston College, which is neither a college (it's a university) nor in Boston (it's in Chestnut Hill), is a large Jesuit school whose greatest strengths lie in its schools of business, nursing, and education. On the other hand, the liberal arts, while good, are "not as strong as they are reputed to be," according to one area college counselor. In all academic areas, BC pursues the Jesuit ideals of developing the intellect and serving the community. The Jesuit spirit is particularly evident in the school's optional PULSE program, which allows students to combine courses in philosophy and ethics with community service in order to "address the relationship of self and society, the nature of community, the mystery of suffering, and the practical difficulties of developing a just society." Other optional course sequences, such as Perspectives on Western Culture and the Faith, Peace, and Justice Program, provide students with the opportunity to concentrate a sizable part of their undergraduate study on global social, philosophical, and theological questions. One drawback of BC is its size; as at many large institutions, students here complain that professors are often inaccessible and that administrative chores, such as registration, "suck."

■ **Life** BC was at one time considered a party school, but the results of our survey give no indication that this is still the case. Students here reported an average amount of beer and drug consumption: BC students are not teetotalers, but neither are they the party animals they were once reputed to be. The campus is officially dry, but students report that local bars that will serve them can be found ("A fake ID is key!" reported one student). BC has no fraternities or sororities, but the lack of a Greek system does not diminish the number of parties, which are plentiful during weekends. Intercollegiate and intramural sports are popular on-campus activities, and many students become involved in community-service-oriented organizations. Downtown Boston, with its vital, college-oriented night life, is only twenty minutes away by car or public transportation.

■ **Students** Despite a relatively large minority population (19 percent, or approximately 2,800 students), BC students consider themselves a homogeneous group. One student (inaccurately) reported, "People here are all white Irish Catholic beer-drinking clones and are damn proud of it, too." Agreed another, "People think BC is very homogeneous, but you come here because you *want* to be around people like yourself." Perhaps this misconception arises from the large Catholic population, the underrepresentation of black students (only three percent of the population), and the fact that "BC is a very cliquish place. As a result, you have to be extremely dynamic in order to make the most of it."

BOSTON COLLEGE

Admissions

The admissions office reports, "Boston College seeks a student body with a diversity of talents, attitudes, backgrounds, and interests to produce a vital community atmosphere. As a Jesuit institution, Boston College also chooses responsible and concerned students who are interested in the ideals of commitment and service to others." The most important factors in your application here are "high school courses taken and the program represented by your transcript," as well as your grades in those courses. Also important are standardized test scores, followed, in decreasing order of importance, by letters of recommendation, essays, extracurricular activities, and interview. No high school courses are required, but the admissions office "recommends that students pursue a strong college-preparatory program." All applicants must complete the SAT and three achievements (English comp, Math I or II, and a third test of your choice). Applicants to Boston College most often also apply to Georgetown, Boston U., Holy Cross, Villanova, and Notre Dame.

Financial Aid

The financial aid office at Boston College requires applicants to submit the FAF, a form generated by the school, their parents' most recent tax return, and a Federal Validation form. BC awards merit grants to athletes (last year, 3% of the students received one; average value: $13,956) and those who have demonstrated academic excellence (number not available; maximum value: $6,845). The school "suggests a variety of parent alternative loans (including PLUS, TERI, EXCEL, ABLE, and Family Education) and the SLS for independent students." The deadline listed below is a *priority* deadline.

A note from the Boston College Admissions Office:

"Boston College students enjoy the quiet, suburban atmosphere of Chestnut Hill, with simple access to the cultural and historical richness of Boston. Junior Year Abroad and Scholar of the College Program offer students flexibility within the curriculum. Facilities opened in the last 10 years include the O'Neill Library, Robsham Theater Arts Center, Conte Forum (sports), and a chemistry center.

"Ten Presidential Scholars enroll in each freshman class with a half-tuition scholarship irrespective of need, and funding is available to meet full demonstrated need. These students, selected from the top 1% of the Early Notification applicant pool, participate in the most rewarding intellectual experience offered at the University."

ADMISSIONS FACTS

Competitiveness Rating:	**91**
% of applicants accepted:	45
% acceptees attending:	38

FRESHMAN PROFILE

Average verbal SAT:	568*
Average math SAT:	624*
Average ACT:	NA
Graduated top 10% of class:	76
Graduated top 25% of class:	96
Graduated top 50% of class:	99

DEADLINES

Early decision/action:	NA
Early dec./act. notif.:	11/1, 11/15
Regular admission:	1/25
Regular adm. notif.:	4/15

APPLICANTS ALSO LOOK AT

and often prefer:
U. Notre Dame
Cornell U.

and sometimes prefer:
Fairfield U.
Villanova U.
Syracuse U.
U. Vermont

and rarely prefer:
U. Connecticut
U. New Hampshire

ADDRESS

Undergraduate Admissions
Chestnut Hill, MA 02167
617-552-3100

FINANCIAL FACTS

In-state tuition ($):	13,690
Out-of-state tuition ($):	13,690
Room & board ($):	6,150
FA application deadline:	2/1
% frosh receiving FA:	61
PT earnings per yr. ($):	2,000

TYPE OF AID: % of students ($)

FA of some kind:	57 (NA)
Need-based grants:	36 (6,801)
Merit-based grants:	NA
Loans:	45 (4,785)
Work study:	16 (1,300)
Student rating of FA:	78

BOSTON UNIVERSITY

CAMPUS LIFE

Quality of Life Rating: 77

Type of school:	private
Affiliation:	none
Environment:	city

STUDENT BODY

FT undergrad enrollment:	13,822
% male/% female:	47/53
% out-of-state:	79
% live on campus:	54
% African-American:	4
% Asian:	12
% Caucasian:	78
% Hispanic:	4
% foreign:	9
% transfers:	4

WHAT'S HOT
location
dorm safety
interaction

WHAT'S NOT
campus appearance
intramural sports
doing all assigned reading
religious clubs
attending all classes
small labs and seminars

ACADEMICS

Academic Rating: 76

Calendar:	semester
Student/teacher ratio:	15/1
% doctorates:	82
Profs interesting:	75
Profs accessible:	76
Hours of study per day:	2.74

MOST POPULAR MAJORS BY %

Business & Management:	22
Social Sciences:	18
Communications:	15

What do students think about Boston University?

■ **Academics** Even though BU is a private institution, the school shares a lot in common with many popular public institutions. For one thing, with 20,000 undergrads, BU is a *really big* school. The diversity of programs available here is amazing (the school offers majors in over 80 categories). The bureaucracy one must navigate if something goes wrong is daunting. And it's easy to get overlooked here. Said one student, "One must be aggressive and independent; you can get lost in the crowd if you don't participate in school activities." Said another, "BU is supposedly dedicated to celebrating the individual, but at a school of 20,000 this is an oxymoron." A good academic program is always within your grasp: bragged one undergrad, "BU is an incredible university, and its resources are extraordinary (and they'd better be because of the price one pays to go here)." Business is the most popular major here. Engineering and basic studies both received praise for the individual attention their students get. The College of Liberal Arts, on the other hand, while good, is seen as "too large and impersonal" by many of its students. Still, if students don't aggressively pursue quality, they can easily find themselves mired in mediocrity. Most of their classmates are lax about studying (fewer than two and three-quarters hours a day), and one complained that "the school offers too many 'high school-level' classes for kids who aren't as talented academically, but the kid's parents are rich enough to send their children to a 'respectable' university, when in fact they are paying $23,000 to go to high school all over again."

■ **Life** Said one student, "BU is located in one of the best cities in which to receive an education. There are at least 100,000 other students in the metropolitan area during the school year." Another insisted that "if you are a BU student you *have* to take advantage of the city. There is so much to do and so many things to see. Boston is the main reason I came to BU." BU's campus is not much to brag about: it's big, spread out, and has a highway running through the middle of it. Students told us that "at BU people love to hook up," an activity made difficult by the school's strict dorm visitation rules (a major bone of contention with the students).

■ **Students** Students' biggest gripe has to do with the level of seriousness with which some of their classmates attack their work. Said one, "A lot of people here don't take the education seriously. Some are only here to find a spouse who will make them financially secure…it's sad because they bring down BU's reputation and potential to be an extraordinary college." Students here feel strongly that they are part of a diverse and harmonious community, although the school does not have an exceptionally large minority population. A noticeable portion of the student body comes from affluent Boston suburbs.

BOSTON UNIVERSITY

Admissions

The admissions office at Boston University considers the following components of your application to be of equal importance: "overall quality of the high school transcript" (i.e., GPA and rigor of program), standardized test scores, and essays. Of less importance, but still considered, are letters of recommendation, extracurricular activities, and interviews. Boston University requires no specific high school courses, but does recommend a college preparatory curriculum, including a full compliment of math, science, and foreign language courses. Applicants must submit scores for either the SAT or ACT. Applicants to Boston University most often also apply to Georgetown, Cornell, University of Pennsylvania, Harvard, and Boston College.

Financial Aid

BU requires financial aid applicants to complete the FAF. Last year, the average need-based grant was $9,445, and the average loan was $2,730 (primarily Stafford Loans, which were recommended to 86% of all FA recipients). BU awarded athletic scholarships to 2% of all undergrads (average scholarship: $18,635) and academic scholarships to 6% (average scholarship: $7,668). A variety of other scholarships were offered (including awards for music and theatre performance, visual art portfolios, dependents of firefighters or Methodist clergy, and ROTC) to 7% of all undergrads (average award: $7,116). Twenty-one percent of all undergrads participated in BU's work-study program. The March 1 deadline is priority only; there is no closing date.

A note from the Boston University Admissions Office:

"Founded in 1839, Boston University is a major, private university located in the historic Back Bay area of Boston. The University is made up of 15 Schools and Colleges, offering more than 250 degree programs. The individual departments, Schools and Colleges serve as smaller communities within the larger framework of the University. Together they form an exciting, varied, and unified teaching and research institution. The University is a recognized educational leader in health care, science, engineering, communications, management, education, the fine arts and many other fields. The breadth of the University's educational opportunities allows students to pursue virtually every academic interest they may have.

"Boston University is coeducational and nonsectarian. Its 100-acre campus extends from the historic Back Bay section of Boston along the south bank of the Charles River."

ADMISSIONS FACTS

Competitiveness Rating:	84
% of applicants accepted:	67
% acceptees attending:	47

FRESHMAN PROFILE

Average verbal SAT:	536
Average math SAT:	594
Average ACT:	26
Graduated top 10% of class:	41
Graduated top 25% of class:	77
Graduated top 50% of class:	98

DEADLINES

Early decision/action:	11/15
Early dec./act. notif.:	NA
Regular admission:	1/15
Regular adm. notif.:	rolling

APPLICANTS ALSO LOOK AT

and often prefer:
Harvard/Radcliffe College
Rochester Inst. of Tech.
U. Notre Dame

and sometimes prefer:
Syracuse U.

and rarely prefer:
U. New Hampshire
Rutgers U./Rutgers College

ADDRESS

Undergraduate Admissions
881 Commonwealth Ave.
Boston, MA 02215
617-353-2300

FINANCIAL FACTS

In-state tuition ($):	15,950
Out-of-state tuition ($):	15,950
Room & board ($):	6,320
FA application deadline:	3/1
% frosh receiving FA:	70
PT earnings per yr. ($):	2,000

TYPE OF AID: % of students ($)

FA of some kind:	58 (NA)
Need-based grants:	NA (9,445)
Merit-based grants:	NA
Loans:	NA (2,730)
Work study:	21(NA)
Student rating of FA:	74

BOWDOIN COLLEGE

CAMPUS LIFE

Quality of Life Rating:	**90**
Type of school:	private
Affiliation:	none
Environment:	suburban

STUDENT BODY

FT undergrad enrollment:	1,344
% male/% female:	57/43
% out-of-state:	83
% live on campus:	90
% African-American:	4
% Asian:	3
% Caucasian:	88
% Hispanic:	3
% foreign:	3
% transfers:	1

WHAT'S HOT
food
dorm comfort
registration
leftist politics
catalog
overall happiness
profs outside class
profs teach upper levels

WHAT'S NOT
dating
diversity
profs lecture a lot
religion

ACADEMICS

Academic Rating:	**90**
Calendar:	semester
Student/teacher ratio:	11/1
% doctorates:	95
Profs interesting:	84
Profs accessible:	89
Hours of study per day:	3.47

MOST POPULAR MAJORS BY %

Social Sciences:	43
Life Sciences:	13
Visual & Performing Arts:	8

% GRADS WHO PURSUE

Law:	5
MBA:	3
Medicine:	8
M.A., etc.:	15

What do students think about Bowdoin College?

■ **Academics** Bowdoin College is working hard to bolster its image. Explained one student, "right now it seems that Bowdoin is in the midst of a mid-life crisis. The grading system has changed (to the conventional letter-grade system), fraternities will be gone in a couple of years, the administration is new and the school is recruiting brighter, more independent, intellectual students. I've only been here a year and a half but it has changed a lot for the better, and also a little for the worse." While students are mostly pleased with the changes, some bristle at certain of the administration's aggressive moves, particularly the dismemberment of the Greek system. One student complained that "taking away all of the students' free choice seems to be high on the administration's agenda. It hurts the educational process greatly." Like many small schools, Bowdoin provides its students with a homey atmosphere and lots of personal attention. Students respond by studying hard (almost three-and-a-half hours a day) and succeeding after graduation: nearly one third proceed on to graduate school, with a surprising number (8 percent) going on to medical school.

■ **Life** Bowdoin is located in Brunswick, Maine, a small town surrounded by gorgeous mountains and streams. Students gave the location below average grades, but noted that "you are easily within one hour of great rock climbing, rafting, kayaking, hiking, or any outdoor activity you could possibly want. There is even inexpensive skydiving (for amateurs) only a half hour away." Claimed one booster, "Bowdoin is a college for those who enjoy the outdoors, parties, and a good education." Not everyone, however, agrees. Explained one student, Bowdoin is "a wonderful place to grow intellectually, but the social sphere is very stifling and 'elite,' with little to do during the limited time students have to take breaks (especially if they have no cars). The administration is now in the process of eliminating the fraternity system, one of the few social outlets on campus." As is often the case at small schools, students rarely "date"; they either settle into long relationships or...well, as one student put it, "As for dating, Bowdoin is the world's most expensive contraceptive." Both intercollegiate and intramural sports are popular: summed up one undergrad, "Most students are athletic and interested in the outdoors." A final note: Bowdoin's cafeterias serve up some of the nation's best food!

■ **Students** The students at Bowdoin agree that theirs is "not a diverse community," but are quick to add that "the students want it to be diverse and the administration is 'seeking diversity.'" Such assertions fall in line with the students self-proclaimed liberal politics. The large and vocal liberal faction has its detractors: wrote one student, "Most students are liberal until they graduate, then they become investment bankers." Most students are wealthy New Englanders, but, as one student explained, "Despite what was said in one college guide book I had, Bowdoin students do *not* all look alike."

BOWDOIN COLLEGE

Admissions

Bowdoin's annual viewbook states that "The Admissions Committee focuses a great deal of its attention on each candidate's academic record, intellectual interests, and overall ability to thrive in a challenging academic environment...To enhance the educational scope and stimulation of the Bowdoin community, special consideration is given...to applicants who represent a culture, region, or background that will contribute to the diversity of the College. Added consideration...is also given to candidates who have demonstrated talents in leadership, communication, social service, and other fields that will contribute to campus life..." Standardized test scores are an *optional* part of your application to Bowdoin: the school will look at your test scores if you submit them, but will not hold it against you if you do not. Music and art applicants should submit cassette tapes/slides of their work.

Financial Aid

The financial aid office at Bowdoin College requires applicants to submit the FAF, a form generated by the school, and their parents' most recent tax return. All aid at Bowdoin is awarded on the basis of need only. Merit grants are available, however, for Bowdoin graduates who continue to graduate and professional schools. Bowdoin participates in "a full range of federal and private student and parent" loan programs.

A note from the Bowdoin College Admissions Office:

"Throughout the years, speakers and writers have told us what Bowdoin has meant to them. Some were student Commencement speakers, from Henry Wadsworth Longfellow of the Class of 1825 to three speakers from the Class of 1991. Some looked back on their Bowdoin days from the vantage point of fame or success—Civil War generals Joshua Lawrence Chamberlain and Oliver Otis Howard, Arctic explorers Robert E. Peary and Donald B. MacMillan, current Senate majority leader George Mitchell and Maine Senator William Cohen, and 1984 Olympic champion Joan Benoit Samuelson, to name a few.

"Bowdoin today boasts nearly two centuries of devotion to "the common good." It has earned exceptional loyalty on the part of its students and alumni, as evidenced by an unusually high retention rate (90 percent of students graduate within five years) and by one of the highest rates of alumni support in the country."

ADMISSIONS FACTS

Competitiveness Rating:	**96**
% of applicants accepted:	27
% acceptees attending:	48

FRESHMAN PROFILE

Average verbal SAT:	NA
Average math SAT:	NA
Average ACT:	NA
Graduated top 10% of class:	79
Graduated top 25% of class:	97
Graduated top 50% of class:	100

DEADLINES

Early decision/action:	11/15
Early dec./act. notif.:	NA
Regular admission:	1/15
Regular adm. notif.:	NA

APPLICANTS ALSO LOOK AT

and often prefer:
Brown U.
Dartmouth College
Cornell U.
Amherst College
Middlebury College

and rarely prefer:
Colby College
Colgate U.
Bates College
U. Mass–Amherst

ADDRESS

Undergraduate Admissions
Brunswick, ME 04011
207-725-3100

FINANCIAL FACTS

In-state tuition ($):	16,070
Out-of-state tuition ($):	16,070
Room & board ($):	5,590
FA application deadline:	3/1
% frosh receiving FA:	40
PT earnings per yr. ($):	630

TYPE OF AID: % of students ($)

FA of some kind:	60 (NA)
Need-based grants:	25 (12,050)
Merit-based grants:	NA
Loans:	39 (2,200)
Work study:	32 (900)
Student rating of FA:	77

BRANDEIS UNIVERSITY

Waltham, MA

What do students think about Brandeis University?

■ **Academics** Brandeis University is one of the rare schools that manage to function well both as a research center and as an undergraduate institution. The school's research orientation attracts some of the nation's top scholars; the school's dedication to undergraduate education guarantees that those scholars teach college students. Of the stellar faculty, students report that "there are some AMAZING professors, and a few (but very few) turkeys." More surprising, given the emphasis on research, is that "the professors are extremely caring and very, very accessible." Brandeis produces a large number of pre-professionals—one in six students goes on to law school, one in 11 to medical school—without skimping on traditional liberal arts and science studies. In fact, some students find Brandeis' distribution requirements (math, science, humanities, and foreign language) excessive: they take at least two semesters to complete. Overall, however, students appreciate the school's academic philosophy. Wrote one student, "the liberal principles on which this university was founded provide an atmosphere conducive for the inter-relation of different ideas, values, cultures, and lifestyles. Anyone with an open mind will love this place, anyone with a closed mind will hate it." Pre-med, economics, English, and Near Eastern and Jewish studies are among the many excellent majors here.

■ **Life** Most Brandeis students concede that social life at their school is slow. Warned one student, "there *is* an opportunity to meet wonderful people here and have a good time, but *don't* come if you're looking for a party school." Another asserted that the school is "great socially, but only if you get involved (clubs, etc.). You've got to find your social life, because it won't find you." Brandeis has an underground Greek scene, but there is an "open animosity" toward the Greeks among administrators and many students. A new athletic center "has added a much-needed outlet for non-academic activity"; students who don't feel like working out often go there to watch the Boston Celtics practice. Of Brandeis's home city, one student wrote: "Waltham is a blue collar area, but it does have a lot of good stores. It's easy to get to downtown Boston, but it's still 45 minutes away." Students also noted that junkets to Boston are invariably expensive, but also necessary if you want to maintain your sanity on this academically intense campus.

■ **Students** Nearly two thirds of Brandeis' undergraduates are Jewish. Commented one student, "At other schools, everyone may look different, but they often think exactly the same. We all look the same, but since heritage is the draw, the political and social ideas are *vastly* different." "Informed," "open-minded," "liberal," and "socially committed" are terms that appeared frequently in students' descriptions of each other; so too, unfortunately, did "spoiled" (Brandeis is one of the country's most expensive schools). Students are liberal socially and politically, and, by their own account, very accepting of diversity and alternative lifestyles.

BRANDEIS UNIVERSITY

Admissions

Brandeis admissions requirements include an "application, transcript, personal statement, teacher recommendation, and scores from the SAT and three Achievement tests, one of which must be English, or the ACT." An interview is recommended but not required. The school's promotional material also states that "Our applicants usually have taken the most challenging courses their schools offer, and Advanced Placement credit is available. Most have also shown evidence of personal leadership and service to the community." Brandeis recommends that applicants have completed four years of English and three years each of a foreign language, math, and science.

Financial Aid

The financial aid office at Brandeis University requires applicants to submit the FAF, a form generated by the school, and their parents' most recent tax return. The financial aid told us that "Brandeis meets the full 'calculated' need of all students who apply by the stated deadlines. Brandeis offers an extensive work program for students who want to work regardless of financial need." The school awards merit-based grants on the basis of academic excellence (in 1991–92, 8% of the students received one; average value: $7,000). In 1991–92, the loans most frequently drawn by students were Stafford (41%; $2,645), Perkins (20%; $1,100); and PLUS (3.6; $3,655). Forty-two percent of all freshmen last year received an aid package, the average value of which was $15,000.

A note from the Brandeis University Admissions Office:

"Brandeis is a private nonsectarian university located in Waltham, Massachusetts, just nine miles west of Boston. Founded in 1948 by the American Jewish community, Brandeis University attract bright and highly motivated students from culturally diverse backgrounds. In its four-decade history, Brandeis has rapidly moved to the forefront of American higher education, combining two important traditions: the dedication to teaching characteristic of a small college and the facilities and superb faculty associated with a research university."

ADMISSIONS FACTS

Competitiveness Rating:	**84**
% of applicants accepted:	67
% acceptees attending:	27

FRESHMAN PROFILE

Average verbal SAT:	580*
Average math SAT:	633*
Average ACT:	NA
Graduated top 10% of class:	48
Graduated top 25% of class:	85
Graduated top 50% of class:	98

DEADLINES

Early decision/action:	1/1
Early dec./act. notif.:	NA
Regular admission:	2/1
Regular adm. notif.:	4/15

APPLICANTS ALSO LOOK AT

and often prefer:
Cornell U.
Columbia U.
Colgate U.
Vassar College

and sometimes prefer:
Union College
Tufts U.
SUNY Binghamton
Clark U.

and rarely prefer:
Boston U.

ADDRESS

Undergraduate Admissions
Waltham, MA 02254-9110
617-736-3500

FINANCIAL FACTS

In-state tuition ($):	16,085
Out-of-state tuition ($):	16,085
Room & board ($):	6,250
FA application deadline:	2/15
% frosh receiving FA:	48
PT earnings per yr. ($):	1,500

TYPE OF AID: % of students ($)

FA of some kind:	44 (14,700)
Need-based grants:	41 (11,400)
Merit-based grants:	8 (7,000)
Loans:	43 (3,500)
Work study:	34 (1,400)
Student rating of FA:	83

BRIGHAM YOUNG UNIVERSITY

CAMPUS LIFE

Quality of Life Rating: **90**

Type of school:	private
Affiliation:	Mormon
Environment:	city

STUDENT BODY

FT undergrad enrollment:	26,421
% male/% female:	50/50
% out-of-state:	68
% live on campus:	10
% African-American:	<1
% Asian:	1
% Caucasian:	97
% Hispanic:	1
% foreign:	5
% transfers:	3

WHAT'S HOT

marriage
religion
working a job
conservative politics
town-gown relations
food
dorm safety
intercollegiate sports
administration (overall)

WHAT'S NOT

drinking/drugs
gay community
small classes (overall)
fraternities/sororities
diversity

ACADEMICS

Academic Rating: **74**

Calendar:	other
Student/teacher ratio:	18/1
% doctorates:	79
Profs interesting:	79
Profs accessible:	75
Hours of study per day:	3.4

MOST POPULAR MAJORS BY %

Business & Management:	17
Letters/Literature:	12
Communications:	10

What do students think about Brigham Young University?

■ **Academics** Brigham Young University is the official school of the Church Of Latter Day Saints (Mormons), and this affiliation pervades every facet of the school. All students, Mormon and non-Mormon alike, must agree to forego drugs, alcohol, pre-marital sex, tobacco, coffee, and tea. Church attendance is required; and a dress code is enforced. As one student explained, "to understand BYU, one must know the culture of the Church. The campus is kept immaculately clean, the Church is discussed every day, students go for weeks not seeing anyone smoke, and the big social event is church." The focus on religion, unsurprisingly, carries over into the classroom, where students must complete seven religion courses (among many other distribution requirements). Furthermore, many men take two years off after freshman year to serve as missionaries. Students do eventually find time to pursue secular studies, however: business and management, communications, engineering are the most popular among the myriad of programs offered at this large university. Several students expressed concern over the lack of academic freedom—"Opportunities for creativity and expression are limited to those opinions that comply with university and church standards. Sometimes it's *very* frustrating," wrote one—but most students willingly accept and even welcome those limits. Students report that classes can be large, but graded the administration remarkably efficient for a school of this size. Concluded one student, "BYU is great, but it's not for everyone. It successfully combines religious and secular education. Some people may feel pressured by the environment—it's intense here—but the rewards are really worth it."

■ **Life** Students at BYU "do not party, they do not drink, smoke or have sex." Extracurricular activities include those related to the church—community service and proselytizing, for example—sports, and seeking a mate. Marriage is the top priority of many BYU undergrads. Wrote one student, "this place is also known as 'Breed-em Young' University. After you go out with somebody once, you are 'seeing' them. After the second date, you are 'dating' and after the third date you are referred to as 'practically engaged.'" Provo, Utah, the surrounding town, "is not exactly the cure for boredom," but students find it pleasant and friendly, and the nearby mountains provide plenty of opportunities for skiing, hiking, and other outdoor activities. Social life revolves around the Church ("on Sunday the entire campus turns into a huge multi-building church. Every auditorium and lecture hall is converted into a chapel," reported one student). Intercollegiate sports, particularly football, are also extremely popular.

■ **Students** Brigham Young, needless to say, is not a very diverse university, nor does it aspire to be. Wrote one student, "the student body is Mormon, thinks Mormon, acts Mormon, and looks Mormon. Outsiders have trouble integrating because of cultural differences." Students do come from all over the world and from all different socio-economic strata, however.

BRIGHAM YOUNG UNIVERSITY

Provo, UT

Admissions

Applicants to Brigham Young must submit a completed application form (which includes several essays), ACT scores, a high school transcript, and a "student commitment" report to be completed by a clergyman (during or after an interview with the applicant). Applicants are required to have completed the following high school courses: four years of English, two years of math, and one year each of laboratory science, social science, foreign language, and humanities. The admissions office takes into consideration the number of AP and college prep courses applicants have successfully completed. Applicants with special talents, creativity, or prior participation in an LDS seminary program also receive special consideration. The school's catalog notes that "BYU is committed to the concept that thoughtful and consistent study of the scriptures is vital to the preparation of those desiring to enter BYU."

Financial Aid

The financial aid office at Brigham Young University requires applicants to submit either the FFS or the AFSA, as well as a form generated by the school. BYU awards merit grants on the basis of athletic ability (average value last year: $375), academic excellence ($5,500) and "performance and talent" ($250). The school assists students seeking Stafford, PLUS, and SLS loans. Long-term, low interest loans are available directly from the university. Although work-study is not offered at the school, BYU does provide part-time employment to 8,000 students a year.

Excerpt from Brigham Young University's promotional materials:

"The mission of Brigham Young University—founded, supported, and guided by The Church of Jesus Christ of Latter-Day Saints—is to assist individuals in their quest for perfection and eternal life. That assistance should provide a period of intensive learning in a stimulating setting where a commitment to excellence is expected and the full realization of human potential is pursued.

"All instruction, programs, and services at BYU, including a wide variety of extracurricular experiences, should make their own contribution toward the balanced development of the total person. Such a broadly prepared individual will not only be capable of meeting personal challenge and change but will also bring strength to others in the tasks of home and family life, social relationships, civic duty, and service to mankind."

ADMISSIONS FACTS

Competitiveness Rating:	**80**
% of applicants accepted:	76
% acceptees attending:	79

FRESHMAN PROFILE

Average verbal SAT:	NA
Average math SAT:	NA
Average ACT:	26
Graduated top 10% of class:	45
Graduated top 25% of class:	78
Graduated top 50% of class:	98

DEADLINES

Early decision/action:	NA
Early dec./act. notif.:	NA
Regular admission:	2/15
Regular adm. notif.:	rolling

APPLICANTS ALSO LOOK AT

and often prefer:
Boston U.
U. Texas–Austin

and rarely prefer:
UC Berkeley
U. Michigan
U. Connecticut
U. Washington
Lewis and Clark College
UC San Diego
Grinnell College

ADDRESS

Undergraduate Admissions
Provo, UT 84602
801-378-2507

FINANCIAL FACTS

In-state tuition ($):	2,000
Out-of-state tuition ($):	3,000
Room & board ($):	3,160
FA application deadline:	3/1
% frosh receiving FA:	50
PT earnings per yr. ($):	2,900

TYPE OF AID: % of students ($)

FA of some kind:	45 (NA)
Need-based grants:	NA
Merit-based grants:	NA
Loans:	NA
Work study:	NA
Student rating of FA:	86

BROWN UNIVERSITY

CAMPUS LIFE

Quality of Life Rating:	**87**
Type of school:	private
Affiliation:	none
Environment:	city

STUDENT BODY

FT undergrad enrollment:	5,587
% male/% female:	52/48
% out-of-state:	97
% live on campus:	85
% African-American:	7
% Asian:	11
% Caucasian:	77
% Hispanic:	4
% foreign:	10
% transfers:	1

WHAT'S HOT

diversity
college radio station
deans
overall happiness
marijuana
living on campus
gay community accepted

WHAT'S NOT

Top 40
dating
attending all classes
doing reading
in-class discussion

ACADEMICS

Academic Rating:	**85**
Calendar:	semester
Student/teacher ratio:	14/1
% doctorates:	98
Profs interesting:	82
Profs accessible:	75
Hours of study per day:	2.87

MOST POPULAR MAJORS BY %

Social Sciences:	43
Letters/Literature:	26
Life Sciences:	16

% GRADS WHO PURSUE

Law:	6
MBA:	1
Medicine:	10
M.A., etc.:	13

What do students think about Brown University?

■ **Academics** Brown University has several unconventional policies intended to create and sustain a non-restrictive, low pressure academic atmosphere in which learning, not getting good grades, is most important. For one, Brown imposes no curricular requirements on its students, providing them with almost limitless freedom to craft their own academic programs. Brown's unconventional approach extends to its grading policy as well. Students here may choose between two grading systems: the ABC/No Credit option (if a student earns a grade below a "C," the course simply does not show up on the transcript); and the Satisfactory/No Credit option (like Pass/Fail without the fail). To judge by the responses to our survey, Brown students appreciate their school's initiatives. Wrote one student, "Brown is awesome. It cares about education, the students, and the community." Another added, "Our curriculum allows us to experiment with many different types of courses in an amazing variety of topics." While Brown students take their studies as seriously as their counterparts at the other Ivies, the grading system and academic philosophy allows them to enjoy minimal stress. As one student put it, "of all the Ivy League schools, Brown seems to me the most well-rounded. The work is hard, but by no means are the students moles who live in the library stacks. The students are friendly and outgoing and enjoy an exciting social life." All departments are reportedly excellent here, but particularly noteworthy are the pre-medical and eight-year medical programs: between them they send 10 percent of all graduates on to careers in medicine.

■ **Life** Brown is located in the city of Providence, but is tucked away in a quaint corner that has more of a "college town" feel. Downtown Providence is easily accessible, although students are less than enthusiastic about the city. For real urban fun, Brown students prefer road trips to New York and Boston. Students enjoy an active party scene, although lately the "administration has cracked down on fraternities and sororities, banned bars, kegs, and other fun things, and therefore has made the social scene more difficult." Student arts and political organizations are also popular.

■ **Students** Brown students have a reputation for liberalism that is only partly borne out by our survey. While students here are significantly left of center, they don't begin to approach their counterparts at, say, Reed College and Wesleyan University. As one student wrote, "Don't be misled when they tell you Brown is liberal—remember we're talking liberal *for the Ivy League*!!!" Still, Brown's healthy p.c. contingent led one conservative student to complain that "Brown's reputation is such that every feminist wanna-be and every radical is attracted to the 'p.c.' movement here. Unfortunately, p.c. is the scourge of Brown, since it stifles everybody's freedom for the sake of what's considered 'right.' It's McCarthyism all over again." Students agree that the student body is ethnically and socially diverse; Brown attracts a 23 percent minority population.

BROWN UNIVERSITY

Admissions

Brown University's undergraduate catalog states that the "desirable" secondary school curriculum is as follows: four years of English, three years of math, three years of a foreign language, two years of lab science (to be taken after freshman year), two years of history (one of them being American history), one year of art, and one elective. Familiarity with computers, particularly with a programming language, is considered a plus. All applicants must submit scores from the SAT or ACT and three Achievement tests.

Financial Aid

The financial aid office at Brown University requires applicants to submit the FAF, a form generated by the school, and their parents' most recent tax return. Brown offers no merit-based grants; all aid from the school is based on demonstrated need and includes scholarships, loans, and a part-time job. Brown University participates in the College Work Study program, the SEOG, and Perkins loan program.

Excerpted from Brown University promotional materials:

"Brown University is located in the City of Providence, the capital of Rhode Island, at the head of Narragansett Bay. The main campus of the University is on College Hill in a residential area overlooking the center of the city.

"In the words of Dr. Henry Merritt Wriston, Brown's eleventh President (1937–55), "The central business of the University is the increase of knowledge, the inculcation of wisdom, the refinement of emotional responses, and the development of spiritual awareness." The Corporation of the University, in fulfilling this purpose, continues to follow the policy of maintaining a university-college of liberal arts, securing at Brown many of the advantages of both the small college and the large university.

"Brown is a coeducational institution drawing men and women from all over the United States and many foreign countries to participate in the academic and extracurricular life of an Ivy League university, with a faculty concerned about the intellectual growth of its students, and an attractive campus close to an urban center."

ADMISSIONS FACTS

Competitiveness Rating:	**96**
% of applicants accepted:	23
% acceptees attending:	50

FRESHMAN PROFILE

Average verbal SAT:	610
Average math SAT:	670
Average ACT:	28
Graduated top 10% of class:	80
Graduated top 25% of class:	92
Graduated top 50% of class:	99

DEADLINES

Early decision/action:	11/1
Early dec./act. notif.:	12/1
Regular admission:	1/1
Regular adm. notif.:	4/1

APPLICANTS ALSO LOOK AT

and often prefer:
Stanford U.

and sometimes prefer:
Swarthmore College
Oberlin College
Smith College

and rarely prefer:
Amherst College
Tufts U.
Georgetown U.
Williams College
Bowdoin College

ADDRESS

Undergraduate Admissions
Providence, RI 02912
401-863-2378

FINANCIAL FACTS

In-state tuition ($):	16,256
Out-of-state tuition ($):	16,256
Room & board ($):	5,219
FA application deadline:	1/1
% frosh receiving FA:	32
PT earnings per yr. ($):	1,300

TYPE OF AID: % of students ($)

FA of some kind:	40 (NA)
Need-based grants:	NA
Merit-based grants:	NA
Loans:	NA
Work study:	NA
Student rating of FA:	84

BRYN MAWR COLLEGE

CAMPUS LIFE

Quality of Life Rating: **85**

Type of school:	private
Affiliation:	none
Environment:	city

STUDENT BODY

FT undergrad enrollment:	1,182
% male/% female:	0/100
% out-of-state:	85
% live on campus:	92
% African-American:	4
% Asian:	10
% Caucasian:	76
% Hispanic:	2
% foreign:	9
% transfers:	3

WHAT'S HOT

gay community accepted
dorm comfort
honesty
interaction
food
studying hard
deans
college theater groups
leftist politics
small classes (overall)

WHAT'S NOT

fraternities/sororities
beer
intramural sports
dating

ACADEMICS

Academic Rating: **89**

Calendar:	semester
Student/teacher ratio:	10/1
% doctorates:	97
Profs interesting:	92
Profs accessible:	93
Hours of study per day:	4.03

MOST POPULAR MAJORS BY %

Social Sciences:	32
Letters/Literature:	17
Foreign Languages:	11

% GRADS WHO PURSUE

Law:	15
MBA:	2
Medicine:	13
M.A., etc.:	20

What do students think about Bryn Mawr College?

■ **Academics** The women of Bryn Mawr work *hard*. Students reported an average of four hours of study every day, and told us that attending all classes is very important. Said one student, "Each woman is challenged to do more work than she thought possible. The workload is like an asymptote, which approaches the x-axis but just never reaches it. The work gets closer and closer to being completed, but somehow there's always something left to do." Said another, "You must take Bryn Mawr seriously, because it takes you very seriously! This school is not for everyone; it is for women who enjoy difficult challenges." Sometimes the pressure gets to be a bit much: as one student put it, "The atmosphere is over-saturated with *STRESS*. Everyone is a big-time achiever and nearly everyone is trying to be the "model student." Fortunately, many factors contribute to alleviate the tension. Professors are great and very helpful. Administrators also received high marks, and students noted that their classmates, while high-strung, are "very supportive, caring, and tolerant of each other." Classics, sociology, English, and pre-med are among the majors that received students' praise (over one quarter of the students go on to either law school or med school); the fine arts departments, however, are said to be weak.

■ **Life** Although Bryn Mawr is an all-women's college, the school maintains a close relationship with co-ed Haverford, which is two miles away. Many Haverford men take classes at Bryn Mawr and vice versa. Still, many Bryn Mawr students complained that their social lives left a little to be desired. Said one, "The only drawback is the lack of the male species. Sure, Haverford *boys* live and take classes here, but they are not real men." Another reported, "One gets easily bored here—thank God for junior year abroad!" Still, other Bryn Mawrtyrs (as they sometimes call themselves) feel the school "gives us a much-needed distance from the idea that women cannot live without men, and shows us that we don't need to put up with them when they act like jerks."

■ **Students** Who is the "Bryn Mawr" woman? Says one student, "if you like people who are talented, unique, interesting, from diverse backgrounds, appreciative of many cultures, and dedicated to both academics and fun, come here. If you can stand living with 1500 stubborn women, come here. If you want challenging courses but hate cutthroat grade competition, and prefer students who help each other in classes, come here. If you like tea, puns, African dance, classical music, and/or Metallica, come here." Students pride themselves on the diversity and harmony of their student body, and consider themselves politically left-of-center and tolerant of others. Said one, "if you are Republican, anti-gay, etc. you will quickly see that you are in the minority." There is a visible gay population, which seemed so natural to students that few bothered to mention it in their comments (except for the one who wrote "Lots o' dykes! Hooray! Yipee!").

BRYN MAWR COLLEGE

Bryn Mawr, PA

Admissions

The admissions office reports that "admission to Bryn Mawr is not based on any arbitrary set of criteria which specify, for example, that applicants must have taken a prescribed set of subjects in secondary school or must exceed certain cut-offs on the SAT or in their class rank. Instead, we believe that your own particular background, experiences, and accomplishments should serve as the basis of our consideration in your application. In reviewing your [application], we will be searching for answers to such questions as: Have you taken fullest advantage of what was available to you in school and community? Have you elected to take a challenging set of courses, even when it meant risking a lower grade? Are you prepared to contribute to and profit from a college community which thrives on testing new ideas and sharing old ones?" Applicants to Bryn Mawr are often also applicants to Wellesley, Smith, Swarthmore, Brown, and Yale.

Financial Aid

Bryn Mawr requires a FAF, your parents' most recent tax return and a form generated by the financial aid office. Grants are entirely based on need (there are no merit-based awards). According to the FA office, "Eligibility for aid and admissions decisions are determined separately. We cannot aid every admissible applicant." Thirty-one percent of the class of '95 received an award of some kind, with the average value being $11,151 (about half of the class applied for aid). Perkins loans were recommended to 10% of all undergrads last year, at an average value of $1,300; Stafford loans went to 40% of all undergrads, with an average value of $2,800. Bryn Mawr also recommends its own institutional loans to about 25% of all undergrads (average value: $500). Seventy percent of all students work on campus.

A note from the Bryn Mawr Admissions Office:

"Nearly a third of Bryn Mawr's undergraduates major in the sciences. We rank first among liberal arts colleges in the number of women physics majors (23 times the national average) and our students are 3–5 times more likely to major in science or math than women nationally. Bryn Mawr ranks first in the nation in percentage of graduates who get Ph.D.s in the humanities and fourth in all fields—remarkable for any college but especially so for one our size: fewer than 1200 undergraduates. Bryn Mawr has two coeducational graduate schools and the faculty in arts and sciences teach freshman as well as Ph.D. candidates. The College uses no teaching assistants and with a student-teacher ratio of 10:1, undergraduates enjoy close relationships with the faculty including working with them on research and co-authoring publications."

ADMISSIONS FACTS

Competitiveness Rating:	**91**
% of applicants accepted:	60
% acceptees attending:	40

FRESHMAN PROFILE

Average verbal SAT:	640
Average math SAT:	630
Average ACT:	NA
Graduated top 10% of class:	70
Graduated top 25% of class:	95
Graduated top 50% of class:	99

DEADLINES

Early decision/action:	11/15, 1/1
Early dec./act. notif.:	NA
Regular admission:	1/15
Regular adm. notif.:	4/10

APPLICANTS ALSO LOOK AT

and often prefer:
Brown U.
Yale U.

and sometimes prefer:
Vassar College
Swarthmore College
Mt. Holyoke College
Haverford College
Skidmore College

and rarely prefer:
Smith College

ADDRESS

Undergraduate Admissions
Bryn Mawr, PA 19010-2899
215-526-5152

FINANCIAL FACTS

In-state tuition ($):	15,250
Out-of-state tuition ($):	15,250
Room & board ($):	5,850
FA application deadline:	1/15
% frosh receiving FA:	37
PT earnings per yr. ($):	900

TYPE OF AID: % of students ($)

FA of some kind:	41 (9,963)
Need-based grants:	43 (10,000)
Merit-based grants:	NA
Loans:	NA
Work study:	70 (1,100)
Student rating of FA:	84

BUCKNELL UNIVERSITY

CAMPUS LIFE

Quality of Life Rating: 89

Type of school:	private
Affiliation:	none
Environment:	suburban

STUDENT BODY

FT undergrad enrollment:	3,373
% male/% female:	55/45
% out-of-state:	69
% live on campus:	84
% African-American:	2
% Asian:	2
% Caucasian:	92
% Hispanic:	2
% foreign:	3
% transfers:	2

WHAT'S HOT

Grateful Dead
administration (overall)
deans
Top 40
dorm comfort
doing all the reading
studying hard
profs in class
library
intercollegiate sports
conservative politics

WHAT'S NOT

diversity
working a job
religion

ACADEMICS

Academic Rating: 83

Calendar:	4-1-4
Student/teacher ratio:	15/1
% doctorates:	87
Profs interesting:	93
Profs accessible:	81
Hours of study per day:	3.89

MOST POPULAR MAJORS BY %

Social Sciences:	28
Business & Management:	16
Engineering:	15

% GRADS WHO PURSUE

Law:	12
MBA:	6
Medicine:	7
M.A., etc.:	20

What do students think about Bucknell University?

■ **Academics** Bucknell University, affectionately known as "the Bubble" for its idyllic, secluded atmosphere, deserves the respect it commands in many areas. Students take pride in their commitment to academics, and indeed must work hard to maintain good standing, especially in the most difficult majors (management, economics, engineering, natural sciences). Competition for grades here is quite high, and some consider it a bit unhealthy. Warned one student, "we're in the cutthroat zone—be careful!" All the hard work and back stabbing pay off hefty dividends: nearly half of Bucknell's graduates proceed on to some graduate program (one quarter go on to law, medical, or business school). The respect students have for their professors, whom they rate quite highly, extends also to the administration of Bucknell. Students display an uncommon warmth toward those who run the place, except when it comes to their enforcement of drinking laws (see "Life," below). Bucknell students dole out high marks to their deans, bursar, and registrar.

■ **Life** Although life at Bucknell can be so isolated that some students complain of "losing sight of what is going on in the rest of the world," overall it is a very happy Bubble. Students love their picture-perfect Georgian campus, and the rural town of Lewisburg (pretty much considered "theirs" as well: as one student reported, "the community clearly revolves around the university") provides an exciting and old-fashioned complement to the school. Fraternities and sororities are very important at Bucknell, though some assert that the Greeks are "overly active" and that other social options do not abound on campus. Indeed, several students complained that the "only outlet on weekends is getting really drunk," despite the university's attempt to crack down on underage drinking with "strict alcohol policies. Wrote one student, "I *know* it's the state law, but without drinking there's no social life here." Sports of all kinds are extraordinarily popular here; students rate their intercollegiate sports teams (especially basketball) as "great!" and intramurals garner lots of zealous participation. Bucknell even sports an 18-hole golf course that's "fantastic," and many other first-rate athletic facilities.

■ **Students** Although students here claim that interaction among ethnic groups is easy and relaxed, there are unfortunately few minority students with whom that assertion can be tested. Bucknell is "*very* homogeneous!" with a mere eight percent minority population. Students are politically conservative, and "too conformist" for some. The gay population here is neither very visible nor very well accepted. One student notes, "If your wardrobe consists of J. Crew, L.L. Bean, Eddie Bauer, or Victoria's Secret, chances are you'll be right at home."

BUCKNELL UNIVERSITY

Admissions

According to Bucknell's undergraduate catalog, the admissions committee evaluates "the quality of the written application which the student submits; the secondary school curriculum of the applicant, with emphasis on both content and performance; aptitude for college study as reflected by the SAT or the ACT; the written recommendation from the secondary school counselor or principal on behalf of the applicant; school and community activities and indications of special talents; and evidence of strong personal qualities of character, leadership, and personality." No set high school curriculum is prescribed; however, students who plan to major in engineering or science should have had at least three years of mathematics, including "substantial work in trigonometry," and should have taken one unit of chemistry or physics (it is strongly recommended that they have taken at least three years of science, including both chemistry and physics). All applicants must submit scores from either the SAT or ACT. An interview is highly recommended.

Financial Aid

The financial aid office at Bucknell University requires applicants to submit the FAF, a form generated by the school, and their parents' most recent tax return. Bucknell does not offer merit-based scholarships. Bucknell's financial aid financial assistance bulletin lists the Stafford loan, Perkins loan, and several university-sponsored loans as the options for students who borrow to finance their education.

A note from the Bucknell Admissions Office:

"As one of the top private liberal arts colleges in the nation, Bucknell University provides an unusual array of choices for its students— from traditional majors such as history, economics, and anthropology to programs in animal behavior, environmental studies, Japanese and East Asian studies, and international relations—from arts, humanities, social sciences, and sciences to professionally oriented programs in engineering, education, business, and music. As a result, Bucknell students have many more options than are usually found in a school of 3,300 students. Bucknell prepares students for the challenges of the 21st century. Whether students plan to begin their careers immediately or go on to professional or graduate schools, professors and administrators are there to help them. Bucknell strives to help its students use their skills and talents, to reason and comprehend, and to interact and communicate with global citizens in an increasingly complex society."

ADMISSIONS FACTS

Competitiveness Rating:	**88**
% of applicants accepted:	55
% acceptees attending:	27

FRESHMAN PROFILE

Average verbal SAT:	568*
Average math SAT:	617*
Average ACT:	NA
Graduated top 10% of class:	59
Graduated top 25% of class:	92
Graduated top 50% of class:	99

DEADLINES

Early decision/action:	12/1
Early dec./act. notif.:	1/1
Regular admission:	1/1
Regular adm. notif.:	4/1

APPLICANTS ALSO LOOK AT

and often prefer:
Middlebury College
Duke U.
Northwestern U.

and sometimes prefer:
Boston U.
Colgate U.
Villanova U.
Penn State U.
Lehigh U.

and rarely prefer:
Lafayette College

ADDRESS

Undergraduate Admissions
Lewisburg, PA 17837
717-524-1101

FINANCIAL FACTS

In-state tuition ($):	15,550
Out-of-state tuition ($):	15,550
Room & board ($):	3,825
FA application deadline:	2/15
% frosh receiving FA:	60
PT earnings per yr. ($):	1,200

TYPE OF AID: % of students ($)

FA of some kind:	60 (NA)
Need-based grants:	NA
Merit-based grants:	NA
Loans:	NA
Work study:	NA
Student rating of FA:	72

UNIVERSITY OF CALIFORNIA—BERKELEY

Berkeley, CA

What do students think about UC Berkeley?

■ **Academics** By most yardsticks, UC Berkeley is, quite simply, the nation's finest public university. "Huge, competitive, wonderful," is how one area counselor characterized the school. Many of its academic programs are superb—particularly noteworthy are the engineering program, all hard sciences, and the English and history departments (but all departments are reportedly strong)—and the faculty is universally recognized as stellar. Academic rigor and competitiveness are the norm here. Seventy percent of Berkeley students are bound for some graduate program almost immediately after graduation. Berkeley is not without its detractors, however. One area counselor wrote that the school is "definitely not recommended for undergraduate study." That's because the emphasis is on research and graduate programs here; undergrads are accordingly often shortchanged when it comes to interaction with faculty. Classes can be extremely large (some lecturers speak to 1,000 or more students), and the bureaucratic hassles one can encounter here (registration, dealing with the bursar, getting the right courses) are not for the thin-skinned. Many students felt that the administration's attitude is one of "indifferent hostility." In general, Berkeley offers a "very big, impersonal, survival-oriented education," one mitigated by "an intellectual/creative/irreverent atmosphere."

■ **Life** Since the turbulent days of the 1960s, "Cal" and the surrounding city of Berkeley have maintained a tradition of activism that continues to affect student life. One sophomore explained, "There is no city in the world that is more concerned with being politically correct. Our homeless population is cared about, our paper and cans are recycled, and we celebrate Indigenous Peoples' Day instead of Columbus Day. If you have a cause, people will listen to you." The campus itself is idyllic, but the surrounding neighborhood is not. One student warned, "the homelessness and squalor on Telegraph Hill are difficult for some to get used to." Most students, however, have to get used to them. On-campus housing is scarce, so many students live off-campus. Some choose to live in the nine student-run co-ops near campus. Others go the way of the Greeks, who are "very close-knit." A vast array of extracurricular options are available to students; politically oriented groups of all persuasions are quite popular. For those who need to get away from campus, the city of Berkeley is always lively and interesting. A bit farther is San Francisco, and the dedicated road tripper can be skiing in Nevada or surfing in L.A. within a few hours.

■ **Students** Ethnic diversity at Berkeley is "impressive," and includes large Asian and Hispanic populations. Some students complained of a "fragmented" atmosphere, but most feel that there is a great deal of interaction among all groups. The gay community is large, visible and well-accepted. For many, the most valuable benefit of Cal is increased awareness of world issues. For better or for worse, "no one leaves Berkeley unchanged."

UNIVERSITY OF CALIFORNIA–BERKELEY

Berkeley, CA

Admissions

To be considered at Berkeley, California residents must have 15 academic credits, including four years of English, three of math, two of a foreign language, and one each of lab sciences and history (an extra year of everything but English is recommended). Residents must either have a 3.3 GPA or do well on a standardized test (the lower the GPA, the better the SAT/ACT score has to be—a detailed chart on this subject, called the "eligibility index," is available from admissions). Non-residents must have taken the same courses but must earn a 3.4 average (the "eligibility index" applies to residents only). Any student who fails to meet the academic requirements may gain admission on the basis of test scores alone if 1) his/her combined SAT is 1300 or higher (ACT composite: 31 or higher), *and* 2) his/her combined achievement scores exceed a minimum score (1650 for residents, 1730 for non-residents), and none is lower than 500. Berkeley applicants often also often apply to UCLA, UC San Diego, and Stanford.

Financial Aid

The financial aid office at UC Berkeley requires applicants to submit the SAAC (Student Aid Application for California). Successful applicants may be requested to submit their parents' most recent tax return. In 1991–92, UC Berkeley students received merit grants on the basis of athletic ability (2% received one; average value: $7,043) and academic ability (average value: app. $1,400). The UC University system also administers "a wide range of scholarships, endowed by private individuals, that are limited to students who meet special requirement related to hometown, ethnic background, choice of major, etc." All UC FA applicants must submit applications for a PELL Grant *and* for a Cal Grant (Cal Grant A or B). In 1991–92, the most popular loan programs with UC Berkeley students were Stafford (20%; $2,542), Perkins (8%; $1,269), and SLS (2%; $2,542).

A note from the University of California–Berkeley Admissions Office:

"One of the top public universities in the nation and the world, the University of California–Berkeley offers a vast range of courses and a full menu of extracurricular activities. Berkeley's academic programs are internationally recognized for their excellence. Undergraduates can choose one of 100 majors. Or if they prefer, they can design their own. Many departments are first-rate, including sociology, mathematics, physics, poets, and scholars, and award-winning researchers who comprise Berkeley's faculty. Access to one of the foremost university libraries enriches studies. There are 23 specialized libraries in campus and distinguished museums of anthropology, paleontology, and science."

ADMISSIONS FACTS

Competitiveness Rating:	**95**
% of applicants accepted:	38
% acceptees attending:	42

FRESHMAN PROFILE

Average verbal SAT:	555
Average math SAT:	644
Average ACT:	NA
Graduated top 10% of class:	95
Graduated top 25% of class:	100
Graduated top 50% of class:	100

DEADLINES

Early decision/action:	NA
Early dec./act. notif.:	NA
Regular admission:	11/30
Regular adm. notif.:	3/15

APPLICANTS ALSO LOOK AT

and often prefer:
Stanford U.

and sometimes prefer:
Tufts U.
Amherst College
Oberlin College
UC Los Angeles
UC Santa Barbara
UC Santa Cruz

and rarely prefer:
Occidental College
UC Davis

ADDRESS

Undergraduate Admissions
Berkeley, CA 94720
415-642-3175

FINANCIAL FACTS

In-state tuition ($):	2,678
Out-of-state tuition ($):	10,377
Room & board ($):	7,800
FA application deadline:	3/2
% frosh receiving FA:	30
PT earnings per yr. ($):	2,400

TYPE OF AID: % of students ($)

FA of some kind:	48 (4,700)
Need-based grants:	36 (2,486)
Merit-based grants:	25 (1,947)
Loans:	24 (2,876)
Work study:	8 (1,833)
Student rating of FA:	68

UNIVERSITY OF CALIFORNIA–DAVIS

Davis, CA

CAMPUS LIFE

Quality of Life Rating:	**80**
Type of school:	public
Affiliation:	none
Environment:	suburban

STUDENT BODY

FT undergrad enrollment:	16,587
% male/% female:	48/52
% out-of-state:	4
% live on campus:	25
% African-American:	4
% Asian:	19
% Caucasian:	59
% Hispanic:	8
% foreign:	1
% transfers:	9

WHAT'S HOT

college newspaper
profs lecture a lot
town-gown relations
intramural sports
caring about politics
overall happiness
library

WHAT'S NOT

small classes (overall)
in-class discussion
deans
studying hard

ACADEMICS

Academic Rating:	**81**
Calendar:	quarters
Student/teacher ratio:	20/1
% doctorates:	97
Profs interesting:	70
Profs accessible:	70
Hours of study per day:	2.5

MOST POPULAR MAJORS BY %

Social Sciences:	18
Life Sciences:	16
Engineering:	11

% GRADS WHO PURSUE

Law:	NA
MBA:	NA
Medicine:	NA
M.A., etc.:	36

What do students think about UC Davis?

■ **Academics** Because of its rural location, UC Davis remains a "low-profile" campus within the UC system despite its ever-growing academic recommendation. Once known almost exclusively for its veterinary program, Davis is now a leading research university in many areas, including chemistry, biology, agriculture, and viticulture (the cultivation of wine). In the liberal arts and sciences, students reported that English, international studies, psychology, and foreign languages are among the many strong departments. According to many respondents, the excellent academics are enhanced by a low-pressure academic atmosphere; as one student explained, "UC Davis presents a strong alternative to the fast-paced, frenetic college education complete with riots and other assorted distractions (such as those one may find at, say, Berkeley). Best of all, the academics are just as good as those at Berkeley or Stanford." Although students here reported that they study fewer hours than their counterparts at other schools in this book, many respondents warned: "Don't worry that you won't be challenged academically: courses are tough and the quarter system is very demanding." Professors here received below-average marks for accessibility and teaching ability, but, among professors at similar schools (large research-oriented universities), they compare favorably. Classes are often huge and the administration is sluggish, but students told us that they are generally pleased with the school: as one student put it, "Getting into classes usually means going through hell, but overall, my college experience has been excellent."

■ **Life** "Friendly," "laid-back," and "peaceful" are words students repeatedly use to describe the Davis community. Explained one student, "Davis is a dream school; the city is a perfect college town, the campus is beautiful, and you don't need a car because everyone rides a bike everywhere. The weather here is close to ideal." For some, the town of Davis is a little small (although several students complimented its cafes and "awesome music scene"), but students can find plenty of action on campus. (Explained one, "Some people complain there isn't enough to do here, but if you get involved in organizations or sports, you will find there is more to do here each week than you have time for.") Furthermore, as one student pointed out, "We're centrally located, with the beach, San Francisco, Sacramento, Napa Valley, Lake Berryessa, and awesome skiing all within a two-hour-or-less-drive." The school is not without its social imperfections—students report, "The campus tends to be divided among Greeks, students of color, and everyone else (although interactions are neither uncommon nor, for me, uncomfortable)"—but most students find a comfortable niche and settle into it.

■ **Students** With a 41 percent minority population, Davis has a truly diverse student body. Students are also "politically aware," and, as a group, drift to the left of center. Many of the students are from the Bay area, and nearly all are native Californians.

UNIVERSITY OF CALIFORNIA–DAVIS

Davis, CA

Admissions

To be considered at Davis, California residents must have 15 academic credits, including four years of English, three of math, two of a foreign language, and one each of lab sciences and history (an extra year of everything but English is recommended). Residents must either have a 3.3 GPA or do well on a standardized test (the lower the GPA, the better the SAT/ACT score has to be—a detailed chart on this subject, called the "eligibility index," is available from admissions). Non-residents must have taken the same courses but must earn a 3.4 average (the "eligibility index" applies to residents only). Any student who fails to meet the academic requirements may gain admission on the basis of test scores alone if 1) his/her combined SAT is 1300 or higher (ACT composite: 31 or higher), and 2) his/her combined achievement scores exceed a minimum score (1650 for residents, 1730 for non-residents), and none is lower than 500.

Financial Aid

The financial aid office at UC Davis requires applicants to submit the SAAC (Student Aid Application for California). Successful applicants may be requested to submit their parents' most recent tax return. In 1991–92, UC Davis students received merit grants on the basis of academic ability (in 1990–91, about 1% of students received one; average value: $500). The UC University system also administers "a wide range of scholarships, endowed by private individuals, that are limited to students who meet special requirement related to hometown, ethnic background, choice of major, etc." All UC FA applicants must submit applications for a PELL Grant *and* for a Cal Grant (Cal Grant A or B). In 1991–92, the most popular loan programs with UC Davis students participated in the following loan programs: Stafford, Perkins, SLS/PLUS, USL, and JKL.

Excerpted from University of California–Davis promotional materials:

"The quality of undergraduate instruction is a prime concern of the faculty, students, and administration at Davis. Creative teaching and academic innovation are encouraged by several programs, including the Distinguished Teaching Awards (for which students can nominate outstanding faculty members), and a $25,000 prize for undergraduate teaching and scholarly achievement (believed to be among the largest of its kind in the nation). *Student Viewpoint,* a student-written and published evaluation of classes and instructors, is compiled each year from course questionnaires completed by students.

"UCD has long been known for teaching and research in agricultural sciences. The reputation of the Davis campus in many other fields has advanced as Davis has moved into the ranks of the top 20 general research universities in the United States."

ADMISSIONS FACTS

Competitiveness Rating:	77
% of applicants accepted:	66
% acceptees attending:	33

FRESHMAN PROFILE

Average verbal SAT:	501
Average math SAT:	587
Average ACT:	NA
Graduated top 10% of class:	NA
Graduated top 25% of class:	NA
Graduated top 50% of class:	NA

DEADLINES

Early decision/action:	NA
Early dec./act. notif.:	NA
Regular admission:	11/30
Regular adm. notif.:	rolling

APPLICANTS ALSO LOOK AT

and often prefer:
UC Los Angeles
UC Berkeley

and sometimes prefer:
UC Santa Barbara
UC Santa Cruz
U. Washington

and rarely prefer:
UC San Diego
UC Irvine
UC Riverside

ADDRESS

Undergraduate Admissions
Davis, CA 95616
916-752-2971

FINANCIAL FACTS

In-state tuition ($):	2,463
Out-of-state tuition ($):	7,699
Room & board ($):	5,015
FA application deadline:	2/1
% frosh receiving FA:	38
PT earnings per yr. ($):	1,500

TYPE OF AID: % of students ($)

FA of some kind:	51 (NA)
Need-based grants:	29 (1,670)
Merit-based grants:	NA
Loans:	NA
Work study:	9 (NA)
Student rating of FA:	NA

UNIVERSITY OF CALIFORNIA–IRVINE

Irvine, CA

What do students think about UC Irvine?

■ **Academics** The social scene at UC Irvine is so dead that even when students are discussing academics, they feel compelled to mention it: "excellent education, terrible social life" is a comment we heard over and over again from UCI undergrads. The school is best known for its biology department—"very competitive and challenging, but the rewards are great if you're a survivor" said one bio major. The results *are* impressive: the school sends an astonishing 17 percent of its graduates on to medical school. The ecological sciences department is also popular; science students in general noted that excellent facilities and numerous opportunities to participate in research among UCI's chief advantages. Outside the sciences, academics are less challenging: students here study an average of two hours, forty minutes a day, which is pretty low. Students also complained about inaccessible profs—a common complaint at research-oriented universities like UCI—and large classes. Of those departments outside the sciences, economics, English, and political science are said to be the strongest. All UCI students must complete "breadth requirements," meaning that they must take three courses each in the natural sciences, social sciences, and humanities to graduate. Honors programs are available in most areas of study (although, curiously, not in the natural sciences).

■ **Life** Because well over half of UCI students commute, social life is slow. "To meet people one must take an active role, joining a club or going Greek," said one student. Said another, "there is little school spirit or unity unless you're in a frat or sorority. We need a football team!" About fifteen percent of UCI students go Greek, but frats and sororities don't have their own houses, so even this "essential" part of UCI social life is limited in what it can contribute. "School functions are numerous," reported one student, but none of our other respondents voiced an enthusiasm for them. The beach is close by, and nighttime parties there are not uncommon. If you like yuppie diversions, there's Irvine ("clean, safe, and not too exciting"). The beach is only five miles from campus, a fact that led one student to assert that UCI is "a great school if you want to ride some tasty waves and catch a hair-raising buzz." Excellent skiing within an hour's drive, as is the city of Los Angeles.

■ **Students** More than one third of UCI's students are Asian, and less than half are white, providing for a truly diverse student body. Unfortunately, since there's little in the way of a social scene, interaction is minimal: interracial animosity is reportedly "not a problem" here. Irvine students are pretty conservative, but mostly they don't care about politics. Ninety-seven percent are from California, with many coming from affluent Orange County.

UNIVERSITY OF CALIFORNIA–IRVINE

Irvine, CA

Admissions

To be considered at Irvine, California residents must have 15 academic credits, including four years of English, three of math, two of a foreign language, and one each of lab sciences and history (an extra year of everything but English is recommended). Residents must either have a 3.3 GPA or do well on a standardized test (the lower the GPA, the better the SAT/ACT score has to be—a detailed chart on this subject, called the "eligibility index," is available from admissions). Non-residents must have taken the same courses but must earn a 3.4 average (the "eligibility index" applies to residents only). Any student who fails to meet the academic requirements may gain admission on the basis of test scores alone if 1) his/her combined SAT is 1300 or higher (ACT composite: 31 or higher), and 2) his/her combined achievement scores exceed a minimum score (1650 for residents, 1730 for non-residents), and none is lower than 500.

Financial Aid

The financial aid office at UC Irvine requires applicants to submit the SAAC (Student Aid Application for California). Successful applicants may be requested to submit their parents' most recent tax return. In 1991–92, UC Irvine students received merit grants on the basis of athletic ability (1% received one; average value: $3,053) and academic ability (3%; $738). The UC University system also administers "a wide range of scholarships, endowed by private individuals, that are limited to students who meet special requirement related to hometown, ethnic background, choice of major, etc." All UC FA applicants must submit applications for a PELL Grant *and* for a Cal Grant (Cal Grant A or B). In 1991–92, the most popular loan programs with UC Irvine students were Stafford (21%; $2,559), Perkins (5%; $1,623), and PLUS (3%; $3,404).

Excerpted from University of California–Irvine promotional materials:

"UCI offers programs designed to provide students with a foundation on which to continue developing their intellectual, aesthetic, and moral capacity. The programs and curricula are based on the belief that a student's collective university experience should provide understanding and insight which are the basis for an intellectual identity and lifelong learning.

"An important aspect of the educational approach at UCI is the emphasis placed on student involvement in independent study, research, and the creative process as a complement to classroom study. Independent research in laboratories, field study, involvement in writing workshops, and participation in fine arts productions are normal elements of the UCI experience."

ADMISSIONS FACTS

Competitiveness Rating:	**76**
% of applicants accepted:	59
% acceptees attending:	22

FRESHMAN PROFILE

Average verbal SAT:	466
Average math SAT:	568
Average ACT:	NA
Graduated top 10% of class:	NA
Graduated top 25% of class:	NA
Graduated top 50% of class:	NA

DEADLINES

Early decision/action:	NA
Early dec./act. notif.:	NA
Regular admission:	11/30
Regular adm. notif.:	rolling

APPLICANTS ALSO LOOK AT

and often prefer:

UC Berkeley
UC Davis
UC Los Angeles
UC Riverside
Stanford U.

and sometimes prefer:

USC
UC San Diego
UC Santa Cruz
UC Santa Barbara

ADDRESS

Undergraduate Admissions
Irvine, CA 92717
714-856-6703

FINANCIAL FACTS

In-state tuition ($):	1,875
Out-of-state tuition ($):	8,291
Room & board ($):	4,719
FA application deadline:	3/2
% frosh receiving FA:	NA
PT earnings per yr. ($):	1,386

TYPE OF AID: % of students ($)

FA of some kind:	40 (5,666)
Need-based grants:	36 (5,825)
Merit-based grants:	4 (1,508)
Loans:	24 (3,067)
Work study:	9 (1,165)
Student rating of FA:	78

CAMPUS LIFE

Quality of Life Rating:	*80*
Type of school:	public
Affiliation:	none
Environment:	city

STUDENT BODY

FT undergrad enrollment:	24,207
% male/% female:	49/51
% out-of-state:	7
% live on campus:	17
% African-American:	7
% Asian:	24
% Caucasian:	47
% Hispanic:	16
% foreign:	2
% transfers:	8

WHAT'S HOT

college newspaper
location
rap/hip-hop
intercollegiate sports
diversity
profs lecture a lot
doing all the reading
leftist politics
library

WHAT'S NOT

deans
catalog
financial aid
profs in class
small classes (overall)

ACADEMICS

Academic Rating:	*81*
Calendar:	quarters
Student/teacher ratio:	17/1
% doctorates:	100
Profs interesting:	67
Profs accessible:	69
Hours of study per day:	3.19

MOST POPULAR MAJORS BY %

Economics:	12
Psychology:	11
Political Science:	10

% GRADS WHO PURSUE

Law:	NA
MBA:	NA
Medicine:	NA
M.A., etc.:	60

What do students think about UCLA?

■ **Academics** Like most large universities, UCLA offers a lot to those who are "capable of taking advantage of things. Opportunities to learn, do research, and have fun are present in great quantity." Students agreed that UCLA is best for the go-getter: wrote one, "To gain the most from this place, one must take advantage of the plethora of activities (internships, research with professors, sororities and fraternities, community service programs…)." If you fit the bill, however, UCLA offers a veritable universe of quality programs at cut-rate prices. Popular and reportedly excellent departments include economics, psychology, sociology and political science/government. Pre-med related hard sciences, liberal arts, and performing and creative arts (the film/television programs are among the nation's best) are also substantial. Classes can be large, but complaints about classrooms the size of shopping malls and inaccessible profs were rare for a school of this size: more characteristic was the comment, "Occasionally classes are hard to get into, but the professors get the information across and classes aren't inhibited by their large sizes." Complaints about bureaucratic red-tape were more common. Said one student, "I feel like a hapless microbe swimming through a quagmire of numbers, unknown faces, and bureaucracy." The situation is exacerbated by the fact that "like all universities, UCLA is experiencing financially difficult times."

■ **Life** "Talk about diversity, Los Angeles is the epitome of a diverse culture," wrote one student. All that diversity is there for the taking by UCLA students, provided they have cars: public transportation, said one succinct student, "sucks." LA is a major city with much in the way of night life and "wonderful weather," and not surprisingly, students gave their location a big thumbs-up. Those who stay on campus find it "a great place to get involved. Due to its size, almost anyone can find a particular niche to fit in." Agreed another, "UCLA's size helps it offer a huge variety of extracurricular activities. There's always something to do here." There is an active Greek scene and it's pretty easy to find parties any night of the week, but, given the enormity of the school, it's also easy to avoid them if you want. Students can choose from hundreds of clubs and community-service organizations. Intercollegiate sports, especially football and basketball, are *huge;* "I bleed blue and gold," wrote one student, expressing a popular sentiment.

■ **Students** As one student explained, "UCLA is the great melting pot of the West!" Fewer than half of UCLA's student body is white. Almost one quarter are Asian; Hispanics make up the next largest minority group, and there are over 1500 black students as well. Students report a moderately well-blended and copacetic community, although several complained that self-imposed racial segregation is too common. The political mainstream is left-of-center, but with 24,000+ students, every political view is well-represented. Over nine tenths of the students are from California.

UNIVERSITY OF CALIFORNIA–LOS ANGELES

Los Angeles, CA

Admissions

To be considered for UCLA, California residents must have 15 academic credits, including four years of English, three of math, two of a foreign language, and one each of lab sciences and history (an extra year of everything but English is recommended). Residents must either have a 3.3 GPA or do well on a standardized test (the lower the GPA, the better the SAT/ACT score has to be—a detailed chart on this subject, called the "eligibility index," is available from admissions). Non-residents must have taken the same courses but must earn a 3.4 average (the "eligibility index" applies to residents only). Any student who fails to meet the academic requirements may gain admission on the basis of test scores alone if 1) his/her combined SAT is 1300 or higher (ACT composite: 31 or higher), *and* 2) his/her combined achievement scores exceed a minimum score (1650 for residents, 1730 for non-residents), and none is lower than 500. UCLA applicants often also often apply to USC, Stanford, Cal State, and Harvard.

Financial Aid

The financial aid office at UCLA requires applicants to submit the SAAC (Student Aid Application for California). Successful applicants may be requested to submit their parents' most recent tax return. In 1991–92, UCLA students received merit grants on the basis of athletic ability (1.4% received one; average value: $7,644) and academic ability (42%; $2,966). The UC University system also administers "a wide range of scholarships, endowed by private individuals, that are limited to students who meet special requirement related to hometown, ethnic background, choice of major, etc." All UC FA applicants must submit applications for a PELL Grant *and* for a Cal Grant (Cal Grant A or B). UCLA participates in the following loan programs: Stafford, PLUS, SLS, Nellie Mae, Terri, and Concern.

A note from University of California–Los Angeles Admissions Office:

"UCLA has earned a worldwide reputation for the excellence of its academic programs, the achievements of its students and faculty, and the beauty of its campus. Acclaimed both as a major public university and a major research university, UCLA is at once distinguished and dynamic, academically rigorous and responsive.

"UCLA is generally considered among the nation's top half-dozen universities and one of the two leading public universities campuses. It is the only institution among the nation's leading research universities that was established in the 20th century.

"With some 35,000 student and more than 18,000 faculty and staff, the UCLA has no equal in the ethnic and cultural diversity of its student body, its faculty and staff, and its curricular and extracurricular offerings. "

ADMISSIONS FACTS

Competitiveness Rating:	**90**
% of applicants accepted:	43
% acceptees attending:	37

FRESHMAN PROFILE

Average verbal SAT:	513
Average math SAT:	612
Average ACT:	NA
Graduated top 10% of class:	NA
Graduated top 25% of class:	NA
Graduated top 50% of class:	NA

DEADLINES

Early decision/action:	NA
Early dec./act. notif.:	NA
Regular admission:	11/30
Regular adm. notif.:	3/7

APPLICANTS ALSO LOOK AT

and sometimes prefer:

UC Berkeley

and rarely prefer:

UC Santa Barbara
UC Irvine
UC Davis
UC San Diego
UC Riverside
UC Santa Cruz
Santa Clara U.

ADDRESS

Undergraduate Admissions
405 Hilgard Ave.
Los Angeles, CA 90024
213-825-3101

FINANCIAL FACTS

In-state tuition ($):	1,686
Out-of-state tuition ($):	8,102
Room & board ($):	4,850
FA application deadline:	3/2
% frosh receiving FA:	42
PT earnings per yr. ($):	NA

TYPE OF AID: % of students ($)

FA of some kind:	40 (NA)
Need-based grants:	NA (1,400)
Merit-based grants:	NA
Loans:	38 (4,000)
Work study:	6 (NA)
Student rating of FA:	65

UNIVERSITY OF CALIFORNIA–RIVERSIDE

Riverside, CA

CAMPUS LIFE

Quality of Life Rating:	**73**
Type of school:	public
Affiliation:	none
Environment:	city

STUDENT BODY

FT undergrad enrollment:	6,892
% male/% female:	46/54
% out-of-state:	3
% live on campus:	35
% African-American:	3
% Asian:	27
% Caucasian:	58
% Hispanic:	10
% foreign:	1
% transfers:	5

WHAT'S HOT

suitcase syndrome
profs lecture a lot
working a job

WHAT'S NOT

location
living on campus
intercollegiate sports
caring about politics

ACADEMICS

Academic Rating:	**83**
Calendar:	quarters
Student/teacher ratio:	14/1
% doctorates:	99
Profs interesting:	70
Profs accessible:	71
Hours of study per day:	2.98

MOST POPULAR MAJORS BY %

Business Administration:	15
Biology:	10
Psychology:	7

What do students think about UC Riverside?

■ **Academics** Probably because of its location, UC Riverside remains a second or third choice for students who wish to attend a University of California campus. Students most often cited the fact that they did not get into UCLA as their reason for attending UCR. Still, Riverside has a lot to offer, and in certain respects, even surpasses its more famous sister campuses. It is the smallest of the UC campuses—much smaller than all others except Santa Cruz. Yet it is large enough to offer a broad range of academic choices. The biomedical program puts 24 students a year on track for a degree from UCLA medical school (in one year less than it would take otherwise). Liberal arts programs have a solid reputation, and business/management and natural science programs are popular. Like most UC schools, Riverside is a research center, but since Riverside's student body is relatively small, its undergraduates are afforded more opportunities to participate in their professors' research projects. Said one Riverside undergrad, "Our school doesn't have the resources of UCLA, its size or prestige. But you learn well here."

■ **Life** Riverside is out in the middle of the desert. There's not a lot to do here—"Socially, the surrounding area is so dead that the Denny's closes at night" is how one student put it. Students must rely on each other for entertainment, unless they want to climb in their cars and drive the hour or so it takes to get somewhere more interesting, such as Los Angeles and the beaches to the west, or the mountains to the east. Dormitory and fraternity parties are common (about 15 percent of the students go Greek), and UCR students seem to enjoy themselves without getting loaded: alcohol consumption here is very low, particularly for a secular school. Dorm space accommodates only about one third of Riverside's undergrads, but cheap off-campus housing is reportedly easy to come by. The sports program, while not particularly well supported, has some standout teams; most noteworthy are the men's and women's karate teams, which have won six national championships.

■ **Students** The average Riverside student is *truly* the average college student: of the 67 questions we asked every student on this survey, UCR students' responses were close to the national average for 61 of them. In most categories, they were just a little less happy than their counterparts elsewhere, and by all indications seem a pretty apathetic group. "UC Riverside has a wonderful, if fairly homogeneous, student body" claims one student; counters another, "Riverside is a place for rich kids with BMWs and money to spend on mass Greek activities, not for those who are politically aware or interested in changing the world for the better—those students should go to UCLA or Berkeley." The school has sizeable Asian and Hispanic populations.

UNIVERSITY OF CALIFORNIA–RIVERSIDE

Riverside, CA

Admissions

To be considered at Riverside, California residents must have 15 academic credits, including four years of English, three of math, two of a foreign language, and one each of lab sciences and history (an extra year of everything but English is recommended). Residents must either have a 3.3 GPA or do well on a standardized test (the lower the GPA, the better the SAT/ACT score has to be—a detailed chart on this subject, called the "eligibility index," is available from admissions). Non-residents must have taken the same courses but must earn a 3.4 average (the "eligibility index" applies to residents only). Any student who fails to meet the academic requirements may gain admission on the basis of test scores alone if 1) his/her combined SAT is 1300 or higher (ACT composite: 31 or higher), *and* 2) his/her combined achievement scores exceed a minimum score (1650 for residents, 1730 for non-residents), and none is lower than 500. UC Riverside applicants often also apply to UC Irvine, UCLA, and California Polytechnic, Pomona.

Financial Aid

The financial aid office at UC Riverside requires applicants to submit the SAAC (Student Aid Application for California). Successful applicants may be requested to submit their parents' most recent tax return. In 1991–92, UC Riverside students received merit grants on the basis of academic ability (numbers not available). The UC University system also administers "a wide range of scholarships, endowed by private individuals, that are limited to students who meet special requirement related to hometown, ethnic background, choice of major, etc." All UC FA applicants must submit applications for a PELL Grant *and* for a Cal Grant (Cal Grant A or B). The UC Riverside general catalog lists only two loan options for students: the Perkins loan and a university-sponsored loan.

A note from the University of California–Riverside Admissions Office:

"University of California, Riverside combines the excellence and diversity of a major university with the supportive and friendly atmosphere of a smaller campus. Students may choose from over 50 challenging majors within the College of Humanities and Social Sciences, the college of Natural and Agricultural Sciences, and the College of Engineering. An undergraduate Honors Program is available. The park-like campus is accessible to southern California cities, beaches, mountains, and desert resorts. On campus, students may choose among over 130 student clubs and organizations, plus intercollegiate and intramural sports. Campus tours are available throughout the year. Under the Host program, prospective students may visit as the guest of a current student."

ADMISSIONS FACTS

Competitiveness Rating:	71
% of applicants accepted:	74
% acceptees attending:	21

FRESHMAN PROFILE

Average verbal SAT:	450
Average math SAT:	542
Average ACT:	23
Graduated top 10% of class:	NA
Graduated top 25% of class:	NA
Graduated top 50% of class:	NA

DEADLINES

Early decision/action:	NA
Early dec./act. notif.:	NA
Regular admission:	11/30
Regular adm. notif.:	3/15

APPLICANTS ALSO LOOK AT

and often prefer:
UC Davis
UC Berkeley
UC Los Angeles

and sometimes prefer:
Brigham Young U.
U. San Diego
UC Santa Barbara
USC
UC Santa Cruz

and rarely prefer:
UC Irvine

ADDRESS

Undergraduate Admissions
900 University Avenue
Riverside, CA 92521-0118
714-787-3411

FINANCIAL FACTS

In-state tuition ($):	2,943
Out-of-state tuition ($):	10,374
Room & board ($):	5,430
FA application deadline:	3/2
% frosh receiving FA:	51
PT earnings per yr. ($):	1,300

TYPE OF AID: % of students ($)

FA of some kind:	51 (NA)
Need-based grants:	NA
Merit-based grants:	NA
Loans:	NA
Work study:	6 (NA)
Student rating of FA:	75

UNIVERSITY OF CALIFORNIA–SAN DIEGO

La Jolla, CA

CAMPUS LIFE

Quality of Life Rating: 82

Type of school:	public
Affiliation:	none
Environment:	city

STUDENT BODY

FT undergrad enrollment:	14,392
% male/% female:	53/47
% out-of-state:	8
% live on campus:	30
% African-American:	3
% Asian:	20
% Caucasian:	59
% Hispanic:	10
% foreign:	1
% transfers:	5

WHAT'S HOT

intramural sports
food
profs lecture a lot

WHAT'S NOT

small lectures
bursar
college theater groups
attending all classes
intercollegiate sports

ACADEMICS

Academic Rating: 81

Calendar:	quarterly
Student/teacher ratio:	18/1
% doctorates:	92
Profs interesting:	67
Profs accessible:	70
Hours of study per day:	2.86

MOST POPULAR MAJORS

Political Science
Psychology
Economics

% GRADS WHO PURSUE

Law:	NA
MBA:	NA
Medicine:	NA
M.A., etc.:	30

What do students think about UC San Diego?

■ **Academics** Because the huge University of California San Diego is divided into five smaller colleges (all five offer a full complement of liberal arts and science courses; they differ mostly in terms of curricular requirements), students here feel they receive the benefits of attending both a small college and a large university. Said one, "Due to the separate colleges, one is able to be in small surroundings and also, when desired, a larger university setting. It's easy to meet people in one's smaller college, and it's also a lot more fun in the midst of the larger college atmosphere." Warned another student, "Make sure that you attend the college that best fits your career goals, otherwise you'll have to stick around trying to finish requirements you don't need for your major." UCSD is a world-class research center with all the benefits and drawbacks that implies. On the upside, academics are rigorous, and professors are often hard at work on some major medical, science, or engineering project. The downside is that some of these professors are reportedly not great teachers, while others' interests lie in advanced research, not in basic undergraduate subject matter. Hard sciences, math, and engineering dominate the academic scene, but there are also plenty of social science and art students. Reported one undergrad, "It's a school for the more serious-minded student who has long-term goals in mind."

■ **Life** There is no consensus on the quality of social life at UCSD. On the one hand are students like the one who told us that "there are many social opportunities for the outgoing student." On the other hand are those who told us, "Don't go to UCSD if you're looking for a good time. It's Nerdville!" Most would agree with the student who reported, "Here, academics are emphasized more than anything else, although extracurricular activities are a must for anyone who does not want to be classified as a deadbeat or a study bum. Overall, the location is beautiful and the weather is a great addition to our learning environment." The Greek system is "growing rapidly" and is hoping to provide housing in the near future. On-campus social life is slow, partly because the school's 'dry campus' policy is vigorously enforced by campus security, but intramural sports are very popular. The area is safe and near the beach, and the weather is amazing.

■ **Students** UCSD has a large minority population made up mostly of Asian and Latino students. Students here are serious; said one, "I was surprised how studious the school environment is. In general I would say it is very mellow, low-key, and casual with a 'whatever' attitude. People need to loosen up and have more fun." Another told us that "if you are really into computers, you'll fit in." Commenting on the looks of UCSD women, one man reported, "There's a saying I've heard around: 9 out of 10 girls in California look good, the 10th goes to UCSD." A female student countered: "although you've probably seen the baseball and water polo teams in YM magazine, not one quarter of the guys come close to that level of desirability."

UNIVERSITY OF CALIFORNIA–SAN DIEGO

La Jolla, CA

Admissions

To be considered at San Diego, California residents must have 15 academic credits, including four years of English, three of math, two of a foreign language, and one each of lab sciences and history (an extra year of everything but English is recommended). Residents must either have a 3.3 GPA or do well on a standardized test (the lower the GPA, the better the SAT/ACT score has to be—a detailed chart on this subject, called the "eligibility index," is available from admissions). Nonresidents must have taken the same courses but must earn a 3.4 average (the "eligibility index" applies to residents only). Any student who fails to meet the academic requirements may gain admission on the basis of test scores alone if (1) his/her combined SAT is 1300 or higher (ACT composite: 31 or higher), *and* (2) his/her combined achievement scores exceed a minimum score (1650 for residents, 1730 for nonresidents), and none is lower than 500.

Financial Aid

The financial aid office at UC San Diego requires applicants to submit the SAAC (Student Aid Application for California). Successful applicants may be requested to submit their parents' most recent tax return. In 1991–92, UC San Diego students received merit grants on the basis academic ability (numbers not available). The UC University system also administers "a wide range of scholarships, endowed by private individuals, that are limited to students who meet special requirement related to hometown, ethnic background, choice of major, etc. " UC San Diego participates in the following loan programs: Stafford, PLUS, SLS. University-sponsored loans are also available. The deadline listed in the FA sidebar is a *priority* deadline.

A note from the University of California–San Diego Admissions Office:

"UCSD is recognized for the exceptional quality of its academic programs. In 1986, the Ford Foundation cited UCSD as one of the six top public institutions in the country based upon the strength and balance of our academic programs, the proportions of undergraduates who go on to earn Ph.D.'s and the ethnic diversity of the student body.

"One feature that sets UCSD apart from most universities in the United States is that its family of five colleges—Revelle, Muir, Third, Warren, and Fifth— are modeled on the Cambridge and Oxford systems found in Great Britain. This arrangement allows our students to enjoy the benefits of a large university without the disadvantages of size found in many of today's 'mega-universities.' Each college offers a distinctive curriculum that allows our students to choose an academic program that best suits their individual interests and educational plans. At UCSD, students have a choice about *what* they learn, and *how* they learn."

ADMISSIONS FACTS

Competitiveness Rating:	**92**
% of applicants accepted:	53
% acceptees attending:	25

FRESHMAN PROFILE

Average verbal SAT:	532
Average math SAT:	617
Average ACT:	NA
Graduated top 10% of class:	90
Graduated top 25% of class:	100
Graduated top 50% of class:	100

DEADLINES

Early decision/action:	NA
Early dec./act. notif.:	NA
Regular admission:	11/30
Regular adm. notif.:	rolling

APPLICANTS ALSO LOOK AT

and often prefer:
Stanford U.
UC Berkeley
UC Los Angeles

and sometimes prefer:
UC Davis

and rarely prefer:
UC Riverside
UC Irvine
UC Santa Barbara
UC Santa Cruz

ADDRESS

Undergraduate Admissions
La Jolla, CA 92093-0337
619-534-0087

FINANCIAL FACTS

In-state tuition ($):	2,463
Out-of-state tuition ($):	10,162
Room & board ($):	6,152
FA application deadline:	5/1
% frosh receiving FA:	41
PT earnings per yr. ($):	NA

TYPE OF AID: % of students ($)

FA of some kind:	31 (NA)
Need-based grants:	NA
Merit-based grants:	NA
Loans:	NA
Work study:	NA
Student rating of FA:	68

UNIVERSITY OF CALIFORNIA–SANTA BARBARA

Santa Barbara, CA

CAMPUS LIFE

Quality of Life Rating:	**84**
Type of school:	public
Affiliation:	none
Environment:	city

STUDENT BODY

FT undergrad enrollment:	15,975
% male/% female:	50/50
% out-of-state:	5
% live on campus:	22
% African-American:	3
% Asian:	11
% Caucasian:	71
% Hispanic:	11
% foreign:	4
% transfers:	7

WHAT'S HOT

marijuana
good-looking students
intramural sports
beer
food

WHAT'S NOT

catalog
diversity
small lectures
interaction
living on campus
deans
religion
college theater groups

ACADEMICS

Academic Rating:	**79**
Calendar:	quarters
Student/teacher ratio:	19/1
% doctorates:	94
Profs interesting:	68
Profs accessible:	73
Hours of study per day:	2.84

MOST POPULAR MAJORS BY %

Business & Management:	16
Social Sciences:	10
Psychology:	9

% GRADS WHO PURSUE

Law:	19
MBA:	8
Medicine:	7
M.A., etc.:	43

What do students think about UC Santa Barbara?

■ **Academics** UC Santa Barbara's academic reputation is not as well developed as its social reputation (see "Life," below). As one student put it, "Because of the amount of partying going on, the university's image is sometimes tarnished regarding the quality of education. Personally, I think this school balances academics and social life really well." Most students agree, although few who come here aren't previously aware of the school's reputation. UCSB is a large university which provides students the opportunity to pursue almost any academic avenue. Economics is the most popular choice, and the school "has many state-of-the-art facilities for science majors, especially physics, marine biology, engineering, and geology," reported one undergrad. Complaints focused on the quality of instruction— "UC schools are top-notch in research, but I must say the undergrad curriculum can be rather dry, due to the system's goal of research over teaching"— and the quarterly schedule of classes—"quarters go by way too fast for effectively studying the liberal arts," said one English major. As at many large universities, it can sometimes be a chore to get courses you need to graduate and to cut through bureaucratic red tape when you have to deal with administrators.

■ **Life** UCSB is a party school! Students here drink more, do more drugs, and lust after each other more than students anywhere else. "It's easy to have too much fun and not enough school," said one student, although another reported that "UCSB offers a quiet atmosphere during the week when I need to study, but it turns into a raging party on the weekends when I need to let loose." It takes a good deal of self-restraint for a student to get through UCSB in four years. Not only are there parties, but also the beach—which is on campus!!—and the perennially amazing weather. Many students live off-campus in the notorious Isla Vista, accommodating to party animals but off-putting to those squeamish about non-stop partying (said one resident, it "gets really loud and old after about a month.") A not-atypical student attitude: "UCSB would be a great place if you didn't have to study."

■ **Students** "Warning: everyone here is blonde," is how a UCSB student characterized his classmates. Said another, students here are "not as stuffy as at UC Davis nor is it as bizarre as at UC Santa Cruz." Like most large schools, there are lots of sub-communities here, and the trick is finding the folks you fit in with. Despite a 25 percent minority population, groups of different ethnicity do not mix particularly well. "Outside of a pretty campus and an education, the community of Santa Barbara has nothing to offer African-Americans," complained one black student. Added an Asian student, "this school is not ethnically diverse at all, but I'm getting used to it."

UNIVERSITY OF CALIFORNIA–SANTA BARBARA

Santa Barbara, CA

Admissions

To be considered for UC Santa Barbara, California residents must have 15 academic credits, including four years of English, three of math, two of a foreign language, and one each of lab sciences and history (an extra year of everything but English is recommended). Residents must either have a 3.3 GPA or do well on a standardized test (the lower the GPA, the better the SAT/ACT score has to be—a detailed chart on this subject, called the "eligibility index," is available from admissions). Non-residents must have taken the same courses but must earn a 3.4 average (the "eligibility index" applies to residents only). Any student who fails to meet the academic requirements may gain admission on the basis of test scores alone if 1) his/her combined SAT is 1300 or higher (ACT composite: 31 or higher), *and* 2) his/her combined achievement scores exceed a minimum score (1650 for residents, 1730 for non-residents), and none is lower than 500.

Financial Aid

The financial aid office at UC Santa Barbara requires applicants to submit the SAAC (Student Aid Application for California). Successful applicants may be requested to submit their parents' most recent tax return. In '89–'90, over 10,000 UC Santa Barbara students received more than $82 million in aid. Ninety funds are available from the federal government, the State of California, the UC Board of Regents, and various private sources. All UC financial aid applicants must submit applications for a PELL Grant *and* for a Cal Grant (Cal Grant A or B).

A note from the University of California–Santa Barbara promotional materials:

"The University of California, Santa Barbara, is a major research institution offering undergraduate and graduate education in the arts, humanities, sciences and technology, and social sciences. Large enough to have excellent facilities for study, research, and other creative activities, the campus is also small enough to foster close relationships among faculty and students. The total student population is about 18,500, with 16,500 undergraduates and 2,000 graduate students. The faculty numbers more than 900.

"A member of the most distinguished system of public higher education in the nation, UC Santa Barbara is committed equally to excellence in scholarship and instruction. Through the General Education program, students acquire good grounding in the skills, perceptions, and methods of a variety of disciplines. In addition, because they study with a research faculty, they not only acquire basic skills and broad knowledge but are exposed to the imagination, inventiveness, and intense concentration that scholars bring to their work."

ADMISSIONS FACTS

Competitiveness Rating:	**76**
% of applicants accepted:	59
% acceptees attending:	25

FRESHMAN PROFILE

Average verbal SAT:	496
Average math SAT:	579
Average ACT:	NA
Graduated top 10% of class:	NA
Graduated top 25% of class:	NA
Graduated top 50% of class:	NA

DEADLINES

Early decision/action:	NA
Early dec./act. notif.:	NA
Regular admission:	11/30
Regular adm. notif.:	3/15

APPLICANTS ALSO LOOK AT

and often prefer:
UC Los Angeles
UC Berkeley

and sometimes prefer:
UC Riverside
Loyola Marymount U.
UC Davis
Pomona College
UC Santa Cruz

and rarely prefer:
UC Irvine

ADDRESS

Undergraduate Admissions
Santa Barbara, CA 93106
805-893-2485

FINANCIAL FACTS

In-state tuition ($):	2,372
Out-of-state tuition ($):	10,071
Room & board ($):	5,368
FA application deadline:	3/2
% frosh receiving FA:	25
PT earnings per yr. ($):	NA

TYPE OF AID: % of students ($)

FA of some kind:	32 (NA)
Need-based grants:	NA
Merit-based grants:	NA
Loans:	NA
Work study:	NA
Student rating of FA:	70

UNIVERSITY OF CALIFORNIA–SANTA CRUZ

Santa Cruz, CA

CAMPUS LIFE

Quality of Life Rating: **86**

Type of school:	public
Affiliation:	none
Environment:	suburban

STUDENT BODY

FT undergrad enrollment:	8,755
% male/% female:	44/56
% out-of-state:	5
% live on campus:	45
% African-American:	3
% Asian:	8
% Caucasian:	72
% Hispanic:	10
% foreign:	1
% transfers:	8

WHAT'S HOT

Grateful Dead
gay community accepted
leftist politics
marijuana
campus appearance
caring about politics

WHAT'S NOT

fraternities/sororities
small classes (overall)
deans
intercollegiate sports
dating
religion
diversity
hard liquor

ACADEMICS

Academic Rating: **97**

Calendar:	quarters
Student/teacher ratio:	19/1
% doctorates:	97
Profs interesting:	82
Profs accessible:	83
Hours of study per day:	3.54

MOST POPULAR MAJORS BY %

Letters/Literature:	21
Psychology:	14
Life Sciences:	13

What do students think about UC Santa Cruz?

■ **Academics** The 9000+ students (mostly native Californians) of UC Santa Cruz describe their school as "a public school with alternative educational values." This truly unique university takes several steps beyond convention to provide its students with a private school experience at public school prices. For one, letter grades are optional; all students receive instead written evaluations of their course work. Also, students do not pre-register for courses; instead, they are given a two-week "shopping period" to decide which courses they want (which practically eliminates the time-consuming "drop-add" process most university students endure). Professors are unusually accessible for those at a public institution. The system works: students here work harder and report a higher level of satisfaction with their educations than most public school students. As one student put it, "this school takes care of its undergraduates better than other universities." A broad range of majors are popular here: English, psychology, marine biology, political science, and visual arts are just some of the many excellent departments at this "little big school."

■ **Life** UCSC features one of the nation's most beautiful campuses. Wrote one student, "I fell in love with this campus the first time I visited it. Could a school be more beautiful?" Another student said of the vast, heavily wooded site that "both the location and environment are very conducive to learning." The campus provides ample opportunities for outdoor activities such as hiking and bicycling. UCSC is a big Deadhead school, and controlled substances, particularly marijuana, are the party implements of choice: neither drinking nor the few "underground" fraternities here seem to be terribly popular. Many noted that the most distinctive quality of life issue at UCSC is the students' laid-back attitude. Wrote one, "the non-competitive atmosphere here is great. It allows students to interact on both a social and academic level." Explained another, "I wanted to study and work hard so I could attend law school immediately after graduation, and I've had no trouble doing that. Others choose to hang out, have fun, and design their own major, and they also have no trouble."

■ **Students** The UCSC student body leans way to the left politically; only thirteen campuses in our survey were more liberal. Students agree there could be more ethnic diversity here despite a 28 percent minority population. Black students are particularly underrepresented, and several warned that it's difficult for blacks to find a comfortable spot in the predominantly white hippie UCSC community. Wrote one, "Many of the students here seem to be prisoners of the sixties. I'm an African-American from Los Angeles and coming here I experienced a *total* culture shock. Over the years I've managed to find a niche with other students of color. We're trying to change the direction of this community to make it more accessible to students who aren't devout Bob Dylan fans." Student acceptance of gay classmates here was the second highest of any public university.

UNIVERSITY OF CALIFORNIA–SANTA CRUZ

Santa Cruz, CA

Admissions

To be considered for UC Santa Cruz, California residents must have 15 academic credits, including four years of English, three of math, two of a foreign language. and one each of lab sciences and history (an extra year of everything but English is recommended). Residents must either have a 3.3 GPA or do well on a standardized test (the lower the GPA, the better the SAT/ACT score has to be—a detailed chart on this subject, called the "eligibility index," is available from admissions). Non-residents must have taken the same courses but must earn a 3.4 average (the "eligibility index" applies to residents only). Any student who fails to meet the academic requirements may gain admission on the basis of test scores alone if 1) his/her combined SAT is 1300 or higher (ACT composite: 31 or higher), *and* 2) his/her combined achievement scores exceed a minimum score (1650 for residents, 1730 for non-residents), and none is lower than 500.

Financial Aid

The financial aid office at UC Santa Cruz requires applicants to submit the SAAC (Student Aid Application for California). Successful applicants may be requested to submit their parents' most recent tax return. In 1991–92, UC Santa Cruz students received merit grants on the basis of academic ability (17% of Santa Cruz students received one; average value: $1,968). The UC University system also administers "a wide range of scholarships, endowed by private individuals, that are limited to students who meet special requirement related to hometown, ethnic background, choice of major, etc." All UC FA applicants must submit applications for a PELL Grant *and* for a Cal Grant (Cal Grant A or B). In 1991–92, the most popular loan programs with UC Santa Cruz students were Stafford (22%; $2,529), Perkins (7%; $1,482), and SLS/PLUS (3%; $3,404). The FA office wrote that "Financial aid resources at our school are insufficient to cover 100%…of the non-resident tuition." In other words, non-Californians are not guaranteed a package that meets 100 percent of their need. The deadline listed in the FA sidebar is a *priority* deadline.

A note from the University of California–Santa Cruz Admissions Office:

> "UC Santa Cruz's dual commitment to rigorous undergraduate education and research is affirmed by its outstanding libraries, computer facilities, and studios for the creative and performing arts, and a new natural sciences building that expands state-of-the-art biology, biochemistry and biophysics labs. UCSC's rich curriculum leaves its graduates with the impress of a strong liberal arts education—an understanding of the many social, historical, and scientific developments that shape the world."

ADMISSIONS FACTS

Competitiveness Rating:	**73**
% of applicants accepted:	73
% acceptees attending:	26

FRESHMAN PROFILE

Average verbal SAT:	515
Average math SAT:	556
Average ACT:	NA
Graduated top 10% of class:	NA
Graduated top 25% of class:	NA
Graduated top 50% of class:	NA

DEADLINES

Early decision/action:	NA
Early dec./act. notif.:	NA
Regular admission:	11/30
Regular adm. notif.:	rolling

APPLICANTS ALSO LOOK AT

and often prefer:
Stanford U.
UC Los Angeles
UC Berkeley

and sometimes prefer:
UC Davis
UC Riverside
UC Santa Barbara

and rarely prefer:
Santa Clara U.
Scripps College
U. Colorado at Boulder

ADDRESS

Undergraduate Admissions
1156 High Street
Santa Cruz, CA 95064
408-459-4008

FINANCIAL FACTS

In-state tuition ($):	2,573
Out-of-state tuition ($):	10,272
Room & board ($):	5,500
FA application deadline:	3/2
% frosh receiving FA:	32
PT earnings per yr. ($):	1,000

TYPE OF AID: % of students ($)

FA of some kind:	35 (5,582)
Need-based grants:	28 (2,960)
Merit-based grants:	NA (1,850)
Loans:	26 (2,690)
Work study:	29 (1,509)
Student rating of FA:	78

CALIFORNIA INSTITUTE OF TECHNOLOGY

Pasadena, CA

CAMPUS LIFE

Quality of Life Rating: *73*

Type of school:	private
Affiliation:	none
Environment:	city

STUDENT BODY

FT undergrad enrollment:	810
% male/% female:	79/21
% out-of-state:	67
% live on campus:	80
% African-American:	2
% Asian:	22
% Caucasian:	62
% Hispanic:	3
% foreign:	10
% transfers:	3

WHAT'S HOT

studying hard
financial aid
interaction
in-class lectures
small labs and seminars
honesty
administration (overall)
campus access

WHAT'S NOT

fraternities/sororities
marijuana
in-class discussion
dating
attending all classes
profs in class

ACADEMICS

Academic Rating: *95*

Calendar:	trimester
Student/teacher ratio:	3/1
% doctorates:	98
Profs interesting:	59
Profs accessible:	75
Hours of study per day:	4.62

MOST POPULAR MAJORS BY %

Engineering:	60
Physical Sciences:	26
Life Sciences:	6

% GRADS WHO PURSUE

Law:	NA
MBA:	NA
Medicine:	5
M.A., etc.:	55

What do students think about Caltech?

■ **Academics** It's not even close: Caltech students work harder than students at any other school in the country, MIT included. Students here reported four and two-thirds hours of study a day, nearly a *half-hour* more than the closest competitor (MIT, of course). Wrote one student, "this place calls for a special student. He or she must be arduous, intelligent, and able to handle a lot of stress. I mean a *lot* of stress." In return for their hard work and stress, students get what's arguably the best and certainly the most intimate technical undergraduate education available anywhere: Caltech's faculty-student ratio is a remarkable three to one. "The small size of Caltech offers a great many advantages," wrote one student. "The professors hold the undergraduate students in high regard, and almost every professor will insist on unproctored take-home exams administered under the honor code." Another advantage of the school's small size: "Independent research opportunities abound right from the start of freshman year." Freshmen are required to take all courses "pass/fail," allowing them time to "get on par with one another by sophomore year." Over half the students major in one of eight engineering fields; the majority of the rest specialize in physics. Students told us that faculty are unusually accessible outside the classroom but gave them very poor grades for their teaching skills. Summed up one student overall: "If you like (or think you like) science or engineering, don't come here: they will beat it out of you really, really quickly. Only the masochistic, extremely well-prepared willing to forego a social life do well here. If you do come to Caltech, however, you will be extremely well prepared after graduation, and you can revel in the fact that you will have become one bad-ass academic stud."

■ **Life** "Come here to study, not to have a good time," wrote one student, explaining succinctly why Caltech students ranked among the nation's least happy in their college environment. With what spare time they can muster, students hang out on a beautiful campus ("a lovely location when you have the time to enjoy it") and participate in a fairly active intramural sports program. A unique housing system "combines the features of dorms and the Greek system. After a 'shopping week,' students are matched with 'specialty houses,' each with a different personality: some emphasize sports, others different social activities and attitudes." A four-to-one male-female ratio effectively squelches any shot Caltech might have at a normal social situation.

■ **Students** One third of Caltech's students are minorities; well over half are Asian. Students are "extremely intense. This place is not for the weak of heart. Death by science." Faculty and student body are still predominantly male, and several women complained that sexism is a problem. Wrote one, "The campus as a whole is very unsupportive of the needs of women and minorities. It's not just the professors; the students view women as second-class scientists."

CALIFORNIA INSTITUTE OF TECHNOLOGY

Pasadena, CA

Admissions

The admissions office reports that "we have no formulas. Students must demonstrate, beyond mere academic success, a clear enthusiasm for math or science, and personal qualities that show that she or he will make a positive contribution to campus life." High school curriculum, letters of recommendation, and SAT/Achievement test scores are most important (Math II, English Composition, and one science—biology, chemistry, or physics—are the required achievements) and are "truly of equal importance"; less important, but essential nonetheless, are extracurricular activities and essays. Applicants must have completed four years of math, four years of English, chemistry, physics, and US history. Students who apply here most often also apply to MIT, UC Berkeley, Princeton, and Harvard. Good luck!

Financial Aid

California Institute of Technology requires financial aid applicants to complete the FAF, and to submit a copy of their parents' most recent tax return. In '91–'92, the average need-based grant was $11,400, and the average loan was $2,500 (60% of all undergrads took out office-recommended loans). Caltech awards no athletic scholarships, but last year awarded academic scholarships to 5% of all undergrads (average scholarship: $9,000). No other merit-based scholarships are awarded. Forty-nine percent of all undergrads participated in Caltech's work-study program. The February 1 deadline is priority only; there is no closing date.

A note from the Caltech Admissions Office:

"At Caltech we look for the qualities that any fine university seeks in its applicants. Our students are serious about their academic achievement, as well as being actively involved in the campus community. The quality that sets our students apart is an extra measure of curiosity about how the world works and an extra measure of creativity in approaching the answer to their questions."

ADMISSIONS FACTS

Competitiveness Rating:	**100**
% of applicants accepted:	30
% acceptees attending:	43

FRESHMAN PROFILE

Average verbal SAT:	650
Average math SAT:	750
Average ACT:	NA
Graduated top 10% of class:	98
Graduated top 25% of class:	100
Graduated top 50% of class:	100

DEADLINES

Early decision/action:	10/15
Early dec./act. notif.:	12/10
Regular admission:	1/1
Regular adm. notif.:	3/15

APPLICANTS ALSO LOOK AT

and often prefer:
Stanford U.
Harvard/Radcliffe College
Princeton U.

and sometimes prefer:
MIT
UC Berkeley
Harvey Mudd College
Georgia Tech
Rensselaer Polytech

and rarely prefer:
Virginia Polytech

ADDRESS

Undergraduate Admissions
1201 E. California Blvd.
Pasadena, CA 91125
818-356-6341

FINANCIAL FACTS

In-state tuition ($):	14,100
Out-of-state tuition ($):	14,100
Room & board ($):	4,358
FA application deadline:	2/1
% frosh receiving FA:	70
PT earnings per yr. ($):	1,000

TYPE OF AID: % of students ($)

FA of some kind:	70 (NA)
Need-based grants:	NA (11,400)
Merit-based grants:	NA
Loans:	NA (2,500)
Work study:	49 (NA)
Student rating of FA:	96

CALIFORNIA POLYTECHNICAL INSTITUTE

San Luis Obispo, CA

CAMPUS LIFE

Quality of Life Rating:	**82**
Type of school:	public
Affiliation:	none
Environment:	urban

STUDENT BODY

FT undergrad enrollment:	15,798
% male/% female:	58/42
% out-of-state:	1
% live on campus:	17
% African-American:	2
% Asian:	6
% Caucasian:	76
% Hispanic:	9
% foreign:	1
% transfers:	NA

WHAT'S HOT

working a job
conservative politics
location
overall happiness
college newspaper
profs teach upper levels
marriage
dating

WHAT'S NOT

diversity
dorm comfort
living on campus
gay community visible
cost of living
interaction

ACADEMICS

Academic Rating:	**80**
Calendar:	quarters
Student/teacher ratio:	18/1
% doctorates:	80
Profs interesting:	90
Profs accessible:	90
Hours of study per day:	3.18

MOST POPULAR MAJORS BY %

Engineering:	24
Business and Mgmnt:	12
Architecture:	9

% GRADS WHO PURSUE

Law:	NA
MBA:	NA
Medicine:	NA
M.A., etc.:	11

What do students think about Cal Poly–San Luis Obispo?

■ **Academics** California Polytechnic State University in San Luis Obispo stands out among the Cal State schools both for its competitive admissions (the most competitive in the State system) and for its distinctive, pragmatic approach to technical study. Cal Poly emphasizes a hands-on approach to practical problem solving for all students ("The focus on campus is industry-related knowledge, not a research grant or thesis," reported one undergrad), including freshmen: in fact, applicants must declare an intended major and begin a course of study pursuant to that major during their first semester. Architecture and engineering are the best known majors here, although agribusiness/agricultural sciences are also reputedly excellent. The business school, furthermore, is beginning to establish a reputation comparable to that of other schools here. Liberal arts majors are also available: English and journalism students in our survey expressed satisfaction with their programs. Students reported that, despite the enrollment of over 16,000, "the academic standards are high, and the classes are small." Several also noted that "The most attractive quality of Cal Poly is the professors' commitment to the undergraduate students and their learning." To others, however, Cal Poly's most attractive quality is its tuition, cheap for everyone but positively a steal for state residents. The mix of quality programs and affordability led many students in our survey to comment that Cal Poly is "a great deal for students."

■ **Life** Students gave San Luis Obispo surprisingly good grades for a small town. Wrote one, "If there was more industry here in SLO, I would never leave! It is a beautiful town with friendly people"; another described it as "a homey college town with quaint coffee shops and restaurants." Another student noted that the school is "located halfway between the Bay area and Los Angeles, so it provides a meeting place for Northern and Southern California students. Also, it is located 15 minutes from the beach and is surrounded by green hills with grazing cows." Social life is reportedly "laid back" and "unexciting" despite an active Greek scene and the relative bounty of free time students enjoy (by technical school standards, the three hours a day students study here is very reasonable). Notably lacking from student surveys were any of the desperate expressions of stress and frustration that were so common at other tech schools. In fact, students reported themselves to be among the nation's happiest student bodies, making them by far the happiest architecture and engineering students in the country.

■ **Students** Cal Poly draws its student body almost entirely from in-state. Despite a 24 percent minority population, students report that the school is "not ethnically diverse"; Hispanics and Asians both constitute substantial populations. Students are generally "quite conservative, mostly Republican," and very practical and goal-oriented. Men outnumber women by an almost three to two margin, which is not too lopsided for a tech school.

CALIFORNIA POLYTECHNICAL INSTITUTE

San Luis Obispo, CA

Admissions

California Polytech uses the following formula to determine whether a candidate is admitted: multiply your high school GPA (on a 0 to 4 scale: add one point to your grade in each honors-level course) by 800 plus your combined SAT score. If you took the ACT, multiply your GPA by 200 and add ten times your ACT composite score. The cut-offs for California residents are 2800 (SAT) or 694 (ACT); for non-residents, the cut-offs are 3402 (SAT) or 842 (ACT). Successful applicants must also have completed the following high school curriculum: four years of English, three years of math (algebra I and II and geometry), two years of a foreign language, one year each of lab science, US history, and art, and three years of academic/arts electives.

Financial Aid

The financial aid office at Cal Polytech–SLO requires applicants to submit the Student Aid Application for California (SAAC). The school offers merit grants awarded on the basis of academic excellence, athletic ability, and special skill in the arts. Last year, students took out the following loans: Stafford (22% took one; average value: $2,853), Perkins (4%; $1,600), and SLS/PLUS (3%;$3,153). Fewer than 1% of the students borrowed on the Collins, EPA, Nissin, and Outside Education loan programs.

Excerpted from California Polytechnic Institute promotional materials:

"From row crops to computers, Cal Poly believes the best way for someone to learn something is to *do* it. That's been the school's philosophy since it began. "Learn by doing," the university calls it.

"Cal Poly students gain invaluable first-hand experience both on campus and off. Course work emphasizes it, with a high proportion of lab work, field work and special projects culminating in a senior project. On-campus opportunities such as the daily student-run newspaper and real-world agricultural enterprise projects make hands-on learning a daily reality, not just a catch phrase. Off-campus work with government agencies and major national corporations—for both academic credit and a salary—is available through various programs that include the largest Cooperative Education Program in the Western United States. Many student activities are designed to give students an additional chance to apply what's learned in the classroom.

"With its approach to education and success in applying it, Cal Poly has built a solid statewide and national reputation. The proof of success is the eagerness of recruiters from business and industry to hire Cal Poly graduates, the support well-known corporations have given its programs, and the loyalty of its alumni."

ADMISSIONS FACTS

Competitiveness Rating:	**85**
% of applicants accepted:	31
% acceptees attending:	70

FRESHMAN PROFILE

Average verbal SAT:	458
Average math SAT:	536
Average ACT:	NA
Graduated top 10% of class:	NA
Graduated top 25% of class:	NA
Graduated top 50% of class:	NA

DEADLINES

Early decision/action:	NA
Early dec./act. notif.:	NA
Regular admission:	11/30
Regular adm. notif.:	2/28

APPLICANTS ALSO LOOK AT

and often prefer:
UC Davis

and sometimes prefer:
UC Berkeley
UC Santa Cruz
UC Los Angeles
UC Santa Barbara

ADDRESS

Undergraduate Admissions
San Luis Obispo, CA 93407
(805)756-2792

FINANCIAL FACTS

In-state tuition ($):	1,191
Out-of-state tuition ($):	4,943
Room & board ($):	4,146
FA application deadline:	3/1
% frosh receiving FA:	19
PT earnings per yr. ($):	NA

TYPE OF AID: % of students ($)

FA of some kind:	32 (NA)
Need-based grants:	NA
Merit-based grants:	NA
Loans:	NA
Work study:	NA
Student rating of FA:	NA

119

CARLETON COLLEGE

CAMPUS LIFE

Quality of Life Rating:	**88**
Type of school:	private
Affiliation:	none
Environment:	suburban

STUDENT BODY

FT undergrad enrollment:	1,707
% male/% female:	52/48
% out-of-state:	76
% live on campus:	85
% African-American:	4
% Asian:	6
% Caucasian:	87
% Hispanic:	2
% foreign:	1
% transfers:	1

WHAT'S HOT

gay community accepted
college radio station
college theater
intramural sports
alternative rock
students interact
leftist politics
profs outside class
registration
profs in class
dorm comfort
overall happiness

WHAT'S NOT

fraternities/sororities

ACADEMICS

Academic Rating:	**88**
Calendar:	trimester
Student/teacher ratio:	9/1
% doctorates:	82
Profs interesting:	90
Profs accessible:	91
Hours of study per day:	3.62

MOST POPULAR MAJORS BY %

English:	13
Political Sciences:	11
History:	11

% GRADS WHO PURSUE

Law:	6
MBA:	2
Medicine:	5
M.A., etc.:	27

What do students think about Carleton College?

■ **Academics** Carleton College is an excellent liberal arts college, the Midwestern "equivalent of Swarthmore and Wesleyan," according to one area college counselor. Its student body is among the most academically accomplished in the country, its faculty is excellent and "very caring," and it maintains strong departments in a wide range of liberal arts, creative arts, and sciences. So how come most people haven't heard of it? One student explained, "Carleton's biggest problem, perhaps its only problem, is intellectual insecurity. This college recruits the best students from the region and the nation. But, because of its remote location, it's a little-known institution. As a result, students here tend to take themselves way too seriously in order to compensate for the school's lack of nation-wide respect." "Intense" is a word many students used to describe the academic environment. Said one student, "Once you clue into the fact that everyone is stressed out, and everyone works on homework eight hours a day, and no one has a life, then you start to enjoy Carleton." A trimester schedule results in frequent exams, further adding to the high pressure environment.

■ **Life** Carleton is located in the middle of rural Minnesota, so, unsurprisingly, students pursue their leisure activities on campus. Fortunately, the school sponsors lots of movies, concerts, and other social events: wrote one student, "Only at Carleton can you attend a Bach concert, a kegger, and the Nude Olympics all on the same night." Students actively participate in theater groups, the college radio station, and a very popular intramural sports program. On party nights, the student body is often augmented by visitors from nearby St. Olaf. Concluded one student, "There's so much to do on campus, it doesn't matter what's going on in Northfield!" Drinking is a popular pastime, so much so that one student wrote that "Carleton has a social scene based on alcohol. We're kind of like a state school where the classes are actually rewarding (by the way, we're a little pretentious)." And snobby, too! A final note: it gets really, *really* cold here during winter trimester. Fortunately, a tunnel system connects many academic and residence buildings.

■ **Students** Despite its small size and remote location, Carleton attracts students from all over the country. This is due both to Carleton's academic reputation and to its aggressive recruitment policies. Although geographic diversity is not a problem, ethnic diversity is another matter; there are no more than 100 students of any single minority group here. Complained one Black student, "I was extremely misinformed about the cohesion, size, and strength of the multicultural community here. I suspect the college intentionally misrepresents itself to minority students, and I feel betrayed." Students describe themselves as politically liberal, but more than a few detractors described their classmates as "'wanna-be' liberals…rich kids who like to pretend they're poor." Students report a high level of tolerance for alternative lifestyles.

CARLETON COLLEGE

Northfield, MN

Admissions

The admissions office reports that "of importance [in the admissions process] are superior academic achievement, as demonstrated in the applicant's school record and scores on required entrance; personal qualities and interests; participation in extracurricular activities; and potential for development as a student and a graduate of the College." High school curriculum, letters of recommendation, and the application essay weigh most heavily in the school's assessment of your application; standardized test scores, extracurricular activities, and an interview are less important. Applicants are "strongly recommended" to have completed four years of English, three years of math and social studies, and two years of natural sciences. Either the SAT or the ACT is required, and three achievements are recommended. An "interim" early decision plan is available: applications are due January 15; notification is made by February 15.

Financial Aid

The financial aid office at Carleton requires applicants to submit the FAF (FFS for Minnesota residents) and a copy of their parents' most recent tax return. Carleton awards no merit grants; all assistance is awarded on the basis of need only. Last year Carleton recommended Stafford loans for 43% of its financial aid recipients; the school also recommends the Perkins loan and a loan sponsored by the school.

A note from the Carleton College Admissions Office:

"Carleton's admission committee makes its decisions on a need-blind basis. Our financial aid policy is one which meets the full demonstrated need of every admitted student. About 60% of our students spend at least one academic term off campus for credit, most of them abroad. Financial aid may be applied to international study programs. More than 75 percent of our graduates eventually go to graduate or professional school. Carleton is second of all liberal arts colleges in the number of its graduates receiving Ph.D.'s in the sciences, math, and social science in 1985-90, first counting the sciences and math only."

ADMISSIONS FACTS

Competitiveness Rating:	**92**
% of applicants accepted:	47
% acceptees attending:	35

FRESHMAN PROFILE

Average verbal SAT:	620*
Average math SAT:	663*
Average ACT:	29*
Graduated top 10% of class:	70
Graduated top 25% of class:	93
Graduated top 50% of class:	99

DEADLINES

Early decision/action:	11/15
Early dec./act. notif.:	12/15
Regular admission:	2/1
Regular adm. notif.:	4/15

APPLICANTS ALSO LOOK AT

and often prefer:
Amherst College
U. Pennsylvania
Swarthmore College

and sometimes prefer:
Wesleyan U.
Haverford College
Vassar College
St. Olaf College

and rarely prefer:
Reed College
U. Minnesota

ADDRESS

Undergraduate Admissions
One North College Street
Northfield, MN 55057
507-663-4190

FINANCIAL FACTS

In-state tuition ($):	16,170
Out-of-state tuition ($):	16,170
Room & board ($):	3,324
FA application deadline:	3/1
% frosh receiving FA:	58
PT earnings per yr. ($):	1,580

TYPE OF AID: % of students ($)

FA of some kind:	59 (NA)
Need-based grants:	52 (7,045)
Merit-based grants:	NA
Loans:	47 (2,500)
Work study:	NA (1,050)
Student rating of FA:	94

CARNEGIE MELLON UNIVERSITY

Pittsburgh, PA

CAMPUS LIFE

Quality of Life Rating:	**76**
Type of school:	private
Affiliation:	none
Environment:	city

STUDENT BODY

FT undergrad enrollment:	4,195
% male/% female:	69/31
% out-of-state:	61
% live on campus:	80
% African-American:	5
% Asian:	18
% Caucasian:	52
% Hispanic:	3
% foreign:	6
% transfers:	2

WHAT'S HOT

gay community visible
studying hard
alternative rock
college theater groups
gay community accepted

WHAT'S NOT

intercollegiate sports
requirements are easy
campus appearance
suitcase syndrome

ACADEMICS

Academic Rating:	**83**
Calendar:	semester
Student/teacher ratio:	9/1
% doctorates:	86
Profs interesting:	75
Profs accessible:	74
Hours of study per day:	3.79

MOST POPULAR MAJORS

Elec.& Comp. Engineering
Math./Computer Science
Architecture

% GRADS WHO PURSUE

Law:	5
MBA:	7
Medicine:	5
M.A., etc.:	13

What do students think about Carnegie Mellon University?

■ **Academics** Carnegie Mellon University is a school that excels in two seemingly disparate fields, engineering and the fine arts. Drama, architecture, and hard sciences are also popular and top quality. CMU is for best suited to the ambitious student already focused on his/her career choice: as one put it, "Carnegie Mellon is the place to go if you know what you want to study, if you are an overachiever, and if you like to work a lot. You won't get a classic liberal arts education here, but you will most definitely be prepared for life after college!" Students here do work hard—over three and three-quarters hours a day—and told us the work is challenging as well as time consuming in all departments. Most, however, feel the hard work will pay off in the near future. Said one, "Although the workload is quite intense, a CMU education provides many employment opportunities that students from other schools do not have." Classes are relatively small and professors are average, which makes them better than most profs at other research-oriented schools.

■ **Life** According to one undergrad, "Carnegie Mellon gets a bad social rap because of the 3:1 male:female ratio and the large computer geek population. The first isn't as big a problem as it seems; the second is." Social life is hindered by the enormous workload students undertake and by the competitiveness of the students. Said one, "Six hours of sleep a night is a treat! Four hours is the norm. Is it cutthroat here? CMU? Naah…(just a touch of sarcasm here)." Still, students do find time to hang out with friends and drink a few beers occasionally. Students gave Pittsburgh decent marks, and a few really were enthusiastic about the city. Wrote one, "I think Pittsburgh is a great city to go to school in, and I grew up in New York City." Perhaps by way of explaining why the lopsided male-female ratio wasn't a problem, another added that "Pittsburgh has a lot of attractive women, strangely enough!" Students are not big on school spirit or their Division III athletic teams; one complained that "students lack the school pride that adds a touch of community to other school's campuses."

■ **Students** Because the school attracts both hard-core scientists and hard-core artists, the student body has "a strange mix of nerds and posing art majors on campus." Most would agree that their classmates make CMU a "very exciting place to be, because there is so much talent and thinking going on." The school has a large minority population, much of which is Asian. Politically the students are split. Wrote one who identified himself as "left-wing," "On this campus, students are either politically radical or politically reactionary. There is very little in between. CMU has active feminist and gay movements, as well as loud and generally violent anti-abortion groups, frat boys, and ROTC. If you like a good political fight, CMU is the place to be." The students want you to know two more things: (1) "CMU is about more than bagpipes!"; and (2) "nobody here calls each other 'fruits' and 'vegetables'!"

CARNEGIE MELLON UNIVERSITY

Pittsburgh, PA

Admissions

The admissions office reports that it uses "no cut-offs, no formulas" in assessing its applicant pool. High school curriculum and grades are the most important components of your application here; standardized test scores, essays, letters of recommendation, extracurricular activities and, finally, interviews are also considered. Either the SAT or ACT are required, as are three achievement tests. Curricular requirements vary depending on which school you apply to; art students, for example, must submit a portfolio, while engineering students must have completed four years of math and science. Students applying to Carnegie Mellon most often also apply to Cornell University.

Financial Aid

The financial aid office at Carnegie Mellon University requires applicants to submit the FAF, a form generated by the school, and copies of their and their parents' most recent tax returns and W-2 forms. CMU provides "a small number" of merit-based awards for "students who succeed academically and artistically, receive strong recommendations, contribute to their communities, and demonstrate leadership." CMU students borrow on the Stafford, Perkins, and PLUS/SLS loan programs.

A note from the Carnegie Mellon Admissions Office:

"Carnegie Mellon is a private, co-educational university with approximately 4,300 undergraduates, 2,500 graduate students, and 425 full-time faculty members. The university's 103-acre campus is located in the Oakland area of Pittsburgh, five miles east of downtown.

"The university is composed of seven colleges: the Carnegie Institute of Technology (engineering); the College of Fine Arts; the College of Humanities and Social Sciences (combining liberal arts education with professional specializations); the Graduate School of Industrial Administration (undergraduate business is Industrial Management); the Mellon College of Science; the School of Computer Science; and the School of Urban and Public Affairs.

"Admission to Carnegie Mellon is competitive and based on an evaluation of each student's academic or artistic potential. Applicants must submit a high school transcript, recommendations, SAT or ACT scores, TOEFL, and the result of three achievement tests. Applicants to the departments or art, design, drama, or music must show a portfolio or an audition."

ADMISSIONS FACTS

Competitiveness Rating:	**85**
% of applicants accepted:	65
% acceptees attending:	26

FRESHMAN PROFILE

Average verbal SAT:	577*
Average math SAT:	643*
Average ACT:	29*
Graduated top 10% of class:	53
Graduated top 25% of class:	86
Graduated top 50% of class:	97

DEADLINES

Early decision/action:	12/1
Early dec./act. notif.:	1/15
Regular admission:	2/1
Regular adm. notif.:	4/15

APPLICANTS ALSO LOOK AT

and often prefer:
Cornell U.
Tufts U.
U. Pennsylvania

and sometimes prefer:
Case Western Reserve U.
Washington U.

and rarely prefer:
U. Pittsburgh
Boston U.
Syracuse U.
Penn State U.

ADDRESS

Undergraduate Admissions
5000 Forbes Avenue
Pittsburgh, PA 15213-3890
412-268-2082

FINANCIAL FACTS

In-state tuition ($):	15,250
Out-of-state tuition ($):	15,250
Room & board ($):	5,110
FA application deadline:	3/1
% frosh receiving FA:	62
PT earnings per yr. ($):	1,300

TYPE OF AID: % of students ($)

FA of some kind:	63 (NA)
Need-based grants:	NA
Merit-based grants:	NA
Loans:	NA
Work study:	NA
Student rating of FA:	78

CASE WESTERN RESERVE UNIVERSITY

Cleveland, OH

What do students think about Case Western Reserve?

■ **Academics** Case Western Reserve is actually two schools in one: the university in its present state was formed by the union of Western Reserve College (a traditional liberal arts and social sciences college) and the Case Institute of Technology (engineering and physical sciences). While engineers make up the largest student group (40 percent of the student body), students report that "Case is not the 'slide rule' school anymore, and many different groups exist here." Applicants are admitted to CWRU and "enter" one of the two colleges when they declare their majors. This merging of student bodies is mostly a formality, though, since freshmen must choose one of three core curricula, each of which leads toward or away from the engineering program. Students report that business and management, pre-medical studies, art history, and nursing are among the strongest, largest programs here. Case's engineering programs, however, are the standouts. Academics are rigorous, the pressure is intense ("there is a high amount of stress"), and the work load is heavy. "One comes to CWRU to learn, learn, and, if you are outgoing, learn some more." Engineers reported that professors are poor teachers even by engineering school standards: said one, "Professors talk over our heads, then look at us in disbelief if we ask questions, as if we didn't belong in class if we didn't understand the material. Then they ignore your question and go on with their lecture." Out of this boot camp-like atmosphere, however, come some of the nation's leading, and highest-paid, engineers.

■ **Life** CWRU was formed of two distinct campuses built with no eye toward joining them, explaining why one student wrote that "the campus looks like the work of one psychotic architect." Although Case and Western Reserve aren't physically separated, "the campus is very divided: Case Core, Reserve Core; North Side, South Side; Frats, GDIs." Most students agree that "social life is lacking" here. Said one, "As far as having fun goes, you have to make it happen for yourself." Men outnumber women two to one, making dating and a "normal" social scene difficult. Said one man of the social scene, "The best part of campus life is dorm roommates and suite mates. It's great to stay up until three in the morning, just bullshitting and playing instruments loudly." There is an active Greek system, and intramural sports are among the popular diversions. So too is downtown Cleveland, which is close by. For an urban campus, CWRU boasts an abundance of trees and relaxing open spaces.

■ **Students** Nearly one quarter of CWRU's students are minorities, and students reported that their classmates are diverse in social background and attitudes as well. The large engineering population tends to make this student body more conservative than most, and most students view their degrees as a means toward a lucrative career, rather than an end to itself. Still, several students reported a surprising absence of cutthroat competition: "People are willing to help each other out here," reported one student.

CASE WESTERN RESERVE UNIVERSITY

Cleveland, OH

Admissions

The admissions office reports that "admission is highly competitive...we look at each student's credentials very carefully. While your standardized test scores tell us something about you, your high school grades (and the difficulty of the courses you've taken), counselor recommendation, extracurricular activities, and personal interests and goals tell us even more...every tub on its own bottom." On-campus interviews are "encouraged but not required for admission." Applicants are expected to have completed 16 units of academic course work, including four years of English, three years of math, and one year of lab science. Two to four years of a foreign language is "strongly encouraged." Prospective math and science majors, furthermore, must have completed further course work in their intended fields. Case requires either the SAT or the ACT, and three achievements (English composition must be one). Applicants to Case are often also applicants to Rochester, Carnegie Mellon, Ohio State, Miami of Ohio, and Northwestern.

Financial Aid

Case Western requires a FAF and your most recent tax return. Academic grants are awarded (currently 39% of all undergrads have academic grants, at an average value of $5,936). The FA office provided financial aid to 91% of incoming freshman last year, with an average award of $13,200. The office states, "All students from Ohio and from other states (e.g., Pennsylvania, Connecticut, Delaware, Massachusetts and Vermont) with portable state grant programs should apply for their state's assistance." CWRU recommends Perkins loans (last year to 18% of undergrads, with an average value of $1,273), Stafford loans (46%; $2,646) and their own university loans (25%; $3,116). The school also offers a tuition stabilization program, through which a family can pay all four years of tuition in advance, and not face future increases. A University loan at 8% simple interest is available with a repayment period of up to ten years.

A note from the Case Western Reserve University Admissions Office:

"CWRU offers majors in 60 fields of engineering, humanities, arts, social sciences, natural and applied sciences, management and nursing. With the exception of nursing (where students must also be admitted to the school of nursing), all these programs are available through our admission door. Students are admitted based on general academic merit, not intended major."

ADMISSIONS FACTS

Competitiveness Rating:	**85**
% of applicants accepted:	86
% acceptees attending:	35

FRESHMAN PROFILE

Average verbal SAT:	570*
Average math SAT:	643*
Average ACT:	28*
Graduated top 10% of class:	70
Graduated top 25% of class:	88
Graduated top 50% of class:	97

DEADLINES

Early decision/action:	1/5
Early dec./act. notif.:	NA
Regular admission:	3/1
Regular adm. notif.:	NA

APPLICANTS ALSO LOOK AT

and often prefer:
U. Minnesota
Marquette U.

and sometimes prefer:
Carnegie Mellon U.
Boston U.

and rarely prefer:
Ohio State U.
Purdue U.
Penn State U.

ADDRESS

Undergraduate Admissions
University Circle
Cleveland, OH 44106-1712
216-368-4450

FINANCIAL FACTS

In-state tuition ($):	13,600
Out-of-state tuition ($):	13,600
Room & board ($):	4,930
FA application deadline:	2/1
% frosh receiving FA:	80
PT earnings per yr. ($):	1,100

TYPE OF AID: % of students ($)

FA of some kind:	86 (12,688)
Need-based grants:	74 (9,473)
Merit-based grants:	39 (5,936)
Loans:	54 (4,659)
Work study:	38 (1,576)
Student rating of FA:	87

CATHOLIC UNIVERSITY OF AMERICA

Washington, DC

CAMPUS LIFE

Quality of Life Rating:	***83***
Type of school:	private
Affiliation:	Roman Catholic
Environment:	city

STUDENT BODY

FT undergrad enrollment:	3,008
% male/% female:	43/57
% out-of-state:	94
% live on campus:	70
% African-American:	5
% Asian:	3
% Caucasian:	88
% Hispanic:	4
% foreign:	7
% transfers:	6

WHAT'S HOT

location
religion
college theater groups
living on campus

WHAT'S NOT

fraternities/sororities
library
gay community visible
town-gown relations
diversity
doing all assigned reading

ACADEMICS

Academic Rating:	***76***
Calendar:	semester
Student/teacher ratio:	12/1
% doctorates:	78
Profs interesting:	72
Profs accessible:	78
Hours of study per day:	3.2

MOST POPULAR MAJORS BY %

Pub. Affairs & Protective Svcs.:	14
Engineering:	13
Health Sciences:	13

% GRADS WHO PURSUE

Law:	7
MBA:	3
Medicine:	2
M.A., etc.:	20

What do students think about Catholic University?

■ **Academics** Although it's the official university of the Roman Catholic Church in America, Catholic U. has a lot more than religious study to offer. Strong programs include drama, music, architecture, nursing, and pre-professional studies: almost one third of all graduates go on to grad school within a year. Students enjoy a close-knit academic community, one united by religion and a demanding core curriculum. Said one freshman, "The students live in a nurturing and supportive environment. I especially enjoy my small classes and the individual attention I receive." Another student noted that "professors and administrators are extremely helpful and available. The president of the university lives in the residence halls. All administrators frequently take part in student activities, and really know many of the students." CUA requires its liberal arts and sciences students (who make up the majority of undergraduates) to complete a particularly comprehensive core curriculum; these requirements chew up approximately half the credits necessary for graduation, leaving students with relatively few opportunities to take elective courses. Students rated their library tenth worst in the country; fortunately, D.C. is home to the Library of Congress, which is excellent. The workload here is average for most students; those in the Honors Program, however, work hard and enjoy smaller, "seminar-style" classes. Selection for the Honors Program is based on high school GPA and SAT scores..

■ **Life** The major quality of life issue at Catholic is its location. On the upside, Washington is a great college town, home not only to Catholic but also to American, Georgetown, George Washington, and Howard. The downside, however, is Catholic's neighborhood, which drew numerous complaints from our respondents. "Dangerous" is the word most frequently used to describe the northeast D.C. area surrounding campus. Downtown Washington is easily accessible by subway. Washington provides the setting for much of CUA's social life; the city "has excellent bars," said one student. The school's religious affiliation notwithstanding, drinking is very popular here. "Because all activities on campus are dry," explained one student, "few students attend them. This forces students off-campus...resulting in more muggings and crimes." Fraternities and sororities are practically non-existent. Contrary to what one might expect, the students are not conservative romantically; in fact, student responses to questions on the subject clung to the national average.

■ **Students** The student body is homogeneous: almost nine-tenths of the students are Catholic, and the same percentage is white. Many of the students are parochial school graduates. Those who fit in report happily that there's "a real sense of community at CUA." Those who don't may feel ostracized. One noted that her classmates were "much too conservative and condescending to anyone who chooses to be unique." Student participation in on-campus activities is low, and there is very little "rah-rah" school spirit here.

CATHOLIC UNIVERSITY OF AMERICA

Washington, DC

Admissions

The admissions office reports that "we are looking for a well-rounded student [who demonstrates a] balance between academics, activities, and community service. High school GPA, standardized test scores, and extracurricular activities are all considered the most important components of the application, although the school adds that "students are evaluated on the whole application package." Applicants must have completed four years of English and social studies, three years of science (at least one lab science), two years of a foreign language, and one year of fine arts/humanities. The SAT and three achievements are required. Students who apply to Catholic University most often also apply to Villanova, Georgetown, and Boston College.

Financial Aid

The financial aid office at the Catholic University of America requires applicants to submit the FAF and a form generated by the school. CUA awards merit grants based on academic excellence, intended program of study, birthplace, and special talent (e.g., music). Furthermore, all 30 U.S. archdioceses award one full, four-year scholarship every year. A family scholarship provides a tuition discount to families whenever more than one sibling is attending CUA on a full-time basis. CUA sponsors its own loan program, and encourages students to take out loans under the Stafford and Perkins loan programs.

A note from the Catholic University of America Admissions Office:

"The Catholic University of America's friendly atmosphere, rigorous academic programs and emphasis on time-honored values attract students from most states and more than 100 foreign countries. Its 142-acre, tree-lined campus is 10 minutes from the nation's capitol. Distinguished as the national university of the Catholic Church in the United States, CUA is the only institution of higher education established by the U.S. Catholic bishops. Students from all religious traditions are welcome.

"CUA offers undergraduate degrees in more then 50 major areas. With Capitol Hill and Smithsonian Institute minutes away via the Metrorail rapid transit system, students enjoy a residential campus in an exciting city of historical monuments, theaters, ethnic restaurants and parks.

"Students participate in internships at the White House, Supreme Court, congressional offices, government agencies, law firms, health organizations, and corporations."

UNIVERSITY OF CHICAGO

What do students think about the University of Chicago?

■ **Academics** If you're serious about getting a rigorous undergraduate education and can tolerate a slow social scene in a dreary neighborhood, you can't do much better than University of Chicago. The school puts students through their paces with a demanding core curriculum that constitutes half the credits necessary for an undergraduate degree. These mandatory courses in humanities, mathematics, science, and foreign languages, when coupled with major requirements, leave little room in the undergrad schedule for electives. When students do take electives, however, it's usually in graduate level courses (grads make up more of the university's population than do the undergrads): "thus," concluded one undergrad, "an academically motivated undergraduate can receive a very stimulating education." Students here recognize that few other schools extend this much respect to their undergrads. Said one, "This school treats its undergrads like grad students. If a student is ready and willing to put the kind of intensity into his/her schoolwork that's required here, then it can be very rewarding." Be aware that expectations are also very high. The school is on a quarterly schedule, which tends to make courses go by a little quickly, and also more easily facilitates semesters off for work and travel.

■ **Life** Chicago is a wonderful city, but Hyde Park, where UC is located, is not one of its most hopping spots. Nor is it one of the city's safest, but, given its reputation, student complaints about the neighborhood were surprisingly few. Because students here are extremely studious and competitive, social life is sub-par. One undergrad summed up life at UC this way: "A small school surrounded by poor ghettoes on Chicago's South Side with few women in the student body or the faculty hardly makes for an enjoyable social situation. When you consider also the stoic design of the buildings and the Chicago weather, and you'll see that there is very little reason for being here unless the academic situation wasn't nearly perfect (and it is nearly perfect—at least in the physics department)."

■ **Students** Chicago students have a well-known "geek" reputation. Said one gleefully, "The U of Chicago is the place where even a geek/loser/nerd can fit in." A classmate disagreed: "The people here, although widely described as geeks, are down-to-earth and tend to get to know each other as people rather than judging by appearances. People here talk about real things—there is real intellectual thought going on even outside of classes." Chicago students are very intense, and perhaps a little unkempt—"It's not so much that students are unattractive here as that they care less about appearances," said one student. Yet one student countered that image: "I'm sick of hearing people complain about the women here being ugly—they're not; in fact, some people prefer the way women look when they don't make a three-foot hole in the ozone layer every morning preparing their hair so they can look like Barbie dolls." So there! To sum it all up: "A small college, full of brilliant neurotics in the midst of a great city."

UNIVERSITY OF CHICAGO

Chicago, IL

Admissions

The University of Chicago requires prospective students to complete an application that includes: high school transcript, a letter of recommendation, several essays, and results of either the SAT or the ACT. Although the school requires no specific high school curriculum, the admissions office strongly suggests that applicants complete a rigorous college prep curriculum including four years of English, and three years each of math, science, a foreign language, and social studies. An interview, while not required, is recommended. Applicants to University of Chicago most often also apply to Harvard, Columbia, Yale, Princeton, and Northwestern.

Financial Aid

Those applying for financial assistance from the University of Chicago are required to submit the FAF and a form generated by the school. The school offers merit-based grants to those with outstanding academic records (including some full scholarships), and also offers grants to those with talents in athletics, music, drama, and the arts. Need-based grants traditionally make up two thirds of financial aid packages, with the rest of demonstrated need met by loans and part-time employment.

Excerpted from University of Chicago promotional materials:

"While Chicago faculty design and teach the curriculum, they do so with the expectations that students will play an active role at every stage of the educational process. A superior education can be obtained by all students who attend the College of the University of Chicago—but it's up to the individual student to secure it. The Chicago curriculum is designed to give students access to the entire world of knowledge and to lead them to an appreciation of the possibilities of human achievement. A Chicago education develops individual powers of judgment and expression and equips students to ask fresh questions and to pursue them on their own. The challenge of a Chicago education is not only to acquire tools and knowledge but also to raise questions about the ends for which they should be used. This is what Chicago means by "liberal education": it is an education for free persons."

ADMISSIONS FACTS

Competitiveness Rating:	**93**
% of applicants accepted:	46
% acceptees attending:	34

FRESHMAN PROFILE

Average verbal SAT:	630
Average math SAT:	670
Average ACT:	29
Graduated top 10% of class:	70
Graduated top 25% of class:	93
Graduated top 50% of class:	100

DEADLINES

Early decision/action:	11/1
Early dec./act. notif.:	12/1
Regular admission:	1/15
Regular adm. notif.:	4/15

APPLICANTS ALSO LOOK AT

and often prefer:
Harvard/Radcliffe College
Swarthmore College
Columbia U.

and sometimes prefer:
Northwestern U.
Johns Hopkins U.

and rarely prefer:
Loyola U.–Chicago
U. Illinois
U. Rochester

ADDRESS

Undergraduate Admissions
1116 E. 59th Street
Chicago, IL 60637
312-702-8650

FINANCIAL FACTS

In-state tuition ($):	15,945
Out-of-state tuition ($):	15,945
Room & board ($):	5,685
FA application deadline:	2/1
% frosh receiving FA:	66
PT earnings per yr. ($):	2,200

TYPE OF AID:	% of students ($)
FA of some kind:	62 (NA)
Need-based grants:	NA
Merit-based grants:	NA
Loans:	NA
Work study:	NA
Student rating of FA:	81

CITY UNIVERSITY OF NEW YORK—HUNTER COLLEGE

New York, NY

CAMPUS LIFE

Quality of Life Rating:	**71**
Type of school:	public
Affiliation:	none
Environment:	city

STUDENT BODY

FT undergrad enrollment:	8,039
% male/% female:	28/72
% out-of-state:	6
% live on campus:	1
% African-American:	23
% Asian:	11
% Caucasian:	43
% Hispanic:	22
% foreign:	3
% transfers:	NA

WHAT'S HOT

working a job
in-class discussion
interaction among students
studying hard
diversity
leftist politics
location

WHAT'S NOT

profs outside class
profs in class
administration (overall)
campus appearance
dorm safety
liquor
library

ACADEMICS

Academic Rating:	**66**
Calendar:	semester
Student/teacher ratio:	17/1
% doctorates:	83
Profs interesting:	34
Profs accessible:	38
Hours of study per day:	3.43

MOST POPULAR MAJORS BY %

Social Sciences:	40
Health Sciences:	14
Psychology:	14

% GRADS WHO PURSUE

Law:	NA
MBA:	NA
Medicine:	NA
M.A., etc.:	37

What do students think about Hunter College?

■ **Academics** Hunter College has long prided itself on offering solid educational opportunities to those who would be unable to get them otherwise. Originally founded as a women's-only teacher's college, Hunter now serves students of both genders and of all interests and ages. Among the strongest departments at Hunter's main, upper-East Side campus are English, urban planning, social sciences (particularly political science), pre-medical sciences, and education. The downtown campus contains the Brookdale Health Sciences Center, home of the outstanding Hunter-Bellevue school of nursing. Hunter-Bellevue wins raves from its students; they are proud to be part of "one of the top nursing schools in the country." Students here, most of whom hold jobs outside of school, are disciplined and practical-minded about their studies; they study hard and take academics very seriously. They expect the same from the faculty and administration. Unfortunately, those who run the college disappoint students in many ways. Students complained about their professors' teaching performance and accessibility, giving them low ratings overall. The administration, deans and bursar also received low marks. Areas of frustration included registration, financial aid, counseling, course selection, and facilities, especially the library. Furthermore, city and state fiscal problems have caused class size to increase and quality of service to decrease further.

■ **Life** Hunter College, almost exclusively a commuter school, does have the only residence hall in the entire CUNY system. Hunter's campuses are situated conveniently for commuters from all areas of New York City, provided they take public transportation (parking is impossible). Students cited location as one of the main assets of their school. Because life in New York is so expensive, however, most students remain at home, coming in just for classes. This is not to say that the social scene at Hunter is dead. Indeed, there are many student organizations active on campus, including a proportionally large number of political groups. Some students wish there were "more parties and sports," and one with a clear case of midwinter blues complained: "No sun, no sand, no fun!" Typical collegiate partying is in short supply here, although there is "a great deal of camaraderie," especially among nursing students. However, intercollegiate and intramural sports, particularly basketball, are popular. In general, Hunter's urban campuses tend to empty out on weekends.

■ **Students** Students here praised their school for its great ethnic and social diversity. Minority students make up over 50 percent of the student body. A large number of merit scholarships help to attract quality students regardless of financial need. Most students are quite liberal politically, and people with all kinds of lifestyles, viewpoints, and preferences can find acceptance at Hunter.

CITY UNIVERSITY OF NEW YORK–HUNTER COLLEGE

New York, NY

Admissions

Applicants to Hunter College may be admitted either as "regular" freshmen, or as SEEK (Search for Education, Elevation, and Knowledge) students. Students wishing to enter the school as freshmen must meet the following minimum requirements: a high school academic average of 80; a combined SAT score of 900; and, placement in the top third of his/her high school graduating class. SEEK students need not meet these minimum requirements; the SEEK program, which "helps economically and educationally disadvantaged students," provides its students "intensive academic services," possibly including "a stipend for educational expenses." Both types of students must submit a full application, including high school transcript and SAT scores.

Financial Aid

The financial aid office at Hunter College requires applicants to submit the CAFSSA (CUNY Application for Federal and State Student Aid). Hunter offers a number of merit-based grants on the basis of academic excellence. Need-based grants come from a number of sources, many of which are specifically earmarked for New York State residents. Among these are scholarships for future teachers, minority students, and children of deceased/disabled public servants (veterans, police, etc.).

Excerpted from Hunter College promotional materials:

"Hunter College, the second oldest college in The City University of New York, is a coeducational, fully accredited college, with a large and diverse faculty in the liberal arts and sciences and in several professional schools. In most of its programs the College offers both undergraduate and graduate degrees.

"Originally called Normal College, the school was founded in 1870 by Thomas Hunter to educate young women who wished to be teachers. Its growth to its present size and complexity was gradual. The institution took its present name in 1914. Evening classes were begun in 1917. Graduate studies were introduced in 1921 for both men and women, and in 1964 the entire College became coeducational.

"Hunter's total enrollment is over 19,500. Of these about 8,000 are full-time undergraduates. An additional 7,000 part-time students are divided between degree and non-degree programs. Over 4,000 graduate students are studying in arts and sciences and teacher education programs and at the Schools of Social Work, Health Sciences and Nursing."

ADMISSIONS FACTS

Competitiveness Rating:	**67**
% of applicants accepted:	66
% acceptees attending:	41

FRESHMAN PROFILE

Average verbal SAT:	NA
Average math SAT:	NA
Average ACT:	NA
Graduated top 10% of class:	NA
Graduated top 25% of class:	NA
Graduated top 50% of class:	NA

DEADLINES

Early decision/action:	NA
Early dec./act. notif.:	NA
Regular admission:	1/15
Regular adm. notif.:	rolling

APPLICANTS ALSO LOOK AT

and sometimes prefer:
CUNY–Queens College
NYU
Fordham U.

and rarely prefer:
SUNY Stonybrook
CUNY–City College
Iona College

ADDRESS

Undergraduate Admissions
695 Park Avenue
New York, NY 10021
212-772-4490

FINANCIAL FACTS

In-state tuition ($):	1,450
Out-of-state tuition ($):	4,050
Room & board ($):	1,600
FA application deadline:	5/31
% frosh receiving FA:	NA
PT earnings per yr. ($):	NA

% FT RECEIVING (AVG.AMT.($)):

FA of some kind:	72 (NA)
Need-based grants:	NA
Merit-based grants:	NA
Loans:	NA
Work study:	NA
Student rating of FA:	60

CITY UNIVERSITY OF NEW YORK—QUEENS COLLEGE

Flushing, NY

CAMPUS LIFE

Quality of Life Rating:	**73**
Type of school:	public
Affiliation:	none
Environment:	city

STUDENT BODY

FT undergrad enrollment:	6,636
% male/% female:	44/56
% out-of-state:	6
% live on campus:	0
% African-American:	10
% Asian:	10
% Caucasian:	49
% Hispanic:	10
% foreign:	5
% transfers:	NA

WHAT'S HOT

commuting
working a job
diversity
library
town-gown relations
dating
interaction among students

WHAT'S NOT

registration
drinking
catalog
profs outside class
studying hard
administration (overall)

ACADEMICS

Academic Rating:	**77**
Calendar:	semester
Student/teacher ratio:	11/1
% doctorates:	99
Profs interesting:	69
Profs accessible:	61
Hours of study per day:	2.80

What do students think about Queens College?

■ **Academics** Many people consider Queens College the finest school in the CUNY (City University of New York) system. Students rated their courses overall as "excellent." Particularly noteworthy departments are English, music, accounting, computer science, biology, and chemistry. The constantly improving facilities also garner praise, especially the first-rate library building. Areas of complaint mostly have to do with the faculty and administration: students gave their professors low marks for teaching prowess and accessibility, and slammed the administration for inefficiency (registration is a red-tape nightmare, many classes are overcrowded, "not enough advising" is available, and too often the course catalog does not accurately reflect the course offerings). Budget problems in the CUNY system, New York City, and New York State have caused service to diminish while tuition charges rise, causing predictable dissatisfaction among students. However, students still considered their school a bargain, given the overall value of their curriculum and facilities.

■ **Life** Queens College, like others in the CUNY system, is a commuter school. There are no dorms at all, so most students live at home, although many find housing nearby, perhaps in order to avoid parking hassles. Most students here must work at some type of job outside of school. Perhaps this necessity contributes to the lack of a typical collegiate party atmosphere. The social scene is "quiet," and mostly centered around "hanging out in the student union or cafeteria." Recently, however, more structured social activities have been promoted; concerts, parties, and other student-government-sponsored events are on the rise. Dating in the traditional sense is very popular as well, as life at this commuter college does not completely end after class. Sports are also now receiving more attention at Queens; the college boasts over 20 NCAA Division II teams, including a strong men's tennis team. The campus is "very safe, and pretty clean," quite a compliment for an urban New York school. In general, many extracurricular and social options exist here for students who have the desire to go after them, but most still opt for weekends at home.

■ **Students:** One of the greatest attributes of Queens College is its diversity. All types of students come here in droves. Minority students make up over half the school's population. There is also a "high foreign student population," and the school's affordability, as well as its considerable merit-based scholarship offerings, allows students of all income levels to enroll. The political climate reflects the heterogeneity of the students: neither liberal nor conservative, but accepting of different points of view. Queens College students can leave after four years with a solid education behind them, as well as the invaluable experience of interaction with virtually all kinds of people.

CITY UNIVERSITY OF NEW YORK–QUEENS COLLEGE

Flushing, NY

Admissions

Applicants to Queens College may be admitted either as "regular" freshmen, or as SEEK (Search for Education, Elevation, and Knowledge) students. Students wishing to enter the school as freshmen must meet the following minimum requirements: a high school academic average of 80; a combined SAT score of 900; and, placement in the top third of his/her high school graduating class. SEEK students need not meet these minimum requirements; the SEEK program, "designed to serve, with distinction, academically underprepared and economically disadvantaged students," provides its students "support through financial assistance, academic instruction, tutorial assistance, and counseling services." Both types of students must submit a full application, including high school transcript and SAT scores.

Financial Aid

The financial aid office at Queens College requires applicants to submit the CAFSSA (CUNY Application for Federal and State Student Aid). Queens offers a number of merit-based grants on the basis of academic excellence. Need-based grants come from a number of sources, many of which are specifically earmarked for New York State residents. Among these are scholarships for future teachers, minority students, and children of deceased/disabled public servants (veterans, police, etc.).

Excerpted from Queens College promotional materials:

"Queens College, called 'World Class' by the *London Times,* is dedicated to the idea that a great education should be accessible to talented young people of all backgrounds—ethnic and financial. It is a global gathering place for ideas. The College's colorful kaleidoscope of tongues, talents, and cultures—66 different native languages are spoken here—provides an extraordinary educational environment. A strong liberal arts curriculum assures students education for a full career and a full life. Opportunities abound with special programs developed for honors students; students in pre-law, pre-med, and business; adults; 'fresh start' students; foreign language speakers. In all their diversity, students come first."

ADMISSIONS FACTS

Competitiveness Rating:	*67*
% of applicants accepted:	61
% acceptees attending:	55

FRESHMAN PROFILE

Average verbal SAT:	500
Average math SAT:	570
Average ACT:	NA
Graduated top 10% of class:	NA
Graduated top 25% of class:	NA
Graduated top 50% of class:	NA

DEADLINES

Early decision/action:	NA
Early dec./act. notif.:	NA
Regular admission:	rolling
Regular adm. notif.:	rolling

APPLICANTS ALSO LOOK AT

and sometimes prefer:

Fordham U.
Hofstra U.
St. Johns U.
CUNY–Hunter College
SUNY Albany
SUNY Binghamton
SUNY Buffalo
SUNY Stonybrook

and rarely prefer:
NYU

ADDRESS

Undergraduate Admissions
65-30 Kissena Boulevard
Flushing, NY 11367
718-997-5600

FINANCIAL FACTS

In-state tuition ($):	1,800
Out-of-state tuition ($):	5,100
Room & board ($) ($):	NA
FA application deadline:	5/31
% frosh receiving FA:	NA
PT earnings per yr. ($):	NA

TYPE OF AID: % of students ($):

FA of some kind:	NA
Need-based grants:	NA
Merit-based grants:	NA
Loans:	NA
Work study:	NA
Student rating of FA:	70

CLAREMONT COLLEGES—CLAREMONT McKENNA COLLEGE

Claremont, CA

CAMPUS LIFE

Quality of Life Rating:	**83**
Type of school:	private
Affiliation:	none
Environment:	city

STUDENT BODY

FT undergrad enrollment:	850
% male/% female:	62/38
% out-of-state:	45
% live on campus:	95
% African-American:	5
% Asian:	13
% Caucasian:	72
% Hispanic:	8
% foreign:	4
% transfers:	2

WHAT'S HOT

small lectures
administration (overall)
profs outside class
campus easy to get around
deans
living on campus
caring about politics
small labs and seminars
profs teach intros

WHAT'S NOT

fraternities/sororities
gay community visible
marriage
diversity
religion

ACADEMICS

Academic Rating:	**89**
Calendar:	semester
Student/teacher ratio:	11/1
% doctorates:	95
Profs interesting:	87
Profs accessible:	92
Hours of study per day:	3.3

MOST POPULAR MAJORS BY %

Economics:	28
Government:	15
International Relations::	7

% GRADS WHO PURSUE

Law:	16
MBA:	2
Medicine:	4
M.A., etc.:	8

What do students think about Claremont McKenna?

Note: The Claremont Colleges are five small undergraduate schools (Claremont McKenna, Harvey Mudd, Pitzer, Pomona, and Scripps) and one graduate school sharing a central location and facilities. Each school serves a distinct purpose and maintains its own faculty and campus. Cross-registration among colleges is encouraged.

■ **Academics** Claremont McKenna College is a "liberal arts college with a particular emphasis on public affairs." This emphasis attracts a pre-law constituency: one in eight CMC students goes on to law school. Government, economics, and international affairs are the most popular majors at this school, although liberal arts and science majors are not uncommon. Most students agree that the nearly unlimited access to professors is CMC's greatest asset. Wrote one student, "Student/professor interaction is the unique characteristic of CMC. The professors are available as teachers, counselors, and peers." Students here truly enjoy a small-school setting while reaping the benefits of a university. While classes are small and personal contact with professors is optimal, CMC's association with the Claremont Colleges provides students an unusual breadth of courses and opportunities for research projects. Course work here is difficult: all students must complete a general education sequence that includes calculus, science, writing, literature, a foreign language, and three courses in CMC's strongest area, the social sciences. In addition, all students must complete a Senior Thesis. Many students take advantage of the school's Study Abroad program, which sends students to 22 different countries all around the globe. One student summed up the school this way: "CMC has more diverse opportunities for students to explore—but students must take the initiative. The rest is easy because professors and administration are very supportive."

■ **Life** Despite its association with the four other undergraduate schools, CMC still feels very much like a small college to its students. Explained one, "a small school grants you advantages: direct contact with professors, small class size, guaranteed housing. It does get constricting, however, seeing the same faces over and over." The small-school atmosphere, coupled with an unfavorable male-female ratio (approximately two to one), leads to what most students agree is a dormant dating scene. Wrote one, "the competition for girls is intense and social events turn into 'rat races' to get together with a girl. That's why the CMC motto is Drunk. Alone. Again." Drinking is an extremely popular recreational activity—"Non-alcoholic activities are null," complained one student, as are intercollegiate sports. Student gave the city of Claremont low grades, but Los Angeles is only an hour away by car.

■ **Students** Over one quarter of CMC's students are minorities, with Asians making up about half the minority population. Still, students graded the student body "not diverse," perhaps because most students share a competitive spirit and a career orientation.

CLAREMONT COLLEGES–CLAREMONT McKENNA COLLEGE

Claremont, CA

Admissions

The admissions offices reports that "each application is reviewed in terms of subjects taken, grades earned, class ranking, and recommendations from the secondary school attended. The committee looks at the kind of intellectual challenges an applicant has faced and how they were handled....Although the majority of students admitted to CMC have combined SAT scores of 1200 or better, no minimum score requirements exist....Non-academic activities considered by the committee include leadership in school or community activities; evidence of exceptional contribution in a constructive extracurricular activity; or unusual interest in some aspect of the social sciences." Applicants are expected to have completed four years of English, at least three years of math, at least two years of foreign language and science, and one year of history. Applicants to CMC most often also apply to UCLA, UC–Berkeley, Stanford, UC–San Diego, Georgetown, Pomona, and UPenn.

Financial Aid

Claremont McKenna College requires financial aid applicants to complete the FAF, the SAAC (Student Aid Application for California) and to submit a copy of their parents' most recent tax return. In '91–'92, the average need-based grant was $8,954, and the average loan was $2,950 (42% of all undergrads took out loans). CMC last year awarded academic scholarships to 11% of all undergrads (average scholarship: $8,954). No other merit-based scholarships were awarded. Twenty-eight percent of all undergrads participated in CMC's work-study program.

A note from the Claremont McKenna College Admissions Office:

"CMC's mission is clear: to educate students for meaningful lives and responsible leadership in business, government, and the professions. While many other colleges champion either a traditional liberal arts education with emphasis on intellectual breadth, or training that stresses acquisition of technical skills, CMC offers a clear alternative. Instead of dividing the liberal arts and the working world into separate realms, education at CMC is rooted in the interplay between the world of ideas and the world of events. By combining the intellectual breadth of the liberal arts with the more pragmatic concerns of public affairs, CMC students gain the vision, skills, and values necessary for leadership in all sectors of society."

ADMISSIONS FACTS

Competitiveness Rating:	92
% of applicants accepted:	41
% acceptees attending:	35

FRESHMAN PROFILE

Average verbal SAT:	600
Average math SAT:	660
Average ACT:	28
Graduated top 10% of class:	68
Graduated top 25% of class:	91
Graduated top 50% of class:	99

DEADLINES

Early decision/action:	12/1
Early dec./act. notif.:	1/10
Regular admission:	2/1
Regular adm. notif.:	4/1

APPLICANTS ALSO LOOK AT

and sometimes prefer:
Pomona College
UC Berkeley
U. Penn
Franklin & Marshall College
Babson College

and rarely prefer:
UC Los Angeles
UC San Diego
UC Davis
UC Irvine

ADDRESS

Undergraduate Admissions
890 Columbia Ave
Claremont, CA 91711
714-621-8088

FINANCIAL FACTS

In-state tuition ($):	14,710
Out-of-state tuition ($):	14,710
Room & board ($):	5,180
FA application deadline:	2/1
% frosh receiving FA:	61
PT earnings per yr. ($):	1,000

TYPE OF AID: % of students ($):

FA of some kind:	76 (NA)
Need-based grants:	NA (8,954)
Merit-based grants:	NA
Loans:	NA (2,950)
Work study:	28 (NA)
Student rating of FA:	87

CLAREMONT COLLEGES—HARVEY MUDD COLLEGE

Claremont, CA

CAMPUS LIFE

Quality of Life Rating:	**71**
Type of school:	private
Affiliation:	none
Environment:	suburban

STUDENT BODY

FT undergrad enrollment:	562
% male/% female:	81/19
% out-of-state:	53
% live on campus:	95
% African-American:	1
% Asian:	19
% Caucasian:	72
% Hispanic:	4
% foreign:	1
% transfers:	1

WHAT'S HOT

studying hard
interaction among students
living on campus
small classes (overall)
campus easy to get around
profs teach upper-level
    courses

WHAT'S NOT

fraternities/sororities
dating
requirements easy
intercollegiate sports
campus appearance
overall happiness
location

ACADEMICS

Academic Rating:	**89**
Calendar:	semester
Student/teacher ratio:	8/1
% doctorates:	96
Profs interesting:	72
Profs accessible:	88
Hours of study per day:	4

MOST POPULAR MAJORS BY %

Engineering:	60
Physical Sciences:	30
Mathematics:	10

% GRADS WHO PURSUE

Law:	NA
MBA:	NA
Medicine:	NA
M.A., etc.:	45

What do students think about Harvey Mudd College?

Note: The Claremont Colleges are five small undergraduate schools (Claremont McKenna, Harvey Mudd, Pitzer, Pomona, and Scripps) and one graduate school sharing a central location and facilities. Each school serves a distinct purpose and maintains its own faculty and campus. Cross-registration among colleges is encouraged.

■ **Academics** Harvey Mudd College offers undergraduate programs in engineering, biology, chemistry, physics, mathematics, and computer science. Harvey Mudd is committed to producing "highly competent engineers and scientists with an understanding of the impact of their work on the rest of society," a goal the school achieves through several unique programs. One is an unusually large number of humanities requirements. The other is the "clinic" program, which sends engineering students (who make up the majority here) to work for three semesters as problem solvers for area companies and industries. What really sets Harvey Mudd apart from other science schools, however, is the quality of instruction. "I like the fact that there are no student- or TA-taught courses," wrote one engineer. "The profs are all here to teach, not to research. It has also been really incredible to work with so many brilliant students who have similar interests and still have a real sense of humor." Commented one physics major, "The biology, chemistry, and physics teachers are unparalleled. Math and engineering faculties are not so good, but engineering professors suck everywhere." Students reported that "the work is intense, the stress level is high." One student elaborated, "I have a friend whose favorite activity after taking a test is to play a record of a Saturn V launch at high volume while bending over and screaming at the top of his lungs. This activity is an excellent example of how students respond to the pressures of this school." Many students here "develop a negative attitude toward the school" which they lose only after graduation, when all their hard work begins to pay off. As one student put it, "Survival at this school is an effort. If you can't take a challenge, don't come here."

■ **Life** Harvey Mudd students have little time for a social life; when free time is available, intramural sports and drinking are two popular outlets for blowing off steam. As for relations with the opposite sex, one man reported that "attitudes about sex here are divided; some just aren't interested and will probably die virgins, others are passionately in favor of it. We are handicapped a lot by our male–female ratio (four to one)." What most makes life bearable here, according to one student, "are the people—students and faculty are generally intelligent, highly motivated people."

■ **Students** About one fourth of the students here are minorities, with Asians making up the lion's share of the minority population. Students describe their student body as "not diverse." Reported one engineer, "this is a great school if you're the nerdy social misfit of your high school. However, if you like fun or free time, go somewhere else!"

CLAREMONT COLLEGES—HARVEY MUDD COLLEGE

Admissions

The most important parts of your application to Harvey Mudd are your course selection and GPA. From Harvey Mudd's brochure: "Each fall we expect about 1,100 applications for an entering class of 168. To enroll 168 freshmen, we'll admit about 450 students. Serious candidates for admission should take all the English, science and math they can. Foreign language, history and other social sciences are also important, but if you're in a solid "college prep" program, you'll have plenty of courses in those fields. If you have the opportunity to take accelerated, Advanced Placement or International Baccalaureate courses—take them. Do all that you can do to make your senior year as tough as possible. Not only do we want excellent students in math and science, but we want multi-dimensional students at Harvey Mudd as well. We're very interested in students with outside activities, musical talent, athletics and leadership responsibilities, but not at the expense of your classroom performance in your senior year!" All students applying must submit scores from the SAT and three Achievement tests (including English Composition and Math level II). At least one year of Calculus is required, and at least one year each of chemistry and physics is highly recommended.

Financial Aid

Financial aid applicants to Harvey Mudd College must complete the FAF (in-state applicants should complete the SAAC) and a form generated by HMC's financial aid office. Merit scholarships available include excellence in academics and leadership; minority scholarships are also offered. HMC sponsors National Merit Scholarships, and annually over 30% of the freshman class are National Merit Scholars. Furthermore, according to HMC's brochure, "About 75% of our students receive financial aid with the typical financial aid package covering about half of our total expenses. In addition to scholarships, HMC students receive low interest educational loans and part-time on campus employment."

A note from the Harvey Mudd College Admissions Office:

"Harvey Mudd College was founded in 1955. Its mission is to educate undergraduate men and women in a rigorous academic environment, focusing on mathematics, science, and engineering, and also to provide a rich background in the humanities and social sciences... Small classes, the excellent faculty, and exceptional students create a setting that is conducive to both teaching and learning.

"In addition to the advantages that all small colleges share, Harvey Mudd has the advantage of being a part of the Claremont Colleges system... Students in the Claremont Colleges share many opportunities in course offerings, facilities, and extracurricular activities."

ADMISSIONS FACTS

Competitiveness Rating:	**96**
% of applicants accepted:	54
% acceptees attending:	38

FRESHMAN PROFILE

Average verbal SAT:	660
Average math SAT:	740
Average ACT:	NA
Graduated top 10% of class:	89
Graduated top 25% of class:	94
Graduated top 50% of class:	99

DEADLINES

Early decision/action:	12/1
Early dec./act. notif.:	mid-Jan
Regular admission	2/1
Regular adm. notif.:	4/1

APPLICANTS ALSO LOOK AT

and often prefer:
UC Berkeley
Caltech

and sometimes prefer:
Stanford U.
Georgia Tech
RPI
Cooper Union

and rarely prefer:
Wooster Polytech
Virginia Polytech

ADDRESS

Undergraduate Admissions
301 East 12th Street
Claremont, CA 91711
714-621-8011

FINANCIAL FACTS

In-state tuition ($):	14,490
Out-of-state tuition ($):	14,490
Room & board ($) ($):	5,890
FA application deadline:	2/1
% frosh receiving FA:	79
PT earnings per yr. ($):	1,000

TYPE OF AID: % of students ($):

FA of some kind:	76 (NA)
Need-based grants:	NA
Merit-based grants:	NA
Loans:	NA
Work study:	NA
Student rating of FA:	73

CAMPUS LIFE

Quality of Life Rating:	**79**
Type of school:	private
Affiliation:	none
Environment:	city

STUDENT BODY

FT undergrad enrollment:	740
% male/% female:	48/52
% out-of-state:	55
% live on campus:	95
% African-American:	8
% Asian:	7
% Caucasian:	66
% Hispanic:	12
% foreign:	6
% transfers:	3

WHAT'S HOT

Grateful Dead
gay community accepted
marijuana
financial aid
small lectures
interaction among students
small classes (overall)
college theater
library
leftist politics
profs in class

WHAT'S NOT

fraternities/sororities
campus appearance
studying hard

ACADEMICS

Academic Rating:	**84**
Calendar:	semester
Student/teacher ratio:	10/1
% doctorates:	100
Profs interesting:	88
Profs accessible:	89
Hours of study per day:	2.74

MOST POPULAR MAJORS BY %

Psychology:	16
Social Sciences:	14
Multi/Interdisciplinary Studies:	13

% GRADS WHO PURSUE

Law:	8
MBA:	7
Medicine:	5
M.A., etc.:	30

What do students think about Pitzer College?

Note: The Claremont Colleges are five small undergraduate schools (Claremont McKenna, Harvey Mudd, Pitzer, Pomona, and Scripps) and one graduate school sharing a central location and facilities. Each school serves a distinct purpose and maintains its own faculty and campus. Cross-registration among colleges is encouraged.

■ **Academics** Pitzer College, founded in 1963 as an alternative women's school, is now a co-ed college whose curriculum "emphasizes the social and behavioral sciences, particularly psychology, sociology, anthropology, and political sciences." Pitzer is by far the most liberal of the Claremont Colleges, and its students are marked by their openness to progressive ideas and educational approaches. Wrote one student, "I think Pitzer has a great deal to offer the new generation of socially informed students. Here one learns through questioning and interactions with the professors' explanations, but ultimately forms his/her own conclusions. If higher education is the process of gaining multiple perspectives on various issues, Pitzer must be at the top of the heap." Besides the previously mentioned majors, history, economics, linguistics, and the arts are also popular fields with students. Students gave their professors excellent grades, calling them "very friendly, and stimulating." To other Claremont students, Pitzer is "the easy school." One undergrad wrote "Pomona students joke: 'How many Pitzer students does it take to screw in a light bulb? One, and s/he'll probably get credit for it!' But it's totally false; I get better grades in my Pomona classes than I get here." There is some truth to the school's reputation: our survey showed that Pitzer students work considerably less hard than their counterparts at the other four schools. Still, you can't argue with the results: half of Pitzer's graduates go on to a professional or academic graduate program.

■ **Life** Pitzer is the Claremonts' undisputed "hippie" school, although several students reported that "there seem to be fewer and fewer hippies in every entering class." A laid-back, Californian, "liberal social atmosphere" predominates. Students told us they enjoy a "very strong sense of community, but one that encourages individuality." Pitzer students seem to have none of the problems other Claremont students have finding parties and good times. Drinking and drugs are very popular, the school's new, stricter alcohol and drug policy notwithstanding. Reported one student, "the new policy, ironically, makes drinking more of a challenge, hence more fun." One often-mentioned event here is Kahoutek, a spring music and crafts festival that evokes the school's sixties spirit.

■ **Students** Pitzer students consider their student body "a diverse community based on rallying causes, listening to hippy music, and commenting on creative bong-designs!" In other words, despite a large minority population, "everyone here is pretty much the same." Students with strong, leftist political beliefs fit in here; only a few students complained that "people tend to be a little self-righteous about issues at times."

Admissions

From Pitzer's *Viewbook*: "Keep a couple of things in mind as you complete your admission application. First, success at Pitzer will come to those students with academic ability, maturity, and independence. Second, show us the ways in which you feel you can both profit from and contribute to the Pitzer community." High emphasis is placed on the essays in Pitzer's application: "Because people demonstrate their strengths in different ways, the Admission Committee does not expect essays to be answered in the same ways...." There are two essays in the application: the regular essay, and a "supplemental essay." All applicants must submit SAT or ACT scores. The recommended high school curriculum should include four years of English, at least three years each of a foreign language, science and social studies/history, and at least three years of mathematics. Accepted students at Pitzer are given the option to defer entry for a year to "pursue a non-academic goal"; they must submit a letter explaining what they plan to do during the year of deferral.

Financial Aid

Financial aid applicants to Pitzer are required to complete the FAF (California residents should compete the SAAC). All aid awarded by Pitzer is based solely on financial need. Students are expected to apply for any state, federal, or private awards for which they may be eligible. Applicants should have submitted all materials by February 1. Notification of awards occurs in April.

A note from the Pitzer College Admissions Office:

"Pitzer is about opportunities. It's about possibilities. The students who come here are looking for something different from the usual: take two courses from column A, two courses from column B, and two courses from column C. That kind of arbitrary selection doesn't make a satisfying education at Pitzer. So we look for students who want to have an impact on their own education, who want the chief responsibility—with help from their faculty advisors—in designing their own futures.

"That may sound like an unusual approach, but Pitzer is a young college, one used to taking chances and used to thinking about old things in new ways. In the words of our founding president, "We thought a new college with an emphasis on the social and behavioral sciences had a mandate to change the universe." Our students are looking for *opportunities* and are excited about *possibilities* because they feel that mandate."

ADMISSIONS FACTS

Competitiveness Rating:	**81**
% of applicants accepted:	49
% acceptees attending:	30

FRESHMAN PROFILE

Average verbal SAT:	550
Average math SAT:	580
Average ACT:	26
Graduated top 10% of class:	35
Graduated top 25% of class:	70
Graduated top 50% of class:	98

DEADLINES

Early decision/action:	12/1
Early dec./act. notif.:	1/1
Regular admission:	2/1
Regular adm. notif.:	4/1

APPLICANTS ALSO LOOK AT

and often prefer:
UC Berkeley
Stanford U.

and sometimes prefer:
Oberlin College
Middlebury College
UC Davis
Occidental College
UC Los Angeles

and rarely prefer:
UC Santa Cruz
UC San Diego

ADDRESS

Undergraduate Admissions
1050 North Mills Avenue
Claremont, CA 91711-6114
714-621-8129

FINANCIAL FACTS

In-state tuition ($):	14,992
Out-of-state tuition ($):	14,992
Room & board ($):	5,836
FA application deadline:	2/1
% frosh receiving FA:	50
PT earnings per yr. ($):	1,200

TYPE OF AID: % of students ($)

FA of some kind:	50 (16,600)
Need-based grants:	NA
Merit-based grants:	NA
Loans:	NA
Work study:	NA
Student rating of FA:	95

CAMPUS LIFE

Quality of Life Rating:	*81*
Type of school:	private
Affiliation:	none
Environment:	city

STUDENT BODY

FT undergrad enrollment:	1,387
% male/% female:	53/47
% out-of-state:	56
% live on campus:	97
% African-American:	5
% Asian:	14
% Caucasian:	67
% Hispanic:	10
% foreign:	4
% transfers:	1

WHAT'S HOT

financial aid
gay community accepted
leftist politics
small labs and seminars
living on campus
profs outside class
cost of living
profs in class

WHAT'S NOT

marriage
religious clubs
dating
Top 40
attending all classes

ACADEMICS

Academic Rating:	*89*
Calendar:	semester
Student/teacher ratio:	9/1
% doctorates:	95
Profs interesting:	88
Profs accessible:	90
Hours of study per day:	3.16

MOST POPULAR MAJORS BY %

Economics:	9
English:	9
Government:	9

% GRADS WHO PURSUE

Law:	10
MBA:	9
Medicine:	9
M.A., etc.:	47

What do students think about Pomona College?

Note: The Claremont Colleges are five small undergraduate schools (Claremont McKenna, Harvey Mudd, Pitzer, Pomona, and Scripps) and one graduate school sharing a central location and facilities. Each school serves a distinct purpose and maintains its own faculty and campus. Cross-registration among colleges is encouraged.

■ **Academics** Pomona College, the most prestigious school in the Claremont cluster, offers a "traditional liberal arts program." Area college counselors report that the school is "academically superior across the board," and students enrolled in a myriad of departments expressed satisfaction with their academic programs. Students begin their studies here in freshman seminars (interdisciplinary courses intended to develop students' analytical and writing abilities). Students must also fulfill general education requirements that can take all of freshman and sophomore years to complete. Afterwards, students "concentrate" in one field, culminating in a comprehensive exam or senior project which must be completed successfully to graduate. Most students relish the challenges given them here. Explained one, "the opportunities for a motivated, directed student are endless." Student-teacher interaction is plentiful ("Professors are accessible, easy to talk to, and willing to help. One of my upper-division math classes had about 15 people in it and I was surprised how big it was," wrote one student) and the students themselves have healthy attitudes toward study. Reported one, "competitiveness here comes from within; people are very supportive of each other."

■ **Life** Many students told us that Pomona's biggest social problem is that students depend too heavily on the campus for their social lives. Said one, "The terrarium effect is really prevalent here. Pomona students in general seem more interested in seeking out the biggest possible beer blast than in taking advantage of the great entertainment possibilities available in L.A. It's like we're in a bubble: if L.A. weren't nearby, no one would even notice." Those who stay on campus are dissatisfied because the administration recently implemented a strict drug and alcohol policy. "Not much in the way of drugs here beyond the 'magic weed,'" explained one student. "The social scene is declining because of fascist alcohol policies imposed by our conservative government." The school does provide the resources for many extracurricular clubs ("But if you want to get involved you'll have to make the first step; no one will come looking for you," wrote one student). Immediately outside the campus is the city of Claremont, "boring, small, and predominantly white."

■ **Students** Pomona students have a well-deserved reputation for arrogance. (Wrote one, "Q: How many Pomona students does it take to screw in a light bulb? A: One: he holds it and waits for the world to revolve around him.") Several students reported that "the average student here is very intelligent and very cynical and knows how to complain well." Politically the campus leans to the left, with the students divided between the "politically correct" and the extremely cynical.

CLAREMONT COLLEGES—POMONA COLLEGE

Admissions

Pomona College uses "no formulas, no cut-offs" to eliminate prospective students. High school curriculum and grades are weighted most heavily in the admissions committee's decisions, followed in importance by standardized test scores, essays, extracurricular activities, letters of recommendation, and interview. Admissions are extremely competitive here, and the admissions office expects applicants to have completed a rigorous college preparatory curriculum in high school. Students must submit scores for either the SAT or ACT. Applicants to Pomona most often also apply to Stanford, Harvard, Yale, and UC–Berkeley. Note: two thirds of Pomona students are public school graduates, a relatively high proportion for a school this competitive.

Financial Aid

The financial aid office at Pomona College requires applicants to submit the FAF, a form generated by the school, and their parents' most recent tax return. The school awards all grants are awarded on the basis of need. In 1991–92, students took advantage of Stafford loans (33% of students took one; average value: $2,838), Perkins loans (6.8%; $2,314), and loans from the school (7%; $2,864). Just over half of incoming freshmen in 1991–92 received a financial aid package, the average value of which was $15,000.

A note from the Pomona College Admissions Office:

"Pomona College is recognized as one of the nation's premier liberal arts colleges. Founded in 1887, Pomona provides excellence in undergraduate instruction in the natural sciences, social sciences, humanities, and fine arts. With a commitment to undergraduate study, its outstanding faculty, accomplished students, extraordinary facilities, and residential character ensure an educational experience second to none.

"The College enrolls 1,375 students and has a student/faculty ratio of less than 10:1. The average class size of 14 offers students the opportunity to become full participants in the learning process. High value is placed on the interaction between teacher and student; most classes are taught as seminars. In challenging one another and their professors, Pomona students develop skills in analytical and critical thinking.

"Pomona is located in Claremont, California, 35 miles east of Los Angeles. It is the founding member of The Claremont Colleges: five undergraduate colleges and a graduate school on adjacent campuses, cooperating to broaden the intellectual, social and cultural resources available to their students."

ADMISSIONS FACTS

Competitiveness Rating:	**93**
% of applicants accepted:	36
% acceptees attending:	36

FRESHMAN PROFILE

Average verbal SAT:	640
Average math SAT:	690
Average ACT:	NA
Graduated top 10% of class:	79
Graduated top 25% of class:	96
Graduated top 50% of class:	100

DEADLINES

Early decision/action:	11/15
Early dec./act. notif.:	12/15
Regular admission:	1/15
Regular adm. notif.:	4/10

APPLICANTS ALSO LOOK AT

and often prefer:
Harvard/Radcliffe College
UC Berkeley
Stanford U.

and sometimes prefer:
UC Davis
Wesleyan U.
Williams College
Dartmouth College
Claremont McKenna College

and rarely prefer:
Pitzer College

ADDRESS

Undergraduate Admissions
333 N. College Way
Claremont, CA 91711-6312
714-621-8134

FINANCIAL FACTS

In-state tuition ($):	14,800
Out-of-state tuition ($):	14,800
Room & board ($) ($):	6,150
FA application deadline:	2/11
% frosh receiving FA:	53
PT earnings per yr. ($):	1,300

TYPE OF AID: % of students ($):

FA of some kind:	51 (15,250)
Need-based grants:	50 (11,338)
Merit-based grants:	NA
Loans:	NA
Work study:	44 (1,678)
Student rating of FA:	95

CLAREMONT COLLEGES–SCRIPPS COLLEGE

Claremont, CA

CAMPUS LIFE

Quality of Life Rating:	**83**
Type of school:	private
Affiliation:	none
Environment:	city

STUDENT BODY

FT undergrad enrollment:	627
% male/% female:	0/100
% out-of-state:	53
% live on campus:	95
% African-American:	3
% Asian:	11
% Caucasian:	75
% Hispanic:	8
% foreign:	3
% transfers:	3

WHAT'S HOT

small classes (overall)
gay community accepted
honesty
campus appearance
living on campus
in-class discussion
leftist politics

WHAT'S NOT

fraternities/sororities
intramural sports
profs lecture a lot

ACADEMICS

Academic Rating:	**88**
Calendar:	semester
Student/teacher ratio:	9/1
% doctorates:	100
Profs interesting:	89
Profs accessible:	89
Hours of study per day:	3.33

MOST POPULAR MAJORS BY %

Social Sciences:	30
Visual & Performing Arts:	19
Letters/Literature:	16

% GRADS WHO PURSUE

Law:	10
MBA:	5
Medicine:	3
M.A., etc.:	40

What do students think about Scripps College?

Note: The Claremont Colleges are five small undergraduate schools (Claremont McKenna, Harvey Mudd, Pitzer, Pomona, and Scripps) and one graduate school sharing a central location and facilities. Each school serves a distinct purpose and maintains its own faculty and campus. Cross-registration among colleges is encouraged.

■ **Academics** Scripps College is an undergraduate women's school "well known for its core curriculum in the humanities, as well as for its emphasis on inter-disciplinary study." Because it is part of the Claremont Cluster, Scripps is a good choice "for women who want a women's school but also want the advantages of co-ed," according to one area counselor. One student reported that this association also "gives you the opportunity to experience a small school but still have the benefits of a large college," as well as "a choice of classes that's endless." English, economics, political science, international affairs, and dramatic and studio arts are among the most popular majors here. Ethnic and women's studies are also reportedly excellent, leading one woman to comment that "Scripps is an interesting place to explore being a feminist. It provides a strong foundation to develop as a modern woman." Students give their professors good grades, noting that "they are willing, even eager, to help any student who approaches him/her with a problem." Students feel that the administration is a little overprotective, however, "very anal and old fashioned; I feel like they want to baby-sit us." Scripps offers students ample opportunities to study abroad, an option several students recommended. Wrote one, "Scripps is a small college and gets boring pretty quickly. If you get tired of studying and hanging out at keggers all the time, go to Europe for a year."

■ **Life** Scripps women are generally negative about the quality of social life here. Some feel that the all-women's environment "is very unnatural. I feel like we're becoming desocialized." Others blame the lackluster social scene on "the enormous emphasis on academics and doing well. I don't feel there is an equal balance between social life and school work." Still others complain about the administration and its "harsh alcohol policy," and some point to the town of Claremont ("boring"). Students did mention some positives. Said one, "You can't beat studying for finals while basking by the pool in the warm California sun." Others noted that "despite being a women's college, there is no shortage of men because of the five colleges." Given students' generally downbeat attitude about life on campus, surprisingly few students take advantage of the nearby Los Angeles social scene.

■ **Students** Scripps students report a lack of diversity in their student body, despite a 25 percent minority population. "Most students here are somewhat elitist and very capitalistic," explained one. Several did note the benefits of the single-sex environment, though, writing that "the all-female support group on campus creates a home away from home." As at all the Claremont Colleges, the students here are bright and motivated: well over half move on to advances programs after graduation.

CLAREMONT COLLEGES–SCRIPPS COLLEGE

Claremont, CA

Admissions

Scripps College selects students who are "intellectually curious and exemplify academic aptitude and motivation, ability and creativity, personal involvement, talents and interests, and potential for success." The most heavily weighed factor in your admissions package is your high school GPA, followed (in order of importance) by your standardized test scores, interview, letters of recommendation and extracurriculars. The recommended high school course of study includes four years of English, three years of social studies, the equivalent of a third-year level of a foreign language or two years each of two foreign languages, three years of lab science and four years of mathematics. Applicants must take the SAT or ACT, and must submit a graded paper from a junior- or senior-year English class. Achievement tests, while optional, are *strongly* recommended, English composition in particular. An interview is also advised, though not required. Students who apply to Scripps also often apply to Pomona, UC San Diego, UC Berkeley, UCLA, and Occidental.

Financial Aid

The financial aid office at Scripps College requires applicants to submit the FAF and the SAAC (Student Aid Application for California). The school awards merit grants on the basis of academic performance only. Scripps students took out federally-sponsored loans (36% of the students took them; average value: $3,250), private bank loans (11%; $3500), and loans provided by the school (2%; $2280). Forty-five percent of all freshmen in the 1991–92 class received a financial aid package, the average value of which was $17,174. The FA deadline listed below is Scripps's *priority* deadline; the school's closing deadline is March 2.

A note from the Scripps Admissions Office:

"At Scripps we believe that learning involves much more than amassing information. The truly educated person is one who can think analytically, communicate effectively, and make confident, responsible choices. Scripps classes are small (the average class size is 15) so that they foster an atmosphere where students feel comfortable participating, testing old assumptions and exploring new ideas. Our curriculum is based on the traditional components of a liberal arts education: a set of general requirements in a wide variety of disciplines including foreign language, natural science and writing; a multicultural requirement; a major that asks you to study one particular field in depth; and a variety of electives that allows considerable flexibility. What distinguishes Scripps from other liberal arts colleges is an emphasis on interdisciplinary courses."

ADMISSIONS FACTS

Competitiveness Rating:	**84**
% of applicants accepted:	70
% acceptees attending:	29

FRESHMAN PROFILE

Average verbal SAT:	564
Average math SAT:	590
Average ACT:	26
Graduated top 10% of class:	57
Graduated top 25% of class:	86
Graduated top 50% of class:	98

DEADLINES

Early decision/action:	11/15
Early dec./act. notif.:	12/15
Regular admission:	2/1
Regular adm. notif.:	4/1

APPLICANTS ALSO LOOK AT

and often prefer:
UC Berkeley
Pitzer College
UC Santa Cruz

and sometimes prefer:
UCLA
Occidental College
Pomona College
UC San Diego

ADDRESS

Undergraduate Admissions
1030 Columbia Avenue
Claremont, CA 91711
714-621-8149

FINANCIAL FACTS

In-state tuition ($):	14,700
Out-of-state tuition ($):	14,700
Room & board ($) ($):	6,200
FA application deadline:	2/1
% frosh receiving FA:	47
PT earnings per yr. ($):	1,200

TYPE OF AID: % of students ($):

FA of some kind:	47 (16,305)
Need-based grants:	NA (13,530)
Merit-based grants:	10 (5,500)
Loans:	NA (3,358)
Work study:	44 (1,350)
Student rating of FA:	87

143

CAMPUS LIFE

Quality of Life Rating: **77**

Type of school: private
Affiliation: none
Environment: city

STUDENT BODY

FT undergrad enrollment: 2,139
% male/% female: 44/56
% out-of-state: 62
% live on campus: 67
% African-American: 3
% Asian: 4
% Caucasian: 74
% Hispanic: 2
% foreign: 9
% transfers: 4

WHAT'S HOT

marijuana
small labs and seminars
interaction among students
dorm comfort
gay community accepted

WHAT'S NOT

location
fraternities/sororities
college radio station
town-gown relations
religious clubs
working a job

ACADEMICS

Academic Rating: **82**

Calendar: semester
Student/teacher ratio: 13/1
% doctorates: 97
Profs interesting: 81
Profs accessible: 80
Hours of study per day: 2.04

MOST POPULAR MAJORS BY %

Psychology: 22
Gov't & International Rel.: 10
Business Management: 8

% GRADS WHO PURSUE

Law: 10
MBA: 2
Medicine: 7
M.A., etc.: 13

What do students think about Clark University?

■ **Academics** "Individualism" is the buzz-word at Clark University: students frequently cited their autonomy in their comments to us. Clark is "a good choice, unless you're the kind of person who must fit into a particular crowd or have constant supervision," said one student. "Clark's the kind of place individuals come to contribute themselves to education and 'college life'." Another lauded the university as "allowing the perfect opportunity to find one's self." Psychology and geography are the two most famous departments here, although study in economics and political science are quite popular. Social science and natural science departments are generally considered stronger than the liberal arts here (except for the English department, which is quite good). Although a research university, Clark has many more undergraduate students than graduate students, allowing undergraduates to participate to an unusually large degree as research assistants. An added plus is that classes are small, so it's easier to get individual attention. Said one business management major, "my freshman year all of my classes had fewer than 20 students. I love Clark!" Clark is a member of the Worcester Consortium, which allows undergraduates to take courses at any of nine other schools in the area.

■ **Life** Life at Clark means dealing with life in Worcester (pronounced "Woostah," like you're in a Pepperidge Farms ad), where, evidently, never is heard an encouraging word. "Worcester sucks, it is one step away from a demilitarized zone," explained one student. Another was a bit more specific: "Basically, two or three Clarkies get mugged or attacked a week by locals. Most of these attacks occur on or near campus. That really gives a person a nice, warm, safe feeling!" There are no fraternities or sororities here. This, combined with the apparent unfriendliness of Worcester, leads to a pretty dull social life. "If you don't drink or do drugs, that cuts out about 85% of your fun," is how one student summed it all up. The consensus: "Don't come to Clark for girls, location, or the parties." Fortunately, Boston is only 40 miles away and is easily accessible by bus.

■ **Students** As one student put it, "Clark boasts having one of the most diverse student populations around; this, however, is an understatement." Most of the diversity is provided by foreign nationals. Asian-Americans make up only four percent of the student body, African-Americans three percent, and Hispanics two percent. Hanging out with so many international students "really opens your eyes to different cultures." Still, students complained that their classmates were cliquish—an almost inevitable result of the fractured social life here (see "Life," above). Clark students are famous for their apathy, and some seem strangely proud of this: said one, "I get really sick of that infamous Clark apathy, but hey, what can you do?"

CLARK UNIVERSITY

Admissions

Clark University considers your high school grades (in tandem with your curriculum) and letters of recommendation the most important components of your application. Essays, school/community activities, and standardized test scores are also considered important. An interview is recommended but not required; your performance during that interview is considered, but is less important than any other part of your application. Either the SAT or the ACT is required; foreign students must also submit TOEFL scores. Students who apply to Clark most often also apply to Boston University, Boston College, Tufts, Brandeis, and the University of Vermont.

Financial Aid

Clark requires a FAF and, after your initial award, a copy of your parents' most recent tax return. Two percent of all undergrads in '91–'92 received an academic grant (average value: $5,000). Clark's FA office states that it meets full demonstrated need for all eligible applicants; limited aid is offered to international students. Fifty-eight percent of last year's freshmen received an award of some kind (60% applied). The average freshman award was $13,500. Clark recommends Perkins loans (last year's figures: 34% of full-time undergrads; average value of $1483), Stafford loans (40%; $2,921), and other miscellaneous loans (1%; $5,367).

A note from the Clark University Admissions Office:

"Richard P. Traina, President of Clark University, will tell you that at Clark, 'A good idea is the best credential you can have,' that whatever the problem, independent-minded individuals with good ideas are key to the solution. What else should you know about Clark? First, it's the *smallest* research university in the country; for Clark's students this means they get the *power* of a national leader in research and the *hands-on attention* of a small school. Second, Clark is perhaps the most *international* school of its kind in the world—in its entering students, its curriculum, and the experiences of its faculty. Third, it is a *passionate and committed* place. Research and teaching aim very deliberately at crucial social issues—no flinching, no equivocating, no holds barred. Finally, Clark takes its students very seriously; we expect them to work very hard and to have a great deal of fun at it. Too challenging? Perhaps you should look elsewhere. Captured your imagination? Then maybe you should find out if you're a Clarkie at heart!"

ADMISSIONS FACTS

Competitiveness Rating:	**78**
% of applicants accepted:	70
% acceptees attending:	22

FRESHMAN PROFILE

Average verbal SAT:	517*
Average math SAT:	577*
Average ACT:	NA
Graduated top 10% of class:	33
Graduated top 25% of class:	71
Graduated top 50% of class:	97

DEADLINES

Early decision/action:	12/1
Early dec./act. notif.:	1/1
Regular admission:	2/15
Regular adm. notif.:	4/1

APPLICANTS ALSO LOOK AT

and often prefer:
Tufts U.
Vassar College

and sometimes prefer:
NYU
Syracuse U.
U. New Hampshire
Wheaton College
U. Mass–Amherst

and rarely prefer:
Boston U.

ADDRESS

Undergraduate Admissions
950 Main Street
Worcester, MA 01610-1477
508-793-7431

FINANCIAL FACTS

In-state tuition ($):	15,000
Out-of-state tuition ($):	15,000
Room & board ($) ($):	4,500
FA application deadline:	2/1
% frosh receiving FA:	50
PT earnings per yr. ($):	1,300

TYPE OF AID: % of students ($):

FA of some kind:	50 (12,800)
Need-based grants:	45 (9,455)
Merit-based grants:	2 (5,000)
Loans:	44 (3,993)
Work study:	34 (1,249)
Student rating of FA:	80

CLARKSON UNIVERSITY

Potsdam, NY

CAMPUS LIFE

Quality of Life Rating: **76**

Type of school:	private
Affiliation:	none
Environment:	suburban

STUDENT BODY

FT undergrad enrollment:	2,925
% male/% female:	79/21
% out-of-state:	30
% live on campus:	77
% African-American:	1
% Asian:	3
% Caucasian:	96
% Hispanic:	1
% foreign:	4
% transfers:	7

WHAT'S HOT

dorm safety
living on campus
catalog
registration
conservative politics

WHAT'S NOT

gay community visible
working a job
college newspaper
library
caring about politics
gay community accepted
marijuana

ACADEMICS

Academic Rating: **78**

Calendar:	semester
Student/teacher ratio:	16/1
% doctorates:	90
Profs interesting:	72
Profs accessible:	79
Hours of study per day:	2.95

MOST POPULAR MAJORS BY %

Engineering:	67
Business & Management:	22
Computer & Info. Sciences:	3

% GRADS WHO PURSUE

Law:	NA
MBA:	4
Medicine:	NA
M.A., etc.:	4

What do students think about Clarkson University?

■ **Academics** For Northeasterners who are looking for a solid engineering education but would rather do without the intense competition of at MIT and RPI, Clarkson may be the place. Explained one CU undergrad, "the level of competitiveness here is very low. Students are willing to help you at all times—it's not a fight to see who is the best, it's more of a 'let's all get through this together' kind of thing." Others agreed that "there's no cut-throat atmosphere, which makes life easier." Two thirds of Clarkson's students are engineers; practically all the rest study business and management (the notable exception is a small group of pre-meds). Professors are helpful and accessible, particularly for those at an engineering-intensive school. Said one student, "The professors here are very interested in the successful progress of their students. Professors will work with students in a way that is unique, from what I've been told about major universities." Academics are challenging but not unreasonably demanding: students put in about three hours of study a day outside the classroom. Required courses, which include liberal arts courses as well as basic math and computer sciences, are considered difficult. Administrators received good grades across the board.

■ **Life** Potsdam is a remote town near the Canadian border. Winters are long and cold, and the setting can be discouraging for newcomers. One senior told us that "almost everyone I've talked to says that during the first year he wanted to transfer out, but by the time he graduated he thought Clarkson was the best and was happy he stayed. Clarkson and even Potsdam grow on you." Men outnumber women three to one. This led one student to write that "Clarkson can appear to be a place where 'the men are men, and so are the women,' but you just have to meet the right people. Downtown [Potsdam] is key! It gives you a chance to meet new people and interact with SUNY Potsdam students. Fraternity life and the bars are the things to do!" Clarkson boasts a student-run television station, which, according to one student, is "one of the best in the country (WCKN TV 31). It's entirely owned and operated by the students with very little faculty involvement, yet we rival 'professional' stations." The hockey team is excellent, and other winter sports are understandably popular.

■ **Students** Clarkson's student body is 96 percent white. With fewer than two hundred minority classmates, minority students can feel a little out of place. One student complained that many of his classmates "have small-town, upstate New York mentalities. There are lots of 'brains' but very few intellectuals." All the same, students are generally friendly and easygoing: said one student, "People here don't think they're above anyone else—that's what's so great about them."

CLARKSON UNIVERSITY

Admissions

Clarkson University uses no cutoffs or formulas in considering its applicants. The school's catalog notes, "In addition to superior scholastic achievement, consideration is given to personal qualities, participation in meaningful extracurricular or out-of-school activities, leadership, and other information that may indicate successful completion of a college career." Clarkson first looks at your high school GPA and your standardized test scores. Following these, in order of importance, are your letters of recommendation, interview (optional, but recommended), extracurriculars, and essays. Either SAT or ACT scores must be submitted, and applicants are urged, but not required, to take Achievements as well. The preferred high school curriculum should encompass 16 units of secondary work, including: for the schools of Engineering and Science, four units of English and mathematics, three to four units of science, with one unit each of chemistry and physics; for the Schools of Management, Liberal Studies and the Industrial Distribution Program, four units of English, three units of mathematics, and one unit of science (for Industrial Distribution, an extra year of math is recommended, and the science unit should be physics). Applicants to Clarkson often also apply to RPI, Rochester Tech, Cornell, SUNY Buffalo, and Syracuse.

Financial Aid

Applicants for financial aid at Clarkson University must complete the FAF and submit copies of their parents' and their own tax returns. Last year, Clarkson awarded a variety of merit-based scholarships, including athletic grants to 1% of its undergrads (average value, $18,400), and academic scholarships to 9% (average value: $1,250). Approximately 2% of all undergrads received an alumni grant, ranging in value from $1,000 to $2,000. In addition to recommending Stafford and Perkins loans, Clarkson offers its own institutional loans and its own Parent Loan program. February 1 is the priority deadline for FA applications; February 15 is the closing date.

A note from the Clarkson Admissions Office:

"If you could capture the character of a university with a single event, a good bet for Clarkson would be its entry in the 1990 SUNRAYCE USA: a car powered by the sun, created by a team of students applying state-of-the-art technology that surpassed the best efforts of larger (but less ingenious) institutions.

"Clarkson is a school where brain power turns into action—and action becomes accomplishment. Bright students come to Clarkson. They work hard. They play hard. And they graduate with a degree that's worth money in the marketplace and status in a graduate school."

ADMISSIONS FACTS

Competitiveness Rating:	**75**
% of applicants accepted:	87
% acceptees attending:	27

FRESHMAN PROFILE

Average verbal SAT:	519
Average math SAT:	616
Average ACT:	NA
Graduated top 10% of class:	44
Graduated top 25% of class:	72
Graduated top 50% of class:	87

DEADLINES

Early decision/action:	12/1
Early dec./act. notif.:	12/15
Regular admission:	3/15
Regular adm. notif.:	rolling

APPLICANTS ALSO LOOK AT

and often prefer:
RIT
SUNY Buffalo
RPI
U. Vermont

and sometimes prefer:
U. Connecticut
U. Rochester
Alfred U.
Lehigh U.

and rarely prefer:
Syracuse U.

ADDRESS

Undergraduate Admissions
Potsdam, NY 13699
315-268-6480

FINANCIAL FACTS

In-state tuition ($):	13,380
Out-of-state tuition ($):	13,380
Room & board ($):	4,732
FA application deadline:	2/15
% frosh receiving FA:	85
PT earnings per yr. ($):	650

TYPE OF AID: % of students ($):

FA of some kind:	85 (NA)
Need-based grants:	77 (3,831)
Merit-based grants:	NA
Loans:	73 (4,943)
Work study:	15 (NA)
Student rating of FA:	81

CLEMSON UNIVERSITY

Clemson, SC

CAMPUS LIFE

Quality of Life Rating: **80**

Type of school:	public
Affiliation:	none
Environment:	suburban

STUDENT BODY

FT undergrad enrollment:	12,280
% male/% female:	57/43
% out-of-state:	32
% live on campus:	55
% African-American:	7
% Asian:	NA
% Caucasian:	91
% Hispanic:	NA
% foreign:	NA
% transfers:	NA

WHAT'S HOT

intercollegiate sports
intramural sports
conservative politics
religion
dating
town-gown relations
overall happiness
hard liquor
beer

WHAT'S NOT

TAs teach intros
food
gay community accepted
studying hard
small classes (overall)

ACADEMICS

Academic Rating: **70**

Calendar:	semester
Student/teacher ratio:	19/1
% doctorates:	79
Profs interesting:	68
Profs accessible:	68
Hours of study per day:	2.56

MOST POPULAR MAJORS BY %

Business & Management:	28
Engineering:	21
Education:	11

% GRADS WHO PURSUE

Law:	5
MBA:	21
Medicine:	8
M.A., etc.:	67

What do students think about Clemson University?

■ **Academics** Clemson University is the school for South Carolinians who want to put their careers on track while also enjoying beautiful mountain scenery, easy-going classmates, and top-notch college football. More than one quarter of the students pursue business and management majors; pre-medicine and engineering are also popular, as is education. Considering the school's size, access to professors is good. Explained one student, "for a big university the classes are very small, similar to high school classes, except biology and chemistry, which can reach about 150 students." However, as one student warned, "lately classes are getting larger due to budget cuts, and tuition is definitely on the rise!" Professors received below-average marks, especially from pre-meds and engineers, "mostly because so many don't speak English very well," according to one student. Students definitely take a laid-back approach to study—their two and a half hours a day of studying ranked among the bottom five percent—but the school is nonetheless "great for people who want to get away from the fast-paced urban life while still getting a good education." Cost is a major drawing card: even for those from out of state, this public university charges an extremely affordable tuition.

■ **Life** You'd have a hard time finding a group of people anywhere who care more about football than do Clemson students. Many students wrote "GO TIGERS!!" across the bottom of their surveys, and it's this undying devotion to football that fuels students' ardent school spirit. Beyond football games, social options are limited. Even the school's most vociferous boosters admit the lack of variety. Wrote one, "in the fall after football games there is a lot to do, but in the spring it gets pretty dull." Parties are relatively easy to come by, however. As one student wrote, "there are not a whole lot of enriching cultural events, but the people are friendly and there's something going on every night of the week." Area bars, frats, and dorms are popular sites for getting together and drinking, although lately the school has begun to enforce drinking age laws pretty vigorously. One student complained, "by trying to eliminate alcohol on campus, the administration is cutting its own throat. People come here for the academics *and* because it's a party school, but the level of fun has definitely dropped." Visitation restrictions in single-sex dorms are also strictly enforced. The location provides excellent recreation opportunities: reported one student, "Good weekend getaways are just an hour away. We've got the mountains for skiing close by."

■ **Students** Over two thirds of the students are native South Carolinians. Over 90 percent are white, but almost all the rest are black, so there is a sizeable black population here. Students are very conservative politically—they ranked fourteenth most conservative in the country. They are also quite religious and tend toward conformity. "Variety is hidden or ousted" complained one student. Within those parameters, the student body is laid-back and friendly in the Southern tradition.

CLEMSON UNIVERSITY

Admissions

The admissions office reports that "admission is competitive and based primarily upon high school curriculum, grades, class standing, and SAT scores. An applicant's intended major and state residency also receive consideration." Applicants must have completed four years of English, three years of social studies and mathematics (a fourth year is strongly recommended), two years of lab sciences (one year each of two different lab sciences, chosen from biology, chemistry, or physics; also, a third year is strongly recommended), two years of foreign language, a year of physical education or ROTC, and one year of either advanced math or computer science (or a half-year of each), and one year of either world history, geography, or Western civilization. Students who apply to Clemson most often also apply to UNC–Chapel Hill, Georgia Tech, NC State, and University of South Carolina.

Financial Aid

Applicants for financial aid at Clemson University must complete the FAF. In '91–'92, Clemson awarded a variety of merit-based scholarships, including athletic grants to 4% of its undergrads (average value: $4,750), and academic scholarships to 15% (average value: $1,200). In addition to Stafford loans and Perkins loans, Clemson recommends PLUS, SLS, and a number of private loans.

Excerpted from Clemson University promotional materials:

"Clemson is a land-grant, state-supported university. Clemson University is accredited by the Commission on Colleges of the Southern Association of Colleges and Schools to award the Bachelor's, Master's, Specialist, and Doctor's degrees. Curricula are accredited by Accreditation Board for Engineering and Technology, American Assembly of Collegiate Schools of Business, Computing Sciences Accreditation Board, Council on Accreditations of the Nation and Park Association, National Architectural Accrediting Board, National Council for Accreditation of Teacher Education, National League for Nursing, and Society of American Foresters.

"The sixty-eight undergraduate and ninety-seven graduate degree programs under the colleges of Agricultural Sciences, Architecture, Commerce and Industry, Education, Engineering, Forest and Recreation Resources, Liberal Arts, Nursing, Sciences, and Graduate School form the background of training for the hundreds of occupations and professions in which Clemson graduates engage. The University is organized on a basis whereby it retains clear entity through the interrelationships of colleges and departments, providing a well-balanced fundamental and general education program."

ADMISSIONS FACTS

Competitiveness Rating:	**77**
% of applicants accepted:	68
% acceptees attending:	48

FRESHMAN PROFILE

Average verbal SAT:	480
Average math SAT:	555
Average ACT:	NA
Graduated top 10% of class:	38
Graduated top 25% of class:	72
Graduated top 50% of class:	95

DEADLINES

Early decision/action:	NA
Early dec./act. notif.:	NA
Regular admission:	rolling
Regular adm. notif.:	rolling

APPLICANTS ALSO LOOK AT

and often prefer:
UNC–Chapel Hill
Duke U.

and sometimes prefer:
Furman U.
James Madison U.
U. South Carolina
Wake Forest U.
Vanderbilt U.

and rarely prefer:
U. Florida
Auburn U.

ADDRESS

Undergraduate Admissions
105 Sikes Hall
Clemson, SC 29634-4024
803-656-2287

FINANCIAL FACTS

In-state tuition ($):	2,623
Out-of-state tuition ($):	7,001
Room & board ($):	3,153
FA application deadline:	2/1
% frosh receiving FA:	59
PT earnings per yr. ($):	1,000

TYPE OF AID: % of students ($):

FA of some kind:	52 (NA)
Need-based grants:	15 (1,575)
Merit-based grants:	NA
Loans:	28 (2,175)
Work study:	4 (NA)
Student rating of FA:	73

COLBY COLLEGE

Waterville, ME

CAMPUS LIFE

Quality of Life Rating: 92

Type of school:	private
Affiliation:	none
Environment:	rural

STUDENT BODY

FT undergrad enrollment:	1,711
% male/% female:	50/50
% out-of-state:	32
% live on campus:	94
% African-American:	2
% Asian:	3
% Caucasian:	92
% Hispanic:	2
% foreign:	2
% transfers:	1

WHAT'S HOT

overall happiness
Grateful Dead
campus appearance
dorm safety
profs outside class
profs in class
financial aid
food
cost of living
college theater
administration (overall)

WHAT'S NOT

fraternities/sororities
diversity
location

ACADEMICS

Academic Rating: 85

Calendar:	4-1-4
Student/teacher ratio:	10/1
% doctorates:	79
Profs interesting:	93
Profs accessible:	94
Hours of study per day:	3.26

MOST POPULAR MAJORS BY %

English:	15
Government:	13
Economics:	9

% GRADS WHO PURSUE

Law:	3
MBA:	1
Medicine:	3
M.A., etc.:	14

What do students think about Colby College?

■ **Academics** "The best things about Colby College," wrote one student, "are the excellence and approachability of the professors." This respect for the faculty prevails throughout the student body. Professors are warmly described over and over as "committed," "outstanding," "always available," and so on. Particularly impressive are the fields of "government and economics; students would be hard pressed to find better departments in comparable colleges." English and other liberal arts majors are also popular, and the school also has a small but dedicated contingent of visual and performing arts students. Colby, a small college nestled quaintly in Waterville, Maine, has often received praise for its dedicated faculty and "surprisingly intellectual" student body. Its history has been dotted with various pioneering moves such as the admission of women in 1871 (making it the first co-ed institution in the Northeast), and the establishment of an enrichment program for its students called "Jan Plan." This program allows students to study non-traditional academic subjects or intern during the month of January (and year-round for top seniors), and the experience generates rave reviews.

■ **Life** Colby students reported a very high level of satisfaction with their lives at Colby. They love their beautiful, secluded campus, they love outdoor sports even during the "frozen tundra" winter months in Maine, they love their classes, and all in all, they consider Colby "a really groovy place" to spend four years. Even the food here gets respect. Wrote one student, the dining halls "are always thinking of new ways to feed the herds. 'Tuesday wok night' is a favorite." A slight flaw in this collegiate utopia may be the pervasiveness of mind-altering substances in Colby's social life ("If you don't drink or smoke drugs, Colby will not be a very fun place"). Despite a "strict but weakly enforced" alcohol policy, students can actually "get beer delivered to the doorstep from local shops in town." If you're not careful, some say, life can be "a drunken blur." A testimony to the importance of alcohol on campus is that it's reportedly not uncommon for there to be a "keg party at 9:00 A.M. on Saturday morning; this is an age-old Colby tradition called a Doghead." If you're up for the lifestyle described as typical here, Colby might be the place for you. As one student summed up, "we work intensely, party with determination, work out religiously, and spend what leisure time is left recuperating." A final note: Colby has no officially sanctioned Greek system, but a small "underground" fraternity scene does exist.

■ **Students:** "OK, so we're not too diverse," one student wryly admitted; the few minority students who attend Colby tend to "segregate themselves" from the white mainstream—some students feel that some new blood to "shake up the comfortable middle-class world constructed here" would be welcome. Certainly the Colby administration is striving for a more heterogeneous student body.

COLBY COLLEGE

Admissions

The admissions office reports that "applicants are evaluated on the basis of academic ability and achievement, as well as on such attributes as intellectual promise, excitement for learning, maturity, character, and social conscience. The quality of a candidate's preparation is judged by academic record, personal essays and interviews, references, and school and community activities. There are no 'cut-offs' of any sort." Applicants are recommended to have completed four years of English, three years of a single foreign language, two years of lab science, three years of "college prep" math, and two years of history/social sciences. Colby requires either the SAT and three achievements (including English composition), or the ACT. Students applying to Colby most often also apply to Dartmouth, Williams, Bowdoin, Middlebury, and Bates.

Financial Aid

Colby requires a FAF, a copy of your parents' most recent tax return and a form generated by its financial aid office. All grants are need-based only. Colby practices need-blind admissions, and the FA office notes, "Private outside scholarships reduce packaged student's loan; only if the total outside scholarships exceed the packaged loan is the institutional grant affected." In other words, if you can find money on your own, it will be reduced from your loan awards, not your scholarship award. Last year, 42% of the freshman class received an award of some kind, with the average value being $13,240. Perkins loans were recommended for 20% of all undergrads in the '91–'92 academic year (average value: $1,860), Stafford loans for 26% ($2,180) and other miscellaneous loans for 2% (2,035). Although forms are due postmarked by 1/15/93, the FAF is not due until 2/1.

A note from the Colby College Admissions Office:

"As the 12th oldest independent college of liberal arts in the nation, Colby values the tradition of liberal learning and has maintained and enriched its core curriculum. The Colby Plan, adopted in 1989, embraces a series of ten educational precepts reflecting the Faculty's sense of the principal elements of a liberal education. They are intended as a guide for course choices and as a framework for education beyond college. Recent program changes include a renewed emphasis in the natural sciences and enhanced opportunities for study abroad. Students praise the faculty for its strong commitment to teaching and to close interaction beyond the classroom. Colby replaced its fraternity system—abolished in 1984—with a system of four residential commons which has increased opportunity for leadership and participation in campus governance for both men and women. Colby's campus, in central Maine, is generally regarded as one of the most handsome in the nation."

ADMISSIONS FACTS

Competitiveness Rating:	**89**
% of applicants accepted:	41
% acceptees attending:	32

FRESHMAN PROFILE

Average verbal SAT:	580
Average math SAT:	620
Average ACT:	27
Graduated top 10% of class:	54
Graduated top 25% of class:	90
Graduated top 50% of class:	100

DEADLINES

Early decision/action:	11/15
Early dec./act. notif.:	12/15
Regular admission:	1/15
Regular adm. notif.:	4/1

APPLICANTS ALSO LOOK AT

and often prefer:
Syracuse U.
Bowdoin College
Colgate U.
Bates College

and rarely prefer:
St. Lawrence U.
U. New Hampshire
Bucknell U.
Dickinson College
U. Mass–Amherst

ADDRESS

Undergraduate Admissions
Waterville, ME 04901
207-872-3168

FINANCIAL FACTS

In-state tuition ($):	15,710
Out-of-state tuition ($):	15,710
Room & board ($):	5,350
FA application deadline:	1/15
% frosh receiving FA:	75
PT earnings per yr. ($):	1,400

TYPE OF AID: % of students ($):

FA of some kind:	70 (13,000)
Need-based grants:	37 (10,475)
Merit-based grants:	NA
Loans:	47 (2,394)
Work study:	33 (1,400)
Student rating of FA:	90

COLGATE UNIVERSITY

Quality of Life Rating: **86**

Type of school:	private
Affiliation:	none
Environment:	suburban

STUDENT BODY

FT undergrad enrollment:	2,680
% male/% female:	54/46
% out-of-state:	63
% live on campus:	65
% African-American:	5
% Asian:	5
% Caucasian:	84
% Hispanic:	2
% foreign:	2
% transfers:	1

WHAT'S HOT

deans
college radio station
dorm safety
campus appearance
hard liquor
marijuana
small labs and seminars
dorm comfort
profs in class
intramural sports

WHAT'S NOT

dating
marriage
interaction among students
location

ACADEMICS

Academic Rating: **90**

Calendar:	semester
Student/teacher ratio:	12/1
% doctorates:	95
Profs interesting:	89
Profs accessible:	89
Hours of study per day:	2.97

MOST POPULAR MAJORS BY %

Social Sciences:	49
Letters/Literature:	13
Life Sciences:	6

% GRADS WHO PURSUE

Law:	10
MBA:	2
Medicine:	5
M.A., etc.:	13

What do students think about Colgate University?

■ **Academics** Colgate University is a small upstate New York liberal arts school with a solid reputation both for academics and social life. One student described Colgate's student body as "characterized by highly intelligent underachievers who enjoy an active social life." Administrators have recently beefed up academic and admissions requirements, thereby improving the school's already excellent programs and student body. Political science, the most popular major, is reportedly the least demanding; among the other popular majors, English, economics, and psychology students reported the most demanding curricula. One student noted that "the outdoor education program is great. We take first-year students out during the year for activities such as hiking, rock climbing, winter camping, and ice climbing. Minimal impact camping and survival are offered for credit." All students must take general education courses, which cover introductory material in the liberal arts and sciences. All professors, regardless of their field of expertise, teach all "gen ed" courses, leading one student to complain that "the interdisciplinary approach to 'gen ed' results in biology professors teaching *The Odyssey*. They end up teaching things that they remember from high school."

■ **Life** Colgate is a party school: students wrote that they "work hard and party hard" so many times that it could be the unofficial school motto. Fraternities and sororities play an important role, one which the administration is trying to curtail through stricter enforcement of drinking policies and frat regulations. Not surprisingly, students resent these incursions, since many were attracted to the school by its famous freewheeling party atmosphere. There is no shortage of extracurricular activities: said one undergrad, "This is a place where almost anyone can make a difference, whether they wish to excel in music, art, theatre, or sports." A community service group, "Volunteer Colgate," is run by students and offers a wide range of volunteer options—from literacy programs to a project aimed at building houses for the homeless. The school is located in a remote area, but many students regard this as an asset. Wrote one, "We're located in the middle of a beautiful farm area. A trek on cross-country skis brings one to overgrown apple orchards, crumbling stone walls, and glades with bubbling springs where deer prints dot the snow."

■ **Students** Colgate has a 16 percent minority population. Most students feel that there's a certain sameness about their classmates. Wrote one, "everyone here was captain of their football, lacrosse, or field hockey team in high school, or was student government president or yearbook editor." The atmosphere is congenial: said one student, "The other students are really friendly and easy to get along with. Unfortunately, this can be chalked up to the homogeneity of the campus." The minority population is comprised mostly of blacks and Asians. Blacks and whites agreed that black students remain alienated from the social mainstream.

COLGATE UNIVERSITY

Admissions

The admissions office reports that candidates are chosen "for the qualities of talent and intellect they can contribute to the college community. Academic achievement, reflecting a student engaged with both ideas and learning, is important…but Colgate also values the student with interests that reflect a disposition to curiosity and commitment, as well as a sympathy and excitement for the spirit of intellectual pursuits. Well-developed special interests, talents, and skills of all kinds can be a significant part of an admissions application. In addition, Colgate is committed to attracting people who represent a diversity of intellectual perspective as well as economic, racial, religious, and geographic background." Colgate prescribes no particular high school courses, but looks for "strong preparation in the humanities, social sciences, mathematics, physical and biological sciences." Colgate applicants are also often applicants to Cornell, Middlebury, Hamilton, U. Penn, Bucknell, and Dartmouth.

Financial Aid

Colgate requires a FAF, a copy of your most recent tax return (parents' and student's) and a form generated by its financial aid office. All grants are need-based only. Colgate's FA office states "Scholarships, work opportunities and loan funds are…awarded on the basis of academic qualifications, total performance, character, and demonstrated need" to accepted students whose personal and family resources are inadequate to meet the cost of a Colgate education. Forty-two percent of last year's freshman class received some type of award; the average value was $7,990. Colgate recommended Perkins loans to 14% of last year's undergrads (the average value was $1,540), Stafford loans to 28% ($2,665) and PLUS loans to 27% ($3,682).

A note from the Colgate Admissions Office:

"Colgate is a private college of 2,200 enormously able students. The faculty is committed to liberal education in its purest sense. Admissions looks for students who typically have 'done well' academically, but more to the point, have a clearly visible, independent, intellectual fire. We spend a lot of time with teacher recommendations and look for commitment to something (in or out of the classroom) with an obvious passion."

ADMISSIONS FACTS

Competitiveness Rating:	**90**
% of applicants accepted:	43
% acceptees attending:	31

FRESHMAN PROFILE

Average verbal SAT:	599*
Average math SAT:	652*
Average ACT:	29*
Graduated top 10% of class:	60
Graduated top 25% of class:	90
Graduated top 50% of class:	98

DEADLINES

Early decision/action:	1/15
Early dec./act. notif.:	rolling
Regular admission:	1/15
Regular adm. notif.:	3/31

APPLICANTS ALSO LOOK AT

and often prefer:
Princeton U.
Dartmouth College
Bowdoin College

and sometimes prefer:
Hamilton College
Lehigh U.
Middlebury College

and rarely prefer:
Bucknell U.
Lafayette College

ADDRESS

Undergraduate Admissions
Hamilton, NY 13346
315-824-1000

FINANCIAL FACTS

In-state tuition ($):	16,012
Out-of-state tuition ($):	16,012
Room & board ($):	5,070
FA application deadline:	2/1
% frosh receiving FA:	55
PT earnings per yr. ($):	1,000

TYPE OF AID: % of students ($):

FA of some kind:	43 (7,990)
Need-based grants:	43 (7,479)
Merit-based grants:	NA
Loans:	33 (NA)
Work study:	29 (1,232)
Student rating of FA:	84

UNIVERSITY OF COLORADO—BOULDER

Boulder, CO

What do students think about University of Colorado?

■ **Academics** There are plenty of students at University of Colorado–Boulder, whose attitude is summed up by the one who wrote, "I chose this school because I love to ski." And, while UC–Boulder is located in one of the most desirable locations in the nation, one undergrad warned that "if you plan on coming here just for fun, forget it! The classes are definitely challenging." Regional college counselors agreed that "the school's academics are underrated." Business and management majors are extremely popular and reputedly excellent; the engineering school also garners praise for its programs. The school is large enough and good enough to provide solid offerings in most traditional college majors—political science, psychology, pre-medical sciences were all noted in our survey—as well as in newer disciplines ("the film studies program is growing in big steps."). The school's ability to serve the needs of practically everybody led one student to note that "if it's sixties, it's UC–Boulder; if it's seventies, it's UC–Boulder; if it's 2010, it's UC–Boulder." On the downside, classes can be enormous, especially introductory classes, and some feel that in general the school is "too large to cater to individual needs and this should be understood by prospective students." The administration is "a huge bureaucracy," wrote one student, who then added, "but once you get used to it, this is a great place to be."

■ **Life** UC–Boulder offers an "incredibly high quality of life, both academically and off-campus." The location, right next to the Rockies, is "an 'outdoorsy' person's paradise, with all the best hiking, skiing, and mountain biking available." Students ranked the city among the nation's top ten college sites, noting that Boulder is a "beautiful, environmentally aware town" and that "Denver is a 30-minute drive, so great music and clubs are never far away." The school's huge size allows for "unlimited extracurricular activities"; one student noted that "we have tons of clubs, a great Greek system, and lots of athletics." Students enjoy a very active party and dating scene, leading one student to characterize the UC–Boulder experience as a "four-year vacation." Intercollegiate sports are so popular that several respondents complained they were *too* popular: wrote one, "Football is far too important here. The coach makes more than the governor of the state." That coach is as controversial as his salary: he made the news in the spring of '92 with his hard-line public proclamations against gays.

■ **Students** Minority representation is low at UC–Boulder. Reported one student, "Although there are unfortunately few minorities on this campus, the student body is very varied in its opinions, values, and social practices." Another explained that "you'll find everything here from big-city folks to granolas, from Greeks to acid heads." A few students disparagingly noted the prevalence of "trust-fund babies" on campus, but most comments about classmates were positive. Many respondents commended their fellow students for their open-mindedness.

UNIVERSITY OF COLORADO–BOULDER

Boulder, CO

Admissions

The most recent University of Colorado–Boulder catalog reports, "prospective students are considered on an individual basis relative to a prediction of academic success in the college to which they apply. The strongest indicators are appropriate course preparation, grades earned in those courses, class rank, and the results of either the SAT or the ACT." Applicants who rank in the top 20 percent of their high school class, have at least a 3.3 GPA, and score above an 850 on the SAT are extremely likely to gain entry here. A chart detailing the likelihood of applicants with various backgrounds appears in the school's catalog; go to the library and check it out for more details on your likelihood of admission here. Minimum high school curricular requirements vary from school to school: all require 16 units of academic study, four years of English; three years each of science and math; and two years each of social studies and a foreign language.

Financial Aid

The financial aid office at University of Colorado requires applicants to submit either the FAF, the FFS, or the Singlefile need-analysis form. A school promotional brochure sent to prospective students reports that "About half of our students receive financial aid. We attempt to meet your financial need through a combination of loans, work-study awards, and grants....The average financial aid award for all students, both residents and non-residents, was $5,800. We also offer a scholarship search service that helps identify grants and scholarships for which you may be eligible." Merit grants are awarded to those gifted in academics, athletics, and the arts.

A note from the University of Colorado Admissions Office:

"At UC–Boulder, you'll share in the excitement of a major research university with an outstanding academic reputation. One of only 29 public institutions belonging to the prestigious Association of American Universities, Boulder's academic excellence is matched by the beauty of its campus and its scenic location. While at Boulder, you'll have the opportunity to learn from faculty who are among the best in their fields, such as Professor Thomas Cech, who won the 1989 Nobel Prize in Chemistry.

"Our students—just over 25,000—come from all 50 states and over 80 foreign countries to enroll in our nine colleges and schools. About 46 percent of them are women and 54 percent men. Colorado residents make up 55 percent of freshmen and 66 percent of all students."

ADMISSIONS FACTS

Competitiveness Rating:	**76**
% of applicants accepted:	74
% acceptees attending:	39

FRESHMAN PROFILE

Average verbal SAT:	507*
Average math SAT:	570*
Average ACT:	25*
Graduated top 10% of class:	32
Graduated top 25% of class:	69
Graduated top 50% of class:	94

DEADLINES

Early decision/action:	NA
Early dec./act. notif.:	NA
Regular admission:	2/15
Regular adm. notif.:	NA

APPLICANTS ALSO LOOK AT

and often prefer:
Northwestern U.
UC Santa Cruz
Stanford

and sometimes prefer:
U. Oregon
U. Vermont

ADDRESS

Undergraduate Admissions
Boulder, CO 80309
303-492-6301

FINANCIAL FACTS

In-state tuition ($):	2,382
Out-of-state tuition ($):	10,360
Room & board ($):	3,507
FA application deadline:	4/1
% frosh receiving FA:	NA
PT earnings per yr. ($):	NA

TYPE OF AID: % of students ($):

FA of some kind:	NA
Need-based grants:	NA
Merit-based grants:	NA
Loans:	NA
Work study:	NA
Student rating of FA:	76

COLORADO COLLEGE

Colorado Springs, CO

CAMPUS LIFE

Quality of Life Rating: **84**

Type of school:	private
Affiliation:	none
Environment:	city

STUDENT BODY

FT undergrad enrollment:	1,876
% male/% female:	50/50
% out-of-state:	65
% live on campus:	66
% African-American:	2
% Asian:	3
% Caucasian:	88
% Hispanic:	4
% foreign:	3
% transfers:	4

WHAT'S HOT

Grateful Dead
small classes (overall)
in-class discussion
leftist politics
intramural sports
marijuana
campus easy to get around
overall happiness
alternative rock
gay community accepted
financial aid

WHAT'S NOT

diversity
religion
town-gown relations

ACADEMICS

Academic Rating: **84**

Calendar:	other
Student/teacher ratio:	13/1
% doctorates:	93
Profs interesting:	87
Profs accessible:	88
Hours of study per day:	3.31

MOST POPULAR MAJORS BY %

Social Sciences:	32
Letters/Literature:	26
Life Sciences:	11

% GRADS WHO PURSUE

Law:	5
MBA:	2
Medicine:	3
M.A., etc.:	20

What do students think about Colorado College?

■ **Academics** Colorado College takes a different approach to the academic calendar. Rather than have students take four or five courses at a time throughout a semester, CC breaks each semester into three-and-a-half week blocks, during which students take one course, intensively. At the end of each block, students get a four day "block break" to cleanse the palate of their minds before starting in on their next course. "There are only two types of students who graduate from here," reported one undergrad, "those who love the block plan and those who are neutral about it. Those who hate it, leave." Students report that the block plan is excellent for liberal arts and social science studies. Said one, "This is the place to study history or political science. The block plan allows you to immerse yourself and thoroughly understand an issue or time period." Performing arts and independently designed majors are also popular. Hard science courses, however, "tend to be too rapid and challenging on the block plan." Said one student of the block plan: "Not having to sit and listen to boring lectures for an hour is a godsend! Instead, you are given the opportunity to participate actively in discussion for two to four hours a day. It's hard to adjust to the intense academics here at first, but after a while it's easy." Students agree that, overall, classes and professors are excellent, and report that they enjoy "both a relaxed atmosphere and stimulating academics."

■ **Life** Nestled among the Rocky Mountains, CC has a beautiful setting that promotes serenity. "Colorado is the greatest place to attend school," wrote one student. "Even when I am stressed about a test, I just look at the mountains and feel 100 percent better." Explained another, "This area of the country is alive and beautiful. Between field courses and heavy duty backpacking, there's a lot to learn here if you care to." During block breaks, students get to take advantage of the natural surroundings, which they prefer to their host town of Colorado Springs (also home to the Air Force Academy). Explained one student, "Living in the middle of a military town, there are occasional conflicts outside of campus. We're pretty removed from the town." Students are active in intramural sports and extracurricular organizations, which are reportedly numerous. Despite the intensity of their studies, they also find time to unwind and party. Beer and pot are both very popular with most students. The Greeks play an active, but not oppressive, role in CC's social universe.

■ **Students** CC attracts a large share of liberal students. One wrote that "there's a very conscientious, environmentally active group here. Most recently students raised over $1000 for the legal defense of CC students arrested in a logging protest." Only one third of the students are natives of Colorado; the rest come from all over the country ("there's a strong New England boarding school element," reported one student). Several students feel that the lack of ethnic diversity here is an issue the administration should address.

COLORADO COLLEGE

Admissions

The admissions office reports that CC "seeks students who demonstrate academic excellence, uncommon talents and interests, and a commitment to the idea of a liberal arts education. Economic and geographic diversity and the potential for making significant contributions to the college community are also factors considered for admission." High school record is considered the most important component of your application here, followed, in decreasing order of importance, by essays, standardized test scores, extracurricular activities, and letters of recommendation. Applicants are required to have completed 16 units of academic course work in high school; most successful applicants "have earned 17 or 18." Either the SAT or the ACT is required. Applicants to Colorado College most often also apply to Middlebury, Lewis and Clark, University of Puget Sound, Stanford, Brown, Pomona, Carleton, and University of Colorado–Boulder.

Financial Aid

Colorado College requires either the FAF or the FFS for freshmen applying for aid (the former is preferred). Returning students must also fill out a form generated by the financial aid office. The school gives out merit grants; last year, grants were awarded for chemistry (at an average value of $13,665, to 1% of the student body), national merit ($750, 1%), and athletics ($13,705, 2%). In 1991, 47% of all freshmen received some type of financial aid; the average award value was $12,058. Colorado College recommended Perkins loans to 22% of its undergrads, at an average value of $1,566, and Stafford loans to 39%, at an average value of $2,721.

A note from the Colorado College Admissions Office:

"The academic Block Plan and an unusually dedicated teaching faculty create a distinctive liberal arts college. Under the Block Plan, students have numerous opportunities for independent projects and classes may take nearly unlimited time for field work. Intensive study on one subject and a friendly, engaging atmosphere produce a unique learning environment. Professors spend more time with students than under a traditional semester, and the small classes (14 average) allow for supportive relationships to develop between faculty and students."

ADMISSIONS FACTS

Competitiveness Rating:	**85**
% of applicants accepted:	50
% acceptees attending:	36

FRESHMAN PROFILE

Average verbal SAT:	553*
Average math SAT:	607*
Average ACT:	27*
Graduated top 10% of class:	45
Graduated top 25% of class:	84
Graduated top 50% of class:	98

DEADLINES

Early decision/action:	12/1
Early dec./act. notif.:	12/31
Regular admission:	2/1
Regular adm. notif.:	4/1

APPLICANTS ALSO LOOK AT

and often prefer:
Stanford U.
Carleton College

and sometimes prefer:
Reed College
Occidental College
Macalester College

and rarely prefer:
U. Vermont
Kenyon College
Lewis and Clark College

ADDRESS

Undergraduate Admissions
14 E. Cache La Poudre
Colo. Springs, CO 80903-9972
719-389-6344

FINANCIAL FACTS

In-state tuition ($):	13,655
Out-of-state tuition ($):	13,655
Room & board ($):	3,530
FA application deadline:	2/1
% frosh receiving FA:	56
PT earnings per yr. ($):	1,200

TYPE OF AID: % of students ($):

FA of some kind:	53 (12,000)
Need-based grants:	NA
Merit-based grants:	4 (NA)
Loans:	NA
Work study:	22 (1,000)
Student rating of FA:	87

COLORADO SCHOOL OF MINES

Golden, CO

CAMPUS LIFE

Quality of Life Rating: **73**

Type of school:	public
Affiliation:	none
Environment:	city

STUDENT BODY

FT undergrad enrollment:	1,575
% male/% female:	80/20
% out-of-state:	28
% live on campus:	35
% African-American:	1
% Asian:	2
% Caucasian:	92
% Hispanic:	4
% foreign:	9
% transfers:	1

WHAT'S HOT

town-gown relations
attending all classes
studying hard

WHAT'S NOT

college radio station
good-looking students
marijuana
working a job
requirements easy
Grateful Dead
gay community accepted
rap/hip-hop
in-class discussion
overall happiness
dating

ACADEMICS

Academic Rating: **81**

Calendar:	semester
Student/teacher ratio:	13/1
% doctorates:	90
Profs interesting:	73
Profs accessible:	75
Hours of study per day:	3.7

MOST POPULAR MAJORS BY %

Engineering	85
Physical Sciences:	10
Mathematics:	5

% GRADS WHO PURSUE

Law:	2
MBA:	3
Medicine:	1
M.A., etc.:	10

What do students think about Colorado School of Mines?

■ **Academics** For Coloradans seeking a career in engineering, math, or science, Colorado School of Mines is a natural first choice. A state school, CSM provides state residents (who make up two thirds of the student body) with a first-rate education at public school prices. CSM offers so much in the way of quality programs and career placement services, however, that even a Tennessee native wrote that CSM "is really one of the last great deals in America." According to CSM, 86 percent of its 1991 graduates were placed in jobs or graduate programs by graduation day, and the school projected 95 percent placement within six months. Students concur: reported one, "CSM is *a lot* of work, but the job placement rate makes it worth it." Another student elaborated, "The best thing about the school is the cooperation with industry. The career placement center has a very high placement rate for both summer and permanent jobs relating to one's own field. With their help, I was able to get a summer job at a precious metals refinery in South Africa. This opportunity will help my future in metallurgical engineering immensely." As you might expect, course work at CSM is both intellectually demanding and time-consuming. Student stress is common, and most students agree that "the work is extremely tough to keep up with. Once you fall behind it is all over with for the semester." Particularly demanding is the Engineering Practices Introductory Course Sequence (EPICS), an engineering core curriculum that it drives away a good number of freshmen every year ("Most professors want at least one fourth of their students to fail or drop," wrote one student). Those who endure enjoy a "high level of student/ faculty interaction. The profs are great and most have a sense of humor, especially in the chemistry department." Stellar departments include geological, petroleum, and mining engineering, chemistry, and mining. Summed up one student: "if you want to be an engineer and a good one, come here. If you're looking for a fun time and easy classes—don't."

■ **Life** Most of students' time at CSM is spent in classrooms, libraries, and labs. After classes are over, students here study, on average, almost four hours a day. Wrote one student, "the social life isn't here at this school, but that's not what most people attend this school for. Most are here for a useful education." When the pressure gets to be too much, students can travel to Denver (15 miles away) or head for the Rockies. Boulder is also close by. Said one student, "If you are looking for a party, CU in Boulder is only 20 minutes away; but one cannot party too much or he'll wind up at CU permanently." A four-to-one male-female ratio further hampers efforts at a "normal" social life.

■ **Students** CSM students "come for a secure future" and are "very academically inclined." Some would even say that "people here are generally geeky." Minority representation is minimal. CSM's state sponsorship guarantees a large home state population, but the school's excellent reputation also draws students from all over the world.

COLORADO SCHOOL OF MINES

Admissions

The admissions office reports that "we look at each applicant using a balance of courses, GPA, SAT/ACT scores, and other factors." High school curriculum and GPA and standardized test scores are reportedly the most important components of your application here, but the admissions office also considers extracurricular activities, letters of recommendation, and essays. An interview is not part of the application process. Applicants are required to have completed four years of English, two years of algebra, one year of geometry, one year of advanced math (including trig), and two years each of history/social studies and lab science. Colorado School of Mines requires either the SAT or the ACT. Applicants to Mines most often also apply to University of Colorado–Boulder, Colorado State, Stanford, University of Texas–Austin, and MIT.

Financial Aid

Colorado School of Mines requires either the FAF or the FFS for freshmen applying for aid along with a form generated by the financial aid office. The school gives out merit grants for academic and athletic excellence. Last year, 20% of all undergrads received academic grants, at an average value of $3,000; 20% received athletic grants as well, at an average value of $2,500. Seventy-two percent of the class of '95 received some type of financial aid, with the average award being $6,000. CSM recommended Perkins loans to 20% of all undergrads (average value: $1,200), Stafford loans to 55% of all undergrads (average: $3,200) and its own institutional loan to 15% of undergrads (average: $1,200). The April 19 deadline is a priority date, not a hard deadline; CMU guarantees it will meet 100% of need for all on-time applicants.

A note from the Colorado School of Mines Admissions Office:

"CSM has an international reputation for education in materials, minerals, and resource science and engineering. In addition, we have growing programs in environmental sciences and the interdisciplinary study of engineering."

ADMISSIONS FACTS

Competitiveness Rating:	**83**
% of applicants accepted:	86
% acceptees attending:	40

FRESHMAN PROFILE

Average verbal SAT:	540
Average math SAT:	640
Average ACT:	27
Graduated top 10% of class:	55
Graduated top 25% of class:	85
Graduated top 50% of class:	100

DEADLINES

Early decision/action:	NA
Early dec./act. notif.:	NA
Regular admission:	8/1
Regular adm. notif.:	rolling

APPLICANTS ALSO LOOK AT

and often prefer:
Stanford U.
MIT

and sometimes prefer:
Colorado State U.
U. Texas–Austin

and rarely prefer:
U. Colorado–Boulder
U. Denver

ADDRESS

Undergraduate Admissions
1500 Illinois St.
Golden, CO 80401
303-273-3220

FINANCIAL FACTS

In-state tuition ($):	3,718
Out-of-state tuition ($):	10,304
Room & board ($):	3,770
FA application deadline:	4/19
% frosh receiving FA:	85
PT earnings per yr. ($):	1,100

TYPE OF AID: % of students ($):

FA of some kind:	72 (6,000)
Need-based grants:	48 (4,000)
Merit-based grants:	45 (2,500)
Loans:	60 (3,700)
Work study:	50 (750)
Student rating of FA:	81

COLUMBIA UNIVERSITY

New York, NY

CAMPUS LIFE

Quality of Life Rating:	**86**
Type of school:	private
Affiliation:	none
Environment:	city

STUDENT BODY

FT undergrad enrollment:	4,789
% male/% female:	55/45
% out-of-state:	69
% live on campus:	96
% African-American:	8
% Asian:	11
% Caucasian:	74
% Hispanic:	7
% foreign:	4
% transfers:	<1

WHAT'S HOT

location
gay community visible
gay community accepted
diversity
leftist politics
campus is easy to get
  around
classical music
caring about politics

WHAT'S NOT

administration (overall)
intramural sports
registration
top 40
intercollegiate sports

ACADEMICS

Academic Rating:	**90**
Calendar:	semester
Student/teacher ratio:	7/1
% doctorates:	91
Profs interesting:	79
Profs accessible:	73
Hours of study per day:	3.15

MOST POPULAR MAJORS

English
History
Political Science

% GRADS WHO PURSUE

Law:	26
MBA:	14
Medicine:	8
M.A., etc.:	27

What do students think about Columbia University?

■ **Academics** Coursework at Columbia is challenging, most notably for a number of required courses. These courses, known as the core curriculum, demand that students spend a good deal of time mastering Western classics. The core is difficult, as one student noted: "Columbia promised the core would change my life. It did; now I have no life." High-quality instruction in just about any field is available to students, and world-renowned scholars can be found in nearly every department. However, don't expect the individual attention that you might receive at a small college. "You can enrich your mind here, but good luck finding an advisor who knows your name," complained one student. Several students complained about professors who are more interested in their graduate students and their own research than in their undergrad courses. Overall, however, students reported their professors were good teachers; class size also got high marks. The administration received poor grades. "Aside from the core curriculum, Columbia has one more requirement: Bureaucracy I, a four-year course in surviving the trials of mountains of red tape," said one student. "Be prepared for many frustrating episodes with the registrar, bursar, and library if you go here." Almost half of Columbia's graduates move on to professional schools within a year; one in four undergrads is a future lawyer! The engineering school is also world-class.

■ **Life** Ask Columbia students what they love most about their school and almost all will say New York City. A whopping 84 percent rated New York a great place to go to school—that from a notoriously iconoclastic student body. "No other city gives students the street-smarts, awareness, and overall life experience," gushed one student. As another pointed out, "Where else can you eat Ethiopian food one night, see *The Will Rogers Follies* the next, catch a Lizzie Borden film the next…" Because the city offers many opportunities for extracurricular activity and entertainment, school organizations and frats play a relatively small role at Columbia. One student complained that there is "very little campus life and school spirit," and several athletes bemoaned the fact that student support of teams is poor. "If you're looking for the typical all-American college scene," said one, "this is not the place for you."

■ **Students** The Columbia student body is still among the more left-leaning in the nation, although many students told us that this isn't as true as it once was. Students gave themselves high marks in ethnic diversity/interaction, and openness/acceptance of alternative lifestyles, all hallmarks of a liberal student body. A growing conservative population finds its liberal classmates self-righteous. "Too many 'I'm gonna change the world' people," said one such student. Minorities make up about one fourth of Columbia's student body.

COLUMBIA UNIVERSITY

New York, NY

Admissions

The admissions office reports that "no cut-offs" are used to eliminate applicants from the applicant pool. High school curriculum and grades are the most important component of your application here; essays and letters of recommendation are considered next most important, and extracurricular activities, an interview, and standardized test scores are also considered, but are less important. Applicants are required to have completed a minimum of three years of English, two years each of science and social studies, and three years of math. Two years of foreign language is "preferred." Columbia requires either the SAT or the ACT, as well as three achievement tests. Students applying to Columbia most often also apply to Harvard, Yale, Princeton, Stanford, Brown, and University of Pennsylvania.

Financial Aid

The financial aid office at Columbia University requires applicants to submit the FAF and a form generated by the school. All financial aid is awarded on the basis of need. Loan options listed in the Columbia Bulletin include: Stafford, Perkins, university-sponsored, PLUS/SLS, and Share. Last year the *New York Times* reported that, because of a large budget deficit, in 1992-93 Columbia would no longer guarantee meeting 100 percent of incoming freshmen's demonstrated need.

A note from the Columbia College Admissions Office:

"Located in the world's most international city, Columbia College offers a diverse student body a solid and broad liberal arts curriculum foundation coupled with more advance study in specific departments."

ADMISSIONS FACTS

Competitiveness Rating:	**96**
% of applicants accepted:	28
% acceptees attending:	43

FRESHMAN PROFILE

Average verbal SAT:	610*
Average math SAT:	667*
Average ACT:	NA
Graduated top 10% of class:	79
Graduated top 25% of class:	93
Graduated top 50% of class:	100

DEADLINES

Early decision/action:	11/1
Early dec./act. notif.:	12/15
Regular admission:	1/1
Regular adm. notif.:	4/15

APPLICANTS ALSO LOOK AT

and often prefer:
Duke U.
Stanford U.

and sometimes prefer:
Dartmouth College
Tufts U.

and rarely prefer:
Wesleyan U.
SUNY Binghamton
Vassar College
Barnard College

ADDRESS

Undergraduate Admissions
212 Hamilton Hall
New York, NY 10027
212-854-2521

FINANCIAL FACTS

In-state tuition ($):	15,500
Out-of-state tuition ($):	15,500
Room & board ($):	8,500
FA application deadline:	2/1
% frosh receiving FA:	48
PT earnings per yr. ($):	1,700

TYPE OF AID: % of students ($):

FA of some kind:	50 (NA)
Need-based grants:	NA
Merit-based grants:	NA
Loans:	NA
Work study:	NA
Student rating of FA:	73

UNIVERSITY OF CONNECTICUT

CAMPUS LIFE

Quality of Life Rating:	**72**
Type of school:	public
Affiliation:	none
Environment:	rural

STUDENT BODY

FT undergrad enrollment:	12,307
% male/% female:	48/52
% out-of-state:	14
% live on campus:	75
% African-American:	4
% Asian:	4
% Caucasian:	89
% Hispanic:	3
% foreign:	<1
% transfers:	5

WHAT'S HOT

rap/hip-hop
intercollegiate sports
Top 40
college newspaper
interaction among students
cost of living
diversity

WHAT'S NOT

TAs teach intros
location
administration (overall)
registration
TAs teach upper levels
campus easy to get around
financial aid

ACADEMICS

Academic Rating:	**74**
Calendar:	semester
Student/teacher ratio:	15/1
% doctorates:	87
Profs interesting:	72
Profs accessible:	72
Hours of study per day:	2.87

MOST POPULAR MAJORS BY %

Economics:	8
English:	8
Psychology:	6

% GRADS WHO PURSUE

Law:	NA
MBA:	NA
Medicine:	NA
M.A., etc.:	15

What do students think about UConn?

■ **Academics** Once known as an agricultural school, University of Connecticut is, in the words of one student, "More than the cow/agriculture school down the road; it is now an admired institute of learning in the arts and sciences." The school has enhanced its reputation by developing a strong engineering program (which attracts 10 percent of the student body) and solid undergraduate business departments (16 percent of the students pursue business majors). In fact, the other popular majors, English and psychology, are about as far from agricultural studies as one can get. As at most large universities, "The choices are unlimited and if you utilize your resources, you really can get the best of all worlds." Or, as another student put it, "There is a lot here but nobody will hold your hand and show it to you." Student complaints centered almost entirely on the effects of recent state education budget cuts, which "have been creating a lot of bureaucratic difficulties." Explained one student, "Larger classes, fewer professors, and loss of accreditation in some areas, uncleanliness of the campus and frustration of students are all visible at UConn."

■ **Life** Storrs, Connecticut is hardly cosmopolitan. Wrote one student, "I'd really love Storrs if I were able to eat hay and lay eggs. As it is, the ducks seem to have the most fun here. You can tell by all the quacking every morning." Another called the town "a very poor location that does not offer *any* off-campus entertainment." While most students would agree (they gave the town a grade of D+), many would counter that the university itself offers "a diverse range of extracurricular activities and opportunities to enhance the students' college career." Wrote another, "You have to get involved! Join cheerleading, take advantage of the extensive study-abroad program, go scuba diving, or become an athlete. Do anything but sit on your butt and complain. And then you'll enjoy UConn." Students are ardent sports fans, and although "basketball is clearly the most important sport," many will tell you that "UConn sports is more than just men's basketball: our soccer, hockey, and women's basketball teams are all well followed." Drinking is a very popular way to pass the time, but one student warns that "there are only three bars anywhere near campus: I call it the 'three-bar rotation.'" When students get tired of hanging around Storrs, "Hartford is only 45 minutes away, and we are a short train ride from Boston or New York City."

■ **Students** Most UConn students are in-state students, and nearly nine-tenths are white. But there are approximately 500 blacks, 500 Asian, and 375 Latinos, so minority students will find decent-sized minority communities, especially important given that the school is out in the boondocks. Discussing student body demographics, a student who had transferred from an expensive private college wrote, "My previous school had nothing but a bunch of rich yuppies who liked the Dead. I love UConn; it's much more like the real world."

UNIVERSITY OF CONNECTICUT

Storrs, CT

Admissions

The admissions office reports that "no formulas or cut-offs are used. Every application is read by *at least* one person." High school curriculum and GPA are considered most important, followed, in order of importance, by standardized test scores, essays, letters of recommendation, extracurricular activities, and an interview (optional). Applicants must have completed four years of English, Algebra I and II, geometry, and two years each of lab science, social studies, and foreign language (a third year of language is recommended). Music and theater majors, furthermore, must audition. UConn requires the SAT. Admissions are decided on a rolling basis. Applicants to UConn often also apply to URhode Island, UMass, UNew Hampshire, Boston U, Syracuse, Fairfield, and Boston College.

Financial Aid

The financial aid office at University of Connecticut requires applicants to submit the FAF and a form generated by the school. Merit-based scholarships are available to National Merit Scholars and athletes; many other specialized scholarships are awarded by departments and alumni associations (for a complete listing, get the school catalog). UConn lists the Stafford and Perkins loan options in its catalog.

A note from the University of Connecticut Admissions Office:

"Located in the wooded hills of Northeastern Connecticut, the University of Connecticut offers tremendous educational opportunities to talented students. An education at the university is a study in contrasts: small school opportunities at a major university, excellent liberal arts foundation with the opportunity to continue in professional, specialized fields and the advantage of a major university in a rural setting.

"The university's location lends itself to many things—a collegiate setting, a comfortable existence, academics, athletics and rural opportunities. Yet at the same time the UConn is accessible to Hartford (1/2 hour), Boston (1 1/2 hours), or New York (2 1/2 hours).

"The University of Connecticut is a blend of people, ideas and opportunities."

ADMISSIONS FACTS

Competitiveness Rating:	**74**
% of applicants accepted:	62
% acceptees attending:	33

FRESHMAN PROFILE

Average verbal SAT:	485
Average math SAT:	551
Average ACT:	NA
Graduated top 10% of class:	24
Graduated top 25% of class:	64
Graduated top 50% of class:	91

DEADLINES

Early decision/action:	NA
Early dec./act. notif.:	NA
Regular admission:	4/1
Regular adm. notif.:	rolling

APPLICANTS ALSO LOOK AT

and often prefer:
Tufts U.

and sometimes prefer:
Boston College
Villanova U.
Providence College
Fairfield U.

and rarely prefer:
Bentley College
Clarkson U.

ADDRESS

Undergraduate Admissions
Storrs, CT 06269
203-486-3137

FINANCIAL FACTS

In-state tuition ($):	3,191
Out-of-state tuition ($):	7,991
Room & board ($):	4,522
FA application deadline:	2/15
% frosh receiving FA:	30
PT earnings per yr. ($):	NA

TYPE OF AID: % of students ($):

FA of some kind:	50 (NA)
Need-based grants:	NA
Merit-based grants:	NA
Loans:	NA
Work study:	NA
Student rating of FA:	69

CONNECTICUT COLLEGE

New London, CT

CAMPUS LIFE

Quality of Life Rating:	**82**

Type of school:	private
Affiliation:	none
Environment:	suburban

STUDENT BODY

FT undergrad enrollment:	1,660
% male/% female:	45/55
% out-of-state:	82
% live on campus:	98
% African-American:	4
% Asian:	5
% Caucasian:	87
% Hispanic:	3
% foreign:	6
% transfers:	2

WHAT'S HOT

cost of living
living on campus
dorm safety
requirements easy
good-looking students
small labs and seminars
leftist politics
college theater groups
overall happiness
beer

WHAT'S NOT

fraternities/sororities
location
religion

ACADEMICS

Academic Rating:	**84**

Calendar:	semester
Student/teacher ratio:	12/1
% doctorates:	90
Profs interesting:	82
Profs accessible:	85
Hours of study per day:	3.2

MOST POPULAR MAJORS BY %

History:	12
Government:	11
English:	10

% GRADS WHO PURSUE

Law:	3
MBA:	6
Medicine:	3
M.A., etc.:	11

What do students think about Connecticut College?

■ **Academics** Connecticut College's greatest asset, according to one student, is "the fact that such diverse departments are strong. Arts, drama, and dance attract a certain type of student, philosophy and psychology another, and a strong athletics department attracts yet another type." It is in fact surprising that such a small school could provide quality education in so many areas: although the arts department is its best-known and best (its lack of film courses not withstanding), the school also features an excellent center for international studies as well as uniformly solid liberal arts and social sciences departments. A broad-based set of core requirements prevents students from escaping UConn without some understanding of literature, history, and hard sciences. What students seem to appreciate most, however, is the small, homey atmosphere of the school. Wrote one: "On the plus side, members of the faculty are readily accessible and one does not get lost in the crowd. Also, our campus has several small dining halls, providing a better environment for getting together with friends or profs. This does, of course, have its down side: there are few secrets on a campus of 1600 people."

■ **Life** One student summed up Connecticut College social life this way: "There's a big emphasis on drinking, which I don't like. Every Thursday (when the weekend starts) there's a dance party and the drinking starts. It continues through Saturday night. Sometimes there's even a keg for Monday night football." Agreed another, "Academically, UConn is close to perfect. But social life (basically drinking and/or dancing) gets a little monotonous." The sameness of social life isn't helped by the town of New London ("it's *dull*!") or by the lack of fraternities. New York and Boston are each about two hours away by car, a little too far for regular visits but close enough for the occasional road trip. Students are active in intramural sports and provide a strong support base for their Division III teams. For the community minded, "the school has some great volunteer programs."

■ **Students** Although Connecticut College has a 13 percent minority population, the small student body (fewer than 1,700) translates into a total minority population of about 200. Fewer than 100 Asian students make up the largest minority group. Many of the white students seem to be cut from the same mold; wrote one, "The student body at first seems very homogeneous—middle-class, white, WASPy. It takes a lot of time to locate all the interesting and unusual people—they tend to be hidden in the woodwork." Several students ragged on their classmates for their complacency: wrote one, "Most of the people here are prep school kids who are smart but lazy or unmotivated. As a public school student I feel a bit out of place. If you plan to bring a car, it better be a Saab—the unofficial car of Connecticut College." Students are politically farther to the left than most.

CONNECTICUT COLLEGE

Admissions

High school curriculum is the most important component of your application here. Essays are next-most important (the admissions office reports that "because the Honor Code is such an important part of campus life, we have a question about living with an honor code on our application for admissions"). Letters of recommendation, standardized test scores, extracurricular activities, and an interview are all considered as part of the application. Applicants are required to have completed a "standard college prep" curriculum; the admissions office adds that "most have done honors or Advanced Placement." The SAT is required, as are three achievement tests. Students who apply to Connecticut College most often also apply to Trinity, Colby, Bates, Vassar, and Colgate.

Financial Aid

Connecticut College requires freshmen applying for aid to submit a FAF, a copy of their parents' most recent tax return, a form generated by Connecticut's financial aid office, and, if applicable, divorced/separated statements, a business/farm supplement, and most recent W-2 statements. No merit-based grants are given. Last year, 42% of freshmen received some form of financial aid; the average award value was $14,858. Connecticut recommended Perkins loans to 8% of all undergrads in '91–'92 (average value: $1,750), Stafford loans to 34% ($2,697) and its own institutional loans to 2% ($2,479).

A note from the Connecticut College Admissions Office:

"Distinguishing characteristics of the diverse student body at this small, highly selective college are honor and tolerance. Student leadership is pronounced in all aspects of the college's administration from exclusive jurisdiction of the Honor Code and dorm life through active representation on the President's academic and administrative cabinets. Differences of opinion are respected and celebrated as legitimate avenues to new understanding. Students come to Connecticut College seeking opportunities for independence and initiative and find them in abundance."

ADMISSIONS FACTS

Competitiveness Rating:	**89**
% of applicants accepted:	45
% acceptees attending:	30

FRESHMAN PROFILE

Average verbal SAT:	590*
Average math SAT:	630*
Average ACT:	NA
Graduated top 10% of class:	53
Graduated top 25% of class:	NA
Graduated top 50% of class:	NA

DEADLINES

Early decision/action:	11/15
Early dec./act. notif.:	12/10
Regular admission:	1/15
Regular adm. notif.:	4/1

APPLICANTS ALSO LOOK AT

and often prefer:
Vassar College
Bowdoin College
Tufts U.

and sometimes prefer:
Colgate U.
Trinity College
U. Vermont
Bates College

and rarely prefer:
Colby College
U. Connecticut

ADDRESS

Undergraduate Admissions
Route 32 North
New London, CT 06320
203-439-2200

FINANCIAL FACTS

In-state tuition ($):	16,080
Out-of-state tuition ($):	16,080
Room & board ($):	5,370
FA application deadline:	2/15
% frosh receiving FA:	44
PT earnings per yr. ($):	1,000

TYPE OF AID: % of students ($):

FA of some kind:	43 (12,479)
Need-based grants:	41 (10,354)
Merit-based grants:	NA
Loans:	44 (2,479)
Work study:	39 (945)
Student rating of FA:	81

COOPER UNION

CAMPUS LIFE

Quality of Life Rating:	**75**
Type of school:	private
Affiliation:	none
Environment:	city

STUDENT BODY

FT undergrad enrollment:	916
% male/% female:	70/30
% out-of-state:	30
% live on campus:	0
% African-American:	5
% Asian:	23
% Caucasian:	63
% Hispanic:	5
% foreign:	4
% transfers:	4

WHAT'S HOT

location
gay community accepted
interaction among students
financial aid

WHAT'S NOT

cost of living
campus appearance
intercollegiate sports
Grateful Dead
hard liquor
marijuana
dating
working a job
profs outside class
overall happiness

ACADEMICS

Academic Rating:	**85**
Calendar:	semester
Student/teacher ratio:	7/1
% doctorates:	NA
Profs interesting:	74
Profs accessible:	70
Hours of study per day:	3.65

MOST POPULAR MAJORS

Chemical Engineering
Electrical Engineering
Fine Arts

% GRADS WHO PURSUE

Law:	1
MBA:	2
Medicine:	3
M.A., etc.:	47

What do students think about Cooper Union?

■ **Academics** In 1991, Cooper Union for the Advancement of Science and Art was again named *Money* magazine's best buy in college education. Chances are it will continue to win that distinction *ad terminum*, because Cooper students pay only $300 in annual fees. Explained one student, "Cooper Union was founded on the principle that all persons should receive an education regardless of financial situation, race, religion, or sex. Thus, anyone accepted to the Union receives a full scholarship." There is a catch: Cooper offers studies only in art, architecture, and engineering. Each discipline has its own school, and, according to one student, "the three schools are in disunion. Each is its own empire, unfortunately discouraging inter-school activity." Engineering students gave their school glowing recommendations. One commented that "engineering profs take real good care of you;" another noted that cutthroat competitiveness was notably absent from his classmates. Concluded a third, "if you can survive on three hours of sleep a night and enjoy challenging work that prepares you for an engineering career better than any other school in the US, then Cooper is for you." Art students enjoy the intellectually challenging approach their instruction takes. Reported one, "you will get sick of post-structuralism, you will criticize post-modernists, and you will talk about art more in a week than the average person does in 10 years." Still, students had their complaints. Academic gripes centered on the inaccessibility of professors and the sometimes oppressive intensity of fellow students. But, as one student summed up, "You can't beat a free ride on a fancy train!"

■ **Life** Cooper is in the heart of Greenwich Village—"it's the little school next to NYU"—the center of night life for New York's counterculture. Wrote one student, "You'll never get bored in New York, if you have any free time to enjoy it." Cooper lacks a traditional college community, in part because its facilities are so small (there is *no* campus) and in part because relations between the three schools are so fractured. An extremely unfavorable male-female ratio further detracts from the social scene here. Students joke about their unconventional college experience. "If you enjoy intercollegiate sports, you can choose from billiards, bowling, ping-pong, or, if you're athletic, fencing," wrote one student. But their answer to the question "how happy are you here?" reveals that Cooper Union students wish their college experience were a little more normal. Their answer was well below the national average—not what you'd expect from students at one of the nation's most elite institutions.

■ **Students** Over one third of Cooper's students are minority students; of them, well over half are Asian. Black and Hispanic populations are small. The students are admittedly eccentric—"this place would be horrid for a "normal" person," wrote one art student—although the engineers who make up the majority here are more conventional and goal-oriented than the artists and architects.

COOPER UNION

Admissions

The admissions office reports that it uses no cutoffs, "but all numbers (GPA, SATs, math achievement, physics, or chemistry achievement) are included in the admissions formula for engineers." Requirements vary according to the school: all applicants must have completed four years of English, two years of history, one year of math and one year of science. Architects need three years of mathematics (trigonometry is required); engineers need three and a half years of math (trig required), a year of physics and a year of chemistry. Cooper considers all applicants on the basis of high school curriculum and grades, letters of recommendation, and essays. SAT scores are important for engineers; a home test and portfolio are important for artists and architects. Applicants to Cooper most often also apply to MIT, Columbia, Cornell University, NYU, and UC Berkeley.

Financial Aid

Cooper Union's financial aid numbers differ from those of most other schools in one drastic respect: full tuition is paid for by scholarship. Room and board costs for New York City tend to make up some of the difference, however. Cooper requires submission of a FAF, most recent tax return, and a form generated by the Cooper financial aid office. No merit-based grants are given. Forty-one percent of the class of '95 received some form of financial aid, with an average award value of $3,000. In the '91–'92 academic year, Cooper recommended Stafford loans to 19% of all undergrads (average loan value: $3,700), SLS/PLUS loans to 3% ($3,500), and Perkins loans to 1% ($1,000). The 4/15/93 deadline date is an *in office* date, not a postmarked date.

A note from the Cooper Union Admissions Office:

"Each of the three schools, Architecture, Art and Engineering, adheres strongly to preparation for its profession and is committed to a problem-solving philosophy of education in a unique, tuition-free environment. A rigorous curriculum and group projects reinforce this unique atmosphere in higher education and contribute to a strong sense of community and identity in each school.

"With McSorley's Ale House and Joseph Papp's Public Theater nearby, The Cooper Union remains at the heart of the city's tradition of free speech, enlightenment, and entertainment. Cooper's Great Hall has hosted national leaders, from Abraham Lincoln to Booker T. Washington, from Mark Twain to Samuel Gompers, from Susan B. Anthony to Betty Friedan."

ADMISSIONS FACTS

Competitiveness Rating:	**95**
% of applicants accepted:	20
% acceptees attending:	63

FRESHMAN PROFILE

Average verbal SAT:	570
Average math SAT:	720
Average ACT:	NA
Graduated top 10% of class:	NA
Graduated top 25% of class:	NA
Graduated top 50% of class:	NA

DEADLINES

Early decision/action:	12/1
Early dec./act. notif.:	12/23
Regular admission:	1/1
Regular adm. notif.:	4/1

APPLICANTS ALSO LOOK AT

and often prefer:
Cornell U.
UC Berkeley

and sometimes prefer:
Columbia U.
Harvey Mudd College
MIT
Georgia Tech

and rarely prefer:
RIT

ADDRESS

Undergraduate Admissions
Cooper Square
New York, NY 10003-7183
212-353-4120

FINANCIAL FACTS

In-state tuition ($):	0
Out-of-state tuition ($):	0
Room & board ($):	10,820
FA application deadline:	4/15
% frosh receiving FA:	40
PT earnings per yr. ($):	1,500

TYPE OF AID: % of students ($):	
FA of some kind:	NA
Need-based grants:	41 (2,800)
Merit-based grants:	NA
Loans:	23 (2,733)
Work study:	6 (1,200)
Student rating of FA:	100

CORNELL UNIVERSITY

CAMPUS LIFE

Quality of Life Rating: **84**

Type of school:	private
Affiliation:	none
Environment:	suburban

STUDENT BODY

FT undergrad enrollment:	12,420
% male/% female:	56/44
% out-of-state:	48
% live on campus:	49
% African-American:	5
% Asian:	12
% Caucasian:	75
% Hispanic:	5
% foreign:	5
% transfers:	1

WHAT'S HOT

food
dorm comfort
studying hard
college newspaper
library
dorm safety
campus appearance
leftist politics

WHAT'S NOT

bursar
living on campus
religion
interaction among students
town-gown relations

ACADEMICS

Academic Rating: **86**

Calendar:	semester
Student/teacher ratio:	11/1
% doctorates:	90
Profs interesting:	76
Profs accessible:	72
Hours of study per day:	3.79

MOST POPULAR MAJORS BY %

Engineering	18
Agribusiness & Agri. Production	16
Social Sciences	13

% GRADS WHO PURSUE

Law:	9
MBA:	1
Medicine:	4
M.A., etc.:	13

What do students think about Cornell University?

■ **Academics** As one student aptly put it, "Cornell University is known as the easiest Ivy to get into and the most difficult to stay in." Our survey showed that no other Ivy League student body works harder, bearing out claims that "the profs expect blood from you, and mostly they get it." Cornell is also unique among the Ivies in that it is not an entirely private university. Three schools, agriculture and life sciences, human ecology, and industrial and labor relations, are publicly funded, and at these schools in-state tuition is about one third that charged students in the Ivy schools. Industrial and labor relations and veterinary sciences are tops among the public divisions; among the private ones, engineering, hotel management, and the liberal arts departments are all first-rate. The pre-medical program is also highly regarded, but one student warned that, even by Cornell standards, "competition among pre-meds is cutthroat." Students must apply to one of the seven divisions of the school, but transferring among them is commonplace.

■ **Life** Social life at Cornell is stifled somewhat by the abundant workload. Explained one student, "there is very little time to do anything except study. When there are a few free moments, most student pack in as much fun or sleep as they can stand because they don't know when they'll get the opportunity again!" Said another student, the "isolated setting makes it the most charming Ivy League school, but it also makes it more intense, since there's only the school here." The setting is beautiful, sort of like a state park with academic buildings. The most striking features are the gorges, legendary as the sites of stressed-out suicides. Students wrote that rumors of Cornell being the suicide capital of academia "are highly embellished." The weather is dreary, "overcast, raining, sleeting, and generally ugly—we say 'it's Ithacating,'" wrote one student. Because of its remote location and because students have "little interaction with the town 'down the hill,'" frats play an important role on the social scene. Drinking is popular but difficult: "the administration is *really* strict on underage drinking," explained one student. Among intercollegiate sports, "hockey, lacrosse, and wrestling are big time"; participation in intramural sports is above average, and the area offers plenty of opportunities for lovers of the outdoors and winter sports.

■ **Students** Almost one quarter of the Cornell student body is made up of minority students. About half of those are Asians, and the rest are evenly split between blacks and Latinos. Cornell's blend of Ivy League private divisions and state-funded public divisions creates a uniquely diverse student body. Wrote one undergrad, "Cornell is the definition of diversity in its student body, faculty, and opportunities."

CORNELL UNIVERSITY

Admissions

Cornell University maintains seven distinct undergraduate divisions, each of which has its own admissions requirements: all divisions are extremely competitive. All applicants are required to submit their high school transcript, a personal statement, letters of recommendations, and scores for either the SAT or the ACT (applicants to most divisions must also take three achievements, including English Composition). All divisions strongly suggest that an applicant's high school transcript reflect the pursuit of a rigorous college prep curriculum; such a curriculum should include the maximum number of courses possible in English, social studies, and foreign language. Math, science, and pre-med applicants should also have completed the maximum number possible of science and math courses. New York State residents receive preferential treatment from the admissions offices of Cornell's public divisions.

Financial Aid

Those seeking financial assistance from Cornell University are required to submit the FAF, a form generated by the school, and a copy of their parents' most recent tax return. Cornell offers no merit-based grants; all aid is awarded on the basis of need only. One of the unique features of financial aid here is "the Cornell Tradition," an alumni-endowed program that provides extra assistance to students who are willing to work to fund a portion of their education. The typical aid package meets all demonstrated need; grants constitute about 70 percent of the package, with the rest made up by loans and part-time work. The deadline in the financial aid sidebar is a *priority* deadline.

A note from the Cornell College Admissions Office:

"In 1978 Cornell adopted a One-Course-At-A-Time academic calendar. Using this distinctive calendar, students and faculty focus their best effort on a single course for three and a half weeks. At the end of that time, students take a four-day break and then enroll in their next class. The academic programs at Cornell are quite rigorous and the atmosphere is informal, encouraging extensive interaction between students and faculty. Classes are capped at 25 students and oral and written participation by each student is important. Cornell attracts serious students that love to learn but also know how to enjoy themselves. Students are involved in more than 60 campus clubs and organizations."

ADMISSIONS FACTS

Competitiveness Rating:	**96**
% of applicants accepted:	30
% acceptees attending:	49

FRESHMAN PROFILE

Average verbal SAT:	610*
Average math SAT:	670*
Average ACT:	NA
Graduated top 10% of class:	82
Graduated top 25% of class:	95
Graduated top 50% of class:	99

DEADLINES

Early decision/action:	11/1
Early dec./act. notif.:	12/15
Regular admission:	1/1
Regular adm. notif.:	4/15

APPLICANTS ALSO LOOK AT

and sometimes prefer:
Williams College
Wesleyan U.
U. Pennsylvania

and rarely prefer:
Amherst College
Purdue U.
Indiana U.
Tulane U.
U. Mass–Amherst
U. Rochester

ADDRESS

Undergraduate Admissions
410 Thurston Avenue
Ithaca, NY 14850-2488
607-255-5241

FINANCIAL FACTS

In-state tuition ($):	16,214
Out-of-state tuition ($):	16,214
Room & board ($):	5,336
FA application deadline:	2/15
% frosh receiving FA:	47
PT earnings per yr. ($):	1,370

TYPE OF AID: % of students ($):

FA of some kind:	43 (NA)
Need-based grants:	NA
Merit-based grants:	NA
Loans:	NA
Work study:	NA
Student rating of FA:	71

CREIGHTON UNIVERSITY

CAMPUS LIFE

Quality of Life Rating: **77**

Type of school:	private
Affiliation:	Jesuit
Environment:	city

STUDENT BODY

FT undergrad enrollment:	3,576
% male/% female:	44/56
% out-of-state:	55
% live on campus:	47
% African-American:	3
% Asian:	4
% Caucasian:	88
% Hispanic:	2
% foreign:	3
% transfers:	5

WHAT'S HOT

marriage
religion
town-gown relations
conservative politics
small labs and seminars
bursar
alternative rock

WHAT'S NOT

college radio station
rap/hip-hop
gay community visible
in-class discussion
religious clubs

ACADEMICS

Academic Rating: **79**

Calendar:	semester
Student/teacher ratio:	13/1
% doctorates:	83
Profs interesting:	83
Profs accessible:	78
Hours of study per day:	3.6

MOST POPULAR MAJORS BY %

Nursing:	22
Psychology:	9
Biology:	8

% GRADS WHO PURSUE

Law:	10
MBA:	2
Medicine:	10
M.A., etc.:	19

What do students think about Creighton University?

■ **Academics** As one student explained, "Getting into Creighton University isn't as hard as getting into Harvard or Yale. But staying here takes a lot of work!" This mid-sized Catholic university propels the pre-professionally minded students who make up the majority at Creighton. Undergrads study over three-and-a-half hours a day here and take class attendance very seriously. Over one quarter of the students pursue degrees in pre-medical sciences and another quarter study business and administration, with almost half those students proceeding to earn MBAs and MDs after graduation. Regardless of their majors, Creighton students must complete a rigorous set of liberal arts core requirements that account for over one third of the courses they take here. Instruction bears a strong Catholic inclination, which suits most students fine. Wrote one, "One of the main reasons I chose Creighton is for its Jesuit education. I have learned a lot about myself and life in general thanks to Creighton." Students reported that few classes are taught by TAs and gave good marks to professors in all departments. An Honors Program rewards top students with smaller classes, courses that take a comprehensive approach to understanding the arts and sciences, and the opportunity to conduct an independent research project during Senior year.

■ **Life** Students gave Omaha poor grades, in part because the neighborhood in which the school is located is somewhat marginal and in part because Omaha is not terribly exciting as cities go. It's a good place to buy some insurance or a juicy steak, but, according to most students, that's about it. Social life revolves around the Greek system and drinking, although neither seem to exert excessive influence on students: most are truly serious about their studies here. Men enjoy a very favorable male-female ratio (9:11), and students of both sexes report an active dating scene and list marriage high among their priorities. The cost of living at Creighton is surprisingly high. Students reported average weekly out-of-pocket expenses of $60 (excluding rent and groceries), the eighth highest amount reported in our survey. Number one on Creighton students' wish list: "If only we had a football team."

■ **Students** Creighton's solid reputation draws students from a wide geographic radius. Fewer than half the students are from Nebraska. Over two thirds of the students are Catholic, and the Catholic influence on academics remains a big drawing card for the university. Twelve percent of Creighton's undergrads are minority students. Approximately 150 Asian students make up the single largest minority population. The student body is religious and generally very conservative politically and socially; alternative lifestyles are predictably frowned upon here.

CREIGHTON UNIVERSITY

Omaha, NE

Admissions

The admissions office reports that it uses no 'cut-offs' nor formulas in considering applicants." High school GPA is the most important element in your application here; the admissions office then considers, in order of importance, standardized test scores, letters of recommendation, the quality of courses you took in high school, and extracurricular activities. Essays and interviews are not part of the Creighton application process. Applicants must have completed three years of English, algebra plus one more year of math, and six years of courses that can include a combination of English, foreign language, math, social science, and natural science classes. Applicants to Creighton most often apply also to UNebraska–Lincoln, UNebraska–Omaha, Marquette, Drake, Notre Dame, Northeast Missouri State, St. Louis University, Colorado State, and University of Iowa.

Financial Aid

Creighton's financial aid office writes that the university "is committed to making our quality education affordable. Recognizing the demands on family budgets today, we want to help you find the resources you need to fund your education." Creighton only requires submission of the FAF from financial aid applicants. No merit-based grants are awarded. Fifty-four percent of the class of '95 applied for some form of financial aid, and while the percent who received aid was not available, the average award value was $8,830. Creighton recommended Perkins loans (average value: $1,738) and Stafford loans (average not available) to undergrads in the '91–'92 academic year. Applications are accepted at any time; the April 1 deadline is for priority consideration.

A note from the Creighton University Admissions Office:

"Considered the most comprehensive university of its size in the nation, Creighton University in Omaha, Nebraska, attracts students from all 50 states and more than 45 foreign countries. At Creighton, 6,000 students study among nine different schools and colleges including professional schools in medicine, dentistry, pharmacy, and law.

"Undergraduates number 3,700 and choose from nearly 50 majors that range from atmospheric science and occupational therapy to creative writing, theater, and management information systems. The university has a strong reputation for pre-professional study in the health sciences.

"Creighton is a co-educational, Jesuit institution that offers many financial aid and scholarship opportunities."

ADMISSIONS FACTS

Competitiveness Rating:	67
% of applicants accepted:	90
% acceptees attending:	38

FRESHMAN PROFILE

Average verbal SAT:	NA
Average math SAT:	NA
Average ACT:	24
Graduated top 10% of class:	27
Graduated top 25% of class:	52
Graduated top 50% of class:	82

DEADLINES

Early decision/action:	NA
Early dec./act. notif.:	NA
Regular admission:	8/1
Regular adm. notif.:	rolling

APPLICANTS ALSO LOOK AT

and often prefer:
Iowa State U.

and sometimes prefer:
U. Notre Dame
U. Colorado at Boulder

and rarely prefer:
U. Iowa
Marquette U.
Texas A&M U.
DePaul U.
U. Wisconsin–Madison

ADDRESS

Undergraduate Admissions
California St at 24th
Omaha, NE 68178
402-280-2703

FINANCIAL FACTS

In-state tuition ($):	8,716
Out-of-state tuition ($):	8,716
Room & board ($):	3,798
FA application deadline:	4/1
% frosh receiving FA:	60
PT earnings per yr. ($):	1,200

TYPE OF AID: % of students ($):

FA of some kind:	75 (NA)
Need-based grants:	NA (1,600)
Merit-based grants:	NA
Loans:	NA
Work study:	NA (1,901)
Student rating of FA:	75

UNIVERSITY OF DALLAS

Irving, TX

CAMPUS LIFE

Quality of Life Rating:	**83**
Type of school:	private
Affiliation:	Roman Catholic
Environment:	city

STUDENT BODY

FT undergrad enrollment:	1,013
% male/% female:	46/54
% out-of-state:	35
% live on campus:	60
% African-American:	2
% Asian:	7
% Caucasian:	75
% Hispanic:	10
% foreign:	7
% transfers:	8

WHAT'S HOT

religion
financial aid
small lectures
interaction among students
town-gown relations
profs in class
college theater groups
profs outside class
honesty
studying hard

WHAT'S NOT

fraternities/sororities
campus appearance
library
food

ACADEMICS

Academic Rating:	**85**
Calendar:	semester
Student/teacher ratio:	12/1
% doctorates:	93
Profs interesting:	94
Profs accessible:	89
Hours of study per day:	3.63

MOST POPULAR MAJORS BY %

Letters/Literature:	20
Life Sciences:	19
Psychology:	15

% GRADS WHO PURSUE

Law:	7
MBA:	9
Medicine:	10
M.A., etc.:	24

What do students think about the University of Dallas?

■ **Academics** "Traditional" is the word UD students use to describe their school's approach to academics. As one explained, "UD is so enamored of the roots of Western thought that newer disciplines, such as psychology, are viewed with some suspicion. Don't look for an anthropology department, much less women's studies." If you are looking for just such a traditional liberal arts education, UD, an affiliate of the Roman Catholic church, is an excellent place to get one. A demanding core curriculum guarantees that students are exposed to the classics of European literature, as well as to science and math. Almost all students spend their sophomore year at the school's Rome campus (an experience students uniformly praise). Then there are the professors here, whom UD students ranked in the top 15 percent in the nation. Said a typical student, "The professors are wonderful. They frequently fraternize with the students in the capuccino bar and the cafeteria. During the Clarence Thomas hearings, I had lunch twice with my politics professor (at his initiation) and discussed the hearings." Explained another, "The professors, in addition to teaching us, expect that we can also teach them. It creates an atmosphere that compels the students to strive for excellence." All departments are good, but many students singled out the English department for its excellence. The school's results are impressive: about one fourth of its graduates go on to professional schools within a year of graduation, and another fourth go on to other graduate schools. About the only negative we heard was that the library is inadequate; many students prefer studying in local restaurants, and they use SMU's library for research.

■ **Life** University of Dallas is *not* a party school, as students kept reminding us. Said one, "If you like personal attention and don't want to feel like a number, this is the place for you. If you require a large social scene, sports, or fraternities/sororities (there are none at UD), go elsewhere." Although drinking is not unheard of here, social life revolves around academics: many students' idea of a good time is staying up all night drinking coffee and discussing Plato and Nietzsche. The small student body creates a Peyton Place atmosphere. Reported one student, "Anyone armed with a video camera could easily compile a soap opera here without *ever* distributing a script." The campus is "really ugly, but this matters little in the big picture," said a typical student.

■ **Students** Only about three quarters of the students at UD are Catholic, but almost all are religious and conservative. "The student body is composed of all sorts, but those seeking a strong religious community can easily find it," said one student. "Many students attend daily mass; this is a school where you can actually have a strong faith (Catholic or otherwise) and not be a nerd." Students here are self-confident: several students agreed with the one who called her classmates "some of the smartest, wittiest, and overall entertaining people you'll ever meet." Liberals have a tough go of it here. "I'm pro-choice and people here wear me out about it," said one student.

Admissions

According to its undergraduate catalog, the University of Dallas "seeks high school students who have pursued a curriculum of college preparatory courses including English, social studies, mathematics, science, and a foreign language. Applicants pursuing a discipline in the sciences should have four years of mathematics. Depth in foreign language is advised....Although the University is flexible in its admission standards, applicants...should be in the upper half of their graduating class and should present satisfactory scores from the College Entrance Examination Board or the American College Testing Program [SAT or ACT; all applicants must submit scores from one or the other]. The Admission Committee treats each applicant as an individual and is especially watchful for areas of individual accomplishment and talent." Priority date for consideration is March 1.

Financial Aid

Financial aid applicants to University of Dallas must complete the FAF or FFS and a form generated by U. of Dallas' financial aid office. The office writes, "We encourage all students to apply for need-based aid as well as merit aid. Many students are pleasantly surprised at the aid we are able to make available to them, especially during their semester in Rome." Ninety-three percent of the class of '95 received some form of aid; the average value was $8,878. In '90–'91, 47% of all undergrads received academic grants (the average value was $2,884); 1% of all undergrads received a language grant (the average value was $4,138); and 2% received an art/drama grant (average value: $4,990). The average Perkins loan was $980 taken out by 29% of all undergrads), the average Stafford loan was $2,778 (taken by 50%), and the average of PLUS and SLS loans was $3,374 (taken by 7%).

Excerpted from *University of Dallas promotional materials:*

"Quite unabashedly, the curriculum at the University of Dallas is based on the supposition that truth and virtue exist and are the proper objects of search in an education.

"The curriculum further supposes that this search is best pursued through an acquisition of philosophical and theological principles on the part of a student and has for its analogical field a vast body of great literature—perhaps more extensive than is likely to be encountered elsewhere—supplemented by a survey of the sweep of history and an introduction to the political and economic principles of society. An understanding of these subjects, along with an introduction to the quantitative and scientific world view and a mastery of a language, is expected to form a comprehensive and coherent experience, which, in effect, governs the intellect of a student in a manner which develops independence of thought in its most effective mode."

ADMISSIONS FACTS

Competitiveness Rating:	**79**
% of applicants accepted:	80
% acceptees attending:	50

FRESHMAN PROFILE

Average verbal SAT:	541
Average math SAT:	566
Average ACT:	25
Graduated top 10% of class:	45
Graduated top 25% of class:	76
Graduated top 50% of class:	98

DEADLINES

Early decision/action:	12/1
Early dec./act. notif.:	1/15
Regular admission:	5/1
Regular adm. notif.:	rolling

APPLICANTS ALSO LOOK AT

and often prefer:
U. Texas–Austin
U. Denver

and sometimes prefer:
U. Texas–Dallas
U. Texas–Arlington
Southern Methodist U.

ADDRESS

Undergraduate Admissions
1845 E. Northgate, Univ. Station
Irving, TX 75062-4799
214-721-5266

FINANCIAL FACTS

In-state tuition ($):	8,150
Out-of-state tuition ($):	8,150
Room & board ($):	4,000
FA application deadline:	3/1
% frosh receiving FA:	95
PT earnings per yr. ($):	1,608

TYPE OF AID: % of students ($):

FA of some kind:	75 (7,716)
Need-based grants:	65 (2,006)
Merit-based grants:	50 (3,009)
Loans:	60 (3,174)
Work study:	31 (1,445)
Student rating of FA:	97

DARTMOUTH COLLEGE

CAMPUS LIFE

Quality of Life Rating: **93**

Type of school:	private
Affiliation:	none
Environment:	rural

STUDENT BODY

FT undergrad enrollment:	3,788
% male/% female:	57/43
% out-of-state:	98
% live on campus:	99
% African-American:	6
% Asian:	8
% Caucasian:	77
% Hispanic:	3
% foreign:	6
% transfers:	<1

WHAT'S HOT

food
dorm safety
dorm comfort
honesty
library
campus appearance
intercollegiate sports
town-gown relations
profs outside class
profs in class
fraternities/sororities
beer

WHAT'S NOT

dating
alternative rock

ACADEMICS

Academic Rating: **88**

Calendar:	quarters
Student/teacher ratio:	12/1
% doctorates:	90
Profs interesting:	88
Profs accessible:	88
Hours of study per day:	3.23

MOST POPULAR MAJORS

Letters/Literature:	16
Psychology:	8
Engineering:	7

% GRADS WHO PURSUE

Law:	6
MBA:	2
Medicine:	5
M.A., etc.:	10

What do students think about Dartmouth College?

■ **Academics** It's no breeze getting through Dartmouth College, and those who succeed here truly apply themselves. Still, among all the Ivy League student bodies we surveyed, Dartmouth students wrote the least about their academic programs; they also wrote the most about social conditions on campus. Don't conclude that these students disregard their studies. It's just that they perceive school work as a chore to be completed, and completed well, so they can get on with their social lives. This practically anti-intellectual attitude might well be summed up by the student who wrote, "The faculty here really seems to care...about what I have no idea." The challenging academic program features distribution requirements that oblige students to take four courses each in the natural sciences, social sciences, and humanities. Students must also demonstrate writing and foreign language proficiency. Political science, economics and English are among the most popular of the uniformly fine departments here. Students also offered praise to the foreign language departments, computer science, and engineering. Students gave their professors excellent marks (the best in the Ivy League).

■ **Life** "Football games, fraternity parties, ice sculptures—Dartmouth's all around atmosphere and 'study hard, party hard' philosophy cannot be beat!" summed up one student. Fraternity parties are the mainstays of social life here, and while administrators have tried to curtail the Greeks' influence, they have had little success. A new campus alcohol policy prohibits kegs at parties at dorms and at school-recognized fraternities, and while our survey results indicate that students still drink regularly, the policy has some students up in arms. Complained one frat member, "The fraternities have taken the brunt of the administration's assault on drinking. The system is fighting back, but I do not see change in the near future." The social scene is "very male-oriented. If you're looking for male bonding, strong athletics, hard drinking and lots of studying, Dartmouth is the place." Beyond the campus confines, "There is not much to do, but Hanover is a quaint, charming town. The countryside is beautiful and there are tons of outdoor activities. We own our own ski mountain 20 minutes from campus." The campus is gorgeous, and the food is the sixth best in the country.

■ **Students** While hardly the most conservative students in the nation, Dartmouth students do fall to the right of center. Although one student noted that "our conservative reputation is overrated: all political, ethical, and moral groups are represented," much more common were comments such as "don't come here if you are liberal, artsy, or anti-social; you won't enjoy yourself." Complained one detractor, "I've had a difficult time here because of my reluctance to adopt a pretentious, pseudo-friendly, beer-loving exterior. Those who stray from the prototype are seen as flaunting their uniqueness. There is no in-between." Nearly one fourth of the students are minorities, with Asians and blacks making up a large portion of the minority population.

DARTMOUTH COLLEGE

Admissions

The admissions office reports, "Admissions to Dartmouth is highly selective. The competition for admission is a function of both the number of applicants as well as their outstanding credentials....A large and well qualified applicant pool offers Dartmouth the opportunity to enroll a freshman class that is not only very capable but also broad in the variety of backgrounds, talents, and interests represented." High school curriculum/GPA is most important to Dartmouth admissions, followed, in descending order of importance, by standardized test scores, extracurricular activities, letters of recommendation, essays, and interview. Dartmouth requires no specific high school courses but urges applicants "to undertake the strongest course of study available at his or her secondary school." Applicants must take the SAT or ACT, and three achievements. Dartmouth applicants most often also apply to Harvard, Princeton, Yale, Stanford, Williams, and Amherst.

Financial Aid

The financial aid office at Dartmouth College requires applicants to submit the FAF, a form generated by the school, and their parents' most recent tax return. The school awards grants on the basis of need only. Students may borrow money from the school under a variety of plans, one of which (the Dartmouth Educational Association loan) defers repayment until after graduation. Dartmouth students also take out Stafford, Perkins, PLUS, and SHARE loans. In its most recent bulletin, the school reported that the financial aid office "occasionally" creates a waiting list for admitted students; in other words, the school does not *guarantee* that it can meet the need of all accepted applicants.

Excerpted from Dartmouth College promotional materials:

"Today Dartmouth's mission is to endow its students with the knowledge and wisdom needed to make creative and positive contributions to society. The College brings together a breadth of cultures, traditions, and ideas to create a campus that is alive with ongoing debate and exploration. The educational value of such discourse cannot be underestimated. From student-initiated roundtable discussions that attempt to make sense of world events, to the late night philosophizing in a dormitory lounge, Dartmouth students take advantage of their opportunities to learn from each other.

"The unique benefits of sharing in this interchange are accompanied by a great sense of responsibility. Each individual's commitment to the 'Principles of Community' assures the vitality of this learning environment."

ADMISSIONS FACTS

Competitiveness Rating:	**94**
% of applicants accepted:	27
% acceptees attending:	52

FRESHMAN PROFILE

Average verbal SAT:	630*
Average math SAT:	683*
Average ACT:	NA
Graduated top 10% of class:	82
Graduated top 25% of class:	85
Graduated top 50% of class:	92

DEADLINES

Early decision/action:	11/15
Early dec./act. notif.:	12/15
Regular admission:	1/1
Regular adm. notif.:	4/15

APPLICANTS ALSO LOOK AT

and often prefer:
Princeton U.
Yale U.

and sometimes prefer:
Amherst College
Wesleyan U.
Columbia U.
Duke U.

and rarely prefer:
Cornell U.
Northwestern U.
Middlebury College

ADDRESS

Undergraduate Admissions
Hanover, NH 03755
603-646-2875

FINANCIAL FACTS

In-state tuition ($):	16,230
Out-of-state tuition ($):	16,230
Room & board ($):	5,160
FA application deadline:	2/1
% frosh receiving FA:	37
PT earnings per yr. ($):	1,500

TYPE OF AID: % of students ($):

FA of some kind:	50 (NA)
Need-based grants:	37 (NA)
Merit-based grants:	NA
Loans:	NA
Work study:	NA
Student rating of FA:	85

DAVIDSON COLLEGE

CAMPUS LIFE

Quality of Life Rating: **89**

Type of school:	private
Affiliation:	Presbyterian
Environment:	city

STUDENT BODY

FT undergrad enrollment:	1,499
% male/% female:	56/44
% out-of-state:	70
% live on campus:	92
% African-American:	5
% Asian:	4
% Caucasian:	90
% Hispanic:	1
% foreign:	4
% transfers:	1

WHAT'S HOT

honesty
food
small lectures
town-gown relations
administration (overall)
financial aid
profs outside class
small labs and seminars
deans
profs in class
studying hard

WHAT'S NOT

marijuana

ACADEMICS

Academic Rating: **90**

Calendar:	semester
Student/teacher ratio:	12/1
% doctorates:	96
Profs interesting:	93
Profs accessible:	94
Hours of study per day:	3.81

What do students think about Davidson College?

■ **Academics** Davidson College scores high marks with its students in many areas, but most noteworthy is their enthusiasm for their professors. In class and out, Davidson professors make the grade. As one student said, "The individual attention one receives at Davidson is overwhelming and well worth the tuition. A student receives whatever assistance he needs from a genuine professor, not from some teaching assistant." Another told us, "Communication with professors here is amazingly effective and always insightful." And necessary, too, to keep up with the workload. Students study, on average, close to four hours a day (*not* including classes): very few student bodies work any harder. Davidson offers pre-professional course sequences for those interested in law, medicine, business, and engineering; engineers may also participate in a 3-2 B.A./B.S. program. Other notable features of a Davidson education are the core curriculum (which heavily emphasizes the social and natural sciences) and the option to pursue a two-year, five-course interdisciplinary Humanities program, in which students focus on the central texts of a specific period in Western history and study central themes as they recur throughout Western art and literature.

■ **Life** Students who apply here know that they will be taking on an enormous workload, and most relish the challenge. "I see Davidson as a place where the students have managed to find a balance of work and play," reported one student. "We spend a *lot* of time studying, but our extracurricular activities keep us sane." More than a few students, however, thought the pressure was a little unhealthy. One wrote that "the academic pressures here at times can be overwhelming. Students at Davidson live on the edge—they study hard, play and party hard and over-commit themselves to many different extracurricular activities." The work load is made a bit more bearable by the school's honor code, which allows students to take exams on their own: it also allows them to leave their dorm rooms open without fear of losing their stereos. Does it work? One student's response was typical of her classmates' attitudes: "I laughed as I answered the question about cheating. No one on the outside can believe it, but the Honor Code at Davidson works. It is a very important part of our school and we are extremely proud to live by it."

■ **Students** Davidson's size and remote location make for a tight-knit college community. As one student told us, "There is *no* anonymity, so you have to like an environment where you're going to know by name two thirds of the people you pass on the way to class—and probably the name of the person they hooked up with last weekend as well." The upside of this is reported by one student: "Here, I don't feel like just another number in a computer." Students gave their classmates high marks, calling them open, friendly, and fun, but also agreed that the student body is a little conservative and homogeneous. One student summed up the Davidson experience this way: "If you are looking for a politically inactive, conservative campus and the best possible liberal arts education in the world, then Davidson is the place for you."

DAVIDSON COLLEGE

Admissions

The admissions office reports that "All our applicants are high achievers in terms of [high school and test performance]....We look for well-developed talents in areas such as athletics and art; we consider commitment and leadership; we seek ethnic and geographic diversity; we expect appreciation and respect for the Honor Code." Davidson first considers your GPA (in academic courses only), then, in descending order of importance, letters of recommendation, essays, extracurricular activities, standardized test scores (either SAT or ACT is accepted), interview, and achievement scores (which are optional). Applicants are required to have completed 16 academic units, including four years of English, three years of math, two years of a foreign language, and a year of history. Further studies in math, science, and foreign language are strongly recommended. Applicants to Davidson most often also apply to UNC–Chapel Hill, Duke, Wake Forest, UVA, and Washington and Lee.

Financial Aid

Financial aid applicants to Davidson must complete the FAF and a form generated by Davidson's FA office. About 10% of the students in each freshman class are awarded "Honor Scholarships." Recipients are selected from the entire applicant pool, not only those who have applied for financial aid. Selection is based on "academic promise, leadership ability, character, and promise of contribution to society." The Honor award stipends range from $350 to $3,000 and are renewable pending academic requirements being met. Five percent of students in each freshman class receive "Merit Scholarships"; some of the recipients include: the winner of an interview competition, students showing advanced musical or orchestral talent; students with exceptional abilities who plan to major in business or chemistry; and applicants who plan to be ordained in the Christian ministry. North Carolina Grants are available to legal residents of the state (in '88–'89, the average value of this grant was $1,100). Davidson's FA office recommends Perkins and Stafford loans. Approximately 300 students have on-campus jobs to help finance their educations.

A note from the Davidson Admissions Office:

"Students are attracted to Davidson for a variety of reasons. The academic program demands high achievement balanced by a full complement of extracurricular activities, providing excellent preparation for graduate study. The Honor Code remains central to the life of the College, making possible open stacks in the library and self-proctored tests and examinations. Classes are small, professors easily accessible, and facilities state of the art."

ADMISSIONS FACTS

Competitiveness Rating:	**92**
% of applicants accepted:	37
% acceptees attending:	55

FRESHMAN PROFILE

Average verbal SAT:	580
Average math SAT:	620
Average ACT:	28
Graduated top 10% of class:	72
Graduated top 25% of class:	92
Graduated top 50% of class:	100

DEADLINES

Early decision/action:	11/1
Early dec./act. notif.:	12/15
Regular admission:	2/1
Regular adm. notif.:	4/1

APPLICANTS ALSO LOOK AT

and often prefer:
Duke U.
U. NC Chapel Hill

and sometimes prefer:
College of William & Mary
Wake Forest U.
Vanderbilt U.

and rarely prefer:
Rhodes College
North Carolina State U.

ADDRESS

Undergraduate Admissions
P.O. Box 1719
Davidson, NC 28036
704-892-2230

FINANCIAL FACTS

In-state tuition ($):	11,954
Out-of-state tuition ($):	11,954
Room & board ($):	3,853
FA application deadline:	2/1
% frosh receiving FA:	63
PT earnings per yr. ($):	1,000

TYPE OF AID: % of students ($):

FA of some kind:	62 (NA)
Need-based grants:	NA
Merit-based grants:	NA
Loans:	NA
Work study:	NA
Student rating of FA:	95

UNIVERSITY OF DAYTON

Dayton, OH

CAMPUS LIFE

Quality of Life Rating: **88**

Type of school:	private
Affiliation:	Roman Catholic
Environment:	city

STUDENT BODY

FT undergrad enrollment:	5,969
% male/% female:	51/49
% out-of-state:	42
% live on campus:	85
% African-American:	4
% Asian:	1
% Caucasian:	90
% Hispanic:	1
% foreign:	1
% transfers:	NA

WHAT'S HOT

religion
food
overall happiness
administration (overall)
intramural sports
Grateful Dead
dorm comfort
beer
hard liquor
conservative politics

WHAT'S NOT

gay community visible
studying hard
caring about politics

ACADEMICS

Academic Rating: **73**

Calendar:	trimester
Student/teacher ratio:	17/1
% doctorates:	78
Profs interesting:	80
Profs accessible:	83
Hours of study per day:	2.7

MOST POPULAR MAJORS

Business & Management:	20
Communications:	14
Engineering:	13

% GRADS WHO PURSUE

Law:	4
MBA:	4
Medicine:	4
M.A., etc.:	25

What do students think about University of Dayton?

■ **Academics** Students at University of Dayton repeatedly emphasize two aspects of the UD experience. One is the sense of community they enjoy. Wrote one, "the best thing about UD is how much the faculty, staff, and administration are dedicated to academics. Professors are very willing to see students individually. The faculty even voted to lower their raises for next year in order to put more money into financial aid." The other is the active party scene. "We were cited as the #1 party school by *Playboy* and *USA Today*," wrote one student (for more, see "Life," below). Students agree that UD is a school for the career-oriented and pre-professional student; liberal arts take a back seat here to business and management, engineering, communications, and education. Like most Catholic schools, UD has a broad set of general education requirements. Students reported that they studied an average of two-and-three-quarters hours a day, which places them among the bottom 25 percent of students we surveyed. For those looking for a greater challenge, UD offers both a University Scholars Program, which offers enrollees special classes, seminars, and symposiums (about 20 percent of UD undergraduates participate in the program), and an even more rigorous Honors Program. Honors students, who make up only three percent of the undergraduate population, follow a prescribed four-year, interdisciplinary curriculum that culminates in a senior thesis.

■ **Life** UD is an apparent oxymoron, a Catholic party school. Explained one student, "UD is like a very conservative parent with rebellious children." Although a few students reported that the administration is beginning to crack down on drinking ("the school is shutting us down abruptly, not gradually," wrote one *very* upset undergrad), the vast majority reported that the party continues here. One student joked that UD is "a drinking institution with a learning problem"; wrote another, "There is a tremendous amount of pressure here to drink beer excessively." Fraternities and sororities, surprisingly, are not the dominant presence they are on most "party" campuses. Students enjoy intramural and intercollegiate sports and participate actively in campus clubs and community-service organizations. The city of Dayton received below-average marks from UD undergrads, but students did report that relations with locals are amiable. Commuters complained that "parking on campus is a constant battle between campus security and students; be prepared to spend money."

■ **Students** About three quarters of UD's students are Roman Catholic. Just over half are from Ohio. Minority enrollment at this school of approximately 6,000 is negligible: approximately 240 blacks constitute the best-represented group. The student body is among the nation's 14 most politically conservative. One student described it as "politically conservative but socially liberal—what a mix!"

178

UNIVERSITY OF DAYTON

Dayton, OH

Admissions

The admissions office reports that "all applications are reviewed on an individual basis with no formulas or cut-offs, but we do plan to keep our SAT/ACT score ranges similar from year to year. College preparatory courses in high school are important, and an interview is encouraged." UDayton considers high school curriculum and grades most important, followed in order of importance by standardized test scores, extracurricular activities, essays, letters of recommendation, and an interview. Applicants must have completed four years of English, three years each of math, science, and social studies, two years of a foreign language, and one year of art. Some programs have further requirements. UDayton requires either the ACT or SAT. Applicants to UDayton often also apply to Ohio State, Miami University, UCincinnati, and Xavier.

Financial Aid

The financial aid office at University of Dayton requires applicants to submit the FAF, a form generated by the school, and their parents' most recent tax return. The school awards merit scholarships on the basis of athletic ability (2% of the students received one; average value: $6,750), academic ability (21%; $3,178), and special talent in music and the visual arts (less than 1%; average value: $2,687). In 1991–92, University of Dayton recommended Stafford loans for 84% of all financial aid recipients; the school also recommends students for the Perkins loan.

A note from the University of Dayton Admissions Office:

"There is a university which combines the best of big schools and small schools. It has become one of the most appealing of the Midwest's private, comprehensive universities. The University of Dayton is medium-sized, residential, and respected as one of the nation's leading Catholic universities. Since 1850, talented students have responded to the UD challenge to learn, lead and serve. This is a university dedicated to helping students realize their dreams."

ADMISSIONS FACTS

Competitiveness Rating:	**65**
% of applicants accepted:	85
% acceptees attending:	38

FRESHMAN PROFILE

Average verbal SAT:	487
Average math SAT:	552
Average ACT:	25
Graduated top 10% of class:	24
Graduated top 25% of class:	41
Graduated top 50% of class:	79

DEADLINES

Early decision/action:	NA
Early dec./act. notif.:	NA
Regular admission:	rolling
Regular adm. notif.:	rolling

APPLICANTS ALSO LOOK AT

and often prefer:
Miami U.
U. Notre Dame

and sometimes prefer:
Ohio State U.

and rarely prefer:
Marquette U.
Indiana U.
U. Illinois
U. South Carolina
Purdue U.
Carnegie Mellon U.

ADDRESS

Undergraduate Admissions
300 College Park Drive
Dayton, OH 45469
513-229-4411

FINANCIAL FACTS

In-state tuition ($):	9,030
Out-of-state tuition ($):	9,030
Room & board ($):	3,760
FA application deadline:	3/31
% frosh receiving FA:	85
PT earnings per yr. ($):	1,200

TYPE OF AID: % of students ($):

FA of some kind:	80 (NA)
Need-based grants:	43 (2,649)
Merit-based grants:	NA
Loans:	40 (2,982)
Work study:	23 (1,500)
Student rating of FA:	78

DEEP SPRINGS COLLEGE

CAMPUS LIFE

Quality of Life Rating:	**94**
Type of school:	private
Affiliation:	none
Environment:	rural

STUDENT BODY

FT undergrad enrollment:	26
% male/% female:	100/0
% out-of-state:	88
% live on campus:	NA
% African-American:	NA
% Asian:	NA
% Caucasian:	NA
% Hispanic:	NA
% foreign:	NA
% transfers:	0

WHAT'S HOT

working a job
in-class discussion
food
small classes (overall)
students interact
studying hard
profs outside class
location
profs in class
campus appearance
overall happiness

WHAT'S NOT

dating
intercollegiate sports
beer

ACADEMICS

Academic Rating:	**89**
Calendar:	other
Student/teacher ratio:	3/1
% doctorates:	NA
Profs interesting:	96
Profs accessible:	92
Hours of study per day:	3.75

MOST POPULAR MAJORS BY %

(Not available)

What do students think about Deep Springs College?

■ **Academics** Men looking for *the* unconventional undergraduate experience, look no further: Deep Springs College provides that experience to its few students. This two-year college (enrollment: 26) furnishes students with an intense, challenging work load that includes not only academics but ranch work as well. Deep Springs is located on a remote desert ranch on which labor is mandatory. Here's how it works: students attend small, discussion-oriented classes in the morning, then spend the afternoons working their jobs, during which the classroom discussions of the morning are often continued. Jobs include such unglamorous titles as ditch digger and general laborer. One lucky guy gets to be a cowboy. According to the school, "the labor program is not a way for students to pay for their time [here]…nor is its purpose to teach skills. The labor program exists to help students develop self-discipline, self-reliance, and an awareness of their responsibilities to the…community." Students play a role in every aspect of the school's governance, from assigning work to recommending courses to reviewing and deciding upon admissions applications. For those suited to this type of life, Deep Springs "helps students gain a perspective on and understanding of the way things work in any community" and "forces you to succeed, to fail, and to evaluate yourself. It is a place where you can realize your full potential." Summed up one student: "higher education was born of a need for something beyond manual labor, but that intermediary step was lost in intervening years. Deep Springs was born of the need to re-establish the complete progression." After two years, students transfer to more conventional four-year colleges, among which are often included the nation's top schools.

■ **Life** As one student put it, "we give up beer and women for 60 miles of sand." (Actually, according to several students, while "it is against rules to drink alcohol during the school term, on our breaks drinking is common.") Television, drugs, and contact with anyone but the Deep Springs community are other things students here forsake. Leaving campus, except for urgent family matters and ranch business, is prohibited. Explained one student, "Students have a love/hate relationship with the school. The absence of women is frustrating, socially, morally, and intellectually. Drugs and alcohol have no place in a schedule jammed with academics, labor, and student government. Coffee and cigarettes are good." The surrounding area, while devoid of civilization and its diversions, is breathtaking in its beauty and accommodating to skiers and hikers.

■ **Students** Deep Springs provides full scholarships for all students, so economic background is no barrier to acceptance here. The student body is largely white (there are a couple of Asians and Hispanics, but no black students), liberal, and extremely bright (Deep Springs accepts only one of every 13 applicants). One student reported, "Most years there is one gay student on campus. Homophobia doesn't exist here."

DEEP SPRINGS COLLEGE

Deep Springs, CA

Admissions

The Deep Springs admissions process is "…a two-part applications process, with Part One due on November 15, and Part Two due January 15, if accepted. Interviews are a mandatory part of Part Two." At Deep Springs, the most important part of your application process is the interview, followed by your essays, GPA, extracurriculars, standardized test scores and letters of recommendation, in descending order of importance. Students are required to take the SAT or ACT. No specific high school courses are required, but "AP courses are looked upon with favor." Deep Springs applicants also often apply to Harvard, Yale, Cornell and the University of Chicago.

Financial Aid

Admission to Deep Springs includes full room, board and tuition for two years, subject to review after the first year. Last year, all enrolled students received a full merit-based academic scholarship of $22,000. Admission is on a need-blind basis.

A note from the Deep Springs College Admissions Office:

"Founded in 1912, Deep Springs College lies isolated in a high desert valley of California, 30 miles from the nearest town. Its enrollment is limited to 26 students, each of whom receives a full scholarship valued at over $20,000 covering tuition, room and board. The students engage in a rigorous academic program, govern themselves, and participate in the operation of the cattle and alfalfa ranch which is owned by the school. After two or three years, they transfer to other schools to complete their studies. Students regularly transfer to Berkeley, Cornell, Harvard, and Yale. Students make up eight of the ten members of the Applications Committee."

DENISON UNIVERSITY

Granville, OH

CAMPUS LIFE

Quality of Life Rating: **80**

Type of school:	private
Affiliation:	none
Environment:	suburban

STUDENT BODY

FT undergrad enrollment:	2,015
% male/% female:	48/52
% out-of-state:	72
% live on campus:	97
% African-American:	5
% Asian:	3
% Caucasian:	91
% Hispanic:	1
% foreign:	3
% transfers:	1

WHAT'S HOT

college radio station
good-looking students
small lectures
Grateful Dead
living on campus
financial aid
profs outside class
small classes (overall)
campus appearance

WHAT'S NOT

dorm safety
dorm comfort
interaction among students
diversity

ACADEMICS

Academic Rating: **80**

Calendar:	4-1-4
Student/teacher ratio:	13/1
% doctorates:	80
Profs interesting:	88
Profs accessible:	92
Hours of study per day:	3.36

MOST POPULAR MAJORS BY %

Economics:	15
English:	14
History:	11

% GRADS WHO PURSUE

Law:	6
MBA:	NA
Medicine:	4
M.A., etc.:	20

What do students think about Denison University?

■ **Academics** Until recently, Denison had a reputation as a party school, and it was common knowledge that students could breeze through many of their courses. This is no longer true: wrote one student, "Academics are becoming increasingly more stringent; our goal of becoming 'little Dartmouth' is coming together well." Another reported that "this semester professors were told to 'get tough or get lost,' which eliminated most of the blow-off courses." Denison is a university in name, but in fact it's a small liberal arts college. Small classes, caring, personable professors, and rigorous academics take precedent over prestige-garnering research and publication. Psychology, English, and economics are among the most popular of the many strong departments here; the school also has its fair share of pre-meds and the engineering department is, according to one electrical engineer, "powerful!" Students work hard at their studies, which include a demanding battery of core courses.

■ **Life** The Greeks play a huge role in the Denison social universe—the school ranked twelfth among all schools in this book in terms of the importance of frats and sororities to campus life. Said one student, "If you aren't in a fraternity or sorority, your social life is non-existent." Without the Greeks, most students fear, DU would have no social life. One student explained, "There is a lack of social alternatives here at Denison. It's not necessarily the fault of the administration, but rather it's because the school is located in small-town central Ohio." Accordingly, moves by the university to reign in Greek excesses have been viewed with apprehension by all students. Said one, "A lot of pressure has been put on the Greeks to make reforms. However, since Greek life is the ONLY social scene within a 10-mile radius, Greeks have really come together in a joint effort to remain an active part of Denison." University efforts notwithstanding, DU remains a party school, although students agree that the partying gets less intense annually. "If you come looking for a constant party scene, you'll be about five years too late," said one student. There are plenty of opportunities for students to participate in clubs and organizations: intramural sports, the school paper, and especially the radio station are very popular. Said one student, "Denison is the perfect size for getting involved in different activities and feeling a real part of the campus community. It is also big enough to offer a wide variety of classes and activities, and wonderful opportunities."

■ **Students** Denison students are pretty cynical about the make-up of their student body. Said one, "Denison does not allow for great diversity of social background. If you come here, prepare to conform to the image of upper class, wealthy, and well-bred." Another wrote: "Denison is still a haven for rich, underachieving prep schoolers, but the student body *is* changing. Recent additions include: students who *like* to study, those *against* the Greek system, and those whose names *aren't* Skip or Bailey." Over 90 percent of the students are white.

DENISON UNIVERSITY

Admissions

The admissions office reports that "each application is reviewed on the individual student's merits. The quality of your academic performance and your GPA in your junior and senior years are the most important factors. Important also is the quality, rather than the quantity, of your extracurricular accomplishments." After high school record, Denison considers, in order of importance, standardized test scores, essays, extracurricular activities, interviews, and letters of recommendation. Applicants are recommended to have completed four years of English, and three years each of math, science, social studies, and a foreign language. Art students must also submit a portfolio of their work. Denison requires either the SAT or ACT. Applicants to Denison most often also apply to Miami of Ohio, Wittenberg, Ohio Wesleyan, Kenyon, Dickinson, and Bucknell.

Financial Aid

Applicants for financial aid at Denison must complete the FAF and a form generated by the Denison FA office. At the time of the first deposit, tax forms must be submitted as well. Part of Denison's extremely well-organized financial aid brochure is a detailed chart which illustrates average awards, grants and family contributions for the class of '95, broken down by family income range Scholarships offered to freshmen for academic performance (Denison awarded academic scholarships to 14% of its students last year, with an average scholarship value of $6,297), special talents and financial need. Minority and Ohio state or county resident-based scholarships are also available.

A note from the Denison University Admissions Office:

"Denison University's concern for the success of each student is reflected in freshman transition programs, such as June Orientation and Freshman Studies, and excellent academic support services, which get first-year students off to a strong start. In small classes—many of them seminar size—active learning is the norm. Faculty are committed to sharing their own high academic standards and to helping students attain them through a strong faculty-based advising system. Unique opportunities to do original research with faculty members, and state-of-the-art equipment in the sciences, set Denison apart from other undergraduate schools. Writing is an integral component of most courses. Outside the classroom, more than 60 student-run organizations offer students many options for developing leadership skills. and the uncommon natural beauty of the campus and its meticulously maintained facilities make Denison a beautiful place to learn."

ADMISSIONS FACTS

Competitiveness Rating:	**73**
% of applicants accepted:	70
% acceptees attending:	24

FRESHMAN PROFILE

Average verbal SAT:	520*
Average math SAT:	567*
Average ACT:	26*
Graduated top 10% of class:	32
Graduated top 25% of class:	56
Graduated top 50% of class:	87

DEADLINES

Early decision/action:	1/1
Early dec./act. notif.:	1/20
Regular admission:	2/1
Regular adm. notif.:	4/1

APPLICANTS ALSO LOOK AT

and often prefer:
Northwestern U.
DePauw U.
Miami U.
Kenyon College

and sometimes prefer:
Ohio State U.
Vanderbilt U.
Skidmore College
Hobart/William Smith College
Ohio Wesleyan U.

ADDRESS

Undergraduate Admissions
Box H
Granville, OH 43023
614-587-6276

FINANCIAL FACTS

In-state tuition ($):	14,050
Out-of-state tuition ($):	14,050
Room & board:	4,010
FA application deadline:	4/1
% frosh receiving FA:	33
PT earnings per yr. ($):	1,000

TYPE OF AID: % of students ($)

FA of some kind:	50 (NA)
Need-based grants:	32 (11,500)
Merit-based grants:	NA
Loans:	26 (1,794)
Work study:	23 (1,150)
Student rating of FA:	92

UNIVERSITY OF DENVER

Denver, CO

What do students think about the University of Denver?

■ **Academics** University of Denver is a place where business and pleasure can be successfully mixed. The school's business and management programs, which claim over half the student body, are all reputedly excellent. And while the proximity of the nation's best ski resorts present a potential major distraction, most students seem to find the time to get their work done before hitting the slopes—the average student puts in over three hours of study a day and takes class attendance and assignments fairly seriously. Music, communications, foreign languages and hotel management are among the other recommended departments here, and one sophomore bragged that "this is probably one of the few universities in the nation where undergraduates work directly with doctors involved in such things as ozone depletion and global warming." All students must complete a broad set of core requirements covering basic humanities, social science, and natural science materials. Students gave their professors average grades; explained one Russian/communications double major, "The faculty and teaching here are mixed, ranging from excellent to horrible." Note: DU runs on a quarterly schedule, so terms go by very quickly.

■ **Students** Many DU students are skiing fanatics, and more than a few choose the school for its location. "You don't need to know how to ski when you come here," wrote one student, "but you better be ready to learn." Explained another, "skiing and partying are big. If you have time, you go to class." The social scene centers on fraternity parties ("The Greek system is huge!" reported one student) and an active dating circuit. Although students at similarly sized schools often complain that their surroundings become claustrophobic at times, DU students have no such complaints, probably because they are located on the outskirts of a major city. In fact, students reported that they enjoy the small student body ("Everywhere you go on campus, including parties, social functions, the cafeteria, etc., you see someone that you know," explained one student. "That is very comforting."). Several students complained that the school could use a football team, but no other complaints were reported by more than one student. Summed up one respondent: "If you enjoy outdoor activities and a small campus, then DU is great. You're only an hour from the mountains. Most freshmen have a more active social life than an academic one, but then, not all of them come back."

■ **Life** The student body of DU is pretty homogeneous: Asians, blacks, and Hispanics combined make up fewer than 10 percent of the population. Wrote one black student, "DU offers little or no attraction for minority students. The school is in a metropolitan area, which means it should have more minority students, but it seems that the school makes little effort to attract minority students from the community." DU does a good job of attracting students from diverse locations however: fewer than one third of the students are from in state, and about one twelfth are from overseas.

UNIVERSITY OF DENVER

Admissions

From the University of Denver's undergraduate catalog: "The University of Denver seeks in prospective students serious educational aims and high standards of scholarship and personal character. The Committee on Admissions selects students whose backgrounds show that enrollment at the University of Denver will be mutually rewarding....In selecting the freshman class, the Committee on Admission considers all available information, including evidence of academic maturity and independence, general contributions to the school and the community, extracurricular activities and leadership....The secondary school record is the most significant document in the application." The recommended high school curriculum includes four years of English, three to four years of mathematics, and a minimum of two years each of social and natural sciences. Foreign language preparation is also recommended. Applicants must submit SAT or ACT scores.

Financial Aid

The financial aid office at University of Denver requires applicants to either submit the FAF or the FFS. Nearly 20 percent of the undergraduate population receive merit scholarships, which are available to all students regardless of need and which are awarded on the basis of academic accomplishment, skill in the arts, athletic achievement, and intended/declared major. Residents of the state of Colorado are also eligible for several merit- and need-based grants. Overall, about half the students receive some form of financial assistance.

A note from the University of Denver Admissions Office:

"The University of Denver is located in an important growth area of the United States, one in which the population will expand enormously during the next decade. We also see evidence of major industrial growth as well. This extensive expansion leads us to ask ourselves what we must, as an institution of higher education, be prepared to do in order to maintain a leadership role. The answers to the problem are not easy, but we invite students who are eager to join us in forming solutions.

"The faculty at the University of Denver will have a voice in identifying the direction in which we will go. The excitement they bring to the classroom through their teaching as well as the research they undertake will help answer immediate questions while raising others which are more complex. The University is not a static place, and all members of the academic community will make contributions to its progress."

ADMISSIONS FACTS

Competitiveness Rating:	**67**
% of applicants accepted:	75
% acceptees attending:	33

FRESHMAN PROFILE

Average verbal SAT:	468
Average math SAT:	425
Average ACT:	23
Graduated top 10% of class:	30
Graduated top 25% of class:	56
Graduated top 50% of class:	83

DEADLINES

Early decision/action:	12/1
Early dec./act. notif.:	1/1
Regular admission:	3/1
Regular adm. notif.:	rolling

APPLICANTS ALSO LOOK AT

and sometimes prefer:
U. Puget Sound
U. Colorado–Boulder
U. Vermont

and rarely prefer
Boston U.
Dartmouth College

ADDRESS

Undergraduate Admissions
MRB #107 University Park
Denver, CO 80208-0132
303-871-2036

FINANCIAL FACTS

In-state tuition ($):	12,852
Out-of-state tuition ($):	12,852
Room & board:	4,206
FA application deadline:	2/20
% frosh receiving FA:	57
PT earnings per yr. ($):	1,400

TYPE OF AID: % of students ($)

FA of some kind:	52 (NA)
Need-based grants:	NA
Merit-based grants:	NA
Loans:	NA
Work study:	NA
Student rating of FA:	94

DEPAUL UNIVERSITY

CAMPUS LIFE

Quality of Life Rating:	*82*
Type of school:	private
Affiliation:	Roman Catholic
Environment:	city

STUDENT BODY

FT undergrad enrollment:	5,946
% male/% female:	46/54
% out-of-state:	17
% live on campus:	25
% African-American:	12
% Asian:	6
% Caucasian:	74
% Hispanic:	7
% foreign:	<1
% transfers:	11

WHAT'S HOT

location
suitcase syndrome
working a job
small lectures
attending all classes
interaction among students

WHAT'S NOT

library
fraternities/sororities
campus appearance
college newspaper
religious clubs

ACADEMICS

Academic Rating:	*78*
Calendar:	quarters
Student/teacher ratio:	13/1
% doctorates:	84
Profs interesting:	81
Profs accessible:	79
Hours of study per day:	2.94

MOST POPULAR MAJORS BY %

Accounting:	15
Communications:	6
Computer Science:	6

% GRADS WHO PURSUE

Law:	12
MBA:	25
Medicine:	2
M.A., etc.:	28

What do students think about DePaul University?

■ **Academics** DePaul University is a Catholic school with a pre-professional emphasis. Business administration, accounting, management, and marketing are popular majors here, as are computer science and political science (a popular choice with pre-law students). DePaul also boasts a nationally renowned drama department. Said one drama major, "We have one of the finest theater schools anywhere, which means there is plenty of talent abounding here." The campus is home to the Blackstone Theatre, which allows DePaul drama students ample opportunities to perform. Although a medium-sized school, DU offers several of the benefits of a small college. Classes are usually small, and professors take genuine interest in their students' progress. Said one student, "The best thing about DePaul is the student-teacher ratio. You really get to know your professors." Reported another, "The instructors set high standards, and encourage us to do the same and not do things by way of the status quo." The quarterly academic schedule drew some complaints ("It does not allow students the time for play"), as did the number and difficulty level of required liberal arts courses. The library also received low grades (a new one is currently under construction), and the facilities in general were viewed as "archaic." The school is divided into two campuses: downtown (at "the Loop"), where most of the pre-professional studies take place, and uptown (Lincoln Park) for liberal arts and science students.

■ **Life** Because three quarters of the students commute, DePaul "lacks a typical college atmosphere." Clubs and the Greeks fill the social void for many who live on campus. Said one student, "there is a club here for everyone. The DePaul Community Service Association is very popular, as is the Residence Hall Council. There's a walking club and even an Elvis Lives Club." Those who live at DePaul are housed at the Lincoln Park campus. The neighborhood around it is not unlike Washington, D.C.'s Georgetown; although it's a little preppy for some tastes, it offers a lot in the way of clubs, record stores, and inexpensive dining. Beyond Lincoln Park is the rest of Chicago, "a terrific city with a lot of culture and history; it's also Partytown USA." Chicago also provides pre-professional students plenty of internship opportunities, opportunities arranged for by the university. The campuses themselves are unspectacular: reported one student, "We need more grass (lawn, that is)."

■ **Students** About half of DePaul's students are Catholic. Many of the students are from Chicago's less-affluent suburbs and were "not really aware of the city" before attending DePaul. One Hispanic woman explained that "although DePaul is located in the city, it caters to the suburbs. I would say that in all my classes I have been the only Latina and the only person born and raised in the city." For the most part, however, students have praise for their classmates, characterizing them as "helpful," and "sociable." Students here are liberal and particularly open-minded for those attending religious schools.

DEPAUL UNIVERSITY

Admissions

The admissions office reports, "No cutoffs or formulas are used in considering applicants. A student's total academic record and extracurricular or co-curricular activities are considered." DePaul considers your high school GPA most important, followed, in order of descending importance, by standardized test scores, extracurricular activities, letters of recommendation, interview, and essays. DePaul requires no specific high school classes, but does recommend a college preparatory curriculum including three years each of math and science, and two years of a foreign language. DePaul requires either the SAT or the ACT and recommends three achievements. Applicants to DePaul are often also applicants to Loyola–Chicago, Northwestern, UIllinois–Urbana, UIllinois–Chicago, UChicago, Indiana U, and Notre Dame.

Financial Aid

DePaul University requires the FAF. The financial aid office awards merit-based grants to approximately one third of the student body; merit grants are awarded on the basis of academic excellence (to 28% of students; the average award is $2600), "talent" (5%, $2350), and athletics (2%, $7280). Slightly over half the students received need-based grants last year. DePaul recommends the Stafford loan (last year to 36% of all undergraduates, at an average value of $2680) and the Perkins loan (4%, $1450). All in all, 75% of all freshmen, and 69% of all undergraduates, received some form of financial aid in 1991.

A note from the DePaul University Admissions Office:

"DePaul University is a growing urban Catholic institution. DePaul has an enrollment of 16,414 students in bachelor, Masters and Doctoral programs, making it the second largest Catholic school in the United States. The university continues to grow physically as well. At the Lincoln Park campus, three new residence halls have opened in the past four years, the new library is slated to open next fall and the University recently acquired the 1,400-seat Blackstone Theater. At DePaul's downtown campus, the University just purchased the Goldblatt building, a 14-story structure for the business and law school. DePaul continues to emphasize teaching ability as a priority for faculty selection. All DePaul students take advantage of the cultural, business and educational opportunities of the city of Chicago."

ADMISSIONS FACTS

Competitiveness Rating:	**74**
% of applicants accepted:	68
% acceptees attending:	38

FRESHMAN PROFILE

Average verbal SAT:	495
Average math SAT:	533
Average ACT:	23
Graduated top 10% of class:	30
Graduated top 25% of class:	63
Graduated top 50% of class:	92

DEADLINES

Early decision/action:	11/15
Early dec./act. notif.:	12/1
Regular admission:	rolling
Regular adm. notif.:	rolling

APPLICANTS ALSO LOOK AT

and often prefer:
I.I.T
Northeastern U.
U. Chicago
Northwestern U.

and sometimes prefer:
U. Notre Dame
Boston U.
U. Illinois
Loyola U.–Chicago

and rarely prefer:
Purdue U.

ADDRESS

Undergraduate Admissions
25 E. Jackson Blvd.
Chicago, IL 60604-2287
312-362-8300

FINANCIAL FACTS

In-state tuition ($):	9,342
Out-of-state tuition ($):	9,342
Room & board:	4,332
FA application deadline:	5/1
% frosh receiving FA:	70
PT earnings per yr. ($):	1,500

TYPE OF AID: % of students ($)

FA of some kind:	69 (6,380)
Need-based grants:	52 (5600)
Merit-based grants:	NA
Loans:	NA
Work study:	20 (1,200)
Student rating of FA:	78

DePAUW UNIVERSITY

Greencastle, IN

What do students think about DePauw University?

■ **Academics** Several features that set DePauw University apart from the "small liberal arts school" pack. One is the Winter semester, a month-long term in which students pursue "many outstanding opportunities to do things you can't do in the classroom." Wrote one student, "during the Winter term I've had friends who interned at hospitals, law firms, and went on Mission trips. I stayed on campus to learn production and news aspects of the college radio station." Another unique aspect of student life is the pronounced level of participation in community service: according to one student, "The level of volunteer involvement with the community is amazing." Students get involved "through their church or through the campus ministries center." In most other ways a conventional liberal arts school, DePauw offers excellent, challenging programs in letters and social sciences (several respondents noted that the new media-studies center is very good). Students enjoy a great deal of contact with professors: wrote one, "The teachers could not be more accessible. The caring academic environment makes it impossible for someone to slip through the cracks unless he or she wants to." DePauw students are encouraged to participate in the overseas studies program, which sends students practically everywhere in the world.

■ **Life** Despite the school's many assets, DePauw students ranked only in the middle of the national pack in terms of overall satisfaction with their school. A major source of dissatisfaction is the limited array of social options. There is essentially one: the Greek system. Nearly everybody goes Greek, and while this arrangement is satisfactory to many, it also has its share of detractors. Wrote one student, "The campus is extremely Greek and the social system is hardly navigable without the correct Greek letters on your chest." Wrote another, "If there was another school just like DePauw, but without the Greek system, I'd be much happier there." The town of Greencastle is "much too rural" and "offers little in terms of entertainment." Positive aspects of life at DePauw include a popular intramural sports program ("Intramurals are more popular spectator sports than the college-affiliated programs"), an excellent college radio station, and the food. Of the last, one student wrote, "With apologies to Mom, the food here is better than what I get at home. After all, it's tough to beat a Belgian waffle maker, self-serve ice cream, salad bar and all around first-class 'grub' with all the fixings."

■ **Students** Several students told us that DePauw has recently stepped up efforts to attract minority students. One student reported, "I have close friends from Argentina, South Africa, and Hawaii. It's a much healthier environment this way." Still, the predominant tone of the student body remains wealthy and WASPy. Wrote one black student, "DePauw is a good school, but academics are only a part of education. DePauw students are rich and often ignorant of other racial and ethnic backgrounds, which makes it a chore for other groups to interact. We constantly have to tolerate their ignorance!" Another student wrote that "the student body is divided by fraternity, sorority, race, and politics. The place is socially fragmented."

DePauw University

Admissions

The admissions office reports that "each candidate is considered individually. We look for students who demonstrate depth as well as breadth in their high school curriculums and extracurriculars." High school grades and quality of classes are considered most important, as are letters of recommendation and essays. Also important, but less so, are standardized test scores, extracurricular activities, and interviews. Applicants are required to have completed four years of English, at least two years of a foreign language, and three years (with a fourth recommended) of each of the following: math, social science, and natural science (two or more years of lab science required). DePauw requires either the SAT or the ACT. Students applying to DePauw most often also apply to Indiana University, Miami of Ohio, Denison, Purdue, and Northwestern.

Financial Aid

Applicants for financial aid at DePauw must complete the FAF and submit a copy of their parents' tax form to the financial aid office. Last year 16% of DePauw's students received academic scholarships, with an average value of $5,500. Achievement-based scholarships are available for music performance (last year: 1% of undergrads, average value $4,500), and for several "planned majors," including sociology, psychology, science, journalism, communications, art, music, medicine, dentistry and veterinary medicine. Minority achievement scholarships are also available. Indiana residents who demonstrate need may apply for various residence-based grants which are offered; in '90–'91, the maximum award of this nature was $5,713. In addition to PLUS, Perkins and Stafford loans, DePauw has its own loan program, which offers loans of up to $2,500 per year.

A note from the DePauw University Admissions Office:

"A love for learning; a willingness to serve others; the reason and judgment to lead; an interest in engaging worlds you don't know; the courage to question your assumptions; and a strong commitment to community—in sum, these describe DePauw University students. Preprofessional and career exploration opportunities coexist with the liberal arts and are encouraged through Winter Term in which 700 students regularly participate in off-campus internships. This represents more students in experiential learning opportunities than at any other liberal arts college in the nation. Other innovative programs include the Honor Scholar Program as well as the Management Fellows, Media Fellows, and Science Research Fellows (Programs), which all include a semester-long internship in the junior year."

ADMISSIONS FACTS

Competitiveness Rating:	**78**
% of applicants accepted:	84
% acceptees attending:	38

FRESHMAN PROFILE

Average verbal SAT:	543*
Average math SAT:	600*
Average ACT:	25*
Graduated top 10% of class:	40
Graduated top 25% of class:	74
Graduated top 50% of class:	97

DEADLINES

Early decision/action:	12/1
Early dec./act. notif.:	1/7
Regular admission:	2/15
Regular adm. notif.:	4/1

APPLICANTS ALSO LOOK AT

and often prefer:
Northwestern U.

and sometimes prefer:
Oberlin College
Washington U.

and rarely prefer:
Ohio Wesleyan U.
Vanderbilt U.
Rhodes College
Lake Forest College
U. Illinois

ADDRESS

Undergraduate Admissions
313 South Locust Street
Greencastle, IN 46135-0037
317-658-4006

FINANCIAL FACTS

In-state tuition ($):	12,288
Out-of-state tuition ($):	12,288
Room & board:	4,420
FA application deadline:	2/15
% frosh receiving FA:	62
PT earnings per yr. ($):	876

TYPE OF AID: % of students ($)

FA of some kind:	49 (NA)
Need-based grants:	10 (11,762)
Merit-based grants:	NA
Loans:	43 (2,925)
Work study:	20 (NA)
Student rating of FA:	83

DREW UNIVERSITY

CAMPUS LIFE

Quality of Life Rating:	**80**
Type of school:	private
Affiliation:	Methodist
Environment:	suburban

STUDENT BODY

FT undergrad enrollment:	1,395
% male/% female:	43/57
% out-of-state:	44
% live on campus:	95
% African-American:	4
% Asian:	3
% Caucasian:	90
% Hispanic:	3
% foreign:	3
% transfers:	4

WHAT'S HOT

college theater
gay community accepted
college radio station
alternative rock
small labs and seminars
gay community visible
living on campus
leftist politics
requirements easy
cost of living

WHAT'S NOT

fraternities/sororities

ACADEMICS

Academic Rating:	**81**
Calendar:	semester
Student/teacher ratio:	13/1
% doctorates:	79
Profs interesting:	84
Profs accessible:	86
Hours of study per day:	3.25

MOST POPULAR MAJORS BY %

Letters/Literature:	12
Psychology:	11
Visual & Performing Arts:	7

% GRADS WHO PURSUE

Law:	5
MBA:	1
Medicine:	2
M.A., etc.:	20

What do students think about Drew University?

■ **Academics** Area college counselors agree that Drew University is a "little-known gem;" wrote one, "This school gets lost in the crowd, but people who go here love it." A small liberal arts school that is nearly unknown outside its region, Drew is working to earn a reputation commensurate with its competitive student body and innovative programs. To accomplish this, the school hired a famous president, former New Jersey governor Tom Kean, who not only attracts attention to the school but also "is extremely active in the student body, and makes a concerted effort to get to know each student personally." High-profile innovations here include the Computer Initiative and Knowledge Initiative programs, which together provide every student with a computer, computer training, and access to an information and communications network: Drew students can E-Mail professors and each other, and can access the library card catalog from their dorm rooms. Political science, psychology, and the liberal arts are popular and reportedly excellent, as is the drama program, and students happily reported that "Drew is a no-pressure kind of place." Students gave good grades to their professors, but, President Kean not withstanding, found fault with the administration. Explained one student, "In general, the students and faculty are great. The administration, however, makes the IRS seem friendly and government seem well run by comparison."

■ **Life** Social life at Drew is reportedly "low-key." Wrote one student, "You have to want to do something at Drew. It won't pound your door down. If you want to have fun, you have to find it. If you want to work, you have to lock your door and do it. The choices are all yours." The school does offer several excellent extracurricular opportunities, however, including a well-funded theater program, a popular radio program, movies, and intramural sports. Despite the school's strict "no drinks for minors" policy and the absence of a Greek system (wrote one student, "This is not a school for those looking to join a Delta-fascist frat!"), students report that parties and drinks are fairly easy to come by. Students reported a moderately active dating scene despite the fact that "the male-female ratio is awful"(about two to three). Overall, student satisfaction with life at Drew is high, in large part because "there is a great sense of community on campus." For those interested in a less intimate, less friendly setting, New York City is only 40 miles away and is easily accessible by public transportation or by car.

■ **Students** In recent years, Drew has stepped up efforts to recruit students from outside its immediate area. Still, more than half its students are natives of New Jersey, and many others come from Delaware, Pennsylvania, and New York. The minority population is small, but the minority students we heard from reported no problems and consider themselves happy at Drew. Students ranked themselves left of center politically and accepting of alternative lifestyles: wrote one student, "The school's atmosphere allows any student to be him/herself."

DREW UNIVERSITY

Admissions

From Drew's undergraduate catalog: "Class rank, secondary school record, recommendations, and test scores are evaluated in the admissions process. The University is also interested in the student as an individual—the special strengths, talents, and extracurricular activities of each applicant are considered...Rank in the highest quarter of the secondary school class in desirable. Secondary school preparation should consist of at least four units of English, three units of college preparatory mathematics, two units of foreign language, two units of history/social studies, and two years of laboratory science, plus three additional units of academic course work, totaling 16 units." Mathematics, physics, and chemistry majors should take an additional year of mathematics. All applicants must submit test scores from three Achievements (including English composition) and either the SAT or ACT.

Financial Aid

Financial aid applicants to Drew University must complete the FAF and a form generated by Drew's financial aid office. Last year, 65% of the class of '95 received some form of aid; the average package value was $16,916. Twelve percent of all undergrads received institutional and state grants; the average grant value was $8,405. Among the scholarships available are those for minorities and academic merit. Drew's financial aid office notes, "We package grant assistance first, then self-help." Incentive programs to attract special students include Middle Income Achievement Awards and Thomas H. Kean Awards.

Excerpted from Drew University promotional materials:

"'Drew University commits itself to being an intimate and significant community,' said a 1980 mission description by the University's Long-Range Planning Committee. Its three schools, each with separate missions, share a common purpose: to increase and transmit knowledge of all aspects of human life. The University distinguishes itself...by its high academic standards, by the strength of its commitment to ethical values, by its global awareness, and by its assumption that all knowledge is interrelated. Drew strives to give concise expression to these commitments in its curriculum, in the quality of its teaching, in the extra-classroom student life, and in the encouragement of its life-long learning. Because each generation re-creates the nation, Drew's objective is education for responsible citizenship and leadership."

ADMISSIONS FACTS

Competitiveness Rating:	**79**
% of applicants accepted:	76
% acceptees attending:	23

FRESHMAN PROFILE

Average verbal SAT:	558
Average math SAT:	599
Average ACT:	NA
Graduated top 10% of class:	50
Graduated top 25% of class:	70
Graduated top 50% of class:	93

DEADLINES

Early decision/action:	1/15
Early dec./act. notif.:	within 3 wks.
Regular admission:	2/15
Regular adm. notif.:	4/1

APPLICANTS ALSO LOOK AT

and sometimes prefer:
George Washington U.
Penn State U.
Fairfield U.
U. Rochester
Franklin and Marshall College

and rarely prefer:
Rutgers U./Rutgers College
Hofstra U.
SUNY Purchase
U. Minnesota

ADDRESS

Undergraduate Admissions
36 Madison Avenue
Madison, NJ 07940-4063
201-408-3739

FINANCIAL FACTS

In-state tuition ($):	16,104
Out-of-state tuition ($):	16,104
Room & board:	4,476
FA application deadline:	3/1
% frosh receiving FA:	74
PT earnings per yr. ($):	1,200

TYPE OF AID: % of students ($)

FA of some kind:	63 (12,772)
Need-based grants:	48 (8,833)
Merit-based grants:	12 (8,405)
Loans:	30 (3,700)
Work study:	20 (856)
Student rating of FA:	81

DREXEL UNIVERSITY

Philadelphia, PA

What do students think about Drexel University?

■ **Academics** Drexel University, like Bentley and Northeastern, provides its largely pre-professional undergraduate students with a noteworthy "co-op" program. "Co-op" finds students employment in the professions they seek to enter for almost half their five-year stay at Drexel. Exclaimed one student, "There is no substitute for co-op. It's absolutely the best thing a college education can offer: experience. It lets you know what you are spending your 60K for." Although a few students complained that their co-op jobs were "menial," most students find the experience extremely beneficial. Students also liked the fact that, upon arrival, they immediately began to study in the field on their choosing: said one, "You are thrown into the thick of your major right from the beginning: you don't have to wait until junior year to realize if you like it or not." The school is on a quarterly schedule, which creates a high-pressure academic environment. Perhaps that's why students responded unenthusiastically to the question, "How happy are you here?" Professors and administrators received low grades.

■ **Life** Drexel is located in the heart of Philadelphia, not far from University of Pennsylvania. Although, in the words of one undergrad, "The neighborhood leaves much to be desired," we heard no complaints about local crime. One student told us that "the campus has good security; I always feel safe." School spirit is largely absent here. Students have several explanations for this. Said one, "the lack of popular athletics and the city environment hinder school spirit." Another student suggested that the rigors of the quarterly schedule make it difficult to participate in any extracurricular activities. The social scene is slow, in part because of a 2:1 male:female ratio, and in part because many of the students commute or leave campus nearly every weekend. One respondent reported that "if you live on campus and are not affiliated with a fraternity or if you don't have a girlfriend, you can forget about a social life." Of course, it's not like Drexel students are stranded in the mountains: Philadelphia is a major city that offers plenty in the way of museums, shopping, sports, and nightlife to those who venture off campus.

■ **Students** Drexel attracts a pretty diverse student body: almost one in ten students is black, and there is also a sizeable Asian population. The typical student is male, conservative, and anxious to succeed in the "real world." Most liberal arts majors feel out of place here; one complained that "the average Drexel student leads a life of quiet following, taking notes and not asking questions. They use co-op as their substitute for real life—since when was Xeroxing real life?" For the engineers and business students who make up the majority of the student body, however, the atmosphere is ideal. As one explained, "Drexel prepares you for the cutthroat corporate world of all for me, 'nothing for you' competition and the 'every man for himself' attitude of the '90s."

DREXEL UNIVERSITY

Admissions

The admissions office reports that "Each candidate is considered individually on the basis of contributions to school and community, academic potential, and achievements as indicated by secondary school records and test results, as well as interest in Drexel." Drexel first considers high school GPA, then, in descending order of importance, standardized test scores, interview, extracurricular activities, letters of recommendation, and essays. Applicants are expected to have completed "a well-rounded college preparatory or academic program," in which "English, mathematics (through trigonometry), and science are important components." Music candidates, furthermore, must audition. All applicants must submit results for either the SAT or the ACT. Applicants to Drexel most often also apply to Penn State, Temple, Villanova, LaSalle, and University of Delaware.

Financial Aid

Financial aid applicants to Drexel must complete the FAF. Drexel has a co-op plan which helps a large number of upperclass students meet their financial obligations. Merit scholarships offered include the President's Freshman Scholarship Program (which awards outstanding incoming students, based on their high school achievements), and Performing Arts Scholarships (recipients must perform in organizations at Drexel. A number of major-related endowed scholarships are also available. The FA office recommends Stafford, PHEAA-HELP, SLS and PLUS loans. The deadline for priority consideration is May 1.

A note from the Drexel University Admissions Office:

"The goal of every Drexel major is to prepare you for success in the professional world or in graduate school. For this reason, the Drexel education goes beyond in solid coursework. It places a high priority on firsthand experience on completing your own design projects, research, or original creative work. And it stresses technology—understanding the innovations that are reshaping the world, even in areas that haven't traditionally been seen as 'high-tech.' Along the way, it provides plenty of personal help to make sure you succeed. The cooperative education, or co-op, is the added dimension that really sets Drexel apart. Through co-op, you switch between periods of full-time studies on campus and periods of full-time professional employment. What also sets Drexel apart is the use of computers. Each student has personal access to a Macintosh. In virtually every career area, from chemistry to corporate communication, one of the most important tools professionals use to do their jobs is the computer. Drexel students use the Macintosh extensively, preparing for lifetime of working with computers after they graduate."

ADMISSIONS FACTS

Competitiveness Rating:	**65**
% of applicants accepted:	91
% acceptees attending:	37

FRESHMAN PROFILE

Average verbal SAT:	486*
Average math SAT:	526*
Average ACT:	NA
Graduated top 10% of class:	21
Graduated top 25% of class:	50
Graduated top 50% of class:	82

DEADLINES

Early decision/action:	11/15
Early dec./act. notif.:	1/2
Regular admission:	3/1
Regular adm. notif.:	NA

APPLICANTS ALSO LOOK AT

and often prefer:
U.S. Coast Guard
American U.
Boston U.

and sometimes prefer:
U. Maryland
Temple U.
Lehigh U.

and rarely prefer:
Villanova U.
Penn State U.
Northeastern U.

ADDRESS

Undergraduate Admissions
32nd and Chestnut Streets
Philadelphia, PA 19104
215-895-2400

FINANCIAL FACTS

In-state tuition ($):	10,288
Out-of-state tuition ($):	10,288
Room & board:	5,030
FA application deadline:	none
% frosh receiving FA:	80
PT earnings per yr. ($):	NA

TYPE OF AID: % of students ($)

FA of some kind:	76 (NA)
Need-based grants:	NA
Merit-based grants:	NA
Loans:	NA
Work study:	NA
Student rating of FA:	66

DUKE UNIVERSITY

Durham, NC

What do students think about Duke University?

■ **Academics** Duke students are the happiest in the nation. And why not? They attend one of the best universities in the country (said one student, "we all know it's number one!"), have access to incredible resources, inhabit a beautiful campus, and, best of all, don't work all that much harder than their peers at much less prestigious universities. In fact, the number of hours the average Duke student puts in each day—about three hours and ten minutes—is below the national average (not what you'd expect at one of *the* top schools). The undergraduate division of the school is divided in two, with a School of Engineering for engineers and the Trinity College of Arts and Sciences for everyone else. Political science, economics, history, and engineering are the favorite majors of this largely pre-professional student body, although departments are uniformly excellent. Almost half the students go on to grad school: 25% attend law school and 9% medical school. Most of the graduate programs here are world-class, yet undergrads did not report that they felt shunted aside in favor of research or graduate students.

■ **Life** Duke is divided into two main campuses separated by a mile of woodland: a shuttle bus carries students from one to the other. The campus is one of the nation's most beautiful, complete with Gothic architecture, sprawling lawns, and a forest. Durham is not popular with the students, except in the summer, when the minor league Durham Bulls play baseball and the city hosts the American Dance Festival. That hardly matters, though, since students are quite happy to spend all their time on campus. Fraternities and sororities are popular and host lots of parties; their challenging studies notwithstanding, Duke students can always find time for a few brews. The student body's first love, however, is sports, especially basketball: the Blue Devils are a perennial Division I powerhouse, and took two consecutive national championships in the early '90s. One student summed up life here this way: "When I came to visit as a prospect, a friend told me that Duke was a place where people 'work hard and play hard.' At the time that statement meant virtually nothing to me. In retrospect, it's incredibly accurate. I can't think of any other university with this incredible combination of academics, social life, weather, and Division I sports."

■ **Students** The student body here is "intellectual, yet cool, fun, and relaxed," according to one sophomore. The typical student is conservative, affluent, and white; there is a 17 percent minority population. Because of its national reputation, Duke attracts students from all over, so the student body is more diverse than that at the typical Southern school. Interaction between ethnic groups is practically non-existent, although one black student reported that "the racial situation is better here than at most Southern schools." One quality all students here share is that they are extremely bright: 90 percent graduated in the top 10 percent of their high school classes.

DUKE UNIVERSITY

Durham, NC

Admissions

Duke's *Profile* for the class of '95 notes, "Every application is reviewed by two or more readers before the candidate is presented to the full Admissions Committee. Candidates are rated on a one to five scale (with five as the highest rating) on six different categories: quality of the academic program, performance in secondary school coursework, recommendations, personal qualities, performance on standardized tests, and quality of the essays. While applicants are reviewed by the Admissions Committee by school and by region, there are no school or regional quotas." All students must either submit ACT scores or submit SAT and English Composition Achievement scores. Engineering candidates who don't take the ACT must also submit a Math I or II Achievement score. High school curriculum should include four years of English, three years of foreign language, three years of math, three years of science and two years of social studies/history."

Financial Aid

Financial aid applicants to Duke are required to complete the FAF and submit a copy of their parents' most recent tax return. The financial aid office writes, "The Duke Pledge: If you're admitted, Duke will meet 100 percent of your demonstrated financial need for all four of your undergraduate years." The average Duke freshmen receives an aid package of $11,664. One percent of Duke students last year received an AB Duke Scholarship, with an average value of $14,527, and about the same number received North Carolina Special Scholarships, each with an average value of $8,547. In '91–'92, 19% of Duke's undergrads took out Perkins loans (average value: $1,185), and the same number took out Stafford loans (average: $1,933). Duke requests that FAF materials be mailed to CSS by 2/1/93.

A note from the Duke University admissions office:

"Duke, a privately supported, church-related (Methodist) university, has over 9,000 students enrolled in degree programs. These students represent nearly every state and many foreign countries. Duke has more than 60,000 alumni in all fifty states and in many foreign countries.

"The Duke University motto, *Erudito et Religio*, reflects a fundamental faith in the union of knowledge and religion, the advancement of learning, the defense of scholarship, the love of freedom and truth, a spirit of tolerance, and a rendering of the greatest service to the individual, the state, the nation, and the church. Through changing generations of students, the objective has been to encourage individuals to achieve, the extent of their capacities, an understanding and appreciation of the world in which they live, their relationship in it, their opportunities, and their responsibilities."

ADMISSIONS FACTS

Competitiveness Rating:	**97**
% of applicants accepted:	33
% acceptees attending:	45

FRESHMAN PROFILE

Average verbal SAT:	627*
Average math SAT:	680*
Average ACT:	30*
Graduated top 10% of class:	90
Graduated top 25% of class:	99
Graduated top 50% of class:	99

DEADLINES

Early decision/action:	11/1
Early dec./act. notif.:	12/15
Regular admission:	1/1
Regular adm. notif.:	4/15

APPLICANTS ALSO LOOK AT

and often prefer:
Brown U.

and sometimes prefer:
Dartmouth College
Davidson College
Emory U.

and rarely prefer:
Wake Forest U.
Vanderbilt U.
College of William & Mary
Georgia Tech

ADDRESS

Undergraduate Admissions
2138 Campus Drive
Durham, NC 27706
919-684-3214

FINANCIAL FACTS

In-state tuition ($):	14,700
Out-of-state tuition ($):	14,700
Room & board:	4,960
FA application deadline:	2/1
% frosh receiving FA:	38
PT earnings per yr. ($):	1,700

TYPE OF AID: % of students ($)

FA of some kind:	38 (11,199)
Need-based grants:	27 (10,342)
Merit-based grants:	NA
Loans:	NA
Work study:	25 (1,494)
Student rating of FA:	76

DUQUESNE UNIVERSITY

CAMPUS LIFE

Quality of Life Rating: **77**

Type of school:	private
Affiliation:	Roman Catholic
Environment:	city

STUDENT BODY

FT undergrad enrollment:	3,926
% male/% female:	44/56
% out-of-state:	18
% live on campus:	66
% African-American:	4
% Asian:	2
% Caucasian:	88
% Hispanic:	1
% foreign:	1
% transfers:	4

WHAT'S HOT

suitcase syndrome
Top 40
location
attending all classes
doing all the reading

WHAT'S NOT

library
gay community visible
Grateful Dead
bursar

ACADEMICS

Academic Rating: **73**

Calendar:	semester
Student/teacher ratio:	17/1
% doctorates:	75
Profs interesting:	78
Profs accessible:	81
Hours of study per day:	3.09

MOST POPULAR MAJORS BY %

Business & Management:	29
Health Sciences:	19
Education:	13

% GRADS WHO PURSUE

Law:	8
MBA:	12
Medicine:	2
M.A., etc.:	28

What do students think about Duquesne University?

■ **Academics** Duquesne University is a Roman Catholic school serving a serious-minded, career-oriented student body. Almost a third of the students here study business and management. Students in the pharmacy department claim it's the university's best, while psychology, occupational therapy, and physical therapy also received students' accolades. DU's professors received good grades, and many respondents noted how helpful instructors were outside the classroom. Strong academics and supportive professors help the school overcome several shortcomings. The biggest problem is the library, described as "confusing, outdated, worthless—and poorly lit" by one student. Said another, "as for the library, plan on spending a lot of time at the University of Pittsburgh." Students also complained that, despite the school's moderate size, it's easy to get lost in the crowd: wrote one, "Duquesne is a good school if you know what you want to major in and what kind of classes you need to take. If you don't know exactly what you need, don't expect to get any help from an advisor." Registration, financial aid, and bill-paying all rated low on the national scale. Finally, students disliked the fact that there are "hidden" charges, such as student activities fees: wrote one undergrad, "everything here is à la carte—be prepared to spend a lot to get the whole deal."

■ **Life** Duquesne has made major alterations to the campus in recent years, and students are split on the issue of their campus' appearance: one wrote that it was "beautiful, and getting more so every year," while another (who felt money to upgrade campus beauty could be better spend on the library and science labs) said the changes made the school "look like an amusement park." Commuters, of whom there are many, complained that the parking situation is "terrible." The large commuter population contributes to Duquesne's subdued social scene. One student referred to DU as "the social black hole of Pittsburgh," and others voiced such opinions as "if you're not planning on going home every weekend, don't come here. There is no weekend life." Residents must deal with restrictive dorm policies ("You can't even sneeze in the dorms without getting in trouble") and a mentality that "treats all sex-related subjects as taboo, even though the students desperately need information." Still, the school is located "in the coolest part of the city (Pittsburgh). We are right downtown and have access to everything." Fraternities and sororities are popular, and students participate actively in intramural sports.

■ **Students** Over half of Duquesne's students are Catholic. Minority populations are small. Although foreign nationals make up only one percent of the student body, they are clearly a noticeable presence, because many students complained of the preferential treatment they felt internationals received.

DUQUESNE UNIVERSITY

Pittsburgh, PA

Admissions

The most recent Duquesne course catalog states that "in general, admission [to the university] is based upon past academic performance, scholastic ability, and personal character." Applicants are expected to have graduated in the upper three fifths of their high school class "and [to have] demonstrated exemplary personal conduct in that institution." Duquesne requires a high school curriculum of 16 academic units, including four years of English, eight years total of social studies, science, math, and language, and four years of electives. Applicants to pharmacy or pre-health programs must have completed seven years of math and science combined. Applicants must submit scores for either the SAT or the ACT; music students must audition.

Financial Aid

The financial aid office at Duquesne requires applicants to submit either the FAF or the FFS and a form generated by the school. Duquesne offers merit-based grants for scholastic promise and for exceptional skill in music, art, and athletics. Sophomores, juniors, and seniors are also eligible for a number of competitive scholarships (both need and merit are considered in awarding these scholarships). The school's course catalog recommends the following loan programs: Perkins, Stafford, Nursing, Health Professions, Alcoa, Gulf, Kershgens, and Power. Duquesne's most recent course catalog notes, "The Financial Aid Office *attempts* to provide aid equal to the need for all student applicants [their emphasis]."

A note from the Duquesne University Admissions Office:

"Duquesne students bring diverse backgrounds and talents to the campus community. There is no typical Duquesne student; they come from nearly every state in the nation and more than 70 foreign countries; their ages range from 17 to 77.

"There are, however, several important factors shared by all Duquesne students which receive individual consideration in admissions decisions.

"Duquesne carefully evaluates high school records and performance when considering candidates. This serious approach to academics is reflected in the fact that nearly 50 percent of last year's freshmen ranked in the top fifth of their high school class, and more than 90 percent were in the top three fifths. The University is also interested in your personal character and extracurricular activities and achievements."

ADMISSIONS FACTS

Competitiveness Rating:	**68**
% of applicants accepted:	89
% acceptees attending:	43

FRESHMAN PROFILE

Average verbal SAT:	453*
Average math SAT:	517*
Average ACT:	22
Graduated top 10% of class:	31
Graduated top 25% of class:	58
Graduated top 50% of class:	87

DEADLINES

Early decision/action:	11/15
Early dec./act. notif.:	12/15
Regular admission:	7/1
Regular adm. notif.:	rolling

APPLICANTS ALSO LOOK AT

and often prefer:
West Virginia U.
Penn State U.

and sometimes prefer:
Ohio State U.
Marquette U.

and rarely prefer:
U. Pittsburgh

ADDRESS

Undergraduate Admissions
600 Forbes Avenue
Pittsburgh, PA 15282
412-434-6220

FINANCIAL FACTS

In-state tuition ($):	8,850
Out-of-state tuition ($):	8,850
Room & board:	4,318
FA application deadline:	NA
% frosh receiving FA:	78
PT earnings per yr. ($):	1,700

TYPE OF AID: % of students ($)

FA of some kind:	75 (NA)
Need-based grants:	NA
Merit-based grants:	NA
Loans:	NA
Work study:	NA
Student rating of FA:	72

197

ECKERD COLLEGE

CAMPUS LIFE

Quality of Life Rating: **81**

Type of school:	private
Affiliation:	Presbyterian
Environment:	city

STUDENT BODY

FT undergrad enrollment:	1,342
% male/% female:	47/53
% out-of-state:	69
% live on campus:	80
% African-American:	2
% Asian:	2
% Caucasian:	92
% Hispanic:	3
% foreign:	9
% transfers:	4

WHAT'S HOT

interaction among students
financial aid
alternative rock
small lectures
dating
campus is easy to get
   around

WHAT'S NOT

fraternities/sororities
food
library
religious clubs

ACADEMICS

Academic Rating: **81**

Calendar:	4-1-4
Student/teacher ratio:	11/1
% doctorates:	84
Profs interesting:	83
Profs accessible:	84
Hours of study per day:	3.61

MOST POPULAR MAJORS BY %

Management:	18
Biology:	15
Psychology:	12

% GRADS WHO PURSUE

Law:	8
MBA:	12
Medicine:	8
M.A., etc.:	20

What do students think about Eckerd College?

■ **Academics** Looking for a challenging, progressive liberal arts education that doesn't include bitter-cold Northeast winters? Some like-minded students have chosen Eckerd College in St. Petersburg, Florida. Given this school's unique blend of personal attention, quality studies, and beautiful surroundings, you have to wonder why more haven't done the same. A powerful sense of community influences the Eckerd experience. Students here enjoy close contact with their professors. (Wrote one, "The chance to interact with professors is probably what's best about Eckerd. Profs are all very accessible here.") Furthermore, the school has an Academy of Senior Professionals, made up of retired doctors, lawyers, businessmen, etc., who lead seminars in their professional fields and also attend undergraduate classes with the "younger" students. Eckerd also has a mandatory January term, during which students pursue independent study. All students at Eckerd undergo a tough battery of core requirements, including several inter-disciplinary seminars and courses in verbal and quantitative proficiency. One enthusiastic student asserted that "this school offers the best, I mean the best, all-around education." As proof, he might have mentioned that almost half the undergraduates here proceed to graduate school within a year of graduation. Pre-professional studies are strong, as are education and the marine sciences.

■ **Life** The student who wrote that "Eckerd is a country club" couldn't have been referring to the food (it rated among the worst in the country) or the level of academic intensity (students here take their work very seriously). Perhaps she was referring to the marina campus with a beach "five minutes away by foot," or to the "awesome" weather, or perhaps to the "laid-back, non-competitive atmosphere." A family atmosphere prevails here; students are even allowed to have pets in some dorms. The school is small, and because of that, according to one student, "one can participate in many different kinds of activities. In the four years I've been here, I've gotten involved in the school newspaper, T.V. station, radio station, student government, chorus, theater, and faculty committees. I never could have done that at a huge institution." Drinking is very popular; one student reported that "most, if not all, of our activities revolve around alcohol." The city of St. Petersburg, unfortunately, "has nothing to do. Tampa has clubs and other stuff, but you need a car to get there."

■ **Students** Eckerd's small student body is almost entirely made up of white students; the minority population is eight percent, or about one hundred students. Fewer than one third of the students are from Florida; many others come from the Northeast. Three quarters of the students receive financial aid, so the student body does have economic diversity. One student noted that "the student body is very well balanced, diversified, and accepting while at the same time most students share an interest and concern with the natural environment."

ECKERD COLLEGE

St. Petersburg, FL

Admissions

The admissions office at Eckerd College writes, "We do not use cut-off points or statistical formulae. We do review carefully all materials submitted by an applicant, whether we required/requested them or not. Beyond the solid academic credentials, we are seeking evidence of leadership and service." Eckerd first considers an applicant's high school GPA and the selection and quality of high school courses taken. After these, in order of importance, are extracurriculars, essays, letters of recommendation, and standardized test scores. All applicants must take either the SAT or ACT, and should have completed at least four years of English, three years of lab science, three years of history /social science, two years of foreign language, and math through Algebra II. Applicants to Eckerd also often apply to U. of Florida, Rollins, Stetson, U. of Miami, Florida State, and U. of South Florida.

Financial Aid

The financial aid office at Eckerd College requires either the FAF or the FFS (the FAF is the preferred form). The school awards merit scholarships for a wide range of skills including athletics, academics, and artistic talent. Last year 82% of all students accepted for the freshman class applied for financial aid, and all but a handful received an award of some kind.

A note from the Eckerd College Admissions Office:

"Eckerd College students come from 49 states and 54 countries. They are attracted to this international environment and participate extensively in our study abroad programs. International business and international studies majors are popular here. Eckerd is located in a beautiful, tropical, waterfront setting which has enabled us to develop one of the strongest marine science majors in the country. New marine science and necropsy labs are currently under construction. Eckerd students share a sense of community and enjoy considerable freedom for individual decision making. Volunteer service is common for Eckerd students, and many are deeply involved in social, political, and environmental issues. We characterize Eckerd students as 'competent givers'."

ADMISSIONS FACTS

Competitiveness Rating:	**72**
% of applicants accepted:	68
% acceptees attending:	36

FRESHMAN PROFILE

Average verbal SAT:	512
Average math SAT:	554
Average ACT:	24
Graduated top 10% of class:	31
Graduated top 25% of class:	58
Graduated top 50% of class:	86

DEADLINES

Early decision/action:	NA
Early dec./act. notif.:	NA
Regular admission:	rolling
Regular adm. notif.:	rolling

APPLICANTS ALSO LOOK AT

and often prefer:
Rollins College
U. Florida

and sometimes prefer:
Stetson U.
U. Miami
Florida State U.

and rarely prefer:
U. of South

ADDRESS

Undergraduate Admissions
4200 54th Street South
St. Petersburg, FL 33711
813-864-8331

FINANCIAL FACTS

In-state tuition ($):	12,900
Out-of-state tuition ($):	12,900
Room & board:	3,210
FA application deadline:	NA
% frosh receiving FA:	75
PT earnings per yr. ($):	1,000

TYPE OF AID: % of students ($)

FA of some kind:	80 (8,700)
Need-based grants:	43 (7,782)
Merit-based grants:	36 (8,200)
Loans:	41 (3,538)
Work study:	30 (1,000)
Student rating of FA:	88

EMERSON COLLEGE

CAMPUS LIFE

Quality of Life Rating:	**75**
Type of school:	private
Affiliation:	none
Environment:	city

STUDENT BODY

FT undergrad enrollment:	1,912
% male/% female:	39/61
% out-of-state:	60
% live on campus:	50
% African-American:	5
% Asian:	1
% Caucasian:	92
% Hispanic:	2
% foreign:	4
% transfers:	9

WHAT'S HOT

college radio station
college theater groups
gay community accepted
location
small classes (overall)
alternative rock
marijuana
leftist politics
in-class discussion

WHAT'S NOT

intercollegiate sports
intramural sports
studying hard
administration (overall)
religion

ACADEMICS

Academic Rating:	**69**
Calendar:	semester
Student/teacher ratio:	17/1
% doctorates:	65
Profs interesting:	76
Profs accessible:	76
Hours of study per day:	2.54

MOST POPULAR MAJORS BY %

Communications:	67
Visual & Performing Arts:	17
Letters/Literature:	14

What do students think about Emerson College?

■ **Academics** Emerson Collee is named after 19th century scholar Charles Wesley Emerson, but, considering the school's emphasis on communication, it could just as easily be named after the company that dominated radio manufacturing during that medium's "Golden Age." Although 14 percent of the students major in liberal arts, communications and performing arts are Emerson's specialty. According to many of the students, Emerson is "the best hands-on school in America for students of television, film, theater, writing, and radio." Said another, "experience is what Emerson is all about." Accordingly, students devote relatively little time to conventional college studying (e.g. reading, writing papers, etc.). That doesn't mean they're not devoted to their school work, though. "We compete like hell," wrote one student. "Emerson is the Ivy League for misfits." Students are extremely satisfied with class sizes ("more than ideal") and the quality of their classmates. (Wrote one public relations major, "The talent here is endless. I've never been so happy.") On the negative side, students have an unusually contentious relationship with the school's administration, whom they portray as unresponsive to student input. Given the artistic temperament of the typical student and the unwieldy price tag for attending Emerson, it's easy to see how such frustrations could arise.

■ **Life** One of Emerson's great drawing cards is the city of Boston, to which students gave high marks. Reportedly, however, the school is planning to move out to the suburbs in the not-too-distant future. For the time being, at least, the school remains "a great institution for an individual who doesn't mind exchanging a city for no campus." Time outside the classroom is often spent working in the school's radio and television stations and theatres, although students also find the time to hit the town. There is, surprisingly, a Greek scene here; unsurprisingly, the school's athletic teams are practically ignored by students.

■ **Students** Emerson students perceive themselves as outsiders. Said one, "Emerson is a school for people who didn't fit in in high school. We're all misfits and freaks." Wrote another, "at Emerson there's a certain freedom of thought and expression. You could go to classes naked if you really wanted to and people would probably accept it…well, *maybe* not." A few dissenters accused their fellow students of being posers. Said one, "Emerson definitely needs more hippies and mellow-seeking individuals. The people here are mainly concerned with what is not important, that is, looks and talk." Students claim diversity, but the student body is 92 percent white. In terms of politics, as one student put it, "the mainstream remain politically correct." There is a considerable gay population.

EMERSON COLLEGE

Admissions

Most important in your application to Emerson is your record of academic achievement. Emerson's undergraduate catalog states that, "under normal circumstances," freshman applicants are expected to have completed four years of English, and at least two years each of mathematics, science, and social science. In addition, two years of a single foreign language are recommended. All applicants must submit SAT or ACT scores. Interviews are not required, but are strongly recommended. Admissions decisions are made on a rolling basis, so applicants are encouraged to submit their materials as early in the senior year as possible. Priority is given to applications received by February 1.

Financial Aid

The financial aid office at Emerson College requires applicants to submit the FAF, a form generated by the school, their parents' most recent tax return, and supporting materials "as requested by the aid officer." The school awards merit grants on the basis of previous academic achievement; a few partial scholarships are also available to writers and those involved in the dramatic arts. Last year, Emerson students borrowed on the following loan programs: Stafford, Perkins, FEL, PLUS, SLS, and TERI. Several installment tuition-payment plans are available.

Excerpted from Emerson College promotional materials:

"Founded in 1880 by Charles Wesley Emerson, noted preacher, orator and teacher, Emerson has grown into a college offering its more than 2,600 students comprehensive undergraduate and graduate curricula in the communication arts and sciences and the performing arts. From the original concentration on oratory have evolved specialization in such fields as mass communication (radio and television broadcasting, film and journalism), theatre arts, communication studies, communication disorders, American culture and communication, writing, literature and publishing.

"As the issues facing business, industry and government grow larger and more complex, effective communication will grow more important, even crucial. Emerson today is preparing to educate those men and women who will bear the burden of that communication in the next century. Emerson college is accredited by New England Association of Schools and Colleges, Inc., and is a member of the Council of Graduate Schools."

ADMISSIONS FACTS

Competitiveness Rating:	**65**
% of applicants accepted:	71
% acceptees attending:	35

FRESHMAN PROFILE

Average verbal SAT:	501
Average math SAT:	490
Average ACT:	NA
Graduated top 10% of class:	16
Graduated top 25% of class:	44
Graduated top 50% of class:	81

DEADLINES

Early decision/action:	NA
Early dec./act. notif.:	NA
Regular admission:	rolling
Regular adm. notif.:	4/1

APPLICANTS ALSO LOOK AT

and sometimes prefer:

Boston U.

NYU

Syracuse U.

and rarely prefer:

U. Mass–Amherst

Ithaca College

ADDRESS

Undergraduate Admissions
100 Beacon Street
Boston, MA 02116
617-578-8600

FINANCIAL FACTS

In-state tuition ($):	12,695
Out-of-state tuition ($):	12,695
Room & board:	7,207
FA application deadline:	3/1
% frosh receiving FA:	75
PT earnings per yr. ($):	1,700

TYPE OF AID: % of students ($)

FA of some kind:	75 (NA)
Need-based grants:	NA (5,719)
Merit-based grants:	7 (2,400)
Loans:	55 (5,535)
Work study:	30 (1,300)
Student rating of FA:	82

CAMPUS LIFE

Quality of Life Rating:	**83**
Type of school:	private
Affiliation:	Methodist
Environment:	city

STUDENT BODY

FT undergrad enrollment:	4,635
% male/% female:	47/53
% out-of-state:	75
% live on campus:	68
% African-American:	7
% Asian:	5
% Caucasian:	82
% Hispanic:	2
% foreign:	4
% transfers:	2

WHAT'S HOT

location
food
gay community visible
dorm comfort
financial aid
college newspaper
hard liquor

WHAT'S NOT

intercollegiate sports
interaction
attending all classes

ACADEMICS

Academic Rating:	**84**
Calendar:	semester
Student/teacher ratio:	13/1
% doctorates:	94
Profs interesting:	73
Profs accessible:	73
Hours of study per day:	3.15

MOST POPULAR MAJORS

Biology
Business
Psychology

% GRADS WHO PURSUE

Law:	12
MBA:	5
Medicine:	10
M.A., etc.:	22

What do students think about Emory University?

■ **Academics** Emory University has been touted as the South's "up-and-coming" contender for Ivy League students for so long that one student complained, "I am sick and tired of Emory being simply an up-and-coming school. It is already one of the nation's truly great undergraduate programs." Backing up this assertion is Emory's impressive record with graduate schools: nearly half of Emory's graduates proceed to some graduate program, and nearly one in 10 goes on to medical school. "Pre-med is by far the most popular path for students, making this a very cutthroat university," wrote one student. Also impressive are the university's constantly expanding facilities, particularly in the physical and life sciences. All Emory students must complete a variety of distribution requirements with an emphasis on literature, history, and aesthetics: between these and mandatory major courses, Emory students spend more than half their tenure fulfilling requirements. Teachers received average grades. Explained one student, "there are some REAL TEACHERS who connect and interact with their students, and there are some lemons. I recommend taking the initiative to find out who the good teachers are and scheduling accordingly." Most students agree that Emory is a Southern anomaly in that it has an "unusually fast-paced faculty and student body." One frequent knock on the university, in fact, is that it's a pre-professional factory. Wrote one student, "academically, this school is challenging but not intellectually stimulating. One is hard-pressed to find an intellectual group of students discussing a political or academic issue. It seems like they're more concerned with their GPAs than with what they've learned."

■ **Life** Emory provides its students with both the comfort of an expansive, wooded campus and access to Atlanta, the South's version of a Northern city. While the city of Atlanta "has a lot to offer students," most students seem content to confine their social lives to campus. The Greek system is dominant, to the chagrin of many. Wrote one student, "the Greek system detracts from the quality of the school—I can say this because I'm in a sorority (because it seems like a necessity, not because it's my first priority)." Agreed another, "I'm in a sorority because if I wasn't, I'd know very few people." Students told us that intramural sports and clubs are popular diversions. Said one, "there are countless opportunities to participate in diverse extracurricular activities such as clubs and school-sponsored social events." Leftist political groups "are pretty active, which is necessary because of the number of conservative jerks that abound here."

■ **Students** Emory has cornered the Southern market on Jewish students, New Jerseyites, and New Yorkers. Wrote one native Ohioan, "it's hard to hear a Southern accent here above all the New York twangs." Minority students are fairly well represented. There is a large and active gay community. One member wrote, "while there is a homophobia problem, it's liberating to be part of such an active community."

EMORY UNIVERSITY

Atlanta, GA

Admissions

The admissions office reports that "admissions at Emory is very selective. The Admissions Committee evaluates applicants on the basis of secondary school records, SAT or ACT scores, and recommendations from teachers and counselors." Applicants are required to have completed four years of high school English, two years of algebra and one of geometry, and a minimum of two years of a foreign language. Furthermore, at least two years of social science, three years of lab science, and another year of math are strongly recommended. Emory "seeks student who have not only academic ability, but also taken and diversity. Students are encouraged to provide an overall view of themselves in their application, including extracurricular activities and interests and academic goals." Students who apply to Emory most often also apply to Duke, Vanderbilt, Washington U., UVA, UNC–Chapel Hill, and Tulane.

Financial Aid

Applicants for financial aid at Emory must complete the FAF and submit a copy of their parents' tax form. Last year about 13% of Emory's entering freshmen received academic scholarships, with an average value of $11,000. Emory's merit scholarships include "Courtesy" scholarships, for employee dependents, and scholarships for children of Methodist clergy. The average values of these last year were, for "courtesy," $14,580 (full tuition), and for Methodist children, $6,561. In addition to Stafford loans, Emory offers "Title IV" loans, and many state and private loans. One interesting note: the work-study program includes jobs in off-campus organizations such as the Centers for Disease Control and the Carter Presidential Center. Priority deadline is February 15.

A note from the Emory University Admissions Office:

"The combination Emory offers you is really a rarity in today's college marketplace. As an Emory student, you can still have the benefits of a small liberal arts college, such as intimacy and personal attention, while enjoying the wider opportunities found in a major university. Emory College is the four-year undergraduate division of the university and provides a broad, rigorous liberal arts curriculum. At the same time, Emory University, with its nine major divisions, numerous centers for advanced study, and a host of prestigious affiliated institutions, provides the larger context, thus enriching your total college experience."

ADMISSIONS FACTS

Competitiveness Rating:	**81**
% of applicants accepted:	66
% acceptees attending:	29

FRESHMAN PROFILE

Average verbal SAT:	570
Average math SAT:	630
Average ACT:	27
Graduated top 10% of class:	33
Graduated top 25% of class:	80
Graduated top 50% of class:	93

DEADLINES

Early decision/action:	11/15
Early dec./act. notif.:	12/15
Regular admission:	2/1
Regular adm. notif.:	4/1

APPLICANTS ALSO LOOK AT

and often prefer:
U. Pennsylvania
Northwestern U.
Duke U.

and sometimes prefer:
Wake Forest U.
Washington U.
Dartmouth College

and rarely prefer:
Tufts U.
Southern Methodist U.

ADDRESS

Undergraduate Admissions
409 Administration Bldg.
Atlanta, GA 30322
404-727-6036

FINANCIAL FACTS

In-state tuition ($):	14,580
Out-of-state tuition ($):	14,580
Room & board:	4,532
FA application deadline:	4/1
% frosh receiving FA:	53
PT earnings per yr. ($):	1,300

TYPE OF AID: % of students ($)

FA of some kind:	53 (NA)
Need-based grants:	32 (8,000)
Merit-based grants:	NA
Loans:	43 (2,645)
Work study:	25 (1080)
Student rating of FA:	89

EUGENE LANG COLLEGE

New York, NY

What do students think about the Eugene Lang College?

■ **Academics** The Eugene Lang College, the undergraduate division of the New School for Social Research, is best suited to the needs of independent, politically progressive undergraduates whose interests lie primarily in the liberal arts and social sciences. Within those tight parameters, Lang serves its students superbly, providing them with both limitless autonomy in fashioning their curricula (there are no required courses) and a tremendous amount of personal attention, as all classes are taught in seminar format with class sizes limited to 16. Wrote one student, "Students are treated with respect; there is almost no supervision, so one must take total responsibility for success." Most students concentrate in writing and literature after freshman year, although other fields of concentration, ranging from the conventional (such as political science and history) to the unconventional (political anthropology, science, technology and power) are also available. Lang's faculty is necessarily limited, by the school's small size (only 300 students) but students can supplement their Lang studies with courses at Cooper Union, Parsons School of Design, Mannes School of Music, and NYU. Courses at the New School's Adult Division and Graduate Faculty are also open to all but freshmen. The school's unconventional approach is not for everyone: explained one discouraged undergrad, "What have I learned here? I understand how society works, that I have no place in it, and that few job opportunities await me upon graduation. Take note: very few credits from here are transferable, should you decide to leave." Still, most students here thrive on the school's alternative approach and would probably be less happy anywhere else. Summed up one, "This is a place where education is something you claim and desire on your own. Learning isn't thrust upon you—you seize it!"

■ **Life** Explained one student, "There is very little social interaction between Lang students once they are out of the dorms, which for most students is after freshman year." Another added, "If you don't live in a dorm, you won't make friends easily." In short, there is no campus social life at Lang. Most students claim that their best friends are people outside the school. Fortunately, Lang is located in the heart of New York's Greenwich Village, "an excellent place for students." Bars, shops, and all varieties of night life are plentiful and within walking distance of the building that *is* Lang's "campus." About New York City, another student noted that "internships in all fields (from shipbuilding to fashion, business and finance to music, etc.) are readily available to Lang students."

■ **Students** The vast majority of Lang students define the concept of "politically correct." One student complained that students are "overwhelmingly 'politically correct'; it sometimes borders on absurdity." Said another, "Students are certainly not politically diverse. The uniformity of political thought is somewhat depressing." The minority population is scant, prompting several complaints from both white and minority respondents.

EUGENE LANG COLLEGE

Admissions

The admissions office reports: "The College seeks students who combine inquisitiveness and seriousness of purpose with the ability to engage in a distinctive, rigorous liberal arts program." Admissions adds further that "We do not use any 'cut-offs.' Each applicant is evaluated on the merit of academic and supporting credentials. A two-part ranking is created as a result." High school curriculum/GPA is the most important component of your application here, followed, in order of decreasing importance, recommendation, essays, interview, test scores, and extracurricular activities. Arts students must complete a home exam and submit a portfolio; jazz applicants must audition. The school requires no specific high school courses, but suggests "adequate preparation [including] English, history, social science, foreign languages, math, and science." Applicants must submit SAT, ACT, or achievement test scores. Applicants to Eugene Lang are often also applicants to NYU, Hampshire, Bard, Sarah Lawrence, and Bennington.

Financial Aid

Financial aid for the Eugene Lang College and the Parsons School of Design is administered through the offices of its parent university, the New School for Social Research. The financial aid office requires applicants to submit the FAF, a form generated by the school, and their parents' most recent tax return. The school reports that "Scholarship decisions are based on a combination of need and merit." Lang/Parsons students last year participated in the following loan programs: Stafford (60% of the students took such a loan; average value: $3,100), Perkins (20%; $1,000), and SLS (5%; $4,000).

A note from the Eugene Lang College Admissions Office:

"Eugene Lang College offers students an innovative approach to a liberal arts education, combining the stimulating classroom activity of a small, personal college with the rich resources of a dynamic, urban university, the New School of Social Research. It offers a rigorous yet flexible academic program, individually designed in consultation with a faculty advisor. Within the College, classes are conducted in small seminars of no more than 15 students. Our small class size allows you to participate in energetic and thoughtful discussions. You will find that your ideas are welcomed and your most creative thinking is encouraged in this setting.

"The liberal arts curriculum of Eugene Lang College is innovative and creative: many Lang courses explore topics that cross traditional academic boundaries and approach classic texts and traditional subjects from new perspectives. It is challenging and demanding; the small classes, the emphasis on reading primary texts, the use of writing and revision as a way of learning—these are hallmarks of the Lang educational program."

ADMISSIONS FACTS

Competitiveness Rating:	**70**
% of applicants accepted:	85
% acceptees attending:	37

FRESHMAN PROFILE

Average verbal SAT:	550
Average math SAT:	520
Average ACT:	24*
Graduated top 10% of class:	21
Graduated top 25% of class:	61
Graduated top 50% of class:	88

DEADLINES

Early decision/action:	11/15
Early dec./act. notif.:	12/15
Regular admission:	2/1
Regular adm. notif.:	4/1

APPLICANTS ALSO LOOK AT

and often prefer:
Bennington College
CUNY–Hunter
CUNY–Brooklyn College

and sometimes prefer:
Bard College
Sarah Lawrence College

and rarely prefer:
Reed College
Hampshire College

ADDRESS

Undergraduate Admissions
65 West 11th Street
New York, NY 10011
212-229-5600

FINANCIAL FACTS

In-state tuition ($):	11,794
Out-of-state tuition ($):	11,794
Room & board:	4,460
FA application deadline:	rolling
% frosh receiving FA:	NA
PT earnings per yr. ($):	NA

TYPE OF AID: % of students ($)

FA of some kind:	NA (9,000)
Need-based grants:	58 (3,143)
Merit-based grants:	NA
Loans:	NA
Work study:	30 (2,000)
Student rating of FA:	86

FAIRFIELD UNIVERSITY

Fairfield, CT

What do students think about Fairfield University?

■ **Academics** Independent college counselors from the Connecticut area told us that Fairfield University, "like many Catholic schools, is making remarkable improvements." Several cited the school's excellent business programs, and most mentioned the school's beautiful campus. For whatever reason, Fairfield students are pleased with what the school offers: they ranked among the top 30 percent among the nation's happiest student bodies. Fairfield offers the rigors and intimacy of a private school education at a cost that is low for a private school (although still very high by public school standards). A demanding core curriculum requires students to receive an extremely broad education, including, of course, religious instruction (this is, after all, a Jesuit school). Classes are small; professors are relatively good teachers and make themselves reasonably accessible outside the classroom. Career and pre-professional majors are popular here, as are English and political science.

■ **Life** Fairfield students have a reputation as drinkers, a reputation borne out by the results of our survey. Wrote one student, "When it comes to social life, non-alcoholic events are rare and unexciting when they do occur." Life doesn't begin and end in bars and dorm parties, however; as one student told us, "If you like to drink, Fairfield is the place to be. Also, for people who do not drink, there are several events throughout the week to keep them happy. It is a well-rounded university." Intramural and intercollegiate sports are popular, and opportunities to become involved in Catholic religious and community service groups abound. There are no fraternities or sororities. Students gave Fairfield high marks in several quality-of-life categories, rating the campus beautiful and easy to get around, and the dorms safe and comfortable. Students gave low marks to the food and to the town of Fairfield, although several recommended the nearby beach on Long Island Sound enthusiastically.

■ **Students** Fairfield is over 90 percent white, and most students fit the "white, preppy, Catholic" mold pretty well. As one student explained, "Fairfield is extremely homogeneous and the student body, on the whole, is not very accepting of non-traditional Irish Catholic viewpoints." Said another bluntly, "You can almost count on your hand the number of black students and most of them are here on basketball scholarships." Most students mentioned the lack of diversity among students, and many trashed their fellow students as "closed-minded yuppie wannabes." So many of our respondents complained about this typical Fairfield student that we had to wonder how many "typical Fairfield students" there could be. More likely, Fairfield students see their classmates weaknesses more readily than they see their own. No wonder one student wrote that "unity among students at Fairfield is definitely not one of the university's strong points." Ironically, students identified themselves as being pretty religious: whatever virtues they may be cultivating, charity is not large among them.

FAIRFIELD UNIVERSITY

Fairfield, CT

Admissions

The admissions office at Fairfield University looks primarily at your high school curriculum and transcript. Extracurricular activities are considered next most important, followed in importance by standardized test scores and letters of recommendations. Neither essays nor an interview are part of the Fairfield application process. Applicants are required to have completed four years of English, three years each of science and math, and two years of a foreign language. Either SAT or ACT results are required. Achievement exams, while not required, are recommended to facilitate class placement of those accepted. Applicants to Fairfield most often also apply to Boston College, Providence College, Villanova, and University of Connecticut.

Financial Aid

Fairfield requires financial aid applicants to complete the FAF and, after the award is confirmed, to submit copies of their own and their parents' tax forms. Last year Fairfield awarded athletic scholarships to 54 students with an average value of $12,500. Three percent of all undergrads received an academic scholarship (average value not available), and awards for merit in glee club and drama went to 11 students (average value: $1,950). Twenty-five percent of all undergrads took out Stafford loans (average value: $2,970) in '91–'92.

A note from the Fairfield University Admissions Office:

"Fairfield University says of itself that its primary objectives are to develop the creative intellectual potential of its students and to foster in them ethical and religious values and a sense of social responsibility. Fairfield recognizes that learning is a lifelong process and sees the education which it provides as a foundation upon which its students may continue to build within their chosen areas of scholarly study or professional development. It also seeks to foster in its students a continuing intellectual curiosity and a desire for self-education which will extend to the broad range of areas to which they have been introduced in their studies.

"The key to the lifelong process of learning which Fairfield seeks to foster is its core curriculum (60 credits), designed to introduce all students to the broad range of liberal learning. The core helps some students discover where their interests truly lie and conveys a broad understanding that makes them more flexible even in their areas of specialty.

"All members of the faculty at Fairfield teach. This is their primary responsibility, one that is not trimmed for research interests. Classes are never taught by graduate students. Senior professors teach many introductory courses, sure evidence of the faculty's commitment to teaching."

ADMISSIONS FACTS

Competitiveness Rating:	**82**
% of applicants accepted:	49
% acceptees attending:	31

FRESHMAN PROFILE

Average verbal SAT:	521
Average math SAT:	586
Average ACT:	25
Graduated top 10% of class:	35
Graduated top 25% of class:	77
Graduated top 50% of class:	98

DEADLINES

Early decision/action:	12/1
Early dec./act. notif.:	1/1
Regular admission:	3/1
Regular adm. notif.:	4/1

APPLICANTS ALSO LOOK AT

and often prefer:
Georgetown U.
College of the Holy Cross
Trinity College
Boston College

and sometimes prefer:
Villanova U.
Fordham U.
U. Mass–Amherst
U. Connecticut

and rarely prefer:
Syracuse U.

ADDRESS

Undergraduate Admissions
North Benson Road
Fairfield, CT 06430-7524
203-254-4100

FINANCIAL FACTS

In-state tuition ($):	12,650
Out-of-state tuition ($):	12,650
Room & board:	5,350
FA application deadline:	2/1
% frosh receiving FA:	65
PT earnings per yr. ($):	1,200

TYPE OF AID: % of students ($)	
FA of some kind:	65 (NA)
Need-based grants:	35 (5,700)
Merit-based grants:	NA
Loans:	NA
Work study:	7 (1,200)
Student rating of FA:	72

FISK UNIVERSITY

CAMPUS LIFE

Quality of Life Rating: **70**

Type of school:	private
Affiliation:	Church of Christ
Environment:	city

STUDENT BODY

FT undergrad enrollment:	891
% male/% female:	28/72
% out-of-state:	80
% live on campus:	95
% African-American:	96
% Asian:	3
% Caucasian:	<1
% Hispanic:	<1
% foreign:	5
% transfers:	NA

WHAT'S HOT

rap/hip-hop
small lectures
religion
leftist politics
doing all assigned reading
attending all classes
cost of living
dating

WHAT'S NOT

diversity
intramural sports
alternative rock
intercollegiate sports
food

ACADEMICS

Academic Rating: **72**

Calendar:	semester
Student/teacher ratio:	15/1
% doctorates:	78
Profs interesting:	87
Profs accessible:	79
Hours of study per day:	3.36

MOST POPULAR MAJORS BY %

Business & Management:	20
Law:	15
Life Sciences:	10

% GRADS WHO PURSUE

Law:	10
MBA:	10
Medicine:	20
M.A., etc.:	20

What do students think about Fisk University?

■ **Academics** Although it may not be as famous as Howard or Tuskegee universities, Fisk boasts a record its main competitors for black students can't touch: over half of Fisk's graduates go on to graduate school within a year of graduation. It is much smaller than either of those other two schools, and admissions accordingly are more competitive. Despite its small size, an excellent, well-rounded education is readily available at Fisk, as Fiskites constantly reminded us. "Educationally, Fisk is an excellent school," reported one undergrad. "The professors really care about us as students and as people. The personal attention we receive from our instructors is great. Fisk provides me with the small classroom atmosphere and the role models I need to succeed." Black perspectives are emphasized in all classes; one student told us that "Fisk University teaches young black Americans not only how to survive in the future but also how our ancestors survived the past." The liberal arts are popular here, as are business administration and pre-law programs. Most complaints we heard concerned administrators ("very uncooperative," said one student) and the fact that "a lack of resources restricts complete educational enrichment." Also, it can be difficult to study at the library, which serves as a campus social center. Still, few schools are attended by such adamant boosters (see "Students," below).

■ **Life** The most attractive aspect of life at Fisk is the sense of community fostered by its size. "Fisk has a family-type atmosphere. Students here interact well with each other, as well as with members of the community," is how one student put it. The campus is currently undergoing necessary renovations: both the dorms and campus received low marks from students. Also, the food here is bad, even by institutional standards (students ranked their food 16th worst of all the schools we surveyed). Unlike most city dwelling students, Fiskites are not crazy about their hometown of Nashville. One student informed us that "it's hard to do anything outdoors because we are located in a bad area, but we still have fun in the dorms."

■ **Students** Although the administration, social life, and living conditions could be better, Fisk students almost unanimously sing the praise of their university: "Fisk...forever!" is their rallying cry. Comments such as "I'll send my children to Fisk and their children, too, if it is left up to me" were the rule rather than the exception. Students feel that, when all is said and done, they are getting an excellent education in an African-American setting, and that the importance of that cannot be overemphasized. The typical Fiskite is politically liberal, socially conservative, religious, serious about study, and holds his fellow students in high regard. As one student summed it up, "Fisk University, like many others, has its problems. On the whole, though, it is excellent, and I can honestly say that the best and the brightest of the black community are being educated here."

FISK UNIVERSITY

Admissions

Fisk University "seeks to enroll men and women who will benefit from a liberal arts experience, designed to equip them for intellectual and social leadership. It is the policy of Fisk University to grant admission to applicants showing evidence of adequate preparation and the ability to successfully pursue college studies at Fisk." The Fisk application includes an essay. Fisk requires applicants to have successfully completed the following high school curriculum: four years of English; one year each of algebra, geometry, foreign language, history, lab science; and six years of academic electives. Letters of recommendation from a principal, headmaster, counselor or teacher "in regard to your academic ability, motivation, character, citizenship, and leadership qualities" are strongly recommended. Applicants are required to take either the SAT or the ACT.

Financial Aid

The financial aid office at Fisk University requires applicants to submit the FAF and a form generated by the school. Fisk awards merit grants for scholastic excellence. The following criteria must be met by any Fisk scholarship recipient: a minimum high school GPA of 3.0; a minimum score on the SAT of 950 (combined) or, on the ACT, 23 (composite); and, rank in the upper third of his/her graduating class. Last year, Fisk students borrowed on the following loan programs: Stafford, Perkins, and PLUS/SLS.

A note from the Fisk University Admissions Office:

"Founded in 1866, the University is coeducational, private, and one of America's older historically black universities. It serves a national student body, with an enrollment of more than 900 students for academic year 1990–91. (There are two residence halls for men and three for women.) The focal point of the 40-acre campus and architectural symbol of the University is Jubilee Hall, the first permanent building for the education of blacks in the South. The Victorian-Gothic structure is named for the internationally renowned Fisk Jubilee Singers, who continue their tradition of singing the Negro spiritual. The original Jubilee Singers toured this country and abroad in 1871. Their selflessness is the saga of Fisk.

"From its earliest days, Fisk has played a leadership role in the education of African-Americans. Faculty and alumni have been among America's intellectual, artistic, and civil leaders. Among them are W.E.B. DuBois, the great social critic and cofounder of the NAACP, and the distinguished artist of the Harlem Renaissance, Aaron Douglas, who taught at Fisk. In proportion to its size, Fisk continues to contribute more alumni to the ranks of scholars pursuing doctoral degrees than any other institution in the United States."

ADMISSIONS FACTS

Competitiveness Rating:	**76**
% of applicants accepted:	60
% acceptees attending:	47

FRESHMAN PROFILE

Average verbal SAT:	422
Average math SAT:	447
Average ACT:	20
Graduated top 10% of class:	40
Graduated top 25% of class:	75
Graduated top 50% of class:	99

DEADLINES

Early decision/action:	NA
Early dec./act. notif.:	NA
Regular admission:	6/15
Regular adm. notif.:	rolling

APPLICANTS ALSO LOOK AT

and often prefer:
Howard U.
Morehouse College
Spelman College

and sometimes prefer:
Vanderbilt U.
Penn State U.

and rarely prefer:
Clark U.

ADDRESS

Undergraduate Admissions
1000 17th Ave. North
Nashville, TN 37208
615-329-8666

FINANCIAL FACTS

In-state tuition ($):	4,950
Out-of-state tuition ($):	4,950
Room & board:	3,050
FA application deadline:	4/20
% frosh receiving FA:	70
PT earnings per yr. ($):	1,100

TYPE OF AID: % of students ($)

FA of some kind:	83 (NA)
Need-based grants:	NA
Merit-based grants:	NA
Loans:	NA
Work study:	NA
Student rating of FA:	80

UNIVERSITY OF FLORIDA

CAMPUS LIFE

Quality of Life Rating: **81**

Type of school:	public
Affiliation:	none
Environment:	urban

STUDENT BODY

FT undergrad enrollment:	22,904
% male/% female:	53/47
% out-of-state:	9
% live on campus:	28
% African-American:	6
% Asian:	4
% Caucasian:	82
% Hispanic:	6
% foreign:	2
% transfers:	11

WHAT'S HOT
dating
college newspaper
intercollegiate sports
good-looking students
profs lecture a lot
hard liquor
Top 40
rap/hip-hop
beer
marijuana

WHAT'S NOT
small classes (overall)
studying hard
profs outside class
profs in class

ACADEMICS

Academic Rating: **76**

Calendar:	semester
Student/teacher ratio:	17/1
% doctorates:	99
Profs interesting:	78
Profs accessible:	82
Hours of study per day:	2.96

MOST POPULAR MAJORS BY %

Business & Management:	18
Communications:	13
Social Sciences:	12

What do students think about the University of Florida?

■ **Academics** Excellent programs in career-track majors and the unbeatable Florida weather are among the assets that draw 25,00 undergraduates to the University of Florida each year. Popular, top-notch majors include business, journalism, engineering, education, and a pre-medical program that benefits from the presence of fine dental and medical schools within the university system. While the school's size allows it to present a limitless range of studies, it also makes undergraduates feel like they are "a number, not a name." Explained one student, "UF is primarily a research university. As a result, underclassmen traditionally wind up in large classes taught by TAs. Classes have been made even larger by the state budget crisis. The self-motivated student can navigate these problems, however, and the resources here seem without bounds." The library, for example, is excellent, although students complain that, for too many students, it serves as a social center ("People talk so loud in the libraries that I sometimes can't fall asleep," noted one undergrad). Students also complain, "The bureaucracy is a mess, but you only have to deal with it once or twice a semester, and the reasonable price of the school makes up for the hassle," and also that state budget cuts have "made necessary upper-level classes hard to get. Don't come here if you want to graduate on time!"

■ **Life** "UF is not the 'party-ville' that it used to be," wrote one student (one can only imagine how it *used* to be: the school ranked fourth on our list of party schools, based on our survey data). Perhaps she was referring to the fact that "Campus officials are cracking down on the Greeks, and beer is no longer available at every corner if you're under 21 (as it once was)." Still, alcohol and drug use are reportedly still widespread. The Greeks, while "powerful," primarily serve only one segment of the population; explained one student, "The Greeks are popular with the rich and upper class; they are way too expensive for the average Joe." For everyone else, there's the campus ("beautiful and wonderful to walk or bike around"), a plethora of extra-curricular activities (including a very well-respected student newspaper and television station), a "great intercollegiate sports program," and the town of Gainesville, which students described as "an easy town to spend a lot of time in, once you get used to its offbeat rhythms, to which many UF dropouts-turned-locals will no doubt attest." Added another student, "The town has a great art museum, professional theater, and other great culture because of the university." Popular road-trip destinations include "amusement parks, historical sites, and recreation sites (beaches, springs, etc.); they're nearby and great for day trips or weekends."

■ **Students** Students reported that the UF student body, which has an 18 percent minority population, "is diverse, but there is little mixing between racial groups—strong political ideals on both extremes divide many groups." Nearly all the students are native Floridians.

UNIVERSITY OF FLORIDA

Gainesville, FL

Admissions

According to the University of Florida undergraduate catalog, applicants should have taken four units of English (three of which include substantial writing requirements), three units of math (including Algebra I and II and Geometry), three units of natural science (including two lab sciences), three units of social science, and two units of foreign language. An additional four units of electives should be taken, to add up to a total of nineteen units of college preparatory work. An overall C average (minimum) is also required. Students will be judged on "grades, test scores, educational objective and pattern of courses completed, rank in class, school recommendation, and personal record." While no grade or test score assures admission, more than 50 percent of each entering class of undergrads at the University have a B+ or better average, and have scored over 500 on the SAT verbal section, and more than 75 percent have scored over 500 on the SAT math section. All applicants must submit SAT or ACT scores.

Financial Aid

Financial aid applicants to University of Florida must complete the FAF and a form generated by U. of Florida's financial aid office. A full 62-page booklet ("Gator Aid") is available to explain applicants' options. Twenty percent of the class of '95 received some form of aid; the average value was $4,700. In '90–'91, 7% of all undergrads received athletic grants; the average value was $1,088. Thirteen percent of all undergrads received Florida Student Grants, which are awarded for academic promise and financial need to Florida residents. The average grant value was $1,100. Overall, over 14,000 grants were awarded, with an average value of $1,225. A large number of loans ('90–'91 average: $2,103) and scholarships ('90–'91 average: $1,828) are available, as are over 7,000 jobs.

Excerpted from University of Florida promotional materials:

"University of Florida students—numbering more than 34,000 in fall 1988—came from 108 countries (1,500 foreign students), all 50 states, and every one of the 67 counties in Florida. The ratio of men to women is 54–46. One third are freshmen and sophomores and 40 percent juniors and seniors. A total of 5,296, or 16 percent of the student body, are graduate students.

"Approximately 2,000 black students and 1,700 Hispanic students attend UF. Ninety percent of the entering freshmen rank above the national mean of scores on standard entrance exams taken by college-bound students. In 1988, UF ranked 4th in the nation among public universities in the number of new National Merit and Achievement Scholars in attendance."

ADMISSIONS FACTS

Competitiveness Rating:	**85**
% of applicants accepted:	67
% acceptees attending:	43

FRESHMAN PROFILE
Average verbal SAT:	541
Average math SAT:	615
Average ACT:	NA
Graduated top 10% of class:	53
Graduated top 25% of class:	85
Graduated top 50% of class:	100

DEADLINES
Early decision/action:	NA
Early dec./act. notif.:	NA
Regular admission:	2/1
Regular adm. notif.:	3/15

APPLICANTS ALSO LOOK AT

and often prefer:
Georgia Tech
Tulane U.
Florida State U.

and sometimes prefer:
Clemson U.
West Virginia U.
U. South Florida

and rarely prefer:
Howard U.
U. Miami

ADDRESS
Undergraduate Admissions
226 Tigert Hall
Gainesville, FL 32611
904-392-3261

FINANCIAL FACTS

In-state tuition ($):	1,475
Out-of-state tuition ($):	5,612
Room & board:	3,950
FA application deadline:	4/15
% frosh receiving FA:	70
PT earnings per yr. ($):	1,100

TYPE OF AID: % of students ($)
FA of some kind:	83 (3,860)
Need-based grants:	NA
Merit-based grants:	NA
Loans:	NA
Work study:	NA
Student rating of FA:	NA

211

FLORIDA STATE UNIVERSITY

Tallahassee, FL

CAMPUS LIFE

Quality of Life Rating:	*77*
Type of school:	public
Affiliation:	none
Environment:	city

STUDENT BODY

FT undergrad enrollment:	19,106
% male/% female:	46/54
% out-of-state:	21
% live on campus:	20
% African-American:	7
% Asian:	2
% Caucasian:	85
% Hispanic:	4
% foreign:	2
% transfers:	12

WHAT'S HOT

dating
profs lecture a lot
intercollegiate sports
living on campus
marijuana
hard liquor
religious clubs

WHAT'S NOT

studying hard
dorm comfort
TAs teach intros
small classes (overall)
in-class discussion
profs in class
caring about politics

ACADEMICS

Academic Rating:	*72*
Calendar:	semester
Student/teacher ratio:	NA
% doctorates:	80
Profs interesting:	68
Profs accessible:	70
Hours of study per day:	2.39

MOST POPULAR MAJORS BY %

Business & Management:	27
Social Sciences:	15
Education:	14

What do students think about Florida State University?

■ **Academics** Florida State University is a school better known for its party atmosphere than its academics. Even its adamant defenders, of which there are many among the student body, rarely mention the quality of the academics without also mentioning the quality of their leisure time. "Florida State University is an excellent school for those seeking higher education balanced by a good time," wrote one student. "Classes are great, but this school is so much fun it's sometimes hard to get motivated," reported another. Serious students here must contend with the temptation to emulate their classmates, who tend to take it easy academically, and the hospitable climate and surroundings. For the strong-willed, however, an excellent education is available at a bargain-basement price. FSU's strengths are definitely in pre-professional and career-oriented programs: business, education, engineering, nursing, and hotel management are among the strongest departments. Performing arts are also excellent, particularly music and theater. Students gave their professors sub-par grades but noted that the quality of instruction varies widely from department to department. One political science major noted that "professors are kind and considerate and care about students' understanding material rather than just memorizing for a test." In all departments, classes are very large, particularly on the introductory levels.

■ **Life** Maybe it's the weather, maybe it's the laid-back, friendly atmosphere, and maybe it's the nationally ranked football and basketball teams, but for whatever reason, FSU students have a *lot* of school spirit. Wrote one typical booster, "FSU is the essence of college and a dream come true. To be a Seminole is to be a true red-blooded American, regardless of race or heritage." Sports are "really popular," both for spectators and participants: FSU has an active intramural program. The Greek system is a major presence in the social scene, but students don't need fraternity parties as an excuse to have a good time. Wrote one student, "Florida State is definitely a party school. Take for instance Mardi Gras in New Orleans: about half the school was there." Students gave Tallahassee below-average marks, although they enjoy its proximity to beaches and national parks.

■ **Students** Over three quarters of FSU students are native Floridians. Minorities make up 15 percent of the student body. Blacks make up half the minority population, which translates into roughly 1500 black students; other minorities are more sparsely represented. Because FSU is particularly lenient in accepting transfer credit from junior and community colleges, many students arrive here as sophomores and juniors: transfers make up 12 percent of the student body. Several of our respondents noted that, because the student body is so large, it is easy for students to finde a comfortable niche here.

FLORIDA STATE UNIVERSITY

Tallahassee, FL

Admissions

Admission to Florida State is easier for Florida residents than for out-of-state applicants. Residents should have a "B" average in high school and have scored at least a 1050 on the SAT (combined) or a 25 on the Enhanced ACT. Out of state residents "must meet somewhat higher standards." All applicants must have completed the following high school curriculum: four years of English; three years of math (algebra I and II and geometry), natural science, and social studies; two years of the same foreign language; and, four years of academic electives. Interviews are not required, and there is no essay question on the application. Performing arts students must audition.

Financial Aid

The financial aid office at Florida State University requires applicants to submit the FFS or the FAF (the FFS is preferred), and a form generated by the school. FSU offers merit grants which are awarded "on a competitive basis to students who display high academic achievement in high school or at one of the Florida public community colleges through the AA degree." Scholarships for gifted athletes, artists, musicians, and dramatic artists are also available.

A note from the Florida State University Admissions Office:

"Florida State University's heritage of service and scholarship began in 1857 when the Florida Legislature established "The Seminary West of the Sewannee." Since those early days, Florida State has evolved into a comprehensive research institution offering undergraduate, graduate, advanced graduate, and professional programs of study; conducting extensive research; and providing service to the public.

"The University's primary role is to serve as a center for advanced graduate and professional studies while emphasizing extensive research and providing excellence in undergraduate programs. Florida State is a thriving educational institution of national and international reputation serving over 28,000 students from all 50 states and over 100 foreign countries."

ADMISSIONS FACTS

Competitiveness Rating:	**81**
% of applicants accepted:	61
% acceptees attending:	36

FRESHMAN PROFILE

Average verbal SAT:	517
Average math SAT:	580
Average ACT:	25
Graduated top 10% of class:	50
Graduated top 25% of class:	90
Graduated top 50% of class:	90

DEADLINES

Early decision/action:	NA
Early dec./act. notif.:	NA
Regular admission:	3/1
Regular adm. notif.:	rolling

APPLICANTS ALSO LOOK AT

and sometimes prefer:
Georgia Tech
Wake Forest U.

and rarely prefer:
U. Florida
Stetson U.
U. Colorado–Boulder

ADDRESS

Undergraduate Admissions
Tallahassee, FL 32306
904-644-6200

FINANCIAL FACTS

In-state tuition ($):	1,491
Out-of-state tuition ($):	5,630
Room & board:	3,408
FA application deadline:	3/1
% frosh receiving FA:	46
PT earnings per yr. ($):	1,500

TYPE OF AID: % of students ($)

FA of some kind:	42 (NA)
Need-based grants:	NA
Merit-based grants:	NA
Loans:	NA
Work study:	NA
Student rating of FA:	74

FORDHAM UNIVERSITY

Bronx, NY

CAMPUS LIFE

Quality of Life Rating: 85

Type of school:	private
Affiliation:	Roman Catholic
Environment:	city

STUDENT BODY

FT undergrad enrollment:	5,083
% male/% female:	50/50
% out-of-state:	50
% live on campus:	70
% African-American:	4
% Asian:	2
% Caucasian:	83
% Hispanic:	6
% foreign:	3
% transfers:	NA

WHAT'S HOT

religion
conservative politics
suitcase syndrome
overall happiness
campus appearance
campus easy to get around
interaction
location

WHAT'S NOT

fraternities/sororities
town-gown relations
honesty
studying hard

ACADEMICS

Academic Rating: 79

Calendar:	semester
Student/teacher ratio:	15/1
% doctorates:	95
Profs interesting:	77
Profs accessible:	81
Hours of study per day:	2.9

MOST POPULAR MAJORS BY %

Business & Management:	20
Letters/Literature:	15
Psychology:	11

% GRADS WHO PURSUE

Law:	20
MBA:	5
Medicine:	10
M.A., etc.:	45

What do students think about Fordham University?

■ **Academics** One independent college counselor accurately characterized Fordham as "an all-purpose Catholic university." Students pursue a broad spectrum of studies: business, hard sciences, and the liberal arts all attract their fair share. A demanding core curriculum provides, according to one biology major, "a solid liberal arts core, backed by one of the best science departments in the state." Students gave Fordham good grades for class size. Although they gave their professors only average grades, many students commented that profs are helpful and friendly. FU maintains two campuses: one is large, beautiful, and in the Bronx; the other is small, institutional, and near New York City's Lincoln Center. Explained one student, "One of the best things about Fordham is that there are two campuses. It is very easy to take advantage of opportunities on both campuses, as there is an inter-campus transportation system." For pre-professionals, New York City provides plenty of internship opportunities.

■ **Life** Fordham's main campus is in the Bronx, and the relative merits and drawbacks of this location was the subject of many students' essays. While most students agreed that the campus itself was safe and self-contained, many felt that some of the immediately surrounding neighborhoods were dangerous. Said one, "Fordham is great!! That is, if you don't mind the garbage, the noise, the muggings, and occasionally falling asleep to the sound of gunshots." The biggest problems occur at night: students enjoy the area bars and are not always cautious enough when returning home. Said one student, "You have to be smart about where you go at night." Still, there is a Little Italy nearby that is safe and chock full of excellent restaurants. The Botanical Gardens and the Bronx Zoo, both of which are spectacular, are very close by. And, of course, there's Manhattan, accessible by subway or by the school-run shuttle bus. The Bronx campus is "absolutely beautiful—trees, old buildings, etc. It's hard to believe it's in the middle of the Bronx!" Students who wish to stay on campus will find "enough activities, clubs, and organizations to suit anyone's needs." Many students get involved in neighborhood affairs by joining community service groups. Sports are popular, and the school's baseball team is top-notch.

■ **Students** The typical Fordham student is bright, conservative, and Catholic. There is some friction between residents and commuters: residents tend to view commuters as "working class," and commuters see residents as stuck-up parochial school graduates. The real problem is that these two populations rarely get the chance to interact, so each group's preconceived notion of the other is almost never challenged. The conservatism of students and administrators can, at times, get oppressive: explained one student, "Since this is a Jesuit institution, not all viewpoints get expressed, particularly liberal ones about gays and premarital sex."

FORDHAM UNIVERSITY

Admissions

According to its most recent catalog, Fordham's Admissions Committee "looks for evidence of academic ability demonstrated through high school performance and college entrance examination scores as well as for personal characteristics such as strength of character, intellectual and extracurricular interests, special talents, and potential for growing and developing within the environment and academic programs offered" at the school. Interviews are recommended but not required. Applicants must submit scores for either the SAT or the ACT and are required to have completed the following high school curriculum: four years of English; three years of math; two years of social studies and foreign language; and, one year of science (note: pre-med/science students must have completed two additional years of science and an additional year of math). Applicants are encouraged to take more than the required number of courses in these areas, when possible.

Financial Aid

The financial aid office at Fordham University requires applicants to submit the FAF and a form generated by the school. Non-need grants are awarded on the basis of intended course of study, place of residence, academic excellence, and athletic skill. Fordham encourages students who need to borrow to take advantage of the following programs: Stafford, Perkins, and PLUS/SLS.

Excerpted from Fordham College promotional materials:

"Fordham College, since its founding in 1841, was for 133 years a college for men. In 1974, by a merger with Thomas More College, a Fordham University coordinate college for women established in 1964, it became a coeducational college. As a four-year liberal arts college, it strives for the fullest development of the intellectual, volitional, and aesthetic faculties of the student through a carefully integrated yet flexible liberal arts curriculum that includes concentration in a particular field of study. This curriculum is designed to develop the faculty of clear and critical thinking and of correct and forceful expression; it seeks to impart a knowledge of scientific principles and skills, an awareness of historical perspective, an understanding of the contemporary world, and an intelligent appreciation of religious, philosophical, and moral values.

"In addition, the College wants to inspire in students a desire to contribute to the culture and civilization in which they live and to form in them a trained capacity for the service of their country. It believes that these purposes are largely secured through adherence to a well-organized curriculum of study committed to the hands of mature scholars and administered according to high standards of performance."

ADMISSIONS FACTS

Competitiveness Rating:	**73**
% of applicants accepted:	73
% acceptees attending:	36

FRESHMAN PROFILE

Average verbal SAT:	525
Average math SAT:	550
Average ACT:	NA
Graduated top 10% of class:	33
Graduated top 25% of class:	59
Graduated top 50% of class:	90

DEADLINES

Early decision/action:	11/1
Early dec./act. notif.:	12/15
Regular admission:	2/1
Regular adm. notif.:	3/15

APPLICANTS ALSO LOOK AT

and often prefer:
SUNY Binghamton
Columbia U.

and sometimes prefer:
SUNY Albany
SUNY Stonybrook
Villanova U.
Boston College

and rarely prefer:
St. Johns U.
Iona College
Hofstra U.

ADDRESS

Undergraduate Admissions
East Fordham Road
Bronx, NY 10458
212-579-2133

FINANCIAL FACTS

In-state tuition ($):	10,950
Out-of-state tuition ($):	10,950
Room & board:	6,700
FA application deadline:	2/15
% frosh receiving FA:	80
PT earnings per yr. ($):	1,200

TYPE OF AID:	% of students ($)
FA of some kind:	80 (NA)
Need-based grants:	NA
Merit-based grants:	NA
Loans:	NA
Work study:	NA
Student rating of FA:	74

CAMPUS LIFE

Quality of Life Rating:	**78**
Type of school:	private
Affiliation:	none
Environment:	city

STUDENT BODY

FT undergrad enrollment:	1,807
% male/% female:	55/45
% out-of-state:	68
% live on campus:	68
% African-American:	3
% Asian:	7
% Caucasian:	87
% Hispanic:	2
% foreign:	4
% transfers:	1

WHAT'S HOT

college radio station
deans
profs are outside class
small classes (overall)
registration
attending all classes
care about politics
library

WHAT'S NOT

gay community visible
diversity
food
religion
overall happiness

ACADEMICS

Academic Rating:	**85**
Calendar:	semester
Student/teacher ratio:	11/1
% doctorates:	96
Profs interesting:	87
Profs accessible:	92
Hours of study per day:	3.24

MOST POPULAR MAJORS BY %

Letters/Literature:	14
Business & Management:	12
Physical Sciences:	9

% GRADS WHO PURSUE

Law:	10
MBA:	1
Medicine:	7
M.A., etc.:	13

What do students think about Franklin and Marshall?

■ **Academics** Franklin and Marshall is the type of small liberal arts college—Bates and Davidson are of the same type—at which students develop a boot-camp attitude toward schoolwork. They perceive the workload as insurmountable yet attempt it anyway; they work their tails off for grades even though they know that "there will be floods in the Sahara before a professor gives an 'A'; and they develop a love-hate relationship with the institution that puts them through this grueling ordeal. Take, for example, their attitude toward professors. Students are quick to praise them ("The main drawing card is that teachers are interesting and sociable both in and out of class," wrote a typical student), but will just as quickly turn around and lambast them for the difficulty of their assignments. "Academically, this school is *too* difficult," complained one student; said another, "some professors don't grade papers, they *de*grade them." They'll commend the administration in one breath ("We have a caring and dynamic administration: lines of communication with students are well-established and maintained," said one), then turn around and criticize it for its insensitivity in the Greek system. In our survey, students expressed relative dissatisfaction with their lives at F&M, yet a whopping 93 percent of freshmen return for sophomore year. Why do they endure? They'll tell you it's for the school's prestigious reputation; then, in true F&M fashion, complain about the school's national anonymity. Said one student, "I wouldn't mind the work so much if the school was better known. I'm tired of saying, 'I go to F&M,' and having people ask me, 'Where?' For the workload and the difficulty, I feel people should know *exactly* where F&M is."

■ **Life** Student life at F&M has traditionally centered around the Greek system, and this continues to be the case, the administration's withdrawal of official recognition not withstanding. "Without fraternities," wrote one student, "this school would be as exciting as watching old people eat." The town of Lancaster certainly offers little in the way of college-style entertainment, unless hanging out at a shopping mall or touring the Pennsylvania Dutch country (home of the Amish) is your idea of college fun. On campus, interest in sports is dampened by "the worst athletic facilities on the Eastern Seaboard," although one student noted that "there's much to be said about the fairly accessible 24-hour bowling facilities" (but then, oddly, failed to elaborate). Aspiring DJs, take note: the F&M radio station ranked seventh most popular in the nation.

■ **Students** Almost half of F&M's small minority population is made up of Asians; blacks and Hispanics make up most of the other half. Students are predominantly white, ambitious, and "on the whole conservative, though they like to think they are liberal." Students' most common complaint about their classmates was that "most are too wrapped up in their future or what their parents want them to do to enjoy what's around them."

FRANKLIN AND MARSHALL COLLEGE

Lancaster, PA

Admissions

According to Franklin and Marshall's undergraduate catalog, "Selection is based upon several criteria, the quality of the student's secondary school record being the most important. The best preparation for study at Franklin & Marshall is a pre-college program providing fundamental training in the arts, English language, foreign language, history, literature, mathematics, and science. It is highly recommended that a student have a combination of strong English language courses and literature courses, three to four years of a modern or classical foreign language, four years of mathematics resulting in a readiness for beginning college calculus, at least two years of historical study, three years of study in the natural sciences, and one or two semester-long courses in the areas of music, theatre or art. The Admissions committee also recommends that students take at least four academic courses during their senior year. Other factors considered in a student's evaluation are participation in extracurricular activities, standardized test scores, recommendations, a demonstrated interest in the College, and information concerning the student's personality and character." All applicants must submit a score from the English Composition Achievement test, and either the SAT or ACT. An interview is not required (except for Early Decision applicants who live "within a reasonable distance of the College"), but it is strongly recommended.

Financial Aid

Financial aid applicants to Franklin and Marshall College must complete the FAF and a form generated by F&M's financial aid office, and submit a copy of their parents' most recent tax return. In '91–'92, 47% of the entering class of '95 received some form of aid; the average package value was $12,270.

ADMISSIONS FACTS

Competitiveness Rating:	**81**
% of applicants accepted:	59
% acceptees attending:	27

FRESHMAN PROFILE

Average verbal SAT:	567*
Average math SAT:	623*
Average ACT:	NA
Graduated top 10% of class:	39
Graduated top 25% of class:	73
Graduated top 50% of class:	93

DEADLINES

Early decision/action:	2/1
Early dec./act. notif.:	rolling
Regular admission:	2/10
Regular adm. notif.:	4/1

APPLICANTS ALSO LOOK AT

and often prefer:
U. Pennsylvania
Hamilton College
College of William & Mary

and sometimes prefer:
Skidmore College
Washington U.
Colgate U.
Tufts U.

and rarely prefer:
Boston U.
Gettysburg College

ADDRESS

Undergraduate Admissions
P.O. Box 3003
Lancaster, PA 17604-3003
717-291-3951

FINANCIAL FACTS

In-state tuition ($):	20,885
Out-of-state tuition ($):	20,885
Room & board:	NA
FA application deadline:	3/1
% frosh receiving FA:	60
PT earnings per yr. ($):	1,200

TYPE OF AID: % of students ($)

FA of some kind:	67 (14,705)
Need-based grants:	30 (13,797)
Merit-based grants:	NA
Loans:	NA
Work study:	29 (1,350)
Student rating of FA:	82

FURMAN UNIVERSITY

Greenville, SC

What do students think about Furman University?

■ **Academics** Furman University is a small Baptist school best known for its lush campus (see "Life," below) and the fact that it hosts the Southern Baptist Convention every year. But Furman is also an excellent academic institution, especially for the pre-professional-minded student: well over 40 percent of the school's undergraduates proceed from here to graduate programs within a year of graduation. Political science and business are by far the most popular majors, but pre-medical majors, the visual and performing arts, and English are all considered strong by undergraduates. All students must complete a wide range of distribution requirements, which include both a religion course and an African or Asian studies course (the latter is the school's concession to multiculturalism). Students report that "Academically, Furman is rather strenuous; however, the professors are extremely helpful and accessible."

■ **Life** Students refer to Furman as "the Country Club of the South" because of its large, well-manicured campus and sports facilities (tennis courts, softball fields, and an 18-hole golf course). Not surprisingly, students here are unusually athletic, and sports, both intramural and intercollegiate, are very popular. School-sponsored activities, while numerous, are less popular because the campus is dry. (Wrote one student, "The school needs to open up a bit and get rid of this dry campus, but other than that everyone is really friendly.") Other on-campus regulations include a strict intervisitation schedule (complained one student, "The rules here are hell—visiting hours are outrageous, they barely even exist"). Social life centers around the fraternities and women's "social clubs" located off campus, whose parties provide a haven for drinkers. Extracurricular clubs and community service groups located on campus also serve as social nuclei: as one student put it, "At Furman, you don't have to be involved in the Greek system to be part of the social scene." All in all, Furman is "a very close-knit community in a country club setting," but only for those who can live within the administration's precepts; as one student who couldn't cope put it, "For the typical Furman student, the big issues are whether condoms should be on campus and how many Baptist teachers there are. It's prison."

■ **Students** Furman's religious orientation and small minority population are contributing factors toward what most students would admit is a "pretty homogeneous student body." One student characterized her classmates this way: "The majority of students are very religious, study all the time, and are conscientious about finding a life-time partner." Most students are "narrowly focused on doing well and preparing their futures for success," which led one to report, "Students are academically and socially successful, though, as a whole, somewhat lacking in depth." Furman students are among the 20 most conservative and five most religious student bodies we surveyed, and, unsurprisingly, "The gay lifestyle at Furman is met with hostility and extreme moral disapproval."

FURMAN UNIVERSITY

Admissions

The admissions office reports, "Selection is based upon the type of courses taken in high school, grades earned, scholastic rank in class, test scores, and other personal information. Neither academic record nor ability is of itself sufficient qualification for the admission of any applicant." Curriculum and standardized test scores are the most important components of your application here; essays and extracurricular activities are also considered. Applicants are required to have completed "a strong college preparatory course of study," which must include four years of English, algebra I and II, geometry, three years of social science, and at least two years each of natural sciences and a foreign language. Furthermore, "students should have four or more academic credits a year on the advance or honors level." Furman requires either the SAT or the ACT. Applicants to Furman most often also apply to Wake Forest, UNC–Chapel Hill, Vanderbilt, Emory, Davidson, and Clemson.

Financial Aid

Financial aid applicants to Furman must complete the FAF and a form generated by Furman's financial aid office. Scholarships available include those based on academic, artistic, or athletic merit, departmental concentration, and minority or residential status. A number of scholarships and low-interest loans are available to students who plan to teach in South Carolina schools upon graduation.

A note from the Furman University Admissions Office:

"Furman University offers an excellent liberal arts education and quality of life. Outside the classroom, the university places a high value on community service. Furman is regularly recognized as one of the nation's top educational bargains."

ADMISSIONS FACTS

Competitiveness Rating:	**82**
% of applicants accepted:	72
% acceptees attending:	39

FRESHMAN PROFILE

Average verbal SAT:	533*
Average math SAT:	587*
Average ACT:	NA
Graduated top 10% of class:	53
Graduated top 25% of class:	85
Graduated top 50% of class:	96

DEADLINES

Early decision/action:	12/1
Early dec./act. notif.:	late Dec.
Regular admission:	2/1
Regular adm. notif.:	3/15

APPLICANTS ALSO LOOK AT

and often prefer:
Washington and Lee U.

and sometimes prefer:
Wake Forest U.
U. South Carolina
Vanderbilt U.

and rarely prefer:
Wofford College
Georgia Tech
Clemson U.
Auburn U.

ADDRESS

Undergraduate Admissions
Poinsett Highway
Greenville, SC 29613
803-294-2034

FINANCIAL FACTS

In-state tuition ($):	10,720
Out-of-state tuition ($):	10,720
Room & board:	1,888
FA application deadline:	2/1
% frosh receiving FA:	65
PT earnings per yr. ($):	1,000

TYPE OF AID: % of students ($)

FA of some kind:	65 (NA)
Need-based grants:	NA
Merit-based grants:	NA
Loans:	NA
Work study:	NA
Student rating of FA:	77

George Mason University

CAMPUS LIFE

Quality of Life Rating: **75**

Type of school:	public
Affiliation:	none
Environment:	city

STUDENT BODY

FT undergrad enrollment:	9,498
% male/% female:	44/56
% out-of-state:	12
% live on campus:	21
% African-American:	6
% Asian:	10
% Caucasian:	78
% Hispanic:	3
% foreign:	3
% transfers:	14

WHAT'S HOT

suitcase syndrome
working a job
diversity
religious clubs
dating
interaction among students

WHAT'S NOT

library
registration
catalog
administration (overall)
studying hard
small classes (overall)

ACADEMICS

Academic Rating: **73**

Calendar:	semester
Student/teacher ratio:	15/1
% doctorates:	85
Profs interesting:	78
Profs accessible:	72
Hours of study per day:	2.72

MOST POPULAR MAJORS BY %

Business:	19
Engineering:	9
Biology:	6

% GRADS WHO PURSUE

Law:	2
MBA:	3
Medicine:	NA
M.A., etc.:	18

What do students think about George Mason University?

■ **Academics** George Mason University, a Virginia state school located southwest of Washington, D.C., has been building its reputation as an up-and-coming powerhouse for quite a while. The general consensus among students is that "Mason is getting better and better every year." Its strong and constantly improving faculty is described by students as "fairly crunchy but highly dedicated." Solid, competitive programs in economics, business, and communications help foster the perception of this school as a major new force in higher education. However, not all its majors are standouts, or even particularly strong; the School of Arts and most liberal arts departments were the subjects of several students' complaints. It is true that Mason has been growing unevenly. New facilities, which are being built as quickly as the university can afford (examples are the new Center for the Arts and the Patriot Center), also support the school's slick image of progress. Unfortunately other important resources like the library are still substandard, and students are not pleased. The administration has trouble keeping up with all the growth here. Students gave it low marks for running the school smoothly. Registration is considered a miserable experience, classes fill up too quickly and too often do not correspond to what is printed in the catalog. Classes are considered too large, and to some, "greatly overrated." Despite these quirks, however, Mason has demonstrated a tremendous surge in quality over the past few years, and should not be overlooked.

■ **Life** George Mason is "basically a commuter school, but if you never live on or near campus you really miss out." The administration is aiming to increase the number of campus dwellers by building new dorms, but for the time being most people still drive to school and scramble for parking spaces. Greek organizations dominate the social scene on campus ("Fraternity life is the only life"), and off-campus partying mostly takes place in private houses and apartments, with lots of drinking the main attraction. Some just don't have time to party ("Working and living off campus take up a lot of the time that could be spent socializing"), but those that do seem content. D.C. is close (about half an hour away) and accessible without a car.

■ **Students** George Mason boasts a student body that is "incredibly diverse." It is a source of pride here that if "one group steps on another's toes...the whole campus becomes involved. The dispute is resolved quickly and satisfactorily." Three percent of the student body is made up of foreign nationals, and most agree that "the international community makes things very interesting."

GEORGE MASON UNIVERSITY

Fairfax, VA

Admissions

The admissions office reports that "there are no minimum test scores or GPA. A student's profile for admissions decisions is made up of a combination of student's academic curriculum, performance in those courses (i.e., GPA), best test scores and essay, achievements, and extracurricular activities." GPA, curriculum, and standardized test scores are computed into a "selection index which represents a weighted value for the criteria used for admissions; the essay is evaluated independently" of the formula. Letters of recommendation are required but considered relatively unimportant; an interview is not part of the admissions process. Applicants are required to have completed four years of English, three years of math (through Algebra II), three years of social studies, and two years of a foreign language. Students must submit either SAT or ACT scores. GMU applicants also regularly apply to Virginia Tech and George Washington.

Financial Aid

The financial aid office at George Mason University requires applicants to submit the FAF. George Mason administers a number of merit-based grants awarded for academic excellence and for athletic ability. Need-based grants are also available, as are loans through the Stafford, Perkins, PLUS, and SLS loan programs. The deadline listed in the FA sidebar is a *priority* deadline.

A note from the George Mason University Admissions Office:

"'To build a great university, get good people first; the bricks and mortar will follow.' George Mason University President George Johnson is fond of saying that. He sees it as the university's philosophy. People are what makes GMU special. A young, energetic university, the outstanding quality of the faculty and students has made George Mason what it is today—a progressive, innovative institution that has "scratched and clawed" its way to the top of the ladder.

"Distinguished Clarence J. Robinson Professor Roger Wilkins, Pulitzer Prize-winning journalist and former assistant U.S. attorney general, loves to say, 'At George Mason, you will never be told, "No, you can't do that here." Instead, we say, "Let's do it. Let's try it and see what happens."'

"George Mason's students bring a wide variety of experiences with them to school. Representatives from more than 120 countries and the United States make up a very diverse student body. This diversity fosters a better understanding of people from other cultures. Our students have found that the school's diversity prepares them for life in the outside world by giving them a global education."

ADMISSIONS FACTS

Competitiveness Rating:	**65**
% of applicants accepted:	83
% acceptees attending:	41

FRESHMAN PROFILE

Average verbal SAT:	503
Average math SAT:	560
Average ACT:	NA
Graduated top 10% of class:	10
Graduated top 25% of class:	36
Graduated top 50% of class:	76

DEADLINES

Early decision/action:	1/15
Early dec./act. notif.:	1/31
Regular admission:	2/1
Regular adm. notif.:	4/1

APPLICANTS ALSO LOOK AT

and often prefer:
College of William & Mary
Drexel U.
Georgetown U.
Texas Christian U.
U. Virginia

and sometimes prefer:
James Madison U.
Virginia Polytech

ADDRESS

Undergraduate Admissions
Fairfax, VA 22030
703-993-2400

FINANCIAL FACTS

In-state tuition ($):	2,988
Out-of-state tuition ($):	4,476
Room & board:	4,750
FA application deadline:	3/1
% frosh receiving FA:	41
PT earnings per yr. ($):	NA

TYPE OF AID: % of students ($)

FA of some kind:	26 (NA)
Need-based grants:	NA
Merit-based grants:	NA
Loans:	NA
Work study:	NA
Student rating of FA:	71

GEORGE WASHINGTON UNIVERSITY

Washington, DC

CAMPUS LIFE

Quality of Life Rating: **84**

Type of school:	private
Affiliation:	none
Environment:	city

STUDENT BODY

FT undergrad enrollment:	5,792
% male/% female:	48/52
% out-of-state:	85
% live on campus:	50
% African-American:	6
% Asian:	8
% Caucasian:	77
% Hispanic:	3
% foreign:	10
% transfers:	5

WHAT'S HOT

requirements are easy
marijuana
location
Grateful Dead
dorm safety

WHAT'S NOT

studying hard
library
living on campus
bursar
honesty
intramural sports

ACADEMICS

Academic Rating: **76**

Calendar:	semester
Student/teacher ratio:	16/1
% doctorates:	91
Profs interesting:	71
Profs accessible:	75
Hours of study per day:	2

% GRADS WHO PURSUE

Law:	9
MBA:	3
Medicine:	3
M.A., etc.:	9

What is life like at George Washington University?

■ **Academics** Politics is the hot ticket at GW. The school is located in downtown DC, just a few blocks down the street from the White House, so both the faculty and guest-lecturer rosters are well populated with government bigwigs. "Where else can you attend lectures by political aides and notables, where else can you be taught by an aide to four presidents?" asked one undergrad. Not surprisingly, the international affairs and pre-law programs are strong, too: one in 10 graduates goes on to law school within a year. Students reported that they study only two hours a day, lowest in the country, reaffirming the school's reputation as a party school and raising the question of how demanding the course work is. The library gets low marks—"the miniscule amount of information available there is generally obsolete and extremely difficult to locate"—but students have access to the Library of Congress, America's library.

■ **Life** As at most urban schools, the predominant influence on quality of life at GW is the city itself. One student explained it: "DC provides a wealth of opportunities for work and entertainment." Like NYU, BU, and many other "downtown" schools, GW has no discernible campus. School spirit and a strong sense of community among students are, accordingly, low. "Much of the school is split up into cliques," explained one senior, "such as Deadheads, fraternities, ROTCs, internationals, African-Americans, and the leftover malcontents. And, sorry, I forgot the left- and right-wingers, the most tedious of all." "The majority of people here love to party," said another, "but they don't party together." Fortunately, the student body is diverse enough that, eventually, students find where they 'fit in.'" Warning to those who think all city dwellers are libertines: a relatively large proportion of students come here looking to get married. Dorms are reportedly comfortable and safe, which will definitely be news to alumni.

■ **Students** "Many people describe GW as a segregated melting pot," reported one student. Indeed, GW has a pretty diverse student body, particularly heavy on international students. "We have everything from the NY/Long Island fraternity contingent to Arab/Middle East oil barons and diplomats," is the way one woman put it. She didn't mention African-American students, who make up only six percent of the student body. The school has a large contingent of '90s-style hippies—pot-smoking, Deadhead preppies, and lots of their detractors. A comment we commonly heard at other schools was "the students are so friendly here." Not at GW: what we most often heard here was that "students all have attitudes." Don't say you weren't warned.

GEORGE WASHINGTON UNIVERSITY

Washington, DC

Admissions

George Washington considers your high school curriculum to be of primary importance when evaluating your application. GPA is next most important, followed in order of importance by letters of recommendation, standardized test scores, essays, and extracurricular activities. Applicants must submit either SAT or ACT scores. Engineering applicants must have completed Algebra II, chemistry, and phsyics; otherwise, no high school courses are required, although a standard "college-prep curriculum" is recommended. Applicants to George Washington most frequently also apply to American, Georgetown, Boston University, University of Maryland–College Park, and Syracuse University. Note: most wait-listed students are eventually admitted here.

Financial Aid

The financial aid office at George Washington University requires applicants to submit the FAF and tax returns *and* W-2 forms for both themselves and their parents. GW awards merit grants on the basis of athletic ability (4% of the students received one last year; average value: 13,744), academic excellence (12%; 4,136), and special talent (e.g. debate, cheerleading, art; 2%; $3,833). Last year, GW recommended Stafford loans for 42% of all financial aid recipients. The deadline listed in the FA sidebar is a *priority* deadline.

A note from the George Washington University Admissions Office:

"At GW, we welcome students who show a measure of impatience with the limitations of traditional education. At many universities, the edge of campus is the 'real world,' but not at GW, where our campus and Washington, D.C. are seamless. We look for bold, bright students who are ambitious, energetic, and self-motivated. Here, where we are so close to the centers of thought and action in every field we offer, we easily integrate our outstanding academic tradition and faculty connections with the best internship and job opportunities of Washington, D.C. A generous scholarship and financial assistance program attracts top students from all parts of the country and the world. This year, 122 National Merit, National Hispanic Scholar, and National Achievement finalists joined the freshman class."

ADMISSIONS FACTS

Competitiveness Rating:	**76**
% of applicants accepted:	81
% acceptees attending:	24

FRESHMAN PROFILE

Average verbal SAT:	540
Average math SAT:	590
Average ACT:	27
Graduated top 10% of class:	34
Graduated top 25% of class:	67
Graduated top 50% of class:	93

DEADLINES

Early decision/action:	11/15
Early dec./act. notif.:	12/15
Regular admission:	2/1
Regular adm. notif.:	4/1

APPLICANTS ALSO LOOK AT

and often prefer:
Georgetown U.
U. Virginia
Boston U.
Emory U.

and sometimes prefer:
Tufts U.
U. Vermont
NYU

and rarely prefer:
American U.
Catholic U. of America

ADDRESS

Undergraduate Admissions
Washington, DC 20052
202-994-6040

FINANCIAL FACTS

In-state tuition ($):	14,600
Out-of-state tuition ($):	14,600
Room & board:	6,356
FA application deadline:	3/1
% frosh receiving FA:	55
PT earnings per yr. ($):	NA

TYPE OF AID: % of students ($)

FA of some kind:	30 (NA)
Need-based grants:	31 (9,175)
Merit-based grants:	NA
Loans:	NA (3,875)
Work study:	8 (1,300)
Student rating of FA:	72

GEORGETOWN UNIVERSITY

Washington, DC

CAMPUS LIFE

Quality of Life Rating:	**85**
Type of school:	private
Affiliation:	Jesuit
Environment:	city

STUDENT BODY

FT undergrad enrollment:	5,579
% male/% female:	49/51
% out-of-state:	97
% iive on campus:	80
% African-American:	8
% Asian:	5
% Caucasian:	73
% Hispanic:	5
% foreign:	9
% transfers:	5

WHAT'S HOT

location
caring about politics
deans
small labs and seminars
working a job
honesty
administration (overall)
religion
conservative politics

WHAT'S NOT

fraternities/sororities
dating
marijuana
intramural sports

ACADEMICS

Academic Rating:	**83**
Calendar:	semester
Student/teacher ratio:	14/1
% doctorates:	89
Profs interesting:	81
Profs accessible:	79
Hours of study per day:	3.08

MOST POPULAR MAJORS BY %

Business & Management:	17
Letters/Literature:	10
Foreign Languages:	8

% GRADS WHO PURSUE

Law:	12
MBA:	4
Medicine:	5
M.A., etc.:	15

What do students think about Georgetown University?

■ **Academics** Georgetown University is made to seem smaller than it is by the division of the school into five self-contained undergraduate schools. Students must apply to the subdivision of their choice, so, as one student explained, "you have to know what you want to do before you get here." These schools are: Arts and Sciences, Business Administration, Nursing, Foreign Service, and Language and Linguistics. One foreign services student explained that "the five schools tend to divide the student body. The School of Foreign Service thinks of itself as superior to the other schools, but I guess all the schools think that way. There's a lot of stratification." Another SFS student apparently confirmed that characterization when he wrote that "this school is the absolute best if you are interested in international affairs. The SFS curriculum is comprehensive and constantly being updated to respond to changes. Plus, the internships that Washington, D.C., has to offer are unparalleled." All students must take certain core requirements, among them courses in the liberal arts and religious studies. Our respondents agreed that professors were good teachers who generally made themselves available after class, that classes were small, and that the administration does a good job running the school. Although it's affiliated with the Catholic church, students agree that Georgetown "does not push Catholicism upon its students," at least not in the classroom (see "Life," below).

■ **Life** Students here love their surroundings: they gave both the campus and the District of Columbia high marks. The immediate neighborhood, Georgetown, is teeming with expensive shops and fern bars: it's a piece of yuppie heaven on earth. There is no Greek life here, and students report that dating is infrequent. Social life revolves around campus clubs and organizations ("Some college students just go to class at college. Here at GU, they place more emphasis on activities"), Georgetown athletics (the Hoya basketball team is very popular), and the surrounding city. Several students complained that the school's Catholic affiliation can put a damper on on-campus socializing. Said one, "The Catholic Church is at times intrusive, which leaves the school behind the times on a few important issues. What kind of school discourages premarital sex but doesn't have married housing?"

■ **Students** Georgetown students are conservative. Explained one, "GU can be a really fun school for liberals—there are *so many* conservatives to annoy and argue with!" Another student put this spin on the subject: "It's the conservative Ken and Barbie school of the East coast. If it wasn't for the prevailing apathy on campus, the liberals would be feeling mighty paranoid." Yet even though students are predominantly Catholic and conservative, our respondents acknowledged a visible gay population and a pretty high level of acceptance for them. Students are bright but not intellectual: one described his classmates as "intelligent, determined, and ambitious; they tend to put more emphasis on pre-professionalism than on pure academics." The school has a sizeable minority population, and nearly one in ten is a foreign national.

GEORGETOWN UNIVERSITY

Admissions

The admissions committee at Georgetown University looks first at your high school GPA and the quality of your curriculum. It then considers, in descending order of importance: standardized test scores, extracurricular activities, essays, interview, and letters of recommendation. The school requires either the SAT or the ACT and three achievement exams, of which English Composition must be one. Applicants are required to have completed the following high school curriculum: four years of English, three years each of science and math, and two years of a foreign language. According to the school, applicants to Georgetown most often also apply to Duke, University of Pennsylvania, University of Virginia, Cornell, and Harvard.

Financial Aid

The financial aid office at Georgetown University requires applicants to submit the FAF and "certain documentation to verify the information on [the] original application." All aid at Georgetown is awarded on the basis of need only: need-based grants "range in value from $500 to more than $12,000 per academic year." The school's financial aid brochure suggests that students pursue the following loan options: Stafford, Perkins, Nursing (for nursing students only), PLUS, DC Consern, and SHARE.

Excerpted from Georgetown University promotional materials:

"Georgetown University is an institution of a national and an international cast. It is located in close proximity to the nation's government and to the international organizations which have roots in Washington. Not surprisingly it attracts faculty and students from all parts of the nation and from many areas of the world. It wished to continue to do so.

"Georgetown is committed to a view of reality which reflects Catholic and Jesuit influences. It neither wishes nor expects all its members to be Catholic, but it does assume that all of them share a basic, widely accepted view of humankind. It sees all men as essentially equal, as endowed with a human dignity always to be respected. It sees its own function as being the service of humankind through teaching, through research, and through other activities that properly flow from these. In particular it wishes these convictions as to the dignity of the individual to be manifested in all its campus life; it believes that, as far as possible, the relationships among faculty, students, and administrators should be personal ones. It seeks to open its arms, in the fullest sense of ecumenism, to those of all beliefs and races."

ADMISSIONS FACTS

Competitiveness Rating:	**93**
% of applicants accepted:	29
% acceptees attending:	50

FRESHMAN PROFILE

Average verbal SAT:	591
Average math SAT:	639
Average ACT:	28
Graduated top 10% of class:	68
Graduated top 25% of class:	91
Graduated top 50% of class:	99

DEADLINES

Early decision/action:	11/1
Early dec./act. notif.:	12/15
Regular admission:	1/10
Regular adm. notif.:	4/1

APPLICANTS ALSO LOOK AT

and often prefer:
Duke U.
Yale U.
Stanford U.

and sometimes prefer:
U. Chicago
U. Pennsylvania
Cornell U.

and rarely prefer:
Syracuse U.
Tulane U.
Emory U.

ADDRESS

Undergraduate Admissions
37th and O Streets NW
Washington, DC 20057
202-687-3600

FINANCIAL FACTS

In-state tuition ($):	15,510
Out-of-state tuition ($):	15,510
Room & board:	5,732
FA application deadline:	1/10
% frosh receiving FA:	61
PT earnings per yr. ($):	2,200

TYPE OF AID: % of students ($)

FA of some kind:	85 (NA)
Need-based grants:	NA
Merit-based grants:	NA
Loans:	NA
Work study:	NA
Student rating of FA:	80

GEORGIA INSTITUTE OF TECHNOLOGY

What do students think about Georgia Tech?

■ **Academics** The Georgia Institute of Technology provides its students with a relatively 'low impact' engineering program. While students at other technical schools study over four hours a day, Tech students reported a manageable three hours of daily study. Tech is by no means an easy school, its students emphasized in their essays, but, the demands it makes on students are apparently less rigorous than other top tech schools. The academic atmosphere here, however, is of an intensity to rival that at other tech schools. Students describe their classmates as "very competitive. Sometimes that's hard to deal with because people are unwilling to help each other; they want to 'make the curve' and let the others bring the curve down." Students also complained that exams are unnecessarily difficult. The "shaft" is a term students frequently use to describe the tests and grades they receive. Most students here are engineers, but Tech has recently made efforts to broaden its major offerings. The College of Management now attracts one fifth of the students, and the school has beefed up its programs in international affairs and in "science, technology, and culture," which prepares students for "communications positions in government and industry that involve interface among science, technology, and social concerns." Tech's reputation and location in downtown Atlanta, a popular corporate headquarters site, make internships for Tech students readily available. Nearly 3,000 undergrads participate in the co-op program, in which they spend alternate quarters attending Tech and working an internship. The program adds an extra year to the undergraduate program. As one student told us, "Tech offers a great opportunity to advance in the business world, if you are willing to put the effort into it."

■ **Life** In terms of social opportunities, Tech has no rival among top engineering schools. For one thing, "It's in the middle of downtown Atlanta, so if there isn't anything doing on campus, Atlanta has plenty to offer." Most often, however, there is "something doing" on campus. Wrote one student, "There are plenty of opportunities for students to get involved on campus: Greek organizations, student government, theater, sports, etc." The Greek system is very active here, hosting parties which attract women from other area schools (somewhat, but not entirely, offsetting the three-to-one male-female ratio at Tech). Furthermore, "Tech has great athletic programs and lots of school spirit!" Our survey supports the student who asserted that "alcohol and drug consumption at Tech is much higher than one would expect, because of the incredible stress that each individual faces every day." While still a far cry from a party school, Tech students unwind almost as often as "normal" college students, making them an anomaly in the engineering world.

■ **Students** Tech boasts a sizable minority population (19 percent), but students reported that interaction between groups is sub-par. Two thirds of the students are from in-state, not surprising given the extremely low tuition charge to Georgia natives.

GEORGIA INSTITUTE OF TECHNOLOGY

Atlanta, GA

Admissions

Aspiring Georgia Tech students may apply to enter the school at the beginning of any academic quarter. The application deadline for summer and fall quarters is February 1; for the winter quarter, October 1; and for spring quarter, January 1. Applicants must take either the SAT or the ACT; achievement tests are not required, but their results can be used to gain advanced placement in English and chemistry. Applicants are expected to have completed the following high school curriculum: four years each of English and math, three years of science, and two years each of a foreign language and history. The application requires neither an essay nor letters of recommendation; it does require that applicants designate a planned major, however. Applicants who are Georgia residents are given preference over those from out-of-state.

Financial Aid

The financial aid office at Georgia Tech requires applicants to submit the FAF or Singlefile. Georgia Tech's application bulletin states that the school "offers a variety of financial aid programs to assist students in meeting normal college expenses; however, the amount of aid granted seldom meets all educational expenses. The student, family, and other outside sources will have to supplement any financial assistance." Merit grants are awarded for academic excellence. Note that, while students may apply for admission for any of the four quarters, financial aid is awarded during the spring only; regardless of the quarter during which you enter the school, your financial aid application must reach the school by March 1 prior to matriculation.

A note from the Georgia Tech Admissions Office:

"Within the past five years, Georgia Tech has developed innovative degree programs based on what our undergraduate customers told us they wanted, and we put those programs in place in record time. We are in the process of reorganizing the student services offices, such as financial aid, admissions, registration, etc., to eliminate the bureaucratic roadblocks, so that you spend your time studying, not standing in lines. We are also expanding housing on campus.

"By 1996, President John P. Crecine expects to increase the number of faculty to allow more interaction between students and faculty....The strength of Georgia Tech depends on the success of its graduates; therefore, it is our responsibility to provide convenient student services and stimulating classes....In the end, these advancements for Georgia Tech mean smaller classes, more variety in course work, better living conditions, higher academic standards for our undergraduate students, and, after all, isn't that what you're looking for in a university?"

ADMISSIONS FACTS

Competitiveness Rating:	**89**
% of applicants accepted:	69
% acceptees attending:	40

FRESHMAN PROFILE

Average verbal SAT:	538
Average math SAT:	649
Average ACT:	NA
Graduated top 10% of class:	80
Graduated top 25% of class:	95
Graduated top 50% of class:	100

DEADLINES

Early decision/action:	NA
Early dec./act. notif.:	NA
Regular admission:	2/1
Regular adm. notif.:	rolling

APPLICANTS ALSO LOOK AT

and often prefer:
UC Berkeley
Duke U.

and sometimes prefer:
U. NC– Chapel Hill

and rarely prefer:
Carnegie Mellon U.
Clemson U.
Auburn U.
U. Florida
Emory U.
Virginia Polytech

ADDRESS

Undergraduate Admissions
225 North Avenue N. W.
Atlanta, GA 30332
404-894-4154

FINANCIAL FACTS

In-state tuition ($):	2,118
Out-of-state tuition ($):	6,279
Room & board:	3,255
FA application deadline:	3/1
% frosh receiving FA:	35
PT earnings per yr. ($):	2,500

TYPE OF AID: % of students ($)

FA of some kind:	40 (NA)
Need-based grants:	NA
Merit-based grants:	NA
Loans:	NA
Work study:	NA
Student rating of FA:	68

GETTYSBURG COLLEGE

Gettysburg, PA

What do students think about Gettysburg College?

■ **Academics** Gettysburg College was created in 1832 as a Lutheran school. Although no longer attended solely by Lutherans, and although the church affiliation is mostly nominal, vestiges of the school's religious origins remain. There's an honor code, for one thing; there is also, as one student reported, the school's "strong commitment to the liberal arts and the moral dimension of learning." Gettysburg believes all undergraduates should receive a varied academic program, and, accordingly, students here spend nearly three semesters completing a vast range of distribution requirements. Gettysburg's chief asset is its dedicated faculty, which, coupled with its favorable student-teacher ratio, provides students with lots of personal attention. Wrote one student, "The professors are down to earth and easy to talk to. I even had a professor buy me a beer at one of the bars that students go to. We talked about everything but classes and school!" Academics are of high quality but not overly demanding, despite the administration's recent efforts to toughen up performance requirements. As one student explained, "Gettysburg provides a challenging academic curriculum while still allowing students time to become involved in a wide variety of activities." Business and management is a favorite field of this career-oriented student body; English, pre-medical sciences, and psychology are also popular and reportedly first-rate.

■ **Life** Gettysburg is, of course, the home of the famous Civil War battle and Lincoln's subsequent famous speech. As a result, students encounter a lot of tourists, especially during the early part of the fall term and the end of the spring term. Said one student, "The town of Gettysburg would be great if it actually had something in it from this century." Area bars welcome the students, but most extracurricular activities seem to take place on campus. Students report that participation in clubs and organizations in high. The Greek system is very popular but, by one student's account, "Not 'do or die.' The same goes for alcohol use." All in all, social life is described as "active," "fun," and "laid back," although students warn, "You have to remember to balance it with academics." Because of the small, affluent student body, some students feel Gettysburg is "very much like a prep school. Almost everyone knows everything about you, especially the bad stuff." "The campus itself," reported one student, "is beautiful and adds to the academic atmosphere."

■ **Students** Gettysburg's student body is overwhelmingly white, affluent, and conservative. Wrote one student, "It's frustrating that the student body isn't too diverse, but the college is making an effort to change that and it shows." That effort isn't reflected in the numbers yet, as a glance at the student body demographics (in the "Campus Life" sidebar) indicates. Concluded one student about her classmates, "Students here are used to being catered to by their parents; they're unaware of the real world and have *no* clue about the value of money. But, besides that, they are great!"

GETTYSBURG COLLEGE

Admissions

The admissions office reports that "students can expect a careful, individual review of their applications. We particularly value: 1) high school achievement, including the choice of challenging courses; 2) personal qualities and talents which will contribute to the community. Evidence of leadership, creativity, integrity, commitment, and service to community are welcomed." Standardized test scores, letters of recommendation, and essays are also seriously considered. An interview is recommended but not required. Applicants are expected to have completed a "full college preparatory program." Either the SAT or the ACT is required; international students must also take the TOEFL. Applicants to Gettysburg College most often also apply to Bucknell, Dickinson, Frankin and Marshall, and Lafayette.

Financial Aid

Gettysburg requires financial aid applicants to submit the FAF and a copy of their parents' tax forms. The average total award for the class of '95 was $12,635. This was broken down as follows: average loan, $1,990; average grant, $9,405; average employment, $1,240. Gettysburg awards no merit-based scholarships. According to the school's brochure, the qualifications for assistance, in addition to need, are "academic ability, academic achievement, and promise of contributing to the College community as a student and citizen." The school offers several loan programs, some for all students and others earmarked specifically for Lutherans.

A note from the Gettysburg College Admissions Office:

"Four major goals of Gettysburg College to best prepare students to enter the 21st century include:

"First, to accelerate the intellectual development of our first-year students by integrating them more quickly into the intellectual life of the campus;

"Second, to use interdisciplinary courses combining the intellectual approaches of various fields to encourage students to develop multidimensional skills needed to deal effectively with the complexity of modern life;

"Third, to help students develop an international perspective through course work, study abroad, association with international faculty, and a variety of extracurricular activities; and

"Fourth, to encourage students to develop (1) a capacity for independent study by ensuring that all students work closely with individual faculty members on an extensive project during their undergraduate years and (2) the ability to work with their peers by making the small group a central feature of college life."

ADMISSIONS FACTS

Competitiveness Rating:	**82**
% of applicants accepted:	61
% acceptees attending:	25

FRESHMAN PROFILE

Average verbal SAT:	530
Average math SAT:	592
Average ACT:	26
Graduated top 10% of class:	42
Graduated top 25% of class:	78
Graduated top 50% of class:	99

DEADLINES

Early decision/action:	2/1
Early dec./act. notif.:	rolling
Regular admission:	2/15
Regular adm. notif.:	4/1

APPLICANTS ALSO LOOK AT

and often prefer:
James Madison U.
College of William & Mary

and sometimes prefer:
Lehigh U.
Bucknell U.
Hobart/William Smith College
U. Delaware

and rarely prefer:
Penn State U.
Muhlenberg College

ADDRESS

Undergraduate Admissions
Gettysburg, PA 17325-1486
717-337-6100 or (800) 431-0803

FINANCIAL FACTS

In-state tuition ($):	16,500
Out-of-state tuition ($):	16,500
Room & board:	3,470
FA application deadline:	2/1
% frosh receiving FA:	55
PT earnings per yr. ($):	1200

TYPE OF AID: % of students ($)

FA of some kind:	55 (NA)
Need-based grants:	40 (8,200)
Merit-based grants:	0
Loans:	16 (3,000)
Work study:	16 (1020)
Student rating of FA:	91

CAMPUS LIFE

Quality of Life Rating:	**86**
Type of school:	private
Affiliation:	none
Environment:	suburban

STUDENT BODY

FT undergrad enrollment:	255
% male/% female:	47/53
% out-of-state:	85
% live on campus:	50
% African-American:	2
% Asian:	1
% Caucasian:	<1
% Hispanic:	1
% foreign:	<1
% transfers:	45

WHAT'S HOT

in-class discussion
gay community accepted
small classes (overall)
leftist politics
food
interaction among students
cost of living
doing all the reading
profs in class
overall happiness

WHAT'S NOT

fraternities/sororities
sports
drinking
administration (overall)

ACADEMICS

Academic Rating:	**78**
Calendar:	semester
Student/teacher ratio:	15/1
% doctorates:	63
Profs interesting:	95
Profs accessible:	94
Hours of study per day:	3.39

MOST POPULAR MAJORS BY %

Psychology	25
Education	20
Letters/Literature	20

What do students think about Goddard College?

■ **Academics** Goddard College, a self-proclaimed alternative school, is definitely not "typical, traditional, or boring." Classes are "small discussion groups in which everyone participates. There are no grades or exams, which alleviates any pressure that interferes with the business of learning." Students enjoy exceptionally close relationships with their professors, whom they respect and rate very highly as teachers. Written evaluations substitute for grades, and most students value the individual attention they receive. But, as one student aptly writes, "Beware, ye pre-professionals!" Goddard is "not about getting a marketable degree"; the emphasis here is on more holistic values like "relearning to be sensitive, integrated human beings who love life on this planet too much to abandon themselves to the materialism of the modern world." Many feel that since students must be "independent, self-directed and focused to attend—there's not much handholding here," coming to Goddard "right after high school is not a good idea. The environment is better suited to older, more experienced students." Some complain about the administration, but students give the deans and even the bursar high marks overall. If prospective students are "willing to look at life, community and education from a whole new perspective," Goddard may prove to be just the place for them.

■ **Life** Of great importance at Goddard are "rounded education and rounded lives." Community action is promoted here, and everyone must work for the college in some constructive way several hours per week. Because of Goddard's tiny size, each individual has a "tremendous opportunity" to get involved in various activities, including the popular school newspaper and radio station. Social life is mostly centered around the dorms, and can get pretty laid-back; wild parties, drinking, and promiscuity are not really among Goddard students' priorities. Religious activity is not popular, although many students cite "spiritual and/or pagan clubs" as well attended. The campus itself is quite beautiful and secluded. Skiing trails are nearby, and there are plenty of places to hike. Students rate themselves as very happy overall. Even the cafeteria food is considered high-quality (which may be one reason the college president frequently lunches with students there). Connoisseurs of rural life especially like Goddard's quiet atmosphere.

■ **Students** It is safe to say that this school "would be an uncomfortable place for a person with a conservative background." Despite the cultural homogeneity of the population (a black student comments, "I am *the* diverse ethnic type"), there are alternative lifestyles aplenty. Many people here are "gay/lesbian/bisexual and proud of it." Goddard prides itself on its opposition to "isms: sexism is challenged openly and daily, as are racism and classism."

GODDARD COLLEGE

Admissions

The admissions office reports that "Goddard aims to bring students into the college, not keep them out. Admissions criteria have to do with an applicant's interest in attending Goddard, readiness to do so, and willingness to embrace the evolving Goddard educational program fully. Underlying these must be a thorough understanding of what Goddard is and is not, what the curriculum and programs can and cannot offer." Essays are the most important component of your application here, followed, in decreasing order of importance, by a personal interview (required), letters of recommendation, high school curriculum/GPA, extracurricular activities, and standardized test scores (SAT or ACT scores are requested but not required). Goddard requires the completion of no specific high school courses, only that applicants "have graduated from high school or earned a high-school equivalency certificate (GED)."

Financial Aid

The financial aid office at Goddard College requires applicants to submit the FAF and a copy of their parents' most recent tax return. Besides conventional aid programs—grants, loans, and work-study—Goddard offers a fourth option called "the Goddard Investment," which, according to the school's most recent catalog, is "a grant made with the understanding that the grantee will pay it back at some future time: in cash, in services, or in material goods." The same catalog reports that "Students must also apply for funds to charitable, union, civic, religious or other groups in their home communities that give educational grants, and to relatives. Aid funds are limited..." The deadline listed in the FA sidebar is a *priority* deadline.

A note from the Goddard College Admissions Office:

"Goddard is a small, coeducational liberal arts college that has an international reputation for appealing to the creative, independent student. Its commitment is to adventurous, capable persons who want to make their own educational decisions and work closely with the faculty. Individually designed programs can be pursued on or off campus."

ADMISSIONS FACTS

Competitiveness Rating:	**68**
% of applicants accepted:	90
% acceptees attending:	51

FRESHMAN PROFILE

Average verbal SAT:	NA
Average math SAT:	NA
Average ACT:	NA
Graduated top 10% of class:	NA
Graduated top 25% of class:	NA
Graduated top 50% of class:	NA

DEADLINES

Early decision/action:	NA
Early dec./act. notif.:	NA
Regular admission:	rolling
Regular adm. notif.:	rolling

APPLICANTS ALSO LOOK AT

and often prefer:
New College
Reed College
Oberlin College

and sometimes prefer:
Antioch College
Hampshire College
College of the Atlantic
Bennington College

and rarely prefer:
Marlboro College

ADDRESS

Undergraduate Admissions
Plainfield, VT 05667
802-454-8311

FINANCIAL FACTS

In-state tuition ($):	12,280
Out-of-state tuition ($):	12,280
Room & board:	4,120
FA application deadline:	3/1
% frosh receiving FA:	NA
PT earnings per yr. ($):	NA

TYPE OF AID: % of students ($)

FA of some kind:	60 (NA)
Need-based grants:	NA
Merit-based grants:	NA
Loans:	NA
Work study:	NA
Student rating of FA:	91

GOLDEN GATE UNIVERSITY

San Francisco, CA

CAMPUS LIFE

Quality of Life Rating:	**69**
Type of school:	private
Affiliation:	none
Environment:	city

STUDENT BODY

FT undergrad enrollment:	483
% male/% female:	44/56
% out-of-state:	16
% live on campus:	0
% African-American:	11
% Asian:	14
% Caucasian:	68
% Hispanic:	7
% foreign:	16
% transfers:	NA

WHAT'S HOT

suitcase syndrome
interaction
location
working a job
small lectures
diversity
attending all classes
town-gown relations
small labs and seminars
requirements are easy

WHAT'S NOT

intramural sports
college radio station
college theater groups
intercollegiate sports

ACADEMICS

Academic Rating:	**80**
Calendar:	trimester
Student/teacher ratio:	10/1
% doctorates:	47
Profs interesting:	81
Profs accessible:	68
Hours of study per day:	3.01

MOST POPULAR MAJORS BY %

Business & Management:	60
Computer Science:	15
Communications:	10

What do students think of Golden Gate University?

■ **Academics** In nearly every aspect, Golden Gate University is atypical of the schools included in this book. Most of its undergraduates study part-time, and many were out of high school for several years before returning to college; it has no campus or campus life to speak of; and, with two-thirds of its students in graduate programs, its orientation is decidedly toward graduate, not undergraduate, study. Golden Gate has several excellent qualities to recommend it, however. For one, the school is located in downtown San Francisco, certainly an exceptional place to spend four years. Second, it attracts a bright, motivated, and unusually diverse student body. Finally, and most importantly, Golden Gate offers fine undergraduate business programs, distinguished by their small classes, capable faculties, and cooperative program; Golden Gate's Cooperative Education and Internship Program allows students to spend alternate trimesters studying and working in the San Francisco business community. The only complaint we heard from the students we surveyed here was that "this school's reputation isn't nearly as good as it should be, given the quality of instruction I receive here." Students praised their professors ("Their frequent use of case studies at this university will be very useful when we graduate and get our career jobs," wrote one), the administration ("The staff are very helpful, from admissions and the library to the career center: everyone is willing to help"), and the fact that "the school allows the motivated student to get a good degree quickly."

■ **Life** As one student put it, "Don't come here for the football team, because we don't have one. We don't even have a cheerleader squad. We come here to learn and eventually to become prominent figures in our society." Students certainly don't come here for the social life, because there is none. Most of the mainstays of typical college life—parties, drinking, sports, clubs—simply don't exist here (complained one student, "It would be nice to have a campus and some social events every now and then.") Furthermore, the school offers no housing, so students are provided with few opportunities to meet outside the classroom. Fortunately, the school is in downtown San Francisco, a city with a very active social life of its own. Off-campus housing is available but, unfortunately, expensive, as is most everything else: students report that cost of living expenses here are extremely high. As one student summed it up, "Golden Gate is an excellent college choice if you are looking forward to studying, not partying."

■ **Students** Golden Gate boasts a 32 percent minority population. Students reported that interaction among students of different ethnicities and backgrounds is frequent, despite the lack of school-supported venues in which students can congregate. To no one's surprise, the student body at this business-oriented school is politically conservative (although less so than at other similar schools).

GOLDEN GATE UNIVERSITY

Admissions

According to Golden Gate University's most recent catalog, the school considers "academic record at other institutions, scores on any required tests, motivation, and educational objectives" in assessing an applicants "ability to benefit from [the school's] educational programs." High school GPA is the most important factor in admissions decisions; a GPA of 3.0 is required (3.2 for applicants to the schools of accounting and taxation). In lieu of a high school diploma, Golden Gate accepts the GED (minimum score on any section: 40; average on all sections: 45) or a passing grade on the California High School Proficiency exam. Standardized tests are not required.

Financial Aid

The financial aid office at Golden Gate University requires applicants to submit the Student Aid Application for California. Non-need based grants are awarded on the basis of previously demonstrated academic excellence and intended area of study; some grants are also set aside specifically for minority students. California residents are eligible for Cal Grants A, B, and C, and must apply for these in order to be considered for aid from the school. The school catalog suggests the following loan options: Stafford, PLUS, SLS, Perkins, and the Golden Gate University loan. The university loan "seldom exceeds $1,500 a year." The deadline listed below is a priority deadline.

Excerpted from Golden Gate University promotional materials:

"Golden Gate University is one of the leading centers for higher education in business, public administration and law in the western United States. More students earn M.B.A. degrees from Golden Gate University each year than from any other university in Northern California. Among the University's alumni are men and women who hold top decision making positions in organizations throughout the world.

"A pioneer in the case-study method of instruction, Golden Gate University is recognized for its practical approach to professional education. The faculty is comprised of full-time academics and career professionals who have advanced degrees and extensive experience in their fields and in the classroom.

"The University is a private, nonprofit institution accredited by the Western Association of Schools and Colleges. Golden Gate's combined enrollment totals some 9,000 students."

Competitiveness Rating:	**75**
% of applicants accepted:	72
% acceptees attending:	71

FRESHMAN PROFILE

Average verbal SAT:	NA
Average math SAT:	NA
Average ACT:	NA
Graduated top 10% of class:	NA
Graduated top 25% of class:	NA
Graduated top 50% of class:	NA

DEADLINES

Early decision/action:	NA
Early dec./act. notif.:	NA
Regular admission:	7/1
Regular adm. notif.:	rolling

APPLICANTS ALSO LOOK AT
and sometimes prefer:
San Francisco State U.

ADDRESS
Undergraduate Admissions
536 Mission Street
San Francisco, CA 94105-2968
415-442-7800

FINANCIAL FACTS

In-state tuition ($):	6,336
Out-of-state tuition ($):	6,336
Room & board ($):	0
FA application deadline:	2/15
% frosh receiving FA:	20
PT earnings per yr. ($):	5,000

TYPE OF AID: % of students ($)

FA of some kind:	20 (NA)
Need-based grants:	NA
Merit-based grants:	NA
Loans:	NA
Work study:	NA
Student rating of FA:	NA

GOUCHER COLLEGE

Baltimore, MD

What do students think about Goucher College?

■ **Academics** As one student at the formerly all-women's Goucher College explained, "We're still struggling to get an identity because we only went co-ed in 1987." Certain components of the school's new identity are already in place, chief among which are a commitment to a broad-ranging liberal arts core curriculum, excellent pre-medical science departments, and an "amazing, very friendly and extremely accessible" faculty. All students must complete distribution requirements covering eight academic disciplines. One student noted that the core places "a strong emphasis on liberal arts and writing proficiency." Several students described the pre-med program as "fantastic." Dance, English, communications, and women's studies also drew students' praise. The students saved their kindest words for the faculty. Wrote a typical respondent, "The best thing about Goucher is the professors. They treat us with respect. We have their home phone numbers and call them by their first names." Students ranked the professors here among the top five percent in the nation for out-of-class accessibility. With a nine-to-one student-faculty ratio, classes are "generally small" and in-class discussions are a major part of most courses.

■ **Life** Students describe the prevailing atmosphere at Goucher as "intimate." Explained one, "building friendships and getting to know people is extremely easy"; said another, "because the school is so small, the rumor mill is always buzzing. You've got to watch what you do and who you do it with. But tight friendships and honest relationships are the advantage." While many complained that "social life is limited because of the school's size and the male-female ratio (currently one to three)," there are, according to one student, "plenty of opportunities for involvement in organizations. We have everything from a gay/lesbian organization to a math and computer science club." The Goucher administration is currently working to build a competitive intercollegiate athletic program. As one student explained, "the future path is towards intercollegiate athletic recognition to complement the already-recognized academic excellence." The campus is located in Towson, an upscale suburb north of Baltimore, and students agreed that it provided an excellent setting for studies. Wrote one, "on campus it's like you're in the country, but outside the gates is a great city."

■ **Students** Goucher is a predominantly white school—its 13 percent minority population translates into roughly 100 students. One student characterized her classmates as "mostly liberal and open-minded." One of her conservative classmates agreed, writing "If you are a right winger and want to know what it feels like to be in the minority, come here; it's like sleeping in the enemy's camp. Not a day will go by that your ideals are not challenged. After you leave here, you'll be able to argue anything with anyone."

GOUCHER COLLEGE

Admissions

Goucher's admissions policy is to "seek excellent students with a diversity of talents, ambitions, backgrounds, and experiences. Personal qualities are weighed along with academic potential as demonstrated by secondary school and standardized test records." Applicants are required to take either the SAT or the ACT; three achievement exams, while not required, are strongly recommended, as is an interview. Letters of recommendation are required. Applicants must have completed at least 14 units of college prep courses, including two years of a single foreign language and three years of science. Note: Goucher is looking to even out its lopsided male-female ratio, so men *may* have an easier time than women gaining admission here.

Financial Aid

The financial aid office at Goucher College requires applicants to submit the FAF, a form generated by the school, and a copy of your parents' most recent tax return. Merit grants are awarded to "exceptional students" and to applicants with special talents in the arts, music, or drama. Most merit grants are four-year awards and are automatically renewed, provided recipients meet minimum academic requirements. A college-sponsored loan is available to those who demonstrate need (values range from $200 to $2,000); the school's financial aid brochure also recommends all major federally and privately funded loan programs for those needing further assistance. The deadline listed in the FA sidebar is a *priority* deadline.

A note from the Goucher College Admissions Office:

"At the heart of a Goucher education are two important elements: an outstanding faculty committed to the craft of teaching and the college's core curriculum—based on the idea of a common body of knowledge that every educated person should possess.

"But unlike many degree programs with core components, Goucher's program is extremely flexible, offering a wide range of courses through which students can complete the eight required areas of study.

"Goucher students receive support to help them do their best while working toward a degree. A 9:1 student:faculty ratio assures students that professors will be accessible to them. Our "Pre-Major Advising Program" eases the transition to college life. Goucher also helps with the adjustment to college-level work through its innovative writing center, where students receive assistance with their writing at all stages of the composing process. For students interested in pre-professional programs, the college offers specialized advising meetings during fall orientation."

ADMISSIONS FACTS

Competitiveness Rating: 67
% of applicants accepted: 71
% acceptees attending: 33

FRESHMAN PROFILE
Average verbal SAT: 540
Average math SAT: 560
Average ACT: NA
Graduated top 10% of class: 30
Graduated top 25% of class: 55
Graduated top 50% of class: 67

DEADLINES
Early decision/action: 12/1
Early dec./act. notif.: 12/15
Regular admission: 2/1
Regular adm. notif.: 4/1

APPLICANTS ALSO LOOK AT

and often prefer:
Syracuse U.
U. NC– Chapel Hill
Connecticut College

and sometimes prefer:
Hobart/William Smith College
Allegheny College
Muhlenberg College
Gettysberg College

and rarely prefer:
Agnes Scott College
Adelphi U.

ADDRESS
Undergraduate Admissions
Dulaney Road
Baltimore, MD 21204
301-337-6100

FINANCIAL FACTS

In-state tuition ($): 12,685
Out-of-state tuition ($): 12,685
Room & board: 5,700
FA application deadline: 2/15
% frosh receiving FA: 70
PT earnings per yr. ($): 1,200

TYPE OF AID: % of students ($)
FA of some kind: 68 (NA)
Need-based grants: NA
Merit-based grants: NA
Loans: NA
Work study: NA

Student rating of FA: 90

GRINNELL COLLEGE

CAMPUS LIFE

Quality of Life Rating: **89**

Type of school:	private
Affiliation:	none
Environment:	suburban

STUDENT BODY

FT undergrad enrollment:	1,251
% male/% female:	52/48
% out-of-state:	83
% live on campus:	87
% African-American:	4
% Asian:	5
% Caucasian:	83
% Hispanic:	1
% foreign:	5
% transfers:	2

WHAT'S HOT

gay community accepted
leftist politics
college radio station
food
students interact
administration (overall)
small classes (overall)
profs outside class
college theater
overall happiness
profs in class

WHAT'S NOT

fraternities/sororities
location

ACADEMICS

Academic Rating: **86**

Calendar:	semester
Student/teacher ratio:	10/1
% doctorates:	83
Profs interesting:	90
Profs accessible:	93
Hours of study per day:	3.38

MOST POPULAR MAJORS

Biology
Economics
English

% GRADS WHO PURSUE

Law:	5
MBA:	NA
Medicine:	4
M.A., etc.:	23

What do students think about Grinnell College?

■ **Academics** The state of Iowa is, by Midwestern standards, a bastion of liberalism, and nowhere in the state is this more apparent than at Grinnell College. As one out-of-state student put it, "I wanted a school with lots of non-mainstream thought and action. Believe it or not, I found it in the middle of Iowa." An unconventional approach to undergraduate education is evidenced by the school's lack of a core curriculum (one student wrote approvingly, "Having no core curriculum allows students to expand their knowledge in fields of interest outside of their majors") and the large degree of autonomy allowed students in both academic and social pursuits. As at many small liberal arts schools, students here enjoy small classes and enthusiastic, dedicated professors (who teach all classes; Grinnell uses no teaching assistants). Reported one undergrad, "The small classes are a real plus here; they allow for more active discussion, since people don't feel so intimidated about speaking out. Also, professors are very accessible and eager to help students." Students also gave high marks to the administration, a rare achievement for a school with a left-leaning student body. One student wrote, "Advisors try to help as much as possible without getting on your case." Best of all, despite the school's excellent academic reputation, many students reported, "This is a very laid-back school *without* competition among students. This creates an atmosphere most conducive to learning."

■ **Life** Although Grinnell is a "very intellectual" school, life here doesn't begin and end in the classroom. As one student put it, "Students are serious about classes, but have a healthy balance of other activities. Everyone has at least one major extracurricular activity." Arts-related extracurriculars, such as the radio station, newspaper, and theater groups, are particularly popular. Of theater, one student wrote that, while theatrical facilities are "far from great," students have "ample opportunity to experiment with improvisational theater, participate and shows, and direct their own productions." Grinnell has no Greek system (said one student, "The Greek system is generally loathed by the student body"), but this deficiency has no noticeable effect on the party scene: students reported above-average use of beer, liquor, and marijuana here.

■ **Students** Wrote one undergrad, "Grinnell seems to be a haven for students who were unique in some way in high school. This makes for a very diverse, very interesting campus." One student warned that "Grinnell has traditionally been a commune-like haven for left-thinking intellectuals who work hard and play hard. However, recently the 'play hard' students have been replaced by more militant 'p.c.' students, creating a more hostile and boring campus life." Tolerance of alternative lifestyles, unsurprisingly, is high; one student told us, "The atmosphere on campus for lesbians and gays is exceptionally *excellent*. As an out lesbian, this is extremely important to me. The town's people, however, are not pleased."

GRINNELL COLLEGE

Admissions

At Grinnell College, the admissions committee first considers your high school GPA. This is followed by your essays, letters of recommendation, extracurriculars, and standardized test scores, all of which are considered roughly equally. Less important than these is your interview (which is optional, but recommended). All applicants are required to submit a score from either the SAT or ACT. They should also have completed four years of English, three years of mathematics, three years of science, three years of social studies/history and, if possible, two years of a foreign language. Students who apply here also often apply to Carleton, Oberlin, Macalester, Northwestern, and Brown.

Financial Aid

The financial aid office at Grinnell requires applicants to submit the FAF. The school's most recent catalog states, "The amount of financial assistance awarded is based primarily upon the applicant's need while the *kind* of assistance is determined by either need and/or academic qualifications." The catalog also notes that "more than 550 students work off-campus," earning between $100 and $1,200 per school year."

A note from the Grinnell Admissions Office:

"Grinnell students are involved and committed—committed to academic work and involved in community and volunteer service. Students are independent and can exercise that independence in Grinnell's open-style curriculum. Grinnell hopes to produce individualism, social commitment, and intellectual self-awareness in its graduates."

ADMISSIONS FACTS

Competitiveness Rating:	**86**
% of applicants accepted:	69
% acceptees attending:	31

FRESHMAN PROFILE

Average verbal SAT:	602
Average math SAT:	634
Average ACT:	28
Graduated top 10% of class:	59
Graduated top 25% of class:	86
Graduated top 50% of class:	97

DEADLINES

Early decision/action:	12/1
Early dec./act. notif.:	1/15
Regular admission:	2/1
Regular adm. notif.:	3/15

APPLICANTS ALSO LOOK AT

and sometimes prefer:
U. Iowa
Carleton College
Washington U.
Oberlin College
Kenyon College
Macalester College

and rarely prefer:
U. Minnesota
Denison U.

ADDRESS

Undergraduate Admissions
Grinnell, IA 50112
515-269-3600

FINANCIAL FACTS

In-state tuition ($):	13,424
Out-of-state tuition ($):	13,424
Room & board:	3,868
FA application deadline:	3/1
% frosh receiving FA:	71
PT earnings per yr. ($):	900

TYPE OF AID: % of students ($)

FA of some kind:	69 (NA)
Need-based grants:	NA
Merit-based grants:	NA
Loans:	NA
Work study:	NA
Student rating of FA:	92

GUILFORD COLLEGE

CAMPUS LIFE

Quality of Life Rating: **86**

Type of school:	private
Affiliation:	Quaker
Environment:	city

STUDENT BODY

FT undergrad enrollment:	1,368
% male/% female:	49/51
% out-of-state:	65
% live on campus:	85
% African-American:	5
% Asian:	2
% Caucasian:	88
% Hispanic:	1
% foreign:	5
% transfers:	9

WHAT'S HOT

college radio station
Grateful Dead
leftist politics
in-class discussion
small classes (overall)
town-gown relations
college theater
gay community accepted
campus easy to get around
interaction among students
doing all the reading
attending all classes

WHAT'S NOT

fraternities/sororities
Top 40

ACADEMICS

Academic Rating: **75**

Calendar:	semester
Student/teacher ratio:	17/1
% doctorates:	77
Profs interesting:	89
Profs accessible:	89
Hours of study per day:	3.63

MOST POPULAR MAJORS BY %

Letters/Literature	12
Business & Management	11
Psychology	5

% GRADS WHO PURSUE

Law:	5
MBA:	4
Medicine:	2
M.A., etc.:	10

What do students think about Guilford College?

■ **Academics** Guilford College, a small school steeped in the Quaker tradition, keeps getting better and better. In recent years, the school's reputation has grown right along with its faculty and enrollment. The student body has also become more competitive and diverse. Classes here are small enough to offer abundant individual attention from the "intensely committed and intelligent" professors, and students appreciate the "interactive teaching methods. Instructors are really interested in students' learning the material, not in torturing them." Indeed, the emphasis on education for its own sake (professors "do not experience pressure from the administration to publish" and are therefore free to concentrate on their students) is one of Guilford's great assets. Another is the large degree of autonomy afforded students: Guilford's curriculum contains few distribution requirements, and even these can by bypassed with good scores on AP exams. Students are not entirely on their own—they must work closely with a faculty advisor in fashioning their curricula—but a Guilford education allows students an unusual amount of freedom in pursuing their studies. Also notable is the school's excellent study abroad program, which over 30 percent of the students enjoy for at least one semester. Standout majors are psychology, English, business, and the sciences. Guilford's small size and limited course selection is mitigated by the fact that students may take courses at any of six other Greensboro area schools.

■ **Life** The Quaker tradition at Guilford allows students to have "a distinctive amount of influence" on all campus issues. Decisions are made "by consensus," and "the Senate (student government) can significantly affect policies" of the college. This self-governance encourages cooperation and responsibility, skills many students feel they learn here. ("I feel better able to face the world now, having 'grown up' at Guilford.") The 300-acre campus is Georgian and beautiful, displaying "lots of trees and more bricks than you've ever seen." Most students enjoy living in the dorms, but many feel the need to get away occasionally ("Living on campus isn't bad, but without a car there is no life"). The social life is quiet, perhaps due to the lack of fraternities and sororities, but Guilford does have its share of parties and its share of collegiate drinking. One student complained, "weekends on campus are pretty boring if you're not drunk." For those so inclined, Guilford provides an impressive array of extracurricular activities, among which theater groups, the college radio station and religious clubs are the most popular. Students here are also sports enthusiasts, both as fans of their intercollegiate teams and as participants in an active intramural program.

■ **Students** The general atmosphere at Guilford is one of acceptance. Students come here from all over the world and from many different lifestyles. As one student explained, "You don't ever not belong, no matter who you are, even if you are a white male straight Republican." The typical Guilfordian is politically quite liberal, and very accepting of the large and visible gay community. Overall, students are very happy here, and the Quakers of the '90s seem to be very good at combining tradition with educational progress.

GUILFORD COLLEGE

Admissions

The admissions office at Guilford College told us that, while they use "no cut-offs," they do "combine class rank and SAT combined score to predict the freshman year GPA." Presumably, then, the number yielded by that formula is carefully considered in the admissions process. Also considered, in descending order of importance, are: high school GPA, application essays, standardized test scores, letters of recommendation, extracurricular activities, and an interview (recommended, but not required). Guilford accepts both the SAT and the ACT. Applicants are expected to have completed, while at high school, four years of English, three years each of math and science, and two years of a foreign language. Applicants to Guilford most frequently also apply to UNC–Chapel Hill, Wake Forest, University of Richmond, UVa, Davidson, and UNC–Greensboro.

Financial Aid

The financial aid office at Guilford College requires applicants to submit the FAF and a copy of their parents' most recent tax return. Merit-based grants are awarded for academics and skills in the arts, music, and drama; other scholarships are set aside for Quakers, others for minority students. The Guilford catalog lists the Perkins, Stafford, and TERI loans as the preferred loan options for students. Work-study employment is available.

A note from the Guilford Admissions Office:

"Founded by the Religious Society of Friends (Quakers), Guilford maintains a strong commitment to social concerns. The campus community tends to be diverse, tolerant and friendly. Students have broad opportunities for involvement.

"Guilford offers seven study-abroad programs and tends to have an international emphasis in our curriculum. Average class size is 18; although teaching styles vary, classes tend to be discussion-oriented.

"Admission to Guilford is competitive, but we are interested in the person behind the application and do take unique experiences into account."

ADMISSIONS FACTS

Competitiveness Rating:	**62**
% of applicants accepted:	80
% acceptees attending:	35

FRESHMAN PROFILE

Average verbal SAT:	500
Average math SAT:	520
Average ACT:	23
Graduated top 10% of class:	18
Graduated top 25% of class:	43
Graduated top 50% of class:	70

DEADLINES

Early decision/action:	12//1
Early dec./act. notif.:	12/15
Regular admission:	3/1
Regular adm. notif.:	4/1

APPLICANTS ALSO LOOK AT

and often prefer:
U. NC– Chapel Hill
Duke U.
Swarthmore College
Oberlin College
U. Virginia
Davidson College

and sometimes prefer:
U. Richmond
U. NC–Greensboro
Earlham College

ADDRESS

Undergraduate Admissions
5800 West Friendly Ave.
Greensboro, NC 27410
919-292-5511

FINANCIAL FACTS

In-state tuition ($):	10,270
Out-of-state tuition ($):	10,270
Room & board:	4,500
FA application deadline:	3/1
% frosh receiving FA:	36
PT earnings per yr. ($):	900

TYPE OF AID: % of students ($)

FA of some kind:	37 (NA)
Need-based grants:	NA
Merit-based grants:	NA
Loans:	NA
Work study:	NA
Student rating of FA:	93

GUSTAVUS ADOLPHUS COLLEGE

Saint Peter, MN

CAMPUS LIFE

Quality of Life Rating:	**83**
Type of school:	private
Affiliation:	Lutheran
Environment:	suburban

STUDENT BODY

FT undergrad enrollment:	2,320
% male/% female:	44/56
% out-of-state:	26
% live on campus:	95
% African-American:	2
% Asian:	2
% Caucasian:	95
% Hispanic:	1
% foreign:	2
% transfers:	1

WHAT'S HOT

intramural sports
financial aid
administration (overall)
working a job
intercollegiate sports
studying hard
cost of living

WHAT'S NOT

dating
diversity

ACADEMICS

Academic Rating:	*78*
Calendar:	4-1-4
Student/teacher ratio:	14/1
% doctorates:	77
Profs interesting:	80
Profs accessible:	84
Hours of study per day:	3.67

MOST POPULAR MAJORS BY %

Psychology:	9
Biology:	8
Management:	7

% GRADS WHO PURSUE

Law:	4
MBA:	4
Medicine:	2
M.A., etc.:	20

What do students think about Gustavus Adolphus College?

■ **Academics** Like many other colleges, Gustavus Adolphus requires students to complete a core curriculum. But unlike other schools, Gustavus offers its students a choice of two cores. Curriculum I resembles distribution requirements; students in this program must spend about one-third of their time taking a variety of courses in different liberal arts areas. Curriculum II, open to only 60 freshmen a year, offers fewer courses but presents material in a sequence designed to help students better "develop a comprehensive understanding of global society." Neither curriculum, the school's catalog notes, interferes with a student's ability to study abroad (over 40 percent of the students study overseas for at least one month). Although Gustavus leans heavily on the liberal arts, the school also seems to understand the career-orientation of its students: the school sponsors semester-long and summer internship programs. Internships are also available during the short January term (which some students use to study abroad). Business and education are popular majors here, as are political science, biology, and psychology.

■ **Life** Our respondents reported that Gustavus students enjoy an exceptionally strong sense of on-campus fellowship. Wrote one, "Gustavus is a community. Sometimes there are little family squabbles, sometimes a little stress—but those are the things that keep Gustavus the friendly, supportive community it continues to be." Students actively participate in a variety of student organizations ranging from literary clubs to faith-centered groups (two-thirds of the students are Lutheran). Most popular is the intramural sports program, which involves over 80 percent of the students. Gustavus' Division III sports teams are also popular, especially football and women's tennis and gymnastics. Greek life exists in a slightly abated form; the school does not recognize the Greeks and consequently all fraternities and sororities are "underground." Explained one student, "When I came here I thought frats/sororities didn't exist because people said that they weren't nationally recognized, but they're here and everyone seems to want to be in one." Students complain that the administration tries to curtail partying ("The Gustavus administration has become very conservative and this has taken a lot of the fun out of college") but despite a strict dry campus policy, drinking is widespread. Minneapolis and St. Paul are about an hour and a half away; noted one student, "It helps to have a car here."

■ **Students** The Gustavus student body is predominantly white, Nordic, Lutheran, and from Minnesota. The grade students gave themselves for diversity was twelfth lowest in our survey, so there's no self-delusion here. Said one student, "When Spike Lee spoke in the 2,000-person capacity chapel, all the minority students sat in the two pews in the first row. All the white students sat behind them. There were about 50 students in the first two rows: our ethnic diversity is pathetic." Politically, the student body is slightly left of center.

GUSTAVUS ADOLPHUS COLLEGE

Saint Peter, MN

Admissions

The admissions office reports that "Gustavus is looking for students from differing socio-economic backgrounds who have strong high school records, who are interested in undergraduate research and a strong writing program. Campus interview is an important part of the admissions process. Volunteer activities are also important." Standardized test scores (either the SAT or the ACT) are considered important, as are essays. Applicants are expected to have completed four years of English, social studies, and math, three years of science, and two years of a foreign language. Students who apply to Gustavus Adolphus most often also apply to St. Olaf, University of Minnesota–Twin Cities, Carleton, and University of Wisconsin–Madison.

Financial Aid

Financial aid applicants to Gustavus Adolphus College must complete the FFS or FAF. Ninety-two percent of those who applied for aid in the class of '95 received some form of financial assistance (72% overall). The average award value was $9,273. Last year, 10% of all undergrads received an academic scholarship (average value: $1,102). In '91–'92, 48% of Gustavus's students took out Stafford loans (average value: $2,731), 14% took out Perkins loans (average value: $1,066) and 8% took out PLUS or SLS loans (average value: $3,645).

A note from the Gustavus Adolphus College Admissions Office:

"Gustavus Adolphus College—a national liberal arts college with a strong tradition of quality teaching, committed to the liberal arts, to its Lutheran history, to innovation as evidenced by the 4-1-4 calendar, Curriculum I and II, and the writing program, and to affordable costs with its unique Guaranteed Cost Plan and the Partners in Scholarship Program. Excellent facilities with most recent buildings being Olin Hall of physics and mathematics, Confer Hall for the humanities, and Lund Center for physical education, athletics, and health."

ADMISSIONS FACTS

Competitiveness Rating:	**88**
% of applicants accepted:	86
% acceptees attending:	50

FRESHMAN PROFILE

Average verbal SAT:	517*
Average math SAT:	587*
Average ACT:	25*
Graduated top 10% of class:	38
Graduated top 25% of class:	76
Graduated top 50% of class:	98

DEADLINES

Early decision/action:	11/15
Early dec./act. notif.:	12/1
Regular admission:	4/1
Regular adm. notif.:	5/1

APPLICANTS ALSO LOOK AT

and sometimes prefer:
Macalester College
U. Wisconsin–Madison

and rarely prefer:
U. Minnesota
St. Olaf College
Carleton College

ADDRESS

Undergraduate Admissions
800 College Ave.
Saint Peter, MN 56082
507-931-7676

FINANCIAL FACTS

In-state tuition ($):	10,765
Out-of-state tuition ($):	10,765
Room & board:	2,750
FA application deadline:	3/15
% frosh receiving FA:	65
PT earnings per yr. ($):	1200

TYPE OF AID: % of students ($)

FA of some kind:	65 (7,708)
Need-based grants:	62 (5,843)
Merit-based grants:	NA
Loans:	55 (3,437)
Work study:	57 (1,219)
Student rating of FA:	90

HAMILTON COLLEGE

Clinton, NY

CAMPUS LIFE

Quality of Life Rating: **83**

Type of school:	private
Affiliation:	none
Environment:	suburban

STUDENT BODY

FT undergrad enrollment:	1,641
% male/% female:	53/47
% out-of-state:	51
% live on campus:	99
% African-American:	3
% Asian:	4
% Caucasian:	85
% Hispanic:	3
% foreign:	5
% transfers:	1

WHAT'S HOT

college radio station
living on campus
profs outside class
campus appearance
profs teach intros
small labs and seminars
deans
dorm comfort
marijuana
profs in class
beer

WHAT'S NOT

diversity
dating

ACADEMICS

Academic Rating: **83**

Calendar:	semester
Student/teacher ratio:	11/1
% doctorates:	81
Profs interesting:	86
Profs accessible:	90
Hours of study per day:	3.06

MOST POPULAR MAJORS BY %

Government:	13
English:	11
Economics:	11

% GRADS WHO PURSUE

Law:	5
MBA:	1
Medicine:	3
M.A., etc.:	10

What do students think about Hamilton College?

■ **Academics** Hamilton College may not have the big-name scholars nearby Ivy League institutions have, but the typical Hamilton student realizes s/he's getting something Ivy students don't: an exceptional amount of personal attention from professors. "I believe I have gotten more out of small classes and personal interactions with professors than my friends who have been taught by TAs at Harvard and Princeton," wrote one Hamiltonian. Reported another, "The accessibility of professors is fantastic. Some will invite you over to their homes for dinner and offer you a beer. That's the great thing about being at a small school." Students here pursue popular liberal arts and social science majors: political science, English, and economics have the highest enrollment. Demanding core requirements in a broad range of subjects eat up over one quarter of the credits necessary for an undergraduate degree.

■ **Life** Hamilton is a small school in a small town (Clinton, New York). The closest city is Utica, but most of Hamilton's social life happens within the confines of its two picturesque campuses. Explained one student, "There's always something to do, from school work, to partying (on weeknights, too), to participating in clubs and intramurals, and finally, to attending guest lectures and plays." For many, the setting is perfect (wrote one student, "There is plenty of time during graduate school to enjoy a big university in a city. Come to Hamilton to experience the small college community life"), but it's certainly not for hard-core urbanites. In certain ways, Hamilton is a typical small school: the fraternity system "is very strong"; the dating scene is practically non-existent (socially active students at small schools usually either settle in with one significant other for the duration or just hook up over and over for four years); and drinking is very popular. Wrote one student, "You learn to do two things really well at Hamilton: study hard and stress; and drink hard and puke." When students hurl at home, they do so within the confines of comfortable dorms.

■ **Students** Hamilton students, as one put it, "do tend to be homogeneous—mostly white with money, from prep-schools." Another described what he called "the Hamilton uniform: Dockers, Champion turtlenecks, L.L Bean or Columbia Siri jackets, knit sweaters, something from Land's End and a New England haircut." Added a black student (one of about 50), "if you're not Caucasian, the adjustment here is tremendous. The school has a great deal to offer to many different people, but it needs more diversity. Also, more attention needs to be paid to women's issues here." About 80 international students "help create a more diverse student body. It's a wonderful situation for both local and international students." There appears to be considerable division over political issues: the student body is by and large conservative, but there are enough left-leaning students and faculty to draw majority complaints about political correctness, multi-culturalism, and the existence of a women's studies center.

HAMILTON COLLEGE

Clinton, NY

Admissions

The admissions office at Hamilton told us, "We are looking for academically gifted, talented students who are ready to undertake a rigorous academic program. We place much more weight on the high school performance of an applicant (GPA, rank in class, recommendations) than we do on standardized test scores." The school considers letters of recommendation the second-most important part of your application, then, in descending order of importance: essays, a "sample of expository prose" (i.e., a paper for a class), standardized test scores, extracurricular activities, and interview ("strongly recommended"). Artists and musicians are encouraged to submit portfolios and cassettes. Applicants are required to submit scores for either the SAT or the ACT; three achievements are "strongly recommended." High school curricular requirements include: four years of English, three years each of math and a foreign language, and two years of science. Hamilton applicants most often also apply to Colgate, Cornell, Dartmouth, Middlebury, Williams, and Bates.

Financial Aid

The financial aid office at Hamilton College requires applicants to submit the FAF. All assistance is granted solely on the basis of need; Hamilton offers no merit scholarships. According to the school's most recent brochure for prospects, "In 1989–90 Hamilton awarded more than $5.2 million in scholarship assistance and administered an additional $3.8 million in loans, jobs, and grants. More than 60% of the student body received some financial assistance based on need." Based on these numbers, we approximate the value of the average aid package to be $9,000.

A note from the Hamilton College Admissions Office:

"One of Hamilton's most important characteristics is the exceptional interaction that takes place between students and faculty members. Whether in class or out, they work together, challenging one another to excel. Academic life at Hamilton is rigorous, and emerging from that rigor is a community spirit based on common commitment. It binds together student and teacher, and stimulates self-motivation, thus making the learning process not only more productive but also more enjoyable and satisfying.

"Also characteristic of Hamilton is its comprehensive, well-rounded academic program. Incorporating the arts and the humanities, mathematics and the sciences, and the social sciences, it combines the traditional and time-tested liberal arts with modern-day approaches to them. Through a system of faculty advising, it also provides Hamilton's students with a maximum of choice while at the same time assuring them of a truly liberal education."

ADMISSIONS FACTS

Competitiveness Rating:	**86**
% of applicants accepted:	43
% acceptees attending:	27

FRESHMAN PROFILE

Average verbal SAT:	560*
Average math SAT:	613*
Average ACT:	NA
Graduated top 10% of class:	50
Graduated top 25% of class:	85
Graduated top 50% of class:	97

DEADLINES

Early decision/action:	11/15
Early dec./act. notif.:	12/15
Regular admission:	1/15
Regular adm. notif.:	4/15

APPLICANTS ALSO LOOK AT

and often prefer:
Dartmouth College
Amherst College

and sometimes prefer:
Trinity College
Vassar College
Williams College
Lafayette College
Colgate U.

and rarely prefer:
Bates College
Skidmore College

ADDRESS

Undergraduate Admissions
Clinton, NY 13323-1293
315-859-4421

FINANCIAL FACTS

In-state tuition ($):	16,650
Out-of-state tuition ($):	16,650
Room & board:	4,550
FA application deadline:	2/1
% frosh receiving FA:	62
PT earnings per yr. ($):	1200

TYPE OF AID: % of students ($)

FA of some kind:	63 (9,000)
Need-based grants:	NA
Merit-based grants:	NA
Loans:	NA
Work study:	NA
Student rating of FA:	83

HAMPDEN–SYDNEY COLLEGE

Hampden-Sydney, VA

CAMPUS LIFE

Quality of Life Rating: 94

Type of school:	private
Affiliation:	Presbyterian
Environment:	rural

STUDENT BODY

FT undergrad enrollment:	950
% male/% female:	100/0
% out-of-state:	46
% live on campus:	93
% African-American:	2
% Asian:	1
% Caucasian:	95
% Hispanic:	1
% foreign:	1
% transfers:	2

WHAT'S HOT

town-gown relations
conservative politics
administration (overall)
small classes (overall)
Grateful Dead
caring about politics
profs in class
dating
overall happiness
campus appearance
attending all classes
profs outside class
food

WHAT'S NOT

diversity

ACADEMICS

Academic Rating: 82

Calendar:	semester
Student/teacher ratio:	12/1
% doctorates:	91
Profs interesting:	98
Profs accessible:	91
Hours of study per day:	3.28

MOST POPULAR MAJORS BY %

Economics:	26
History:	17
Political Science:	11

% GRADS WHO PURSUE

Law:	8
MBA:	5
Medicine:	5
M.A., etc.:	10

What do students think about Hampden-Sydney College?

■ **Academics** Tradition, honor, character, gentility: when Hampden-Sydney men describe their school, these are words they invariably use. This small, adamantly Southern all-male liberal arts school is ideally suited to men who wish to "live in the traditions that their predecessors created and learn what it means to become 'good men and good citizens.'" That tradition includes "a strict Honor Code: students accused of wrong-doing are judged by a court of their peers. The system is very effective." It also includes a rigorous set of distribution requirements comprising about half the credits toward graduation. H-S students must take two semesters of English composition (called "The Rhetoric Program"; one student told us the classes had "done wonders for my writing. The program is tedious, yet, once finished, it adds confidence and gives us the ability to express ourselves effectively in writing."). All classes are small and taught by full professors who are "extremely accessible and eager to help—some even get offended if you don't come see them outside of class!" Students also reported a "laid-back, not 'dog eat dog' atmosphere" in class and noted that "The classroom is much more relaxed without the presence of women." Many students pursue pre-business majors, but the liberal arts and social sciences are reportedly uniformly strong. Students enjoy a widely used Study Abroad program that sends students to "over thirty different overseas programs."

■ **Life** Hampden-Sydney has an undeniable country club atmosphere: the campus is gorgeous, the dorms are beautiful, and even the food is good. Greek life, sports, and extracurricular clubs are all central to life at H-S. Explained one student, "With only 950 students, it is very easy to get involved in campus activities, which are important because the college is secluded and all-male." Social life, according to many, is "active. Although the school is all-male, women from nearby schools, such as Sweet Briar and Hollins, visit regularly on weekends." Others, however, complained, "Interacting with the opposite sex can be extremely difficult because the only time you see women is in a purely social context. Therefore, you have to be very comfortable with and confident in your ability to meet and relate to females." Perhaps that's why another student wrote that, "Having an outgoing personality is crucial to social success—introverts will not go far here."

■ **Students** What sort of man goes to Hampden-Sydney? Summed up one student, "This school is a wonderful place for the true Southern gentleman." Added another, "When you arrive in the fall, bring your golf bag and your hunting rifle." Diversity is not a major concern here; the vast majority of students fit the H-S mold and are happy that they do. The student body is the nation's most politically conservative. Oddly, they are also major Dead Heads. One can only imagine the conversations here (Student 1: "Get the government off the back of business!!" Student 2: " Yeah, but...leave that Rain Forest alone!!" [high fives all around]).

HAMPDEN–SYDNEY COLLEGE

Hampden-Sydney, VA

Admissions

The admissions office at Hampden-Sydney considers your high school GPA and curriculum the most important part of your application. The school then considers, in descending order of importance: essays, standardized test scores, letters of recommendation, extracurricular activities, and interview. Applicants must take either the SAT or the ACT, and are expected to have completed the following high school curriculum: four years of English, three years of math, two years each of foreign language and science (at least one lab), and one year of social studies. The school adds, "We encourage applicants to take as many advanced courses in the above academic areas as possible, with a third year of a foreign language and a fourth year of math being especially valuable." Applicants to Hampden-Sydney most often also apply to UVa, Washington and Lee, and James Madison University.

Financial Aid

The financial aid office at Hampden-Sydney requires applicants to submit the FAF. The school awards academic scholarships; last year, six percent of the students received one (average value: $7,534). The most popular loan programs with Hampden-Sydney students last year were: Stafford (21%; $2,732); Perkins (6%; $2,173), and PLUS (8%; $3,757).

A note from the Hampden-Sydney Admissions Office:

"The spirit of Hampden-Sydney is its sense of community. As one of only 950 students, you will be in small classes and find it easy to get extra help or inspiration from professors when you want it. Many of our professors live on campus and enjoy being with students in the snack bar, as well as in the classroom. They give you the best, most personal education possible." A big bonus of small-college life is that everybody is invited to go out for everything, and you can be as much of a leader as you want to be. From athletics, to debating, to publications, to fraternity life, this is part of the process that produces a well-rounded Hampden-Sydney graduate."

ADMISSIONS FACTS

Competitiveness Rating:	**67**
% of applicants accepted:	70
% acceptees attending:	40

FRESHMAN PROFILE

Average verbal SAT:	516
Average math SAT:	569
Average ACT:	25
Graduated top 10% of class:	17
Graduated top 25% of class:	51
Graduated top 50% of class:	75

DEADLINES

Early decision/action:	11/15
Early dec./act. notif.:	12/15
Regular admission:	3/1
Regular adm. notif.:	4/15

APPLICANTS ALSO LOOK AT

and often prefer:
College of William & Mary
U. Virginia

and sometimes prefer:
Washington and Lee U.
James Madison U.
Vanderbilt U.
U. NC– Chapel Hill

and rarely prefer:
Randolph-Macon College

ADDRESS

Undergraduate Admissions
Post Office Box 667
Hampden-Sydney, VA 23943
804-223-4388

FINANCIAL FACTS

In-state tuition ($):	11,316
Out-of-state tuition ($):	11,316
Room & board:	3,797
FA application deadline:	3/1
% frosh receiving FA:	72
PT earnings per yr. ($):	600

TYPE OF AID: % of students ($)

FA of some kind:	87 (6,273)
Need-based grants:	38 (10,939)
Merit-based grants:	6 (7,534)
Loans:	27 (2,938)
Work study:	30 (1,042)
Student rating of FA:	97

HAMPSHIRE COLLEGE

Amherst, MA

CAMPUS LIFE

Quality of Life Rating:	**83**
Type of school:	private
Affiliation:	none
Environment:	rural

STUDENT BODY

FT undergrad enrollment:	1,253
% male/% female:	39/61
% out-of-state:	86
% live on campus:	87
% African-American:	3
% Asian:	4
% Caucasian:	88
% Hispanic:	3
% foreign:	3
% transfers:	15

WHAT'S HOT

gay community accepted
leftist politics
honesty
in-class discussion
alternative rock
Grateful Dead
marijuana
caring about politics
small classes (overall)
profs in class

WHAT'S NOT

fraternities/sororities
intercollegiate sports
college radio station
marriage

ACADEMICS

Academic Rating:	**81**
Calendar:	4-1-4
Student/teacher ratio:	13/1
% doctorates:	91
Profs interesting:	90
Profs accessible:	81
Hours of study per day:	3.7

MOST POPULAR MAJORS BY %

Visual and Performing Arts:	26
Social Sciences:	22
Humanities:	15

What do students think about Hampshire College?

■ **Academics** Students at Hampshire College, a small school known for its philosophy of alternative, self-directed education, responded to our questions with a flood of well-written essays. The unusually high number of thoughtful responses from Hampshire is telling. Students here are used to creative thinking and fluent writing, because those skills are expected of them daily. Hampsters "have no tests, grades, credits or majors. Instead, we have course papers, self and teacher evaluations, the divisional system and concentrations." This unusual academic structure is hailed by many as progressive and challenging. Since students design their own programs, there are "no cheesy English 101 requirements." Rather than "teaching countless empty facts, the system teaches students to think independently and to write well." Warned one student, "Don't think this place is a breeze just because we don't believe in grades. Written evaluations can be harsh, and you'll never write—and *revise*—as many papers anywhere as you will here." All agreed that if a prospective student is not "extremely motivated," s/he should not come to Hampshire. Many artistic types can be found here. Witness the excellent film and photography departments, which are so popular that they "close out students who aren't majors." Most students believe Hampshire's system really works; but others are less satisfied, classifying the school as "*so* alternative that after two years you are trapped in a non-transferable system." A few complain of the administration, calling it "tyrannical and impossible to interact with," but overall student opinion of Hampshire is very high. It is "OK to draw outside the lines here," and most appreciate the opportunity to do just that.

■ **Life** Hampshire "is the drug use, PC, hippie, punk, gay/lesbian, free love, clothing-optional capital of the US college scene," according to one adjective-happy student. Just about anything goes here. Acid is widely accepted, for example (beer is not very popular), but "peer pressure is low. There are plenty of virgin teetotalers who are accepted here." Some are disappointed with the somewhat smothering social life, but most admit to having fun. One wryly remarked, "Hampster relationships are never a problem, if you're one of the dozen or so people who are still whimsical enough to date anyone." Anyone seeking escape can easily slip out to another college (Hampshire is part of the Five College Consortium, which includes Amherst, Smith, Mount Holyoke, and UMass-Amherst).

■ **Students** Hampsters are a very tolerant and accepting group. One said that "gays, lesbians and bisexuals are active and accepted here, but not in a way that limits heterosexuals, many of whom attend LGBA-sponsored dances." Retro clothing and purple, blue, green, orange or non-existent hair are more common here than different shades of skin color, but Hampshire is diverse in its own way.

HAMPSHIRE COLLEGE

Amherst, MA

Admissions

The admissions office reports that "no cut-offs or standardized tests are required for admission. In addition to solid academic preparation, we seek students who wish to participate in shaping their own education, who have intellectual curiosity, and who are self-motivated." Hampshire looks closely at your high school transcript, essays, and record of extracurricular involvement. The school also considers the results of your interview, letters of recommendation, and a sample of your creative work (the submission of which is optional). Applicants are recommended to have completed a college preparatory program and to demonstrate an interest in a specific course of study. ESL students must take the TOEFL. Those who apply to Hampshire most often also apply to Sarah Lawrence, Oberlin, Bard, Bennington, and Reed.

Financial Aid

Financial aid applicants to Hampshire must complete the FAF, and the HCA form generated by Hampshire's FA office. The school offers several scholarships based on "academic merit and leadership potential." These awards are made at the time of admission, and all students are considered for them. The average financial aid *grant* for 1991 entering students was $11,809, and the average overall financial aid package was $14,000. The deadline for priority consideration is *received at Hampshire by February 15*. Applicants are notified of awards by April 1.

A note from the Hampshire College Admissions Office:

"In many ways, Hampshire is like other selective liberal arts colleges. Here you will find approximately 1,250 students, about equally divided between men and women, from 46 states and many foreign countries; a student-faculty ratio of 13:1; the full range of subjects and fields of concentration; and sophisticated equipment and facilities.

"Yet Hampshire offers an extraordinary education. Rather than selecting a major with a predetermined set of required courses, as a Hampshire student you complete three divisions of study built upon your evolving interests and aspirations. Together you and a faculty advisor map out each semester's program, a thoughtful combination of courses, independent study and, if appropriate, field work or an internship. Extensive evaluations for courses and divisional projects—written by faculty who serve as teachers, mentors and examiners—highlight your academic strengths, suggest areas for improvement, and serve as a permanent record of your work at Hampshire."

ADMISSIONS FACTS

Competitiveness Rating: **76**
% of applicants accepted: 51
% acceptees attending: 35

FRESHMAN PROFILE

Average verbal SAT: NA
Average math SAT: NA
Average ACT: NA
Graduated top 10% of class: 29
Graduated top 25% of class: 66
Graduated top 50% of class: 94

DEADLINES

Early decision/action: 12/3
Early dec./act. notif.: 12/7
Regular admission: 2/1
Regular adm. notif.: 4/1

APPLICANTS ALSO LOOK AT

and often prefer:
Bates College
Vassar College

and sometimes prefer:
Reed College
Sarah Lawrence College
Bennington College
Antioch College
New College

and rarely prefer:
Goddard College
Bard College

ADDRESS

Undergraduate Admissions
Amherst, MA 01002
413-549-4600

FINANCIAL FACTS

In-state tuition ($): 17,200
Out-of-state tuition ($): 17,200
Room & board: 4,560
FA application deadline: none
% frosh receiving FA: 47
PT earnings per yr. ($): 1450

TYPE OF AID: % of students ($)
FA of some kind: 47 (14,000)
Need-based grants: NA
Merit-based grants: NA
Loans: NA
Work study: NA

Student rating of FA: 76

247

HARVARD COLLEGE AND RADCLIFFE COLLEGE

Cambridge, MA

CAMPUS LIFE

Quality of Life Rating:	**88**
Type of school:	private
Affiliation:	none
Environment:	city

STUDENT BODY

FT undergrad enrollment:	6,787
% male/% female:	58/42
% out-of-state:	76
% live on campus:	99
% African-American:	8
% Asian:	17
% Caucasian:	66
% Hispanic:	6
% foreign:	6
% transfers:	4

WHAT'S HOT

student interaction
college theater
library
gay community accepted
location
dorm comfort
small labs and seminars
studying hard
administration (overall)

WHAT'S NOT

fraternities/sororities
marijuana
dating
diversity
attending all classes

ACADEMICS

Academic Rating:	**94**
Calendar:	semester
Student/teacher ratio:	8/1
% doctorates:	98
Profs interesting:	78
Profs accessible:	75
Hours of study per day:	3.63

MOST POPULAR MAJORS BY %

Government:	12
English and American History:	9
History:	9

% GRADS WHO PURSUE

Law:	13
MBA:	1
Medicine:	19
M.A., etc.:	29

What do students think about Harvard/Radcliffe?

■ **Academics** Harvard is one of the best academic universities in the country, if not *the* best. If you attend school here, you will learn from world-famous scholars in small classes, do research in excellent facilities, and probably feel privileged to be at the nation's most famous institution. Not surprisingly, Harvard students love everything about their school (although, oddly, they are not among the 10 happiest student bodies in the nation). The school is a hub of intellectual activity in America, home to a distinguished faculty and often host to visiting politicians and scholars. Said one student, "there is always so much going on—lectures, visiting speakers, events—it's just a matter of going out and finding what you want!" Students gave their profs average marks, as students often do at schools with considerable graduate populations. Even those who disliked their instructors, though, were happy with Harvard. Said one, "The resources available for learning (libraries, labs, friends) are the redeeming qualities that make it worthwhile coming here." Said another, "Harvard has all the resources: career services advisors, great people academically and administratively at many different levels. But students must go out and tap these resources themselves—there's not much hand-holding here." Students gave the administration a big thumbs-up. Once discrete all-male and all-female colleges, Harvard and Radcliffe are now separate entities in name only.

■ **Life** One thing that clearly sets Harvard apart from Yale is location. Yale is located in dingy, unfriendly downtown New Haven, while Harvard is in very student-friendly Cambridge, minutes away from Boston. Another difference between the two is quality of dorms. You guessed it: Harvard's are great, Yale's are gross. Partly because of the workload, the staples of social life at most other schools—partying and dating—are relatively uncommon here. Another impediment to social life, according to one student, is that "Harvard makes students work very hard—they have no time to socialize and interact with others—so when placed into social situations, they don't know how to act." There is no Greek system here, but there are several exclusive, upper-crust social clubs (membership by invitation only). Biggest negative of life here: the weather stinks.

■ **Students** The students have a reputation for arrogance. Of course, Harvard students feel they're entitled to be arrogant. "Lots of huge egos, but, unfortunately, many are well deserved," reported one student. "Brilliant" is the word most often used by Harvard students to describe each other; "preppy" is the second-most common description. Still, many students indicated surprise at how heterogeneous the student body here is. A gay student told us that while "there is a rather large proportion of preppy snobs, it's easy to avoid them if you want. Everyone and anyone can find his/her niche among the incredibly diverse students." Said one freshman, "I wholeheartedly recommend applying to all you dweebs out there."

HARVARD COLLEGE AND RADCLIFFE COLLEGE

Cambridge, MA

Admissions

The admissions office reports that "we require the SAT or ACT and also three CEEB achievement tests; we have no 'cut-offs,' nor do we admit students on the basis of test scores alone. Successful applicants normally pursue their school's most rigorous academic programs, with strong results. In making decisions, we consider also extracurricular achievements, recommendations, and interviews." An interview is required. Harvard did not provide information regarding schools with which they share the greatest overlap in applicant pools; our surveys indicated that Yale, Williams, Boston College, Boston University, NYU, Northwestern, Georgetown, and University of Pennsylvania were popular choices among Harvard applicants.

Financial Aid

Harvard/Radcliffe financial aid office requires applicants to submit the FAF, their parents' most recent tax return, and a form generated by the school. The FA office told us that "Our need-blind admissions process and commitment to meeting the full need of all admitted students assures access to students from diverse backgrounds. Our financial aid staff is available to listen to and take into account individual family financial situations." Harvard does not award merit-based grants. Loans recommended last year included the Stafford (taken by 34% of the students; average value: $2,626), Perkins (7%; $3,068), and a loan sponsored by the university (10%; $2,531). The FA application deadline is February 15 for freshmen, April 1 for returning students.

A note from the Harvard/Radcliffe Admissions Office:

"Founded in 1636, Harvard College is the oldest American institution of higher education. For more than 150 years, Harvard's primary function was the training of ministers. By 1872, the College had established five professional schools, and had become the central unit of a large university.

"Radcliffe College was founded in 1879 as an annex to Harvard College. Over the course of a century, the Colleges have developed a partnership. Men and women apply for admission through a joint admissions office for one class of 1600 students, and become candidates for the Bachelor of Arts or Bachelor of Science degree in a liberal arts program.

"Located by the Charles River in Cambridge, Massachusetts, Harvard is 10 minutes from Boston by public transportation. The Cambridge and Boston area is home to numerous museums, professional sports teams, theater companies, and musical ensembles."

ADMISSIONS FACTS

Competitiveness Rating:	100
% of applicants accepted:	18
% acceptees attending:	73

FRESHMAN PROFILE

Average verbal SAT:	663*
Average math SAT:	707*
Average ACT:	NA
Graduated top 10% of class:	90
Graduated top 25% of class:	98
Graduated top 50% of class:	98

DEADLINES

Early decision/action:	11/1
Early dec./act. notif.:	12/20
Regular admission:	1/1
Regular adm. notif.:	4/1

APPLICANTS ALSO LOOK AT

and sometimes prefer:
Princeton U.
Stanford U.
Yale U.

and rarely prefer:
Northwestern U.
Georgetown U.
Amherst U.
Williams College
U. Pensylvania
Swarthmore College

ADDRESS

Undergraduate Adm., Byerly Hall
8 Garden Street
Cambridge, MA 02138
617-495-1551

FINANCIAL FACTS

In-state tuition ($):	15,410
Out-of-state tuition ($):	15,410
Room & board:	5,520
FA application deadline:	2/15
% frosh receiving FA:	67
PT earnings per yr. ($):	1300

TYPE OF AID: % of students ($)

FA of some kind:	67 (NA)
Need-based grants:	43 (11,846)
Merit-based grants:	0
Loans:	44 (2,764)
Work study:	22 (1,500)
Student rating of FA:	86

HAVERFORD COLLEGE

Haverford, PA

CAMPUS LIFE

Quality of Life Rating: **87**

Type of school:	private
Affiliation:	none
Environment:	suburban

STUDENT BODY

FT undergrad enrollment:	1,122
% male/% female:	56/44
% out-of-state:	81
% live on campus:	96
% African-American:	5
% Asian:	8
% Caucasian:	82
% Hispanic:	5
% foreign:	3
% transfers:	1

WHAT'S HOT

gay community accepted
deans
administration (overall)
leftist politics
profs outside class
catalog
profs in class
library
studying hard
small classes (overall)

WHAT'S NOT

cost of living
dating
religion
hard liquor

ACADEMICS

Academic Rating: **91**

Calendar:	semester
Student/teacher ratio:	11/1
% doctorates:	93
Profs interesting:	93
Profs accessible:	94
Hours of study per day:	3.7

MOST POPULAR MAJORS BY %

Social Sciences:	44
Letters/Literature:	13
Life Sciences:	12

% GRADS WHO PURSUE

Law:	7
MBA:	1
Medicine:	10
M.A., etc.:	12

What do students think about Haverford College?

■ **Academics** Haverford College has a well-deserved reputation as one of the finest small colleges in the country. Students here gave high marks to most facets of the academic environment, citing their easy interaction with professors, relatively painless dealings with campus bureaucrats, and satisfaction with the honor code. One student told us that "the Honor Code is probably the most unique thing about Haverford. Students take the code very seriously and on the whole it provides an atmosphere of trust. Many exams are self-scheduled which makes exam period more relaxed." Students stressed the ease of cross-registration at nearby Bryn Mawr. Said one, "The two schools function together as one academic entity." Pre-medical studies are popular here—one in ten students goes on to medical school—as are English, history, and philosophy. Students carry a heavy work load (about three-and-three-quarters hours a day), but most seem comfortable with it and would agree that "Haverford is a wonderful place for the mind to germinate."

■ **Life** Haverford is a great place to study. Just ask any undergrad about social life here and s/he'll tell you: "Haverford is a great place to study." Social life definitely runs second to academics here. Wrote one typical respondent, "It's not a big party school, but you can find good pals to drink with regardless." There is a partying contingent—one member wrote, "One third of us go out drinking on weekends and try to do enough to make up for the other two thirds"—but quiet weekends seem more the rule than the exception. Haverford has no Greek system. For off-campus activity, Philadelphia is only 20 minutes away by train. Many student activities are run jointly with the school down the road. Reported one student, "Haverford is pretty hard to evaluate without taking Bryn Mawr into account. Virtually everything is bi-college." There is a closeness at Haverford that comes from having a small student body (fewer than 1,200). Sometimes that closeness is overwhelming. Wrote one student, "This place can seem a little too small, especially when I realize that I know everyone here by face."

■ **Students** Haverford has an 18 percent minority population, nearly half of which is made up of Asians. Blacks and Hispanics make up the other large minority groups here. Haverford has more men than women, but Haverford/Bryn Mawr combine for a 3:1 female to male ratio. The student body leans to the left, but with its right foot on the ground. One black student called Haverford "a small liberal arts school with a semi-liberal attitude." The honor code affects student relations as well as academics. One student summed it up this way: "Some say the code restricts people in the minority view because they don't want to offend the majority. I think it's just the opposite, the code creates an atmosphere where people are more likely to listen to and respect views which are different from theirs."

HAVERFORD COLLEGE

Haverford, PA

Admissions

According to Haverford's brochure, "The College seeks a diversity of talents, interests, and backgrounds, placing greatest emphasis on academic promise, preparation for college-level work, and the candidate's potential to contribute to Haverford's community." Candidates for admission must take the SAT and three Achievement tests, including English Composition. While an interview isn't required, it is strongly recommended, particularly for applicants within 150 miles of Haverford. The recommended high school curriculum includes four years of English, three years each of foreign language and math, and two years each of science and social science.

Financial Aid

Financial aid applicants to Haverford are required to complete the FAF and a form generated by Haverford's financial aid office. At Haverford, federal and state grants will reduce the amount of your Haverford grant, but for all other outside grants, "the first $500 or 50%, whichever is greater and up to the amount of your loan expectation, will reduce that loan expectation. Any amount above the first $500 or 50% will reduce your Haverford College Grant." 61% of those who applied for aid in the class of '94 received Haverford Grant funds. The average grant for the class of '94 ranged from $14,426 (for families with income below $10,000) to $5,283 (for families with income of $60,000 or above). In the '90–'91 academic year, the first $4,700 of eligibility for aid was automatically met by a combination of job, loan, and summer savings.

A note from the Haverford Admissions Office:

"Haverford strives to be a college in which integrity, honesty, and concern for others are dominant forces. The college does not have many formal rules; rather, it offers an opportunity for students to govern their affairs and conduct themselves with respect and concern for others. Each student is expected to adhere to the Honor Code as it is adopted each year by the Students' Association. Haverford's Quaker roots show most clearly in the relationship of faculty and students, in the emphasis on integrity, in the interaction of the individual and the community, and through the College's concern for the uses to which its students put their expanding knowledge. Haverford's 1,100 students represent a wide diversity of interests, backgrounds and talents. They come from public, parochial and independent schools across the United States, Puerto Rico, and 27 foreign countries. Students of color are an important part of the Haverford community. The Minority Coalition, which includes Asian, Black, and Hispanic students' associations, works with faculty and administration on matters directly concerned with the quality of life at the College."

ADMISSIONS FACTS

Competitiveness Rating:	**94**
% of applicants accepted:	40
% acceptees attending:	34

FRESHMAN PROFILE

Average verbal SAT:	610*
Average math SAT:	657*
Average ACT:	NA
Graduated top 10% of class:	78
Graduated top 25% of class:	96
Graduated top 50% of class:	100

DEADLINES

Early decision/action:	11/15
Early dec./act. notif.:	12/15
Regular admission:	1/15
Regular adm. notif.:	4/15

APPLICANTS ALSO LOOK AT

and often prefer:
Princeton U.
Columbia U.
Yale U.

and sometimes prefer:
Amherst College
Swarthmore College
Williams College
U. Pennsylvania

and rarely prefer:
Vassar College
Middlebury College

ADDRESS

Undergraduate Admissions
370 Lancaster Avenue
Haverford, PA 19041-1392
215-896-1350

FINANCIAL FACTS

In-state tuition ($):	15,992
Out-of-state tuition ($):	15,992
Room & board:	5,400
FA application deadline:	1/31
% frosh receiving FA:	41
PT earnings per yr. ($):	1150

TYPE OF AID: % of students ($)	
FA of some kind:	40 (NA)
Need-based grants:	NA
Merit-based grants:	NA
Loans:	NA
Work study:	NA
Student rating of FA:	96

HENDRIX COLLEGE

Conway, AR

CAMPUS LIFE

Quality of Life Rating: **87**

Type of school:	private
Affiliation:	Methodist
Environment:	city

STUDENT BODY

FT undergrad enrollment:	1,003
% male/% female:	46/54
% out-of-state:	20
% live on campus:	85
% African-American:	6
% Asian:	2
% Caucasian:	90
% Hispanic:	1
% foreign:	2
% transfers:	2

WHAT'S HOT

college radio station
small lectures
alternative rock
gay community visible
college theater groups
cost of living
deans
profs in class
profs outside class
intramural sports
overall happiness

WHAT'S NOT

fraternities/sororities
location

ACADEMICS

Academic Rating: **81**

Calendar:	trimester
Student/teacher ratio:	16/1
% doctorates:	80
Profs interesting:	94
Profs accessible:	93
Hours of study per day:	3.4

MOST POPULAR MAJORS BY %

Social Sciences	19
Business & Management	17
Psychology	12

% GRADS WHO PURSUE

Law:	7
MBA:	3
Medicine:	8
M.A., etc.:	20

What do students think about Hendrix College?

■ **Academics** Hendrix students gave their school high grades in almost every academic category. Full professors, not TAs, teach almost all classes; the profs are great teachers, and are very accessible outside the classroom; the student-teacher ratio is good, and most classes are small; and, most importantly, students ranked high in our "overall happiness" category. Not bad for a small school out in the boondocks! Over one third of Hendrix graduates go on to grad school, including the eight percent who proceed to medical school: "Science classes are openly competitive and pre-med oriented," explained one pre-med. Economics, political science, and liberal arts programs are also popular here. Hendrix's general education requirements are flexible but demanding: while students are afforded a number of choices in fulfilling these, all entail a great deal of work in the fields of Western civilization, humanities, social sciences, natural sciences, and foreign language. Hendrix's trimester schedule, which consists of three nine-week terms, creates a high-pressure atmosphere, as exams are never far off: perhaps that's why one student summed his four years here up as "sort of a 'be all you can be' experience minus the camouflage and combat boots." A final note: Hendrix offers several attractive study abroad options, including the 'Hendrix-in-Oxford' plan, which allows students to spend their junior years at Oxford University in England.

■ **Life** Hendrix is the quintessential small school. It has only 1000 students, and it's located in a town none of the students like, so the students are pretty much stuck with each other. Said one, "Hendrix is fun at the beginning of the year, but in a school of 1000, cliques form rapidly and the social scene slows to a crawl." Drinking to alleviate boredom isn't uncommon at a school where "the idea of a good time during the week is to forego studying to watch a movie." Still, the campus is beautiful and the students, fortunately, like each other. Tininess is not without its benefits; as one student pointed out, "Hendrix's small size gives everyone a chance to participate in the life of the college to the degree they wish." There is no Greek life here, and, according to many of our respondents, students very much want to keep it that way.

■ **Students** For a Southern school, Hendrix is a liberal place. Students seriously value diversity and tolerance, and they definitely stand out among the other residents of Conway. As one student put it, "It's not for every student, but only those willing to be open-minded and experience new ideas, lifestyles, and religious beliefs that often challenge the more conservative, Bible-belt tradition of this area." Explained one Easterner, "It's not as liberal as I imagined, but there is a definite liberal presence." Nine of 10 students are white; still, it wouldn't be a stretch to call Hendrix one of the most progressive institutions of any kind in Arkansas. There is a visible hippy contingent; also accounted for are "redneck reactionaries, metal fans, and poseurs."

HENDRIX COLLEGE

Admissions

From Hendrix's Freshman *Bulletin*: "Admission decisions are based on academic competence and preparation, dedication to learning, and motivation to participate fully in the Hendrix community. As an institution of Arkansas Methodism, Hendrix follows a non-sectarian approach to admissions.... Hendrix College expects students to demonstrate their seriousness of purpose by participating in a college preparatory program throughout their high school careers." The recommended curriculum includes four units of English, three units of social studies, two unit of natural sciences, three units of mathematics, and one year in foreign language. "Particular attention is given to the level of challenge of an applicant's previous course of study and to trends in performance." After the academic record, Hendrix looks at your leadership abilities, special talents and record of involvement "in school, church and community." All students must submit SAT or ACT scores.

Financial Aid

Financial aid applicants to Hendrix are required to complete the FFS. Last year the range of "financial or scholarship assistance" from Hendrix ranged from $100 to $9,645. Several scholarships (including Hays Memorial, Chairman's, Hendrix) are available for academic merit, with awards up to the full cost of tuition. Winning a Dean's, Trustee's, or President's Scholarship is a prerequisite for some of these. In '91–'92, 197 students (approximately 20% of the student body) received academic awards; the average value of these was $1,993. Other merit scholarships are available for leadership and areas of interest. Ten percent of all undergrads received one of these in '91–'92; the average value was $1,245. Priority consideration is given to applications received by April 1.

A note from the Hendrix College Admissions Office:

"Students who choose Hendrix are bright, eager learners. They have high aspirations; many go on to pursue advanced degrees in graduate and professional schools. Each year the average ACT and College Board scores of the incoming class are in the 85th to 90th percentile range nationally.

"But Hendrix students expect more from the school than academic challenge. For most, there is a desire to balance their schedules with other kinds of activity—from ensemble practice to a game of intramural racquetball. Everyone fits in; the small campus engenders a sense of openness and belonging.

"Among the recent graduating class 200 seniors are recipients of offers to study biochemistry at Yale, English at the University of Virginia, electrical engineering at Duke, business administration at Harvard, medicine at John Hopkins, theology at Claremont, and law at Georgetown."

ADMISSIONS FACTS

Competitiveness Rating:	**78**
% of applicants accepted:	89
% acceptees attending:	45

FRESHMAN PROFILE

Average verbal SAT:	515
Average math SAT:	551
Average ACT:	26
Graduated top 10% of class:	49
Graduated top 25% of class:	84
Graduated top 50% of class:	97

DEADLINES

Early decision/action:	NA
Early dec./act. notif.:	NA
Regular admission:	rolling
Regular adm. notif.:	rolling

APPLICANTS ALSO LOOK AT

and often prefer:
Tulane U.
Vanderbilt U.
Rhodes College
Millsaps College

and sometimes prefer:
U. of South

and rarely prefer:
Rhodes College
U. Arkansas

ADDRESS

Undergraduate Admissions
Conway, AR 72032
501-329-6811

FINANCIAL FACTS

In-state tuition ($):	7,050
Out-of-state tuition ($):	7,050
Room & board:	2,775
FA application deadline:	4/1
% frosh receiving FA:	76
PT earnings per yr. ($):	1120

TYPE OF AID: % of students ($)

FA of some kind:	70 (7,266)
Need-based grants:	33 (3,093)
Merit-based grants:	NA
Loans:	40 (3,374)
Work study:	27 (1,122)
Student rating of FA:	75

HIRAM COLLEGE

Hiram, OH

What do students think about Hiram College?

■ **Academics** An excellent biology department—"one of the best in the nation," according to more than one student—sets Hiram apart from the nation's many fine small liberal arts schools. About one fifth of the students here pursue bio degrees, taking advantage of the dedicated faculty and top-notch facilities (including "superior" laboratories and a renowned off-campus field station/greenhouse/nature reserve). Pre-business and liberal arts majors are also strong and popular, although the latter reportedly suffer from a lack of support from the school ("Hiram College, while very strong in the sciences, is in danger of losing the 'arts' in 'liberal arts,'" complained one biology student). Core curriculum requirements are extensive and include two three-quarter interdisciplinary classes: each treats a general academic theme (e.g., "the Idea of the West") and is team-taught by professors from different departments. Students gave the faculty high grades, reporting that they were "very active in student life" and "very easy to reach and willing to help with problems." Students were less pleased with the administration, however; the most frequent complaint concerned its "insensitivity to social and political issues that are important to students." Students also gave the library low marks (construction of a new one is reportedly under way).

■ **Life** Students gave their hometown of Hiram low marks; reported one student, "The biggest entertainment center at Hiram is the local elementary school's playground. We're pretty rural." Students don't let their sedate setting hamper their social lives, though; as one student explained, "Even though the town of Hiram is boring, we create our own good times on weekends and we're able to study without distractions during the week. What more can one ask for?" Hiram has no Greek system, but it does have "social clubs," which are fairly popular and which serve the same function as the Greeks do elsewhere. Cleveland and Akron are less than an hour away by car; wrote one student, "If there is even an inkling for the city and its big lights and fast-paced life, all you have to do is hop in your jalopy and head for any of the numerous surrounding 'Meccas.'" On campus, students experience "a very community-oriented lifestyle. Everyone knows everyone else and it is very much like one big family. This has its advantages and disadvantages, though; everybody knows what everybody else is doing or has done." One major complaint concerned the perceived lack of administration support for social clubs and athletics.

■ **Students** Hiram students are predominantly white and Midwestern; explained one student, "Hiram has a long way to go to create an environment that encourages diversity and supports initiative. Recent changes in the administration indicate that the college is moving in the wrong direction." Students are generally "friendly and very accepting," although they also reported that a visible gay population is not well accepted; "There are more homophobes than you can shake a stick at," complained one gay student.

Hiram College

Admissions

Hiram's admissions office considers your high school curriculum and grades to be the most important component of your application. Standardized test scores are next-most important, followed by letters of recommendation, interview, essays, and extracurricular activities. Applicants are required to have completed four years of English and at least three years each of science and social studies. Two years of a foreign language are recommended. Admissions are awarded on a rolling basis; you know whether you've been accepted by Hiram within a month of sending your application. Applicants to Hiram most often also apply to Miami of Ohio, Ohio Wesleyan, College of Wooster, and John Carroll University.

Financial Aid

The financial aid office at Hiram College requires applicants to submit the FAF. The school awards no merit-based grants; all assistance is awarded on the basis of need only. Last year, the most popular loan among Hiram students was the Stafford loan; 75% of the students took one (average value: $2,000); other popular loans include SLS (25%; $2,000) and Perkins (15%; $800). Hiram administers a school-sponsored loan as well.

A note from the Hiram College Admissions Office:

"Every student can expect a sense of belonging—a sense of community. Hiram's location and setting fosters a very tight-knit community. There are no in-groups and out-groups; no cliques. It is a very friendly community. Politics vary from left to right; student clothing comes in all styles; there is no Hiram "type." All this makes for a pretty tolerant and independent-minded student body—a community in the best sense of the word.

"Our Extra Mural Studies Program is unusual. Unlike most schools, these are *our* programs. Hiram students take Hiram courses abroad, taught by Hiram faculty. The College travels all over the world. Nearly 50 percent of our students take advantage of the EMS program, despite the fact that they are not required to do so.

"Our two field stations are distinctive. The James H. Barrow Field Station is one of only a handful of such facilities in the country. It offers science students—generally biology majors—opportunities to do significant undergraduate research. The second station—Northwoods Station in the Upper Peninsula of Michigan—is a Hiram microcosm: The huge lodge and five or six sleeping cabins were built entirely by Hiram faculty and students. They maintain the station together. The station is the only development on Little Lost Lake. Hiram is also an affiliate of Shoals Marine Laboratory."

ADMISSIONS FACTS

Competitiveness Rating:	**76**
% of applicants accepted:	82
% acceptees attending:	32

FRESHMAN PROFILE

Average verbal SAT:	510
Average math SAT:	540
Average ACT:	25
Graduated top 10% of class:	47
Graduated top 25% of class:	71
Graduated top 50% of class:	94

DEADLINES

Early decision/action:	NA
Early dec./act. notif.:	NA
Regular admission:	4/15
Regular adm. notif.:	rolling

APPLICANTS ALSO LOOK AT

and often prefer:
U. Ohio
Ohio Wesleyan U.

and sometimes prefer
John Carroll U.
College of Wooster

and rarely prefer
Ohio State U.

ADDRESS

Undergraduate Admissions
Hiram, OH 44234-9990
216-569-5169

FINANCIAL FACTS

In-state tuition ($):	11,800
Out-of-state tuition ($):	11,800
Room & board:	3,780
FA application deadline:	3/31
% frosh receiving FA:	85
PT earnings per yr. ($):	1000

TYPE OF AID: % of students ($)

FA of some kind:	85 (12,188)
Need-based grants:	37 (7,141)
Merit-based grants:	7 (5,475)
Loans:	36 (3,646)
Work study:	33 (1,564)
Student rating of FA:	80

HOBART AND WILLIAM SMITH COLLEGES

CAMPUS LIFE

Quality of Life Rating: **82**

Type of school:	private
Affiliation:	Episcopal
Environment:	suburban

STUDENT BODY

FT undergrad enrollment:	1,858
% male/% female:	57/43
% out-of-state:	58
% live on campus:	85
% African-American:	7
% Asian:	2
% Caucasian:	88
% Hispanic:	2
% foreign:	3
% transfers:	3

WHAT'S HOT

Grateful Dead
food
marijuana
deans
good-looking students
profs in class
campus easy to get around
profs outside class
in-class discussion

WHAT'S NOT

town-gown relations
religion
interaction among students
diversity
location

ACADEMICS

Academic Rating: **83**

Calendar:	trimester
Student/teacher ratio:	13/1
% doctorates:	94
Profs interesting:	90
Profs accessible:	90
Hours of study per day:	3.27

MOST POPULAR MAJORS BY %

Social Sciences	39
Letters/Literature	22
Multi/Interdisciplinary Studies	11

% GRADS WHO PURSUE

Law:	6
MBA:	3
Medicine:	5
M.A., etc.:	22

What do students think about Hobart and William Smith?

■ **Academics** Hobart and William Smith Colleges, as mutually dependent yet separate institutions, are able to offer students a unique combination of both coeducational and single-sex environments. The "coordinate system" allows the two schools to "share the same campus and classes," yet operate under the auspices of two "very different" administrations. Female students especially appreciate the emphasis on gender issues at William Smith (the women's school) and the supportive atmosphere of their own college within the larger coed framework. Another unusual characteristic of HWS is its trimester calendar, widely lauded "because it allows students to *concentrate* on only three classes at a time." Quality of course offerings is high, and the professors were universally praised in our surveys for their "excellent" teaching and "great willingness to work with the students." The academic environment here is intimate and caring. A biology student, for instance, reported that "the department prepares each student individually for medical school by putting together the applications, giving mock interviews, and being there for you when you need to ask questions." Some students did cite a lack of academic discipline on campus, but agreed that the dedicated student can get an excellent education without getting too distracted by less-committed classmates.

■ **Life** What was considered in the 1970s and early '80s as "a college that catered to those who followed the Dead and played lacrosse" has definitely changed its image, putting a much higher premium on education. Deadheads and pot-smoking lacrosse players are still a highly visible campus presence, but students report that there seem to be fewer such students every year. One aspect of life that has "changed drastically" in recent times is on-campus alcohol consumption. A senior lamented that "the days of kegs on the quad are gone, and have been replaced by more controlled, less popular drinking." Most students live on campus and some complained that the "segregated nature of the dormitory setup (i.e. single-sex dorms)" adversely affects socializing. Fraternities are relatively important at Hobart, but William Smith forbids sororities altogether. "Hard partying and random hookups" characterize some students' social lives, but others prefer to concentrate on more serene activities. HWS is located "on the banks of historic Seneca Lake in the beautiful Finger Lakes region of New York State," and provides a perfect backdrop for the many outdoorsy types. Students agreed that "the continuous blustery winter weather is miserable, but well worth suffering through to experience the perfect spring."

■ **Students** The typical HWS student is from the Northeast and is white and upper-middle-class. The schools' lack of diversity is one of their very few flaws. One appreciative senior concluded, "Hobart and William Smith Colleges do not give away success; instead, they demand initiative, hard work, enthusiasm, self-discipline, and the ability to appreciate people both as resources and as friends."

HOBART AND WILLIAM SMITH COLLEGES

Geneva, NY

Admissions

The most recent course catalog for Hobart and William Smith Colleges states that candidates for admission "must offer strong and well-balanced secondary school records in addition to evidence of scholastic aptitude. Special talents, as well as involvement in community and school activities, are also considered." The admissions office considers your high school GPA and the quality of courses you took in high school to be the most important part of your application. The school then considers, in descending order of importance, your SAT scores, letters of recommendation, "evidence of special talents," and interview (not required but "expected"). Applicants are expected to have completed a high school curriculum that includes: four years of English, three years of math, two lab sciences, and two years each of history and foreign language. Additional years of study in these areas, when possible, is expected. All in all, 18 academic units should be reflected on your 9th through 12th grade transcript.

Financial Aid

The financial aid office at Hobart and William Smith requires applicants to submit the FAF, a form generated by the school, and their and their parents' most recent tax returns. The school awards six trustee grants every year (value: $10,000) for excellence in academics; all other awards are need-based only. Last year, students borrowed on the following loan programs: Stafford (31% did; average value: $2,850) and Perkins (6%; $2,047). The school's catalog states, "The Colleges assist *as many as possible* of those qualified students who do not have sufficient resources to meet all of their college expenses" (emphasis added).

Excerpted from Hobart and William Smith promotional materials:

"The purpose of Hobart College for men and William Smith College for women is to provide a distinguished liberal arts program of high quality in a diverse community.

"Our history is a record of bringing together the traditional and the innovative. The Colleges have been leaders in the development of general curricula, interdisciplinary teaching, and the interrelation between the rigorous pursuit of intellectual goals and reflection on their social consequences. This task has been undertaken as part of our continuing effort to engage the great tradition of Western thought with the traditions of other cultures and the challenges to those traditions raised by the contemporary world. The faculty is dedicated to the development of a course of study that promotes imagination and curiosity and demands intellectual rigor."

ADMISSIONS FACTS

Competitiveness Rating:	**74**
% of applicants accepted:	62
% acceptees attending:	26

FRESHMAN PROFILE

Average verbal SAT:	530*
Average math SAT:	570*
Average ACT:	26*
Graduated top 10% of class:	30
Graduated top 25% of class:	65
Graduated top 50% of class:	85

DEADLINES

Early decision/action:	1/1
Early dec./act. notif.:	1/15
Regular admission:	2/15
Regular adm. notif.:	4/1

APPLICANTS ALSO LOOK AT

and often prefer:
Colgate U.
Trinty College
Connecticut College
Hamilton College

and sometimes prefer:
Skidmore College
Kenyon College
Gettysburg College
St. Lawrence U.
Union College

ADDRESS

Undergraduate Admissions
Geneva, NY 14456
315-789-5500

FINANCIAL FACTS

In-state tuition ($):	16,077
Out-of-state tuition ($):	16,077
Room & board:	5,166
FA application deadline:	2/15
% frosh receiving FA:	42
PT earnings per yr. ($):	1000

TYPE OF AID: % of students ($)

FA of some kind:	45 (11,066)
Need-based grants:	42 (8,390)
Merit-based grants:	0.3 (10,000)
Loans:	NA
Work study:	20 (1,415)
Student rating of FA:	88

HOFSTRA UNIVERSITY

CAMPUS LIFE

Quality of Life Rating:	**77**
Type of school:	private
Affiliation:	none
Environment:	city

STUDENT BODY

FT undergrad enrollment:	7,167
% male/% female:	45/55
% out-of-state:	27
% live on campus:	60
% African-American:	6
% Asian:	2
% Caucasian:	88
% Hispanic:	3
% foreign:	6
% transfers:	10

WHAT'S HOT

suitcase syndrome
working a job

WHAT'S NOT

cost of living
location
financial aid
studying hard
bursar
profs in class

ACADEMICS

Academic Rating:	**72**
Calendar:	4-1-4
Student/teacher ratio:	17/1
% doctorates:	80
Profs interesting:	65
Profs accessible:	72
Hours of study per day:	2.6

MOST POPULAR MAJORS BY %

Business & Management	14
Marketing & Distribution	14
Computer & Info. Sciences	11

% GRADS WHO PURSUE

Law:	6
MBA:	9
Medicine:	3
M.A., etc.:	49

What do students think about Hofstra University?

■ **Academics** As one Hofstra student put it, "Hofstra should be known as the school that sells success." With business and management, marketing, engineering, television, and computer science as its most popular majors, Hofstra is decidedly career-oriented. The liberal and fine arts aren't neglected, however; the drama program, in particular, is excellent, and other popular liberal arts and sciences (English, psychology, political science, etc.) are strong. Students don't receive much direction from professors and administration; said a typical respondent, "learning at Hofstra is up to the students. There are good classes and professors, you just have to be looking for them." Overall, professors received poor grades for in-class performance: complained one student, "The professors should be a little more patient and understanding. The quality of teaching isn't the best." Most administration categories received low grades. Still, despite its problems, Hofstra has come a long way from the Long Island commuter school it was just 30 years ago; today, the school boasts a state-of-the-art computer center, television and radio stations, a theater, new classrooms, and a day care center, all of which are used to enhance the curriculum and make the school more accessible to all students. No wonder one student bragged that "the school's growing reputation is well-deserved."

■ **Life** Although it was once entirely attended by Long Island commuters, Hofstra is now home to about half its 7000+ undergraduates. Dorms are OK (not great) and difficult to come by, due to the current upswing of the out-of-state population. As the resident population has grown, so has the popularity of fraternities and sororities. Athletic facilities—pools, tennis courts, and fields—are new and high-quality: the New York Jets use them for preseason training. The large campus houses an arboretum, and the entire campus is peppered with plants, trees, and sculpture. Some students find the school's focus on campus beauty excessive: said one, the "administration is overly concerned with appearances, sometimes at the expense of education." Off-campus is the town of Hempstead, which is "neither safe nor clean nor beautiful nor fun"; neighboring towns, accessible by car, are full of hospitable bars. New York City is only 45 minutes away by train, but few students go there regularly. Commuters report that parking on or near campus is difficult.

■ **Students** Almost three quarters of the students are from New York, with a large portion from the immediate area. The school is predominantly white, and blacks complained that they felt "somewhat segregated here." Students are politically conservative (this is Republican Senator Alfonse D'Amato's backyard) and most are focused on career tracks. Although determined to succeed, they are not grubs—they study as much as they need to to get good grades and no more. When those books close, it's Miller time!

HOFSTRA UNIVERSITY

Admissions

Hofstra's undergraduate bulletin states, "The previous record, personal qualities, recommendation of the guidance counselor, and the SAT or ACT are important factors in evaluating the applicant." Additionally, Hofstra recommends four units of English, two of a language, two of mathematics, one of laboratory science, three of history and social studies, and four of electives. Engineering students should have four years of mathematics, and at least one year each of chemistry and physics. Applicants who do not meet these standards will be given "careful consideration by the Admissions Committee to determine from achievements and from assessment of abilities and maturity the probability of success in the chosen program." Admissions for fall semester are rolling, but priority is given to applications received by February 15.

Financial Aid

Financial aid applicants to Hofstra are required to complete the FAF. Hofstra awards scholarships for athletic merit: in '90-'91, 2% of all undergrads received one; the average value was $6,250. Hofstra also awards scholarships for academic merit: in '91-'92, 28% of all undergrads received one; the average value was $4,000. Other scholarships available include Memorial Honor scholarships (entering freshmen in the top 5% of their graduating class with combined SATs over 1350 or ACT of 30—minimum $2,500 per year), Presidential Scholarships (top 20%, SATs 1200 or above, or ACT of 27—minimum $2,000 per year) and Freshman Recognition Scholarships (top 10% SATs 1000–1200 or ACT above 22—minimum $1,500 per year). All of these are renewable if certain criteria are met. A limited number of full-tuition scholarships are also available. In addition to Stafford loans (recommended to 90% of undergrads), Hofstra recommends PLUS loans. Priority deadline is March 1.

Excerpted from Hofstra University promotional materials:

"Founded in 1935 as Long Island's first coeducational college, Hofstra has evolved into a major independent university. Significant indicators of its excellence may be seen in the fact that, among private Island colleges, Hofstra is currently the only one deemed worthy of granting the Phi Beta Kappa distinction; and it is the Island's private school with the most students going on to earn graduate and professional degrees—an important yardstick for rating the academic capabilities of a university's graduates.

"At Hofstra, the emphasis is on developing judgement, flexibility of mind, powers of self-education and insight into human behavior as opposed to mere acquisition of skills. The University's administration and faculty believe these are the most hardy seeds to sow in the rapidly shifting environment of the present and future."

ADMISSIONS FACTS

Competitiveness Rating:	74
% of applicants accepted:	68
% acceptees attending:	28

FRESHMAN PROFILE

Average verbal SAT:	475
Average math SAT:	550
Average ACT:	23
Graduated top 10% of class:	25
Graduated top 25% of class:	62
Graduated top 50% of class:	97

DEADLINES

Early decision/action:	12/1
Early dec./act. notif.:	NA
Regular admission:	2/15
Regular adm. notif.:	rolling

APPLICANTS ALSO LOOK AT

and often prefer:
Cornell U.
Rutgers U./Rutgers College
SUNY Albany
Fordham U.
SUNY Binghamton

and sometimes prefer:
Syracuse U.
SUNY Stonybrook
NYU

ADDRESS

Undergraduate Admissions
1000 Fulton Ave
Hempstead, NY 11550
516-463-6700

FINANCIAL FACTS

In-state tuition ($):	8,570
Out-of-state tuition ($):	8,570
Room & board:	4,930
FA application deadline:	none
% frosh receiving FA:	90
PT earnings per yr. ($):	1000

TYPE OF AID: % of students ($)

FA of some kind:	80 (NA)
Need-based grants:	29 (950)
Merit-based grants:	NA
Loans:	NA (3,200)
Work study:	NA
Student rating of FA:	65

HOLLINS COLLEGE

CAMPUS LIFE

Quality of Life Rating:	**87**
Type of school:	private
Affiliation:	none
Environment:	city

STUDENT BODY

FT undergrad enrollment:	853
% male/% female:	0/100
% out-of-state:	64
% live on campus:	98
% African-American:	2
% Asian:	<1
% Caucasian:	96
% Hispanic:	<1
% foreign:	2
% transfers:	3

WHAT'S HOT

marriage
small lectures
dating
profs outside class
profs in class
honest students
campus appearance
small classes (overall)
campus easy to get around
financial aid

WHAT'S NOT

fraternities/sororities
library
diversity
intramural sports

ACADEMICS

Academic Rating:	**83**
Calendar:	4-1-4
Student/teacher ratio:	10/1
% doctorates:	87
Profs interesting:	92
Profs accessible:	93
Hours of study per day:	3.27

MOST POPULAR MAJORS BY %

English:	14
Psychology:	13
Economics:	12

% GRADS WHO PURSUE

Law:	3
MBA:	2
Medicine:	1
M.A., etc.:	26

What do students think about Hollins College?

■ **Academics** "Tradition is what's great about Hollins College," reported one undergrad at this tiny all-women's school. "It creates an amazing sense of community, from the president to the dining hall staff. Everyone takes pride in the history of Hollins and works to preserve the atmosphere of belonging and openness." Having just celebrated its 150th anniversary, Hollins has had plenty of time to accumulate traditions, as well as time to define and redefine its educational mission. Once considered a finishing school for Southern debutantes, Hollins has recently earned a reputation for helping women develop talents in fields as diverse as business and the creative arts. Liberal arts and social science majors—English, political science, and history, specifically—are most popular here. Psychology is also reportedly strong, as is the creative writing program. Students gave their profs very high grades for both in-class presentation and for accessibility outside the class. Among the unique features of life at Hollins are: an honor code, which allows students to schedule their own exams and take them unproctored; a January term, during which students pursue an independent study, take a seminar, or serve in an internship program; and an unusual emphasis on developing the students' computer skills. Hollins also supports an active study abroad program, but one financial aid student warned that, because of the extra cost involved, "if you're not rich it's almost impossible to take advantage of this opportunity." She also noted that "most services here (computers, student government, phone, cable T.V.) require extra fees. Be forewarned: there are a lot of hidden expenses."

■ **Life** Hollins women obviously must look elsewhere for male companionship, and they do, most often at nearby Washington and Lee or Hampden-Sydney. "For a good social life, road tripping is a must," wrote one woman. As another woman put it, "this is a great place to spend four years, but you have to have a car and the motivation to look places other than campus for opportunities to socialize." The school supports many popular extracurricular clubs and organizations, among which are student government, associational community service, leadership programs, horseback riding, theater, dance, and the literary society. Drinking is more popular here than at most women's colleges, but still does not approach the level it reaches at most co-ed schools. The campus, located beside the Blue Ridge Mountains, is "to die for."

■ **Students** Hollins College is very nearly an all-white school. There are fewer than 40 minority students here, approximately half of whom are black. Wrote one student, "Hollins needs more ethnic and political diversity. The women here are respectful of differing opinions, but unfortunately few such opinions are represented." The typical Hollins women is a politically conservative, affluent, tradition-minded Southerner, although the school is reportedly currently trying to recruit a more diverse student body.

HOLLINS COLLEGE

Admissions

The admissions office reports that "Hollins evaluates student strengths both in and out of the classroom. Greatest weight is given to the student's high school record (GPA, rank in class, and the breadth and depth of student's academic program), school recommendation, and SAT or ACT scores. An assessment is made of the student's writing ability through her responses to essays questions on the application. Hollins looks for indications of special interests and talents...as evidenced by extracurricular interests, volunteer activities, and outside jobs." The school recommends a high school curriculum including four years of English, and three years each of math, foreign language, social studies, and science. Applicants to Hollins also apply most often to Mt. Holyoke, Randolph-Macon Women's College, Vanderbilt, Smith, UNC–Chapel Hill, and University of Richmond.

Financial Aid

The financial aid office at Hollins College requires the FAF and your parents' most recent tax return. Merit based scholarships are awarded on the basis of scholastic ability (to 6% of all students; average value of award: $5800) and leadership (1%, $1500). Hollins recommends Stafford loans (30% of the students take them; average value: $2998), Perkins loans (18%, 1219), and PLUS/SLS/bank loans (6%; $3220). Hollins reports that its awards to upperclassmen are slightly higher than those given to incoming freshmen (average freshman award: $11994)

A note from the Hollins Admissions Office:

"Hollins is a liberal arts college for women dedicated to academic excellence. A spirit of independent inquiry, the free exchange of ideas, and a love of learning characterize the campus community. Hollins is a place where each student is valued. A faculty/student ratio of 1:10 makes it possible for each student's personal aspirations—where she wants to go and what she wants to become—to be taken seriously.

"Graduates of Hollins have become Pulitzer Prize-winning writers, renowned psychologists, award-winning movie producers, surgeons, journalists, business leaders, researchers, aviators, educators, environmentalists, artists, scholars, judges, and college presidents. They have also led rewarding family lives, become leaders in their communities, and participated in activities ranging from exploring the Galapagos Islands to pioneering genetic research on embryos in England to founding the National Down Syndrome Society in New York City. Hollins alumnae overwhelmingly state that their liberal arts education at Hollins prepared them well for their lives."

ADMISSIONS FACTS

Competitiveness Rating:	**61**
% of applicants accepted:	82
% acceptees attending:	40

FRESHMAN PROFILE

Average verbal SAT:	480*
Average math SAT:	515*
Average ACT:	NA
Graduated top 10% of class:	20
Graduated top 25% of class:	40
Graduated top 50% of class:	68

DEADLINES

Early decision/action:	11/15
Early dec./act. notif.:	12/15
Regular admission:	2/15
Regular adm. notif.:	4/15

APPLICANTS ALSO LOOK AT

and often prefer:
Smith College
Vanderbilt
U. NC-Chapel Hill

and sometimes prefer:
Randolph-Macon College
Mt. Holyoke College
Sweet Briar College

ADDRESS

Undergraduate Admissions
P.O. Box 9707
Roanoke, VA 24020
703-362-6401

FINANCIAL FACTS

In-state tuition ($):	11,600
Out-of-state tuition ($):	11,600
Room & board:	4,600
FA application deadline:	3/31
% frosh receiving FA:	63
PT earnings per yr. ($):	1500

TYPE OF AID: % of students ($)

FA of some kind:	58 (12,188)
Need-based grants:	37 (7,141)
Merit-based grants:	7 (5,475)
Loans:	36 (3,646)
Work study:	33 (1,564)
Student rating of FA:	88

COLLEGE OF THE HOLY CROSS

Worcester, MA

CAMPUS LIFE

Quality of Life Rating: **86**

Type of school: private
Affiliation: Roman Catholic
Environment: city

STUDENT BODY

FT undergrad enrollment: 2,655
% male/% female: 50/50
% out-of-state: 64
% live on campus: 80
% African-American: 4
% Asian: 2
% Caucasian: 92
% Hispanic: 2
% foreign: 1
% transfers: 1

WHAT'S HOT

studying hard
religion
small lectures
dorm safety
campus appearance
honesty
profs in class
small classes (overall)

WHAT'S NOT

fraternities/sororities
dating
gay community visible
diversity
location

ACADEMICS

Academic Rating: **86**

Calendar: semester
Student/teacher ratio: 14/1
% doctorates: 93
Profs interesting: 91
Profs accessible: 89
Hours of study per day: 3.96

MOST POPULAR MAJORS BY %

English: 19
Political Science: 13
History: 12

% GRADS WHO PURSUE

Law: 8
MBA: 2
Medicine: 6
M.A., etc.:   9

What do students think about Holy Cross?

■ **Academics** Holy Cross students gave their school high grades in practically every one of our academic categories. Professors teach all courses and received praise both for their skills as instructors and for their accessibility outside the classroom. Wrote one student, "The faculty is totally accessible and unbelievably talented." Academics are challenging—students put in nearly four hours of work a day beyond class attendance—yet none complained that the work was excessive or superfluous. Administrators received high marks, too, and one student told us it was because "they genuinely care about all of us." Concluded one Indiana native, "I can honestly say that Holy Cross is the Notre Dame of New England, with a few differences: HC is half the size, the campus is prettier, [nearby Boston] is more exciting, and we don't have parietals (restricted dorm visitation rights) here. It's a highly competitive, Irish Catholic institution with an excellent football team." Students major in the traditional variety of liberal arts and social science majors, and about one fourth proceed to graduate school within a year of graduation. Holy Cross is a member of the Worcester consortium, which allows students to take classes at any of ten area schools.

■ **Life** As one undergrad explained, "Students here tend to complain about a lot of things, but really, it's all a facade. No one would want to be anywhere else." Indeed, Holy Cross students ranked among the top 10 percent of all student bodies surveyed in terms of overall satisfaction. But they *do* complain. Topping the list of annoyances is the city of Worcester, the nonexistent dating scene, the food, and the lack of diversity among the student body (see "Students," below). Students had positive things to say about the campus, which, reported one, "is so beautiful and secure, you almost forget you're in the city of Worcester." They also reported favorably on the quality and safety of the dorms. Sports, both intramural and intercollegiate, are very popular. Drug usage is minimal, but drinking is not: "This school is 50 percent hard work, 50 percent hangover," wrote one student. Said another, "I have yet to find a student in any department who does not work hard at course work and still does not have an excellent time on weekends." There are no fraternities and sororities.

■ **Students** Over 90 percent of Holy Cross students are white, and the minority population is pretty evenly divided among Asians, Hispanics, and African-Americans, so each individual minority population is small. One student reported that "the administration seems to be concerned with making the school more diverse; more minority-focused scholarships and recruiting plans have surfaced." So far, however, these efforts have had little effect on student body demographics. Most students are Catholic, and there is a visible preppy population: wrote one student, "If you wonder where the Gap and J. Crew families reside, they're here at Holy Cross." If there are any gay students here, their presence is unacknowledged and unwelcome by fellow students.

COLLEGE OF THE HOLY CROSS

Admissions

The admissions office reports that it uses no formulas or cut-offs to eliminate applicants from its applicant pool. Academic record is considered the most important component of your application here; letters of recommendation are also very important, as are standardized test scores. Considered less important (but still considered) are essays, extracurricular activities, and an interview. Applicants must have completed four years of English and math; three to four years of foreign language, natural sciences, and social sciences are "recommended." Applicants must submit scores for the SAT and three achievements, one of which must be English composition. Students applying to Holy Cross most often also apply to Boston College, Fairfield University, Notre Dame, Providence College, and Georgetown University.

Financial Aid

Applicants for financial aid at College of the Holy Cross must complete the FAF. Most aid is need-based (only two students received academic scholarships last year; however, both of those were for full tuition). Each year, according to HC's catalog, "More than 200 entering freshmen are awarded Holy Cross scholarships with stipends ranging from $200 to $15,200, depending on each student's financial need." Scholarships are generally renewed (provided a student still needs financial assistance), but stipends are adjusted based on changes to family financial strength/resources. February 1 is a priority deadline; there is no closing deadline.

A note from the Holy Cross Admissions Office:

"Holy Cross was founded in 1843 by the second Bishop of Boston, Benedict Joseph Fenwick, S.J., and placed under the direction of the Society of Jesus. The oldest Catholic college in New England, it is a community of 2,600 students, half of them men and half women. Few classes exceed an enrollment of 40, and most average around 20. The atmosphere this community of scholars creates, both collectively and separately, is frequently described as welcoming and friendly, where students receive encouragement and support from classmates and professors.

"Because of its academic strength, Holy Cross succeeds in educating the best and the brightest to become tomorrow's leaders. Because of its commitment to social justice, its graduates leave the campus as ethically sensitive adults deeply and personally committed to sharing the gifts they have so generously received from God with others, especially those less fortunate than themselves."

ADMISSIONS FACTS

Competitiveness Rating:	**89**
% of applicants accepted:	43
% acceptees attending:	38

FRESHMAN PROFILE

Average verbal SAT:	580*
Average math SAT:	623*
Average ACT:	NA
Graduated top 10% of class:	60
Graduated top 25% of class:	91
Graduated top 50% of class:	98

DEADLINES

Early decision/action:	11/1
Early dec./act. notif.:	12/15
Regular admission:	2/1
Regular adm. notif.:	4/12

APPLICANTS ALSO LOOK AT

and often prefer:
Dartmouth College
Georgetown U.
U. Notre Dame

and sometimes prefer:
Bowdoin College
Boston College

and rarely prefer:
U. Mass–Amherst
Fairfield U.
Providence College
Villanova U.

ADDRESS

Undergraduate Admissions
College Street
Worcester, MA 01610
508-793-2443

FINANCIAL FACTS

In-state tuition ($):	15,200
Out-of-state tuition ($):	15,200
Room & board:	5,700
FA application deadline:	2/1
% frosh receiving FA:	56
PT earnings per yr. ($):	1105

TYPE OF AID: % of students ($)

FA of some kind:	60 (NA)
Need-based grants:	40 (NA)
Merit-based grants:	NA
Loans:	NA (3,503)
Work study:	41 (1,188)
Student rating of FA:	65

HOWARD UNIVERSITY

CAMPUS LIFE

Quality of Life Rating: **76**

Type of school:	private
Affiliation:	none
Environment:	city

STUDENT BODY

FT undergrad enrollment:	7,400
% male/% female:	39/61
% out-of-state:	74
% live on campus:	40
% African-American:	83
% Asian:	1
% Caucasian:	1
% Hispanic:	1
% foreign:	15
% transfers:	3

WHAT'S HOT

rap/hip-hop
college radio station
college newspaper
good-looking students
dating
leftist politics
religious clubs
religion

WHAT'S NOT

financial aid
registration
gay community visible
administration (overall)

ACADEMICS

Academic Rating: **71**

Calendar:	semester
Student/teacher ratio:	7/1
% doctorates:	47
Profs interesting:	79
Profs accessible:	75
Hours of study per day:	2.94

MOST POPULAR MAJORS

Business
Arts and Science
Communications

% GRADS WHO PURSUE

Law:	NA
MBA:	NA
Medicine:	NA
M.A., etc.:	23

What do students think about Howard University?

■ **Academics** Among the great universities geared predominantly toward serving African-Americans, Howard remains the most famous and arguably the best (see also Fisk, Morehouse, Spelman, and Tuskegee). Instruction here naturally reflects black perspectives (just as, at most universities, instruction reflects white attitudes, albeit without acknowledgment). Said one African-American student, "I'm glad I chose Howard because it taught me a lot about my race." Practical concerns seems to be the main motivating factor when students choose their courses of study: one in five pursues a degree in business administration. Also, because it is attached to an excellent medical school, Howard offers a full complement of pre-med science courses. Its liberal arts departments, however, are also strong. Students had kind words for their professors—"Professors are excellent because they truly care about their students succeeding in school; there are no office hours when it comes to a student needing additional help," said one. They did not have kind words for the administration, which received low marks in every category.

■ **Life** Howard students gave their hometown lower grades than did other DC undergrads, partly because their neighborhood is not entirely safe, and partly because Howard students are more involved with their college experiences than with the city. Said one undergrad, "One of the things I like most about Howard that you don't find at other schools is the school spirit. You don't find as many people at other schools as you do here that are truly happy and excited to attend their school." Dating is the key to social life here, and fraternities and sororities are also very popular. Sitting around and drinking beer, one of the staples of the white college experience, is not popular. Also, Howard continues to have a major housing problem: the school currently guarantees housing for freshman only and can accommodate fewer than half the other students.

■ **Students** Because Howard is such a prominent black institution, some students here feel pressure to present themselves as exemplary students. Explained one: "The things that go on here are the same as what goes on at other schools; just because we are the Mecca doesn't mean we should be put on some kind of pedestal. But when something goes wrong with a Howard student, it's like we just robbed a bank or something. Remember we are human, too." Politically, the student body leans farther to the left than most, and they are a relatively religious group. They are also happy to be at Howard: in terms of happiness, students here ranked in the top third of the schools we surveyed. The male-female ratio is 2:3, giving men a decided advantage in the dating game. Said one man, "Howard is the gateway to meeting the best-looking women in the country."

HOWARD UNIVERSITY

Admissions

The admissions office reports, "The objective of the selection process is to admit those student who, through prior academic performance, evidence the capability of successfully completing a degree program while enrolled at Howard University. All decisions are made on an individual basis... For admission to most majors, a student should have a combined SAT score of 800 or above or ACT composite of 20, rank in the top half of his/her graduation class, or have a 'C+' average." Admissions criteria for the College of Fine Arts and the School of Education are similar but somewhat lower; for the School of Engineering, somewhat higher. High school curriculum requirements also vary from school to school; for details, write the school and ask for the "New Freshman Admission Information" pamphlet. Applicants to Howard most often also apply to Hampton, Spelman, Morehouse, and University of Maryland.

Financial Aid

Howard requires financial aid applicants to complete the FAF. The school offers athletic scholarships (last year, 7% of all undergrads received one; average value, $8,000) and academic scholarships (36% of all undergrads received one; average value, $5,421). Achievement scholarships are also offered for music, drama and art. Renewal of University-based scholarships is subject to students maintaining a 3.0 GPA during the year preceding that for which aid is being sought. The school recommends several loans, including Stafford, Perkins, PLUS, SLS, HEAL, and its own institutional loans.

A note from the Howard University Admissions Office:

"Since its founding, Howard has stood among the few institutions of higher learning where African-Americans and other minorities have participated freely in a truly comprehensive university experience. Thus, Howard has assumed a special responsibility to prepare its students to exercise leadership wherever their interest and commitments take them. Howard has issued approximately 67,000 degrees, diplomas, and certificates to men and women in the professions, the arts and sciences, and the humanities. The University has produced and continues to produce a high percentage of the nation's African-American professionals in the fields of medicine, dentistry, pharmacy, engineering, nursing, architecture, religion, law, music, social work, education and business. There are more than 12,000 students from across the nation and approximately 109 countries and territories attending the University. Their varied customs, cultures, ideas, and interests contribute to the University's international character and vitality. Approximately 2000 faculty members represent the largest concentration of African-American scholars in any single institution of higher education."

ADMISSIONS FACTS

Competitiveness Rating:	**68**
% of applicants accepted:	44
% acceptees attending:	58

FRESHMAN PROFILE

Average verbal SAT:	423
Average math SAT:	456
Average ACT:	19
Graduated top 10% of class:	10
Graduated top 25% of class:	20
Graduated top 50% of class:	100

DEADLINES

Early decision/action:	NA
Early dec./act. notif.:	NA
Regular admission:	4/1
Regular adm. notif.:	rolling

APPLICANTS ALSO LOOK AT

and often prefer:
Morehouse College
Spelman College

and sometimes prefer:
George Washington U.
U. Maryland

and rarely prefer:
Morgan State U.

ADDRESS

Undergraduate Admissions
2400 Sixth St. NW
Washington, DC 20059
202-806-2700

FINANCIAL FACTS

In-state tuition ($):	5,825
Out-of-state tuition ($):	5,825
Room & board:	4,040
FA application deadline:	4/1
% frosh receiving FA:	NA
PT earnings per yr. ($):	1500

TYPE OF AID: % of students ($)

FA of some kind:	80 (NA)
Need-based grants:	34 (1,817)
Merit-based grants:	NA
Loans:	63 (4,000)
Work study:	5 (2,509)
Student rating of FA:	60

UNIVERSITY OF ILLINOIS AT URBANA

CAMPUS LIFE

Quality of Life Rating: **78**

Type of school:	public
Affiliation:	none
Environment:	city

STUDENT BODY

FT undergrad enrollment:	25,489
% male/% female:	57/43
% out-of-state:	6
% live on campus:	33
% African-American:	7
% Asian:	10
% Caucasian:	76
% Hispanic:	4
% foreign:	1
% transfers:	5

WHAT'S HOT

intercollegiate sports
conservative politics
dating
beer
alternative rock

WHAT'S NOT

profs teach intros
small lectures
small labs and seminars
small classes (overall)
profs teach upper levels
registration
financial aid
working a job

ACADEMICS

Academic Rating: **78**

Calendar:	semester
Student/teacher ratio:	12/1
% doctorates:	80
Profs interesting:	72
Profs accessible:	72
Hours of study per day:	3.31

MOST POPULAR MAJORS BY %

Engineering:	20
Business & Management:	15
Social Sciences:	14

% GRADS WHO PURSUE

Law:	4
MBA:	3
Medicine:	NA
M.A., etc.:	20

What do students think about the University of Illinois?

■ **Academics** The University of Illinois attracts an almost entirely in-state student body, but, as one student explained, "that can only be attributed to the cheap price for in-state students. It sure isn't because of the quality of the school." This huge university's greatest assets are its competitive engineering and business programs, but because of its size the school supports many other less-touted but fine programs (mostly career-track majors). Although the University of Illinois is very big, a good education is easily within reach for the student who doesn't need to be led by the hand to find it. True, lecture classes can reach four-digit enrollments, but discussion sections are much smaller. True, students never meet some of their professors, but they do have access to an unbelievable variety of "lectures, seminars, plays, performances, speakers, sports, and other presentations which are readily available for anyone interested." And, the school boasts some of the most studious public school students in the country, in part because one fifth of the student body is made up of engineers. As one student explained, "I came from a small town and was worried about this school's size, but I wouldn't be happier anywhere else. The possibilities are endless." Still, students voiced some of the complaints common at many large schools: those most often mentioned concerned TAs ("You're lucky if your TA speaks English," wrote a finance major) and the time-consuming registration process.

■ **Life** Said one student of the social scene, "It's about as good as you can have in an area that's completely surrounded by farms." Wrote another, "Socially, the university offers an extremely wide variety of ... bars." Still, it's not as if University of Illinois students are completely cut off from civilization: explained one, "Both cities, Champaign and Urbana, are accessible with mass transit and offer decent shopping and dining." An "excellent transportation system" makes cars unnecessary for travelling off-campus. Of course, at a school of 26,000, one rarely needs to leave campus for entertainment. Parties at dorms and off-campus housing are frequent, and fraternities and sororities play a dominant role in the lives of those who go Greek. Students ardently follow their intercollegiate sports teams, the Fighting Illini, particularly in football and basketball. One of the few controversies at the school centers on the team mascot, a Native American chief whom some perceive as an offensive racial stereotype.

■ **Students** Practically every student here is from the state of Illinois. One student reported that, despite the low tuition rates, "For a public school, Illinois students are pretty affluent. Most are seeking a good job and family—the things they were given in their home life." Wrote another, "Because this is a large college, you will find a group to associate with, but you will also have the opportunity to meet people from very diverse backgrounds." Asians make up the largest minority population, Blacks the second largest. Both black and white students reported that race relations are acrimonious. One black student wrote that U of I is "a great school, but the student body and faculty need to be better educated about minorities and their cultures."

UNIVERSITY OF ILLINOIS AT URBANA

Urbana, IL

Admissions

Applicants to the University of Illinois/Urbana must apply to one of eight undergraduate colleges, the School of Social Work, or the Institute of Aviation. Because course requirements differ for these schools and admission is highly competitive, "Each applicant's initial choice of college and curriculum is important and should be carefully considered in consultation with counselors and parents. Due to the great interest in admission to all programs, there usually is not an opportunity for a student to ask for reconsideration of admission for an alternate program after an initial decision has been made." High school course requirements vary greatly from college to college; a detailed breakdown of the four recommended "patterns" of high school curricula is listed in the undergraduate course catalog. Many of the colleges also require additional sources of information ranging from a personal interview to "additional background information" to aptitude tests. Students who are close to meeting the requirements for a particular school and who feel their academic credentials do not adequately reflect their potential are encouraged to complete a "background statement" portion of the application form. All applicants must submit SAT or ACT scores.

Financial Aid

Financial aid applicants to the University of Illinois at Urbana-Champaign must complete the FAF or FFS (preferred). In '91–'92, 57% of the entering class of '95 received some form of aid; the average package value was $3,500. Overall, 59% of all undergrads received a need-based or merit-based grant; the average value was $1,950. A variety of scholarships are available, including those for academic merit, artistic talent, minorities, residency, and athletic ability. The priority deadline for consideration is March 15.

Excerpted from University of Illinois promotional materials:

"Since its founding in 1867, the University of Illinois at Urbana-Champaign has earned a reputation as an institution of international stature. It is recognized for the high quality of its academic programs and the outstanding facilities and resources it makes available to students and faculty, including a library with the third largest academic collection in the country.

"The University of Illinois at Urbana-Champaign is a comprehensive institution offering undergraduate, graduate, and professional degrees in more than 100 fields of study. There are approximately 35,000 students (26,000 undergraduate, 9,000 graduate) and 12,600 faculty and staff members in the University community."

ADMISSIONS FACTS

Competitiveness Rating:	**83**
% of applicants accepted:	77
% acceptees attending:	53

FRESHMAN PROFILE

Average verbal SAT:	520
Average math SAT:	611
Average ACT:	27
Graduated top 10% of class:	58
Graduated top 25% of class:	88
Graduated top 50% of class:	98

DEADLINES

Early decision/action:	NA
Early dec./act. notif.:	NA
Regular admission:	1/1
Regular adm. notif.:	rolling

APPLICANTS ALSO LOOK AT

and sometimes prefer:
Miami U.
U. Kentucky
Loyola U.–Chicago
Purdue U.
Northern Illinois State U.

and often prefer:
Northwestern U.

and rarely prefer:
Illinois State U.
Southern Illinois U.

ADDRESS

Undergraduate Admissions
506 South Wright Street
Urbana, IL 61801
217-333-0302

FINANCIAL FACTS

In-state tuition ($):	2,236
Out-of-state tuition ($):	5,988
Room & board:	3,902
FA application deadline:	none
% frosh receiving FA:	80
PT earnings per yr. ($):	650

TYPE OF AID: % of students ($)

FA of some kind:	85 (NA)
Need-based grants:	33 (2,944)
Merit-based grants:	NA
Loans:	33 (2,845)
Work study:	4 (1326)
Student rating of FA:	68

ILLINOIS INSTITUTE OF TECHNOLOGY

Chicago, IL

What do students think about IIT?

■ **Academics** IIT maintains five undergraduate divisions—one each for engineering, architecture, design, business administration, and sciences and letters—but engineering is by far the school's major drawing card: 80 percent of the undergraduates are engineers. Like most engineering students, the undergraduates of IIT work hard (nearly four hours a day) and must endure an extremely stressful academic environment (so stressful, in fact, that IIT students' answer to the question "How happy are you here?" ranked the lowest in our survey). Besides engineering, architecture and computer science are also reputedly excellent; liberal arts departments, on the other hand, exist almost solely to teach courses required by the core curriculum. That core, which applies to students in all divisions, mandates 12 hours of humanities and 12 hours of social sciences, as well as 12 hours natural science/engineering and eight hours of math (the engineering core demands more hours of science and math). All divisions offer an honors program, and all but design offer five-year graduate/undergraduate degree programs. Co-operative programs are available in most fields, allowing students the opportunity to put their educations in use in the business and research worlds. Research opportunities on campus are also reportedly numerous.

■ **Life** IIT students are uniformly negative about many aspects of life outside their classrooms and labs. Chief among their complaints is the area surrounding the school: IIT, like University of Chicago, is located in the South Side of Chicago, a notoriously run-down neighborhood, and IIT students were certainly thinking of relations with their immediate neighbors when they ranked "town-gown relations" the fourth worst in the country. Positive notes: the school is just across the expressway from Comisky Park (good news for White Sox fans), and is also near the Lincoln Park Zoo and Grant Park; all forms of public transportation make stops right on campus. Students also ranked their campus the nation's third ugliest: Clearly, they were unimpressed that the boxy, urban campus was largely designed by famous architect (and former director of the College of Architecture) Ludwig Mies van der Rohe. Students also reported that they have neither the time nor the opportunities for a "normal" social life—intense academic pressure, the fact that half the students commute and that many others go home every weekend, and a four-to-one male-female ratio create an atmosphere in which there is little dating or partying (what little drinking there is, is most often of the "stress relief," as opposed to "social," variety). Finally, there are the Chicago winters, during which the temperature frequently drops near zero degrees…Kelvin!

■ **Students** IIT draws a good mix of students from different ethnic and social backgrounds. Because the students essentially share the same general academic interests, and because the student body is predominantly male, IIT students can seem a little similar, but, by tech school standards, IIT has a well-balanced student body. Nearly half the students are from out-of-state.

ILLINOIS INSTITUTE OF TECHNOLOGY

Chicago, IL

Admissions

According to its most recent catalog, IIT "considers each application on its individual merits, always looking for superior ability as determined through previous academic records, recommendations, statements by the student, leadership experiences, aptitudes, and goals. The student's record of achievement in high school, however, most often provides the best prediction of success at IIT." Applicants are required to submit scores for either the SAT or ACT, and are expected to have completed the following high school curriculum: 16 units of academic courses, including four units of English, two units of algebra, and one unit each of geometry, history, and a lab science. Engineers are required to have an additional unit of lab science and a half-unit of trigonometry.

Financial Aid

The financial aid office at IIT requires applicants to submit the FAF and a form generated by the school. IIT awards athletic and academic scholarships as well as need-based grants. IIT participates in the Perkins, Stafford, PLUS, and Illinois Guaranteed loan programs. The school also notes that all students can earn money through on-campus employment and through the school's co-op program, which allows students to work full-time and earn college credit for their work.

Excerpted from Illinois Institute of Technology promotional materials:

"IIT is committed to providing undergraduate education of the highest quality. We believe that every one of our students has the ability to make significant contributions to society. Our goal is to help you attain the knowledge, skills, ethical perspective, and motivation you will need to realize that potential.

"Our university is especially well suited to prepare you to seize the opportunities and address the real problems of a rapidly changing, increasingly complex world. The IIT scholars with whom you will study contribute to the nation's intellectual wealth in areas ranging from ethics and management to design processes, mathematical problems, and theoretical physics. Our multicultural student body and our location in the heart of one of America's most ethnically diverse cities make the undergraduate experience an ideal way to prepare for tomorrow's global society.

"As we celebrate our centennial year and look toward the 21st century, we hold fast to the qualities on which our past successes have been built: small size, solid curriculum in liberal arts and technology, private funding, superior students and faculty, and metropolitan location."

ADMISSIONS FACTS

Competitiveness Rating:	**78**
% of applicants accepted:	81
% acceptees attending:	40

FRESHMAN PROFILE

Average verbal SAT:	540
Average math SAT:	550
Average ACT:	25
Graduated top 10% of class:	47
Graduated top 25% of class:	75
Graduated top 50% of class:	95

DEADLINES

Early decision/action:	12/1
Early dec./act. notif.:	1/15
Regular admission:	2/15
Regular adm. notif.:	4/1

APPLICANTS ALSO LOOK AT

and often prefer:
Virginia Polytech
Lafayette College
Washington U.

and rarely prefer:
Purdue U.
Case Western Reserve U.
Southern Illinois U.
Marquette U.

ADDRESS

Undergraduate Admissions
10 W. 33rd Street
Chicago, IL 60616
312-567-3025 or
800-572-1587 (in state)
800-448-2329 (out-of-state)

FINANCIAL FACTS

In-state tuition ($):	12,690
Out-of-state tuition ($):	12,690
Room & board:	4,400
FA application deadline:	4/1
% frosh receiving FA:	84
PT earnings per yr. ($):	1,500

TYPE OF AID: % of students ($)

FA of some kind:	80 (NA)
Need-based grants:	NA
Merit-based grants:	NA
Loans:	NA
Work study:	NA
Student rating of FA:	69

CAMPUS LIFE

Quality of Life Rating:	**75**
Type of school:	public
Affiliation:	none
Environment:	city

STUDENT BODY

FT undergrad enrollment:	17,950
% male/% female:	45/55
% out-of-state:	1
% live on campus:	35
% African-American:	6
% Asian:	2
% Caucasian:	91
% Hispanic:	1
% foreign:	<1
% transfers:	9

WHAT'S HOT

working a job
dating
marriage
rap/hip-hop
attending all classes
caring about politics
Top 40

WHAT'S NOT

small lectures
small labs and seminars
dorm comfort
deans
honesty

ACADEMICS

Academic Rating:	**69**
Calendar:	semester
Student/teacher ratio:	23/1
% doctorates:	73
Profs interesting:	80
Profs accessible:	77
Hours of study per day:	2.86

MOST POPULAR MAJORS BY %

Pre-Business:	7
Elementary Education:	5
Special Education:	4

What do students think about Illinois State University?

■ **Academics** Illinois State University is often overlooked by those who devise national college rankings, in part because its students are nearly all in-staters and in part because its home state is crammed with quality schools. ISU students reported a high degree of satisfaction with their choice, however, and you certainly can't argue with the price of tuition. Students warned that prospects should investigate the quality of their desired major before coming, noting that education, music, speech and mass communication, and business administration are all strong. Several told us that the honor's program is the school's greatest bargain. Full professors teach an unusual number of introductory courses. One student further noted that the "faculty have a stand-up, accept-responsibility attitude. There's no run-around, but rather an attitude of 'if it doesn't work, come back to me and I'll make it work.'" Like most public institutions, ISU is currently suffering the effects of a poor economy and state budget deficits. Complained one student, "There are not enough classes to take and you have a hard time getting into classes that are offered. I have only one required class left but it was closed. I wish the school had more financial stability so things like this wouldn't happen." Red tape is another unfortunate fact of life here. Said one student, "Employees of the university (in all areas) aren't informed of the school's policies and procedures. It's very frustrating." Even with its faults, though, ISU remains a great bargain.

■ **Life** With nearly 20,000 undergraduates, ISU is a huge school. Fortunately it has a self-supporting social scene, because its host town, Normal, is unexciting. "This town is what its name suggests, Normal," is about as close as any student came to complimenting the locale. Several complained that town police strictly enforced drinking laws, making the town an inhospitable social venue for most students. Police policies notwithstanding, drinking is a very popular way to pass leisure time at ISU. A woman who chose ISU over rival Northern Illinois University wrote that ISU has "hot guys, cool parties. Boy, am I glad I didn't go to Northern—their students come here to party! Ha!" For those who wish to avoid the party scene, the school supports plenty of clubs, organizations, and "great programs for those who want to get involved." A final note: "services for the disabled are excellent."

■ **Students** Even though out-of-state students pay only a pittance more than Illinois residents, ISU still attracts an almost entirely in-state student body. A small minority population (less than 10 percent) is made up mostly of black students, and all students report that minority communities socialize among themselves. Said one black student, "The campus is very segregated and as an African-American I can say that most blacks are content with sticking together because the university doesn't seem to care about its minority student population." A white student agreed that "it's rather cliquish here."

ILLINOIS STATE UNIVERSITY

Admissions

Applicants to Illinois State University who rank in the upper half of their high school class and have a composite score of at least 21 on the Enhanced ACT (or who score approximately 1000 on the SAT) gain automatic admission to the school. Students in the bottom half of their high school classes or who have lower standardized test scores are not necessarily rejected, although both poor test scores and poor high school ranking will probably keep you out of ISU. Applicants must have completed four years of English, three years of math, and two years each of a lab science, social studies, electives, and either a foreign language or fine arts. Students who apply to Illinois State most often also apply to University of Illinois, Northern Illinois University, and Southern Illinois University.

Financial Aid

Illinois State University requires financial aid applicants to complete "any of the federally approved need-analysis forms" and a form generated by its own financial aid office. In '90–'91, ISU offered athletic scholarships to 1% of all undergrads with an average scholarship value of $3,304. Eight percent of its students received academic grants (average value: $1,555). Other miscellaneous merit awards went to about 8% of all undergrads, with an average value of $1,245 each. Illinois State recommends PLUS, SLS, Stafford, and Illinois Opportunity Program loans. There's no closing date for FA applications, but the priority deadline is March 1.

A note from the Illinois State University Admissions Office:

"Illinois State University (ISU) was founded in 1857 as the first public institution of higher learning in Illinois. Today, Illinois State University is a comprehensive institution with degree programs at the bachelor's, master's, and doctoral levels. There are more than 21,000 students enrolled at ISU in more than 70 different fields of study housed in 34 academic departments within five colleges. The tree-shaded campus of Illinois State University, covering 850 acres in Normal, is a study of varying architecture, ranging from the castlelike appearance of Cook Hall to the modernistic dominance of the 28-story twin Watterson Towers residence halls. Major classroom buildings are centrally located and are surrounded by the library and recreational, social and residence structures. Most facilities are accessible to the handicapped. ISU has gained nationwide recognition in a recently published book by California educator Martin Nemko entitled *How to Get an Ivy League Education at a Public University*."

ADMISSIONS FACTS

Competitiveness Rating:	**61**
% of applicants accepted:	75
% acceptees attending:	36

FRESHMAN PROFILE

Average verbal SAT:	NA
Average math SAT:	NA
Average ACT:	22
Graduated top 10% of class:	11
Graduated top 25% of class:	36
Graduated top 50% of class:	75

DEADLINES

Early decision/action:	NA
Early dec./act. notif.:	NA
Regular admission:	rolling
Regular adm. notif.:	rolling

APPLICANTS ALSO LOOK AT

and often prefer:
Illinois Wesleyan U.

and sometimes prefer:
Iowa State U.
Northeast Missouri State U.
Indiana U.

and rarely prefer:
U. Illinois
Southern Illinois U.
U. Iowa

ADDRESS

Undergraduate Admissions
Normal, IL 61761
309-438-2181

FINANCIAL FACTS

In-state tuition ($):	2,430
Out-of-state tuition ($):	3,015
Room & board:	2,786
FA application deadline:	none
% frosh receiving FA:	NA
PT earnings per yr. ($):	1542

TYPE OF AID: % of students ($)

FA of some kind:	49 (NA)
Need-based grants:	33 (2,944)
Merit-based grants:	NA
Loans:	33 (2,845)
Work study:	4 (1326)
Student rating of FA:	70

ILLINOIS WESLEYAN UNIVERSITY

Bloomington, IL

CAMPUS LIFE

Quality of Life Rating: **77**

Type of school:	private
Affiliation:	Methodist
Environment:	city

STUDENT BODY

FT undergrad enrollment:	1,744
% male/% female:	46/54
% out-of-state:	14
% live on campus:	88
% African-American:	3
% Asian:	4
% Caucasian:	86
% Hispanic:	2
% foreign:	5
% transfers:	2

WHAT'S HOT

college radio station
town-gown relations
dorm safety
profs teach intros
doing all the reading
cost of living
college theater groups
small lectures

WHAT'S NOT

library
food
overall happiness
intramural sports
hard liquor

ACADEMICS

Academic Rating: **79**

Calendar:	4-1-4
Student/teacher ratio:	NA
% doctorates:	72
Profs interesting:	80
Profs accessible:	79
Hours of study per day:	3.32

MOST POPULAR MAJORS BY %

Social Sciences:	13
Life Sciences:	10
Visual & Performing Arts:	10

% GRADS WHO PURSUE

Law:	5
MBA:	10
Medicine:	5
M.A., etc.:	15

What do students think about Illinois Wesleyan University?

■ **Academics** In 1991, *US News & World Report* named Illinois Wesleyan the #1 regional university for the Midwest. You'd think students would take pride in this achievement, right? Wrong! Most of our respondents used the school's high ranking as a jumping-off point for their own gripes. Many started their essays in this manner: "It's *supposed* to be the best in the area, but…" The old cliché is true: it *is* lonely at the top. How did IWU get there, and why are students trying to bring it back down to earth? First things first: compared to other schools in its class, IWU has very competitive admissions. For a school of its small size, it's also very versatile, strong in the fine arts (particularly drama and music) but also able to send 20 percent of its students on to professional programs (one in 10 goes on to pursue an MBA). Classes are small, and, for a private school, tuition is pretty reasonable. So what's the problem? Mostly it's the perception that the administration, in its eagerness to maintain the school's new-found prominence, is ignoring the needs of the students. Music students complained that new distribution requirements take too much time away from their music studies, and fear that when they graduate they won't be able to compete with conservatory students in the job market. Others complained that important facilities, such as the library, are in disrepair, and others still that financial aid packages were meager; still, one student pointed out, "There's $15 million dollars being invested in a new athletic center—why?" And, while several students positively noted the small class size and instructor accessibility, our survey showed overall student dissatisfaction in these categories. Mel Brooks once said, "it's *good* to be the king!" Well, maybe not.

■ **Life** Many students mentioned the high level of participation in extracurricular clubs here. Wrote one, "People are encouraged to get involved in a wide range of activities, from frats to the scuba club." Students get pretty excited about their Division III sports teams, but intramural sports are not among the many popular extracurriculars. Nor is partying: wrote one student: "This is not a party school. Alcohol rules are strict, and controlled substances are rare." Because the school is so small, it's hard to maintain any degree of anonymity. Wrote one student, "Some students aren't comfortable with the small school 'everyone knows everyone' scene, because one mistake and you can't recover. There's no new social group to go to who doesn't know you or the reputation you just earned." Students gave Bloomington below average grades: explained one, "Usually I enjoy the small-town feel at this school, but weekends can get pretty boring."

■ **Students** IWU students characterized all their classmates as "overwhelmingly conservative," but those who filled out our survey fell to the left of center of the political spectrum. Did we hit the small mother lode of liberals here? More likely, the student body isn't quite as homogeneously white, rich, and Republican as students think. Over three quarters of the students are from in-state, many from the Chicago area. Wrote one out-of-state student, "I'm from Minnesota and I feel like a foreign student."

ILLINOIS WESLEYAN UNIVERSITY

Bloomington, IL

Admissions

Illinois Wesleyan's admissions requirements vary slightly for applicants to its divisions of liberal arts, fine arts, and nursing. The catalog states, "Because of specific liberal arts requirements in all disciplines, each applicant is advised to present a minimum of 15 units of secondary school credit." "Strongly recommended" curricular requirements for all applicants include: four years of English, three years of natural science (two lab), three years of math, three years of foreign language, and two years of social studies. IWU requires that scores for either the SAT or ACT be submitted. An interview is recommended, but not required. Students for the school of fine arts must audition or present a portfolio (whichever is appropriate).

Financial Aid

The financial aid office at Illinois Wesleyan requires applicants to submit the FAF. Merit-based grants are awarded to students who have previously demonstrated academic excellence and to those with talent in music, art, or drama. Other non-need based grants are set aside for pre-ministerial students and for children of Methodist ministers. The most recent IWU catalog lists the following loan options for students: Stafford, Perkins, PLUS, Nursing Student, and IWU-sponsored loans. The office points out that, for its students, "One of the largest sources for funds is through Illinois State Scholarships and Grants. In order to qualify a student must be a resident of the State of Illinois."

Excerpted from Illinois Wesleyan University promotional materials:

"Illinois Wesleyan University strives to provide a liberal education of high quality for all of our students, whether enrolled in the College of Liberal Arts or in one of the professional Schools of Nursing, Art, Music, or Drama. An Illinois Wesleyan education is distinctive in giving a liberal arts direction to the curricula of the professional schools and programs and in allowing liberal arts majors access to a wide variety of professional courses as electives. We believe that our most important educational goal is liberation from ignorance and complacency. Because we assume that the mind is the key to the educated person, we hope to foster during the college years the knowledge, values and skills that will sustain all of us over a lifetime of learning. We intend, moreover, to prepare our students for responsible citizenship and leadership in a democratic society and global community. We want Illinois Wesleyan to reflect the ethnic, racial, and cultural diversity of the world. Above all, whatever their course of studies, we wish to enable Wesleyan graduates to lead useful, creative, fully realized lives."

ADMISSIONS FACTS

Competitiveness Rating:	**86**
% of applicants accepted:	57
% acceptees attending:	34

FRESHMAN PROFILE

Average verbal SAT:	533
Average math SAT:	640
Average ACT:	27
Graduated top 10% of class:	54
Graduated top 25% of class:	88
Graduated top 50% of class:	100

DEADLINES

Early decision/action:	NA
Early dec./act. notif.:	NA
Regular admission:	3/1
Regular adm. notif.:	rolling

APPLICANTS ALSO LOOK AT

and sometimes prefer:
U. Illinois
DePauw U.
Northern Illinois U.
Southern Illinois U.
Illinois State U.

and rarely prefer:
Eastern Illinois U.
Bradley U.

ADDRESS

Undergraduate Admissions
Box 2900
Bloomington, IL 61702
309-556-3031

FINANCIAL FACTS

In-state tuition ($):	11,015
Out-of-state tuition ($):	11,015
Room & board:	3,695
FA application deadline:	3/1
% frosh receiving FA:	89
PT earnings per yr. ($):	1,275

TYPE OF AID: % of students ($)

FA of some kind:	81 (NA)
Need-based grants:	NA
Merit-based grants:	NA
Loans:	NA
Work study:	NA
Student rating of FA:	70

INDIANA UNIVERSITY AT BLOOMINGTON

Bloomington, IN

What do students think about Indiana University?

■ **Academics** It may come as a surprise to some that Indiana University, known mainly for its dominant athletic teams, demonstrates similar prowess in the academic arena. Students particularly praised the "top notch" business and journalism schools, the excellent psychology department, and the world-renowned School of Music. In all departments, students agreed that "the opportunities are there, but size is a big deterrent." Indeed, classes are often huge, even for upperclassmen. Those who are not assertive can easily get lost in the shuffle. Most concurred that professors must be sought out for help and often don't have time to deal with the vast number of students in their courses. One student complained, "It is too bad that this university concentrates so much on professors' publishing records. It's publish or perish." Courses fill up quickly, and registration is a major hassle. Students we asked said, "Our system of registration for classes needs major improvement." If prospective students can deal with the administrative problems inherent in such a large university, however, the benefits are well worth it. Indiana University has quite a lot to offer for its state university price.

■ **Life** Bloomington, Indiana is a "great example of a college town," according to our respondents. Students rated themselves 'very happy' here overall. Students "love the social atmosphere; everybody has fun here!" The campus itself, according to one junior, is "one of the most beautiful places I've ever seen." Athletics are, of course, a very important part of non-academic life. Intercollegiate sports are universally popular—men's basketball, however, is paramount—and intramural programs are also well attended. Social life basically revolves around fraternities and sororities, acceptance to which can be brutally competitive. One of the few complaints we received was that "this school is so Greek; there is a sharp division between the Greeks and everyone else." Another was that the campus can get socially cliquish. Wrote one undergrad, "Students in the different schools are greatly segregated. You are pretty much confined to the school where your major is." Dating in the traditional sense is very common at Indiana, and students claimed to be very happy socially, rating each other as fun-loving and even good-looking as a group.

■ **Students** Indiana University is not a terribly diverse school. Almost all of students are from in-state, and minorities make up only 15 percent of the student body. Still, with an undergraduate population of over 25,000, there are enough people so that everyone can interact with the "wide variety of cultures in the student body." The political climate is basically conservative, as is most of Indiana, but again, anyone can probably find others of similar interests in a place this large. The fine quality of many of the different schools within the university assures a multi-faceted and interesting undergraduate population.

INDIANA UNIVERSITY AT BLOOMINGTON

Admissions

Indiana's bulletin states, "University-bound students should establish a solid foundation at the high school level in English (they require four years), laboratory sciences (one year) and social sciences (two years) if they intend to compete in any academic program offered by Indiana University. Society's increasing demands for mathematical analysis and computing make a broad background in mathematics, including algebra and trigonometry (three years total required), essential for many fields of study. The study of a foreign language is desirable but not required for admission." The admissions office at IU writes that class rank, high school program and grade trends are all weighed equally in the evaluation of an application.

Financial Aid

The financial aid office at Indiana University requires the FAF and, for the 1992–93 academic year only, a form generated by the institution. Applications must be *postmarked* by March 1. The school reports that the average financial aid award for incoming freshmen in 1991–92 was $4,911; 56% of the freshman class received a financial aid award for that year. Indiana University did not provide us with a breakdown of the types of loans taken by its students.

A note from the Indiana University Admissions Office:

"Indiana University is a traditional university located in Bloomington, Indiana. The campus is known for its spacious, wooded beauty, classic limestone buildings and wide variety of trees and flowers. Bloomington is a wonderful college town. Its liberal arts curriculum offers students a wide range of academic options combined with built-in flexibility."

ADMISSIONS FACTS

Competitiveness Rating:	**77**
% of applicants accepted:	75
% acceptees attending:	48

FRESHMAN PROFILE

Average verbal SAT:	470
Average math SAT:	537
Average ACT:	24
Graduated top 10% of class:	34
Graduated top 25% of class:	77
Graduated top 50% of class:	99

DEADLINES

Early decision/action:	NA
Early dec./act. notif.:	NA
Regular admission:	2/15
Regular adm. notif.:	rolling

APPLICANTS ALSO LOOK AT

and often prefer:
U. Notre Dame

and sometimes prefer:
U. Illinois
U. Wisconsin–Madison
U. Iowa
Ohio State U.

and rarely prefer:
Purdue U.
SUNY Buffalo
Wabash College

ADDRESS

Undergraduate Admissions
814 East Third Street
Bloomington, IN 47405
812-855-0661

FINANCIAL FACTS

In-state tuition ($):	2,368
Out-of-state tuition ($):	6,900
Room & board:	3,730
FA application deadline:	3/1
% frosh receiving FA:	64
PT earnings per yr. ($):	NA

TYPE OF AID: % of students ($)

FA of some kind:	67 (NA)
Need-based grants:	NA
Merit-based grants:	NA
Loans:	NA
Work study:	NA
Student rating of FA:	67

UNIVERSITY OF IOWA

Iowa City, IA

CAMPUS LIFE

Quality of Life Rating: **79**

Type of school:	public
Affiliation:	none
Environment:	city

STUDENT BODY

FT undergrad enrollment:	16,396
% male/% female:	48/52
% out-of-state:	28
% live on campus:	30
% African-American:	3
% Asian:	3
% Caucasian:	91
% Hispanic:	1
% foreign:	2
% transfers:	5

WHAT'S HOT

working a job
intercollegiate sports
dating
marriage
college newspaper
gay community visible

WHAT'S NOT

profs teach intros
small lectures
TAs teach upper-level courses
deans
attending all classes
living on campus
studying hard
honest students

ACADEMICS

Academic Rating: **75**

Calendar:	semester
Student/teacher ratio:	17/1
% doctorates:	98
Profs interesting:	70
Profs accessible:	72
Hours of study per day:	2.72

MOST POPULAR MAJORS BY %

Business :	14
Engineering:	8
Pre-Medicine:	6

What do students think about University of Iowa?

■ **Academics** Peppered among the many large Midwestern public universities that capably serve the pre-professional crowd are a few institutions that also do a little more. University of Iowa is just such a school, one that does an excellent job producing the lawyers, doctors, businessmen, engineers, and teachers of tomorrow while also providing one of the region's intellectual centers—"the Athens of the Midwest," as several students described it. Wrote one economics major, "Almost every academic discipline and combination thereof can be found here. Best of all, the students here live and work in a friendly environment where learning is more than just rote memorization—it's learning who you are and how you can best use the skills you gain during your years in Iowa City." Among the university's nationally renowned departments are journalism, English (especially the creative writing program), film theory and production, and molecular biology. Humanities and social science departments are, in general, stronger here than at most schools. Students in the liberal arts college must complete a massive battery of distribution requirements; students in the other schools are allowed to focus more specifically on one area of study. Regardless, the school is tough. Wrote one student, "Graduate in four years? Yeah, right!" As at most large schools, unfortunately, classes are often huge, professors inaccessible, and the bureaucracy running the institution cumbersome. Students report that the generally friendly atmosphere on campus makes some of the school's drawbacks a little easier to bear.

■ **Life** Iowa City is small, but unlike most similar-sized towns, Iowa City receives high marks from students. Wrote one, "Iowa City is the greatest college town in the nation…I feel sorry for anyone who's never been here for a visit." Because the university is the city's chief industry, Iowa City is more accommodating to students than are most small cities. Local bars and clubs provide hospitable diversions for students, who report that drinking is both popular and easy to do, even for those under 21. Intercollegiate sports provide another rallying point for students. Football, wrestling, and basketball are most popular. The Greeks are active but not dominant. The school is so large and so diverse that no one organization or activity could overwhelm social life here. For road trips, Chicago is five hours away by car, "which in the Midwest is just a hop, skip, and a jump," reported one student.

■ **Students** UI's minority population is small. Still, students report that theirs is a diverse student body. "UI is a diverse place in every respect," said one student. "Students here come from a wide variety of social and economic backgrounds, and there are many foreign students, which adds a unique international dimension to the school." Liberal politics is the rule rather than the exception here, although, with nearly 20,000 undergraduates, all perspectives are represented.

UNIVERSITY OF IOWA

Iowa City, IA

Admissions

The admissions office reports that "Iowa residents are admitted to the College of Liberal Arts if they rank in the upper half of their high school graduating class; non-residents are admitted if they rank in the top 30 percent OR residents and non-residents are admitted with an acceptable "admissions index score"—two times ACT composite plus class rank percentile. For 1991–92, admissible index scores were 90 for residents and 110 for non-residents. Criteria for the College of Engineering are higher." Applicants to the College of Liberal Arts must have completed four years of English, three years each of science, math, and social studies, and two years of a foreign language. The school requires either the ACT or the SAT. Applicants to University of Iowa often also apply to Iowa State, University of Northern Iowa, Drake, University of Illinois (Urbana), and Indiana U.

Financial Aid

University of Iowa requires its financial aid applicants to complete its own verification form, either the FAF or FFS, and a copy of the parents' most recent tax return. The FA office writes, "We award on a first-come, first-served basis as files are completed. We do not use the Stafford loan as part of the awards in the aid package—students decide if they want to borrow to meet any remaining need." In '90–'91, 8% of all undergrads received a merit-based scholarship (average value $2,000). Overall, 70% of the class of '95 applied for aid; of those, 65% received an award of some kind. University of Iowa has a rolling FA application deadline. Students who want to apply for aid are encouraged to do so "as soon as possible."

A note from the University of Iowa Admissions Office:

"The University of Iowa has strong programs in the creative arts, being the home of the first Writer's Workshop and now housing the world-renowned International Writing Program. It also has strong programs in communication studies, journalism, political science, English, and psychology, and was the birthplace of the discipline of speech pathology and audiology. It offers excellent programs in the basic health sciences and health care programs, led by the top-ranked College of Medicine and the closely associated University Hospitals and Clinics, the largest university-owned teaching hospital in the United States."

ADMISSIONS FACTS

Competitiveness Rating:	**70**
% of applicants accepted:	85
% acceptees attending:	41

FRESHMAN PROFILE

Average verbal SAT:	NA
Average math SAT:	NA
Average ACT:	24
Graduated top 10% of class:	25
Graduated top 25% of class:	57
Graduated top 50% of class:	90

DEADLINES

Early decision/action:	NA
Early dec./act. notif.:	NA
Regular admission:	5/15
Regular adm. notif.:	rolling

APPLICANTS ALSO LOOK AT

and often prefer:
Northwestern U.

and sometimes prefer:
Illinois State U.
Iowa State U.
Grinnell College
U. Wisconsin–Madison

and rarely prefer:
Cornell College
Indiana U.
U. Missouri–Rolla

ADDRESS

Undergraduate Admissions
Iowa City, IA 52242
319-335-3847

FINANCIAL FACTS

In-state tuition ($):	1,952
Out-of-state tuition ($):	6,470
Room & board:	2,920
FA application deadline:	NA
% frosh receiving FA:	NA
PT earnings per yr. ($):	3,240

TYPE OF AID: % of students ($)

FA of some kind:	70 (NA)
Need-based grants:	38 (1,570)
Merit-based grants:	8 (2,000)
Loans:	NA
Work study:	6 (1,098)
Student rating of FA:	68

IOWA STATE UNIVERSITY

Ames, IA

CAMPUS LIFE

Quality of Life Rating:	**82**
Type of school:	public
Affiliation:	none
Environment:	suburban

STUDENT BODY

FT undergrad enrollment:	19,639
% male/% female:	59/41
% out-of-state:	21
% live on campus:	56
% African-American:	2
% Asian:	2
% Caucasian:	86
% Hispanic:	1
% foreign:	4
% transfers:	6

WHAT'S HOT

fraternities/sororities
dating
top 40
alternative rock
hard liquor
overall happiness
administration (overall)

WHAT'S NOT

small classes (overall)
doing all the reading
caring about politics
living on campus
attending all classes

ACADEMICS

Academic Rating:	**69**
Calendar:	semester
Student/teacher ratio:	18/1
% doctorates:	77
Profs interesting:	65
Profs accessible:	63
Hours of study per day:	3.18

MOST POPULAR MAJORS BY %

Engineering:	20
Business:	15
Art and Design:	10

% GRADS WHO PURSUE

Law:	1
MBA:	1
Medicine:	1
M.A., etc.:	13

What do students think about Iowa State University?

■ **Academics** Iowa State University has earned its reputation as one of the country's leading agricultural schools. But farming and agricultural sciences aren't the only things taught here: career-oriented programs of all types attract the school's 20,000+ students to Ames. About one tenth of the students study agriculture, but a much larger proportion, about one quarter, study business and management; another one-fifth pursue engineering degrees, and one in 10 studies education. Liberal arts studies are also available, as are a myriad of other career-oriented majors: our respondents expressed satisfaction with programs as varied as landscape architecture, speech communication, and graphic design. Students told us that the school was unusually well-run for a large university: they gave good grades in most administrative categories. Said one, "I think the academic advising here is exceptional. Advisors want to know what you want from your education and really help you achieve it." Although professors received only average grades, several students mentioned how helpful instructors were. "The profs really care about teaching you and also care whether you excel," reported one accounting major. Classes of all difficulty levels are too often taught by graduate students, and class sizes are predictably large.

■ **Life** Ames, Iowa is a small town, and its slow pace suits many of ISU's undergraduates. One reported, "Ames is a college town, not a huge metropolis. The people are easy to know and friendly. ISU is the best decision I ever made." Still, if you're looking for big city action, ISU probably won't suit your needs. One undergrad complained that "Iowa State University is a well-thought-out campus without an active campus town surrounding it. If Ames would get its act together and create a working campus/town relationship, maybe enrollment would increase." Des Moines is a half hour away, but most students' social lives begin and end on campus. The campus is beautiful and easy to get around. One student wrote that "from one corner to another is a 13-minute walk; it's so convenient there are hardly any bikes on campus." Another reported, "The campus is absolutely beautiful. There is always something to do—whether you choose a school-related activity or a party." Fraternities and sororities play a major role here: they are more popular at only thirteen other schools included in this book. ISU students aren't sports nuts to the same degree that other students at large universities are, but they do take an active interest in their teams and cherish their rivalry with University of Iowa. Said one, "There is a big interstate rivalry between University of Iowa and Iowa State University, and finally after years of lopsidedness, ISU is taking over. It's about time, ISU!"

■ **Students** ISU students are extremely happy with their choice, particularly for students at a large university. It's probably because of "The school's most unique quality: the friendliness of the students." They must be particularly well adjusted, because they reported an active dating scene despite a pretty lopsided male-female ratio. Students are generally conservative and serious, and the minority population is relatively small.

IOWA STATE UNIVERSITY

Admissions

Iowa State admits all applicants who ranked in the top half of their high school classes. For applicants in the bottom half, they use a formula that ties class rank to ACT/SAT scores. Any student with a composite ACT score of 24 or higher is admitted to Iowa State regardless of class rank, provided that s/he meets the high school curriculum requirements, which are: four years of English, there years of mathematics (including algebra, geometry, and advanced algebra), three years of science (two years of lab sciences), and two years of social studies (including one year of US history and a semester of US government). Applicants to the College of Liberal Arts and Sciences must have an additional year of social studies and two years of a foreign language. Applicants to Iowa State most often also apply to University of Iowa, UIllinois–Urbana, Purdue, Nebraska, and Arizona State.

Financial Aid

Iowa State University requires financial aid applicants to complete either the FFS, FAF, or SingleFile (USAF). Iowa State offers a variety of merit-based scholarships; last year, 17% of all undergrads received an academic scholarship, with an average value of $1,400. Merit scholarships are also awarded for excellence in athletics and performing arts, for minority students (George Washington Carver and National Hispanic Scholarships), and for departmental (planned major) choices. The school maintains a database of 180,000 scholarships available from 20,000 sources.

A note from the Iowa State Admissions Office:

"Iowa State was recognized by *Money Magazine* as 'one of the top college bargains in the United States,' with 'high-quality education at a remarkably low cost.' Along with a strong academic experience, students also have outstanding opportunities for further developing their leadership skills and interpersonal relationships through one of the over 500 student organizations which add to the high quality of campus life and exemplary out-of-class experiences.

"The University has lavished attention on its park-like campus, located on a 1,770-acre tract in the middle of Ames, population 50,000. History and tradition prevail, from the Stanton Campanile, which serenades campus with its carillon bells to the sculptures across campus created by Danish artist, Christian Petersen. High-tech buildings such as the new $12 million Durham Computation Center, the $30 million molecular biology building, and the $13 million athletic/recreation facility add a contemporary and sophisticated feeling to the campus."

ADMISSIONS FACTS

Competitiveness Rating:	**71**
% of applicants accepted:	88
% acceptees attending:	47

FRESHMAN PROFILE

Average verbal SAT:	450
Average math SAT:	530
Average ACT:	25
Graduated top 10% of class:	27
Graduated top 25% of class:	60
Graduated top 50% of class:	96

DEADLINES

Early decision/action:	NA
Early dec./act. notif.:	NA
Regular admission:	8/24
Regular adm. notif.:	rolling

APPLICANTS ALSO LOOK AT

and often prefer:
U. Wisconsin–Madison
U. Michigan

and sometimes prefer:
Kansas State U.
U. Iowa
U. Minnesota

and rarely prefer:
Illinois State U.
Purdue U.
Creighton U.

ADDRESS

Undergraduate Admissions
100 Alumni Hall
Ames, IA 50011-2010
515-294-5836

FINANCIAL FACTS

In-state tuition ($):	1,952
Out-of-state tuition ($):	6,406
Room & board:	2,850
FA application deadline:	3/1
% frosh receiving FA:	65
PT earnings per yr. ($):	1,700

TYPE OF AID: % of students ($)

FA of some kind:	65 (NA)
Need-based grants:	53 (2,200)
Merit-based grants:	NA
Loans:	50 (3,200)
Work study:	2 (2,400)
Student rating of FA:	79

JAMES MADISON UNIVERSITY

Harrisonburg, VA

CAMPUS LIFE

Quality of Life Rating: **82**

Type of school:	public
Affiliation:	none
Environment:	suburban

STUDENT BODY

FT undergrad enrollment:	9,311
% male/% female:	45/55
% out-of-state:	23
% live on campus:	51
% African-American:	9
% Asian:	2
% Caucasian:	87
% Hispanic:	1
% foreign:	1
% transfers:	4

WHAT'S HOT

food
cost of living
college radio station
religious clubs
dorm comfort
good looking students
college newspaper
administration (overall)

WHAT'S NOT

library
working a job
financial aid
doing all the reading
caring about politics

ACADEMICS

Academic Rating: **71**

Calendar:	semester
Student/teacher ratio:	19/1
% doctorates:	74
Profs interesting:	76
Profs accessible:	73
Hours of study per day:	2.95

MOST POPULAR MAJORS BY %

Business & Management:	30
Social Sciences:	14
Education:	10

What do students think about James Madison University?

■ **Academics** James Madison University is a true bargain. Reasonably priced for both in-state and out-of-state students, JMU provides many strong programs in comfortable surroundings to a diverse, friendly student body. Students told us that business and music are the school's standout programs. Liberal arts courses got the big thumbs down ("they're classes for the thirteenth grade") and, while students like the new international relations department, "they still have to work some of the kinks out." The best programs are the most popular: almost one third of the students pursue business and management majors. Like many state schools, James Madison University has had to endure recent home-state fiscal woes. One optimistic student wrote that "JMU, even in the grasp of the death grip of Virginia's state budget cuts, maintains an effective focus on the quality of student life and faculty skills." Others, however, noted signs that academic standards might be suffering. One pointed out what several others also noted, that "the school's population is growing without a proportional increase in teachers and staff, causing larger classes and more competition for spots in popular courses." Complained another: "Tuition is going up and professors are not getting promised raises. Why are we starting new construction projects?" Students also gave low grades to course registration ("It sends everyone running around campus for overrides") and the library.

■ **Life** Harrisonburg, Virginia may not be the nation's entertainment capital, but JMU students don't seem to mind, because the university goes out of its way to provide diversions. "The campus provides a great diversity of students and activities, and it is very easy to become involved in clubs and organizations," wrote one student. Said another, "JMU is always concerned with my entertainment needs. This I like. I have been able to make my own music videos, see movies for free, eat free pizza, be hypnotized, and go roller-skating for free, all in one year...keen!" A sprawling, country club-like campus ("If you love flowers and shrubberies, this is the place to be") is yet another reason students are happy here even though they're out in the sticks. Fraternities play a central but not overwhelming role in social circles; it's possible not to go Greek and still have a life at JMU. Sports are also very popular. When students get tired of the country, they usually head off to Richmond or Washington DC, both within driving distance. One final perquisite: students ranked JMU's food the tenth best in the nation.

■ **Students** The student body of James Madison is nearly nine-tenths white. Almost all minority students are black, however, meaning there are almost 1000 African-American students here. Three quarters of the students are Virginia natives. There must be a solid core of fundamentalists: we got more "John 3:16" essays from here than from anywhere else, religious schools included!

JAMES MADISON UNIVERSITY

Harrisonburg, VA

Admissions

James Madison's admissions office writes that "There are no cut-offs. Our formula allows us to take all applicants into consideration in a very personal and individual manner. Each applicant is evaluated using…six factors (listed below). We make collective admissions decisions, which allows us to admit the best students who apply." The admissions committee at JMU first looks at your program of study and your high school rank. These are followed by standardized test scores, extracurriculars, essays, and letters of recommendation. The SAT is required. While no high-school curriculum is specified, the JMU undergraduate catalog states, "…the applicant with solid achievement in five or more academic courses each of the four years of high school will have a distinct advantage in the admissions process." Applicants to JMU also often apply to Virginia Tech, U. Virginia, and William and Mary.

Financial Aid

James Madison University requires financial aid applicants to complete the FAF. The university awards academic scholarships (in '90–'91, 5% of all undergrads received an academic scholarship) and athletic (4% of all students; average value $4,000). A number of need-based scholarships are available, including JMU's own Foundation Scholarships, the General Undergraduate Scholarship (GUS), which ranges from $800–$2,000 per year (Virginia residents only), Pell Grants, and the College Scholarship Assistance Program ($400–$2,000 per year). In addition to Perkins and Stafford loans, JMU recommends PLUS, SLS, and state-sponsored Edvantage loans. Edvantage is a long-term loan which requires "no income limit or financial need qualification"; you need only pass a credit check.

A note from the James Madison University Admissions Office:

"James Madison University has been described as the 'Ultimate University.' It is a close-knit community that possesses a unique atmosphere the university's current students call the 'JMU Way.' This 'JMU Way' is a special kind of spirit that emphasizes excellence in all aspects of a student's life. Students are challenged both inside and outside the classroom by talented, caring faculty and staff. They are especially challenged by other JMU students, who are extremely friendly, outgoing and actively involved in their own educations. The diversity of individuals who comprise the JMU student body make the most of their college experience by creating and participating in a rich variety of educational, social, and extracurricular programs. A beautiful campus, supportive environment, and strong commitment to a student's preparation for the 21st century combine to make JMU a truly unique institution."

ADMISSIONS FACTS

Competitiveness Rating:	**81**
% of applicants accepted:	43
% acceptees attending:	39

FRESHMAN PROFILE

Average verbal SAT:	512
Average math SAT:	580
Average ACT:	NA
Graduated top 10% of class:	34
Graduated top 25% of class:	72
Graduated top 50% of class:	97

DEADLINES

Early decision/action:	NA
Early dec./act. notif.:	NA
Regular admission:	2/1
Regular adm. notif.:	4/1

APPLICANTS ALSO LOOK AT

and sometimes prefer:
Villanova U.
American U.

and rarely prefer:
Virginia Polytech
West Virginia U.
Clemson U.
Hampden-Sydney College

ADDRESS

Undergraduate Admissions
Harrisonburg, VA 22807
703-568-6147

FINANCIAL FACTS

In-state tuition ($):	3,298
Out-of-state tuition ($):	6,650
Room & board:	4,102
FA application deadline:	3/19
% frosh receiving FA:	38
PT earnings per yr. ($):	1220

TYPE OF AID: % of students ($)

FA of some kind:	47 (NA)
Need-based grants:	12 (2,500)
Merit-based grants:	NA
Loans:	16 (2,600)
Work study:	21 (1,530)
Student rating of FA:	66

JOHNS HOPKINS UNIVERSITY

Baltimore, MD

CAMPUS LIFE

Quality of Life Rating:	**75**
Type of school:	private
Affiliation:	none
Environment:	city

STUDENT BODY

FT undergrad enrollment:	2,986
% male/% female:	63/37
% out-of-state:	80
% live on campus:	50
% African-American:	6
% Asian:	18
% Caucasian:	67
% Hispanic:	2
% foreign:	5
% transfers:	2

WHAT'S HOT
studying hard

WHAT'S NOT
college newspaper
college radio station
requirements are easy
dating
overall happiness
Top 40
in-class discussion
rap/hip-hop
living on campus
town-gown relations

ACADEMICS

Academic Rating:	**88**
Calendar:	4-1-4
Student/teacher ratio:	9/1
% doctorates:	99
Profs interesting:	74
Profs accessible:	72
Hours of study per day:	3.74

MOST POPULAR MAJORS BY %

Social Sciences:	27
Engineering:	24
Life Sciences:	21

% GRADS WHO PURSUE

Law:	10
MBA:	5
Medicine:	30
M.A., etc.:	30

What do students think about Johns Hopkins University?

■ **Academics** Although nearly one in three Johns Hopkins students goes on to medical school, JHU has a lot more to offer than a world-class pre-med program. The English, writing, history, political science and engineering departments are all among the nation's best, and in fact few departments are not strong. Still, pre-med is the marquee major here. As one student explained, "I'm pre-med and there's no place I would rather be. The academics are killer, no joke, but for those few who survive, the world is their oyster." Said another, "The university offers students an excellent opportunity to do research in medicine, physics, biochemistry and other sciences, and consequently make something of their lives." Science majors study with "the brightest minds in their fields" and are offered "unique research opportunities in which they interact with their professors." For all students, academics are "very intense" and course work is "rigorous and demanding": as one history major put it, "Students here have only one thing on their minds: work! work! work! If you aren't prepared for 500-800 pages of reading per week and four term papers in excess of 10 pages then, for God's sake, go elsewhere." Many of our respondents noted that Hopkins is best for those who know what they want before they get to school; as one put it, "Hopkins can be distressing if you are uncertain about what you want to study. The faculty and administration are definitely 'hands off.'"

■ **Life** JHU's undergraduate campus is located in Baltimore's Homewood section, a residential area that provides few social opportunities. Downtown Baltimore is better, with lots of restaurants and a strip of bars known as Fells Point, but you need a car to get there. On-campus social life is slow, both because of the seriousness with which most students attack their studies and because of the unfavorable male:female ratio (almost 2:1). Reported one student, "There is fun to be had at JHU, but it's your responsibility to create it." Another told us that "it is very important to participate in some type of extracurricular activity or school gets boring." Plans to upgrade the student center should improve the social scene somewhat, but interaction between the sexes will probably remain low-key. Students emphasized that they attend JHU for an education, not a social life. Still, they ranked low in terms of overall happiness, and it's not because of the quality of education they receive.

■ **Students** With three quarters of its students going on to some kind of graduate school, Hopkins' student body is certainly an ambitious, hardworking lot. Said one undergrad, "Students here tend to be more self-sufficient, mature, and work-oriented. Professional school plans come easy to a JHU graduate." Pre-meds form their own community: "The opportunities to get stoned and run around campus in one's underthings are of course limited to those in the humanities majors, who have no biochemistry tests to study for," said one. The large pre-professional population explains the relative conservatism of students here.

JOHNS HOPKINS UNIVERSITY

Baltimore, MD

Admissions

Johns Hopkins's most recent catalog reports, unsurprisingly, "Intellectual interests and academic performance are of primary importance in the admissions decision. The Admissions Committee carefully examines each applicant's complete scholastic record and aptitude test results. Recommendations from secondary school officials and other sources about a student's character, intellectual curiosity, seriousness of purpose, and range of extracurricular activities are also considered." Applicants must submit scores for either (1) the SAT and three achievements (preferred), or (2) the ACT, and to have completed a rigorous college-prep curriculum including a minimum of: four years each of English and math; and two years each of a foreign language, science, and social studies (three years of science and social studies is "preferred").

Financial Aid

The financial aid office at Johns Hopkins University requires applicants to submit the FAF. The school awards merit-based grants for those with exceptional talents in the arts, music, academics, and athletics. Hopkins recommends that students demonstrating need take advantage of all federally funded loan programs; the school also sponsors a loan for financial aid recipients. Administered through the SHARE program, Hopkins loans range in value from $2,000 to $20,000 per year.

Excerpted from Johns Hopkins University promotional materials:

"The unique educational philosophy of The Johns Hopkins University was first articulated more than a century ago by Daniel Coit Gilman, the university's first president. Gilman believed that the highest quality education must be carried out in a research environment and that the best training, whether undergraduate or graduate, takes place under the supervision of an active researcher. This belief in the inseparability of education and research has become the distinguishing feature of the university's academic programs.

"The low student-faculty ratio on the Homewood campus is a direct consequence of this educational philosophy, which requires the kind of close interaction between faculty and students that occurs in small seminars, in the supervision required for independent projects, or in the research laboratory. Academic requirements for undergraduates are highly flexible and designed to enhance rather than restrain creativity. As a result, many Hopkins undergraduates quickly find themselves enrolled in advanced seminars, engaged in independent study projects, or incorporated into research teams with faculty, graduate students, and postdoctoral fellows."

ADMISSIONS FACTS

Competitiveness Rating:	*90*
% of applicants accepted:	53
% acceptees attending:	30

FRESHMAN PROFILE

Average verbal SAT:	603
Average math SAT:	684
Average ACT:	30
Graduated top 10% of class:	67
Graduated top 25% of class:	90
Graduated top 50% of class:	98

DEADLINES

Early decision/action:	11/15
Early dec./act. notif.:	12/15
Regular admission:	10/1
Regular adm. notif.:	4/5

APPLICANTS ALSO LOOK AT

and often prefer:
MIT
Harvard/Radcliffe College
U. Virginia
Princeton U.

and sometimes prefer:
Duke U.
U. Pennsylvania

and rarely prefer:
Cornell U.
U. Maryland
Lehigh U.

ADDRESS

Undergraduate Admissions
34th & Charles Streets
Baltimore, MD 21218
301-338-8171

FINANCIAL FACTS

In-state tuition ($):	16,000
Out-of-state tuition ($):	16,000
Room & board:	6,120
FA application deadline:	1/15
% frosh receiving FA:	50
PT earnings per yr. ($):	1,600

TYPE OF AID: % of students ($)

FA of some kind:	60 (NA)
Need-based grants:	NA
Merit-based grants:	NA
Loans:	NA
Work study:	NA
Student rating of FA:	77

JUILLIARD SCHOOL

New York, NY

CAMPUS LIFE

Quality of Life Rating:	**78**
Type of school:	private
Affiliation:	none
Environment:	city

STUDENT BODY

FT undergrad enrollment:	485
% male/% female:	46/54
% out-of-state:	73
% live on campus:	35
% African-American:	6
% Asian:	29
% Caucasian:	60
% Hispanic:	4
% foreign:	23
% transfers:	8

WHAT'S HOT

classical music
college theater
gay community accepted
location
interaction among students
dorm safety
small classes (overall)
diversity
in-class discussion
leftist politics

WHAT'S NOT

fraternities/sororities
cost of living
beer
overall happiness

ACADEMICS

Academic Rating:	**90**
Calendar:	semester
Student/teacher ratio:	4/1
% doctorates:	NA
Profs interesting:	80
Profs accessible:	75
Hours of study per day:	3.75

MOST POPULAR MAJOR BY %

Visual & Performing Arts:	100

What do students think about the Juilliard School?

■ **Academics** As one student explained, "Comparing Juilliard to a university is like comparing Shakespeare to all literature. There's not nearly as much diversity, but it is superb in its small field." Intensity and focus are what characterize this prestigious performing arts institution, which has divisions in music, drama, and dance. The motto here is "practice, practice, practice!," and indeed the competitive atmosphere proves too overwhelming for some aspiring performers ("Sending a freshman to Juilliard is like teaching a baby to swim by throwing it in the ocean," wrote one). Although some find the place cutthroat and stifling (there are tales of students listening at others' practice room doors just to psych them out), many thrive on the pressure because it improves their motivation. One of the most important aspects of the Juilliard School is private instruction. A senior warns, "A good experience at Juilliard is 100 percent contingent on a good relationship with one's private teacher. Going to school here can be traumatic, and it's not worth it without a devoted instructor who gives you weekly lessons. Do not trust reputations; find out what present or recent students say about their teachers." In short, the school can prove to be a very different place for each student, especially since interaction between the divisions is "almost nonexistent." But it has launched many stellar careers, and most students believe their hard work pays off. A dance student sums up: "The schedule is grueling, but the level of technical and performance training here at Juilliard is fantastic. This school is a gem set in the middle of the world's most exciting and inspiring city."

■ **Life** Because the artistic pursuits at Juilliard are "individualistic, personal and intense, the result is not a very active social community," according to students we asked. There is a definite lack, common to most art and music schools, of "normal" college activities (there are no sports here, no fraternities or sororities, few large parties, and no pretty campus through which to stroll). But of course those are not the reasons for coming here. Musical, theatrical and other performances abound daily. The campus is in the middle of New York City, and no one can complain of a lack of social or artistic options there. The social scene at Juilliard itself also seems to be drastically changing since the appointment of a new president, who is very concerned with "actively cultivating a healthy environment" for students. New dorms have just opened, and students hope the improvements will make Juilliard "more accommodating to the human aspect of their lives."

■ **Students** Most students at the Juilliard School are quite liberal, although not overly involved in politics. The campus is ethnically diverse, and is home to people with all kinds of lifestyles. The gay community is large and well-accepted, and despite some students' judgments of their peers as "bizarre," generally all the different creative types who come here can feel comfortable.

JUILLIARD SCHOOL

Admissions

The admissions process at Juilliard is understandably less standard since it is an arts school. The admissions office states, "Applicants to Juilliard in Dance and Music should have had extensive prior training. Drama applicants must demonstrate potential. Admission is based almost entirely on the quality of the audition." The admissions committee first considers that audition. After that, in order of importance, it looks at your high school GPA and your essays. Applicants must have completed high school, but there are no required courses. Applicants whose native language is not English must either take the TOEFL or Juilliard's English Proficiency Exam. Applicants to Juilliard also often apply to the Curtis Institute.

Financial Aid

The financial aid office at The School requires applicants to submit the FAF and a form created by the school. The Juilliard course catalog states that awards are made "on the basis of merit and need combined. The total amount of aid provided, depends on the students artistic promise and school record, and on the financial circumstances of the student and his or her family." The same catalog lists only the Stafford loan, Perkins loan, and university-sponsored loan as loan options recommended by the FA office. An unusual grant, the Gluck Fellowship, is awarded to a number of students who demonstrate the desire to perform in "hospitals, hospices, and similar institutions in New York City."

A note from the Juilliard School Admissions Office:

"The Juilliard School, founded in 1905, is a private college of the performing arts. Degrees are offered through the divisions in Dance, Drama, and Music. Juilliard is located at Lincoln Center, the home of the N.Y. Philharmonic, Metropolitan Opera, N.Y. City Ballet, etc., and Juilliard students interact with these constituencies regularly. A regular series of Master Classes are taught regularly by visiting artists. The faculty consists of renowned teachers/artists. Prominent alumni include: Leontyne Price, opera singer; Itzhak Perlman, violinist; Wynton Marsalis, trumpet player; Kevin Kline, Kelly McGillis, Robin Williams, Christopher Reeve, and Patti LuPone, actors; and Paul Taylor, choreographer."

ADMISSIONS FACTS

Competitiveness Rating:	**93**
% of applicants accepted:	16
% acceptees attending:	64

FRESHMAN PROFILE

Average verbal SAT:	NA
Average math SAT:	NA
Average ACT:	NA
Graduated top 10% of class:	NA
Graduated top 25% of class:	NA
Graduated top 50% of class:	NA

DEADLINES

Early decision/action:	NA
Early dec./act. notif.:	NA
Regular admission:	1/8
Regular adm. notif.:	rolling

APPLICANTS ALSO LOOK AT

and often prefer:
Curtis Institute of Music

and rarely prefer:
Eastman School of Music
New England Conservatory
Manhattan School of Music
Oberlin College

ADDRESS

Undergraduate Admissions
60 Lincoln Center Plaza
New York, NY 10023-6590
212-799-5000

FINANCIAL FACTS

In-state tuition ($):	9,800
Out-of-state tuition ($):	9,800
Room & board:	6,125
FA application deadline:	2/15
% frosh receiving FA:	92
PT earnings per yr. ($):	1000

TYPE OF AID: % of students ($)

FA of some kind:	88 (NA)
Need-based grants:	NA
Merit-based grants:	NA
Loans:	NA
Work study:	NA
Student rating of FA:	67

KALAMAZOO COLLEGE

Kalamazoo, MI

CAMPUS LIFE

Quality of Life Rating: **85**

Type of school:	private
Affiliation:	none
Environment:	city

STUDENT BODY

FT undergrad enrollment:	1,265
% male/% female:	46/54
% out-of-state:	25
% live on campus:	97
% African-American:	3
% Asian:	5
% Caucasian:	90
% Hispanic:	1
% foreign:	3
% transfers:	2

WHAT'S HOT

gay community visible
profs outside class
campus access
cost of living
gay community accepted
profs in class
small classes (overall)
honesty
administration (overall)
caring about politics
overall happiness

WHAT'S NOT

fraternities/sororities
hard liquor
beer

ACADEMICS

Academic Rating: **84**

Calendar:	quarters
Student/teacher ratio:	12/1
% doctorates:	81
Profs interesting:	90
Profs accessible:	91
Hours of study per day:	3.58

MOST POPULAR MAJORS BY %

Business & Management:	26
Life Sciences:	12
Psychology:	12

% GRADS WHO PURSUE

Law:	7
MBA:	6
Medicine:	9
M.A., etc.:	15

What do students think about Kalamazoo College?

■ **Academics** When discussing their experiences at Kalamazoo College, few students remember the same campus, or even the same language. What most consider this school's greatest asset is an imaginative and "really well put together" program called the K Plan, which allows for an unparalleled amount of foreign travel and study by all students who are interested. Most are. Over 90 percent of students "go abroad at least once in their four years at Kalamazoo." The same tuition students pay in Michigan covers all foreign expenses, thanks to an endowment specifically for this purpose, so financial need does not preclude participation in the program. Not everything good about Kalamazoo is off campus. The college itself offers "fast-paced and challenging academics" in a "small, personalized atmosphere" (even smaller than one might think, given the fact that about a quarter of the students are away at any given time). Over one third of Kalamazoo graduates go on to earn degrees beyond their B.A.s; nearly one in ten (!) goes on to medical school.

■ **Life** Many students at Kalamazoo notice a sense of transience about the place. Certainly the population changes dramatically from quarter to quarter, due to students' various global jaunts. Furthermore, Kalamazoo has an unusual housing policy that requires students to participate in a housing lottery every three months or so (one nomadic junior suggested the college "should offer a self-help cassette entitled *Learning to Deal with Moving Anxiety*.") But many students view this campus-in-flux as a benefit, constantly stimulating new friendships and improving coping skills. Kalamazoo is "definitely not a party school (especially after the new [restrictive] alcohol policy)," although many claim to have figured out ways to drink despite the rules. Some simply wait until their trips abroad; one marveled, "You can have a brew in the Hofbrau Haus, slam some vodka in Red Square, and drink tequila south of the border—all while you study and explore foreign cultures." Most students we asked are glad that drinking and Greek life (there is no Greek system here) are not the focus of the campus social life. For whatever reasons, those at K Zoo enjoy simply "having fun with friends, who are always only minutes away," and rate themselves overall as extremely happy.

■ **Students** There is an apt saying on campus: "some people join the Navy to see the world—others just go to Kalamazoo College." This applies not only to the K Plan, but also to the feeling of diversity on the campus itself. This heterogeneous atmosphere belies the low percentage of minority students and the high percentage of Michigan natives. Maybe it is the constantly changing population, or the large number of students with "alternative lifestyles," but students rate themselves highly in terms of their political involvement, and also in their acceptance of the visible gay community. Overall this school is what one disgusted student termed "nauseatingly politically correct." Most students, however, don't feel even a little sick about this.

KALAMAZOO COLLEGE

Admissions

Kalamazoo seeks "able students from diverse geographic, ethnic, social and economic backgrounds—students who are looking for the academic and personal challenge which is offered in the Kalamazoo plan. Probably the most important determinants for admission are intellectual curiosity and motivation." The admissions committee first considers your high school GPA and standardized test scores. These are followed, in order of importance, by extracurriculars, essays, letters of recommendation, and an interview (the interview is optional). All applicants must submit either ACT or SAT scores. The recommended high school curriculum includes four years of English, three years each of mathematics and social sciences and two years of natural sciences. Foreign language study is a plus, but is not required.

Financial Aid

The financial aid office at Kalamazoo College requires applicants to submit the FAF and a form generated by the school. Merit grants, administered through the admissions office, are awarded for academic excellence and leadership qualities. After freshman year, students are eligible for scholarships awarded "on the basis of the results of competitive exams given on campus." Of need-based grants, Kalamazoo's most recent catalog reports, "In cases where funds available are exceeded by student need, funds will be awarded on a first-come, first-served basis."

A note from the Kalamazoo College Admissions Office:

"Kalamazoo College offers studies in the liberal arts and sciences, but the learning doesn't end in the classroom. The 'Kalamazoo Plan' includes an international study program in which 90% of the students participate, a career development field experience in which 85% of the students participate, and the senior individualized project, which is required for all students."

ADMISSIONS FACTS

Competitiveness Rating:	**80**
% of applicants accepted:	87
% acceptees attending:	34

FRESHMAN PROFILE

Average verbal SAT:	530*
Average math SAT:	593*
Average ACT:	27*
Graduated top 10% of class:	54
Graduated top 25% of class:	80
Graduated top 50% of class:	98

DEADLINES

Early decision/action:	NA
Early dec./act. notif.:	NA
Regular admission:	rolling
Regular adm. notif.:	rolling

APPLICANTS ALSO LOOK AT

and often prefer:
Dartmouth College
Duke U.
Georgetown U.

and sometimes prefer:
U. Notre Dame
Northwestern U.

and rarely prefer:
U. Michigan
DePauw U.
Michigan State U.
Albion College

ADDRESS

Undergraduate Admissions
1200 Academy St.
Kalamazoo, MI 49007-3295
616-383-8408

FINANCIAL FACTS

In-state tuition ($):	12,669
Out-of-state tuition ($):	12,669
Room & board:	4,053
FA application deadline:	2/15
% frosh receiving FA:	68
PT earnings per yr. ($):	1050

TYPE OF AID: % of students ($)

FA of some kind:	71 (NA)
Need-based grants:	NA
Merit-based grants:	NA
Loans:	NA
Work study:	NA
Student rating of FA:	84

UNIVERSITY OF KANSAS

Lawrence, KS

CAMPUS LIFE

Quality of Life Rating: 85

Type of school:	public
Affiliation:	none
Environment:	city

STUDENT BODY

FT undergrad enrollment:	18,281
% male/% female:	50/50
% out-of-state:	33
% live on campus:	25
% African-American:	3
% Asian:	2
% Caucasian:	85
% Hispanic:	2
% foreign:	5
% transfers:	5

WHAT'S HOT

location
intercollegiate sports
college radio station
conservative politics
overall happiness
small classes (overall)

WHAT'S NOT

TAs teach intro courses
small lectures
TAs teach upper-level courses
deans
living on campus
registration
profs outside class
profs in class

ACADEMICS

Academic Rating: 73

Calendar:	semester
Student/teacher ratio:	16/1
% doctorates:	92
Profs interesting:	67
Profs accessible:	66
Hours of study per day:	3.05

MOST POPULAR MAJORS BY %

Business & Management:	14
Communications:	14
Social Sciences:	10

What do students think about the University of Kansas?

■ **Academics** University of Kansas is "excellent: the best of the Big Eight," according to one area college counselor. Another concurred, calling the school "a real sleeper, especially for easterners and westerners." Like many large universities, UK offers a tremendously varied assortment of majors and academic options. UK exceeds the norm, however, both in the quantity of excellent programs it provides and in its extremely reasonable tuition. KU is noted for its pre-professional schools, to which one must apply separately. Architecture, engineering, and a unique blend of the two, architectural engineering, are all first-rate, as are the schools of journalism, pharmacy, nursing, and education. Those who are not admitted to the professional schools (and those who submit a general application) are considered for admission into the College of Arts and Sciences (in which an honors program is available, and recommended, for advanced students). Here students must complete nearly two years of distribution requirements (stressing science, math, and the liberal arts) before pursuing their intended major (of which there are over 100 to choose). UK is very much like other large universities when it comes to its administration, however; a typical student reported, "The process of enrolling, paying fees, and receiving the courses required for your particular major is ridiculous! It is far too time-consuming and tedious!" Another student countered, however, "People here complain about things (classes, the newspapers, parking), but this place gets to you. You love and cherish it." "KU has so much to offer, most importantly an excellent education, for a very reasonable price."

■ **Life** With almost 20,000 undergraduates calling KU home, this school truly can offer something to just about everyone. Dorm life is reasonably comfortable and provides students with an instant social base, but many upperclassmen prefer rooming with the Greeks, in "scholarship halls," or in off-campus apartments. Intercollegiate sports are universally popular, especially when a KU team takes on rival Kansas State. So too is the Greek system, to which about one quarter of the students pledge. Students report that parties are easy to come by but not too difficult to avoid, should the urge to study overtake you. Lawrence, Kansas, received high marks from the student body. Several noted that the town is both accommodating to students and conveniently located for road trips to Topeka and Kansas City.

■ **Students** Over two thirds of KU's students are still home-staters. Relatively easy admissions and a cheaper charge for Kansas natives guarantee that things will stay that way through the foreseeable future. KU's minority population is small, but students claim, "The diversity of people and ideas at KU combine to provide an alternative view of life for students searching to broaden their horizons."

UNIVERSITY OF KANSAS

Admissions

All graduates of accredited Kansas high schools are automatically offered admission. The College of Liberal Arts and Sciences at University of Kansas "strongly recommends four years of English, three years of mathematics (including two years of algebra, one half year of geometry, and one half year of trigonometry), two years of foreign language, three years of social studies, and three years of natural science. Students from out of state are required to have at least a "C" average, and all students are recommended to exceed the course distributional minimums, particularly in mathematics and English. All applicants must submit ACT scores.

Financial Aid

Financial aid applicants to the University of Kansas must complete the FFS. A number of scholarships are available, including academic, residence, minority, talent, and athletic scholarships. These range from $100 per year to full tuition. In '89–'90, over 3,300 scholarships were awarded by KU and 291 awarded by the state. The average Stafford loan was $2,102 (taken by 29% of all undergrads) and the average Perkins loan was $1,816 (taken by 5% of all undergrads). Priority date for consideration is March 1.

Excerpted from University of Kansas promotional materials:

"Many undergraduate students have achieved distinction at the University of Kansas. KU has been a leader among public universities in producing national fellowship winners. In recent years KU students have won top honors in national competitions in debate, theatre, aerospace engineering, and international moot court, and have achieved national recognition in medical technology, design, music, journalism, and the sciences.

"More than 70 percent of KU's students are undergraduates. More than 90 percent of KU undergraduates pursue their studies on the Lawrence campus. Total fall enrollment in 1989 was 28,773. In 1989-1990, KU granted approximately 3,500 bachelor's degrees.

"About half of KU's students graduated in the top third of their high school classes. In the fall of 1989, KU ranked 15th among all U.S. public universities in enrollment of National Merit Scholars. KU enrolled 49 new National Merit Scholars, more than twice as many as any other Kansas institution. Twenty-one KU students have become Rhodes scholars; seven have won Truman scholarships; five have become Marshal scholars; two have become Goldwater scholars. KU has had 13 Mellon fellows since the Andrew W. Mellon Foundation established the program in 1982. In 1990, KU stood fourth among public institutions in number of Mellon fellows."

ADMISSIONS FACTS

Competitiveness Rating:	**63**
% of applicants accepted:	85
% acceptees attending:	42

FRESHMAN PROFILE

Average verbal SAT:	NA
Average math SAT:	NA
Average ACT:	23
Graduated top 10% of class:	20
Graduated top 25% of class:	45
Graduated top 50% of class:	75

DEADLINES

Early decision/action:	NA
Early dec./act. notif.:	NA
Regular admission:	2/1
Regular adm. notif.:	rolling

APPLICANTS ALSO LOOK AT

and often prefer:
Kansas State U.

and rarely prefer:
Purdue U.
Texas A & M U.
Indiana U.
Michigan State U.
Centre College

ADDRESS

Undergraduate Admissions
Lawrence, KS 66045-1910
913-864-3911

FINANCIAL FACTS

In-state tuition ($):	1,324
Out-of-state tuition ($):	5,002
Room & board:	2,684
FA application deadline:	3/1
% frosh receiving FA:	32
PT earnings per yr. ($):	2,040

TYPE OF AID: % of students ($)

FA of some kind:	33 (NA)
Need-based grants:	NA
Merit-based grants:	NA
Loans:	NA
Work study:	NA
Student rating of FA:	79

UNIVERSITY OF KENTUCKY

Lexington, KY

What do students think about the University of Kentucky?

■ **Academics** It's hard to tell whether University of Kentucky students take more pride in their school's academic programs or in its basketball teams: undergrads gush over both. "While Kentucky may be known for its shoeless hillbillies," explained one student, "the University of Kentucky is a veritable educational stalwart. And, we have the most loyal basketball following on earth. In fact, a lot of students choose UK, believe it or not, because of the basketball!." Those who register at UK because of its basketball team receive, at no additional cost, the opportunity for an excellent education at bargain-basement prices. Students praised all business and management departments ("We have top-notch instructors" claimed one management major), laying claim to "one of the best accounting programs in the nation." Other popular majors are in career-oriented fields such as communications, health sciences, education, and engineering; the last is perhaps UK's most underrated program. The school requires all students to complete general education requirements, meaning that everyone dabbles at least a little in the liberal arts. Top high school students can qualify for the honors program which, according to one enrollee, "provides students with an exceptional opportunity to obtain an Ivy League education at a state school." Students gave their professors good grades, especially for accessibility outside the classroom. In fact, about the only negatives students commented on were that classes are generally too large and that too many intro courses are taught by TAs. Both of those complaints, though, could be made at any state school, and even at some more expensive, research-oriented private universities.

■ **Life** Only four other student bodies profiled in this book care more about their sports teams than UK students. Football is a big draw and provides the setting for popular tailgate parties, but students save their greatest praise for the basketball team. One student's entire essay consisted of the sentence "Rick Pitino rules my life!" No further explanation seemed necessary to the writer, who must have assumed that everyone in the country knows UK's basketball coach. Students reported that partying is popular but not excessively so; they take the same laid-back approach to academics, studying and attending enough classes to stay on top of things but no more. Students gave the city of Lexington good grades and noted that they were within driving distance of Louisville.

■ **Students** Nearly 90 percent of UK's student body hails from the Bluegrass State. Over 90 percent of the students are white: approximately 600 black students make up the single largest minority population. Students wrote that race relations were good; said one, "I love UK because of the diverse mixture of cultures. I have Pakistani, Jordanian, and Korean friends here." Two percent of the students are foreign nationals. Students are generally conservative both politically and socially.

UNIVERSITY OF KENTUCKY

Lexington, KY

Admissions

From University of Kentucky's brochure: "Admission to the University of Kentucky is offered on a competitive basis to students who can demonstrate the ability to succeed in an academically demanding environment. The admissions policy is based on an evaluation of a student's standardized test scores, high school grade-point average, and completion of a minimum pre-college curriculum [see below]. Student whose scores and grades predict a high probability of achieving a C average or better the freshman year at UK will be accepted automatically. Generally, accepted students are notified on a continual basis throughout the school year. Up to 20 percent of the UK freshman class may be selected form the applications who do not meet the requirements for automatic admission. In addition to standardized test scores, grades, and high school curriculum, the Office of Admissions will consider such factors as extracurricular activities, out-of-class accomplishments, and personal achievement..." All applicants must submit SAT or ACT scores. The recommended high school curriculum includes a minimum of four units of English, three units of mathematics, two units of natural science (chemistry, biology, or physics), two units of social science, and one unit of fine arts.

Financial Aid

Financial aid applicants to the University of Kentucky must complete the KFAF (Kentucky Financial Aid Form). According to UK's brochure, "Academic scholarships are awarded to freshmen on a competitive basis in recognition of outstanding academic performance and potential. These prestigious awards are based on a faculty evaluation of standardized test scores, high school grades, extracurricular activities, and a 500-word essay. A student must have a minimum ACT composite score of 28 (1100 SAT) and a strong high school grade point average." In addition to these scholarships (which are not need-based), a variety of grants, loans, and need-based scholarships are available. Deadline for priority consideration is April 1.

Excerpted from University of Kentucky promotional materials:

"The University of Kentucky offers you an outstanding learning environment and quality instruction through its excellent faculty. Of the 1,606 full-time faculty, 98 percent hold the doctorate degree or the highest degree in their field of study.

"Many are nationally and internationally known for their research, distinguished teaching, and scholarly service to Kentucky, the nation, and the world. Yet, with a student-teacher ratio of only 15 to 1, UK faculty are accessible and willing to answer your questions and discuss your interests."

ADMISSIONS FACTS

Competitiveness Rating:	**72**
% of applicants accepted:	78
% acceptees attending:	51

FRESHMAN PROFILE

Average verbal SAT:	470
Average math SAT:	520
Average ACT:	24
Graduated top 10% of class:	NA
Graduated top 25% of class:	NA
Graduated top 50% of class:	NA

DEADLINES

Early decision/action:	NA
Early dec./act. notif.:	NA
Regular admission:	6/1
Regular adm. notif.:	rolling

APPLICANTS ALSO LOOK AT

and sometimes prefer:
Vanderbilt U.
U. Tennessee–Knoxville
Transylvania U.

and rarely prefer:
U. Illinois
Purdue U.
Ohio State U.
Florida State U.
U. Florida
Indiana U.

ADDRESS

Undergraduate Admissions
Lexington, KY 40506-0032
606-257-2000

FINANCIAL FACTS

In-state tuition ($):	1,620
Out-of-state tuition ($):	4,860
Room & board:	3,734
FA application deadline:	4/1
% frosh receiving FA:	50
PT earnings per yr. ($):	NA

TYPE OF AID: % of students ($)

FA of some kind:	50 (3,700)
Need-based grants:	NA
Merit-based grants:	NA
Loans:	NA
Work study:	NA
Student rating of FA:	86

KENYON COLLEGE

CAMPUS LIFE

Quality of Life Rating: **85**

Type of school:	private
Affiliation:	Episcopal
Environment:	rural

STUDENT BODY

FT undergrad enrollment:	1,503
% male/% female:	49/51
% out-of-state:	77
% live on campus:	99
% African-American:	3
% Asian:	4
% Caucasian:	92
% Hispanic:	1
% foreign:	2
% transfers:	1

WHAT'S HOT

small lectures
dorm safety
deans
profs outside class
small classes (overall)
small labs and seminars
living on campus
profs in class
cost of living
campus appearance

WHAT'S NOT

diversity
working a job
dating
location

ACADEMICS

Academic Rating: **85**

Calendar:	semester
Student/teacher ratio:	11/1
% doctorates:	85
Profs interesting:	92
Profs accessible:	93
Hours of study per day:	3.71

MOST POPULAR MAJORS BY %

English:	26
Political Science:	14
Psychology:	12

% GRADS WHO PURSUE

Law:	10
MBA:	5
Medicine:	10
M.A., etc.:	35

What do students think about Kenyon College?

■ **Academics** Students at Kenyon College ranked their faculty in the top 10 percent in the country for their teaching skills and among the twenty most accessible outside of class. Such are the benefits of attending a small liberal arts college where practically all the professors live near campus. Said one student, "I feel that it's important to stress the student-faculty relationships here. Almost all our faculty hold their Ph.D.s, but that doesn't deter them from interacting in all aspects of life at Kenyon." The English department is universally acclaimed and is so popular that it's difficult for those not majoring in English to get into English classes. Most departments are nearly as good. Students reported that class sizes were excellent and gave administrators very high marks. They also noted that the school encourages students to focus intensively in specific areas of study and to pursue independent studies, both of which help to prepare students for graduate studies. This program suits the needs of Kenyon undergraduates perfectly, as over half go on to graduate school within a year of graduation. Pre-professional tracks are popular: 10 percent of the students go on to study law and another 10 percent pursue medicine.

■ **Life** As one student put it, "Community makes Kenyon. I feel that I know everyone, from the president to my professor's dog Barny." Kenyon is the quintessential small college, where the outside world rarely encroaches on campus life and everyone knows everyone else. For many, Kenyon's size is one of its great assets: as one student told us, "After visiting many universities and large schools I've realized how highly I value Kenyon's close-knit community." Most students live right on campus and rarely go home, so for some the community can get a little *too* close-knit. One student put it this way: "Kenyon is a small place, which leads, after a time, to intensive familiarity (not always a good thing). I went abroad junior year, which was wonderful, and it's really cool how Kenyon supports the Junior Year Abroad program. I think they realize four years here can be a bit much." The town of Gambier "can become very dull very quickly," and a car to facilitate occasional excursions to Columbus or to nearby ski areas is recommended. A night of socializing starts by generally hanging out in the early evening with friends, perhaps drinking some beers or smoking some pot, and then heading over to a frat party later. Steady dating is infrequent, "hooking up" more common. The campus is beautiful, the dorms comfortable.

■ **Students** Kenyon students have, in the past, had a reputation for being apathetic preppies. That seems to be changing, however; reported one senior, "Kenyon has changed a lot in the past four years. There's a different type of student here now, one that's more informed and interested in the world around us." The student body is still predominantly white and affluent, and there's a growing "pseudo-hippie" population.

KENYON COLLEGE

Admissions

The admissions office reports, "We look for students who have taken AP or Honors courses in two or more subjects. Students who have outstanding achievement in activities, e.g. athletics, drama, music, community service, leadership, and sound academic records are given preference." Kenyon considers high school curriculum and grades most important, followed in importance by essays, extracurricular activities, standardized test scores, letters of recommendation, and an interview (not required). Applicants must have completed four years of English, three years of a foreign language, three years of science (two years of a lab science), at least three years of math ("but most successful candidates are in pre-calculus or calculus"), and two years of social studies. Kenyon requires either the SAT or ACT. Applicants to Kenyon most often also apply to Oberlin, Middlebury, Carleton, Miami of Ohio, Denison, Colby, Colgate, and Hamilton.

Financial Aid

The financial aid office at Kenyon College requires applicants to submit the FAF and a copy of their parents' most recent tax return. Merit-based grants are awarded for academic excellence (approximately 5% of students here receive one; average value: $10,320). In 1991–92, the most popular loans taken by students were the Stafford loan (12%; $3,386), the Perkins loan (11%; $1,181), and the PLUS loan (6%; $2,840). The FA office reports, "A Kenyon education is a significant investment in a student's future, an investment that requires commitment, effort, and, often, sacrifice. But the investment is well worth the sacrifice, for the power of the liberal arts and sciences curriculum...will help shape a student and will influence that student throughout his or her life."

Excerpted from Kenyon College promotional materials:

"We at Kenyon College seek through liberal education to enhance our understanding of humanity, society, art, and nature. We expect to develop our awareness of our private capacities and creative talents, even as we seek to improve our ability to formulate our ideas rigorously and communicate them effectively to others. And, while we strive to further our intellectual independence so as to be free of dogmatic thinking, we seek to find a basis for moral judgments in a thorough understanding of both our environment and our cultural heritage."

ADMISSIONS FACTS

Competitiveness Rating:	**83**
% of applicants accepted:	65
% acceptees attending:	29

FRESHMAN PROFILE

Average verbal SAT:	NA
Average math SAT:	NA
Average ACT:	28*
Graduated top 10% of class:	40
Graduated top 25% of class:	74
Graduated top 50% of class:	98

DEADLINES

Early decision/action:	12/1
Early dec./act. notif.:	12/15
Regular admission:	2/15
Regular adm. notif.:	4/1

APPLICANTS ALSO LOOK AT

and often prefer:
U. Michigan
Hamilton College

and sometimes prefer:
Bowdoin College
Oberlin College
Bates College
Carleton College

and rarely prefer:
Hobart/William Smith College
Denison U.

ADDRESS

Undergraduate Admissions
Gambier, OH 43022-9623
614-427-5776

FINANCIAL FACTS

In-state tuition ($):	15,525
Out-of-state tuition ($):	15,525
Room & board:	3,375
FA application deadline:	2/15
% frosh receiving FA:	32
PT earnings per yr. ($):	600

TYPE OF AID: % of students ($)

FA of some kind:	30 (NA)
Need-based grants:	38 (10,500)
Merit-based grants:	5 (10,320)
Loans:	NA (7,407)
Work study:	11 (825)
Student rating of FA:	86

KNOX COLLEGE

CAMPUS LIFE

Quality of Life Rating:	**80**
Type of school:	private
Affiliation:	none
Environment:	city

STUDENT BODY

FT undergrad enrollment:	921
% male/% female:	48/52
% out-of-state:	46
% live on campus:	92
% African-American:	8
% Asian:	8
% Caucasian:	81
% Hispanic:	2
% foreign:	11
% transfers:	4

WHAT'S HOT

financial aid
radio station
in-class discussion
college theater
administration (overall)
Grateful Dead
profs outside class
leftist politics
diversity
cost of living
small classes (overall)

WHAT'S NOT

location

ACADEMICS

Academic Rating:	**83**
Calendar:	trimester
Student/teacher ratio:	10/1
% doctorates:	77
Profs interesting:	91
Profs accessible:	92
Hours of study per day:	3.64

MOST POPULAR MAJORS BY %

Political Science:	9
Chemistry:	8
Economics:	8

% GRADS WHO PURSUE

Law:	6
MBA:	6
Medicine:	5
M.A., etc.:	23

What do students think about Knox College?

■ **Academics** With fewer than 1000 undergraduates, Knox College is a quintessential small liberal arts school, and as such its strengths lie in the personal attention and academic challenges it provides. Probably its greatest strength is its ability to "enliven and personalize academics." To achieve this goal, Kenyon allows, and in fact expects, students to participate in the governance of the school: most faculty and administration boards have student members with voting powers. Students here bestowed extremely high marks on their professors, both for excellent teaching and also for their extraordinary level of accessibility. One student wrote, "Knox is here to meet *your* needs. Professors are always available to speak with you." Another marveled that many students meet with instructors even after courses end. In general, all levels of the administration at Knox display an attitude of caring ("The faculty is extremely responsive to student needs. If they don't respond to a problem, President McCall will fan the flames for the students"). The academic atmosphere is challenging, and requirements are strict ("Medieval monks didn't write as much as we do here"): all students must complete a two-term course sequence in communication and reasoning as well as a broad set of distribution requirements. These rigors pay off for many. One grateful senior wrote, "If I didn't end up at Knox, there's no way I'd be going into a Ph.D. program next year. This school has a way of giving the right intellectual kicks in the butt at the right time." Forty percent of Knox graduates go on to graduate programs.

■ **Life** Galesburg, Illinois, is a small town. As one student put it, "If you're looking for excitement, don't go to college in the middle of a cornfield." The seclusion of the college creates an "intimate" sense of community on campus, however, which many students appreciate. Extracurricular activities abound. Especially popular are theatre groups and the student newspaper. Fraternities and sororities help to liven up the social scene and fortunately engender little bad feeling. According to one student, "the boundary between the Greeks and the rest of the students virtually does not exist." Drinking is rampant and, in some cases, excessive. (A senior commented, "If someone actually remains sober for an extended period of time, their friends start to express concern for their welfare.") We received numerous complaints about the dating scene on campus. The consensus was that "Dating is nonexistent: either you're in a relationship, or you hang out with your buddies and bitch about it." Living conditions are first-rate. The large suites at Knox are among the most luxurious in the nation. One of the few drawbacks to life here is the much-maligned food. (One vegetarian was appalled that "*everything* is fried—corn dogs, tater tots, fried broccoli, and fried apple sticks!"

■ **Students** Although most students at Knox are from the Midwest, many felt that "the diversity is unmatched." Approximately one fifth of the students are minorities, with blacks and Asians making up most of that population. Political activism is not widespread, and disparate viewpoints are generally well accepted on campus.

KNOX COLLEGE

Galesburg, IL

Admissions

The admissions office reports, "Students with initiative, imagination, eagerness for learning, emotional maturity and a willingness to share are best able to benefit from the opportunities available at Knox. Knox seeks a student body that is racially, socially, and culturally diverse; the college values the diversity that varied interests, talents, and backgrounds bring to the campus. With this in mind, Knox reviews each application on an individual basis. Carefully considered are each student's course of study, grades, recommendations, extracurricular activities, essay, talents, personal qualities and results on the ACT/SAT tests. These factors are evaluated in approximately that order of importance." Applicants must have completed a "college preparatory curriculum." Many Knox applicants apply also to University of Illinois, Northwestern, Grinnell, and Beloit.

Financial Aid

The financial aid office at Knox College requires the FAF and a copy of your parents' most recent tax return. Merit-based grants are awarded for academic achievement and special talent in the creative arts. In 1991–92, students took out Perkins loans (23% of the student body; average value, $3,400) and Stafford loans (48%, $2,560). Knox told us that "Knox is committed to meeting the demonstrated financial need of its students. The financial aid office provides individual attention and counseling, as well as information about alternative financing and payment options."

A note from the Knox College Admissions Office:

"Economists talk about the importance of finding your 'niche'—knowing that one special thing you do better than anyone else. At Knox, we specialize in changing people's lives. Knox isn't an elitist school with mile-high hoops for applicants to jump through. We work hard at finding those students who will flourish here and giving them the freedom to do so. The result is a top-notch academic school with a remarkably unpretentious sense of itself. Our students can go anywhere with a Knox degree, and they do. For instance, we're 11th among all liberal arts colleges in the percentage of grads who earn math/science Ph.D.'s and 30th for those becoming business executives. Our student literary magazine has been named the best in the country, and a recent English major argues a case before the U.S. Supreme Court in 1991. But we're not a cutthroat or 'stressed out' place. Every fall, everyone—faculty, students, even the President—gather in front of Old Main to shake hands and welcome each other back. This 100-year-old tradition, known affectionately as 'Pumphandle,' captures perfectly the tone of friendship and mutual regard that marks the Knox experience."

ADMISSIONS FACTS

Competitiveness Rating:	77
% of applicants accepted:	78
% acceptees attending:	33

FRESHMAN PROFILE

Average verbal SAT:	527*
Average math SAT:	573*
Average ACT:	27*
Graduated top 10% of class:	37
Graduated top 25% of class:	70
Graduated top 50% of class:	96

DEADLINES

Early decision/action:	12/1
Early dec./act. notif.:	12/31
Regular admission:	2/15
Regular adm. notif:	3/31

APPLICANTS ALSO LOOK AT

and often prefer:
U. Kansas
Northwestern U.

and sometimes prefer:
Carleton College
Bradley U.
Grinnell College
Beloit College

and rarely prefer:
U. Illinois

ADDRESS

Undergraduate Admissions
Galesburg, IL 61401-4999
309-343-0112

FINANCIAL FACTS

In-state tuition ($):	12,609
Out-of-state tuition ($):	12,609
Room & board:	3,675
FA application deadline:	3/1
% frosh receiving FA:	NA
PT earnings per yr. ($):	900

TYPE OF AID: % of students ($)

FA of some kind:	87 (11,568)
Need-based grants:	70 (8,350)
Merit-based grants:	10 (3,400)
Loans:	50 (3,000)
Work study:	62 (1,122)
Student rating of FA:	97

LAFAYETTE COLLEGE

CAMPUS LIFE

Quality of Life Rating: **78**

Type of school:	private
Affiliation:	none
Environment:	city

STUDENT BODY

FT undergrad enrollment:	1,941
% male/% female:	59/41
% out-of-state:	75
% live on campus:	94
% African-American:	4
% Asian:	2
% Caucasian:	91
% Hispanic:	1
% foreign:	4
% transfers:	1

WHAT'S HOT

college radio station
Grateful Dead
fraternities/sororities
marijuana
campus is easy to get
around
hard liquor
beer

WHAT'S NOT

location
gay community accepted
town-gown relations
diversity
interaction among students

ACADEMICS

Academic Rating: **83**

Calendar:	semester
Student/teacher ratio:	12/1
% doctorates:	94
Profs interesting:	78
Profs accessible:	78
Hours of study per day:	2.93

MOST POPULAR MAJORS BY %

Economics and Business:	22
English:	9
Government and Law:	8

% GRADS WHO PURSUE

Law:	6
MBA:	1
Medicine:	3
M.A., etc.:	10

What do students think about Lafayette College?

■ **Academics** Lafayette College is a fine liberal arts college that also boasts a nationally renowned engineering program. One third of the students pursue engineering degrees: other popular majors include psychology, computer science, business, and liberal arts. All students here must complete a demanding core curriculum that stresses a comprehensive approach to academic subjects: in fact, the mandatory senior seminar is called "An Approach to Synthesis." While students here are satisfied with their academic programs and work hard at them during the week, most also view them as a responsibility to be endured: their real enthusiasm is for social life (see "Life," below), which almost all addressed in their comments to us.

■ **Life** Lafayette has a party-school reputation, one that its students earn Thursday through Sunday nights every week (although some start partying on Wednesday). Drinking and pot-smoking rank high among favored activities here—"I wish I could give 'beer' a higher mark than an 'A'!" one student commented on our grading system. Drinking laws, and the schools efforts to enforce them, seem to have had little impact on consumption. Fraternities and sororities ranked fourth most popular in the country (one of the few schools that nosed Lafayette out of first place is arch-rival Lehigh): if you have any problems with the Greek system, do NOT come here, as social life begins and ends in the Greek houses. Despite the fact that many students come here to enjoy frat life, the school maintains, at best, a polite relationship with the frats. This is one cause of animosity between students and administrators. Another is an enforced meal plan: students are required to pre-pay for $250 worth of food at the "food court" per semester. To add insult to injury, "The price of food is high and the quality is poor." For go-getters, there are plenty of campus groups and organizations to become involved with. The town of Easton "stinks," said one student. "The townies hate the students, but we're up on the hill pretty much segregated from them. The only time we go into town is for restaurants, movies, and bars." The campus is beautiful and easy to get around.

■ **Students** Lafayette has a homogeneous student population. "White, conservative, and preppy" describes most students pretty accurately. A small minority population exists on the fringes—"There isn't even a black frat or sorority" complained one African-American student. If there is a gay population, it's invisible and, by students' accounts, unwelcome. For those who fit the mold, LC provides a very homey atmosphere. Many students voiced the same sentiment as did the one who reported, "There's something on this campus that you can't get a sense of when you read about it in a book. It's almost a feeling of family. When I return from visiting another school, I suddenly feel like I'm home." A 3:2 male-female ratio must make for a pheromone-laced atmosphere at parties.

LAFAYETTE COLLEGE

Admissions

Lafayette's admissions office writes, "While we do not utilize test score "cut-offs" nor formulae in considering applicants, we seek academically motivated students who are anxious to push themselves to excel in an intellectual environment where these challenges are balanced by a wealth of co-curricular and social opportunities." Most important in your application to Lafayette are the level of high-school courses you've taken, and what the admissions office calls "intangible qualities." These are followed, in order of importance by your standardized test scores, extracurriculars, essays and letters of recommendation (roughly equal), and interview. All applicants must take the SAT or ACT and three Achievements, including English Composition with essay and Math 1 or Math 2. Prospective engineering majors must take either the Physics or Chemistry Achievement as well. All applicants should also have completed at least four years of English, three years of math (four for science or engineering majors), and two years each of foreign language and science (physics and chemistry for engineers). Students who apply to Lafayette also often apply of Colgate, Cornell, Bucknell, Lehigh, and Tufts.

Financial Aid

The financial aid office at Lafayette College requires the FAF, a form generated by the school, and, if applicable, a business/farm supplement and a divorced/separated parents statement. Returning students must also submit family tax returns. Lafayette awards one merit grant called the Marquis Scholarship, which entitles students to a three-week intern/study program and carries a $1,000 stipend. In 1991–92, Lafayette students took Stafford loans (26% borrowed on the Stafford program; average value of the loan, $2,535), Perkins loans (8%; $1,457), and institutional loans (3%; $1,706). The FA office adds that "Lafayette offers a $5,000 parent loan (HELP) to all needy families and those whose family contribution does not exceed our aid budget by more than $5,000 dollars. The college pays all interest on the loan while the student is enrolled and the parents have eight years to repay after graduation." Lafayette also told us, "When aid is awarded, we meet 100% of the demonstrated need of the recipient."

A note from the Lafayette College Admissions Office:

"Lafayette College is a highly selective, academically challenging small liberal arts college combined with an engineering department in a very aesthetically pleasing, interpersonal environment."

ADMISSIONS FACTS

Competitiveness Rating:	**88**
% of applicants accepted:	44
% acceptees attending:	27

FRESHMAN PROFILE

Average verbal SAT:	573*
Average math SAT:	633*
Average ACT:	NA
Graduated top 10% of class:	50
Graduated top 25% of class:	85
Graduated top 50% of class:	99

DEADLINES

Early decision/action:	11/1
Early dec./act. notif.:	12/1
Regular admission:	1/15
Regular adm. notif.:	4/1

APPLICANTS ALSO LOOK AT

and often prefer:
U. Pennsylvania
Tufts U.

and sometimes prefer:
Bucknell U.
Lehigh U.
Boston College
Hamilton College
Gettysburg College

and rarely prefer:
Penn State U.

ADDRESS

Undergraduate Admissions
118 Markle Hall
Easton, PA 18042-1770
215-250-5100

FINANCIAL FACTS

In-state tuition ($):	15,475
Out-of-state tuition ($):	15,475
Room & board:	4,900
FA application deadline:	2/15
% frosh receiving FA:	56
PT earnings per yr. ($):	1,000

TYPE OF AID: % of students ($)

FA of some kind:	60 (NA)
Need-based grants:	41 (10,655)
Merit-based grants:	8 (1,000)
Loans:	NA
Work study:	16 (916)
Student rating of FA:	81

LAKE FOREST COLLEGE

Lake Forest, IL

What do students think about Lake Forest College?

■ **Academics** Lake Forest College is a small school whose excellent and caring professors set it apart from the "small liberal arts college" pack. Students uniformly praised their teachers—even those who complained about everything else concluded with a statement such to the effect that "the professors are the best and most valuable asset of this school." Small classes further enhance the LFC experience. An excellent education is certainly available here, but how vigorously students pursue that education is another matter. Because LFC imposes no core curriculum, students are on their own in designing a course of study. Those students who capitalize on the system by pursuing challenging, interesting courses resent the majority of their classmates, who "really need to start taking things a lot more seriously" (see "Students," below). Many Foresters pursue business studies; liberal arts departments are also excellent.

■ **Life** Campus life at LFC means participating in a tiny community. As one student put it, "This school is so small that everyone knows your business before you do." Drinking and drugs continue to make up a big part of student life, even though the school is looking for ways to scale back the partying. Romantically, "People don't seem to date, they just 'hook up'." Chicago is only a half-hour away, so even if you find life on campus unbearable, you might still salvage your social life with frequent trips to the Windy City. A final note: don't be surprised if your roommate takes off to follow the Dead for a week: Deadheads are rampant here.

■ **Students** LFC has a reputation as a prep school dumping ground, a reputation confirmed by our respondents. "This school is for Easterners who went to boarding school and want to appease their parents by going to college. Shallowness is the biggest personality trait," stated one student who didn't fit that demographic mold. Another referred to the prepsters as "pseudo hippies…I've heard them competing about how many thousands they've spent on pot since they got here." Resentment of the—whom the public high school contingent see as the biggest problem with the school—is widespread. On the whole, students are very white and conservative. Cliquishness is the rule, and it's hard to imagine most minority students feeling comfortable in this environment. Said one black student, "I would not recommend black students or any people of color coming here. People here do not care to be involved or address world events like the release of Nelson Mandela or the election of David Duke, and they certainly are not sensitive to issues concerning minorities and homosexuals." Another student explained students' social awareness with this oxymoron: "Apathy runs rampant here."

LAKE FOREST COLLEGE

Admissions

Lake Forest's most recent catalog states, "Criteria for selection include assessment of a student's program of study, academic achievement, aptitude, intellectual curiosity, qualities of character and personality, and activities both within and without the school." Applicants must submit results for either the SAT or the ACT. An interview is recommended, but not required. The school reports, "There are no formal [high school curricular] requirements for entrance to Lake Forest," but "recommends" four years of English, three years of math, study in one or more foreign languages, and two to four years each of science and social studies.

Financial Aid

The financial aid office at Lake Forest College requires applicants to submit the FAF and the form generated by the school. The school's form, the Lake Forest Application for Financial Assistance (LFAFA), may be completed and filed with the school's financial aid office at any time during the year. The College will assess the application and notify students of their estimated financial need within two weeks, thereby providing applicants with "*quick* access to accurate information about the amount of aid for which they may qualify." The school reports, "All aid is based on financial need. Currently, fifty-five percent of the student body receives financial assistance from an annual budget of over six million dollars."

A note from the Lake Forest College Admissions Office:

"There are about 1100 Lake Forest College students. Representing 46 states and 22 foreign countries, students come from all parts of the country and the world. About 10 percent are from American ethnic groups. Lake Forest students represent a wide variety of socioeconomic backgrounds. Some come from affluence, some from disadvantage and most from somewhere in between. Their similarities are more important than their differences, however. Their most common experience is the confidence they share in the future. Together they have come to Lake Forest recognizing that the College provides tremendous opportunities. They know that by putting forth a serious effort and by taking an active role in their education, they will be shaping a more confident and satisfying future.

"Lake Forest College takes its responsibility seriously. It, accordingly, treats students as the adults they are and fosters the principle that responsibility and freedom go hand in hand."

ADMISSIONS FACTS

Competitiveness Rating:	**71**
% of applicants accepted:	71
% acceptees attending:	38

FRESHMAN PROFILE

Average verbal SAT:	487*
Average math SAT:	537*
Average ACT:	24*
Graduated top 10% of class:	27
Graduated top 25% of class:	64
Graduated top 50% of class:	86

DEADLINES

Early decision/action:	2/1
Early dec./act. notif.:	rolling
Regular admission:	2/15
Regular adm. notif.:	late March

APPLICANTS ALSO LOOK AT

and often prefer:
DePauw U.
Connecticut College
Kenyon College

and sometimes prefer:
U. Illinois
Bradley U.
Val Paraiso–Indiana
Hollins College
Cornell College
U. Iowa

ADDRESS

Undergraduate Admissions
Sheridan and College Rd.
Lake Forest, IL 60045
312-234-3100

FINANCIAL FACTS

In-state tuition ($):	13,710
Out-of-state tuition ($):	13,710
Room & board:	3,080
FA application deadline:	3/1
% frosh receiving FA:	56
PT earnings per yr. ($):	1,300

TYPE OF AID: % of students ($)

FA of some kind:	57 (12,575)
Need-based grants:	NA
Merit-based grants:	NA
Loans:	NA
Work study:	NA
Student rating of FA:	97

LEHIGH UNIVERSITY

CAMPUS LIFE

Quality of Life Rating:	80
Type of school:	private
Affiliation:	none
Environment:	city

STUDENT BODY

FT undergrad enrollment:	4,508
% male/% female:	63/37
% out-of-state:	72
% live on campus:	75
% African-American:	2
% Asian:	4
% Caucasian:	90
% Hispanic:	2
% foreign:	2
% transfers:	1

WHAT'S HOT

fraternities/sororities
library
registration
administration (overall)
hard liquor
bursar
beer

WHAT'S NOT

location
town-gown relations
gay community visible
diversity
working a job
interaction among students

ACADEMICS

Academic Rating:	81
Calendar:	semester
Student/teacher ratio:	13/1
% doctorates:	98
Profs interesting:	71
Profs accessible:	78
Hours of study per day:	3.26

MOST POPULAR MAJORS BY %

Engineering:	26
Business & Management:	23
Social Sciences:	11

% GRADS WHO PURSUE

Law:	4
MBA:	NA
Medicine:	2
M.A., etc.:	9

What do students think about Lehigh University?

■ **Academics** Lehigh University maintains a prestigious engineering school, a College of Business and Economics, and a College of Arts and Sciences. By all accounts, the first two are excellent, while the third is "weak." One student expressed what is pretty much the consensus: "We have an incredibly demanding school for engineering and business. Lehigh has been trying to improve its Arts and Sciences, but it is not yet worth the money to come here if you are undecided as to what you're going to study. Computer engineering [*this student's major*] is really tough, but you'll be prepared socially and academically for your future." Engineering and business students agreed that "the courses are quite hard and require many hours of preparation." Students here are extremely achievement-oriented; many take advantage of the numerous accelerated undergraduate/graduate degree programs here, and double-majors and demanding independent studies are also popular. Still, undergrads do not work so hard as to preclude an active social life (see "Life," below). Students gave the administration and library high marks.

■ **Life** At most schools, one or two respondents write us, "At our school, we work hard and party hard." At Lehigh, one out of every 10 students wrote that on his survey. For Lehigh undergrads, "work hard, party hard" is not just a hackneyed cliché, it's a way of life. Social life here is dominated by the Greek system: students ranked the popularity of fraternities and sororities third in the country. Those who live for frat parties are never disappointed. Reported one student, "once Thursday rolls around, the social atmosphere takes the place of academics. The strong Greek system results in free-flowing alcohol and everybody 'hooking up.'" Despite efforts by the state and the school to curb underage drinking, beer and alcohol are still mainstays of life at Lehigh. The Greek houses and a beautiful campus keep most social life on campus, as does the lack of attractions in the town of Bethlehem, a town described as "boring" by the one respondent who mentioned it at all. When campus life gets oppressive, most students blow off steam by travelling to Philadelphia (an hour and a half away) or New York (two hours away).

■ **Students** Lehigh draws its students primarily from Pennsylvania and the rest of the Eastern seaboard. The school has only a small minority population, made up predominantly of Asian students. One Asian student wrote to tell us that they maintain a tight-knit community, participating in activities and trips on an almost weekly basis: by both groups' accounts, interaction between the Asian and White communities is minimal. The predominant feel of the student body is white, conservative, jockish, and affluent. The male to female ratio here is almost two to one, even worse (for men) than at "party school" rival Lafayette.

LEHIGH UNIVERSITY

Bethlehem, PA

Admissions

Lehigh's most recent course catalog reports, "The admissions policy of the university is designed to encourage students with varied backgrounds to consider study at Lehigh....An applicant's full potential as a Lehigh student, including evidence of academic growth and desire to learn, are special qualities that may not be reflected in mere accumulation of [academic] units. Such qualities are considered when appraising applicants." Nonetheless, the university does set out minimum curricular requirements for applicants: four years of English and four years of college prep math (a waiver on math requirements is available to liberal arts applicants), two years of foreign language, and six years of academic electives. Applicants are required to submit results of the SAT and three achievement exams (English Comp and two others for Arts and Sciences students; Math I or II, chemistry or physics, and one more for Engineering and Applied Sciences students).

Financial Aid

The financial aid office at Lehigh University requires applicants to submit the FAF, a form generated by the school, and their parents' most recent tax return. Seven students in each class receive full academic scholarships; other merit grants are available for athletes, students in specific departments, students from specific geographical regions, and those who demonstrate "special potential for significant contributions to the Lehigh experience." The university "guarantees to meet the demonstrated financial need of any applicant, admitted under the regular admissions process, who is a U.S. citizen or permanent resident who complies with the filing deadlines."

Excerpted from Lehigh University promotional materials:

"The primary mission of Lehigh University is to provide excellence in teaching, research, and the application of knowledge for a useful life. In pursuit of this mission Lehigh offers a broad range of high quality programs in the humanities, arts, sciences, engineering, business, and education.

"Lehigh is an independent, coeducational university, with a deep commitment to cultural diversity and human dignity as essential elements of the learning environment. Distinctive elements of a Lehigh education are its balance and strong commitment to a liberal education for a useful life. Through the programs offered by its colleges, academic departments, and interdisciplinary centers and institutes, Lehigh combines the cultural with the professional, the theoretical with the practical, and the humanistic with the technological. In order that Lehigh's graduates become effective and enlightened citizens, the University's rigorous learning environment also provides opportunities for the physical, moral, spiritual, and social development of all students."

ADMISSIONS FACTS

Competitiveness Rating:	**82**
% of applicants accepted:	72
% acceptees attending:	30

FRESHMAN PROFILE

Average verbal SAT:	550*
Average math SAT:	620*
Average ACT:	NA
Graduated top 10% of class:	37
Graduated top 25% of class:	85
Graduated top 50% of class:	99

DEADLINES

Early decision/action:	11/17
Early dec./act. notif.:	12/15
Regular admission:	2/15
Regular adm. notif.:	4/11

APPLICANTS ALSO LOOK AT

and often prefer:
U. Pennsylvania

and sometimes prefer:
Colgate U.
Union College
Boston U.
Villanova U.

and rarely prefer:
Boston College
Penn State U.
Syracuse U.
Gettysburg College

ADDRESS

Undergraduate Admissions
Bethlehem, PA 18015
215-758-3100

FINANCIAL FACTS

In-state tuition ($):	15,650
Out-of-state tuition ($):	15,650
Room & board:	4,940
FA application deadline:	2/8
% frosh receiving FA:	42
PT earnings per yr. ($):	1,000

TYPE OF AID: % of students ($)

FA of some kind:	38 (12,551)
Need-based grants:	36 (8,981)
Merit-based grants:	NA
Loans:	NA
Work study:	20 (1,630)
Student rating of FA:	80

LEWIS AND CLARK COLLEGE

Portland, OR

CAMPUS LIFE

Quality of Life Rating:	**83**
Type of school:	private
Affiliation:	none
Environment:	city

STUDENT BODY

FT undergrad enrollment:	1,851
% male/% female:	44/56
% out-of-state:	70
% live on campus:	47
% African-American:	2
% Asian:	9
% Caucasian:	84
% Hispanic:	2
% foreign:	9
% transfers:	6

WHAT'S HOT

Grateful Dead
location
leftist politics
gay community accepted
marijuana
college radio station
college theater
campus appearance
living on campus
alternative rock

WHAT'S NOT

fraternities/sororities
library
interaction among students
hard liquor

ACADEMICS

Academic Rating:	**80**
Calendar:	quarters
Student/teacher ratio:	22/1
% doctorates:	90
Profs interesting:	83
Profs accessible:	86
Hours of study per day:	3.19

MOST POPULAR MAJORS BY %

Social Sciences:	34
Letters/Literature:	16
Life Sciences:	11

% GRADS WHO PURSUE

Law:	5
MBA:	4
Medicine:	3
M.A., etc.:	20

What do students think about Lewis and Clark College?

■ **Academics** Lewis and Clark College is an excellent liberal arts school whose reputation rests on a variety of strong academic departments, a progressive core curriculum, a popular overseas-studies program, and a dedicated faculty. For a small school, L&C offers a remarkable choice of quality programs. The international affairs department is its most famous, but the school's success in sending students to MBA and MD programs attests to the soundness of its business and pre-medical departments. Students also reported satisfaction with their English and foreign language courses. All students must complete a core curriculum that stresses 'liberal' perspectives, critical thought, and understanding of non-Western culture. This progressive approach permeates all study here. Explained one student, "This is a great place to learn to synthesize material. I don't know where else I could study mitosis and, in another class, turn it into a mime piece for high school students." More than half the students take advantage of the overseas studies program, which sends students virtually everywhere in the world. Best of all, the school foots the bill for the air fare and extra tuition. Students also praised their professors, saying that "they have an obvious love for the subjects they teach." The school runs on an 11-week trimester schedule.

■ **Life** One almost assumes that a campus in the Pacific northwest will be beautiful. In the case of L&C, at least, that assumption is correct. Wrote one student, "The campus is gorgeous. You can just go out and wander around the woods, ravine, or rose garden. The grass is lush and relaxing. It's great fun!" To make matters even better, the school is located on the outskirts of Portland, so students enjoy both serene immediate surroundings and access to a moderately large city. Extracurricular clubs and organizations are popular. Reported one student, "This school allows for a lot of artistic and creative freedom. There are student-directed one-act plays, a student-run radio station and newspaper. These organizations are an active part of the community." There is no Greek system, so students party in dorm rooms or in off-campus apartments. On-campus partying has been somewhat curtailed by the administration's decision to enforce more aggressively Oregon's drinking-age laws, but several students wrote that "the dry campus policy is a joke." Added one, "If only they knew what goes on behind the drawn shades." As is often the case at schools with drinking policies, pot smoking is very popular here.

■ **Students** Explained one student, "This school is mostly white and American, but we do have students who represent any possible philosophical train of thought one can imagine. In other words, our physical diversity is largely homogeneous, but our cultural diversities are widespread." Nearly one in 10 students is Asian, accounting for practically all of the ethnic diversity here. Students are "very friendly and rather on the 'crunchy granola' side," and consider themselves very liberal politically.

LEWIS AND CLARK COLLEGE

Portland, OR

Admissions

Lewis and Clark has two distinct options for application. The first is more "standard," in which the admissions committee looks at a student's GPA and high school curriculum, followed (in order of importance) by standardized test scores, essays, extracurriculars, letters of recommendation, and an interview. There are "no cut-offs or multiple regression formulas." The SAT or ACT is required. The second option is called the "Portfolio Path," in which students are asked to assemble a personal portfolio; suggested materials include, but are not limited to, writing samples (graded essays or term papers, personal journals), science projects or lab reports, samples of work from other classes, and video or other examples of talent in the fine arts. Students who opt for the Portfolio Path may request that their school remove standardized test scores form their transcript. Applicants pursuing either option should have completed four years of English, at least three years each of mathematics, history, and social sciences, and at least two years each of lab sciences and a foreign language. Students with other academic preparation "may be considered if other aspects of their record indicate readiness for Lewis & Clark coursework."

Financial Aid

Financial aid applicants to Lewis and Clark must complete the FAF and submit a copy of their parents' most recent tax return. Four percent of the college's undergrads received academic scholarships in '91–'92. The average value was $3,927. Achievement scholarships were also given to students who showed merit in forensics or music: 2% of all undergrads received such an award; the average value was $1,094. Among the need-based aids available are the Barbara Hirschi Neely scholarships. Ten of these are awarded; each is for the full value of four years' tuition ($54,000). Students are nominated for these scholarships by a counselor, principal, teacher, alumnus, or friend of the College. Preference in selection is given to "students whose interests lie in the sciences and who intend to advance understanding of the natural systems and promote responsible use of resources; or students who possess an unusually keen interest in the history, the arts, and the political and social realities of other nations or cultures, and who show they are prepared to become citizens of the world."

A note from the Lewis and Clark Admissions Office:

"While solidly grounded in the arts and sciences, with strengths in all pre-professional areas, Lewis and Clark is justifiably renowned for its overseas and off-campus programs. Nearly 60% of our graduates participate in these one-term, two-term (quarter), or full-year programs. One of the oldest and largest such programs in the U.S., 1992 is the 30th anniversary of this feature."

ADMISSIONS FACTS

Competitiveness Rating:	73
% of applicants accepted:	80
% acceptees attending:	23

FRESHMAN PROFILE

Average verbal SAT:	507
Average math SAT:	537
Average ACT:	24
Graduated top 10% of class:	31
Graduated top 25% of class:	66
Graduated top 50% of class:	92

DEADLINES

Early decision/action:	NA
Early dec./act. notif.:	NA
Regular admission:	2/1
Regular adm. notif.:	rolling

APPLICANTS ALSO LOOK AT

and often prefer:
Colorado College

and sometimes prefer:
UC Santa Barbara

and rarely prefer:
Reed College
U. Puget Sound
Williamette U.
U. Oregon
UC Santa Cruz

ADDRESS

Undergraduate Admissions
0615 SW Palatine Hill Rd.
Portland, OR 97219
503-768-7040

FINANCIAL FACTS

In-state tuition ($):	13,407
Out-of-state tuition ($):	13,407
Room & board:	4,653
FA application deadline:	2/15
% frosh receiving FA:	73
PT earnings per yr. ($):	1,200

TYPE OF AID: % of students ($)

FA of some kind:	76 (NA)
Need-based grants:	47 (7,125)
Merit-based grants:	NA
Loans:	41 (4,600)
Work study:	25 (840)
Student rating of FA:	89

LOYOLA MARYMOUNT UNIVERSITY

Los Angeles, CA

CAMPUS LIFE

Quality of Life Rating:	**85**
Type of school:	private
Affiliation:	Roman Catholic
Environment:	city

STUDENT BODY

FT undergrad enrollment:	3,716
% male/% female:	44/56
% out-of-state:	22
% live on campus:	53
% African-American:	5
% Asian:	13
% Caucasian:	66
% Hispanic:	15
% foreign:	2
% transfers:	2

WHAT'S HOT

marriage
religion
town-gown relations
college theater
administration (overall)
religious clubs

WHAT'S NOT

doing all the reading
library
Grateful Dead
studying hard

ACADEMICS

Academic Rating:	**77**
Calendar:	semester
Student/teacher ratio:	16/1
% doctorates:	85
Profs interesting:	79
Profs accessible:	86
Hours of study per day:	2.81

MOST POPULAR MAJORS BY %

Business & Management:	28
Communications:	12
Social Sciences:	12

% GRADS WHO PURSUE

Law:	3
MBA:	NA
Medicine:	7
M.A., etc.:	NA

What do students think about Loyola Marymount U.?

■ **Academics** According to an area college counselor, Loyola Marymount University is "small and friendly," a true anomaly in a city that is anything but. "It's not the *most* challenging academically," the same source continued, "but it's still an excellent choice for good students, especially those who underachieved in high school." Our survey results bore out this characterization of LMU. Students here enjoy a challenging but laid-back academic atmosphere, one that is augmented by effective, caring professors with whom one-on-one contact is relatively easy. In response to our survey, students indicated a high degree of satisfaction with LMU, expressing their approval of class sizes, professors, and administrators. Many come here to learn about those art forms indigenous to California (and Los Angeles in particular), namely, film and music production. The College of Business Administration, however, attracts the most students. Studies in all popular liberal arts and social sciences, as well as in engineering, are also available. While requirements vary from major to major, most students are required to complete a core curriculum of humanities, sciences, math, and philosophy/theology courses in order to graduate. Exceptional students may enroll in the honors program, which affords them smaller, more demanding classes and a more prestigious degree upon graduation.

■ **Life** Students describe LMU as "a *small* school in a *big* city." With just over 4,000 undergraduates (and approximately another 1,000 graduate students), Loyola Marymount has "a smallness of the school [that] gives it a family-type atmosphere." Wrote one student, "I can't walk from one side of campus to the other without seeing at least one person I know." Campus life is made even more intimate by the fact that only half the students live on campus. Students report that LMU is "a serious school, yet it is also fun on weekends." Said one, "if you want to drink, LMU's the place!" Greek life is popular, with almost one-fifth the students joining. For those who disdain the Greeks (such as the respondent who wrote "I'm sick of stuck-up frat boys and bouncy sorority bimbos"), there are a wide assortment of extracurricular clubs and organizations, a newspaper and radio station, the school's popular Division I sports teams, an active intramural sports program, and, of course, the city of Los Angeles, which one student described as "exciting, even though it smells a little bit funny." As an added bonus, the school is close to the beach.

■ **Students** LMU does a good job of recruiting minority students: nearly one third of the student body is made up of minorities. Hispanics and Asians make up the largest groups; there are relatively few black students here. Students identified themselves as more religious than most student bodies, not at all unusual at a Catholic school.

LOYOLA MARYMOUNT UNIVERSITY

Los Angeles, CA

Admissions

Loyola Marymount's most recent catalog reports, "The University makes selective and individual decisions, taking into consideration the applicant's secondary school record, national test scores, recommendations, personal characteristics, and relationship to the University. Each applicant is individually evaluated to insure a diversified student population." Applicants must submit scores for either the SAT or the ACT, and all applications must include a recommendation from an official (teacher, principal, counselor, or dean) at his/her previous school. An interview is recommended but not required. The school recommends the following high school curriculum: four years of English, three years each of foreign language, mathematics, and social studies; two years of science; and one year of academic electives.

Financial Aid

The financial aid office at Loyola Marymount requires applicants to submit the FAF and a copy of their parents' most recent tax return. The school offers merit grants for "demonstrated academic achievement" and for "exceptional promise as campus or community leaders." Other non-need based scholarships are available for students from Jesuit or other Catholic high schools. Last year, LMU students drew loans on the following programs: Stafford (36% borrowed such loans; average value: $3,200); Perkins (10%; $2,200); and PLUS/SLS (7%; $3,600).

Excerpted from Loyola Marymount promotional materials:

"The visionary statement which the Trustees adopted in 1976 commits Loyola Marymount University to the following goals:

"To strive toward all our goals within the context of a university that has an institutional commitment to Christianity and the Catholic tradition.

"To provide strong undergraduate humanistic education as an integral part of the academic program of each student.

"To offer sound professional programs on both the undergraduate and graduate level.

"To help the student advance significantly in personal, social, and professional growth through a program of services to students.

"To work toward the formation of a true spirit of community at all levels and in all areas of the University.

"To be at the service of the community beyond the campus, especially in the fostering of a more just society."

ADMISSIONS FACTS

Competitiveness Rating:	**74**
% of applicants accepted:	61
% acceptees attending:	34

FRESHMAN PROFILE

Average verbal SAT:	486
Average math SAT:	543
Average ACT:	NA
Graduated top 10% of class:	34
Graduated top 25% of class:	71
Graduated top 50% of class:	94

DEADLINES

Early decision/action:	NA
Early dec./act. notif.:	NA
Regular admission:	2/1
Regular adm. notif.:	rolling

APPLICANTS ALSO LOOK AT

and often prefer:
UC Davis
Stanford U.
UC Los Angeles

and sometimes prefer:
UC Irvine
UC San Diego
UC Santa Barbara

and rarely prefer:
Santa Clara U.
UC Riverside
Pepperdine U.

ADDRESS

Undergraduate Admissions
Loyola Blvd. at W. 80th St.
Los Angeles, CA 90045
213-338-2750

FINANCIAL FACTS

In-state tuition ($):	11,411
Out-of-state tuition ($):	11,411
Room & board:	6,000
FA application deadline:	2/15
% frosh receiving FA:	63
PT earnings per yr. ($):	1,800

TYPE OF AID: % of students ($)

FA of some kind:	60 (12,551)
Need-based grants:	36 (8,981)
Merit-based grants:	6 (5,500)
Loans:	NA
Work study:	20 (1,630)
Student rating of FA:	82

LOYOLA UNIVERSITY CHICAGO

Chicago, IL

What do students think about Loyola University?

■ **Academics** Chicago's Loyola University is actually five undergraduate institutions in one: the school maintains separate colleges for the arts and sciences, business administration, nursing, education, and continuing education. At the College of Arts and Sciences, the most popular undergraduate division, the curricular centerpiece is the battery of core requirements, so demanding that "it is rather difficult for many students to finish in four years." Students here pursue mandatory studies in theology and philosophy—as you might expect, since Loyola is affiliated with the Roman Catholic church—and also in history, science, mathematics, and writing. Requirements can constitute half the credits toward a B.A., and that doesn't include courses required for one's major. When arts and sciences students do find time for electives, they most often head for the School of Business Administration to take popular courses in marketing and finance. According to area college counselors, the psychology and pre-medical departments are the strongest divisions in Arts and Sciences; counselors also recommended the schools of nursing and business administration. Loyola University has two undergraduate campuses, the Water Tower campus downtown and the Lake Shore campus, which is currently being expanded, on the north side of town. The school recently purchased a third campus in Wilmette. Residents live at Lake Shore.

■ **Life** Loyola is a big commuter school. The university guarantees housing to the 20 percent of its student body from out of state, but almost all the rest end up off-campus. Lots of students go home for the weekend, so the campus goes dead Friday afternoon. One student complained, "The only neighborhood place which offers some amusement is Hamilton's (a bar reminiscent of high school hang-outs like White Castle or the mall)." However, some residents who stick around say that there is "a great diversity of clubs and activities which enable the students to get involved." And of course, students are in Chicago, which is an amazingly cool city (except in winter, when it is an amazingly *cold* city). Frat parties are open to all, and the "Greek-independent" animosity common at many other schools is absent here. Commuters beware: said one, "Parking is a nightmare. Commuters have no chance of finding a spot."

■ **Students** Minority students at Loyola complained that, although they were well represented in the student body, interaction among ethnic groups was practically nonexistent. Said one Latino student, "Although the university is ethnically diverse, the students do not hang together. It looks great on paper, but in reality it is not what it seems," and an African-American woman went so far as to accuse administrators and fellow students of "racism, sexism, and right-wing conservatism." The lack of a conventional college community certainly contributes to students "falling in" with their own rather than reaching out to interact with others, as does the conservatism of the student body. Those who seek to break into new social circles reported that Loyola provided them with great experiences. A little over half the student body is Catholic.

LOYOLA UNIVERSITY CHICAGO

Admissions

The admissions office reports that "as a selective institution, Loyola is looking for applicants with academic achievement in a strong high school curriculum." High school GPA is considered the most important aspect of your application here; standardized test scores are the next-most important; high school curriculum is also considered. Applicants need to have completed a minimum of 15 high school credits, thirteen of which must be academic credits and must include: four years of English, two years of math, one year of social science, and one year of natural science. Applicants to Loyola most often also apply to DePaul, University of Illinois (Chicago and Urbana campuses), Northwestern, Marquette, and University of Chicago.

Financial Aid

Financial aid applicants to Loyola U/Chicago must complete a form generated by its financial aid office and the FAF. Among the scholarships available are: merit scholarships for academic achievement; the Condon scholarship for students who plan to major in Greek or Latin (and who took at least two years in high school); Plocieniak scholarships, for undergrads of Polish descent who are fluent in Polish, scholarships for students planning to major in accounting or nursing; and scholarships for students who demonstrate talent or experience in debate, theatre, or athletics. Loans recommended by the school include Perkins, Stafford, PLUS, SLS, and Loyola's own institutional loans. The priority deadline for application is April 1. All complete files are reviewed in the order of the date they are received.

A note from the Loyola Admissions Office:

"As a national research university, Loyola provides a superb academic program which is distinctive because of its personal approach. Nationally and internationally renowned scholars teach introductory freshman level courses in classes that average 21 students. A special emphasis in our curriculum is placed on the examination of ethics and values as well as a commitment to instill intensive writing skills which will benefit the student throughout his/her life. Despite its large population, Loyola is committed to the individual student, and its programs and policies reflect the importance of community. Students from throughout the nation are attracted to Loyola for the opportunities offered by the University as well as the benefits of studying in Chicago, a world-class city."

ADMISSIONS FACTS

Competitiveness Rating:	**69**
% of applicants accepted:	81
% acceptees attending:	34

FRESHMAN PROFILE

Average verbal SAT:	475
Average math SAT:	521
Average ACT:	23
Graduated top 10% of class:	25
Graduated top 25% of class:	55
Graduated top 50% of class:	89

DEADLINES

Early decision/action:	NA
Early dec./act. notif.:	NA
Regular admission:	7/1
Regular adm. notif.:	rolling

APPLICANTS ALSO LOOK AT

and often prefer:
U. Chicago
Northwestern U.

and sometimes prefer:
U. Illinois
Indiana U.
DePaul U.
Marquette U.
U. Wisconsin–Madison

ADDRESS

Undergraduate Admissions
820 North Michigan Ave.
Chicago, IL 60611
312-915-6500

FINANCIAL FACTS

In-state tuition ($):	9,210
Out-of-state tuition ($):	9,210
Room & board:	4,769
FA application deadline:	none
% frosh receiving FA:	80
PT earnings per yr. ($):	NA

TYPE OF AID: % of students ($)

FA of some kind:	80 (NA)
Need-based grants:	NA
Merit-based grants:	NA
Loans:	NA
Work study:	NA
Student rating of FA:	72

MANHATTANVILLE COLLEGE

CAMPUS LIFE

Quality of Life Rating: 77

Type of school:	private
Affiliation:	none
Environment:	suburban

STUDENT BODY

FT undergrad enrollment:	1,010
% male/% female:	37/63
% out-of-state:	55
% live on campus:	90
% African-American:	8
% Asian:	4
% Caucasian:	71
% Hispanic:	8
% foreign:	11
% transfers:	15

WHAT'S HOT

small labs and seminars
living on campus
small lectures
small classes (overall)
diversity
financial aid
deans
cost of living
profs outside class

WHAT'S NOT

fraternities/sororities
gay community visible
studying hard
library
administration (overall)

ACADEMICS

Academic Rating: **80**

Calendar:	semester
Student/teacher ratio:	12/1
% doctorates:	90
Profs interesting:	84
Profs accessible:	86
Hours of study per day:	2.55

MOST POPULAR MAJORS BY %

Social Sciences:	20
Business & Management:	18
Psychology:	15

% GRADS WHO PURSUE

Law:	15
MBA:	2
Medicine:	7
M.A., etc.:	9

What do students think about Manhattanville College?

■ **Academics** Willingness to take initiative is what sets Manhattanville students apart from the pack. Explained one student, "What makes this a great learning environment is that students are encouraged to get involved and make a difference." Said another, "This is a good school, especially if you are a leader and willing to get involved, willing to change." The school's unusual curriculum demands that students take an active role in designing their educations. Freshmen are assigned advisors and are required to devise a four-year program during their first semester. They must maintain a portfolio of work finished toward the completion of that curriculum; the portfolio is periodically evaluated by a faculty panel. Students continually revise their curricula as their interests change and their perspectives broaden. A standard variety of liberal arts majors are available here, and students tend toward pre-professional pursuits: 15 percent go on to law school. Science courses are said to be weak, mostly because the school is too small to adequately support them, but somehow seven percent of the students proceed from here to medical school. Classes are small and professors are reasonably accessible, but as one student explained, "Responsibility for a good education lies with the student, as it should. Professors are there to facilitate learning to the extent that students want to go."

■ **Life** Manhattanville is located in the suburbs of New York City, about an hour away from Manhattan (where the school was once located). The city is easily accessible by commuter train or by car, although New York City traffic and parking conditions are infamous. Closer to school is White Plains, a typical suburban town with a typically huge shopping mall. The area is home to the headquarters of many large corporations, and internships are reportedly easy to come by. There are no fraternities or sororities, but students have plenty of outlets for partying: beer and alcohol are favorites here. The drinking, coupled with many students' laid-back attitude toward academics, frustrates some of the more serious students. "This isn't college, it's merely a scholastic slumber party!" complained one.

■ **Students** Manhattanville has a remarkably diverse student body for a small private college. Exclaimed one student, "Manhattanville College has an important variety of cultures, religions, and people from all over the world." Eleven percent of the students are foreign nationals, and American students come from all over the county. There is a relatively large black and Hispanic population. However, interaction between whites and minorities is reportedly minimal. One minority student explained, "There is a sharp distinction between the wealthy whites and the minority students (largely of African-American or Hispanic background), which often becomes a stressful situation."

MANHATTANVILLE COLLEGE

Admissions

Manhattanville has two different admissions plans. The first, called Plan I, requires applicant to submit scores from the SAT or ACT. Approximately 90% of the average freshman class opts for Plan I. Plan II applicants replace their SAT and ACT scores with "one substantial example of written academic work," and the results of Achievement tests in English and Mathematics. According to Manhattanville's catalog, "By far the most important consideration in the evaluation process is your secondary school performance, both your grades and the types of courses you have taken. The second most important consideration is the result of standardized testing and/or the quality of academic work submitted if you are applying under Plan II. In addition, recommendations submitted on your behalf are carefully reviewed and extracurricular activities in which you have participated and leadership positions you have held are viewed as another indication of your future contributions to the College."

Financial Aid

Financial aid applicants to Manhattanville are required to complete the FAF or FFS, and a form generated by Manhattanville's financial aid office. Manhattanville offers its own scholarships to freshman, regardless of need, who "demonstrate either exceptional academic performance or a strong aptitude for leadership." The scholarships range from $5,000 to half the cost of one year's tuition. The average award value in '90–'91 was $6,000; in that year, Manhattanville provided over $3.9 million in scholarship assistance to qualified students. The FAF or FFS should be submitted to the appropriate agency by March 1.

A note from the Manhattanville College Admissions Office:

"In the community of learning which is Manhattanville College, there is a genuine concern for the development of each student and a continuing search for excellence. The college's strong desire for beneficial growth continually involves faculty and students in the fostering of this search.

"The Portfolio System, at the undergraduate level, emphasizes student responsibility. Young men and women must submit a coherent plan for their education; they must master the appropriate academic skills; they are urged to enter a period of graduate study and to prepare themselves for a useful contribution to their time and world. It is recognized that this means a strenuous four years. Manhattanville hopes to recruit students with the energy and the courage to undertake such a program."

ADMISSIONS FACTS

Competitiveness Rating:	**71**
% of applicants accepted:	77
% acceptees attending:	31

FRESHMAN PROFILE

Average verbal SAT:	506
Average math SAT:	545
Average ACT:	NA
Graduated top 10% of class:	19
Graduated top 25% of class:	56
Graduated top 50% of class:	93

DEADLINES

Early decision/action:	1/15
Early dec./act. notif.:	2/1
Regular admission:	3/1
Regular adm. notif.:	rolling

APPLICANTS ALSO LOOK AT

and often prefer:
Syracuse U.
Skidmore College
NYU

and sometimes prefer:
SUNY–Purchase
Fordham U.

and rarely prefer:
Mercy College

ADDRESS

Undergraduate Admissions
125 Purchase Street
Purchase, NY 10577
914-694-2200

FINANCIAL FACTS

In-state tuition ($):	12,400
Out-of-state tuition ($):	12,400
Room & board:	5,600
FA application deadline:	3/1
% frosh receiving FA:	65
PT earnings per yr. ($):	1,200

TYPE OF AID: % of students ($)

FA of some kind:	65 (NA)
Need-based grants:	NA
Merit-based grants:	NA
Loans:	NA
Work study:	NA
Student rating of FA:	88

MARLBORO COLLEGE

CAMPUS LIFE

Quality of Life Rating:	**91**
Type of school:	private
Affiliation:	none
Environment:	rural

STUDENT BODY

FT undergrad enrollment:	276
% male/% female:	44/56
% out-of-state:	80
% live on campus:	80
% African-American:	1
% Asian:	4
% Caucasian:	93
% Hispanic:	1
% foreign:	2
% transfers:	10

WHAT'S HOT

gay community accepted
small classes (overall)
food
in-class discussion
interaction among students
doing all the reading
honesty
profs in class
dorm comfort
profs outside class
overall happiness
leftist politics

WHAT'S NOT

fraternities/sororities
intercollegiate sports

ACADEMICS

Academic Rating:	**81**
Calendar:	semester
Student/teacher ratio:	8/1
% doctorates:	53
Profs interesting:	99
Profs accessible:	96
Hours of study per day:	3.48

MOST POPULAR MAJORS

Natural Sciences
Humanities

% GRADS WHO PURSUE

Law:	5
MBA:	NA
Medicine:	5
M.A., etc.:	60

What do students think about Marlboro College?

■ **Academics** Cloistered away in the Vermont mountains is Marlboro College, a tiny school (fewer than 300 students) ideal for free-thinking individualists. Most students choose Marlboro for its Plan of Concentration, a program that requires students to spend their junior and senior years following a self-devised curriculum, culminating in a senior research paper "analogous to a master's thesis." During those last two years, students work individually with professors ("By the time students graduate, they have had many one-on-one tutorials"). Students must also pass a writing proficiency exam, but otherwise, their course of study is left entirely to them. Explained one student, "Most students choose Marlboro because they know 'the plan' will prepare them for graduate school. Classes are informal, yet rigorous, and professors are easy to approach." Students here are well prepared for grad school. By the school's account, over three-quarters proceed from here to advanced degree programs. Students reported a high level of satisfaction with their professors, administration, class availability ("We're guaranteed a class of choice: in some cases, teachers will change the time of their class so that a student with a scheduling conflict can attend") and facilities ("The library, although small, is open 24 hours a day and is run completely on the honor system"). There are no official majors here, but studies cover a remarkably broad range. Joked one student, "You could study African narcoleptic midwifery here if you wanted to."

■ **Life** Marlboro students certainly do not experience a "typical" college lifestyle. Wrote one, "We have no sports, no frats, no sorority houses, and no radio station. This is a small, work-intensive environment. If you are interested in independent thinking, self-motivation, and learning to write well, then you could have a good experience here." Most agree that they enjoy "a laid-back and comfortable atmosphere conducive to learning," but would probably also admit that "if you're not used to isolation and you do not have a car, this little mountain community can be a challenging adjustment." The small community demands that students become involved. Students meet twice weekly, using the "New England town meeting" model to "create and run activities and govern the student body." Organized sports are not popular here (although one student insisted that "co-ed naked broom ball" is), but outdoor activities are. Wrote one student, "December to May is an experience. Bring a sled." Although hard-working, Marlboro students do occasionally take time out to party. Drinking is popular; pot-smoking more so.

■ **Students** Marlboro has a large "pseudo-hippie" population. Wrote one student, "Our school colors are tie-dye." Reported one student, "There's not much ethnic diversity here, but students would welcome it." A Hispanic student agreed, writing, "Because Marlboro is overwhelmingly white and non-ethnic, and because the students here are open-minded and curious, a minority student is given a chance to educate others about his/her culture, mores and language."

MARLBORO COLLEGE

Admissions

Marlboro's admissions office states that there are cut-offs "only for Early Action—students must be in the top 10 percent of their high school class with minimum combined SAT scores of 1200. There are no cut-offs for Regular Decision applicants." The admissions committee first looks at your high school GPA. This is followed (in order of importance) by your standardized test scores, extracurriculars, essays, letters of recommendation, and interview. Students must take the SAT or ACT, and those applying to the College of Liberal Arts and Sciences must take Achievements as well. Applicants should also have completed four years of English, at least three years of mathematics, at least one year of science, and two years of foreign language (certain majors). Marlboro applicants also often apply to Boston College, Notre Dame, Rutgers, Fairfield, and Penn State.

Financial Aid

Marlboro College requires a FAF, a copy of your parents' most recent tax return, and a form generated by its own financial aid office. The school awards no merit-based grants. Last year, 65% of the class of '95 received an award of some kind, with an average value of $9,000–$10,000. The FA office recommended Stafford loans (average value $5,000), PLUS loans ($1,500), and Perkins loans ($1,000). The office makes available "The Financial Aid Estimator," which offers families a preview of their chances for financial aid.

A note from the Marlboro College Admissions Office:

"Marlboro College is unlike any other college in the United States. It is distinguished by its curriculum—praised in higher education circles as unique—by its self-governing philosophy and by its 43-year history of offering a rigorous, exciting, self-designed course of study taught in very small classes and individual tutorials. Marlboro is also distinguished by its size—with 250 students and a student/faculty ratio of 8 to 1, it is one of the nation's smallest liberal arts institutions.

"At Marlboro, students are taught by professors dedicated to teaching, not research. Graduates of Marlboro—over 60 percent of whom pursue graduate-level work—enter careers in academic, business, the arts, and many other fields."

ADMISSIONS FACTS

Competitiveness Rating:	72
% of applicants accepted:	85
% acceptees attending:	46

FRESHMAN PROFILE

Average verbal SAT:	556
Average math SAT:	530
Average ACT:	NA
Graduated top 10% of class:	36
Graduated top 25% of class:	65
Graduated top 50% of class:	85

DEADLINES

Early decision/action:	12/1
Early dec./act. notif.:	12/15
Regular admission:	rolling
Regular adm. notif.:	rolling

APPLICANT ALSO LOOK AT

and often prefer:
Sarah Lawrence College
Bard College
Hampshire College

and sometimes prefer:
Bennington College
Fairfield U.

and rarely prefer:
Goddard College

ADDRESS

Undergraduate Admissions
Marlboro, VT 05344
802-257-4333
800-343-0049

FINANCIAL FACTS

In-state tuition ($):	15,000
Out-of-state tuition ($):	15,000
Room & board:	5,150
FA application deadline:	4/1
% frosh receiving FA:	60
PT earnings per yr. ($):	1,300

TYPE OF AID: % of students ($)

FA of some kind:	60 (8,000)
Need-based grants:	NA
Merit-based grants:	NA
Loans:	NA
Work study:	40 (1,300)
Student rating of FA:	100

MARQUETTE UNIVERSITY

CAMPUS LIFE

Quality of Life Rating: **74**

Type of school:	private
Affiliation:	Roman Catholic
Environment:	city

STUDENT BODY

FT undergrad enrollment:	8,193
% male/% female:	52/48
% out-of-state:	44
% live on campus:	65
% African-American:	4
% Asian:	4
% Caucasian:	89
% Hispanic:	3
% foreign:	4
% transfers:	13

WHAT'S HOT

working a job
marriage
suitcase syndrome
studying hard

WHAT'S NOT

campus appearance
rap/hip-hop
town-gown relations
gay community accepted
living on campus
caring about politics
TAs teach intros
good looking students
overall happiness

ACADEMICS

Academic Rating: **77**

Calendar:	semester
Student/teacher ratio:	15/1
% doctorates:	85
Profs interesting:	71
Profs accessible:	79
Hours of study per day:	3.64

MOST POPULAR MAJORS BY %

Marketing:	7
Political Science:	6
Accounting:	5

% GRADS WHO PURSUE

Law:	4
MBA:	4
Medicine:	2
M.A., etc.:	11

What do students think about Marquette University?

■ **Academics** Area college counselors agree that Marquette University is "a solid pre-professional college." Among the areas of study singled out for excellence, business, nursing, physical therapy, communications, and engineering (especially biomedical engineering) are the most frequently praised. A Jesuit school, Marquette does its best to create a supportive, caring environment for its students, and apparently it succeeds. Students we surveyed gave their professors good grades for after-class accessibility and told us that deans and other administrators are particularly helpful. As a large school, MU also provides great academic diversity and flexibility. Reported one student, "I was interested in developing an interdisciplinary degree in Medieval studies, and I was able to formulate such a program at MU. The academic depth here has been beneficial." While some students who apply here may expect a relaxed academic atmosphere—most schools with national reputations built primarily on sports are perceived as easy by those not attending them—most are quickly disabused of that notion upon arrival. "Marquette has a hard curriculum, and some of the students aren't up to it," explained one undergraduate who survived the distribution requirements, which for most students entail work in mathematics, science, liberal arts, and theology (different divisions of the school have different requirements). For the highly motivated/talented student, Marquette offers an honors program with smaller classes and more rigorous academics.

■ **Life** Marquette is located in downtown Milwaukee, and location is definitely the number one quality-of-life issue at the school. Several area counselors warned that MU is in an unsafe neighborhood, and many of our respondents concurred. Wrote one, "The downtown scene has been problematic because of the nature of this area of the city and the police department's dislike for the students. The social problems of Milwaukee can be a great distraction." Not everyone agrees, however. One student noted that because the school is "located in downtown Milwaukee, there are a lot of things to do. It's unfortunate that most people just don't take the time to find out about them." Students report that, the school's official religious affiliation notwithstanding, drinking is popular, with beer—Milwaukee is one of America's brewing capitals—naturally the beverage of choice. The Greek system barely exists—fewer than five percent of the students pledge—and social life centers around dorm parties, sporting events, and the city.

■ **Students** Marquette has developed a reputation for diversity that is not borne out by its student body demographics: only 11 percent of the students are minorities. "Diversity," wrote one undergraduate, "is well-publicized but superficial." Many of Marquette's students represent the first college-educated generation of their families, and many, accordingly, are career-oriented.

MARQUETTE UNIVERSITY

Admissions

Marquette considers high school rank the most important component of an application. Standardized test scores are also very important, as are high school curriculum, quality of high school attended, and letters of recommendation: essays, interviews, and extracurricular activities are not considered. The school suggests that applicants have completed four years of English, three years of math, two years each of science, social studies, and a foreign language, and at least three other academic courses. Math and science majors are further expected to have taken advanced math and science courses. The admissions office notes that applicants interested in receiving direct freshman entry into the Master's in Physical Therapy program (a six-year program) must meet a strict December 15 deadline; all other admissions are on a rolling basis. Applicants to Marquette are often also applicants to UWisconsin–Madison, Notre Dame, and Northwestern.

Financial Aid

Marquette University requires a FAF and a form generated by its own financial aid office (the latter for new students only). The school awarded academic scholarships to half of its undergraduates in the '91–'92 academic year, with values ranging from $500 to $900. Seventy-six percent of all freshmen received aid, with an average award package of $8,200. While there is no hard deadline for financial aid, the priority date is 3/1. The figure shown in the sidebar for work-study represents students who actually took work-study jobs, not the number of offers made.

A note from the Marquette University Admissions Office:

"Since 1881, Marquette University has stood for excellence in higher education. Marquette challenges students to work toward reaching their potential in every facet of their lives, and therefore offers a well-rounded curriculum with emphasis on the liberal arts, Christian ideals, and humanistic concern for others. Thirty master's degrees, 12 doctorates, law and dental degrees, and approximately 50 undergraduate majors are offered through its 12 colleges, programs and schools. Nearly 90 percent of the faculty hold the Ph.D. or equivalent terminal degrees, and all are expected to teach and to do research. The student/faculty ratio is 15:1.

"Marquette's 8,500 undergraduates hail from all 50 states and more than 70 foreign countries. This diverse, residential student body participates in more than 150 student organizations and a wide range of intramural, club and varsity (NCAA Division I) sports."

ADMISSIONS FACTS

Competitiveness Rating:	**72**
% of applicants accepted:	80
% acceptees attending:	32

FRESHMAN PROFILE

Average verbal SAT:	480
Average math SAT:	538
Average ACT:	25
Graduated top 10% of class:	31
Graduated top 25% of class:	63
Graduated top 50% of class:	91

DEADLINES

Early decision/action:	NA
Early dec./adm. notif.:	NA
Regular admission:	rolling
Regular adm. notif.:	rolling

APPLICANTS ALSO LOOK AT

and often prefer:
Miami U.

and rarely prefer:
Vanderbilt U.
Case Western Reserve U.
Purdue U.
Villanova U.
U. Oklahoma

ADDRESS

Undergraduate Admissions
Milwaukee, WI 53233
414-288-7302

FINANCIAL FACTS

In-state tuition ($):	9,000
Out-of-state tuition ($):	9,000
Room & board:	3,900
FA application deadline:	3/1
% frosh receiving FA:	80
PT earnings per yr. ($):	1500

TYPE OF AID: % of students ($)	
FA of some kind:	80 (NA)
Need-based grants:	60 (3,000)
Merit-based grants:	50 (NA)
Loans:	50 (NA)
Work study:	10 (1,500)
Student rating of FA:	75

UNIVERSITY OF MARYLAND

College Park, MD

What do students think about the University of Maryland?

■ **Academics** While the University of Maryland, College Park remains a fine institution, it is a school in crisis because of massive state budget cuts. Faculty layoffs are pervasive, and certain departments are simply being "dissolved." Some of these are not accepting any more majors, while some smaller, more expensive ones are closing up shop and forcing their students to transfer. Required courses are not offered every semester, and when they are it is a "major hassle" to get into them. Effecting major campus renovations, however necessary, while simultaneously firing lots of professors was not a good public relations move on UMD's part. In short, anxiety levels over the future of the school are high. Other complaints concerned uncomfortably large lecture classes and science/engineering TAs whose command of English is unimpressive. Still, Maryland is not without its merits. For those who qualify for the Honors Program, classes are smaller and much easier to get into. The school has excellent engineering, physics, and economics departments, and theater majors are vocal boosters of their program. And Maryland's core curriculum requires students to fulfill a wide range of distribution requirements and then, during senior year, take two seminars designed to help students integrate these disparate courses into their major fields of study. Finally, our respondents reported that, while some of their classmates "coast through" their four years, many students here are serious about their studies (the school's nickname notwithstanding: see "Life," below).

■ **Life** "Party Park" is how Marylanders have traditionally referred to this campus, and while the school has worked hard to downplay this aspect of its reputation, the fact is that Maryland students still party hard. "A great party school, especially if you are in a sorority or fraternity," said one student—ten percent of the undergrads are in the Greek system. UM students are active boosters of their varsity teams (called the Terrapins), and are particularly enthusiastic about the football, lacrosse, and basketball teams, the last of which is strongly rebounding from a series of scandals and NCAA suspensions. The town of College Park has very little to offer students, but with a student body of 21,500, you're already in a small city while on campus. For those who have cars and money to spend, D.C. is close by and Baltimore is not much further away. Car owners complained to us that legal parking is scarce and that they are regularly ticketed.

■ **Students** Almost three quarters of College Park students are from the state of Maryland. Although the student body is ethnically diverse, different groups generally don't interact. Many students already know each other from high school and easily fall into social groups similar to the ones they had there. With this many classmates, almost any Maryland student will eventually find a social group into which he fits, although finding it may take a bit of time.

UNIVERSITY OF MARYLAND

Admissions

In its catalog, The University of Maryland states that it "maintains a competitive admissions policy, with priority given to those students with the most outstanding academic credentials, and seeks to enroll students who demonstrate the potential for academic success." Although primarily dedicated to the educational needs of Maryland residents, UMCP currently has fifty states, D.C., two territories, and 100 foreign countries represented in its undergraduate population. In order of importance, the admissions committee looks at an applicant's GPA, standardized test scores, extracurriculars, essays, and letters of recommendation. No cut-offs, minimum scores, or formulas are used in the admissions process. All applicants must submit SAT or ACT scores, and should have completed four years of English, three years of history/social science, two years of lab science, three years of mathematics (with a fourth year recommended), and one year of a foreign language. Applicants to UMCP also often apply to U. Delaware, Virginia Tech, and Penn State.

Financial Aid

The financial aid office at University of Maryland, College Park requires applicants to submit the FAF, a form generated by the school, their parents' most recent tax return, and "information as required by Federal Regulations." Athletic scholarships are "awarded through a private foundation"; last year, 443 athletes received an average grant of $6,545. Merit grants are also awarded on the basis of academic ability (547 students; average value: $3,985). State-sponsored scholarships, tuition waivers, and private scholarships are also available, as are major-specific, career-goal-specific, and ethnicity-specific grants. University of Maryland recommends the following loan programs to financial aid recipients: Stafford, PLUS, SLS, and Perkins. The deadline listed in the FA sidebar is a *priority* deadline.

A note from the University of Maryland Admissions Office:

"These are great days at the University of Maryland. Through an act of the state legislature, the university has been designated officially as the state's flagship campus with a mandate to become one of the nation's leading public universities. The effect of that mandate is for individuals from all corners of the university to aspire toward excellence, to think great thoughts, and to become immersed in an educational enterprise of the highest caliber. There is an unmistakable momentum for change and a sense of heightened expectation at College Park—Maryland is choosing quality."

ADMISSIONS FACTS

Competitiveness Rating:	**75**
% of applicants accepted:	61
% acceptees attending:	36

FRESHMAN PROFILE

Average verbal SAT:	504
Average math SAT:	582
Average ACT:	NA
Graduated top 10% of class:	35
Graduated top 25% of class:	51
Graduated top 50% of class:	92

DEADLINES

Early decision/action:	12/1
Early dec./adm. notif.:	rolling
Regular admission:	4/30
Regular adm. notif.:	rolling

APPLICANTS ALSO LOOK AT

and often prefer:
U. NC–Chapel Hill

and sometimes prefer:
SUNY Binghamton
Penn State U.
NYU
Howard U.
George Washington U.

and rarely prefer:
Syracuse U.
U. Delaware

ADDRESS

Undergraduate Admissions
N. Administration Building
College Park, MD 20742-1672
301-314-8385

FINANCIAL FACTS

In-state tuition ($):	2,436
Out-of-state tuition ($):	7,304
Room & board:	4,712
FA application deadline:	2/15
% frosh receiving FA:	66
PT earnings per yr. ($):	NA

TYPE OF AID: % of students ($)

FA of some kind:	48 (NA)
Need-based grants:	28 (993)
Merit-based grants:	NA
Loans:	29 (2,215)
Work study:	3 (NA)
Student rating of FA:	64

UNIVERSITY OF MASSACHUSETTS AT AMHERST

Amherst, MA

CAMPUS LIFE

Quality of Life Rating: **75**

Type of school: public
Affiliation: none
Environment: suburban

STUDENT BODY

FT undergrad enrollment: 17,189
% male/% female: 49/51
% out-of-state: 15
% live on campus: 58
% African-American: 2
% Asian: 3
% Caucasian: 86
% Hispanic: 3
% foreign: 2
% transfers: 7

WHAT'S HOT

gay community visible
marijuana
profs lecture a lot

WHAT'S NOT

administration (overall)
small classes (overall)
food
dorm comfort

ACADEMICS

Academic Rating: **74**

Calendar: semester
Student/teacher ratio: 17/1
% doctorates: 90
Profs interesting: 81
Profs accessible: 73
Hours of study per day: 3.2

MOST POPULAR MAJORS BY %

Business & Management 18
Social Sciences: 16
Communications: 9

What do students think about UMass, Amherst?

■ **Academics** Students disagree about the quality of the education they receive at the University of Massachusetts at Amherst. A disconcerting number, discouraged by tuition hikes and the "loss of classes, professors and library hours," call UMass Amherst a "once-great university going down the tubes." Said one disgruntled student, "Perhaps the best words to describe it are 'substandard' and 'inadequate.'" Still, considerably more remain quite satisfied with their experience: "UMass does a damn good job living up to the strong reputation it has earned," wrote one; the professors, who received good grades for those at a public institution, are, according to one undergrad, "wonderful and very committed to teaching." Once known as "Zoo Mass" for the preponderant party scene there, the school has effectively sobered up its image in the past decade. Respect for UMass as an academic institution has soared since then, as has the annual application rate. Recent budget cuts have hurt, and many students complain about their increased financial burdens. Membership in the Five College Consortium, however, lessens the impact of some of these cuts: students may use not only their own school's resources, but also those of four other highly reputed New England colleges (Amherst, Hampshire, Smith and Mount Holyoke). The popularity of the consortium leads some to say that UMass Amherst offers a private education "with a price a private school can't match." Pre-professional studies—business and management, communication, and engineering—are most popular here.

■ **Life** Although the days of "Zoo Mass" are reputedly over, references to this legendary style of partying abound in students' accounts of their present lives. The less-than-comfortable dorms, which house about half the student population, are sites of much "craziness" on campus: UMass's reputation as a "party school" is tenacious. The social atmosphere is welcoming ("It's a place where anybody can fit in"); fraternities and sororities are available but students say there's no pressure to join. Amherst is considered "a great college town" that offers lots of opportunities for a good time. Many prefer to stay and forge their own fun on campus, however, and the school's large scale affords students plenty of social and extracurricular opportunities. One blissful student described his social life as "better than sex in summer rain." Students agreed, however, "Opportunities don't come to you here; you've got to go out and get them yourself."

■ **Students** Over 80 percent of the students here are Massachusetts natives. 14 percent are minorities, which is a relatively small percentage, and black and Asian populations are infinitesimal. Students are generally very career- and goal-oriented, although, with over 18,000 classmates and potential friends at the four other consortium schools, most students can find others with common backgrounds without looking too hard.

UNIVERISTY OF MASSACHUSETTS AT AMHERST

Amherst, MA

Admissions

University of Massachusetts, Amherst, considers your high school curriculum and GPA the most important component of your application, followed in order of importance by standardized test scores, essays, letters of recommendation, extracurricular activities, and an optional interview. Applicants are expected to have completed four years of English, three years of math, and two years each of science, social studies/history, and a foreign language. UMass requires either the SAT or ACT. Applications are considered on a rolling basis after January 1. Applicants to UMass are often also applicants to Boston College, Boston University, University of New Hampshire, Syracuse, Northeastern, and Tufts.

Financial Aid

The financial aid office at University of Massachusetts requires applicants to submit the FAF and their parents' most recent tax returns. Non-need grants are awarded in the basis of "academic achievement, residency, field of study, or other." Students may also pay tuition on an installment plan (no interest, but a "small, non-refundable fee" is required). The school catalog lists the following loan options: Stafford, Perkins, PLUS, SLS, NELLIE MAE, MELA, TERI, and Shawmut Tuition Credit Line. The catalog also encourages students "to apply as early as possible, beginning January 1."

A note from the University of Massachusetts Admissions Office:

"The University of Massachusetts at Amherst is the largest public university in New England, offering more than 100 majors, 1,200 faculty, and a comprehensive set of campus activities and events. We house 11,000 students on campus in 50 residence halls. We are distinguished by the open diversity of our academic and social/cultural life and by the Five College Consortium, whereby students may take classes and use the facilities of our four great neighbors: Amherst, Smith, Mt. Holyoke, and Hampshire Colleges."

ADMISSIONS FACTS

Competitiveness Rating:	**69**
% of applicants accepted:	76
% acceptees attending:	30

FRESHMAN PROFILE

Average verbal SAT:	478
Average math SAT:	541
Average ACT:	NA
Graduated top 10% of class:	19
Graduated top 25% of class:	53
Graduated top 50% of class:	88

DEADLINES

Early decision/action:	NA
Early dec./adm. notif.:	NA
Regular admission:	2/15
Regular adm. notif.:	4/1

APPLICANTS ALSO LOOK AT

and often prefer:
Dartmouth College

and sometimes prefer:
U. Vermont
U. Wisconsin
Bates College
SUNY Albany

and rarely prefer:
Worcester Polytech
Boston U.
Carnegie Mellon U.

ADDRESS

Undergraduate Admissions
Admissions Center
Amherst, MA 01003
413-545-0222

FINANCIAL FACTS

In-state tuition ($):	2,052
Out-of-state tuition ($):	7,920
Room & board:	3,508
FA application deadline:	3/1
% frosh receiving FA:	70
PT earnings per yr. ($):	1,400

TYPE OF AID: % of students ($)

FA of some kind:	65 (NA)
Need-based grants:	NA
Merit-based grants:	NA
Loans:	NA
Work study:	NA
Student rating of FA:	65

MASSACHUSETTS INSTITUTE OF TECHNOLOGY
Cambridge, MA

What do students think about M.I.T.?

■ **Academics** There's an old M.I.T. joke that goes, "M.I.T. Pick two: work, friends, sleep." By all indications, work is always one of the two choices. On average, M.I.T. students put in four and a quarter hours of studying per day (only Cal Tech work harder). Not surprisingly, students here are under a lot of pressure to perform, and stress is ubiquitous. The school tries to relieve the pressure somewhat—freshmen take all courses pass/fail, and their fail grades are expunged from their records—but the prevalent attitude here was expressed by the sophomore who told us: "I heard this is a great place to go to school and when I have graduated I'm sure I'll agree, but right now, it sucks." Those who can take the pressure benefit from "the best science education in the world, beyond doubt," one supplemented by "amazing resources" and world-famous professors. The Undergraduate Research Opportunities Program (UROP) allows undergrads to earn credit doing research, thereby giving them more autonomy than their peers at most other schools. Students who venture beyond the sciences will find excellent economics, humanities, and political science departments as well. The school offers so much that the opportunities can seem a little daunting: "Getting an education from M.I.T. is like getting a drink from a firehose" is how one student put it. The most common cause for complaint (besides the workload) is the quality of in-class instruction. Explained one student, "Classes are taught at a level to challenge Nobel prizewinners, so its easy to get disillusioned and lost."

■ **Life** For many M.I.T. students, life begins and ends in the labs and libraries. "Cambridge may be great, but who has time to find out?" said one student. The word "hell" came up a distressing number of times in students' descriptions of their surroundings; it's the kind of joke that must have a lot of truth behind it. One student told us that the predominantly male population "requires girls to be bussed in from other colleges for parties. It's funny to see the 'meat trucks' come in with a new load every hour. The parties are composed mainly of dancing, beer drinking, and guys hitting on girls. It can be fun, but it leaves me searching for something more." "Meat trucks," eh? No wonder several students told us that "sexism is pretty bad here."

■ **Students** Will all your classmates at M.I.T. be nerds? More likely you'll find that there are "some pretty scary nerds here at M.I.T., but most people are pretty normal." M.I.T. students are unhappy, particularly for a group of students at one of the nation's most prestigious institutions. For many, the pressure and intensity are overwhelming; said one, "It's too easy to turn into an emotionless machine, just doing problem sets. Only three months into my college career, I am losing my humanity." Minorities make up 42 percent of the student body: M.I.T. is definitely an equal opportunity "hell." Still, when all is said and done, students keep coming here, and very few transfer out. Why subject yourself to this? Explained one student, "Everyone says they hate it and it's too hard, but it's really rewarding to attend school with the smartest people you will ever be around."

MASSACHUSETTS INSTITUTE OF TECHNOLOGY

Cambridge, MA

Admissions

Regarding admissions policy, MIT's promotional literature states that "MIT seeks a diverse, creative, and academically talented freshman class. Each student is granted admission on an individual basis: Intellect, special strengths, character, and goals all bear on the admissions decision." Applicants are required to take either the SAT or the ACT and three achievements, which must include: Math I, II, or IIC; chemistry, physics, or biology; and English composition (or American history, European history, or social studies). An "ideal, though not required" college prep curriculum should include four years of English, two or more years of social studies, math through calculus, three lab sciences, and a foreign language.

Financial Aid

The financial aid office at MIT requires applicants to submit the FAF, a form generated by the school, and their and their parents' most recent tax returns and W-2 forms. MIT does not award merit grants; all assistance is provided on the basis of need only. Last year, the average financial aid package for freshmen was $17,670, $1,220 more than the average package for all undergraduates. The school's promotional literature asserts, "If you are admitted to MIT, we will make *every attempt* to help you afford it through financial aid" (emphasis added).

A note from the M.I.T. Admissions Office:

"The students who come to the Massachusetts Institute of Technology are some of America's—and the world's—best and most creative.

"As graduates, they leave here to make real contributions—in science, technology, business, education, politics, architecture, and the arts. From any class, a handful will go on to do work that is historically significant. These young men and women are leaders, achievers, producers.

"Helping such students make the most of their talents and dreams would challenge any educational institution. MIT gives them its best advantages: a world-class faculty, unparalleled facilities, remarkable opportunities.

"In turn, these student help to make the Institute the vital place it is. They bring fresh viewpoints to faculty research: More than three quarters participate in the Undergraduate Research Opportunities Program (UROP). They play on MIT's 37 intercollegiate teams as well as in its 13 musical ensembles. To their classes and to their out-of-class activities, they bring enthusiasm, energy, and individual style."

ADMISSIONS FACTS

Competitiveness Rating:	**99**
% of applicants accepted:	32
% acceptees attending:	53

FRESHMAN PROFILE

Average verbal SAT:	625
Average math SAT:	735
Average ACT:	31
Graduated top 10% of class:	94
Graduated top 25% of class:	100
Graduated top 50% of class:	100

DEADLINES

Early decision/action:	11/1
Early dec./adm. notif.:	1/1
Regular admission:	1/1
Regular adm. notif.:	4/1

APPLICANTS ALSO LOOK AT

and sometimes prefer:

Yale U.
Harvard/Radcliffe College
Brown U.
Caltech

and rarely prefer:

U. Virginia
Columbia U.
RPI
Carnegie Mellon U.

ADDRESS

Undergraduate Admissions
77 Massachussetts Ave.
Room 4-237
Cambridge, MA 02139-4301
617-253-4791

FINANCIAL FACTS

In-state tuition ($):	16,900
Out-of-state tuition ($):	16,900
Room & board:	5,330
FA application deadline:	1/1
% frosh receiving FA:	56
PT earnings per yr. ($):	1,000

TYPE OF AID: % of students ($)

FA of some kind:	55 (16,450)
Need-based grants:	56 (10,500)
Merit-based grants:	0
Loans:	56 (3,300)
Work study:	NA
Student rating of FA:	78

MIAMI UNIVERSITY–OXFORD CAMPUS

Oxford, OH

CAMPUS LIFE

Quality of Life Rating:	**87**
Type of school:	public
Affiliation:	none
Environment:	suburban

STUDENT BODY

FT undergrad enrollment:	13,669
% male/% female:	47/53
% out-of-state:	28
% live on campus:	50
% African-American:	3
% Asian:	1
% Caucasian:	95
% Hispanic:	1
% foreign:	<1
% transfers:	2

WHAT'S HOT

food
marriage
good looking students
campus appearance
conservative politics
overall happiness
intramural sports

WHAT'S NOT

diversity
interaction among students
small labs and seminars
doing all the reading

ACADEMICS

Academic Rating:	**66**
Calendar:	semester
Student/teacher ratio:	22/1
% doctorates:	80
Profs interesting:	74
Profs accessible:	77
Hours of study per day:	2.96

MOST POPULAR MAJORS BY %

Business & Management:	23
Business and Office Admin:	16
Education:	9

What do students think about Miami University?

■ **Academics** In its more than 180 years of existence, Miami University (located in Ohio, not Florida), has cultivated and maintained its reputation as a "public Ivy League" school. Selective by state university standards, Miami of Ohio offers its students the accouterments many private school students enjoy—excellent, caring professors, and bright classmates—at a reasonable price. Many undergraduate fields of study are quite good, including the highly rated majors in business, accounting and architecture. Pre-professional programs in general are well regarded, as is the School of Interdisciplinary Studies' demanding "Western Program," which incorporates science, social science, and the humanities. Miami's public character shows itself in its large average class size, and in student complaints about the bureaucratic red tape that often plagues state institutions. Registration is a hassle here, and getting into desired classes is often difficult. Professors received good ratings from students, who praised them more for their "great accessibility" than their teaching. Academic pressure is not intense as a rule, although certain majors (accounting, pre-medical sciences) are demanding.

■ **Life** Miami University is often referred to as "Mother Miami" by students frustrated with the numerous campus regulations. One explained, "The administration seems to forget that we are adults, and tightens the reins on our freedom daily. Every incoming freshman should know that the dorms have a visitation policy, and it is strictly enforced." An additional restriction is the campus-wide no-car policy, which hinders some of the more cosmopolitan students ("The closest 'civilization' is at least 30 minutes away"). Many students love the sheltered environment and isolation, however, contending that "once you are on campus, it is hard to leave due to its incredible beauty." Located literally "in the middle of a cornfield," the campus is described as "a haven for red-bricklayers." Social life is dominated by the Greeks ("Although less than half of the students are in fraternities or sororities, the Greek system rules the school"). Off-campus socializing, popular among non-Greeks and those denied dorm rooms, centers around the "uptown" area, where most bars are found. The town of Oxford get little praise from students, who call it "a one-horse town whose horse was just shipped to Elmer's [Glue]." Intramural sports are extremely popular, "especially the hockey and broomball programs." Even the food received strong ratings, which is indicative of the high level of overall student happiness here.

■ **Students** Miami University is neither a multicultural melting pot nor a hotbed of liberal politics. Admittedly a bastion of white conservatism, Miami is "tradition-minded but tolerant of progressive ideas," according to its students. A more diverse student body would be welcome here, and the administration would love them to apply. Students agreed that "Miami offers a lot of exciting and enriching experiences behind its conservative facade."

MIAMI UNIVERSITY–OXFORD CAMPUS

Oxford, OH

Admissions

According to Miami's brochure, "Admission to Miami University is based upon high school performance (class rank, grade point average, and curriculum), test scores (ACT and/or SAT), high school experience and community activities, and recommendation of the high school. In making admission decisions, Miami also considers the diversity of the student body and applicants' special abilities, talents, and achievements. The University believes that the diversity of the student body enhances the quality of education its students receive. Therefore, diversity may include socioeconomic factors, under-enrolled minority group members, career interest, artistic ability, geographical background, and other special characteristics of the population." The expected high school curriculum includes four units of English, three units each of mathematics (including Algebra II), natural science, and social studies (including one unit of history), two units of a single foreign language, and one unit of fine arts. SAT or ACT scores are required.

Financial Aid

Financial aid applicants to Miami are required to complete the FAF and a form generated by Miami's financial aid office. Miami awards athletic scholarships (in '91–'92, 2% of all undergrads received one; the average value was $5,948) and academic scholarships (in '91–'92, 13% of all undergrads received one; the average value was $976). Other awards available include leadership, residency, and minority scholarships. The financial aid office recommends a large variety of loans, including Stafford loans to 33% of all financial aid recipients.

Excerpt from Miami University's promotional materials:

"Miami's primary concern is its students. This concern is reflected in a broad array of efforts to develop the potential of each student. The University endeavors to individualize the educational experience. It provides personal and professional guidance; and it offers opportunities for its students to achieve understanding and appreciation not only of their own culture but of the cultures of others as well. Selected undergraduate, graduate, and professional programs of quality should be offered with the expectation of students achieving a high level of competence and understanding and developing a personal value system. Since the legislation creating Miami University stated that a leading mission of the University was to promote 'good education, virtue, religion, and morality,' the University has been striving to emphasize the supreme importance of dealing with problems relating to values."

ADMISSIONS FACTS

Competitiveness Rating:	*81*
% of applicants accepted:	78
% acceptees attending:	47

FRESHMAN PROFILE

Average verbal SAT:	543*
Average math SAT:	597*
Average ACT:	27*
Graduated top 10% of class:	47
Graduated top 25% of class:	85
Graduated top 50% of class:	98

DEADLINES

Early decision/action:	11/1
Early dec./adm. notif.:	12/15
Regular admission:	1/31
Regular adm. notif.:	3/15

APPLICANTS ALSO LOOK AT

and often prefer:
Northwestern U.

and sometimes prefer:
DePauw U.
Ohio U.
Ohio State U.

and rarely prefer:
Washington U.
Indiana University

ADDRESS

Miami University
Undergraduate Admissions
Oxford, OH 45056
513-529-2531

FINANCIAL FACTS

In-state tuition ($):	3,023
Out-of-state tuition ($):	7,313
Room & board:	3,360
FA application deadline:	1/31
% frosh receiving FA:	45
PT earnings per yr. ($):	NA

TYPE OF AID: % of students ($)

FA of some kind:	42 (NA)
Need-based grants:	19 (1,975)
Merit-based grants:	NA
Loans:	20 (3,470)
Work study:	7 (1224)
Student rating of FA:	75

UNIVERSITY OF MICHIGAN

CAMPUS LIFE

Quality of Life Rating:	*83*
Type of school:	public
Affiliation:	none
Environment:	city

STUDENT BODY

FT undergrad enrollment:	21,815
% male/% female:	53/47
% out-of-state:	30
% live on campus:	40
% African-American:	7
% Asian:	8
% Caucasian:	80
% Hispanic:	3
% foreign:	1
% transfers:	3

WHAT'S HOT

rap/hip-hop
intercollegiate sports
marijuana
hard liquor
location
ethnic diversity

WHAT'S NOT

small classes (overall)
TAs teach intros
deans
attending all classes
dorm comfort
doing all the reading

ACADEMICS

Academic Rating:	*83*
Calendar:	trimester
Student/teacher ratio:	11/1
% doctorates:	93
Profs interesting:	68
Profs accessible:	73
Hours of study per day:	3.12

MOST POPULAR MAJORS BY %

Social Sciences:	21
Engineering:	15
Psychology:	9

What do students think about University of Michigan?

■ **Academics** As one student put it, "Quite simply, U of M is the quintessential state university. It has everything from the rah-rah attitude at football games to Ivy-covered buildings set in a beautiful campus." Although this respondent failed to mention them, the school also has a number of outstanding academic departments scattered among its eleven undergraduate schools. The engineering school, for example, is among the nation's most highly regarded, as is the school of business; in the arts and sciences division, political science, history, and film and video studies drew student accolades. The level of difficulty varies from program to program, but, overall, Michigan students work a little harder than the average public university student and consider their studies challenging; wrote one student, "They say life's a bitch and then you die. Well, Michigan is an all-night cramming session, and then you get a C+." As at most large universities, students are limited in their fields of study only by their imaginations, but often have a hard time finding a full professor to help them with their work. Many courses, including a good number of upper-level classes, are taught by TAs of widely varying didactic skills (complained one biology major, "TAs are often inadequate or do not have full command of the English language."). Students must also contend with long lines for everything from registration to football tickets. The students' grade for the U of M administration was slightly above average for a large school and below average for all schools in our survey; explained one student, "The administration is just bad enough to spark a protest march every once in a while. Cool!"

■ **Life** Social life at U of M has a little of something for everyone: tons of extracurricular clubs, on-campus movies, concerts, and theatrical productions, an active Greek scene, and a successful and hugely popular intercollegiate athletic program (the men's basketball and football teams are widely followed, not only on campus, but by sports fans across the country). The school also has more than a little for the student who likes to party: students reported that drinking and drug use are commonplace. For some socially conservative Midwesterners, the party atmosphere is too much to take; complained one, "U of M is obscenely humanistic. If you're from a conservative background, get ready for a massive change. If you are a moralistic person, good luck maintaining those morals." The most frequent student complaint, however, concerned the campus police: "They don't like us and most of us hate them," is how one student summed up the situation.

■ **Students** U of M has a 20 percent minority population, which, combined with its huge enrollment, means that minority students are well represented. Students reported that racial tensions exist but are "not a major problem... for now." Explained one student, "At Michigan you can be any color, have any sexual orientation, listen to any music, dress any way (hippies to suits), or practice any religion and fit somewhere into a group."

UNIVERSITY OF MICHIGAN

Ann Arbor, MI

Admissions

According to the University of Michigan's bulletin, "...admission is dependent upon a high probability of success in the chosen school or college and the availability of places. Students are encouraged to submit their applications early in the fall of their senior year." Admission requirements vary at U. of M.'s twelve undergraduate schools and colleges (only seven of which admit freshmen). In general, however, admission is selective and is based primarily on "the strength of the applicant's high school background, including the rigorousness of courses selected, the record of academic achievement, special or unique accomplishments, both in and out of the classroom, and the ACT or SAT scores." A "B" average or above in "a rigorous and appropriate college preparatory program" and "standardized test scores comparable to freshmen pursuing similar programs in the University" are expected. All students must submit scores for the SAT or ACT.

Financial Aid

Financial aid applicants to the University of Michigan must complete the FAF and a form generated by the U. of M's financial aid office, and submit a copy of their most recent tax return. Three percent of U. of M's undergrads received an academic scholarship in '90–'91; the average value was $1,120. Three percent received minority-academic scholarships (average value: $2,840) and One percent received scholarships for "special characteristics" (average value: $1,430). Twenty percent of U. Michigan's students took out Perkins loans in '91–'92 (average value: $1,215), Twenty percent took out Stafford loans ($2,125), and Five percent took out PLUS or SLS loans ($3,850).

Excerpted from University of Michigan promotional materials:

"The University of Michigan is continuing its dynamic mission into the twenty-first century—the commitment to diversity. To accomplish our goals, efforts are in place across the campus to meet the challenges of racism, community and change, while preserving the important balance between tradition and preparation for the future. As the University's more than century-old tradition of excellence serves as its foundation, progress toward building a multicultural community is occurring at all levels of the institution.

"The campus engages the participation of individuals from a wide variety of cultures in the life of the University. Students and scholars study and work closely together; the residence halls create a living community where lifelong friendships unfold. In addition, the University community and the Ann Arbor community complement one another—adding even more choices to the long list of available resources."

ADMISSIONS FACTS

Competitiveness Rating:	**88**
% of applicants accepted:	60
% acceptees attending:	44

FRESHMAN PROFILE

Average verbal SAT:	563*
Average math SAT:	630*
Average ACT:	27*
Graduated top 10% of class:	69
Graduated top 25% of class:	93
Graduated top 50% of class:	99

DEADLINES

Early decision/action:	11/15
Early dec./adm. notif.:	12/15
Regular admission:	2/1
Regular adm. notif.:	4/15

APPLICANTS ALSO LOOK AT

and often prefer:
Brown U.
U. Pennsylvania
Dartmouth College

and sometimes prefer:
Tufts U.
Brandeis U.
U. Chicago
U. Notre Dame

and rarely prefer:
Michigan State U.
Kenyon College

ADDRESS

Undergraduate Admissions
1220 Student Activities Bldg.
Ann Arbor, MI 48109-1316
313-764-7433

FINANCIAL FACTS

In-state tuition ($):	3,610
Out-of-state tuition ($):	12,718
Room & board:	3,853
FA application deadline:	2/15
% frosh receiving FA:	60
PT earnings per yr. ($):	2,880

TYPE OF AID: % of students ($)

FA of some kind:	60 (6,300)
Need-based grants:	35 (6,300)
Merit-based grants:	7 (1,970)
Loans:	30 (3,045)
Work study:	10 (1,240)
Student rating of FA:	75

MIDDLEBURY COLLEGE

Middlebury, VT

CAMPUS LIFE

Quality of Life Rating: **85**

Type of school:	private
Affiliation:	none
Environment:	suburban

STUDENT BODY

FT undergrad enrollment:	1,950
% male/% female:	50/50
% out-of-state:	86
% live on campus:	99
% African-American:	3
% Asian:	3
% Caucasian:	90
% Hispanic:	3
% foreign:	9
% transfers:	2

WHAT'S HOT

good looking students
deans
Grateful Dead
small classes (overall)
living on campus
campus appearance
profs outside class

WHAT'S NOT

dating
Top 40
religion
diverse
rap/hip-hop

ACADEMICS

Academic Rating: **87**

Calendar:	4-1-4
Student/teacher ratio:	11/1
% doctorates:	90
Profs interesting:	88
Profs accessible:	91
Hours of study per day:	3.5

MOST POPULAR MAJORS BY %

English:	16
Political Science:	13
History:	12

What do students think about Middlebury College?

■ **Academics** Some schools in New England (and in the West) attract a large number of skiing fanatics. Middlebury College attract students in that category who are also looking for a rigorous liberal arts education. Middlebury students work hard—about three and a half hours a day—and seem genuinely interested in academics for their own sake: foreign languages, English, history, theater, and other non-career-related majors are pursued vigorously here. Pre-med departments are also popular and reportedly excellent. Professors are widely regarded as excellent, especially for their willingness to provide extra help; wrote one student, "Never could I have imagined being able to find professors like these, who are so willing to help you late at night or on the weekends." Middlebury has a January semester, during which students concentrate on one course (usually in a less traditionally academic subject); students report that January is a "heavy ski period." Nearly half the undergrad population takes advantage of the school's Junior Year Abroad program.

■ **Life** Middlebury's mountain setting is "ideal for outdoor activities," particularly jogging, hiking, and skiing (the school has its own slope and lighted cross-country ski trail). Leisure options are otherwise limited; as one student put it, "Don't come to Middlebury if you're seeking an active night life; you have to make your own fun." This situation suits some students perfectly well; explained one such undergrad, "Middlebury may be remote, but our isolation promotes creative social options and terrific friendships." Popular, though not particularly creative, social venues include Greek and dorm parties, at which drinking is often the main attraction: explained one student, "Social life is great for students who drink. But for everyone else, it gets pretty boring at times." Things may soon get boring for drinkers as well; several respondents told us, "Socially, Middlebury is in a transition state. The college is trying to control much of the social life; this is evident in its attempts to abolish fraternities." Students also told us "Dating is non-existent; the closest thing you'll find to a date is going down to Mr. Up's (local watering hole) in a group. Random hook-ups or serious relationships, however, are prevalent."

■ **Students** In response to our question about the diversity of the student body, one Middlebury student responded, "Diversity? Sure! I met a guy who isn't from Boston today. But his dad is a lawyer anyway, so it didn't count." The Middlebury student body is predominantly white, upper middle-class, intelligent, and high-spirited. As one student put it, "Middlebury is not a school for the depressed, brooding, coffee-drinking smoker; it is a school for the stoned Patagonia-wearing skier/hiker. We are a happy and rich sort." Students have "a sense of balance: they work hard and play hard, are moderately physically active, and are politically middle of the road. It's a pretty easy place to be whoever you are (even though most people are pretty much alike)."

MIDDLEBURY COLLEGE

Middlebury, VT

Admissions

The admissions office reports, "Admissions at Middlebury is selective and is based upon academic ability and achievement, community citizenship and leadership, character, and personality. We use no 'cut-off' and no formulae." Middlebury judges applicants based primarily on essays, high school GPA, standardized test scores, and extracurricular activities; letters of recommendation and an optional interview are also considered. Middlebury has no firm requirements for high school curricula but does recommend a rigorous college preparatory curriculum. All applicants must submit scores for either: the SAT and three achievements (one must be English); five achievements; or, the ACT. Applicants to Middlebury most often also apply to Dartmouth, Williams, Amherst, Bowdoin, and Brown.

Financial Aid

Financial aid applicants to Middlebury must complete the FAF and a form generated by Middlebury's financial aid office, and submit a copy of their parents' most recent tax return. In '91–'92, 56% of the freshman class received an award of some kind; the average award value was $12,272. All grants are based on demonstrated financial need. Approximately 66% of undergrads had jobs on campus in '90–'91.

A note from the Middlebury College Admissions Office:

"Middlebury College is often described as an international university masquerading as a small liberal arts college in Vermont. The feeling of internationalism pervades the campus and its programs. The College includes the eight summer language schools, the Bread Loaf School of English, the Bread Loaf Writers' Conference, and undergraduate and graduate programs in Mainz, Madrid, Florence, Paris, and Moscow as well as summer programs at Oxford University and in Santa Fe, New Mexico. Prominent international visitors to the campus are made available to students, from His Holiness the Dalai Lama joining students for lunch in the dining hall, to Bill Moyers, Paul Volcker, Ted Turner, or Ralph Nader and other leaders in politics, government, economics, or literature joining in seminars or evening discussions. The American Collegiate Consortium, the Geonomics Institute and the Salzburg Seminar are three independent international programs on the edge of the campus whose programs also feed into the international character of the College. Middlebury's student body includes students from all 50 states and 60 foreign countries. Its need-blind admissions policy assures equal opportunity for those who qualify for admission."

ADMISSIONS FACTS

Competitiveness Rating:	**90**
% of applicants accepted:	40
% acceptees attending:	35

FRESHMAN PROFILE

Average verbal SAT:	603*
Average math SAT:	643*
Average ACT:	NA
Graduated top 10% of class:	61
Graduated top 25% of class:	86
Graduated top 50% of class:	99

DEADLINES

Early decision/action:	11/15
Early dec./adm. notif.:	12/15
Regular admission:	1/15
Regular adm. notif.:	4/3

APPLICANTS ALSO LOOK AT

and often prefer:
Amherst College
Princeton U.
Yale U.
Williams College
Harvard/Radcliffe College
Dartmouth College

and rarely prefer:
Hamilton College
Skidmore College
St. Lawrence U.
Bowdoin College

ADDRESS

Undergraduate Admissions
Middlebury, VT 05753
802-388-3711

FINANCIAL FACTS

In-state tuition ($):	21,200
Out-of-state tuition ($):	21,200
Room & board:	incl. above
FA application deadline:	2/1
% frosh receiving FA:	37
PT earnings per yr. ($):	NA

TYPE OF AID: % of students ($)

FA of some kind:	35 (11,919)
Need-based grants:	NA
Merit-based grants:	NA
Loans:	NA
Work study:	NA
Student rating of FA:	86

MILLSAPS COLLEGE

CAMPUS LIFE

Quality of Life Rating: **80**

Type of school:	private
Affiliation:	Methodist
Environment:	city

STUDENT BODY

FT undergrad enrollment:	1,134
% male/% female:	53/47
% out-of-state:	50
% live on campus:	70
% African-American:	4
% Asian:	2
% Caucasian:	92
% Hispanic:	1
% foreign:	1
% transfers:	6

WHAT'S HOT

fraternities/sororities
small lectures
Grateful Dead
hard liquor
profs in class
profs teach upper levels
profs teach intros
campus easy to get around

WHAT'S NOT

college radio station
college newspaper
diversity
studying hard
gay community visible
doing all the reading

ACADEMICS

Academic Rating: **76**

Calendar:	semester
Student/teacher ratio:	15/1
% doctorates:	72
Profs interesting:	90
Profs accessible:	83
Hours of study per day:	2.64

MOST POPULAR MAJORS BY %

Business & Management	31
Letters/Literature:	16
Social Sciences:	11

% GRADS WHO PURSUE

Law:	8
MBA:	5
Medicine:	10
M.A., etc.:	17

What do students think about Millsaps College?

■ **Academics** Millsaps College, once unknown outside Mississippi, now boasts a solid reputation throughout the Deep South. Its greatest assets are its fine pre-professional programs and committed faculty. Although some students complained that "Millsaps College is caught up in the lawyer-and-doctor-producing industry," most applauded their school's "rigorous academic environment," which extends to most areas of study. Standout departments are business, premedical sciences, political science, English, music, and history. Although it is possible to get through Millsaps without much strain (some undergrads claim to study very little), this approach is not advocated by the majority. Certainly the students who enroll in the interdisciplinary Heritage program (a year-long Western Civilization survey) can expect to spend a great deal of time in the library. Professors received high marks from students for teaching well and encouraging discussion. Classes are small, and faculty/student interaction is frequent and casual. One student enthused, "The professors are really cool—you often see them roaming down fraternity row with a beer in their hands on weekends." For many, this personalized, informal atmosphere is one of Millsaps' best features.

■ **Life** Millsaps students raved, "Jackson, Mississippi offers a safe, friendly environment for us to learn and party in." There is a "real sense of community" among the small student body. One woman wrote, "Everyone on this campus is super-friendly, and the small campus makes it easier to interact with other students." Participation in extracurricular activities is important; most students "utilize their chances to become involved in Greek societies, various clubs and honorary fraternities, college committees, and intercollegiate and intramural sports." Social life is ruled by the fraternities and sororities, which claim two-thirds of the students as members. Drinking is also integral: students rated the presence of hard liquor as extremely high. This reality runs counter to Millsaps' stated Methodist ideals. The official alcohol policy prohibits any drinking outside of dorm rooms, even for those of age. The general disregard for this stricture demonstrates the looseness of the college's religious ties. Students asserted that "although this is a church-affiliated school, one would not notice if s/he did not know." Although Millsaps boasts some excellent intercollegiate sports teams, athletics are far from being the focus of the campus; more popular are the wide variety of intramurals.

■ **Students** Millsaps is definitely no multicultural melting pot: the school is only four percent black. Griped one student, "The student body is almost completely made up of white, upper-middle-class Southerners." However, as the school's reputation grows, so too does its applicant pool and, it is hoped, its diversity. Students agreed that a spirit of hospitality pervades the campus. One student summed up, "If you are looking for a beautiful, friendly school and greater self-awareness, look at Millsaps College."

MILLSAPS COLLEGE

Admissions

Millsaps' undergraduate catalog states: "Applicants must furnish evidence of: 1) good moral character; 2) sound physical and mental health; 3) adequate scholastic preparation; 4) intellectual maturity." The applicant's high school record should show satisfactory completion of "at least twelve units of English, mathematics, social studies, natural sciences or foreign language. Four units of English should be included." Satisfactory results from the ACT or SAT must also be submitted. Applicants are advised to apply for admission "well in advance of the date on which they wish to enter, particularly if housing accommodations on the campus are desired."

Financial Aid

Financial aid applicants to Millsaps College must complete the FAF or FFS and a form generated by Millsaps' financial aid office, and submit a copy of their parents' most recent tax return. Last year, 68% of the class of '95 received some form of aid; the average value was $9,062. 18% of all undergrads received academic grants; the average value was $4,500. Among the scholarships available are those for minorities, leadership, academic merit and artistic talent.

A note from the Millsaps College Admissions Office:

"Your academic experience at Millsaps begins with Introduction to Liberal Studies, a comprehensive freshman experience. You will be encouraged to develop critical thinking skills, analytical reasoning and independence of thought as preparation for study in your major.

"The interdisciplinary Heritage Program offers a unique approach to the culture and development of society through lectures and small group discussions by a team of faculty who represent a cross-section of the humanities.

"Entering freshmen are primarily taught by full-time, Ph.D. professors. The close relationship between faculty and students encourages classroom participation and enables students to explore their options as they choose a major field of study. Course work in the major may begin as early as the freshman year."

ADMISSIONS FACTS

Competitiveness Rating:	**72**
% of applicants accepted:	84
% acceptees attending:	41

FRESHMAN PROFILE

Average verbal SAT:	520
Average math SAT:	550
Average ACT:	25
Graduated top 10% of class:	34
Graduated top 25% of class:	61
Graduated top 50% of class:	88

DEADLINES

Early decision/action:	NA
Early dec./adm. notif.:	NA
Regular admission:	rolling
Regular adm. notif.:	rolling

APPLICANTS ALSO LOOK AT

and often prefer:
Duke U.
Emory U.

and sometimes prefer:
Vanderbilt U.
Tulane U.
Rhodes College

and rarely prefer:
Hendrix College

ADDRESS

Undergraduate Admissions
1701 North State Street
Jackson, MS 39210
601-974-1050

FINANCIAL FACTS

In-state tuition ($):	9,510
Out-of-state tuition ($):	9,510
Room & board:	3,635
FA application deadline:	3/1
% frosh receiving FA:	68
PT earnings per yr. ($):	600

TYPE OF AID: % of students ($)

FA of some kind:	64 (7,702)
Need-based grants:	64 (5,028)
Merit-based grants:	NA
Loans:	48 (4,000)
Work study:	30 (1,000)
Student rating of FA:	85

UNIVERSITY OF MINNESOTA

CAMPUS LIFE

Quality of Life Rating:	**70**
Type of school:	public
Affiliation:	none
Environment:	city

STUDENT BODY

FT undergrad enrollment:	27,076
% male/% female:	51/49
% out-of-state:	10
% live on campus:	10
% African-American:	3
% Asian:	5
% Caucasian:	85
% Hispanic:	1
% foreign:	2
% transfers:	1

WHAT'S HOT

working a job
suitcase syndrome
leftist politics
profs lecture a lot

WHAT'S NOT

living on campus
deans
campus easy to get around
administration (overall)
profs outside class
overall happiness
catalog
prof's in-class discussion
intramural sports
college theater groups

ACADEMICS

Academic Rating:	**77**
Calendar:	quarterly
Student/teacher ratio:	8/1
% doctorates:	90
Profs interesting:	69
Profs accessible:	61
Hours of study per day:	2.98

MOST POPULAR MAJORS BY %

Science Technologies:	16
Engineering:	12
Business & Management:	10

% GRADS WHO PURSUE

Law:	6
MBA:	5
Medicine:	4
M.A., etc.:	28

What do students think about the University of Minnesota?

■ **Academics** University of Minnesota/Twin Cities is not for everyone (although it's almost big enough to be); if you need a lot of direction and attention, this is not the place for you. "The U," as it is known to its students, "is a great place to get lost." More than 27,000 full-time undergrads, and 41,000+ students overall, populate the two main campuses (St. Paul for students of forestry and agriculture, Minneapolis for just about everything else). You will not meet most of your classmates; you even may not see some of your profs in the flesh, since certain intro classes have up to 500 students and are delivered via television monitors. The upside of the U's enormity is that you can study just about anything you want. If you don't like any of the more than 100 majors offered here, you can even design your own. Most students opt for career-track majors like business and management, journalism, psychology, and engineering. Said one student, "Every instructor is a specialist in his subfield, and the selection of upper division courses is excellent." Another accurately summed up the UMTC academic experience this way: "This is a professional school. You can work hard and have a good time both. If you want to excel here, get lots of advice and never stop asking questions." As is often the case at large universities, students consider most administrative procedures—registration, bill-paying, and dealing with any problems or errors—to be a major hassle. Complained one, "You get a different answer to any one question by going from office to office. No one is sure what the policy or procedures are." Tuition has increased sharply in recent years while services have gotten worse—a common malady of state-funded universities—and as a result, many students have bad feelings about the place.

■ **Life** UMTC is a commuter school; only about 3000 students live on campus. The campus is peppered with comfortable student unions; for those interested, there are close to 500 campus organizations in which to get involved. The main campus is located in Minneapolis, one of America's "alternative rock" capitals, and students often avail themselves of the hopping nightclub scene. As one student put it, "There's always something going on here." Needless to say, it gets very cold during the winter.

■ **Students** Students are mostly white, mostly Minnesotan. The average UMTC student fits the "ethical humanist" mold, but, hey, with 40,000 students you can find everybody from Marxists to John Birchers. Said one student, "Although the catalog claims diversity in the state university system, the majority of students at this campus are white, of Scandinavian-German descent. I'm not sure if [this homogeneity is] because the school is less academically rewarding than others or because it's so damn cold here."

UNIVERSITY OF MINNESOTA

Minneapolis, MN

Admissions

Applicants to the University of Minnesota/Twin Cities are expected to have completed four units of English, three units each of mathematics and science, and two units each of foreign language and lab science. Certain majors demand a more rigorous record, particularly in the areas of math and science. The ACT is not required, but it is strongly recommended. Applicants are judged on high school course achievement (class rank and GPA) and their standardized test scores. These are combined to make an admissions index; other factors which may come under consideration are high school curriculum, minority status, and special talents or activities.

Financial Aid

Financial aid applicants to the University of Minnesota/Twin Cities must complete the FFS. The financial aid office writes that there are thousands of jobs open to undergrads, both on- and off-campus. The average award value for the class of '95 was $4,748. Undergrads received athletic scholarships (average value: $5,770) and merit scholarships (average value: $1,283). U. of Minnesota offers its own institutional loans (average value last year: $1,088). The average value of Federal and State loans taken out by undergrads was $3,216.

Excerpted from University of Minnesota promotional materials:

The University of Minnesota is. . .

"**Empowering.** Offering you boundless opportunities to realize your potential. Opportunities to make important decisions about your future, to take charge of your life. Education for adulthood.

"**Diverse.** Bringing together thousands of people from all over the world into a multicultural, international learning community. Education in an environment that will expand your world. Where you can find your own community, speak your own language, be among friends—whoever you are.

"**Prestigious.** Carrying on a tradition of high distinction and leadership in scholarship, research, academic excellence, and commitment to the personal and intellectual growth of students. Education that matters. A degree that you can be really proud of.

"**Magnetic.** Providing a high-powered, high-energy environment for dynamic sharing of ideas—with room for quiet reflection. Education that will stretch your imagination and take you to the boundaries of knowledge and beyond.

"**Responsive.** Meeting your needs with services and resources that provide both academic and personal guidance and support. Helping you feel connected, nourished. Education with a heart."

ADMISSIONS FACTS

Competitiveness Rating:	**66**
% of applicants accepted:	69
% acceptees attending:	50

FRESHMAN PROFILE

Average verbal SAT:	483
Average math SAT:	560
Average ACT:	24
Graduated top 10% of class:	27
Graduated top 25% of class:	27
Graduated top 50% of class:	81

DEADLINES

Early decision/action:	NA
Early dec./adm. notif.:	NA
Regular admission:	rolling
Regular adm. notif.:	rolling

APPLICANTS ALSO LOOK AT

and often prefer:
St. Olaf College
Iowa State U.

and rarely prefer:
U. Wisconsin–Madison
U. Iowa
Case Western Reserve U.
Syracuse U.
U. Michigan
Michigan State U.

ADDRESS

Undergraduate Admissions
231 Pillsbury Pr. S.E.
Minneapolis, MN 55455
612-625-2008

FINANCIAL FACTS

In-state tuition ($):	3,400
Out-of-state tuition ($):	8,000
Room & board:	3,400
FA application deadline:	None
% frosh receiving FA:	41
PT earnings per yr. ($):	NA

TYPE OF AID: % of students ($)

FA of some kind:	43 (4,200)
Need-based grants:	35 (6,300)
Merit-based grants:	NA
Loans:	NA
Work study:	NA (2,944)
Student rating of FA:	71

UNIVERSITY OF MISSOURI–ROLLA

Rolla, MO

CAMPUS LIFE

Quality of Life Rating:	**72**
Type of school:	public
Affiliation:	none
Environment:	suburban

STUDENT BODY

FT undergrad enrollment:	3,588
% male/% female:	79/21
% out-of-state:	16
% live on campus:	20
% African-American:	4
% Asian:	4
% Caucasian:	83
% Hispanic:	1
% foreign:	3
% transfers:	6

WHAT'S HOT

studying hard
attending all classes
doing all the reading
caring about politics
suitcase syndrome
college radio station
conservative politics

WHAT'S NOT

gay community visible
marijuana
intercollegiate sports
requirements easy
college theater groups
location

ACADEMICS

Academic Rating:	**79**
Calendar:	semester
Student/teacher ratio:	15/1
% doctorates:	91
Profs interesting:	71
Profs accessible:	74
Hours of study per day:	4.04

MOST POPULAR MAJORS BY %

Engineering:	83
Computer & Info. Sciences:	7
Social Sciences:	4

% GRADS WHO PURSUE

Law:	NA
MBA:	NA
Medicine:	NA
M.A., etc.:	30

What do students think about the U. of Missouri, Rolla?

■ **Academics** University of Missouri, Rolla offers a fine engineering education at public school prices. Over 80 percent of the students pursue studies in more than a dozen engineering fields, the most popular of which are electrical, mechanical, and physical. Chemical, civil, and aerospace engineering are among the school's other drawing cards. The program is competitive: "cut" classes (which must be completed for students to proceed to the next level of study) are common and difficult, particularly in the electrical engineering program. Surprisingly, students saved their nicest compliments for their liberal arts instructors. "The English professors are intelligent, well-educated, and determined to provide students with a wide range of literary educational experiences. Unfortunately, the English department is overlooked by those who would classify UMR as a technological university," wrote one engineer. Students also were highly complimentary of the computer science department. As is often the case at engineering schools, most students here work extremely hard and many professors are ineloquent teachers. "This university is more interested in research than in educating the students," complained one student. Remember, however, that this sentiment is common at many private engineering institutions that cost four times as much to attend.

■ **Life** Most Rolla students are engineers, and accordingly, they study almost incessantly—over four hours a day, on average. They do *occasionally* find the time to party, however. One wrote that "during the week, students need to bury their heads in the book, or else they will not make it. But on the weekends there are always plenty of parties." Men outnumber women four to one here, leading one student to explain, "Students would date frequently if they had somewhere to go and someone to go there with." Social opportunities in the town of Rolla consist of "movies, a bowling alley, a couple of bars and campus parties." Not surprisingly, many students go home over the weekend. A student group called the St. Patrick's Board used to plan a Spring blow-out party, but whether this will continue is currently in dispute. One student reported, "Due to recent alcohol-related incidents, our one big party time, St. Patrick's weekend, has lost the recognition and support of the university. The St. Patrick's Board is no more. But, St. Patrick is the patron saint of engineers, therefore the students will still hold onto the tradition strongly and we look forward to this rite of spring, to taking a break from out studies and letting it all hang out." We'll see.

■ **Students** Most students at Rolla are from in-state, and a sizeable number come from the St. Louis area. The student body is predominantly white, male, and conservative. Wrote one student, "This school is pretty midwestern and pretty conservative, and I think the administration would like to keep it that way." One student bragged, "My classmates seems unusually bright and motivated for those at a medium-sized public university. The credentials and abilities of the student body are reminiscent of those of a much more selective institution."

UNIVERSITY OF MISSOURI–ROLLA

Rolla, MO

Admissions

Applicants for admission to the University of Missouri, Rolla are required to take either the SAT or the ACT. The following high school curriculum is required of all applicants: four units of English; three units of mathematics (Algebra I and two higher level classes); two units of science (one of which must be a lab science); two units of social studies; one unit of fine arts; and three additional units of academic electives (it is "strongly recommended" that two units of a foreign language be included in these). The application does not include letters of recommendation or an essay question.

FinancialAid

The financial aid office at University of Missouri, Rolla requires applicants to submit the FFS, and *may* request your parents' most recent tax return and a "verification form." The school awards scholarships to athletes (in 1991–92, 4% of the students got one; average value: $1,717) and to those who have previously demonstrated academic excellence (32%; $1,969). Last year, Rolla recommended Stafford loans for 335 of its financial aid recipients; it also recommended PLUS/SLS and "income contingent" loans for those needing them.

A note from the University of Missouri–Rolla Admissions Office:

"The University of Missouri–Rolla, Missouri's Technological University, is an institution of excitement and challenge. Whatever field you choose (engineering, math, science, humanities or social sciences), as a student at UMR, you are among the chosen few. You will be expected to become a leader in your chosen field as well as in the world around you, and UMR gives you the tools to do that.

"Leaders learn from leaders, and at UMR you will receive personal attention from outstanding faculty members who are themselves leaders in their fields. Classes are small and professors are available if you have any questions.

"Campus life is fun, rewarding and fulfilling. Friendships are easy to develop and will be longlasting. You share a common interest with those around you and there always will be an avenue of discussion."

ADMISSIONS FACTS

Competitiveness Rating:	**75**
% of applicants accepted:	99
% acceptees attending:	49

FRESHMAN PROFILE

Average verbal SAT:	NA
Average math SAT:	NA
Average ACT:	26
Graduated top 10% of class:	44
Graduated top 25% of class:	72
Graduated top 50% of class:	93

DEADLINES

Early decision/action:	NA
Early dec./adm. notif.:	NA
Regular admission:	7/1
Regular adm. notif.:	rolling

APPLICANTS ALSO LOOK AT

and often prefer:
U. Wisconsin–Madison
U. Iowa

and sometimes prefer:
Georgia Tech

and rarely prefer:
Purdue U.

ADDRESS

Undergraduate Admissions
Rolla, MO 65401
314-341-4164

FINANCIAL FACTS

In-state tuition ($):	1,905
Out-of-state tuition ($):	5,703
Room & board:	3,370
FA application deadline:	3/31
% frosh receiving FA:	65
PT earnings per yr. ($):	1,250

TYPE OF AID: % of students ($)

FA of some kind:	60 (NA)
Need-based grants:	27 (1,555)
Merit-based grants:	NA
Loans:	NA (1,550)
Work study:	7 (1,030)
Student rating of FA:	81

MOREHOUSE COLLEGE

Atlanta, GA

CAMPUS LIFE

Quality of Life Rating: **74**

Type of school:	private
Affiliation:	none
Environment:	city

STUDENT BODY

FT undergrad enrollment:	2,582
% male/% female:	100/0
% out-of-state:	78
% live on campus:	55
% African-American:	98
% Asian:	<1
% Caucasian:	<1
% Hispanic:	<1
% foreign:	2
% transfers:	4

WHAT'S HOT

rap/hip-hop
dating
religion
doing reading
leftist politics
location
caring about politics
profs in class

WHAT'S NOT

library
diversity
gay community accepted
beer
administration (overall)

ACADEMICS

Academic Rating: **73**

Calendar:	semester
Student/teacher ratio:	17/1
% doctorates:	71
Profs interesting:	88
Profs accessible:	72
Hours of study per day:	3.53

MOST POPULAR MAJORS BY %

Biology:	11
Engineering:	10
Political Science:	9

% GRADS WHO PURSUE

Law:	6
MBA:	10
Medicine:	14
M.A., etc.:	22

What do students think about Morehouse College?

■ **Academics** Morehouse College, an all-male, (nearly) all-black college in Atlanta, boasts a distinguished list of alumni: Martin Luther King, Julian Bond, Spike Lee, and Leroy Bennett are just some of the school's graduates. Ironically, this impressive list tends to overshadow Morehouse's current achievements. Most people know Morehouse only as "the school King attended." In fact, Morehouse continues to produce the nation's and black community's potential leaders: half of all recent Morehouse graduates went on to pursue a graduate degree. Career-oriented study is the predominant focus of the student body: business and management, pre-medical sciences, engineering, and pre-law studies claim well over half the students. No student, however, can escape Morehouse without a well-rounded liberal arts, sciences, and ethnic studies background: the school's core curriculum, which takes two full years to complete, covers all these subjects. Because Morehouse is a member of the Atlanta University Center, a consortium of seven predominantly black schools, students have a wide variety of course offerings to choose from. Students reported that their professors are excellent teachers but do not always make themselves readily available outside the classroom. Wrote one student, "This school requires a dedication on the part of the student in order to work closely with the faculty." They also complained that administrative chores are unnecessarily difficult. Explained one undergrad, "A word my college should become more familiar with is *organization*!" While recognizing these problems, though, students reported satisfaction with Morehouse. Concluded one student, "there is a true spirit of pride which flows through here. The school's positive effects can be seen in the attitudes of students and faculty. This school teaches you to know yourself."

■ **Life** Students report that their historic campus has seen better days. The campus is currently undergoing renovations, but its current state led one student to comment, "Morehouse is by no means a country club." Even though it is nominally a single-sex school, Morehouse classes are open to all students in the Atlanta University Center, and Morehouse students frequently take classes at the all-women's Spelman College. As a result, social life here is much more lively than at most single-sex institutions. Greek life is popular—too popular, some would claim (see *School Daze*, the film Spike Lee based on his experiences at Morehouse for more information). Atlanta is popular with all its college students, and Morehouse is no exception.

■ **Students** Morehouse draws students from all over the country. Outside the South, the Eastern Seaboard is the most prolific source of Morehouse undergrads. Students are politically progressive but also fairly religious, and therefore socially a little conservative. The typical Morehouse attitude is summed up by the student who wrote "adversity builds character and the hotter the fire, the tougher the steel. If you come to Morehouse, you will either become a man or you will leave, plain and simple."

MOREHOUSE COLLEGE

Admissions

The admissions office at Morehouse provides the following profile of the '91–'92 freshman class: A mean high school GPA of 3.0, mean SAT scores of 480V and 520M, and a mean ACT score of 23. The class represents 40 states and ten foreign countries. Half of the college's current undergraduates (all four years) have graduated in the top 20 percent of their respective high school classes. The admissions committee at Morehouse first looks at your high school GPA, followed by your standardized test scores. After these, in order of importance, come your essays, extracurriculars, letters of recommendation, and interview. All applicants must submit an SAT or ACT score (the SAT is preferred). Applicants should also have completed four units of English, three units of math, two units of natural sciences, and two units of social sciences. Students who apply to Morehouse most often also apply to Howard U., Georgia Tech, U. of Georgia, Hampton U., and U. Maryland/College Park.

Financial Aid

Morehouse College requires only a FAF of its financial aid applicants. Last year the school awarded academic scholarships to 13% of its undergrads, with an average award value of $6,045. These awards are generally made during the admissions process; students must complete FAFs to receive their awards. Talent grants were awarded to 6% of the '91–'92 undergrads, with an average value of $3,726. Morehouse's FA office recommended Stafford loans to 48% of '91–'92 undergrads (average value: $2,892), SLS loans to 5% ($3,666), and Perkins loans to 4% ($1,260). The 4/1/93 deadline is an "in-office" deadline.

A note from the Morehouse College Admissions Office:

"Morehouse College is the nation's only predominantly black, all-male, four-year liberal arts college. It is an independent institution located on a 45-acre campus in Atlanta, Georgia.

"The college was founded in 1867 as the Augusta Institute in Augusta, Georgia, The college was relocated to Atlanta in 1879 as the Atlanta Baptist College and was renamed Morehouse College in 1913.

"Morehouse is committed to educating and developing strong black leaders who will be dedicated to addressing the problems of society. The Morehouse education is designed to serve the three basic aspects of a well-rounded man: the personal, the social, and the professional."

ADMISSIONS FACTS

Competitiveness Rating:	**76**
% of applicants accepted:	43
% acceptees attending:	47

FRESHMAN PROFILE

Average verbal SAT:	450
Average math SAT:	530
Average ACT:	21
Graduated top 10% of class:	35
Graduated top 25% of class:	43
Graduated top 50% of class:	99

DEADLINES

Early decision/action:	10/15
Early dec./adm. notif.:	NA
Regular admission:	2/15
Regular adm. notif.:	4/1

APPLICANTS ALSO LOOK AT

and often prefer:
Georgia Tech

and sometimes prefer:
Fisk College
Clark College
U. Maryland–College Park
Emory U.
U. Georgia
Hampton U.

and rarely prefer:
Howard U.

ADDRESS

Undergraduate Admissions
830 Westview Dr. S.W.
Atlanta, GA 30314
404-215-2632

FINANCIAL FACTS

In-state tuition ($):	5,800
Out-of-state tuition ($):	5,800
Room & board:	4,734
FA application deadline:	4/1
% frosh receiving FA:	70
PT earnings per yr. ($):	1,500

TYPE OF AID: % of students ($)

FA of some kind:	77 (6,337)
Need-based grants:	NA
Merit-based grants:	NA
Loans:	NA
Work study:	14 (1,555)
Student rating of FA:	74

MOUNT HOLYOKE COLLEGE

South Hadley, MA

What do students think about Mount Holyoke College?

■ **Academics** Wrote one Mount Holyoke senior, "When I started applying to colleges, I never assumed I'd be at a women's school, but now I wouldn't trade my experience for the world." Such attitude readjustments are not unusual at Mount Holyoke, the nation's first all-women's college and still one of its most academically challenging and rewarding. Students here enjoy "great and very approachable" professors, a "nurturing and supportive atmosphere," and a gorgeous New England campus. Best of all, Mount Holyoke students agree that their school is a "uniquely challenging" place where "permanent self-confidence and unyielding motivation" are instilled from day one. Opportunities abound to study a wide variety of excellent liberal arts courses in very small classes. Life sciences departments, while small, are also effective enough to send five percent of MHC graduates on to medical school. In general, students here work extremely hard, take their course work very seriously and feel the tough workload rewards them by providing focus. "If you didn't know where you were going when you came, you sure do when you leave!" MHC women are also the nation's second happiest all-female student body (Sweet Briar is number one).

■ **Life** Most Mount Holyoke students love the sense of family they get here: one recalled, "From the first moment…the atmosphere was warm and homey. I felt like I was being baked by Betty Crocker." The all-female environment is a huge plus for many, but takes a little getting used to. Reported one student, "Freshman year I couldn't wait to transfer—by senior year I didn't want to graduate." After making the adjustment to single-sex life, students find intimacy and support plentiful. The college "gives you pure friendship minus the competition for most beautiful/skinniest/most attractive to guys." And of course, "if you want to see men you can just hop on the five-college bus and go to another college." Mount Holyoke is a member of the Five College Consortium, which also includes UMass-Amherst, Smith, Amherst, and Hampshire. Still, the Mount Holyoke way of life isn't for everyone. There "aren't many parties on campus, because of the no-keg rule." While many believe that "by working at your social life you get practice for the real world" and are proud that life does not revolve around parties, drinking, drugs, or boys, others wish the place were more lively. One mourned, "The weekends on campus consist of laundry and *Saturday Night Live*. I suppose that is why there is a transfer club in my dorm (a collection of students determined to escape). I am one of them." Students strongly recommend bringing a car if you can.

■ **Students** Mount Holyoke claims a relatively diverse student body (about 20 percent of the students are minorities), and interaction between everyone is frequent and casual. There are "not as many lesbians as people think. They're very vocal because they can 'get away with it'—that is, not be harassed." Most students here are quite liberal and accepting of the gay community.

MOUNT HOLYOKE COLLEGE

South Hadley, MA

Admissions

Mount Holyoke's most recent catalog reports, "Greatest weight in [admissions decisions] is almost always given to the school record and evaluations, but all information, including test results, special talents, particular goals, and evidence of determination, is studied carefully." The school also notes, "In order to make the college a more truly multiracial community, students from minority groups have been actively sought for a number of years." Applicants must take either (1) the SAT and three achievement tests, or (2) the SAT and the ACT. A personal interview is required. Applicants are expected to have completed the following high school curriculum: four years of English and foreign language; "at least" three years of math and laboratory science; one year of world history; and, courses providing the applicant with "a thorough grounding" in U.S. history. The school has two rounds of early decision admissions; the deadline for the first is November 15, for the second, January 15.

Financial Aid

The financial aid office at Mt. Holyoke requires applicants to submit the FAF, a form generated by the school, and a copy of their and their parents' most recent income tax return. The school awards scholarships on the basis of need only. Last year, almost 65 percent of the students here received some form of financial aid. Seventy-five percent of that aid was awarded in grant form; 17 percent came in the form of loans; and the rest represents money earned by students at work-study and school-funded jobs. Last year, students borrowed Stafford, Perkins, and college-sponsored loans. Needy students may also pay their tuition on an installment plan with no interest accrued (a $70 administrative fee is charged, however).

Excerpted from Mount Holyoke College promotional materials:

"Mount Holyoke's liberal tradition is strengthened by its special commitment to women. This is a time of great testing for women, opportunities for work and experience are vastly increased but real restraints, whether of attitude or of conflicting responsibilities, remain. In a sense every Mount Holyoke woman is a pioneer today, for each is charting new directions in circumstances radically altered from past expectations. As a community dedicated to the education of women, Mount Holyoke creates a sense of continuity and comradeship which adds immeasurably to the confidence and resolve of its students."

ADMISSIONS FACTS

Competitiveness Rating:	**82**
% of applicants accepted:	61
% acceptees attending:	40

FRESHMAN PROFILE

Average verbal SAT:	NA
Average math SAT:	NA
Average ACT:	NA
Graduated top 10% of class:	47
Graduated top 25% of class:	79
Graduated top 50% of class:	97

DEADLINES

Early decision/action:	11/15
Early dec./adm. notif.:	12/15
Regular admission:	2/1
Regular adm. notif.:	4/15

APPLICANTS ALSO LOOK AT

and often prefer:
Dartmouth College

and sometimes prefer:
Wellesley College
Smith College

and rarely prefer:
Skidmore College
U. Mass–Amherst

ADDRESS

Undergraduate Admissions
College Street
South Hadley, MA 01075
413-538-2023

FINANCIAL FACTS

In-state tuition ($):	15,950
Out-of-state tuition ($):	15,950
Room & board:	4,900
FA application deadline:	3/1
% frosh receiving FA:	51
PT earnings per yr. ($):	1,300

TYPE OF AID: % of students ($)

FA of some kind:	60 (NA)
Need-based grants:	NA
Merit-based grants:	0
Loans:	NA
Work study:	NA
Student rating of FA:	97

MUHLENBERG COLLEGE

Allentown, PA

CAMPUS LIFE

Quality of Life Rating: **79**

Type of school:	private
Affiliation:	Lutheran
Environment:	city

STUDENT BODY

FT undergrad enrollment:	1,610
% male/% female:	49/51
% out-of-state:	65
% live on campus:	96
% African-American:	2
% Asian:	5
% Caucasian:	89
% Hispanic:	1
% foreign:	2
% transfers:	2

WHAT'S HOT

campus easy to get around
Top 40
profs teach upper-level courses
Grateful Dead
cost of living
fraternities/sororities
living on campus

WHAT'S NOT

gay community visible
diversity
food
overall happiness

ACADEMICS

Academic Rating: **80**

Calendar:	semester
Student/teacher ratio:	11/1
% doctorates:	81
Profs interesting:	81
Profs accessible:	86
Hours of study per day:	3.02

MOST POPULAR MAJORS BY %

Biology:	12
Psychology:	10
English:	8

% GRADS WHO PURSUE

Law:	8
MBA:	2
Medicine:	12
M.A., etc.:	14

What do students think about Muhlenberg College?

■ **Academics** Given that almost one third of Muhlenberg's small student body pursues business and management majors, one could be forgiven for assuming that business is the only major-league discipline at this school. And, while Muhlenberg's business departments are highly regarded, even more noteworthy (given the school's size) are its life sciences departments and the results they generate: one in every eight Muhlenberg College students proceeds on to medical school. Not surprisingly, several students remarked that "Classes are difficult; there are no easy ones." Besides the rigorous major requirements, Muhlenberg students must also complete a battery of liberal arts-oriented distribution requirements designed to guarantee that the largely pre-professional students here get well-rounded educations. Students reported that the school's size is to their benefit academically ("It is very small, and I like that, because all members of the faculty are extraordinarily accessible"), but that it has a detrimental impact on social life (see "Life," below).

■ **Life** Social life at Muhlenberg can be summed up in two words: fraternity parties. Wrote one student, "The social scene is redundant because all there is to do is go to Greek parties. The student body is too apathetic to come up with innovative and fun activities." Another said simply, "If you don't go Greek, you're a leper." To make matters worse, the administration has recently taken to pressuring the fraternities and sororities into curtailing drinking at their houses. Complained one student, "Fraternities have become more restricted and have to fear for their every move. Let us have a good time while we're still young!" Students describe the atmosphere on campus as friendly—"We are all very close and it's like we are family," gushed one student. Another warned of the flip-side of all that closeness, saying "everyone here knows who you are, what you do and who with." Several students noted that life gets very routine, and one recommended spending junior year abroad because "you'll go suicidally crazy with boredom otherwise." Hometown Allentown received poor grades. "It's a boring hellhole," offered one student, while another described it as "scungy."

■ **Students** Diversity is not one of Muhlenberg's strong suits. There are approximately 100 Asians, 40 blacks, 40 Arabs, and a lot of whites. One student who described himself as "very happy" at Muhlenberg admitted, "We are a homogeneous group. It's just the type of place that you either love or don't." Those who don't usually complain that students are overly conformist. "People here are afraid to look or act differently out of fear of not being accepted," reported one. Not looking different means "dressing like a J. Crew model." Explained another student, "Most people here are wealthy, Republican, apathetic, and snobby."

MUHLENBERG COLLEGE

Admissions

According to the admissions office, "Muhlenberg uses no formulas or cut-offs. The Admissions Counselors read every student's file thoroughly and carefully. We consider all aspects of each student's application including, but not limited to, secondary school record, standardized test scores, extra-curricular activities, teacher recommendations, essay, and the personal interview (not required but highly recommended)." Applicants are required to have completed four years of English, two years of a foreign language, three years of mathematics, two years of science, and two years of history. Applicants must also submit scores for either the SAT or the ACT and achievement tests (English Composition and Math I or II are required). Applicants to Muhlenberg are frequently also applicants to Franklin and Marshall, Gettysburg, Dickinson, Lafayette, Bucknell, and Lehigh.

Financial Aid

Financial aid applicants to Muhlenberg must complete a form generated by its financial aid office and the FAF, and submit a copy of their parents' tax forms. Transcripts for financial aid at each prior institution must also be submitted. Scholarships available include awards for academic performance ($2,000–$7,000) and for dependents of Lutheran pastors (up to one half of tuition). Muhlenberg recommends Stafford, Perkins, PHEAA, HELP, and PLUS loans.

A note from the Muhlenberg Admissions Office:

"Listening to our own students, we've learned that most of them picked Muhlenberg mainly because it has a long-standing reputation for being academically challenging on the one hand, but personally supportive on the other. There's no better reason. And the fact that, as juniors and seniors, they still believe Muhlenberg lives up to that reputation means that it's real. Said one senior, 'It's a very personal atmosphere.' Another added, 'I wasn't a number, I was a person.' It's true. We expect a lot from our students, but we also expect a lot from ourselves. Muhlenberg offers majors in 36 fields; the opportunity for self-designed majors and study abroad; preprofessional programs in law, medicine, education, and the ministry; and combined-degree programs with Duke, Penn, Columbia, and Washington Universities. About one third of our graduates go on immediately to graduate or professional school—many in law or medicine. Other alumni are working for such diverse organizations as AT&T, CBS, Chase Manhattan Bank, Citibank, Dun and Bradstreet, Dell Publishing, Exxon, Greenpeace, Hershey Medical Center, Hoffman LaRoche, IBM, Merrill Lynch, Peat Marwick & Mitchell, Rodale Press, and Xerox."

ADMISSIONS FACTS

Competitiveness Rating:	**79**
% of applicants accepted:	60
% acceptees attending:	29

FRESHMAN PROFILE

Average verbal SAT:	516
Average math SAT:	578
Average ACT:	25
Graduated top 10% of class:	36
Graduated top 25% of class:	71
Graduated top 50% of class:	97

DEADLINES

Early decision/action:	1/15
Early dec./adm. notif.:	2/1
Regular admission:	2/15
Regular adm. notif.:	4/1

APPLICANTS ALSO LOOK AT

and often prefer:
Skidmore College

and sometimes prefer:
Franklin & Marshall College
Bucknell U.
Lafayette College
Gettysburg College
Villanova U.
Lehigh U.

and rarely prefer:
Penn State U.
Susquehanna U.

ADDRESS

Undergraduate Admissions
2400 West Chew Street
Allentown, PA 18104-5586
215-821-3200

FINANCIAL FACTS

In-state tuition ($):	15,115
Out-of-state tuition ($):	15,115
Room & board:	4,260
FA application deadline:	2/15
% frosh receiving FA:	54
PT earnings per yr. ($):	1,000

TYPE OF AID:	% of students ($)
FA of some kind:	52 (NA)
Need-based grants:	NA
Merit-based grants:	NA
Loans:	NA
Work study:	NA
Student rating of FA:	86

New College of the University of South Florida

Sarasota, FL

CAMPUS LIFE

Quality of Life Rating:	**81**
Type of school:	public
Affiliation:	none
Environment:	suburban

STUDENT BODY

FT undergrad enrollment:	520
% male/% female:	48/52
% out-of-state:	48
% live on campus:	52
% African-American:	2
% Asian:	4
% Caucasian:	88
% Hispanic:	3
% foreign:	3
% transfers:	34

WHAT'S HOT

gay community accepted
marijuana
interaction
leftist politics
dorm comfort
alternative rock
small classes (overall)
Grateful Dead
in-class discussion
caring about politics
doing reading
profs in class

WHAT'S NOT

intercollegiate sports
fraternities/sororities

ACADEMICS

Academic Rating:	**85**
Calendar:	semester
Student/teacher ratio:	10/1
% doctorates:	98
Profs interesting:	90
Profs accessible:	88
Hours of study per day:	3.52

MOST POPULAR MAJORS BY %

Psychology:	20
Biology:	15
Literature:	15

What do students think about New College?

■ **Academics** As one student wrote, "New College is a world unto itself: an eclectic student body, a gifted faculty, an intimate and intense academic atmosphere…and all this at a bargain price in the beautiful Florida sunshine." Indeed, New College offers an intimate, 'private' education at public school prices. The tiny, bright student body, combined with NC's excellent faculty and unique "contract" system ("Instead of grades, each student receives a written evaluation in class, along with a pass/fail specification"), makes for a program particularly attractive to the self-motivated. The academic system is "based on student initiative and flexibility; it requires self-reliance and individuality" in order to achieve success. Distribution requirements, and structure in general, are minimal. Many find the lack of guidelines unsettling (hence the relatively high number of non-returning sophomores); so, as many warned, "Don't buy without a test drive (i.e., visit the school before deciding)." Professors were widely praised for their exceptional teaching skills and accessibility. Because the NC system is personalized, academic competition is rare, and as an added bonus, bureaucratic hassles are few. For the student seeking an individualized college experience in the company of a few hundred self-proclaimed "mavericks and rebels," NC could be perfect.

■ **Life** The social scene at New College is as self-directed as the intellectual one ("You are the sole one responsible for your own fun"). There is little interaction with giant USF—New Collegians prefer their own intimate surroundings. Dorms are modern, comfortable, and safe as a rule, but demand exceeds supply. Many students opt to live off campus, where apartments are cheap and plentiful. Typical collegiate activities such as varsity sports and frat parties are nowhere to be found at NC; more common pastimes include casual, open gatherings (featuring lots of music and marijuana) and political debates over coffee. However, some students complained that the administration's recent "crackdown on noise" has all but eliminated the popular outdoor soirees. A drug scene does exist, but peer pressure is virtually nil. One student reported, "Acid and pot are tolerated, and in fact, tolerance as a whole is worshipped as an ideal." The relaxed attitude prevalent here is considered "kooky" by some, but in general students enjoy New College's cozy, unconventional atmosphere.

■ **Students** The diversity of NC is best summed up by the student who wrote, "I know a 14-year-old student and a 32-year-old student, one who studied classical Indian music with a master in India, one who played and traveled with a rock band, one who wants to be an orthodox Jewish rabbi, and one who is now off training for the Olympic handball team." Students are politically liberal as a rule, and commitment to world issues is intense. Alternative lifestyles abound ("Gays, socialists, bisexuals, and anarchists are common"). Students who crave a unique education at a reasonable price should definitely check out New College.

NEW COLLEGE OF THE UNIVERSITY OF SOUTH FLORIDA

Sarasota, FL

Admissions

The New College of the University of South Florida catalog states, "Although New College is among the most selective in the nation, no candidate for admission is arbitrarily excluded from full consideration because of a particular test score or grade point average." The admissions committee first looks at an applicant's high school curriculum and GPA, followed, in order of importance, by standardized test scores, essays, an interview, extracurriculars, and letters of recommendation. The admissions office notes, "We do re-compute GPA on a weighted basis using only academic courses." The SAT or ACT is required, as are two academic recommendations, and a copy of the high school transcript (it is suggested that the school send a "School Profile" with these materials). In addition, all applicants must submit a graded paper from a high school English or history course. The interview is required of applicants within a 100-mile radius of the campus, and optional (but strongly recommended) for others. Applicants to New College of USF also often apply to UC Santa Cruz, Florida State, Rice, Michigan, and Oberlin.

Financial Aid

Financial aid applicants to New College of the University of South Florida must complete the FAF or FFS and submit a copy of their parents' tax forms. Out-of-State students are considered for one year tuition waivers which help make up the difference between in-state and out-of-state tuition rates. New College also offers its own scholarships, as well as scholarships for minorities, and scholarships for graduates of Florida high schools. Furthermore, according to New College's brochure, "…the New College Foundation contributes $1,400 per year toward the cost of education of each New College student. Thus, our low tuition rates reflect a "built-in scholarship" totaling $5,600 over the course of a four-year stay at the College." The priority application deadline is February 1.

A note from the New College Admissions Office:

"New College provides the opportunity to obtain the highest quality education at a state institution price. Students work directly with senior faculty and are often exposed to levels of study not generally found outside of graduate institutions. The student who will do bets at New College is one who is independent, broad-minded, self-confident, and capable of rigorous academic work. The very nature of New College requires one to be dedicated to education and the pursuit of individual growth."

ADMISSIONS FACTS

Competitiveness Rating:	**93**
% of applicants accepted:	33
% acceptees attending:	45

FRESHMAN PROFILE

Average verbal SAT:	660
Average math SAT:	640
Average ACT:	29
Graduated top 10% of class:	37
Graduated top 25% of class:	78
Graduated top 50% of class:	100

DEADLINES

Early decision/action:	NA
Early dec./act. notif.:	NA
Regular admission:	rolling
Regular adm. notif.:	rolling

APPLICANTS ALSO LOOK AT

and often prefer:
Emory U.

and sometimes prefer:
Rice U.

and rarely prefer:
Evergreen State College
U. Florida
Florida State U.
Grinnell College
Antioch College
Eckerd College

ADDRESS

Undergraduate Admissions
New College of U.S.F.
Sarasota, FL 34243
813-355-2963

FINANCIAL FACTS

In-state tuition ($):	1,675
Out-of-state tuition ($):	6,690
Room & board:	3,375
FA application deadline:	6/1
% frosh receiving FA:	NA
PT earnings per yr. ($):	NA

TYPE OF AID: % of students ($)

FA of some kind:	67 (NA)
Need-based grants:	NA
Merit-based grants:	NA
Loans:	NA
Work study:	NA
Student rating of FA:	88

UNIVERSITY OF NEW HAMPSHIRE

Durham, NH

What do students think about the U. of New Hampshire?

■ **Academics** According to one undergraduate, "The University of New Hampshire has made the move toward academics and is trying to shun its 'party school' image." UNH has indeed worked to improve facilities and toughen academic requirements, so that now, according to one undergrad, "UNH is perfect for an undergraduate education. It clearly defines the students' purpose for being here: not to party, but to study and learn." A rigorous and varied core curriculum eats up a fourth of the credits necessary toward graduation (beware: students here have little room in their schedules for elective courses). Professors are extremely helpful for those at a public institution: wrote one molecular biology major, "Professors here are more than willing to sit down and explain the material if you have any questions. Some of my professors have become good friends of mine." Departments earning the most praise from students are English, business, pre-medical sciences, and the nursing program. Student complaints centered mostly on administrative problems: the dean's office, the bursar, and the library all received below average grades. Registration is "a nightmare, and getting classes in popular departments like English is close to impossible." Students also complain about the long semesters. Explained one, "UNH stands for the University of No Holidays. We go back earlier and get out later than any other area schools, which means that kids from other schools scavenge the summer jobs before you do."

■ **Life** UNH still retains some vestiges of its party school days. Wrote one student, "Socially this school is great—my weekends start on Wednesdays too often!" Despite a new dry campus policy, students report that alcohol is popular and accessible; marijuana remains the intoxicant of choice for the considerable 'crunchy' Deadhead population. Students enjoy a wide variety of extracurricular activities: the radio station and school newspaper are popular, as are sports, both intramural and intercollegiate. The frat scene, while popular, is not monolithic, as it is at some schools located in small towns. Students gave Durham below average marks. Explained one student, "The towns surrounding Durham have much to offer students, and Boston is easily accessible. Durham and UNH itself, however, leave much to be desired in terms of the diversity of options available to students."

■ **Students** A whopping 98 percent of UNH students are white. Wrote one student, "The biggest problem at UNH is the lack of ethnic diversity. It's really sad: when you see a black student, you wonder what sports team he's on." The student body is made up of both urbanites and earthy nature lovers, although there are more of the latter. As one student put it, "If you wear Birkenstocks, L.L. Bean and are at all 'crunchy,' you'll fit right in." Students identified themselves as politically left of center and as more politically concerned than most college students.

UNIVERSITY OF NEW HAMPSHIRE

Admissions

According to its undergraduate catalog, admission to the University of New Hampshire is based primarily on "academic achievement and aptitude, as demonstrated by the quality of candidates' secondary school course selection rank in class, recommendations, and the results of [the] SAT." Strong consideration is also given to "character, leadership, and special talents." An applicant's high school curriculum should include four years each of English and mathematics, three years of science, two years of social science, and three years of study in a single foreign language, or more than one year of study in each of two different foreign languages. All applicants must submit SAT scores, and if declaring a major, are encouraged to submit an Achievement test score related to that major.

Financial Aid

The financial aid office at the University of New Hampshire requires applicants to submit the FAF. UNH offers merit-based grants to students with exceptional abilities in academics, athletics, and the creative and performing arts, as well as need-based grants to those who demonstrate need. A little over half of the typical UNH financial aid package is in grant form, with the rest of the package made up of loans and work-study.

Excerpted from University of New Hampshire promotional materials:

"In the 1989–90 academic year, the University of New Hampshire had 11,566 degree candidates enrolled, including 400 in the associate in applied science program of the Thompson School and 172 in the associate in arts program in the Division of Continuing Education. In the Division of Continuing Education, 1,742 special students also were enrolled.

"The University is committed to offering excellent educational programs and opportunities for its students…A faculty member's first responsibility is teaching students. The University considers teaching so important that it engages in regular evaluation of each faculty member's teaching by students and colleagues. Such evaluation is intended to promote excellence in teaching and is used in tenure, promotion, and salary decisions concerning teaching faculty.

"The University also requires its faculty to contribute to the growth of human knowledge through scholarly research and to disseminate that knowledge to the community beyond the campus. Research normally results in the publication of books, articles, or talks given to scholarly associations, while wider dissemination is accomplished, for example, through the Cooperative Extension Service, the public TV station, and various programs for educating professionals."

ADMISSIONS FACTS

Competitiveness Rating:	79
% of applicants accepted:	64
% acceptees attending:	34

FRESHMAN PROFILE

Average verbal SAT:	489
Average math SAT:	556
Average ACT:	NA
Graduated top 10% of class:	31
Graduated top 25% of class:	86
Graduated top 50% of class:	99

DEADLINES

Early decision/action:	12/1
Early dec./act. notif.:	1/15
Regular admission:	2/1
Regular adm. notif.:	4/15

APPLICANTS ALSO LOOK AT

and often prefer:
U. Colorado–Boulder
U. Vermont

and sometimes prefer:
St. Lawrence U.
U. Mass–Amherst
Boston College
Bentley College

and rarely prefer:
Clark U.
Northeastern U.
U. Connecticut

ADDRESS

Undergraduate Admissions
4 Garrison Avenue
Durham, NH 03824
603-862-1360

FINANCIAL FACTS

In-state tuition ($):	3,290
Out-of-state tuition ($):	9,840
Room & board ($):	3,600
FA application deadline:	2/15
% frosh receiving FA:	40
PT earnings per yr. ($):	NA

TYPE OF AID:	% of students ($)
FA of some kind:	50 (NA)
Need-based grants:	NA
Merit-based grants:	NA
Loans:	NA
Work study:	NA
Student rating of FA:	75

New Jersey Institute of Technology

Newark, NJ

What do students think about New Jersey Tech?

■ **Academics** To the in-state students who make up the vast majority of the New Jersey Institute of Technology's student body (and, to a lesser extent, to the tiny out-of-state population), publicly funded NJIT provides "an excellent education for the money." NJIT is notable not only for its reasonable price, but also for its quality programs in engineering (especially mechanical and electrical engineering), mathematics, science, and architecture. The addition of new laboratories and the expansion of current facilities led one student to note that "this school is up-and-coming, and looks like it will continue to grow into the '90s." The school also offers a cooperative education program to its undergraduates, thereby allowing them to make money and gain work experience while earning credit towards their degrees. Students reported that class sizes were small for those at a public institution. They gave their teachers poor marks, both for accessibility outside the classroom and for in-class instruction. TAs were a particular sore point: "They barely speak English," complained one mechanical engineering student. Other complaints concerned class schedules ("Courses are poorly scheduled, making it hard to make all the courses you need and want fit into one schedule") and the school's location (see "Life," below). Summed up one student: "NJIT may not offer the best social life, but it is preparing me for a promising future in the working world."

■ **Life** Students here uniformly agree that NJIT offers little in the way of social distractions. "There is no life on campus, there are no activities, there is no fun," is how one student summed up the situation. There is a fairly active Greek system, a functional intramural sports program, and a popular school newspaper, but the very lopsided male-female ratio (more than four to one) and the large commuter population causes this campus to thin out pretty quickly after classes, and to empty almost entirely over the weekend. Students ranked their host city, Newark, the third worst college location in the country. Many students perceive the surrounding neighborhood as dangerous. Wrote one commuter, "Professors who ask or even insist that students stay several hours beyond class time seem not to realize that Newark is not safe at night." Another caveat for commuters: parking is very difficult to find. Construction is underway on new dormitories and parking facilities, however, which should alleviate some problems.

■ **Students** NJIT has a large minority population: Asians, blacks, and Hispanics make up two fifths of the student body. For many students, as well as for many teachers, English is a second language, leading one sarcastic student to note that "NJIT is great if you want the experience of studying in a foreign country without the expense of going to one." Very few students come here to pursue theoretical studies. Most are interested in translating their hard work here immediately into a conventional, high-paying technical job.

NEW JERSEY INSTITUTE OF TECHNOLOGY

Admissions

The admissions office reports, "New Jersey Institute of Technology considers each applicant on the basis of his/her overall individual merits." In determining an applicant's desirability, the admissions office looks first at high school GPA and standardized test scores. Also considered are extracurricular activities, letters of recommendation, essays, and interview. Applicants must have completed four years of English, at least three years of college prep math (four years for math-related majors), and at least two years of science (lab sciences are preferred). In addition, applicants must take the SAT and the math achievement (Math I or II). Architecture majors must also submit a portfolio. Those applying to NJIT most often also apply to Rutgers, Stevens, Montclair State College, Seton Hall, and Trenton State.

Financial Aid

Financial aid applicants to the New Jersey Institute of Technology must complete the NJFAF and a form generated by NJIT's financial aid office, and must submit a copy of their parents' most recent tax return. In the '90–'91 academic year, 18% of all undergrads received an academic merit award; the average value was $1,480. Four percent of all undergrads took out Perkins loans (average value: $1,235); 33% took out Stafford loans (average: $1,585); 1% took out SLS loans ($3,245); 1% took out PLUS loans ($3,130); and 4% took out NJIT's own institutional loans ($1,190). The average financial aid recipient in the class of '95 received an award of $5,222. A number of major-related and geographic awards and scholarships are available.

A note from the New Jersey Institute of Technology Admissions Office:

"New Jersey Institute of Technology is New Jersey's publicly supported comprehensive technological university providing instruction, research, and public service in engineering, computer science, management, architecture, engineering technology, applied sciences, and related fields. NJIT is composed of four units: Newark College of Engineering, School of Industrial Management, College of Science and Liberal Arts, and School of Architecture. The School of Architecture is the only publicly supported college of architecture in the state.

"NJIT's mission reflects a world vision that considers a fiercely competitive marketplace shaped by rapidly evolving technologies, an ethnically rich workforce, and a fragile environment shared by the entire planet. NJIT's programs prepare students to meet the global challenges of the 21st century."

ADMISSIONS FACTS

Competitiveness Rating:	**73**
% of applicants accepted:	58
% acceptees attending:	49

FRESHMAN PROFILE

Average verbal SAT:	458
Average math SAT:	599
Average ACT:	NA
Graduated top 10% of class:	23
Graduated top 25% of class:	57
Graduated top 50% of class:	90

DEADLINES

Early decision/action:	12/1
Early dec./adm. notif.:	12/31
Regular admission:	4/1
Regular adm. notif.:	rolling

APPLICANTS ALSO LOOK AT

and often prefer:
Rutgers U.
Seton Hall U.
Stevens Tech

and sometimes prefer:
Worcester Polytech
Monclair State U.
Trenton State U.
Virginia Polytech

ADDRESS

Undergraduate Admissions
University Heights
Newark, NJ 07102-9938
201-596-3300

FINANCIAL FACTS

In-state tuition ($):	4,360
Out-of-state tuition ($):	6,880
Room & board:	3,192
FA application deadline:	3/16
% frosh receiving FA:	75
PT earnings per yr. ($):	2,000

TYPE OF AID: % of students ($)

FA of some kind:	77 (6,337)
Need-based grants:	45 (1,285)
Merit-based grants:	18 (1,480)
Loans:	45 (1,610)
Work study:	14 (1,555)
Student rating of FA:	67

NEW YORK UNIVERSITY

New York, NY

What do students think about New York University?

■ **Academics** NYU's greatest strength is diversity, both in its academic programs and student body. Two programs in particular stand out : the Stern Business School and the Tisch Arts Program, both of which serve undergraduates and graduate students. Both are nationally recognized as leaders in their fields, the Tisch program mostly for its film program (alumni include Oliver Stone, Martin Scorsese, and many others). Art history is the best of the many solid liberal arts departments. As one student noted, "NYU is a perfect school if you're not really sure about your career goals. It embraces a wide spectrum of majors." Another put it this way: "I am never bored and could never imagine being in a place less amazing and dynamic than here. NYU is like a miniature United Nations." On the down side, students find many professors cold and give them low marks for in-class and out-of-class performance.

■ **Life** Most of the unhappiness at NYU can be attributed to the school's lack of a campus, which, coupled with its great size, often causes NYU students to feel detached from their school. The administration is faced with the challenge of creating school spirit in a centerless community, and, unfortunately, it doesn't seem up to the task. Students lambasted administrators, most often characterizing them as sluggish bureaucrats interested almost solely in collecting money. "The school is really a money-making proposition for the administration; you're always being charged extra for something," complained one student. "The bureaucracy is crazy," said another. "To accomplish something you get sent to 10 people. The tenth person who has the answer is invariably the first person you talked to." The hefty price tag for attending NYU exacerbates student frustration. Fortunately, there's always Greenwich Village, the heart of the social universe of young New York. "NYU would be a great school if it were in the middle of Death Valley, but it isn't," explained one student from Florida. "It's in the middle of New York City, and that puts it past great, somewhere in the vicinity of orgasmic." NYU's students and New York's inhabitants are a perfect match: both seem most comfortable when they are dissatisfied with something.

■ **Students** NYU's student body is one of the most diverse in the nation. Here are African-Americans, whites, Asians, and Hispanics, commuters and residents, hip urbanites and suburbanites, straights and gays, Jews, Christians, Muslims, Buddhists, and Hindus, all apparently united by one thing: their love/hate relationship with their school. Although NYU students gush about many aspects of the university—the diversity of programs it offers, the diversity of the student body, and Greenwich Village, most notably— they are also a generally unhappy lot. "Post-punk" definitely describes the prevalent attitude.

NEW YORK UNIVERSITY

Admissions

NYU's most recent course catalog reports, "The applicant's capacity for successful undergraduate work is measured through careful consideration of secondary school and/or college records; recommendations from guidance counselors, teachers, and others; and rank in class." NYU requires applicants to submit scores for either the SAT or the ACT. The admissions office recommends the following high school curriculum: four years of English, "with heavy emphasis on writing"; three years of math; two or three years of lab science; three or four years of social studies; and two to three years of a foreign language. Math and language during senior year are "strongly recommended."

Financial Aid

Applicants for financial assistance from NYU must submit the either the FAF, FFS, or the AFSA, as well as a form generated by the school. The most recent NYU bulletin lists several merit grants awarded for scholastic excellence and/or exceptional talents in the arts, but the same source reports that all financial assistance at the school is "based on academic achievement, financial need, and the availability of funds." NYU administers the Perkins loan program, and suggests that students looking to borrow further pursue loans from the Stafford, PLUS, and SLS loan programs. NYU participates in the College Work-Study program.

A note from the New York University Admissions Office:

"NYU is distinctive both in the quality of education we provide and in the exhilarating atmosphere in which our students study and learn. As an undergraduate in one of our seven small to medium-size colleges, you will enjoy a faculty/student ratio of only 1:13 and a dynamic, challenging learning environment which encourages lively interaction between students and professors. At the same time, you will have available to you all the resources of a distinguished university dedicated to research and scholarship at the highest levels, including a curriculum that offers over 2,500 courses and 160 programs of study and a faculty that includes some of the most highly regarded scholars, scientists, and artists in the country.

"New York University is a vital, vibrant community. There is an aura of energy and excitement here; a sense that possibilities and opportunities are limited only by the number of hours in a day. The educational experience at NYU is intense, but varied and richly satisfying. You will be actively engaged in you own education, both in the classroom and beyond."

ADMISSIONS FACTS

Competitiveness Rating:	**87**
% of applicants accepted:	54
% acceptees attending:	44

FRESHMAN PROFILE

Average verbal SAT:	547*
Average math SAT:	597*
Average ACT:	NA
Graduated top 10% HS class:	70
Graduated top 25% HS class:	85
Graduated top 50% HS class:	98

DEADLINES

Early decision/action:	11/1
Early dec./act. notif.:	12/1
Regular admission:	2/1
Regular adm. notif.:	4/1

APPLICANTS ALSO LOOK AT

and often prefer:
Barnard College
Columbia U.

and sometimes prefer:
George Washington U.
Syracuse U.

and rarely prefer:
Hofstra U.
Rutgers U.–Douglass

ADDRESS

Undergraduate Admissions
22 Washington Square North
New York, NY 10011
212-998-4500

FINANCIAL FACTS

In-state tuition ($):	14,860
Out-of-state tuition ($):	14,860
Room & board:	6,538
FA application deadline:	2/15
% frosh receiving FA:	82
PT earnings per yr. ($):	2,100

TYPE OF AID: % of students ($)

FA of some kind:	68 (NA)
Need-based grants:	NA
Merit-based grants:	NA
Loans:	NA
Work study:	NA
Student rating of FA:	70

UNIVERSITY OF NORTH CAROLINA–CHAPEL HILL

Chapel Hill, NC

What do students think about UNC–Chapel Hill?

■ **Academics** For many students, the University of North Carolina at Chapel Hill represents "the true college experience. From theater to tennis, baseball to basketball, academics to amusement, UNC provides students with the ability to discover that life is a test with more questions than answers." Sports and amusement notwithstanding, Chapel Hill's reputation as one of the nation's state universities is based on its first-rate academic offerings; area counselors cited the school's nationally known journalism and business programs, while students noted that classics, English and political science are also strong. On the downside is the school's enormousness. Because of UNC's size, classes are often very large and led by teaching assistants. Students noted that even some upper level classes and labs are crowded. As a rule, opportunities here must be sought out rather than simply handed to students. Professors are available, but only to students who take the initiative to ask for help. Of course, UNC's drawbacks are the same as those at most state universities, and within those parameters UNC remains an excellent school. Its facilities are excellent (the libraries received especially high ratings), its faculty is strong, and its students bright and ambitious.

■ **Life** UNC Chapel Hill is often called "the Southern Part of Heaven." This label aptly describes the stately campus, widely admired for its great beauty and charm. The town of Chapel Hill is also well regarded by students. One wrote, "Chapel Hill is the quintessential college town. It has a small-town atmosphere, but there's plenty to do. There are large cities close by, so there's something for everyone. The campus is beautiful, the people are friendly, the school is academically strong. What more could you want?" This vote of confidence was overwhelmingly affirmed by the students in our survey. Nearly every comment about nonacademic life was positive. (Students even gave themselves high marks for being good-looking.) The social scene is active and extends throughout campus and into town. Fraternities and sororities are popular, but not dominant. Dating in the traditional sense is in, and sports (intercollegiate and intramural) account for lots of extracurricular time. Tarheel men's basketball, in particular, is extremely popular, as are the men's football, lacrosse, and baseball teams. Women's teams in soccer, field hockey, and volleyball are also usually excellent and well supported.

■ **Students** Over three quarters of the students are native to North Carolina. Out-of-state students face much stricter admissions standards, but apply in droves anyway. The political climate on campus is rather moderate, and most people of different backgrounds and lifestyles feel they are accepted. Some minority students complained that "the campus has two very distinct and separate communities, black and white, but the administration is trying to break down some of these barriers." As at many Southern schools, there is a larger-than-average religious contingent among the students.

University of North Carolina–Chapel Hill

Chapel Hill, NC

Admissions

UNC–Chapel Hill uses a formula to determine admissibility of an applicant. The admissions office rates the difficulty of your high school curriculum, then combines that rating with your grades and class rank: that number represents 60 percent of the formula. 20 percent weight is given to standardized test scores; the other 20 percent is made up of extracurricular activities, leadership qualities, and optional recommendations and essays (said to be helpful to the marginal candidate). Admissions requirements are tough for nonresidents: most reportedly have "A" averages in high school, graduate in the top 5 percent of their class, and have an average 1370 combined SAT score. Successful resident applicants have B+/A- averages, are generally in the top 12 percent of their classes, and average 1150 on the SAT. Applicants must complete a traditional college preparatory curriculum.

Financial Aid

Financial aid applicants to University of North Carolina/Chapel Hill must complete the FAF. For students who demonstrate financial need and who have "above average" academic records, UNC awards general scholarships ranging in value from $300 to $1,500 per year. A number of special need-based scholarships are also available: students eligible for these awards include those who show outstanding academic and leadership ability, North Carolina residents, and minorities. The most prestigious of these are the James M. Johnston Awards. Based on academic ability and leadership, stipends range from $200 to the total cost of education. Many recipients of these awards are students in the school of Nursing. "Competitive" scholarships offered include 60 John Mosley Morehead Awards, which are renewable annually, and are designed to cover a full four years of study at the University. Students may not apply for these awards; they must be nominated by their secondary schools. UNC's recommended loans include Perkins, Stafford, and PLUS loans. March 1 is the priority deadline for the FA application. Students whose materials are complete and on file by this date can expect award notification in May.

A note from the University of North Carolina–Chapel Hill Admissions Office:

"What makes UNC–Chapel Hill different from other institutions? Atmosphere of academic rigor mingled with an unpretentious, friendly lifestyle; planetarium; commitment to vital teaching and cutting edge research; socioeconomic diversity; classic residential campus; a permeable honors program; study abroad; diversity permeates social life, classes, and curriculum and paces academic excellence; village-like atmosphere; the University is large enough to grant your individuality yet small enough for you to find your niche; academic quality of the highest caliber yet inexpensive cost; third among public universities in the production of Rhodes Scholars."

ADMISSIONS FACTS

Competitiveness Rating:	**89**
% of applicants accepted:	37
% acceptees attending:	58

FRESHMAN PROFILE

Average verbal SAT:	527
Average math SAT:	584
Average ACT:	NA
Graduated top 10% HS class:	76
Graduated top 25% HS class:	92
Graduated top 50% HS class:	96

DEADLINES

Early decision/action:	12/1
Early dec./act. notif.:	2/15
Regular admission:	1/15
Regular adm. notif.:	4/15

APPLICANTS ALSO LOOK AT

and often prefer:
Princeton U.
Duke U.

and sometimes prefer:
Harvard/Radcliffe College
Brown U.
U. Virginia

and rarely prefer:
North Carolina State U.
U. Maryland
Tulane U.
Rutgers U./Rutgers College

ADDRESS

Undergraduate Admissions
Monogram Bldg. CB#2200
Chapel Hill, NC 27599-2200
919-966-3621

FINANCIAL FACTS

In-state tuition ($):	1,094
Out-of-state tuition ($):	5,761
Room & board:	3,700
FA application deadline:	3/1
% frosh receiving FA:	35
PT earnings per yr. ($):	NA

TYPE OF AID: % of students ($)

FA of some kind:	30 (NA)
Need-based grants:	NA
Merit-based grants:	NA
Loans:	NA
Work study:	NA
Student rating of FA:	79

NORTH CAROLINA STATE UNIVERSITY

Raleigh, NC

What do students think about North Carolina State U.?

■ **Academics** North Carolina State University, plagued recently by scandals involving the academic records of its athletes, has responded to the adversity by renewing its commitment to academic quality and integrity for all its students. Especially in technical areas, NC State is thought of as "an excellent school." Particularly noteworthy departments are engineering, business management, design, architecture, and the top-notch textile school. All students must fulfill distribution requirements that include a number of liberal arts courses, but students reported that most classes stress an analytical, science-oriented approach to their subjects. Although a few respondents reported that the faculty is "very dedicated, helpful, and approachable," the faculty overall got low marks from students for both teaching ability and accessibility. Many classes do tend to be large and crowded, but few students complained. Few arrive here expecting small classes. The overall atmosphere is easygoing. Students we asked admitted that doing "most or all the assigned reading for classes" is not overly important. NC State emphasizes a practical approach to education: an integral part of its undergraduate curriculum is the cooperative education program, which allows students to work for credit outside the classroom.

■ **Life** Intercollegiate sports are an important feature of life at NC State. Wolfpack basketball, football, and soccer each boast thousands of dedicated fans among the student body. Fraternities and sororities are also central to social life, but some who don't like them contend that they are too dominant on campus. "There is too much emphasis on Greek activities," said one friend, "yeah right, I wanna pay $600 a semester to buy a personality and some cheesy friends." But there are enough social activities that avoiding frat parties is not that difficult. One student assured us, "There is so much going on here that anyone should be able to find a place" to have fun. For those who need a break from campus events, the surrounding city has plenty to offer. Students praised Raleigh for its receptiveness to students. In fact, most NC State students end up living in Raleigh as opposed to on campus, because there is not nearly enough dorm space to go around. Drinking is quite prevalent here, and the recent wave of crackdowns on underage drinking doesn't seem to have reached State…yet. Dating in the traditional sense is common, and the lopsided male-female ratio (nearly two to one) is somewhat balanced by the nearby women's colleges in Raleigh.

■ **Students** The large undergraduate population at NC State is "very diverse," despite the disproportionate number of native North Carolinians. The minority population is 17 percent, and the reasonable tuition prices combined with the many different scholarships make it possible for students of all socio-economic backgrounds to attend. The political atmosphere is mostly conservative, but in a school this size, it is easy to find people of all creeds. North Carolina State provides a quality education for the price, and its renewed commitment to academics bodes well for the school's future.

NORTH CAROLINA STATE UNIVERSITY

Raleigh, NC

Admissions

The admissions office reports using "no cut-offs; however, GPAs under 2.5 or SATs under 800 are not competitive as a rule (SATs between 800 and 900 must be accompanied by a very exceptional high school record). Typical successful candidates: B+ GPA, 1000–1200+ SAT and rigorous college prep curriculum." NC State also considers extracurricular activities, essays, letters of recommendation, and an optional interview. Applicants are expected to have completed four years of English, three years each of science (including a lab science) and math (algebra I and II, and geometry), and two years of social science. Two years of both a foreign language and advanced math are strongly recommended. Applicants must submit either SAT or ACT scores. Applicants to NC State often also apply to UNC–Chapel Hill, Georgia Tech, and Virginia Tech.

Financial Aid

Financial aid applicants to North Carolina State University must complete the FAF and a form generated by NC State's financial aid office, and submit a copy of their parents' most recent tax return. Thirty percent of the class of '95 received an award of some kind upon entry; the average award value was $3,315. In '90–'91, the average "merit" grant was $1,625, and the average athletic grant was $5,616. In addition to Perkins and Stafford loans, NC State recommends its own institutional loans. The May 1 deadline is an "in-office" date.

A note from the North Carolina State University Admissions Office:

"North Carolina State University combines the best of several academic worlds. As the largest university in N.C., the academic, extracurricular, cultural, and social opportunities are simply tremendous, yet enrolling in one of our eight undergraduate colleges/schools provides for a more intimate and personal learning experience than is normally associated with a university of 27,000. Further, NCSU's location in Raleigh, the capitol and cultural center of North Carolina, provides student with the vast and varied entertainment opportunities associated with a city of 200,000."

ADMISSIONS FACTS

Competitiveness Rating:	**80**
% of applicants accepted:	64
% acceptees attending:	52

FRESHMAN PROFILE

Average verbal SAT:	486
Average math SAT:	567
Average ACT:	NA
Graduated top 10% HS class:	38
Graduated top 25% HS class:	80
Graduated top 50% HS class:	100

DEADLINES

Early decision/action:	11/1
Early dec./act. notif.:	12/15
Regular admission:	2/1
Regular adm. notif.:	4/1

APPLICANTS ALSO LOOK AT

and often prefer:
U. Tennessee–Knoxville
U. NC Chapel Hill

and sometimes prefer:
Wake Forest U.
U. NC Charlotte

and rarely prefer:
Clemson U.
U. South Carolina
Auburn U.
Georgia Tech
Virginia Polytech

ADDRESS

Undergraduate Admissions
P.O. Box 7103
Raleigh, NC 27695-7103
919-737-2434

FINANCIAL FACTS

In-state tuition ($):	1,126
Out-of-state tuition ($):	5,792
Room & board:	3,030
FA application deadline:	5/1
% frosh receiving FA:	49
PT earnings per yr. ($):	800

TYPE OF AID: % of students ($)

FA of some kind:	37 (NA)
Need-based grants:	NA
Merit-based grants:	NA
Loans:	NA
Work study:	NA
Student rating of FA:	78

UNIVERSITY OF NORTH DAKOTA

Grand Forks, ND

CAMPUS LIFE

Quality of Life Rating:	*79*
Type of School:	public
Affiliation:	none
Environment:	city

STUDENT BODY

FT undergrad enrollment:	10,650
% male/% female:	54/46
% out-of-state:	41
% live on campus:	46
% African-American:	<1
% Asian:	1
% Caucasian:	92
% Hispanic:	<1
% foreign:	3
% transfers:	25

WHAT'S HOT

marriage
working a job
town-gown relations
Top 40
profs lecture a lot
conservative politics
dating
small classes (overall)

WHAT'S NOT

Grateful Dead
living on campus
registration
marijuana
gay community accepted
college theater

ACADEMICS

Academic Rating:	*69*
Calendar:	semester
Student/teacher ratio:	19/1
% doctorates:	69
Profs interesting:	73
Profs accessible:	73
Hours of study per day:	2.97

MOST POPULAR MAJORS BY %

Business & Management:	17
Education:	10
Engineering:	9

What do students think about the U. of North Dakota?

■ **Academics** The University of North Dakota provides "a sound learning environment for students who really want to learn." It is large and well-funded enough to offer state-of-the-art facilities in most areas, yet small enough to allow reasonably sized classes. Respondents reported a surprising number (about 30 percent) of classes with fewer than 20 students. The strongest and most popular department at UND is aviation. The Center for Aerospace Science is highly respected nationwide, and attracts many of the out-of-state students to the school. Business and management departments are also popular and reputedly top-notch, as are most other career-oriented studies (physical and occupational therapy and education, for example). Although UND has a reputation for having a 'relaxed' academic atmosphere, the students we spoke to took their academic responsibilities fairly seriously. Professors received average marks for instruction and accessibility (for those at a large public university). Like most state universities, UND has its share of red tape. Students condemned the poor registration process and gave low ratings to the administration and deans.

■ **Life** Grand Forks, North Dakota, enjoys a pleasant and fruitful relationship with the university it contains. Interaction between students and local residents is described as frequent and friendly. Students told us that they consider "the beautiful people" they attend school with to be a great asset, and appreciate the "polite, trusting and giving" attitude that is prevalent among them. Most come from "small or moderate cities or farming communities" that are "family oriented, and promote religion and hard work." It should come as no surprise, then, that controlled substances are very unpopular here. Drugs are scarce and are frowned upon by most. The social scene centers around fraternities and sororities; although they attract only a small minority of students, they still tend to dominate the party scene because they're the only game in town. As one independent told us, "There really needs to be more things for students to do in their free time." Some other social and extracurricular options are certainly available, but most students go home on the weekends except when there is a major event (such as a hockey game). Be forewarned that winters can get bitterly cold here. It is not unknown for class to be canceled "on minus-60-degree days."

■ **Students** As one student observed, UND is "smack dab in the middle of the Bible Belt, so left-wing or alternative lifestyles are not easily found or accepted." This generalization was borne out by our surveys. Marriage is high on many students' lists of priorities, while tolerance of gays is not. The political climate is conservative, but characterized more by apathy than by right-wing activism. A little more than half the students are from in-state; the minority population is a tiny 8 percent.

UNIVERSITY OF NORTH DAKOTA

Grand Forks, ND

Admissions

All residents of North Dakota or Minnesota who are graduates of accredited or approved high schools are eligible for admission to the University of North Dakota. Candidates who are in the bottom one fourth of their graduating class, and who score lower than 19 on the ACT are strongly encouraged to come to the campus for additional tests and counseling before admission. Candidates from out of state must rank in the upper half of their graduating class to be eligible for admission. All applicants must submit ACT (preferred) or SAT scores. The recommended high school curriculum includes four years of English, three years each of mathematics, science, and social science, and two years of foreign language. Priority consideration is given to applications received by March 1.

Financial Aid

Financial aid applicants to The University of North Dakota must complete the FFS (preferred) or the FAF. Upon request, they must complete a form generated by UND's financial aid office, and submit copies of their parents' most recent tax returns. In '91–'92, 1% of all undergrads received an athletic grant (the average value was $5,730) and 19% of all undergrads received an academic grant (average value: $603). UND Honor Scholarships range in value from $250 to $2,250, and are awarded based on academic merit to nearly 400 freshmen each year. A number of other scholarships (talent, leadership, etc.) are available. Financial aid is not offered until students are admitted to the University.

Excerpted from University of North Dakota promotional materials:

"The University of North Dakota is a coeducational state-supported institution located in Grand Forks, a city with a population of approximately 44,000. The campus is in the center of the Red River Valley, one of the richest farming areas in the world. In addition, UND is responsible for free-standing branch campuses at Devils Lake and Williston.

"The University's academic programs are offered in 130 fields through 13 major academic units: University College (freshmen division), College of Arts and Sciences, Center for Aerospace Sciences, College of Business and Public Administration, School of Engineering and Mines, College of Fine Arts, College for Human Resources Development, College of Nursing, Center for Teaching and Learning, Graduate School, School of Law, School of Medicine, and Division of Continuing Education.

"The campus itself includes nearly 500 acres, including the 152-acre north campus (Bronson property) and the nine-acre UND Energy Resource Center site."

ADMISSIONS FACTS

Competitiveness Rating:	**62**
% of applicants accepted:	87
% acceptees attending:	75

FRESHMAN PROFILE

Average verbal SAT:	NA
Average math SAT:	NA
Average ACT:	21
Graduated top 10% HS class:	NA
Graduated top 25% HS class:	52
Graduated top 50% HS class:	87

DEADLINES

Early decision/action:	NA
Early dec./act. notif.:	NA
Regular admission:	7/1
Regular adm. notif.:	rolling

APPLICANTS ALSO LOOK AT

and often prefer:
U. Nebraska
U. Colorado–Boulder
U. Notre Dame

and sometimes prefer:
Washington U.
U.S.A.F. Academy

and rarely prefer:
U. Minnesota
Marquette U.
U. Wisconsin–Madison

ADDRESS

Undergraduate Admissions
Box 8193
Grand Forks, ND 58202
701-777-3821

FINANCIAL FACTS

In-state tuition ($):	2,146
Out-of-state tuition ($):	5,254
Room & board:	2,455
FA application deadline:	3/15
% frosh receiving FA:	55
PT earnings per yr. ($):	1,400

% FT RECEIVING (AVG.AMT.($)):

FA of some kind:	55 (NA)
Need-based grants:	NA (3,298)
Merit-based grants:	NA
Loans:	30 (2,133)
Work study:	19 (1,140)
Student rating of FA:	70

NORTHEAST MISSOURI STATE UNIVERSITY

Kirksville, MO

What do students think about Northeast Missouri State U.?

■ **Academics** Once a regional teacher's college, Northeast Missouri State University has grown into a nationally recognized university with quality programs in business, communications, and (of course) education. The curriculum here features one of the nation's most comprehensive liberal arts core requirements and stresses the development of communication skills (writing, speaking, etc.) for all students. The school also employs a battery of standardized tests to assess students' progress continually. Many students appreciate what the school provides: "a quality liberal arts and sciences education at an affordable price." They also assert that "the faculty and administration are very involved in individual students' progress, and are always willing to help." They are also proud that NMSU "is in the middle of a renaissance." While they admit that "the development of a liberal arts and sciences culture has caused some growing pains," they also assert that "those who are interested have a wonderful opportunity to shape a new university community." Still, many students here are definitely less than satisfied. Our surveys were filled with complaints about everything from registration ("closed classes are a *real* problem") to courses ("the theme in evaluation for grading purposes is still 'memorize and regurgitate'") to competition for grades ("this is NM Stress U") to the overall mission of the university ("If you want job training come here—if you want an education, DON'T!").

■ **Life** Kirksville, NMSU's home town, gets a bad rap from many of its temporary inhabitants, who cited "extreme culture shock" and a "dearth of activities to relieve the stress of academic work." Nevertheless, some students stuck up for their town. Wrote one enthusiast, "Kirksville is a much better city than most people give it credit for; one must search out its beauty (The Blue Moon Cafe is excellent)." Students here are more involved in religion than at many colleges, and religious clubs are quite popular. The dating scene is very active, and people who have found a comfortable social niche claim to be happy here.

■ **Students** NMSU is not the place to come seeking a paradise of ethnic diversity and harmony. Although a few students believe different groups interact with each other very easily, most believe just the opposite. Wrote one black student, "Our school is completely Eurocentric: a whitewashed faculty with a whitewashed student body." Complained another student, "minority students and organizations do not receive the support of the school community." Most students would agree that "the campus needs to start integrating itself academically. If minorities are good enough to come here and play sports, NMSU should incorporate studies and have guest speakers that deal with different ethnic backgrounds." NMSU's small minority population (8 percent) is made up almost entirely of African-Americans.

NORTHEAST MISSOURI STATE UNIVERSITY

Kirksville, MO

Admissions

Northeast Missouri State's admissions office writes "Northeast has a competitive admission process. There are no strict minimum requirements. All of the (below) criteria are used in considering a student for admission." Members of the entering class of 1991 had an average GPA of 3.40, and an average rank of 81 percent in their high school classes (top 19 percent). The admissions committee first looks at an applicant's standardized test scores, the strength of the high school curriculum ("College preparatory courses carry a greater weight," according to Northeast's general bulletin), GPAs and class rank. These are followed, in order of importance, by extracurriculars, essays, the interview, and letters of recommendation. Either the SAT or ACT may be submitted. The suggested high school curriculum includes four units of language arts and English, three units each of science, social studies (including history) and mathematics, two units of a foreign language and one unit of fine arts. Applicants to NE Missouri State also often apply to U. Illinois–Urbana, Southwest Missouri State, and St. Louis U.

Financial Aid

Financial aid applicants to Northeast Missouri State must complete the FAF or the FFS (the FFS is preferred); certain applicants must also submit a copy of their parents' most recent tax return. The school awarded athletic grants to 3% of its undergrads last year; the average award was $1,853. Thirty-six percent of all undergrads received an academic scholarship; the average value was $1,551. Merit-based scholarships are also awarded for achievements in language, debate, music, art, theatre and leadership. Three percent of '90–'91 undergrads received one of these awards, which averaged $615. NE Missouri State recommends a variety of loans, including Perkins, PLUS, SLS, TERI, and its own institutional loans.

A note from the Northeast Missouri State University Admissions Office:

"Northeast Missouri State University is the premier liberal arts and sciences school for the state of Missouri. The belief that liberal learning is the cornerstone of the undergraduate experience is reflected in every facet of the university.

"Northeast complements this commitment to liberal arts and sciences with the educational philosophy that the acquisition of knowledge and skills is best facilitated in an active learning environment. Northeast has integrated this philosophy through pairing a competitive academic climate with small class sizes, allowing a dynamic, interactive style of instruction."

ADMISSIONS FACTS

Competitiveness Rating:	**80**
% of applicants accepted:	50
% acceptees attending:	38

FRESHMAN PROFILE

Average verbal SAT:	530
Average math SAT:	533
Average ACT:	26
Graduated top 10% HS class:	37
Graduated top 25% HS class:	71
Graduated top 50% HS class:	96

DEADLINES

Early decision/action:	11/5
Early dec./act. notif.:	12/15
Regular admission:	3/1
Regular adm. notif.:	rolling

APPLICANTS ALSO LOOK AT

and sometimes prefer:
Lawrence U.

and rarely prefer:
U. Iowa
Illinois State U.
U. Illinois
Illinois Wesleyan U.
Purdue U.
St. Louis U.

ADDRESS

Undergraduate Admissions
McClain Hall 205
Kirksville, MO 63501
816-785-4114

FINANCIAL FACTS

In-state tuition ($):	1,800
Out-of-state tuition ($):	3,504
Room & board:	2,584
FA application deadline:	4/30
% frosh receiving FA:	88
PT earnings per yr. ($):	572

TYPE OF AID: % of students ($)

FA of some kind:	75 (NA)
Need-based grants:	20 (1,508)
Merit-based grants:	NA
Loans:	30 (2,947)
Work study:	5 (1,020)
Student rating of FA:	80

NORTHEASTERN UNIVERSITY

Boston, MA

CAMPUS LIFE

Quality of Life Rating: 67

Type of School:	private
Affiliation:	none
Environment:	city

STUDENT BODY

FT undergrad enrollment:	13,788
% male/% female:	60/40
% out-of-state:	36
% live on campus:	25
% African-American:	5
% Asian:	3
% Caucasian:	63
% Hispanic:	2
% foreign:	8
% transfers:	17

WHAT'S HOT

requirements are easy
in-class discussion
working a job
studying hard

WHAT'S NOT

campus appearance
TAs teach upper levels
hard liquor
campus easy to get around
overall happiness
attending all classes
beer
college newspaper
doing all assigned reading

ACADEMICS

Academic Rating: 71

Calendar:	quarters
Student/teacher ratio:	16/1
% doctorates:	77
Profs interesting:	70
Profs accessible:	70
Hours of study per day:	3.57

MOST POPULAR MAJORS BY %

Business & Management:	35
Engineering:	16
Allied Health:	8

What do students think about Northeastern University?

■ **Academics** Ask Northeastern students why they chose their university and most mention the cooperative education program first. This five-year B.A. program requires students to spend two of their four quarters each year (after freshman year) at work for one of thousands of employers who participate in the program. Jobs are predominantly in the New England area, although the co-op does send students across the country and even overseas. Explained one student, "Because of co-op, I have had the experience of writing a resume, negotiating for a higher salary, and working in my field. I think this school is underrated." Not surprisingly, studies at the university are predominantly geared towards the professions: over one third of the students are pre-business, and engineering, pharmacology, and physical therapy are also popular. Because the school is huge, it's easy to get lost in the crowd: "You need a lot of self-discipline because it's a big school and basically you're on your own," said one student. Yet for a school of its size, complaints about class size, administration, and inaccessible professors were surprisingly rare. On the contrary, one student told us, "The college of pharmacology is a small college in a large university, so I benefit from both," while another said that "business teachers at Northeastern have worked in the business world, owned businesses, etc., and they teach because they want to help students, not because they need the money."

■ **Life** Social life at Northeastern is strongly influenced by the co-op plan. With students spending one quarter on campus and the next at work, it can be difficult to form deep friendships with classmates. The campus, spread out and ugly, does little to help the situation, nor does the large commuter population. As a result, students find small groups of friends and stick with them: "Social interaction between groups doesn't happen," said one student. The lack of a cohesive social scene probably explains why Northeastern students gave themselves low grades in overall happiness despite their general satisfaction with their academic program. Still, the school is in downtown Boston, the college student's Mecca. Clubs, bars, record and book stores, and Fenway Park are just a stone's throw away.

■ **Students** Students here are pretty serious about the programs they are pursuing. Many slacked off during high school and are attending Northeastern for the direction and discipline it imposes. Students here study hard and don't drink nearly as much as they are reputed to, but they aren't Puritans. They're just a little more focused and conservative than the average college student. Said one, "If you want to drink, go to a less traditional school like Hampshire; if you want to get a job when you graduate, go to Northeastern." Northeastern is yet another school with a good ethnic mix where, sadly, most groups simply don't, or don't get the chance to, interact.

354

NORTHEASTERN UNIVERSITY

Admissions

The admissions office at Northeastern University considers your high school GPA and the quality of courses taken the most important component of your application. It then considers, in descending order of importance: standardized test scores, extracurricular activities, interview, essays, and letters of recommendation. Applicants must submit scores for the SAT and three achievements, of which English composition must be one. The school catalog recommends "an academically challenging secondary school program—one that includes courses in English, mathematics, laboratory science, history, and a foreign language. Proficiency in a foreign language is especially important for applicants interested in study or cooperative placement abroad." According to the school, applicants to Northeastern most often also apply to UMass–Amherst, Boston U., Boston College, Syracuse U., and U. of Rhode Island.

Financial Aid

The financial aid office at Northeastern requires applicants to submit the FAF. The school offers merit scholarships for academic excellence and athletic skill; other non-need-based grants are awarded on the basis of field of study and place of birth. The school's catalog lists the following loan options: Stafford, Perkins, PLUS/SLS, and Nursing Student. The catalog also states, "Awards are made on a first-applied, first aided basis."

A note from the Northeastern University Admissions Office:

"Northeastern University is the acknowledged leader in cooperative education. 'Coop' allows students to alternate classwork with regular periods of paid professional employment related to students' career interests."

ADMISSIONS FACTS

Competitiveness Rating:	**63**
% of applicants accepted:	48
% acceptees attending:	29

FRESHMAN PROFILE

Average verbal SAT:	447
Average math SAT:	504
Average ACT:	21
Graduated top 10% HS class:	15
Graduated top 25% HS class:	38
Graduated top 50% HS class:	68

DEADLINES

Early decision/action:	NA
Early dec./act. notif.:	NA
Regular admission:	1/15
Regular adm. notif.:	rolling

APPLICANTS ALSO LOOK AT

and often prefer:
MIT
Drexel U.
Boston U.

and sometimes prefer:
U. Connecticut
U. Mass–Amherst

ADDRESS

Undergraduate Admissions
360 Huntington Avenue
Boston, MA 02115-9056
617-437-2200

FINANCIAL FACTS

In-state tuition ($):	10,523
Out-of-state tuition ($):	10,523
Room & board:	6,690
FA application deadline:	4/15
% frosh receiving FA:	81
PT earnings per yr. ($):	2,050

TYPE OF AID: % of students ($)

FA of some kind:	64 (NA)
Need-based grants:	NA
Merit-based grants:	NA
Loans:	NA
Work study:	NA
Student rating of FA:	79

NORTHWESTERN UNIVERSITY

Evanston, IL

CAMPUS LIFE

Quality of Life Rating: **89**

Type of School:	private
Affiliation:	none
Environment:	city

STUDENT BODY

FT undergrad enrollment:	7,360
% male/% female:	50/50
% out-of-state:	73
% live on campus:	74
% African-American:	7
% Asian:	11
% Caucasian:	80
% Hispanic:	2
% foreign:	1
% transfers:	2

WHAT'S HOT

college theater groups
overall happiness
library
food
college newspaper
campus appearance
dorm comfort
classical music

WHAT'S NOT

dating
working a job

ACADEMICS

Academic Rating: **90**

Calendar:	quarters
Student/teacher ratio:	8/1
% doctorates:	96
Profs interesting:	78
Profs accessible:	78
Hours of study per day:	3.03

MOST POPULAR MAJORS BY %

Social Sciences:	29
Communications:	15
Health Sciences:	12

% GRADS WHO PURSUE

Law:	12
MBA:	2
Medicine:	11
M.A., etc.:	10

What do students think about Northwestern University?

■ **Academics** When indicating why they chose Northwestern University, many of our respondents noted the diversity of experiences available to the NU undergrad. Said one, "I came to NU because it seemed to have everything I wanted in a perfect package: great theater department with a wide variety of opportunities, strong Greek life, well-respected academic program, and Chicago, Chicago—what a wonderful town!" Academics at Northwestern are first-rate, with the school's programs in engineering, journalism, and theater receiving the praise of our respondents; liberal arts departments are also uniformly strong, while the 11 percent of graduates who proceed to medical school attests to the success of NU's pre-med departments. Still, the school's reputation among college-bound students remains just one notch below the Ivies. Students accepted here and at an Ivy League institution continue consistently to choose the Ivy, although, given the overall satisfaction of NU students (see "Students," below), one could easily wonder why. One NU student did: "When I first came here I was a little disappointed because I'd wanted to go to Princeton. But now—wow! I'm a senior and I wouldn't have gone anyplace else had I known about Northwestern from the start."

■ **Life** As mentioned previously, Chicago is a great town, only half an hour away by public transportation. "Evanston's a bit dull," said one student of the school's suburban setting, "but the easy access to Chicago more than definitely makes up for it." Northwestern scored well in most quality-of-life categories, rating particularly high for its beautiful campus, comfortable dorms, and better-than-edible food. Extracurricular activities are popular here, which, coupled with the reasonable number of hours students study (three hours a day, about the national average), indicates that life at Northwestern doesn't begin and end in the classroom. Dating is not popular here, however. In fact, students' response to the question, "How frequently do students date?" ranked 18th lowest in the nation. It's not that students have no social life; it's just that dating and sex seems to play a pretty small role in it. As one student said, "Most nights there are people going to bars and partying. But if you need to stay in and study, everyone understands and you won't be alone. There seems to be a really good balance between studying and fun." Students had few nice things to say about Chicago winters, which are severe.

■ **Students** Students at Northwestern University scored high in what is arguably the single most important category: overall happiness. Their answer to the question, "How happy are you here?" yielded a 3.6, fifth highest among the schools we surveyed. They are very bright, but in every other way are very much the average college students.

NORTHWESTERN UNIVERSITY

Admissions

The admissions committee at Northwestern University considers applicants on the basis of the rigor of their high school curricula and their GPA, their SAT (or ACT) scores, application essay, extracurricular activities, and a letter of recommendation. An interview, either on-campus or with an alumnus/alumna, is recommended but not required; achievement exams (one of which should be English Composition) are also recommended. NU requires no specific high school curriculum, but strongly recommends that applicants have completed four years of English, three years each of math, science, social studies, and a foreign language. Students who apply to Northwestern most often also apply to University of Chicago, Harvard, Yale, Columbia, Princeton, and Stanford.

Financial Aid

Financial aid applicants to Northwestern must complete the FAF. In '91–'92, Northwestern awarded more than $24 million in need-based grants to its undergraduates; half of the undergraduate body received a Northwestern grant; more than 60% received some form of assistance. In '91–'92, the average freshman who received aid was awarded an overall package worth $13,134; $8,922 in grants, $2,720 in loans, and $1,492 in part-time employment. In addition to need-based grants, athletic, forensic, and music scholarships are available, as are ROTC and various outside scholarships.

A note from the Northwestern University Admissions Office:

"Consistent with its dedication to excellence, Northwestern provides both an educational and an extracurricular environment that enables its undergraduate students to become accomplished individuals and informed and responsible citizens. To the students in all its undergraduate schools, Northwestern offers liberal learning and professional education to help them gain the depth of knowledge that will empower them to become leaders in their professions and communities. Furthermore, Northwestern fosters in its students a broad understanding of the world in which we live as well as excellence in the competencies that transcend any particular field of study: writing and oral communication, analytical and creative thinking and expression, quantitative and qualitative methods of thinking."

ADMISSIONS FACTS

Competitiveness Rating:	**94**
% of applicants accepted:	46
% acceptees attending:	35

FRESHMAN PROFILE

Average verbal SAT:	580
Average math SAT:	670
Average ACT:	28
Graduated top 10% HS class:	82
Graduated top 25% HS class:	96
Graduated top 50% HS class:	100

DEADLINES

Early decision/action:	11/1
Early dec./act. notif.:	1/1
Regular admission:	8/15
Regular adm. notif.:	rolling

APPLICANTS ALSO LOOK AT

and often prefer:
Yale U.
Harvard/Radcliffe College

and sometimes prefer:
U. Chicago
Stanford U.

and rarely prefer:
DePaul U.
Marquette U.
Denison U.
Purdue U.

ADDRESS

Undergraduate Admissions
P.O. Box 3060
1801 Hinman Avenue
Evanston, IL 60204-3060
312-491-7271

FINANCIAL FACTS

In-state tuition ($):	14,370
Out-of-state tuition ($):	14,370
Room & board:	4,827
FA application deadline:	2/15
% frosh receiving FA:	63
PT earnings per yr. ($):	1,500

TYPE OF AID: % of students ($)

FA of some kind:	63 (NA)
Need-based grants:	NA
Merit-based grants:	NA
Loans:	NA
Work study:	NA
Student rating of FA:	83

UNIVERSITY OF NOTRE DAME

Notre Dame, IN

What do students think about the University of Notre Dame?

■ **Academics** The University of Notre Dame is highly respected, not only in the sports arena, but in nearly all academic fields as well. The strongest departments are considered to be in the pre-professional fields. Students told us that the pre-med program, chemical engineering, architecture, and accounting are standouts. The College of Arts and Letters boasts fine programs as well. English and history are among its best. The core curriculum reflects Notre Dame's Catholic tenor: among the usual math, science, and writing requirements are several courses in theology and philosophy. Students receive lots of academic guidance at Notre Dame, especially through Freshman Year of Studies program, which prescribes the entire freshman curriculum. Many appreciate the extra structure, but some find it restrictive. One student complained, "The administration obviously has read Orwell's *1984*." On the whole, the administration gets mixed reviews. Some consider it "slow to respond to the students' needs. The red tape here would make the federal government gawk." Others praise it for running the school smoothly. Registration, for example, is a surprisingly painless process for a school of this size. The faculty is perceived as "taking interest in the students," and overall students rated their academic experiences as "fantastic."

■**Life** The crux of extracurricular life at Notre Dame is definitely sports. One student wrote, "The football games generate incredible energy among the student body; it's truly a religious experience." Religion is also extremely important here. The Catholic tradition of the school is well preserved, and a large majority of the students are practicing Catholics. The emphasis on faith distinctly affects the social atmosphere. One student explained, for instance, that "every sexual issue here is also a spiritual one; sex is more or less out of the question." Long-term relationships are on many people's minds here, according to our surveys. One woman wrote, "Students here pretend that marrying an ND guy isn't important, but many are searching for an MRS degree along with an undergraduate one." To further complicate matters, men outnumber women by almost two to one. Most students live on campus, and submit to strict visitation rules. Many "live in the same dorm for all four years, and the dorm often plays the role of a fraternity/sorority." The Greek system is officially banned at ND. Drugs and smoking are "rarely seen at parties," perhaps due to the strong religious character of the school, but NDers know how to drink, describing themselves as "always the first to crack open a Bud." Some students insist that at Notre Dame, "beer is the fourth member of the Trinity."

■ **Students:** One student summed up quite well: "If you seek true diversity, a Catholic school in Indiana may leave you disappointed. This is a bastion of conservatism, yet that also creates a stable, ethical environment. Notre Dame offers a comfortable atmosphere in which you may find the best friends of your life while getting an excellent education."

UNIVERSITY OF NOTRE DAME

Notre Dame, IN

Admissions

The admissions office reports that it uses no formulas or cut-offs, but adds "we rate the academic and non-academic achievements of each applicant." Notre Dame also suggests that "applicants should take the time to present themselves in a thoughtful, creative way." Class rank, high school curriculum/GPA, and standardized test scores are the most important components of your application here. Also considered, but less important, are essays, letters of recommendation, and extracurricular activities. Interviews are not part of the application process here. Applicants are expected to have completed course work in English, math, science, history, and a foreign language. Notre Dame requires either the SAT or the ACT. Applicants to Notre Dame often also apply to Duke, Georgetown, Boston College, Northwestern, Michigan, and Cornell U.

Financial Aid

The financial aid office at the University of Notre Dame requires applicants to submit the FAF. According to the school, approximately 60 percent of the freshman class applied for financial aid; two thirds of those received an award, the average value of which was $8,425. The school reports, "All financial aid, including scholarship assistance, includes a financial need determination."

A note from the University of Notre Dame Admissions Office:

"Notre Dame is a Catholic university, which means it offers unique opportunities for academic, ethical, spiritual, and social service development. The Freshman Year of Studies program provides special assistance to our students as they make the adjustment from high school to college. The first-year curriculum includes many core requirements, while allowing students to explore several areas of possible future study. Each residence hall is home to students from all classes; most will live in the same hall for all their years on campus. An average of 92 percent of entering students will graduate within five years."

ADMISSIONS FACTS

Competitiveness Rating:	**94**
% of applicants accepted:	37
% acceptees attending:	53

FRESHMAN PROFILE

Average verbal SAT:	572
Average math SAT:	650
Average ACT:	NA
Graduated top 10% HS class:	80
Graduated top 25% HS class:	98
Graduated top 50% HS class:	100

DEADLINES

Early decision/action:	11/1
Early dec./act. notif.:	12/15
Regular admission:	1/8
Regular adm. notif.:	4/10

APPLICANTS ALSO LOOK AT

and often prefer:
Princeton U.
Harvard/Radcliffe College
U. Virginia

and sometimes prefer:
Georgetown U.

and rarely prefer:
Columbia U.
U. Michigan
College of the Holy Cross
Lehigh U.
U. Wisconsin–Madison

ADDRESS

Undergraduate Admissions
Notre Dame, IN 46556
219-239-7505

FINANCIAL FACTS

In-state tuition ($):	13,500
Out-of-state tuition ($):	13,500
Room & board:	3,575
FA application deadline:	2/28
% frosh receiving FA:	65
PT earnings per yr. ($):	1,200

TYPE OF AID: % of students ($)

FA of some kind:	65 (8,190)
Need-based grants:	NA
Merit-based grants:	NA
Loans:	NA
Work study:	NA
Student rating of FA:	79

OBERLIN COLLEGE

CAMPUS LIFE

Quality of Life Rating:	*79*
Type of School:	private
Affiliation:	none
Environment:	suburban

STUDENT BODY

FT undergrad enrollment:	2,423
% male/% female:	48/52
% out-of-state:	88
% live on campus:	65
% African-American:	8
% Asian:	8
% Caucasian:	75
% Hispanic:	3
% foreign:	5
% transfers:	2

WHAT'S HOT

classical music
gay community accepted
library
rap/hip-hop
alternative rock
studying hard
diversity
leftist politics
college theater
profs in class
college radio station
profs teach intro courses

WHAT'S NOT

fraternities/sororities
intercollegiate sports

ACADEMICS

Academic Rating:	*86*
Calendar:	4-1-4
Student/teacher ratio:	13/1
% doctorates:	91
Profs interesting:	92
Profs accessible:	87
Hours of study per day:	3.85

MOST POPULAR MAJORS BY %

English:	15
Biology:	10
Psychology:	7

% GRADS WHO PURSUE

Law:	1
MBA:	NA
Medicine:	1
M.A., etc.:	20

What do students think about Oberlin College?

■ **Academics** Oberlin students rated their college highly in nearly every academic category. An outstanding liberal arts school connected to a world-renowned conservatory of music, Oberlin has something to offer almost everyone. The atmosphere is "academically intense, yet noncompetitive"; classes are challenging and small; and the professors are "*extremely* accessible. You really get a sense that they are eager to meet you and help you with anything they can." The sciences are unusually strong and well-supported for those at a small liberal arts school. Also popular among students are English, performing arts, history, and minority studies Oberlin pioneered race-, gender-, and faith-blind admissions in the U.S. All students must complete a wide array of distribution requirements that include three courses geared toward promoting awareness of cultural diversity. Students study hard during the semester (almost four hours a day), but are offered the chance to lighten up during EXCO, which offers a variety of short, offbeat courses during January. Conservatory students are well integrated into academic life, with many of them opting for Oberlin's popular five-year combined BM/BA program. Over half the students take advantage of opportunities to spend at least one semester off-campus, either in the U.S. or abroad: study in Asia is a particularly popular option here.

■ **Life** One student remarked, "Oberlin is a place where green hair is as common as Levi's in a country and western bar." The college's bohemian, slightly weird image is slowly changing, but this is certainly no place for the uptight prepster. The social scene is atypical as well: there are no fraternities or sororities, and Oberlin undergraduates much prefer political debates, concerts, and plays to drinking or playing sports. Indeed, the enthusiastic responses we received to our questions about theater and music were virtually unparalleled at other colleges. The campus, is described as beautiful and ugly, depending on where you are standing at the moment. The town of Oberlin is small and generally unremarkable and is "surrounded by farmland. We see corn, corn, and more corn," wrote one student. However, Cleveland is not too far away, and students do enjoy a vast array of cultural offerings on campus. Overall, students claimed to be quite happy here, and even some graduating seniors were not overly eager to leave their beloved community.

■ **Students** Oberlin has been described as "the Mecca for the lesbian/gay/bisexual collegiate community." Ethnic diversity, as well as acceptance of all racial and social groups, is very high: over one fourth of the students here are minorities. The student body classified itself as "largely liberal," with a commitment to progressive political issues unusual for Midwesterners. Summed up one student: "If such a thing is possible, the majority of people here conform to non-conformity."

OBERLIN COLLEGE

Admissions

The admissions office reports that it uses no cut-offs or formulas to eliminate candidates for admittance, and adds that "test scores, GPA, recommendations, and application itself are important." Oberlin considers extracurricular activities very important, indicating that they place a premium on finding "well-rounded" students. Interviews are not part of the application process. Applicants must have completed four years each of English and math (beyond Algebra II), three years each of social studies (including history), science, and one foreign language. Applicants must provide scores for either the SAT or ACT.

Financial Aid

Oberlin College requires a FAF of all its financial aid applicants. The school gives out many merit-based grants, including National Merit ('91–'92: 2% of undergrads, average value of $1,021) and Conservatory Deans' Talent (3%; $3,750). Last year, 45% of freshman received aid, with an average award value of $14,347. The FA office at Oberlin notes that full demonstrated need is met for all on-time filers (applications must be *in office* by 2/1, not postmarked). In the '91–'92 academic year, the office recommended Stafford loans to 43% of all undergrads (average value: $3,065), Perkins loans to 29% ($1,115) and its own institutional loans to 3% ($4,286). Admissions is need blind, except for international and wait-list students.

A note from the Oberlin College Admissions Office:

"Since its founding in 1833, the faculty of Oberlin College and its graduates have brought Oberlin national recognition as an institution of academic excellence and rigor—and as an institution with a historic commitment to the most basic of human values. Oberlin was the first college to grant degrees to women and the first to declare its instruction open to all races.

"Oberlin's student body of 2,750 students is national in scope and chosen largely from among the top 10 percent of all graduating students in the country. The college is located in a small town 35 miles from Cleveland, Ohio, surrounded by a green belt of farms and open land. The facilities are exceptional for a school of Oberlin's size: one of the nation's best college art museums, the third largest library collection of any comparable school in the country, two Digital VAX 11/780 computers and a VAX 11/750, extensive music practice and rehearsal facilities, and a modern gymnasium adjacent to 22 outdoor playing fields. The talented students and splendid facilities create what is Oberlin's unique and perhaps most distinguishing feature: the coexistence of a first rate liberal arts college with one of the nation's finest music schools."

ADMISSIONS FACTS

Competitiveness Rating:	**90**
% of applicants accepted:	54
% acceptees attending:	30

FRESHMAN PROFILE

Average verbal SAT:	611
Average math SAT:	638
Average ACT:	28
Graduated top 10% HS class:	66
Graduated top 25% HS class:	88
Graduated top 50% HS class:	100

DEADLINES

Early decision/action:	10/15
Early dec./act. notif.:	1/1
Regular admission:	1/15
Regular adm. notif.:	4/1

APPLICANTS ALSO LOOK AT

and often prefer:
Stanford U.
Wesleyan U.

and sometimes prefer:
Haverford College
Tufts U.
Grinnell College
Williams College
Connecticut College

and rarely prefer:
Carleton College

ADDRESS

Undergraduate Admissions
Oberlin, OH 44074
216-775-8411

FINANCIAL FACTS

In-state tuition ($):	16,375
Out-of-state tuition ($):	16,375
Room & board:	5,155
FA application deadline:	2/1
% frosh receiving FA:	41
PT earnings per yr. ($):	1,450

TYPE OF AID:	% of students ($)
FA of some kind:	46 (14,209)
Need-based grants:	45 (10,050)
Merit-based grants:	NA
Loans:	47 (3,857)
Work study:	45 (1,450)
Student rating of FA:	71

OCCIDENTAL COLLEGE

Los Angeles, CA

What do students think about Occidental College?

■ **Academics** Like many small liberal arts schools, Occidental College offers a talented, dedicated faculty with whom students can work closely on a regular basis. Wrote one student, "the interaction between students and faculty is fantastic! Most profs have their home phone numbers on their office doors in case you need to see them. Some profs have the class over for dinner at the end of the term." The results of such attention are impressive: nearly one third of Oxy's graduates proceed to pre-professional programs within a year, and as many again go on to academic graduate programs. Even more impressive is the fact that Oxy has not tailored its academic program to obtain these results. On the contrary, the school's program demands that students complete a core curriculum so demanding that they are prevented from over-specializing in the field of their choice. For most students, core requirements—which include healthy doses of world culture, as well as math, science, humanities, and foreign language—take a full two years to complete (although a brave few opt for Core II, which allows students to finish all requirements during freshman year). Popular majors include the pre-medical sciences, economics, English, marine biology, and politics. All are reportedly excellent, as are nearly all departments here.

■ **Life** Studies definitely take priority over fun at Occidental. Reported one student, "Wild parties are rare, semi-okay parties occur between 10 p.m. and 1 a.m. on Fridays and Saturdays, but the rest of the time is given to studying." Hanging out with friends and shooting the breeze is considered a good night off from studies. As one student explained, "People here are intelligent and friendly. If you pass someone you don't know, chances are that student will at least say 'hi.' A popular pastime at Oxy is simply sitting around and talking about backgrounds, deep personal feelings, societal issues, etc." Community service and Christian Fellowship activities are also popular. Because the student body is small, Oxy "has the advantages or disadvantages of a family or a small town. If you breathe too loud, your friends will know, but so will your enemies." When life on campus ("which is gorgeous," students agreed) gets boring or oppressive, there's always Los Angeles. Oxy is located in an L.A. neighborhood called Eagle Rock, which students uniformly panned. The fun parts of L.A. (Santa Monica, Venice Beach, Hollywood), however, are within driving distance.

■ **Students** Several Oxy undergrads noted a pervasive p.c. streak among the student body. Said one, "Oxy is very p.c. and frequently tries to 'shove it down' people's throats, but once you look beyond that nonsense, you tend to get used to the outrageousness of students' opinions on issues." Added another, "People are extreme—extremely militant, extremely religious, extremely wild, or extremely apathetic. Whatever you choose to do at Oxy, you'd better do it 99 percent or not at all." Nearly one third of the students are minorities; Asians and Hispanics both constitute sizable on-campus populations.

OCCIDENTAL COLLEGE

Los Angeles, CA

Admissions

From Occidental's undergraduate catalog: "The Committee on Admission looks for students with very strong academic and personal qualifications who demonstrate motivation, accomplishment, involvement, and commitment. The majority of students admitted to the College rank in the upper 5 to 10 percent of their high school classes. Because the individual characteristics of each candidate are considered, no specific formula of grades and scores guarantees admission. Rigor of coursework, grades, test scores, recommendations, and extracurricular activities are all taken into consideration when the freshman class is selected." Applicants should have taken four years of English, three years of a foreign language, three years each of mathematics and social studies, and one year each of biological and physical science. Students interested in science or engineering should include chemistry and physics, and should take an additional year of mathematics. All students are required to submit SAT (preferred) or ACT scores.

Financial Aid

Financial aid applicants to Occidental must complete the FAF and a form generated by Occidental's financial aid office (California residents must complete the SAAC). Sixty-seven percent of the class of '95 received some form of aid upon entry; the average award value was $12,980. Scholarships are available for academic merit, talent and leadership.

Excerpted from Occidental College promotional materials:

"The College is committed to a philosophy of total education. Intellectual capability is a dominant component, but is conceived of as one dimension in a process which includes and stresses personal, ethical, social, and political growth toward maturation as well. The high percentage of students in residence at the College works toward the achievement of this objective.

"Successful Occidental students are self-motivated, independent-minded, and intellectually talented people. They base their judgments upon respect for evidence, ideas, and a deep concern for values, both private and public. They are alert to the possibilities of betterment, in themselves, their college, and their society. Above all, they realize that no education is finished, that they are in college to learn how to learn, so that they may carry on their own education for the rest of their lives."

ADMISSIONS FACTS

Competitiveness Rating:	**86**
% of applicants accepted:	49
% acceptees attending:	33

FRESHMAN PROFILE

Average verbal SAT:	550
Average math SAT:	600
Average ACT:	NA
Graduated top 10% HS class:	57
Graduated top 25% HS class:	85
Graduated top 50% HS class:	97

DEADLINES

Early decision/action:	11/15
Early dec./act. notif.:	12/15
Regular admission:	2/1
Regular adm. notif.:	4/1

APPLICANTS ALSO LOOK AT

and often prefer:

Yale U.
Columbia U.
UC Davis
Pomona College

and sometimes prefer:

UC Berkeley
UC Los Angeles
USC

and rarely prefer:

Pitzer College

ADDRESS

Undergraduate Admissions
1600 Campus Rd.
Los Angeles, CA 90041
213-259-2700

FINANCIAL FACTS

In-state tuition ($):	14,517
Out-of-state tuition ($):	14,517
Room & board:	4,613
FA application deadline:	2/1
% frosh receiving FA:	65
PT earnings per yr. ($):	1,400

TYPE OF AID: % of students ($)

FA of some kind:	63 (14,014)
Need-based grants:	NA
Merit-based grants:	NA
Loans:	NA
Work study:	NA
Student rating of FA:	86

OGLETHORPE UNIVERSITY

Atlanta, GA

What do students think about Oglethorpe University?

■ **Academics** Ask most students to name the most prestigious, most competitive school in Atlanta (or in Georgia, for that matter) and most will instinctively respond, "Emory." Ask them to name another, and many will draw a blank. On the periphery of Atlanta, however, is a small school that inexplicably attracts only the peripheral attention of most South-bound students. That school is Oglethorpe University. The student body receives a rigorous education, particularly in the pre-professional fields, and all Oglethorpe students must complete an unusually demanding and broad-based set of general education requirements, which constitute nearly half the credits required toward education. Despite the pre-professional inclinations of most undergrads, the core demands that students approach school work with an attitude traditionally adopted by students at liberal arts–oriented colleges. Wrote one student, "OU's classes and general atmosphere are extremely academic. Every part of life is open to a multi-political, multi-cultural, objective debate in the quest for truth." Most students agree that "the faculty is superior and clearly is the outstanding reason to attend OU." Others, without detracting from the quality of the faculty, might point to OU's excellent placement record with graduate programs as their chief motivation for attending. Pre-medicine and business majors are by far most popular with the students, although liberal arts and social sciences are also reportedly strong. Students may cross-register at other Atlanta schools when desired courses are not offered at OU.

■ **Life** Students at Oglethorpe gave Atlanta an unqualified thumbs-up, responding positively to its many clubs, restaurants, professional athletic teams, and "excellent weather." On campus, the Greek scene is popular, and parties are frequent. Despite a "dry campus" policy, students report that access to alcohol is often sought after and easily found. Said one student, "I know of no other school that studies and parties with equal intensity. We have the best of both worlds." Support for the school's Division III teams is moderate. Men's basketball and soccer are the most popular teams. Intramural sports are more popular, and most students participate on at least one intramural team. All in all, though, students reported that participation in most extracurricular clubs and activities is below average. Reported one student, "Oglethorpe is a small community, very sheltered from the 'real world.' Campus life is not booming and participation is low in most activities."

■ **Students** Oglethorpe pioneered the admission of black students to non-black universities in the South. Today the black population is only four percent: minority population overall is a more impressive 19 percent. OU works hard to make its education affordable to everyone it accepts—a large majority of students receive some form of financial aid—and students reported that, as a result, students of diverse social backgrounds are well represented.

OGLETHORPE UNIVERSITY

Atlanta, GA

Admissions

According to Oglethorpe's brochure, "Admission...is a selective, yet personalized process....In building each class, Oglethorpe looks beyond academic achievement to find the unique characteristics of each individual. Factors such as talent, interests, and extracurricular achievements of each candidate as well as geographic and ethnic diversity, are strongly considered....Achievement tests, essays, portfolios, or videos are not required for admission purposes but will be considered if submitted. Interviews and campus visits are not required but are strongly recommended." The admissions committee writes that it first looks at the sequence of your coursework and your high school GPA; after these, in order of importance, come your standardized test scores (SAT or ACT accepted), letters of recommendation, extracurriculars, essays, and interview. Admissions are rolling, but priority is given to applications received by March 1.

Financial Aid

Financial aid applicants to Oglethorpe must complete the FAF, FFS, or SingleFile. Oglethorpe notes in its brochure that "many families who do not apply [for financial aid] would have received aid if they had." To encourage families to apply, Oglethorpe offers this intriguing guarantee: the University *guarantees* each enrolling student who applies for financial assistance a minimum award of $100 in grant aid. "We make this offer because we are confident that the results will surprise many families." Payment plans are available, as are a number of scholarships based on considerations such as academic merit, leadership, artistic talent, and religious affiliation/commitment.

A note from the Oglethorpe University Admissions Office:

"Promising students and outstanding teachers come together at Oglethorpe University in an acclaimed program of liberal arts and sciences. Here you'll find an active intellectual community on a beautiful English Gothic campus just 10 miles from the center of Atlanta, capital of the Southeast, site of the 1996 Summer Olympics and home to 2.8 million people. If you want challenging academics, the opportunity to work closely with your professors and the stimulation of a great metropolitan area, consider Oglethorpe, a national liberal arts college in a world-class city."

ADMISSIONS FACTS

Competitiveness Rating:	**81**
% of applicants accepted:	78
% acceptees attending:	33

FRESHMAN PROFILE

Average verbal SAT:	541
Average math SAT:	580
Average ACT:	26
Graduated top 10% HS class:	50
Graduated top 25% HS class:	83
Graduated top 50% HS class:	98

DEADLINES

Early decision/action:	12/1
Early dec./act. notif.:	12/11
Regular admission:	rolling
Regular adm. notif.:	rolling

APPLICANTS ALSO LOOK AT

and often prefer:
Emory U.
Florida State U.

and sometimes prefer:
U. Georgia
U. of the South
Furman U.

ADDRESS

Undergraduate Admissions
4484 Peachtree Road N. E.
Atlanta, GA 30319-2797
404-233-6864

FINANCIAL FACTS

In-state tuition ($):	10,250
Out-of-state tuition ($):	10,250
Room & board:	4,000
FA application deadline:	5/1
% frosh receiving FA:	88
PT earnings per yr. ($):	1,200

TYPE OF AID: % of students ($)

FA of some kind:	85 (NA)
Need-based grants:	NA
Merit-based grants:	NA
Loans:	NA
Work study:	NA
Student rating of FA:	85

OHIO UNIVERSITY

Athens, OH

CAMPUS LIFE

Quality of Life Rating: **81**

Type of School:	public
Affiliation:	none
Environment:	suburban

STUDENT BODY

FT undergrad enrollment:	14,500
% male/% female:	48/52
% out-of-state:	25
% live on campus:	99
% African-American:	7
% Asian:	1
% Caucasian:	80
% Hispanic:	1
% foreign:	8
% transfers:	3

WHAT'S HOT
cost of living
living on campus
doing all the reading
profs lecture a lot
campus appearance

WHAT'S NOT
small lectures
working a job
small labs and seminars
registration
small classes (overall)

ACADEMICS

Academic Rating: **68**

Calendar:	quarters
Student/teacher ratio:	22/1
% doctorates:	76
Profs interesting:	75
Profs accessible:	71
Hours of study per day:	3.09

MOST POPULAR MAJORS BY %

Biology:	6
Accounting:	5
Journalism:	5

% GRADS WHO PURSUE

Law:	5
MBA:	5
Medicine:	5
M.A., etc.:	15

What do students think about Ohio University?

■ **Academics** Ohio University's biggest academic strength is its ability to offer many of its students a private-style education for a reasonable, public-school price. The excellent honors tutorial program allows select students to work more closely with professors than is usually possible at a large university. Standout areas of study include communications and the "renowned journalism school." Also, education and business are both popular and high quality. Distribution requirements have become more rigorous in recent years with the introduction of the "tier" system. Freshmen must conquer Tier I (English, writing and math), while upperclassmen must complete Tier II (assorted subjects including the natural sciences, social sciences, fine arts, Third World studies and humanities), and Tier III (one interdisciplinary course for seniors). Although some classes are quite large, most are reasonable; in fact, students claimed that many classes have fewer than 20 members, particularly once one has completed required and introductory courses. Registration, however, is problematic, with many students (especially underclassmen) running up against closed classes. The faculty and administration received relatively high marks overall.

■ **Life** Students described life at Ohio U. as "extremely nice." The generally relaxed academic atmosphere frees students from the need for intense decompression common at many schools. Some admit to taking this attitude a bit too far. One carefree student wrote, "beer and sex top the list of things to do. At the bottom there is studying." Partying opportunities are rarer now that the university is officially "dry," but a significant portion of students join the fun- and alcohol-loving Greeks each year, and the numerous bars in Athens are usually crowded with students. Despite the official policy, the motto for many remains, "When the load gets tough, the tough get loaded." Ohio U.'s campus is "very attractive." Campus beauty was cited in our surveys as a major asset of the school. Intercollegiate basketball is big, and the intramural scene can get quite intense during the popular flag football and broomball competitions. The fact that Athens, Ohio is far from any kind of urban center contributes to the feeling of isolation some get here, but the flip side for students is the freedom from unnecessary distractions that city students never experience. Students report a high level of happiness despite the lack of nearby skyscrapers, ski resorts or beaches. Most feel that the careers they prepare for here will ultimately allow them plenty of interesting travel.

■ **Students** Most students here are from in-state, and all in all, the OU crowd is fairly homogeneous. Approximately 1,000 blacks make up the only noticeable minority group here; other minority populations are tiny, unless one counts foreign students as a minority. The pre-professional white contingent, on the other hand, is huge. Within the student body, however, interaction is relatively high, and the student body's size enables most everyone at Ohio University to find a satisfying niche.

OHIO UNIVERSITY

Admissions

The admissions office reports that "most successful applicants will rank in the upper quarter of their class, possess a strong college-prep curriculum, and have ACT/SAT scores in the top quarter to top third of national norms (i.e., SATs combined: 1000; ACTs composite score: 23)." High school curriculum and class rank are most important, then standardized test scores. OU also considers essays and extracurricular activities, but not interviews. Applicants are required to have completed four years of English, three years each of math, science, and social studies, and two years of a foreign language. Applicants for the fine arts program may be required to audition or submit a portfolio. Those who apply to OU most often also apply to Miami of Ohio, Indiana University, Michigan State, Ohio State, Bowling Green State, and Penn State.

Financial Aid

The financial aid office at Ohio University requires applicants to submit the FAF, a form generated by the school, and their parents' most recent tax return. The school awards merit scholarships for athletics (2% of the students received one; average value: $4,500) and academic excellence (17%; $800). The school also provides grants targeted specifically for minority students (0.5%; $1,000). Loans are available from the university.

A note from the Ohio University Admissions Office:

"Ohio University is a public institution and was founded in 1804, making it Ohio's first university. Among the 15,000 undergraduate students are representatives from all 50 states and over 100 nations. The university is located in Athens, a classic college town of approximately 20,000 residents, and features a wide variety of cultural and recreational opportunities. The university seeks students who are interested in a residential university setting with over 250 majors from which to choose."

ADMISSIONS FACTS

Competitiveness Rating:	**74**
% of applicants accepted:	78
% acceptees attending:	40

FRESHMAN PROFILE

Average verbal SAT:	500
Average math SAT:	510
Average ACT:	23
Graduated top 10% HS class:	30
Graduated top 25% HS class:	75
Graduated top 50% HS class:	95

DEADLINES

Early decision/action:	NA
Early dec./act. notif.:	NA
Regular admission:	3/1
Regular adm. notif.:	rolling

APPLICANTS ALSO LOOK AT

and often prefer:
Oberlin College

and sometimes prefer:
Penn State U.
Michigan State U.
Ohio State U.
Wittenberg U.

and rarely prefer:
Purdue U.
Indiana U.
U. Dayton

ADDRESS

Undergraduate Admissions
120 Chubb Hall
Athens, OH 45701-2979
614-593-4100

FINANCIAL FACTS

In-state tuition ($):	2,946
Out-of-state tuition ($):	6,291
Room & board:	3,639
FA application deadline:	3/15
% frosh receiving FA:	50
PT earnings per yr. ($):	900

TYPE OF AID: % of students ($)

FA of some kind:	60 (NA)
Need-based grants:	NA (1,030)
Merit-based grants:	NA
Loans:	NA (2,600)
Work study:	NA
Student rating of FA:	80

OHIO STATE UNIVERSITY–COLUMBUS

Columbus, OH

What do students think about Ohio State University?

■ **Academics** Most Ohio State students would agree with the classmate who told us that "OSU has anything and everything both academically and socially." With over 34,000 full-time undergraduates (and another 6,000 part-timers), OSU is more like a small city than it is like most other colleges. As one student explained, "OSU is great not only for academics but also for life. There is such a wide range of ethnic, political, religious, and social beliefs, all of which count and make OSU so diverse." Career-oriented programs—accounting, nursing, engineering, etc.—are uniformly strong. The journalism program also has a good reputation, while engineering and business are among the other popular majors. As an added perk, OSU is extremely affordable. One student complained that "tuition is going up and services, such as the bus system, library hours, and the number of courses offered, are diminishing," but even if fees were to double next year, OSU would remain a bargain. As you might expect at a school with 40,000 undergraduates, classes are frequently huge and professors can be hard to contact personally, but relatively few students complained about these issues. Quite a few undergraduates felt that graduate students taught a distressing number of undergrad courses, however. OSU runs on a quarterly academic schedule.

■ **Life** Getting involved in the OSU community is the key to enjoying one's stay here, and it's something that requires students to take the initiative. Said one, "Because it's so large, you can't expect OSU to come to you—*you* have to get the most out of your education. Getting involved makes a big difference!" Once students become active in an organization, club, or social niche, the school's size ceases to intimidate them. There's something here for everyone, particularly if he or she happens to love intercollegiate sports (*especially* football). There's a very lively social scene, with plenty of drink, drugs, and promiscuity for those who want that, but there are also plenty of ways to avoid that social scene. Explained one student, "to attend this school is to have infinite control over your destiny. You can crouch in your room like Gregor Samsa transformed into a dung beetle, or you can plunge into the infinite sea of faces that each year flood OSU like a tidal wave." Explained another, "This campus is so big, it's tough to categorize anything, except that OSU is justifiably famous for its lines (to pay fees, buy tickets, get classes, etc.)."

■ **Students** One student summed up her experiences at OSU this way: "I have been exposed to an incredible variety of people, an experience I could only have had at a large school. I have met people of many nationalities, religions, and economic backgrounds. Additionally, there is every social group here, from frat rats to progressives to punks to Deadheads to snobs." Another put it more simply: "Because of OSU's size and diversity, you can always find another person like you." Students are politically conservative. They report that both interaction between ethnic groups and acceptance of gays are low.

OHIO STATE UNIVERSITY–COLUMBUS

Columbus, OH

Admissions

The admissions office reports that it "primarily reviews rank in high school, units of college prep courses, activities in high school, special talents, high test scores, contribution to the diversity of the student body, and special circumstances." OSU also considers letters of recommendation; essays and an interview are not part of the application process here. Applicants are required to have completed four years of English, three years of math, two years each of science, social science, and a foreign language, and one year of visual or performing arts. An extra year of math and language are recommended. Applicants must supply scores for either the ACT or SAT for class placement and to earn merit grants. Applicants to OSU most often also apply to Bowling Green State, Ohio U., Miami of Ohio, and University of Cincinnati.

Financial Aid

Financial aid applicants to Ohio State University must complete the FAF. In the '89–'90 academic year, the average financial aid recipient received $1,530 in grants, $2,030 in loans, and $1,080 in campus employment. Special academic-merit scholarships available include the Presidential Scholarship (estimated at $8,300) and the Medalist Scholarship (est. $2,300). Scholarships are also awarded for talent in a variety of areas (including business, landscaping, agriculture, music, art and athletics); for geographic residence; and for minorities. The FA office recommends Stafford, Perkins, PLUS, SLS and HEAL loans, as well as Ohio State's own institutional loans. Application deadline for priority consideration is March 1.

A note from the Ohio State University Admissions Office:

"The Ohio State University is Ohio's leading center for teaching, research, and public service. Our exceptional faculty, innovative programs, supportive services, and our extremely competitive tuition costs make Ohio State one of higher education's best values. Our central campus is in Columbus, Ohio—the state's capital and largest city. About 54,000 students from every county in Ohio, every state in the nation, and over 100 foreign nations are enrolled at Ohio State. Our faculty includes Nobel Prize winners, Rhodes Scholars, members of the National Academy of Sciences, widely published writers, and noted artists and musicians. From classes and residence halls, to concerts and seminars, to clubs and sports and honoraries, to frisbee games on the Oval, Ohio State offers lots of opportunities to develop talents and skills while meeting a variety of people. At Ohio state, you're sure to find a place to call your own."

ADMISSIONS FACTS

Competitiveness Rating:	**63**
% of applicants accepted:	85
% acceptees attending:	42

FRESHMAN PROFILE

Average verbal SAT:	450
Average math SAT:	520
Average ACT:	22
Graduated top 10% HS class:	23
Graduated top 25% HS class:	52
Graduated top 50% HS class:	74

DEADLINES

Early decision/action:	NA
Early dec./act. notif.:	NA
Regular admission:	2/15
Regular adm. notif.:	3/31

APPLICANTS ALSO LOOK AT

and often prefer:
U. Illinois
Syracuse U.
U. Michigan
U. Pittsburgh

and sometimes prefer:
Miami U.

and rarely prefer:
RPI
U. Tennessee–Knoxville

ADDRESS

Undergraduate Admissions
Columbus, OH 43210-1200
614-292-3980

FINANCIAL FACTS

In-state tuition ($):	2,485
Out-of-state tuition ($):	7,359
Room & board:	4,206
FA application deadline:	3/1
% frosh receiving FA:	65
PT earnings per yr. ($):	1,500

TYPE OF AID: % of students ($)

FA of some kind:	35 (NA)
Need-based grants:	NA
Merit-based grants:	NA
Loans:	NA
Work study:	NA
Student rating of FA:	71

CAMPUS LIFE

Quality of Life Rating:	**76**
Type of School:	private
Affiliation:	none
Environment:	city

STUDENT BODY

FT undergrad enrollment:	1,992
% male/% female:	51/49
% out-of-state:	60
% live on campus:	95
% African-American:	4
% Asian:	2
% Caucasian:	86
% Hispanic:	1
% foreign:	7
% transfers:	2

WHAT'S HOT

small lectures
financial aid
profs in class
profs outside class
Grateful Dead
cost of living
profs teach intros
living on campus

WHAT'S NOT

location
town-gown relations
working a job
gay community visible

ACADEMICS

Academic Rating:	**78**
Calendar:	semester
Student/teacher ratio:	14/1
% doctorates:	77
Profs interesting:	87
Profs accessible:	87
Hours of study per day:	3.11

MOST POPULAR MAJORS BY %

Business & Management:	14
Letters/Literature:	12
Social Sciences:	11

% GRADS WHO PURSUE

Law:	8
MBA:	4
Medicine:	5
M.A., etc.:	9

What do students think about Ohio Wesleyan University?

■ **Academics** Ohio Wesleyan University students are aware that their university is on the upswing. In the words of one student, the school's efforts over the last decade to create a more competitive academic atmosphere have resulted in OWU's becoming "one of the best private liberal arts institutions in the Midwest." Midwestern independent college counselors agreed. "Outstanding academics," wrote one; another was enthusiastic about the "excellent teachers." OWU is a medium-sized university that offers a remarkably diverse array of studies. Strong programs include not only the most popular ones—business, English, political science—but also such "off the beaten path" majors as zoology, botany, and urban studies. Small classes and vibrant, accessible professors are the school's other exceptional assets. "Professors here are incredibly helpful," wrote one of the many students who mentioned the teachers as the best thing about OWU. Students reported that the workload was slightly easier than average (compared to the workload at comparable schools). An honors program is available to top students interested in a more challenging curriculum.

■ **Life** Most OWU students, even those deeply immersed in their studies, would probably agree that developing an active social life is crucial to enjoying one's stay at OWU. Several students voiced opinions similar to this classmate's: "Life on OWU's campus revolves more closely around the social than the academic." There are plenty of opportunities on campus; as one student put it, "If you get bored with the social scene here, it is your own fault. There are coffee houses, free campus movies, dances, other campus programming, fraternities, parties, etc. You can always find your group if one scene doesn't 'fit' you." There are also the school's Division III sports teams, which are very popular, and intramural sports. Fraternities and sororities are major players in the social arena. One student complained that "the party scene has been getting lamer ever since the average SAT score went up!" Drinking, however, is still quite popular: said one student, "People mostly do their exercise by lifting 12 ounces." Students gave the town of Delaware poor marks, although several reported that, for a considerable number of undergrads, "Time outside the class revolves around the bars in town." The city of Columbus is "nearby, and it's a good escape."

■ **Students** Although students gave the student body good marks for ethnic diversity, the student population at OWU is predominantly white: fewer than 100 black students make up the single largest minority population. Students reported that interaction among students from different backgrounds is minimal: explained one, "Students tend to be very cliquish." More than half the students are from Ohio with others from surrounding states; the number of students from the East and West coasts is growing, however. There's a sizable Deadhead population.

OHIO WESLEYAN UNIVERSITY

Admissions

Ohio Wesleyan's pamphlet for applicants states, "In addition to your high school record and test scores, we want to know about you. Your school recommendations, activities and talents, and personal self-assessment will be important." The same publication notes that "more than half" the students it accepts achieve a high school GPA between 3.4 and 4.0 and score between 1150 and 1600 on the SAT (between 26 and 36 on the ACT). The remaining admittees are those judged "to have special personal qualities. These students typically flourish at Ohio Wesleyan because they are hard workers." OWU has an Honors Program with more competitive admissions standards.

Financial Aid

The financial aid office at Ohio Wesleyan requires applicants to submit the FAF and a copy of their and their parents' most recent tax returns and W-2 forms. Merit grants are awarded for those who excel in academics, the arts, and/or music. The school reports that, "typically, when all other funding sources are exhausted," it recommends that students draw loans on the following programs: Stafford, PLUS, TERI, and EXCEL.

A note from the Ohio Wesleyan Admissions Office:

"Balance is the key word that describes Ohio Wesleyan. For example:

"50% male, 50% female;

"50% members of Greek life, 50% not;

"National Colloquium Program, Top Division III sports program;

"Small town setting of 22,000, near 16th largest city in U.S. (Columbus, Ohio);

"Excellent faculty/student ratio, outstanding fine and performance arts program."

ADMISSIONS FACTS

Competitiveness Rating:	**72**
% of applicants accepted:	75
% acceptees attending:	29

FRESHMAN PROFILE

Average verbal SAT:	523*
Average math SAT:	573*
Average ACT:	25*
Graduated top 10% HS class:	31
Graduated top 25% HS class:	60
Graduated top 50% HS class:	84

DEADLINES

Early decision/action:	1/4
Early dec./act. notif.:	2/1
Regular admission:	3/1
Regular adm. notif.:	4/1

APPLICANTS ALSO LOOK AT

and sometimes prefer:
Ohio State U.
DePauw U.
Miami U.

and rarely prefer:
Denison U.
Wittenberg U.
Penn State U.

ADDRESS

Undergraduate Admissions
Delaware, OH 43015
800-922-8953

FINANCIAL FACTS

In-state tuition ($):	13,610
Out-of-state tuition ($):	13,610
Room & board:	4,884
FA application deadline:	3/1
% frosh receiving FA:	65
PT earnings per yr. ($):	1,100

TYPE OF AID: % of students ($)

FA of some kind:	65 (NA)
Need-based grants:	39 (8,175)
Merit-based grants:	NA
Loans:	27 (2,440)
Work study:	22 (NA)
Student rating of FA:	87

UNIVERSITY OF OKLAHOMA

Norman, OK

CAMPUS LIFE

Quality of Life Rating: **77**

Type of School:	public
Affiliation:	none
Environment:	city

STUDENT BODY

FT undergrad enrollment:	12,312
% male/% female:	55/45
% out-of-state:	17
% live on campus:	20
% African-American:	6
% Asian:	3
% Caucasian:	83
% Hispanic:	2
% foreign:	3
% transfers:	7

WHAT'S HOT

Top 40
marriage
religious clubs
dating
rap/hip-hop
hard liquor

WHAT'S NOT

profs teach intro courses
studying hard
gay community accepted
profs outside class
profs teach uppers

ACADEMICS

Academic Rating: **72**

Calendar:	semester
Student/teacher ratio:	16/1
% doctorates:	83
Profs interesting:	71
Profs accessible:	67
Hours of study per day:	2.68

MOST POPULAR MAJORS BY %

Business & Management:	24
Communications:	13
Engineering:	11

What do students think about the University of Oklahoma?

■ **Academics** "University of Oklahoma's reputation as a party school coaxed me from the East Coast," explained one Savannah, Georgia native. "Too bad for my GPA," he continued, "that my professors never heard of that reputation." Although it is still possible to get by at OU with only a modicum of work—students reported that studying and class attendance are well below the national average—it's also true that the school is providing more opportunities for the motivated student to challenge him/herself. Full scholarships for National Merit Scholars and an honors program open to students who score above 1100 on the SATs have helped create an atmosphere in which the top student feels more compelled to excel. Business and management programs are reputedly very good, as are engineering programs (studies in petroleum are especially fine, due to the proximity of the oil industry's center). Education majors are also popular. On the down side, OU is in many ways a typical large school: professors vary widely in quality and are uniformly difficult to meet after class ("from my experience I would guess that the student/teacher ratio is 50:1," complained one accounting major); TAs teach a relatively large proportion of courses on all levels; and administrators are overtaxed in managing this small-town sized school. The school's subdivision into 16 smaller colleges seems to make management more difficult. A music education major explained that separate colleges (in this case, music and education) do not coordinate schedules, making it difficult for students taking courses at more than one school to schedule their semesters.

■ **Life** Most OU students still live for football games and frat parties, but at a school this large, "a student can find a campus organization to meet any of his/her interests. Campus leadership, although dominated by the Greek system, is quite diverse." Most students agreed that "life here depends on what group you hang out with. If you want to remain in high school you join a frat or a sorority. If not, it isn't hard to find a niche. We have everything from religious groups to a gay and lesbian society!" Most students enjoy the laid-back town location; explained one city-hater, "The school is beautifully set in Norman, OK. The only disadvantage is how close it is to Oklahoma City. The campus is phenomenally pretty, and I love the school spirit here, with the nationally recognized sports programs."

■ **Students** Well over three quarters of OU's student body are natives of Oklahoma. Minorities constitute 17 percent of the student body, an improvement from past years and a good indication that OU is pursuing its goal of diversifying the student body. Students noted that there is a visible gay presence on campus but also noted that acceptance of the gay community is low.

UNIVERSITY OF OKLAHOMA

Admissions

From the University of Oklahoma's undergraduate catalog: "Admission to the University of Oklahoma is based upon graduation from an accredited high school, completion of a specified curriculum of high school courses, and either high school rank, grade average, or performance on the ACT or SAT. Because success in college is enhanced by solid academic preparation in high school, completion of the following courses in high school is required before entering the University": Four units of English, (choose from grammar, literature, and composition), three units of mathematics (choose from algebra, geometry, trigonometry, math analysis, or calculus), two units of lab science, and two units of history (one of which must be American history). Applicants must also either be in the upper 40 percent of their high school graduating class, or must score in the upper forty percent of the ACT (based on Oklahoma norms) or SAT (based on national norms). For applicants who do not meet these criteria, "full attention will be given to...written comments concerning background and educational goals, personal interviews, as well as letters of recommendation from school counselors, teachers, principals, employers, or supervisors attesting to the applicant's motivation and potential for academic success." All applicants must submit ACT or SAT scores.

Financial Aid

Financial aid applicants to The University of Oklahoma must complete the FFS. In '91–'92, 3% of all undergrads received an athletic grant (the average value was $5,482) and 53% of all undergrads received an academic grant (average value: $1,288). One percent of all undergrads received a merit grant for drama, music, art, band, or choir; the average value of these was $593. Minority and leadership scholarships are also available. In addition to Stafford loans (recommended to about half of all financial aid applicants), U. of Oklahoma recommends PLUS, SLS, and various institutional loans.

Excerpted from University of Oklahoma promotional materials:

"The mission of the University of Oklahoma is to educate outstanding professionals and an enlightened electorate for the state and nation at the baccalaureate, masters, professional and doctoral levels, to carry out research and creative activities for the advancement of knowledge and for the benefit of Oklahoma, and to provide continuing education and public service for the state.

"The University of Oklahoma recognizes, appreciates, and actively pursues its special responsibility to help make Oklahoma a good place in which to live and work. The University is also part of a world community of scholars, and its activities make national and international contributions."

ADMISSIONS FACTS

Competitiveness Rating:	**66**
% of applicants accepted:	97
% acceptees attending:	56

FRESHMAN PROFILE

Average verbal SAT:	NA
Average math SAT:	NA
Average ACT:	23
Graduated top 10% HS class:	NA
Graduated top 25% HS class:	NA
Graduated top 50% HS class:	NA

DEADLINES

Early decision/action:	NA
Early dec./act. notif.:	NA
Regular admission:	8/1
Regular adm. notif.:	rolling

APPLICANTS ALSO LOOK AT

and often prefer:
Washington U.
Rice U.

and sometimes prefer:
Baylor U.
U. Texas–Austin
U. Kansas

ADDRESS
Undergraduate Admissions
1000 Asp Avenue
Norman, OK 73019-0430
405-325-2251

FINANCIAL FACTS

In-state tuition ($):	1,468
Out-of-state tuition ($):	4,218
Room & board:	3,172
FA application deadline:	3/1
% frosh receiving FA:	54
PT earnings per yr. ($):	1,975

TYPE OF AID: % of students ($)

FA of some kind:	51 (NA)
Need-based grants:	36 (2,302)
Merit-based grants:	NA
Loans:	51 (2,836)
Work study:	6 (1,224)
Student rating of FA:	76

UNIVERSITY OF OREGON

CAMPUS LIFE

Quality of Life Rating:	**76**
Type of School:	public
Affiliation:	none
Environment:	suburban

STUDENT BODY

FT undergrad enrollment:	12,385
% male/% female:	47/53
% out-of-state:	19
% live on campus:	20
% African-American:	1
% Asian:	5
% Caucasian:	82
% Hispanic:	2
% foreign:	10
% transfers:	25

WHAT'S HOT

Grateful Dead
marijuana
gay community visible

WHAT'S NOT

living on campus
profs teach intros
small labs and seminars
religion
small classes (overall)

ACADEMICS

Academic Rating:	**69**
Calendar:	quarters
Student/teacher ratio:	NA
% doctorates:	NA
Profs interesting:	72
Profs accessible:	70
Hours of study per day:	3.26

MOST POPULAR MAJORS BY %

Business & Management:	18
Architect. & Environ. Dsgn.:	11
Letters/Literature:	9

% GRADS WHO PURSUE

Law:	13
MBA:	13
Medicine:	7
M.A., etc.:	NA

What do students think about the University of Oregon?

■ **Academics** A beautiful campus and a large "pseudo-hippie" population are the two traits that most obviously distinguish University of Oregon from the typical state-sponsored university. But scratch the surface and you'll find an institution that is unusually serious about academics, particularly for a state school. Students here study over three-and-a-quarter hours a day, placing them among the top twelve hardest-working public school student bodies. Pre-professional majors are popular, with business claiming the most students. Architecture, journalism, and the hard sciences are also excellent. An honors program, which offers classes not available to non-honors students, is available for top-notch students. Facilities are good; one psychology major reported, "My department includes a program that cuts the leading edge in the field of cognitive science and is well supported by neuroscience programs and laboratories." Students complained about class size and the number of introductory courses taught by TAs, but not much else. An unusual number of students told us that coming to this school was a perspective-broadening experience: a typical respondent wrote that "U of O has a progressive attitude toward the free expression of ideas. Here you come face to face with many issues you didn't deal with in high school. You have the opportunity to hear both sides and form an opinion about such issues as homosexuality, p.c., racism, sexism, anti-war attitudes, etc."

■ **Life** The University of Oregon has a beautiful campus, complete with "grassy lawns, quiet walkways, and towering redwood trees." Classes are held in "ivy-covered brick buildings," and dorms are safe but uncomfortable (and hard to come by; most students live in apartments off-campus). Students like the town of Eugene, although some feel that a trip off-campus is "like living Woodstock all over again." A laid-back, stereotypically West Coast vibe permeates the area; it's the kind of place where someone can say, "The karma is good and so are the people," and probably no one will laugh. The weather is awful unless you like rain—no wonder the school's mascot is a duck.

■ **Students** Said one student of her classmates, "Everyone here is either a hippie or from a frat or sorority." The two distinct communities coexist in a mostly peaceful manner, although some conservative students resent the pervasiveness of their liberal classmates' social activism. One complained, "This is a great place unless you study something that offends any long-haired leftist who's a vegetarian." Public protests are not unusual; wrote one respondent, "We have students who protest and students who protest the protests, but there's always someone or another protesting something or other. It's a conscientious campus."

UNIVERSITY OF OREGON

Admissions

The University of Oregon "will admit the best qualified of those applicants who meet the minimum standards." The minimum standards include completing four units of English ("English language, literature, speaking and listening, and writing, with emphasis on writing expository prose during all four years"), three units of mathematics ("first-year algebra and two additional units such as geometry, advanced algebra, trigonometry, calculus, and probability and statistics," two units of science ("one unit in two fields of college preparatory science such as biology, chemistry, physics or earth and physical science; one unit laboratory science is recommended"), three units of social science (one unit of US history, one unit of global studies, and one elective; government is strongly recommended), and two units of college-prep level electives (foreign language is highly recommended, but applicants may also choose from computer science, fine and performing arts, and other areas). Students who have not met these academic requirements may submit scores from College Board Achievement Tests (English, Math I or II, and a third of applicant's choice); a score of at least 410 should be attained on each one. All applicants should also have a 3.00 high school grade point average; those that do not may be admitted based on high standardized test scores. All applicants must submit scores for the SAT or ACT. Finally, "Once students have met minimum standards for admission, we consider such factors as the quality of course work taken in high school, grades earned, grade trend, class rank, and senior year course load. Academic potential, diversity of the student body, and special talents may be considered.

Financial Aid

Financial aid applicants to the University of Oregon must complete the SingleFile (preferred), FFS, or FAF. Scholarships are available from the university and private sources for academic merit, departmental interest, artistic achievement, residency, and minorities. The priority deadline for consideration is February 1.

Excerpted from University of Oregon promotional materials:

"Five generations of outstanding leaders and citizens have studied at the University of Oregon since it opened in 1876. Today's students, like the 300,000 who came before them, have access to the most current knowledge in classes, laboratories, and seminars conducted by active researchers. In turn, by sharing their research through teaching, professors are better able to articulate their findings and to integrate their specialized studies with broader areas of knowledge. Their students learn that knowledge is a vital and changing commodity and that learning should be a lifelong activity."

ADMISSIONS FACTS

Competitiveness Rating:	**64**
% of applicants accepted:	86
% acceptees attending:	65

FRESHMAN PROFILE

Average verbal SAT:	478
Average math SAT:	526
Average ACT:	NA
Graduated top 10% HS class:	29
Graduated top 25% HS class:	NA
Graduated top 50% HS class:	NA

DEADLINES

Early decision/action:	NA
Early dec./act. notif.:	NA
Regular admission:	3/1
Regular adm. notif.:	4/15

APPLICANTS ALSO LOOK AT

and often prefer:
UC Berkeley
U. C Davis

and sometimes prefer:
Washington U.
U. Colorado–Boulder
U. Portland

and rarely prefer:
Oklahoma State U.
Williamette U.

ADDRESS

Undergraduate Admissions
240 Oregon Hall
Eugene, OR 97403-1217
503-346-3201

FINANCIAL FACTS

In-state tuition ($):	2,694
Out-of-state tuition ($):	6,675
Room & board:	2,700
FA application deadline:	3/1
% frosh receiving FA:	45
PT earnings per yr. ($):	2,100

TYPE OF AID: % of students ($)

FA of some kind:	47 (NA)
Need-based grants:	NA
Merit-based grants:	NA
Loans:	NA
Work study:	NA
Student rating of FA:	68

PARSONS SCHOOL OF DESIGN

New York, NY

What do students think about Parsons School of Design?

■ **Academics** Parsons students are "more focused on their careers than are students at a regular university." One student exemplified the Parsons attitude: "Becoming a good and accurate artist is as difficult as becoming a good and accurate neurosurgeon, and the school you attend is vital to how serious and successful you become." Said another, "I highly recommend this school, but only if you have the drive (not just because you 'like' art in high school) and the funds." The prospective commercial and graphic artists, photographers, and architects of Parsons spend almost four hours a day in the studios and libraries. Work is particularly intense during "foundation year," a first-year program during which students are given crash courses in all aspects of design. After foundation year, students focus on their majors, the best known of which is fashion design; among the other popular majors are illustration, photography, and communication design. Professors are "working professionals" who are "energetic, intelligent, and engaging in class," although students wish profs would make themselves more available for extra help. Because tuition is steep and the facilities are old, many students complained that they "expected more—equipment, materials, information—for the money." Also, several students warned that "there aren't many jobs out there for Parsons graduates!"

■ **Life** Parsons lacks most of the accoutrements of the typical college life. Wrote one student, "There really is no campus where students can meet. The social spots are the cafeteria and the library." Said another, there are "very few groups or activities to belong to," while a third told us bluntly that "we don't do advanced high school–type stuff like foot-a-ball 'n' beer. We go to school for a specific end, to learn not to screw around." (With classmates this intense, it's no wonder one student wrote that "we tend to make friends outside the school.") Not surprisingly, "There is no school spirit in Parsons." If students don't mind this lack of a traditional college setting, it's because (1) they're not traditional college students, and (2) they are located in America's art and design capital, New York City. The city offers an abundance of galleries for art students, textile manufacturers for fashion design students, advertising agencies for communications majors, and architecture of practically every style for architecture students. Wrote one student, "New York is a great place to live if you have any money after art supplies. And, if you have any time." Another warned, however, that to survive there, "One has to like conflict, dirt, noise, and anger. The school and the city merge into one experience."

■ **Students** Over one fourth of the students are minorities, and respondents described the student body as "very diverse." Students tend to be "very individualistic; if you have a good sense of your identity, this is the place for you." The school has a considerable gay community; wrote one student, "Heterosexual students often complain how hard it is to find someone to go out with. I think it's easier for gay students because of the close-knit gay community."

PARSONS SCHOOL OF DESIGN

New York, NY

Admissions

According to Parsons' undergraduate catalog, "Each applicant is reviewed individually in light of his or her experience, achievement, and potential for artistic growth. A large portion of the admissions decision is based upon the student's portfolio and home exam. Significant weight is also placed on academic credentials (such as grades, rank in class and test scores)." Although most Parsons' students have had "substantial art preparation" prior to attending the school, some have had "little or none"; Parsons considers artistic potential as well as past achievement. Interviews are required of all applicants who live within 200 miles of New York City. Applicants must submit scores for either the SAT or the ACT. Applicants may provide letters of recommendation but are not required to do so.

Financial Aid

Financial aid for the Parsons School of Design and the Eugene Lang College is administered through the offices of its parent university, the New School for Social Research. The financial aid office requires applicants to submit the FAF, a form generated by the school, and their parents' most recent tax return. The school reports, "Scholarship decisions are based on a combination of need and merit"; all are listed as "need-based" in the FA sidebar. Parsons/Lang students last year participated in the following loan programs: Stafford (60% of the students took such a loan; average value: $3,100), Perkins (20%; $1,000), and SLS (5%; $4,000).

A note from the Parsons School of Design Admissions Office:

"In a world crowded with "multi-purpose" and "comprehensive" colleges and universities, Parsons School of Design has a singular mission: to educate the leadership of tomorrow's art and design communities. Parsons students become polished craftsmen, expert technicians, skilled practitioners. Graduates of this school have more than well-trained hands. *Ideas* lie at the heart of a Parsons education—ideas that inspire creativity, ideas that propel conceptual vision, ideas that change and advance the design process. Art and thought are inseparable at Parsons.

"Parsons' graduates will lead the design and visual art professions during the early twenty-first century. The painters, photographers, sculptors, and craftsmen will enrich our cultural and intellectual environment. The designers will give form and shape and color to our everyday lives—to our homes and offices, our clothes and accessories, our books and magazines, movies and television, our logos, symbols and advertising, our furniture, appliances, and utensils."

ADMISSIONS FACTS

Competitiveness Rating:	**81**
% of applicants accepted:	19
% acceptees attending:	61

FRESHMAN PROFILE

Average verbal SAT:	550
Average math SAT:	520
Average ACT:	NA
Graduated top 10% HS class:	30
Graduated top 25% HS class:	70
Graduated top 50% HS class:	90

DEADLINES

Early decision/action:	12/1
Early dec./act. notif.:	12/15
Regular admission:	rolling
Regular adm. notif.:	rolling

APPLICANTS ALSO LOOK AT

and often prefer:
Cooper Union
Rhode Island School of Design

and sometimes prefer:
NYU

and rarely prefer:
Syracuse U.

ADDRESS

Undergraduate Admissions
66 Fifth Avenue
New York, NY 10011
212-229-8910

FINANCIAL FACTS

In-state tuition ($):	12,500
Out-of-state tuition ($):	12,500
Room & board:	5,000
FA application deadline:	rolling
% frosh receiving FA:	NA
PT earnings per yr. ($):	NA

TYPE OF AID: % of students ($)

FA of some kind:	NA (9,000)
Need-based grants:	58 (3,143)
Merit-based grants:	0
Loans:	NA
Work study:	30 (2,000)
Student rating of FA:	71

UNIVERSITY OF PENNSYLVANIA

Philadelphia, PA

What do students think about University of Pennsylvania?

■ **Academics** University of Pennsylvania is in the odd position of being considered a "second-tier Ivy League school": said one student, "Everyone knows we're just a safety for people who don't get into Harvard, Yale, or Princeton." In other words, Penn is probably the best school-with-an-inferiority-complex in the country. Wharton, its business school, is indisputably among the nation's best; and both the School of Nursing and the School of Engineering and Applied Sciences are top-rate (although "the engineering teachers are incomprehensible," according to one frustrated student). The College of Arts and Sciences, the school's most popular division, is easy only in comparison to the other three. Students were quick to remind us that "Penn is not one school but four, and each school is different." Students in all divisions agree, however, that the work is hard, their fellow students are "self-motivated and *extremely* pre-professional," and their professors are by and large disappointingly impersonal. Wrote one, "Research is the primary concern of professors and administrators; as a result, graduate departments are strong, but the ability to teach undergrads is minimal." With over 9,000 undergraduates, Penn is smaller than only Cornell among the Ivies. Students say that because of Penn's size, "The opportunities for networking are amazing, but you need to actively persist; you will not be spoon-fed opportunities!"

■ **Life** Penn students are certain that they surpass their counterparts at other Ivies in at least one area: social life. "This is the social Ivy," wrote one student; "It's the least nerdy of the Ivies," offered another. Although it may not exactly be "a four-year fiesta with an excellent education as the party favor," as one student claimed, it does seem that while "the students here are serious about their studies, they also know how to relax on weekends and have fun. Penn offers true balance, not often found at colleges." Penn has an active frat scene, plenty of campus clubs and organizations, and a major city waiting beyond its gates. What waits immediately outside those gates, the neighborhood of West Philadelphia, was *the* hottest topic among our respondents. "I really don't feel too safe walking around at night," wrote one. Explained another, "The upper-middle class student body makes us a major target for crime." Others disagreed. "The crime in West Philly gets a lot of bad press," wrote one student, "but, if you're smart, you'll get along just fine." Most students agreed that campus police do an adequate job patrolling the campus and that the dorms are "safe as fortresses." Safety concerns are greatest among the many upperclassmen who live off-campus.

■ **Students** Penn attracts students of all types from around the world. The school has a 29 percent minority population, but one student explained that while "the number of different groups is many, the interactions between them are few." There is a noticeable Long Island contingent, noted several students, and some noted a conformist tendency among the student body. Wrote one, "Penn is one of those places where you are allowed to be yourself…provided that you're just like everyone else!"

UNIVERSITY OF PENNSYLVANIA

Philadelphia, PA

Admissions

The admissions office at the University of Pennsylvania looks first at the quality of your high school curriculum, your GPA, and your class rank. Also considered important are extracurricular activities and letters of recommendation. Penn requires applicants take either the SAT and three Achievements (of which one must be English Composition) or the ACT; the former is preferred. An interview is recommended, but not required. The school requires no specific high school courses, but recommends a rigorous college prep curriculum including four years of English and three years each of math, science, social studies, and a foreign language.

Financial Aid

Those seeking financial assistance from the University of Pennsylvania are required to submit the FAF, a copy of their parents' most recent tax return, and a form generated by the school. All assistance from U Penn is provided on the basis of demonstrated need; the school offers no merit-based grants. The typical aid package from U Penn meets 100 percent of demonstrated need; 70 percent of the package is made up of grants, with the rest made up by loans and part-time work. Those who demonstrate need may also be eligible to participate in an installment payment plan. The deadline listed in the financial aid sidebar is a priority deadline.

Excerpted from University of Pennsylvania promotional materials:

"The University of Pennsylvania combines both tradition and change. From modest beginnings in 1740 as a college for the "complete education" of youth, the University has become one of the foremost multidisciplinary institutions in the nation, a major repository of humanistic and scientific research. Its undergraduate and graduate schools comprise more than 20,000 students and 1,700 faculty, pursuing scores of disciplines in more than 2,500 courses, including 1,500 at the undergraduate level alone."

ADMISSIONS FACTS

Competitiveness Rating:	**94**
% of applicants accepted:	42
% acceptees attending:	49

FRESHMAN PROFILE

Average verbal SAT:	591
Average math SAT:	677
Average ACT:	NA
Graduated top 10% HS class:	83
Graduated top 25% HS class:	96
Graduated top 50% HS class:	100

DEADLINES

Early decision/action:	11/1
Early dec./act. notif.:	12/15
Regular admission:	1/1
Regular adm. notif.:	4/3

APPLICANTS ALSO LOOK AT

and often prefer:
Stanford U.

and sometimes prefer:
Johns Hopkins U.
Cornell U.
Goergetown U.

and rarely prefer:
U. Illinois
Temple U.
Carnegie-Mellon U.
Tufts U.
Lehigh U.

ADDRESS

Undergraduate Admissions
34th and Spruce Street
Philadelphia, PA 19104
215-898-7507

FINANCIAL FACTS

In-state tuition ($):	15,894
Out-of-state tuition ($):	15,894
Room & board:	6,030
FA application deadline:	2/15
% frosh receiving FA:	52
PT earnings per yr. ($):	1,375

TYPE OF AID: % of students ($)

FA of some kind:	53 (NA)
Need-based grants:	NA
Merit-based grants:	NA
Loans:	NA
Work study:	NA
Student rating of FA:	78

PENNSYLVANIA STATE UNIVERSITY

University Park, PA

What do students think about Penn State?

■ **Academics** In nearly all attributes, Pennsylvania State University is the quintessential state-sponsored university. The school provides a reasonably priced education to a large number of students, offers studies in an almost unimaginably wide range of studies, and maintains top departments in some areas, particularly those geared toward career training. Among its many fine departments, those lauded by our respondents include administration of justice, engineering, business, agricultural economics and science, education, computer science ("There are a lot of computers on campus: learn to use them") and meteorology. Overall, students agree that "you can get a great, well-rounded education here; the options are endless." Students also agreed that acquiring that education requires tenacity, because the school's physical and administrative girth make it very easy to become discouraged. One student wrote, "This school is *way* too big to be run efficiently. You have a terrible time scheduling, reaching your professors, and finding classes when you're a freshman." Again, as at most large state-sponsored schools, students can feel neglected by their professors, for whom undergraduates are but one of many responsibilities. Complained one student, "This school is very unconcerned about its students; all it cares about is research." Overall, however, students expressed satisfaction with the school, primarily because of Penn State's appealing blend of low-pressure academics (for most; *not* for engineers and pre-meds, however) and varied social options (see "Life," below).

■ **Life** Because of its huge student population, Penn State offers social opportunities for just about everyone. Explained one student, "The social life here is extremely exciting. State has one million and one things to do, ranging from football games, women's field hockey, parties, Bible study groups, Roy's, Unimart, the library, drinking, test reviews, the Nittany mall, and concerts." The Greeks are unusually popular for a school of this size. Complained one student, "Greek life is overbearing, and those not involved in it see it as childish and annoying, which it is." For Greeks and GDIs alike, drinking is a major part of social life. Wrote one student, "Penn State is a place where 32,000 people are working toward a common goal: to drink a lot of beer and to have a good time!" One student reported that "the bars and liquor stores are all very strict about not selling to people under 21, but there are many ways around them." With nationally ranked teams in football, wrestling, and women's basketball, it should come as no surprise that "PSU completely revolves around sports." Students gave their home town of University Park average marks; several complained that local cops seem to have little else to do but give parking tickets to students.

■ **Students** Most Penn State students are from the Quaker State. A proportionally small minority population (nine percent) still translates into more than 3,000 minority students, leading one student to call PSU "a great place to meet a wide variety of people and cultures."

PENNSYLVANIA STATE UNIVERSITY

University Park, PA

Admissions

According to Penn State's undergraduate catalog, "Each applicant is evaluated on the basis of the high school record and results of the SAT or ACT. This evaluation produces an evaluation index. Admission decisions are made on the basis of a review of the applicant's evaluation index in relation the requested area of enrollment, space availability, and the quality of the credentials presented by other applicants." The minimum secondary school units required vary, depending on the college to which you're applying. Most colleges require four years of English, three years of mathematics, five years of arts/humanities/social studies and foreign language (distribution of these varies for each area of concentration) and three years of science. All applicants must submit SAT or ACT scores. The priority application deadline for the University Park campus is November 30.

Financial Aid

Financial aid applicants to Penn State must complete the FAF (Pennsylvania residents should complete the Pennsylvania State Grant and Federal Student Aid Application). Penn State Academic Grants are available for students who demonstrate academic excellence and financial need. Pennsylvania residents are eligible for PHEAA grants. Various scholarships are available including those based on academic, artistic, or athletic merit, and minority or residential status. Priority consideration is given to financial aid applications received by March 1.

Excerpted from Penn State promotional materials:

"Penn State is a comprehensive, multicampus research university serving all regions of the Commonwealth, as well as the nation and the world, in instruction, research, and service roles that require responsiveness to and support from society's public and private sectors. As a comprehensive land-grant university, Penn State has responsibility for providing a wide array of programs in the professional and technical disciplines as well as a balanced offering of undergraduate and graduate programs in the arts and sciences.

"The University shares with other major research universities the traditional responsibilities to discover, develop, preserve, and disseminate knowledge. Penn State's multicampus system establishes the University as uniquely fitted to maintain extensive continuing education and other public service programs that serve the diverse geographical and economic areas of the state and region."

PEPPERDINE UNIVERSITY

Malibu, CA

CAMPUS LIFE

Quality of Life Rating: **81**

Type of School:	private
Affiliation:	Church of Christ
Environment:	city

STUDENT BODY

FT undergrad enrollment:	2,446
% male/% female:	44/56
% out-of-state:	47
% live on campus:	65
% African-American:	3
% Asian:	6
% Caucasian:	72
% Hispanic:	5
% foreign:	10
% transfers:	5

WHAT'S HOT

religion
marriage
campus appearance
Top 40
location
conservative politics
administration (overall)
profs in class
overall happiness

WHAT'S NOT

hard liquor
cost of living
beer
dorm comfort
doing all the reading

ACADEMICS

Academic Rating: **82**

Calendar:	semester
Student/teacher ratio:	16/1
% doctorates:	95
Profs interesting:	85
Profs accessible:	83
Hours of study per day:	2.86

MOST POPULAR MAJORS BY %

Communications:	30
Business & Management:	24
Social Sciences:	16

What do students think about Pepperdine University?

■ **Academics** Two things immediately set Pepperdine University apart. One is its beach-front location in idyllic Malibu; the other is its affiliation with the Church of Christ, a devout evangelical faith. Non-religious students attracted by the school's setting should be forewarned that the school's stated purpose is "to pursue the very highest academic standards within a context that celebrates and extends the spiritual and ethical ideals of the Christian faith." Pepperdine takes its mission seriously: weekly chapel attendance is mandatory, the core curriculum contains three religion surveys, and all courses emphasize "Christian values." Students who can fit in at such a school are rewarded with excellent academic programs, particularly in pre-professional areas such as communications, business, and computer science. Classes "are small enough that you can really get to know your professors and classmates," and many here would agree that "the excellent teachers, small classes, and beautiful campus are what make this school worthwhile. Pepperdine is very much a follower of ancient academia, because of the active discussions between professors and students."

■ **Life** Pepperdine's campus and location are among the nation's best. One student called the area "a beautiful resort," and few would disagree. Some students even went as far as to claim that "without the beauty of Malibu, Pepperdine would be just another uptight elitist religious school." "Peace and serenity" characterize life on campus. Social life is subdued: the school's religious affiliation results in strict regulations concerning drinking (it's prohibited) and hanging out in your dorm room with members of the opposite sex (the door must remain open). These rules led one student to comment, "For a university dedicated to higher learning, it would be nice to get out of the Middle Ages." And, although Pepperdine accepts students of all faiths, those who are not members of the Church of Christ may find that "religiously this school is not open-minded. It's affiliated with the Church of Christ and therefore doesn't allow any other religious clubs on campus. Students of different faiths have to leave campus if they want to worship; it's a bit unfair." On-campus housing is required for freshmen and sophomores, although a current housing shortage makes it possible to get off-campus sooner, for those so inclined. The small student body further discourages an active social scene. Students reported that "rumors spread here like VD. Classmates are *very* judgmental." Summed up one student: "The frat/sorority scene happens—sports, too—but that's about it."

■ **Students** Pepperdine has a reputation for an upper-class student body that students seemed eager to confirm. "Too many people care whether you are registered in your home city's social register," explained a typical respondent. Minority enrollment here is high. Asians, Pacific Islanders, and Hispanics are each well represented. Students tend to be politically conservative and, not surprisingly, religious.

PEPPERDINE UNIVERSITY

Malibu, CA

Admissions

Pepperdine's admissions office writes, "We have no set cut-offs but 75 percent of our admitted students have a 3.00+ academic GPA (non-weighted, including 9th grade), and a composite SAT of 1000+. Our average is a 3.4, with an 1100 SAT (27 ACT). The committee first examines your high school academic record (including number and kinds of classes taken, GPA and grade trends), followed by your standardized test scores. Next, in order of importance, are your essays, letters of recommendation, interview, and extracurriculars. Community service and volunteer efforts are also considered. While there is no "rigid pattern" of high school requirements, "a strongly emphasized college preparatory program including coursework in speech communication, humanities, foreign language, social science, three years of mathematics, and four years of English is recommended." SAT or ACT scores are required. Applicants to Pepperdine also often apply to UC Berkeley, UCLA, U. of Southern California, Boston College, UC Santa Barbara and the Claremont Colleges.

Financial Aid

Financial aid applicants to Pepperdine must complete the SAAC (or the FAF, if the applicant is from out-of-state), a form generated by Pepperdine's FA office, and submit copies of their parents' and their own tax returns. Loans recommended by the FA office include Perkins, Stafford, PLUS, and SLS loans. California residents are eligible for Cal Grants from the California Student Aid Commission. Cal Grant A is awarded based on financial need and GPA; '90–'91 awards ranged from $600 to $5,250 at Pepperdine. Cal Grant B is awarded based on need only; it provides a living allowance of $1,410 and tuition expenses up to $5,250 per year. The top 5% of Pepperdine's anticipated freshman class typically receive academic awards in the form of Regent's, President's Honors, and Dean's Scholarships. Achievement awards are also available for talent in a variety of areas, including art, athletics, journalism, radio, TV and film, missions, and theatre.

A note from the Pepperdine Admissions Office:

"As a selective university, Pepperdine seeks students who show promise of academic achievement at the collegiate level. However, we also seek students who are committed to serving the University community, as well as others with whom they come into contact. We look for community service activities, volunteer efforts and strong leadership qualities, as well as a demonstrated commitment to academic studies and an interest in the liberal arts."

ADMISSIONS FACTS

Competitiveness Rating:	**82**
% of applicants accepted:	63
% acceptees attending:	39

FRESHMAN PROFILE

Average verbal SAT:	508
Average math SAT:	568
Average ACT:	25
Graduated top 10% HS class:	60
Graduated top 25% HS class:	80
Graduated top 50% HS class:	95

DEADLINES

Early decision/action:	11/15
Early dec./act. notif.:	12/15
Regular admission:	2/1
Regular adm. notif.:	3/15

APPLICANTS ALSO LOOK AT

and often prefer:
UC Berkeley
UC Irvine
U. Colorado–Boulder
USC
Loyola Marymount U.

and sometimes prefer:
UC Santa Barbara

and rarely prefer:
Brigham Young U.

ADDRESS

Undergraduate Admissions
24255 Pacific Coast Highway
Malibu, CA 90263
213-456-4392

FINANCIAL FACTS

In-state tuition ($):	15,230
Out-of-state tuition ($):	15,230
Room & board:	6,070
FA application deadline:	4/1
% frosh receiving FA:	67
PT earnings per yr. ($):	1,200

TYPE OF AID: % of students ($)

FA of some kind:	65 (NA)
Need-based grants:	NA
Merit-based grants:	NA
Loans:	NA
Work study:	NA
Student rating of FA:	84

UNIVERSITY OF PITTSBURGH

Pittsburgh, PA

What do students think about the University of Pittsburgh?

■ **Academics** University of Pittsburgh is a large, research-oriented public university whose greatest attributes are its programs in health sciences and engineering. Said one student, "Pitt has wonderful opportunities for any student interested in the health professions. The University Medical Center consists of four hospitals that all welcome students as volunteers." Explained another, "Pitt is great for those studying anything related to science. The school is a hotbed of research." Pitt has other assets as well: affordability, location, and a broad range of well-maintained programs, particularly in pre-professional fields. However, as is often the case at research centers, many of the students here see their professors as average teachers at best. Also, liberal arts majors can be left feeling like second-class citizens. Complained one black studies/education major, "All Pitt cares about is research and money." Classes are sometimes huge, particularly introductory lecture courses, and often "entail memorizing a lot of information." However, top students seeking individual attention can enter an honors program in which classes are smaller and "students are encouraged to ask questions and solve problems, to think in terms of the subject matter." Students reported that administrative duties like registering for classes, meeting with deans, etc. are particularly unpleasant.

■ **Life** Pitt students love their sports teams and are particularly enthusiastic about football and basketball. The Greek system is alive and well here, but because the university is located in a major city, the Greeks don't dominate the social scene as they do at many small-town institutions. Students like the city of Pittsburgh a lot. Explained one, "Pitt is great because students have their own section of a major city (a neighborhood called Oakland). It's our domain, and no matter what direction you head in, there's always something going on." Oakland is Pittsburgh's cultural center, home to museums, art galleries, concert halls, theaters, and even a mosque. Some complained that the area could be safer (explained one, "Pitt can be a fun-filled campus if you're informed on safety"). Another complained of the weather, "It always rains." Drinking is a popular form of recreation, and students reported that their classmates were sexually active. Many students live off-campus, as dorm space is limited.

■ **Students** The Pitt student body is largely white, middle class, and from Western Pennsylvania. Seven percent of the students are African-American and interaction between whites and blacks is limited. Many students work their way through Pitt, and it is not uncommon for students to take up to six years to get their degrees. Students are politically conservative, but mostly they don't really care: one student dubbed the school "Apathy State U."

UNIVERSITY OF PITTSBURGH

Admissions

The admissions office reports that "applications are reviewed by Committee on a rolling basis and students notified on a rolling basis. The Committee looks at class rank, the quality and level of challenge of courses being taken, grade trends over a four-year period, college entrance examination results, the personal essay, and extracurricular activities, including work." Arts and Sciences majors must have completed four years of English, three years each of math and lab sciences, and one year of social studies; engineers must have completed chemistry, physics, and trig; pharmacists are required to have completed chemistry, biology, and trig; nurses must have completed chemistry and another lab science and two units of math. Either the SAT or the ACT is required. UPittsburgh applicants often also apply to Penn State, Indiana, UPenn, and West Virginia U.

Financial Aid

The financial aid office at University of Pittsburgh requires applicants to submit the FAF and a supplemental form that is part of the admissions application (i.e. all students apply for financial aid as part of the admissions process). The University sponsors a number of merit-based grants, the values of which range from $500 to $9,000. In 1991–92, UPitt distributed 781 such grants, the approximate average value of which was $1,670. Pitt students received a total of 9,550 need-based grants, mostly government-sponsored; the average value of these was $1,532.

A note from the University of Pittsburgh Admissions Office:

"The University of Pittsburgh is ranked one of the top 56 research institutions in the United States by the Association of American Universities. Over 400 degree-granting programs are available from among nine undergraduate and 14 graduate schools and four regional campuses, allowing students a wide latitude of choices, both academically and in setting, style, size, and pace of campus life. The Schools of Engineering, Nursing and Pharmacy offer strong professional programs; the College of Arts and Sciences' highest-ranked departments, nationally, include Philosophy, History and Philosophy of Science, Anthropology, Art History, Chemistry, History, Microbiology, Physics, Psychology, and Spanish. The University Center for International Studies is ranked one of the exemplary international programs in the country by the Council on Learning; and a Semester at Sea program takes students around the world to different ports of call on an ocean liner. Premedical students benefit from association with the University medical center which is the leading organ transplant center in the world; pre-dental students with the Dental School."

ADMISSIONS FACTS

Competitiveness Rating:	*66*
% of applicants accepted:	88
% acceptees attending:	57

FRESHMAN PROFILE

Average verbal SAT:	480*
Average math SAT:	533*
Average ACT:	NA
Graduated top 10% HS class:	27
Graduated top 25% HS class:	64
Graduated top 50% HS class:	94

DEADLINES

Early decision/action:	NA
Early dec./act. notif.:	NA
Regular admission:	rolling
Regular adm. notif.:	rolling

APPLICANTS ALSO LOOK AT

and often prefer:
Drexel U.
Duquesne
U. Delaware

and sometimes prefer:
Clemson U.
Penn State U.
U. South Carolina
Carnegie Mellon U.

and rarely prefer:
Villanova U.
Ithaca College

ADDRESS

Undergraduate Admissions
4200 Fifth Ave.
Pittsburgh, PA 15260
412-624-7488

FINANCIAL FACTS

In-state tuition ($):	4,048
Out-of-state tuition ($):	8,620
Room & board:	3,514
FA application deadline:	3/1
% frosh receiving FA:	73
PT earnings per yr. ($):	1,100

TYPE OF AID: % of students ($)

FA of some kind:	73 (NA)
Need-based grants:	NA (1,532)
Merit-based grants:	NA (1,670)
Loans:	NA (2,500)
Work study:	NA (1,000)
Student rating of FA:	70

PRINCETON UNIVERSITY

CAMPUS LIFE

Quality of Life Rating: **83**

Type of school:	private
Affiliation:	none
Environment:	city

STUDENT BODY

FT undergrad enrollment:	4,497
% male/% female:	61/39
% out-of-state:	86
% live on campus:	98
% African-American:	6
% Asian:	8
% Caucasian:	76
% Hispanic:	4
% foreign:	6
% transfers:	1

WHAT'S HOT

administration (overall)
honest students
library
small labs and seminars
campus appearance
living on campus
registration
dorm safety
leftist politics

WHAT'S NOT

dating
marriage
marijuana

ACADEMICS

Academic Rating: **94**

Calendar:	semester
Student/teacher ratio:	9/1
% doctorates:	99
Profs interesting:	82
Profs accessible:	82
Hours of study per day:	3.21

MOST POPULAR MAJORS BY %

Social Sciences:	42
Letters/Literature:	16
Engineering:	12

% GRADS WHO PURSUE

Law:	10
MBA:	2
Medicine:	8
M.A., etc.:	17

What do students think about Princeton University?

■ **Academics** As one area counselor stressed, "Princeton University offers the best *under*graduate education in the country." Other prestigious institutions feature famous medical, law, and/or business schools, but Princeton has none of these: here, the focus is on the college student. Academic departments are uniformly excellent: particularly noteworthy are engineering ("It has a friendly 'we're in this together' atmosphere—no 'cut throat, kill-the-curve-breaker' competition like at MIT," wrote one engineer), political science, history, religion, and English. Students enjoy a great deal of personal attention thanks to "precepts," once-a-week-small-group discussion meetings with each class's professor or TA. Core distribution requirements guarantee that all students are schooled in the classic academic disciplines (math, natural and social sciences, humanities). A series of independent projects, culminating in a year-long senior thesis, give upperclassmen an unusual amount of autonomy in fashioning their workloads. The amount of work here is "difficult but not overbearing"; in fact, students here study no more than the average student profiled in this book.

■ **Life** Princeton University is located in Princeton, New Jersey, and, as one student explained, "The town and the university are like a divorced couple no longer on speaking terms. They ignore each other and the students suffer. The town offers no student-oriented cafes or amusements within a student's budget. Off-campus housing is exorbitant." Accordingly, social life centers around the beautiful Gothic campus. Underclassmen live in groups of dorms called "colleges," each of which provides meals and sponsors a roster of extracurricular activities. Fraternities exist but are not officially sanctioned and have limited memberships. However, "eating clubs" (which are a lot like fraternities: they provide meals, host parties, and place students in a "sub-community") are crucial. During sophomore year, most students join one of the 13 eating clubs, eight of which choose members by lottery; the other five hand-pick members (in a process called "bicker"). Students explain that there is a "big gulf between residential college underclassmen and upperclassmen in eating clubs." Parties here tend to be "orgies of beer"; explained one student, "If you're not into the drinking scene, your social life could be a bit mundane." Students also actively support their sports teams. Finally: "The most bizarre phenomenon on campus is the popularity of the a cappella singing groups. We have eight of them, seven more than campuses 10 times our size."

■ **Students** Almost a quarter of Princeton's students are minorities. Wrote one Hispanic student, "If you are a minority, you must come here." Several students expressed surprise that their classmates were not nerds ("The guy next door blasting Guns and Roses is probably brilliant; cool people *can* be found here"), but others complained that their classmates were "anti-intellectual: it's not considered cool to talk about your work or seem passionately committed to it." Said another student: "It's a place to grow, but only a place for soul-searching if you step outside the mainstream."

PRINCETON UNIVERSITY

Admissions

From Princeton's undergraduate catalog: "Princeton seeks students of good character who have demonstrated scholastic achievement and capacity for further growth....to identify those candidates who seem best qualified to take advantage of Princeton's academic programs and to select from among them those who will form an undergraduate body with a wide representation of interests, backgrounds and special abilities." The University doesn't require a fixed high school course curriculum; however, the catalog notes, "English, foreign languages, and mathematics are so necessary to intellectual growth and attainment that sustained study of each in secondary school is expected. The following program is desirable: *English*, four years; *foreign languages*, four years of one language (rather than two years each of two languages), preferably continued through the final year of secondary school; *mathematics*, four years." In addition to the courses listed above, "important components of strong preparation" include two years of lab science, two years of history (U.S. plus another country or area), "some study of art or music," and an additional foreign language. It should be noted, however, "The University will give full consideration to an applicant who has been unable to pursue the recommended studies to the full extent if the record otherwise shows clear promise." All applicants must submit SAT or ACT scores, and three Achievements are strongly recommended, as is an alumni interview.

Financial Aid

Financial aid applicants to Princeton must complete the FAF and a form generated by Princeton's financial aid office. Financial aid awards are need-based only. All '91–'92 undergrads who demonstrated need received a grant (1,750 students, about 40% of the undergraduate population). An additional 30% of all undergrads received aid through outside scholarships (merit, ROTC, etc.), loans (mostly Perkins and Stafford, plus Princeton's own institutional loans), and campus employment.

Excerpted from Princeton University promotional materials:

"Methods of instruction [at Princeton] vary widely, but common to all areas of the academic program is a strong emphasis on individual responsibility and the free interchange of ideas. This is displayed most notably in the wide use of preceptorials and seminars, in the provision of independent study for all upperclass students and qualified underclass students, and in the availability of a series of special programs to meet a range of individual interests. The undergraduate college encourages the student to be an independent seeker of information, not a passive recipient, and to assume responsibility for gaining both knowledge and judgement that will strengthen later contributions to society."

ADMISSIONS FACTS

Competitiveness Rating:	**100**
% of applicants accepted:	17
% acceptees attending:	54

FRESHMAN PROFILE

Average verbal SAT:	640
Average math SAT:	700
Average ACT:	NA
Graduated top 10% of class:	89
Graduated top 25% of class:	100
Graduated top 50% of class:	100

DEADLINES

Early decision/action:	11/1
Early dec./act. notif.:	12/15
Regular admission:	1/3
Regular adm. notif.:	4/1

APPLICANTS ALSO LOOK AT

and sometimes prefer:
UC Berkeley
Harvard/Radcliffe College
Yale U.

and rarely prefer:
Columbia U.
Johns Hopkins U.
Wesleyan U.
U. Chicago
U. Pennsylvania
Northwestern U.

ADDRESS

Undergraduate Admissions
Box 430
Princeton, NJ 08544
609-258-3060

FINANCIAL FACTS

In-state tuition ($):	16,670
Out-of-state tuition ($):	16,670
Room & board:	5,311
FA application deadline:	2/1
% frosh receiving FA:	70
PT earnings per yr. ($):	1800

TYPE OF AID: % of students ($)

FA of some kind:	70 (NA)
Need-based grants:	40 (10,500)
Merit-based grants:	NA
Loans:	NA (3,000)
Work study:	NA
Student rating of FA:	83

PROVIDENCE COLLEGE

CAMPUS LIFE

Quality of Life Rating:	**83**
Type of school:	private
Affiliation:	Dominican
Environment:	city

STUDENT BODY

FT undergrad enrollment:	3,805
% male/% female:	48/52
% out-of-state:	85
% live on campus:	64
% African-American:	2
% Asian:	1
% Caucasian:	94
% Hispanic:	2
% foreign:	1
% transfers:	2

WHAT'S HOT

intramural sports
religion
intercollegiate sports
small lectures
caring about politics
overall happiness

WHAT'S NOT

fraternities/sororities
diversity
town-gown relations
dating
gay community accepted
students interact
studying hard

ACADEMICS

Academic Rating:	**76**
Calendar:	semester
Student/teacher ratio:	15/1
% doctorates:	83
Profs interesting:	81
Profs accessible:	83
Hours of study per day:	2.75

MOST POPULAR MAJORS BY %

Business:	35
English:	9
History:	7

% GRADS WHO PURSUE

Law:	8
MBA:	4
Medicine:	3
M.A., etc.:	12

What do students think about Providence College?

■ **Academics** Providence College is a small school run by the Dominican Order of Preachers and attended almost entirely by Catholics. But while the influence of Catholicism on campus life is undeniable, most students' interests lie in more mundane matters: namely, their careers. Fully one third of PC's students are business and management majors. Education, computer science, and pre-medical studies are among the other popular profession-oriented majors. The social sciences (particularly history, political science, and government) and English are also popular. All students must complete a two-year interdisciplinary Western Civilization survey as well as a wide array of distribution requirements. With fewer than 4,000 undergraduates, PC is "rather small, so it sometimes seems like a high school, but the closeness of the students and faculty more than make up for it. You couldn't be 'just a number' if you tried." Academically, most students describe the school as "low pressure." Explained one, "PC has a great reputation, so a PC diploma means a lot; but academically this school is not as difficult as some would have you believe. Hell, my GPA is 3.4, so I'm not complaining." Almost all student complaints here concern the administration, whom students describe as "completely out of touch with students' desires," and "concerned almost solely with appearances to outsiders." To support their claims, students cited recent incidents of campus violence, in which they perceived the administration as more concerned with "keeping the public from learning about them than with figuring out how to prevent similar incidents in the future."

■ **Life** PC students enjoy a full schedule of parties and extracurriculars. As one student put it, "PC provides a good balance between the academic world and the social scene." Another agreed: "If you are looking for a school that offers a great social environment, excellent sports facilities, and a work load that is definitely manageable, PC is the school for you." PC's affiliation with the Dominicans means that all dorms are single-sex and maintain strict visitation rules. Not surprisingly, many upperclassmen move off-campus. The party scene is not hampered by either Dominican oversight or the lack of a Greek system, however. Students report that their classmates are "a bunch of heavy drinkers," and that parties are frequent. "Weekends usually start on Wednesday, by Thursday at the latest," reported one student. PC's Division I sports teams are very popular. The city of Providence itself, however, received low marks, mostly because it is perceived as dangerous.

■ **Students** Nearly every PC student fits the description "white and Catholic." Wrote one student, "We're a friendly group but too homogeneous. The administration is so concerned with its 'Catholic image' that it overlooks the need for student diversity." Many students indicated a large degree of comfort and satisfaction with their classmates. As one senior put it, "I don't feel $70,000 smarter, but I do feel a million dollars richer from the friendships I've made here."

PROVIDENCE COLLEGE

Admissions

According to Providence College's most recent catalog, the school's admissions committee considers "school records, recommendations, and results of standardized ability and achievement tests...The Committee on Admissions gives recognition to students with different talents, contrasting backgrounds, and geographical origins...All candidates are encouraged to broaden their reading outside of class and to take every opportunity to develop their competence in writing. Candidates who cannot demonstrate competence in written English will be at a distinct disadvantage in the competition for admissions." Applicants must submit scores for either the SAT or the ACT, and are expected to have completed the following high school curriculum: four years of English; at least three years of math; three years of a foreign language; two years each of social studies and lab science; and, four additional academic units. Providence runs two rounds of Early Action admissions; the deadline for the first is November 15; for the second, December 15.

Financial Aid

The financial aid office at Providence College requires applicants to submit the FAF. The school awards merit scholarships to athletes (4% of the students here received such an award last year; average value: $10,500) and to pre-meds (about 1%; $17,500). Last year, students borrowed most frequently from the Stafford loan program (32%; $2,968) and the Perkins loan program (13%; $1,900).

Excerpted from Providence College promotional materials:

"Providence College is, and plans to continue to be, a relatively small, coeducational, liberal arts institution of higher learning which is church-related and primarily undergraduate in character. Its mission is to provide all of its students with a variety of opportunities for intellectual growth and personal development, chiefly through the disciplines of the liberal arts and sciences, but also through a living-learning environment which provides programs and activities designed to aid students to discover their aptitudes and develop themselves as productive members of society.

"The College views the cultivation of spiritual, ethical, and aesthetic values as an essential aspect of its mission. It pursues this dimension of its work within the context of the standards of scholarship, the principles of the Judeo-Christian heritage, and the unique Catholic educational tradition of the Dominican Order, from which the College derives its distinctive character."

ADMISSIONS FACTS

Competitiveness Rating:	**73**
% of applicants accepted:	58
% acceptees attending:	37

FRESHMAN PROFILE

Average verbal SAT:	510
Average math SAT:	590
Average ACT:	26
Graduated top 10% of class:	20
Graduated top 25% of class:	50
Graduated top 50% of class:	89

DEADLINES

Early decision/action:	11/15
Early dec./act. notif.:	1/15
Regular admission:	2/1
Regular adm. notif.:	4/15

APPLICANTS ALSO LOOK AT

and often prefer:
College of the Holy Cross
Fairfield U.

and sometimes prefer:
Syracuse U.
U. Vermont
Boston College
U. New Hampshire

and rarely prefer:
U. Connecticut
Boston U.
U. Mass–Amherst

ADDRESS

Undergraduate Admissions
Providence, RI 02918-0001
401-865-2535

FINANCIAL FACTS

In-state tuition ($):	10,935
Out-of-state tuition ($):	10,935
Room & board:	5,000
FA application deadline:	f2/15
% frosh receiving FA:	45
PT earnings per yr. ($):	1400

TYPE OF AID: % of students ($)

FA of some kind:	50 (9,222)
Need-based grants:	45 (5,350)
Merit-based grants:	NA (10,600)
Loans:	40 (2,498)
Work study:	26 (1,650)
Student rating of FA:	69

389

RANDOLPH-MACON COLLEGE

Ashland, VA

What do students think about Randolph-Macon College?

■ **Academics** Randolph-Macon College, located in Ashland, Virginia, boasts a wide variety of solid academic offerings. Students described R-MC as "academically competitive with a very strong liberal arts program." Popular majors include psychology, English, business and management, and biology. Distribution requirements are rigorous, comprising courses in English, math, natural and social sciences, fine arts and foreign languages. Small class size is a plus and contributes to the "family" atmosphere on campus. Students appreciate the fact that "teachers are always willing to help," and wrote that "students are often invited to dine with their professors." Randolph-Macon's 4-1-4 calendar includes a January term, which students may use for nontraditional academic courses, field study, or travel. During the rest of the year, interested students may apply for internships in Washington, D.C., or terms of study at any of the other schools in the Seven College Consortium of Virginia (Washington and Lee, Hampden-Sydney, Sweet Briar, Mary Baldwin, Hollins, or Randolph-Macon Woman's College). Although several students complained that "the administration needs to listen more and be open to the feelings of the students," the undergraduate population as a whole is satisfied with the way the school is run. In general, R-MC offers a challenging, intimate academic setting, complete with an "excellent" faculty that wins high praise from students.

■ **Life** Many students cited the "incredibly personable" attitude prevalent among their peers, as well as the "tight community" atmosphere, as positive aspects of life at R-MC. Although the social scene frequently involves traveling off campus ("Ashland is NOT the center of the universe!"), no one seems to mind—distractions are within easy reach. As one student reported, "You can't beat the location of Randolph-Macon: it's 15 minutes from Richmond, 90 minutes from Virginia Beach, 60 minutes from the Blue Ridge Mountains, and 90 minutes from Washington, D.C. Everything is extremely accessible." The Greeks are popular, and although not everyone loves them ("The frats are always breaking rules"), they do dominate the party scene. The major area concern right now is alcohol: according to students, there are "many conflicts between the administration and the students, as the school is leaning toward more restrictive policies." R-MC undergrads do not appreciate being "forced to go off campus to drink," and there is a movement afoot to found a campus pub for those 21 and over. On the whole, however, students find life at Randolph-Macon quite enjoyable. As one student wrote, "Everyone makes the most, academically and energetically, of their time."

■ **Students** Randolph-Macon is 94 percent Caucasian, with very small black and Asian contingents. There are plenty of "upper-class, nice-dressing Southerners," and student interest in political issues is minimal. Reported one student, "People here didn't care during the Gulf war, but are currently banding together to protest keg restrictions."

RANDOLPH-MACON COLLEGE

Ashland, VA

Admissions

The admissions office reports that "the admissions staff takes the following factors into consideration when evaluating an applicant: high school record, standardized test scores, recommendations, extracurricular activities, and personal qualities. No formulas or arbitrary cut-offs are used. Our approach is highly personal." An interview is not part of the application process here. Applicants are required to have completed a minimum of four years of English, three years each of a foreign language, math, social studies, and physical/biological sciences. All told, a minimum of 16 academic units are required. Students must submit scores for either the SAT or ACT. Applicants to Randolph-Macon most often also apply to James Madison, Hampden-Sydney, Virginia Tech, Mary Washington, and University of Richmond.

Financial Aid

Financial aid applicants to Randolph-Macon must complete the FAF or FFS (the former is preferred). RMC's brochure states that most aid awards are based on the FAF analysis. The college awards scholarships based on "merit and academic and leadership potential." Minority and religious-affiliation scholarships are also offered. In addition to loan programs, interest-free payments plans and Virginia's Tuition Assistance Grant program (Virginia residents only) are available. Priority is given to completed applications received by March 1.

Excerpted from Randolph-Macon College promotional materials:

"Randolph-Macon College is an independent liberal arts college with a broad curriculum designed to allow students considerable freedom in planning their own program. Students here acquire not only the breadth of knowledge traditionally emphasized in a liberal education, but also a sound foundation in a particular field.

"Students receive solid support from advisors, faculty, and peers. The Counseling and Career Center provides personal and career counseling as well as workshops and seminars. The combination of people, programs, and services prepare students for any future, including success in securing a job or in gaining acceptance to graduate or professional school.

"The college offers a wide variety of social and recreational opportunities. A full-time Student Activities Director works in conjunction with over 60 campus organizations to ensure that almost every day, there are activities and events in which students can participate. Forty percent of the students participate in one or more community service activities; 80 percent play intramural sports; 50 percent join a fraternity or sorority; and everyone has a voice in Student Government."

ADMISSIONS FACTS

Competitiveness Rating:	**66**
% of applicants accepted:	66
% acceptees attending:	27

FRESHMAN PROFILE

Average verbal SAT:	497
Average math SAT:	540
Average ACT:	NA
Graduated top 10% of class:	13
Graduated top 25% of class:	40
Graduated top 50% of class:	80

DEADLINES

Early decision/action:	12/1
Early dec./act. notif.:	12/20
Regular admission:	3/1
Regular adm. notif.:	4/1

APPLICANTS ALSO LOOK AT

and sometimes prefer:
James Madison U.
Virginia Polytech
Washington & Lee U.

and rarely prefer:
Hampden-Sydney College
Sweet Briar College
U. Richmond

ADDRESS

Undergraduate Admissions
Ashland, VA 23005
804-752-7305

FINANCIAL FACTS

In-state tuition ($):	10,685
Out-of-state tuition ($):	10,685
Room & board:	4,600
FA application deadline:	3/1
% frosh receiving FA:	71
PT earnings per yr. ($):	800

TYPE OF AID: % of students ($)

FA of some kind:	74 (NA)
Need-based grants:	NA
Merit-based grants:	NA
Loans:	NA
Work study:	NA
Student rating of FA:	85

REED COLLEGE

Portland, OR

What do students think about Reed College?

■ **Academics** In many ways, Reed College epitomizes the ideal of a progressive undergraduate institution. Its students are hard-working, intelligent, and open to unconventional ideas; its philosophy de-emphasizes the traditional (grades, while recorded, are neither reported or discussed; restrictions on student behavior are minimal); and its professors and academic programs constantly challenge the students' preconceptions and capacities for work. As several Reed students noted, "this school is not for everyone." Because of its non-traditional aspects, Reed scares off some potential applicants, and many who do attend leave before graduation. About half of Reed freshman make it through all four years. Students are forthcoming about the school's assets: wrote one, "The classes are tiny and the profs are fantastic. Reed treats you like an adult. Students and faculty are accepting of just about everything. If you want to work really hard, hang out with brilliant, strange, intelligent, and interesting people, Reed is the place." They are equally forthcoming about its less appealing side. As one student wrote, "The ethos here is, if you're not haggard, sleep-deprived, and lonely, you're not living up to your academic potential." The academic program includes an introductory humanities course, an array of general education requirements, and a senior thesis. Academic departments are all reportedly excellent. History, English, and the sciences drew frequent praise. Reed is best for "self-motivated, intelligent students; it's a place of many sticks and few carrots." For those who survive, there is one huge carrot: Reed's excellent reputation among graduate schools (over two thirds of Reed graduates continue on to graduate work).

■ **Life** Explained one student, "When Reedies party, which is generally infrequently, they do so with the same intensity they devote to their studies." Drugs "are kinda big here but everyone's cool about it," and alcohol is also popular. Several students noted that drugs no longer occupy the center of Reed social life, as they did in the 1960s and '70s. Student activism and community service are popular, as are creative outlets (newspaper, literary and political journals, radio station, etc.). Students also noted a number of recreational options in the area: the city of Portland, Mt. Hood, several nearby national parks, and the Pacific Ocean all offer relief from the sometimes pervasive stress.

■ **Students** Reed's student body is the most left-leaning politically included in our survey. Alternative lifestyles—drug usage, homosexuality—are openly accepted here. Frequent gripes against the student body are its lack of political and ethnic diversity ("This school is *so* white!" wrote one Asian student), and its propensity toward cynicism and an obsession with work that borders on the anti-social. As one student put it, "Reed students do things like study or write rather than bathe, eat, sleep or other things that 'normal' humans do. If students' nerves could generate electricity, we might be able to light all of Southern California during finals week."

REED COLLEGE

Admissions

Reed College's most recent admissions bulletin states, "The Committee on Admission takes into account many integrated factors, but academic accomplishments and talents are given the greatest weight in the selection process. Strong verbal and qualitative skills and demonstrated writing ability are important considerations…The Committee on Admission may give special consideration to applicants who represent a particular culture, region, or background that will contribute to the diversity of the college…qualities of character—in particular, motivation, attitude toward learning, and social consciousness—also are important considerations." Reed strongly recommends a college prep curriculum that includes: four years of English, at least two years of a foreign language, three or four years of math, and two or more years each of a lab science and history/ social studies. The school requires applicants to submit scores for either the SAT or the ACT. An interview is "strongly recommended" but not required.

Financial Aid

The financial aid office at Reed College requires applicants to submit the FAF, a form generated by the school. All assistance is need-based; Reed offers no merit scholarships. The school's admissions brochure reports that federally subsidized loans, Perkins loans, and a limited number of Reed College loans are available. The same brochure states that *"While Reed is unable to meet the need of some new freshmen and transfer students*, the College guarantees to meet the full demonstrated need of all continuing students in good academic standing (emphasis added)."

A note from the Reed College Admissions Office:

"Dedication to the highest standards of academic scholarship is central to a Reed education. A well-structured curriculum and small classes with motivated students and dedicated faculty provide the environment in which a student's quest for learning can be given broad rein. Students most likely to derive maximum benefit from a Reed education are individuals who possess a high degree of self-discipline and a genuine enthusiasm for academic work."

ADMISSIONS FACTS

Competitiveness Rating:	**87**
% of applicants accepted:	63
% acceptees attending:	27

FRESHMAN PROFILE

Average verbal SAT:	612
Average math SAT:	635
Average ACT:	29
Graduated top 10% of class:	58
Graduated top 25% of class:	89
Graduated top 50% of class:	98

DEADLINES

Early decision/action:	12/1
Early dec./act. notif.:	12/15
Regular admission:	2/1
Regular adm. notif.:	early April

APPLICANTS ALSO LOOK AT

and often prefer:
Oberlin College
UC Berkeley

and sometimes prefer:
New College
Colorado College

and rarely prefer:
Hampshire College
Grinnell College
UC Santa Cruz
Evergreen College

ADDRESS

Undergraduate Admissions
3203 SE Woodstock Blvd.
Portland, OR 97202-8199
503-777-7511

FINANCIAL FACTS

In-state tuition ($):	16,570
Out-of-state tuition ($):	16,570
Room & board:	4,640
FA application deadline:	3/1
% frosh receiving FA:	41
PT earnings per yr. ($):	675

TYPE OF AID: % of students ($)

FA of some kind:	47 (11,000)
Need-based grants:	NA
Merit-based grants:	NA
Loans:	NA
Work study:	NA
Student rating of FA:	81

RENSSELAER POLYTECHNIC INSTITUTE

Troy, NY

What do students think about RPI?

■ **Academics** Students looking for four carefree years don't usually look to engineering schools first, and for good reason; as the students of Rensselaer Polytechnic Institute demonstrate, pursuing an engineering degree entails single-minded devotion to the task. "I would definitely describe this as a high-pressure school," wrote one student in what may be the understatement of the year. Stress is a way of life for RPI students. Sentiments such as "College is boot camp: deal with it!" were common among students' responses. Students who endure this atmosphere work in excellent facilities with professors who are also important players in the world of research. Electrical engineering is the most popular major, but mechanical and aeronautic engineering are also strong, as is computer science. Business and management courses are also surprisingly strong. Wrote one management major, "Although the School of Management is regarded as 'where the hockey players go,' it has a very good program and is small, which allows for more student/faculty interaction." Due to the pressure, the high tuition, and the sometimes incomprehensible nature of instruction, however, overall satisfaction levels here are low. A typical student complained that "tuition is too high for what we get. The high price causes too much emphasis on grades instead of learning. The result is that nobody cares about anything but money and grades and lots of cheating." Another student wrote that "my main complaint is that RPI makes the transition from high school to college life during freshman year very difficult. During first year the professors were unreachable, many of my labs were taught by foreign TAs so there was a language barrier, and most of my classes were taught as if we were reviewing material rather than learning it for the first time. Oddly, it gets better as you move on. This school supports you least just when you need it most."

■ **Life** Students gave their hometown of Troy low marks. Wrote one woman, "If you like rain, freezing temperatures, and secluded and remote old industrial towns, this is the school for you." She also complained that her male classmates were chauvinists. Perhaps their difficulties interacting with women come from the fact that they rarely see one: the male-female ratio is four to one. Wrote one student, "The social scene is pretty bad due to the male-female ratio, but that happens at nearly all big engineering colleges. Don't worry, though, you'll be out in only four years." The Greeks play "a major part on campus and a major role in many people's social lives." Sports are also popular, both for spectators and participants. One student summed up, "You can get a great education in engineering here and they try hard to get you a job, but if you're looking for fun, excitement, or friends who won't kill you for your homework, go somewhere else or join a fraternity."

■ **Students** As previously mentioned, the student body is overwhelmingly male. Because RPI is a technical school, students are also similar in terms of their interests; nearly all share more than a mild fascination with computers and science. Still, students ranked their student body "very diverse," probably because of the 20 percent minority population.

RENSSELAER POLYTECHNIC INSTITUTE

Troy, NY

Admissions

The admissions office reports that "the admissions staff at Rensselaer does its utmost to ensure that every application receives the time and personal attention it deserves. Each application is carefully examined by two staff members; a final decision is made after the committee has read and discussed the qualifications of the applicants and recommendations made by the first readers." RPI considers high school curriculum and GPA most important in determining an applicant's desirability; standardized test scores (SAT or ACT plus three achievements—English comp, Math I or II, and Chemistry or Physics) are also important. Extracurricular activities and a personal statement are also considered. Applicants are expected to have completed four years of math (calculus is recommended) and chemistry or physics. RPI applicants most often also apply to Cornell U, MIT, Carnegie Mellon, and RIT.

Financial Aid

The financial aid office at Rensselaer Polytech requires applicants to submit the FAF, a form generated by the school, and their parents' tax return. According to the school's catalog, scholarships are offered on the basis of "relative financial need, academic achievement and promise, qualities of character, evidence of willingness to help oneself by working, and participation in community and school activities." Special scholarships awarded on the basis of place of residence, area of study, and other specialized areas (enumerated in the catalog) are also available. RPI participates in the following loan programs: Stafford, Perkins, PLUS, SLS, HELP, and EXCEL.

A note from the Rensselaer Polytechnic Institute Admissions Office:

"Rensselaer is a private, coeducational university made up of the schools of Architecture, Engineering, Humanities and Social Sciences, Management, and Science, all serving undergraduate and graduate students with more than 110 programs. All of Rensselaer's educational programs support, directly or indirectly, its original mission to instruct persons 'in the application of science to the common purposes of life' and its current mandate to provide education for technological leadership."

ADMISSIONS FACTS

Competitiveness Rating:	**84**
% of applicants accepted:	77
% acceptees attending:	28

FRESHMAN PROFILE

Average verbal SAT:	567*
Average math SAT:	643*
Average ACT:	NA
Graduated top 10% of class:	59
Graduated top 25% of class:	83
Graduated top 50% of class:	98

DEADLINES

Early decision/action:	1/1
Early dec./act. notif.:	rolling
Regular admission:	1/15
Regular adm. notif.:	3/7

APPLICANTS ALSO LOOK AT

and often prefer:

Yale U.

MIT

and sometimes prefer:

Lehigh U.

and rarely prefer:

SUNY Binghamton

SUNY Albany

SUNY Buffalo

Syracuse U.

Boston College

Carnegie Mellon U.

ADDRESS

Undergraduate Admissions
Troy, NY 12180-3590
518-276-6216

FINANCIAL FACTS

In-state tuition ($):	15,150
Out-of-state tuition ($):	15,150
Room & board:	5,150
FA application deadline:	2/15
% frosh receiving FA:	72
PT earnings per yr. ($):	1300

TYPE OF AID: % of students ($)

FA of some kind:	68 (NA)
Need-based grants:	NA
Merit-based grants:	NA
Loans:	NA
Work study:	NA
Student rating of FA:	72

UNIVERSITY OF RHODE ISLAND

CAMPUS LIFE

Quality of Life Rating: 71

Type of school:	public
Affiliation:	none
Environment:	suburban

STUDENT BODY

FT undergrad enrollment:	9,588
% male/% female:	47/53
% out-of-state:	36
% live on campus:	39
% African-American:	2
% Asian:	2
% Caucasian:	84
% Hispanic:	1
% foreign:	1
% transfers:	4

WHAT'S HOT

marijuana
dating
Grateful Dead
working a job
suitcase syndrome
school newspaper

WHAT'S NOT

dorm comfort
library
caring about politics
honesty
administration (overall)
food
small seminars and labs
dorm safety

ACADEMICS

Academic Rating: 71

Calendar:	semester
Student/teacher ratio:	14/1
% doctorates:	78
Profs interesting:	72
Profs accessible:	69
Hours of study per day:	2.74

MOST POPULAR MAJORS BY %

Business & Management:	12
Education:	12
Social Sciences:	12

What do students think about the University of R.I.?

■ **Academics** University of Rhode Island is a medium-sized public institution that offers students from within the state a fine education at cut-rate prices. For those from out of state, the price is less of a bargain (although it's still only half what you'd pay at most private universities). Most URI students pursue a pre-professional track. Business, and education are popular majors, and the engineering, pharmacological studies, and nursing departments, which are only slightly less popular, are said to be excellent. As one student explained, "This university is a good school, but it is a typical large university—many students are here only for a party, which brings down the quality of education (see "Life," below)." URI is a typical large university in other ways as well: desirable courses can be extremely difficult to get into, especially for underclassmen; classes are large and professors are often hard to meet with one-on-one; and administrative chores, such as paying bills and meeting with advisors, can be a real hassle. Students gave the library poor grades, but that's because it's currently under construction. Overall, the intensity with which students attack their studies here is below the national average; however, an honors program, open to top-ranked students, offers smaller classes and a more challenging curriculum.

■ **Life** URI is a party school: drinking, drugs, frats, and promiscuous behavior are all extremely popular with the student body. Complained one student, "There is too much drinking on this campus and part of that is due to the lack of alternative social activities. The choice is either a fraternity party or the campus pub." Several students wanted us to know that "URI is better known as 'You Are High.'" The administration is considering a "dry campus" policy, but since "a lot of people go off-campus to party," the move probably won't have a major effect on students' social lives. Students also complained about campus security and the food, and many commuters noted that parking is a real problem: "Local liquor stores and tow trucks make a killing off us," said one student. Several students noted that URI is the ideal size for socializing, "not so big that a student becomes lost and not so small that everyone is aware of everyone else's private business."

■ **Students** Well over half of URI's student body comes from in-state. Those from out of state come from other states on the Eastern Seaboard, particularly New Jersey; said one student, "You would think that you were attending the University of New Jersey, Rhode Island campus." Among the students are "many older, non-traditional undergrads." Although only two fifths of the students live on-campus, URI is not a big commuter school: many students rent cheap, nearby housing along the beach. A final note: URI students are the seventh most apolitical in the nation.

UNIVERSITY OF RHODE ISLAND

Kingston, RI

Admissions

The admissions office reports that "no cut-offs or formulas are used" to eliminate candidates from the applicant pool. The admissions committee looks first at your high school curriculum and the grades you received, then at standardized test scores. Next, in importance, are an interview, extracurricular activities, and letters of recommendation. Essays are not part of the application process. Applicants are required to have completed four years of English, three years of algebra and geometry, and two years of science, history, and foreign language. Furthermore, pharmacy and engineering majors must complete further math and science courses. Music students must audition. University of Rhode Island requires either the ACT or SAT for freshman applicants. Those who apply to URI often also apply to UConn, UNew Hampshire, UMass–Amherst, UDelaware, and Providence College.

Financial Aid

The financial aid office at the University of Rhode Island requires applicants to submit the FAF. In 1991–92, the school awarded merit grants on the basis of athletic ability (22% of the students received such an award; average value: $7,677), academic excellence (13%; app. $1,230), and musical skill (less than 1%; $900). In 1991–92, the financial aid office recommended Stafford loans for 75% of all financial aid recipients; the school also recommends PLUS/SLS loans for those receiving an award.

A note from the University of Rhode Island Admissions Office:

"Like the permanent granite cornerstones that grace its stately buildings, the University of Rhode Island was founded in the lasting tradition of the land-grant colleges and later became one of the original crop of national Sea Grant colleges. Observing its centennial in 1992, the state's largest university prepares its students to meet the challenges of the 21st century."

ADMISSIONS FACTS

Competitiveness Rating:	**65**
% of applicants accepted:	74
% acceptees attending:	27

FRESHMAN PROFILE

Average verbal SAT:	450
Average math SAT:	515
Average ACT:	22
Graduated top 10% of class:	12
Graduated top 25% of class:	44
Graduated top 50% of class:	83

DEADLINES

Early decision/action:	11/1
Early dec./act. notif.:	12/15
Regular admission:	3/1
Regular adm. notif.:	4/15

APPLICANTS ALSO LOOK AT

and often prefer:
U. Mass–Amherst
U. Connecticut

and sometimes prefer:
Boston U.
U. Delaware
U. Vermont

and rarely prefer:
U. Maine
U. New Hampshire

ADDRESS

Undergraduate Admissions
Kingston, RI 02881
401-792-9800

FINANCIAL FACTS

In-state tuition ($):	2,045
Out-of-state tuition ($):	6,550
Room & board:	4,424
FA application deadline:	3/1
% frosh receiving FA:	75
PT earnings per yr. ($):	1,500

TYPE OF AID: % of students ($)

FA of some kind:	82 (NA)
Need-based grants:	31 (2,500)
Merit-based grants:	4 (4927)
Loans:	60 (2,800)
Work study:	8 (1,200)
Student rating of FA:	68

RHODE ISLAND SCHOOL OF DESIGN

Providence, RI

CAMPUS LIFE

Quality of Life Rating:	**82**
Type of school:	private
Affiliation:	none
Environment:	city

STUDENT BODY

FT undergrad enrollment:	1,809
% male/% female:	43/57
% out-of-state:	92
% live on campus:	33
% African-American:	3
% Asian:	9
% Caucasian:	75
% Hispanic:	3
% foreign:	11
% transfers:	10

WHAT'S HOT

gay community accepted
gay community visible
alternative rock
marijuana
studying hard
rap/hip-hop
interaction among students
attending all classes
leftist politics
in-class discussion
profs in class

WHAT'S NOT

financial aid
caring about politics
food

ACADEMICS

Academic Rating:	**78**
Calendar:	4-1-4
Student/teacher ratio:	NA
% doctorates:	NA
Profs interesting:	90
Profs accessible:	70
Hours of study per day:	4.03

MOST POPULAR MAJORS BY %

Architect. & Envirnmntl. Dsgn.:	25
Visual & Performing Arts:	75

% GRADS WHO PURSUE

Law:	NA
MBA:	NA
Medicine:	NA
M.A., etc.:	20

What do students think about RISD?

■ **Academics** The Rhode Island School of Design is one of the nation's finest and most demanding art schools. Students here work hard (they spend over four hours a day in their studios) with a determination that few but those who are certain of their life's goals can muster. Wrote one student, "RISD is pretty intense—long studio hours—lots of people survive on coffee—but I wouldn't choose any other way of life." Said another, "Do NOT go to RISD if you are indecisive about your future. Knowing that you want to go into an art field is recommended, and it also saves time, money, and headaches over transferring to another school." The payoff for all the hard work is the chance to study with excellent teachers (who, however, are only moderately accessible to their students after classes), the use of top-notch facilities, and the opportunity to participate in a community of similarly dedicated, similarly offbeat artists (see "Students," below). Students were uniformly happy with courses in commercial arts, architecture, and fine arts. Their complaints all concerned non-art-related courses. Said one, "There are no business courses, and the liberal arts courses are mostly lame. Cross-registration at Brown is advertised, but it's relatively impossible."

■ **Life** RISD students have a tendency to get a little obsessive about their work, to the extent that many of them don't consider spending much time at leisure activities. One student explained, "Work dominates everyone's center of concerns and many trivial issues, such as parties, slide to secondary places." To most students, this is not a negative: the same student continued, "I love the mentality that accompanies individuals who dedicate their lives to creative areas and that's why I'm here. The environment is alternative to the mainstream and offers unlimited options to explore new fields, philosophies and artistic languages. I just wish more people had the opportunity to experience it." When they do take time off from work, RISD students smoke a ton of pot (ninth most per capita of all student bodies profiled in this book). They give the city of Providence below-average marks.

■ **Students** RISD's student body, in the words of one student, is made up of "lots of loony people all doin' their own thang." Explained another, "The student body here is more accepting of eccentric personalities and strong opinions than most." There is a visible gay population which encounters little prejudice from the straight students. Students lean to the left politically but identify themselves as apathetic. Students come from all over the country, and ten percent are foreign nationals. Some are unhappy with the state of minority representation on campus. Explained one who is active in student government, "Unfortunately, this is an expensive school with very little endowment, so financial aid is limited. As a result, there are not many African-American, Native American, or Hispanic students here." The most frequent negative rap on RISD students: they're arrogant. Said one, "Although it may not seem like it, RISD is a very religious school. Everyone thinks they're God." Among the student bodies profiled here, they are among the top 10 percent in overall happiness with their school.

398

RHODE ISLAND SCHOOL OF DESIGN

Providence, RI

Admissions

Applicants to RISD are required to submit a portfolio of their work (eight to 20 reproductions should be included; a portfolio is not required of architecture students) as well as drawings (on 16"-by-20" white paper, in soft pencil) of a bicycle, an interior or exterior environment, and a subject of their choosing. The admissions committee considers these, as well as applicants' high school transcripts, written statements of purpose, SAT or ACT scores, and letters of recommendation when making its decisions. RISD "urges" applicants to pursue a college preparatory program in high school, including studio art and art history classes whenever possible; architecture applicants should also have completed two years of algebra, one semester of trigonometry, and one year of science (physics preferred).

Financial Aid

The financial aid office at RISD requires applicants to submit the FAF and a copy of their parents' most recent tax return. The school offers several merit scholarships each year to students "who have outstanding academic and visual achievements"; these awards range in value from $500 to $2,500. Need-based grants range in value from $200 to $14,000; "over one quarter of the student body" receive such grants. The school's admissions brochure also lists Perkins, Stafford, and PLUS/SLS loans as options for students who cannot otherwise afford to attend the school.

A note from the Rhode Island School of Design Admissions Office:

"Education at RISD is a blend of long and rich tradition, intellectual stimulation, creativity, and a commitment to the visual arts. Our outstanding faculty forms the cornerstone of a RISD education. With impressive educational backgrounds, scholarship, and professional artistic achievements, RISD faculty members bring great expertise an sensitivity to their teaching. This superb faculty...yield an atmosphere charged with energy. Here, at once, is the freedom to create and the challenge to produce. This experience—and this place—have attracted international recognition, as may be seen from RISD's student body."

ADMISSIONS FACTS

Competitiveness Rating:	**90**
% of applicants accepted:	36
% acceptees attending:	51

FRESHMAN PROFILE

Average verbal SAT:	515
Average math SAT:	550
Average ACT:	NA
Graduated top 10% of class:	21
Graduated top 25% of class:	21
Graduated top 50% of class:	87

DEADLINES

Early decision/action:	12/15
Early dec./act. notif.:	1/31
Regular admission:	2/15
Regular adm. notif.:	4/7

APPLICANTS ALSO LOOK AT

and often prefer:
Cooper Union

and sometimes prefer:
Carnegie Mellon U.
Parsons School of Design

and rarely prefer:
Syracuse U.
Maryland Institute/College of Art

ADDRESS

Undergraduate Admissions
Two College St.
Providence, RI 02903
401-331-3511

FINANCIAL FACTS

In-state tuition ($):	14,036
Out-of-state tuition ($):	14,036
Room & board:	5,892
FA application deadline:	2/15
% frosh receiving FA:	60
PT earnings per yr. ($):	1500

TYPE OF AID: % of students ($)

FA of some kind:	67 (NA)
Need-based grants:	NA
Merit-based grants:	NA
Loans:	NA
Work study:	NA
Student rating of FA:	57

RHODES COLLEGE

CAMPUS LIFE

Quality of Life Rating:	**94**

Type of school:	private
Affiliation:	Presbyterian
Environment:	city

STUDENT BODY

FT undergrad enrollment:	1,332
% male/% female:	46/54
% out-of-state:	63
% live on campus:	77
% African-American:	4
% Asian:	3
% Caucasian:	93
% Hispanic:	1
% foreign:	2
% transfers:	1

WHAT'S HOT

small classes (overall)
town-gown relations
honesty
campus appearance
profs outside class
small lectures
college theater groups
location
doing all the reading
dorm comfort
overall happiness

WHAT'S NOT

gay community visible
marriage
diversity

ACADEMICS

Academic Rating:	**87**

Calendar:	semester
Student/teacher ratio:	12/1
% doctorates:	90
Profs interesting:	92
Profs accessible:	95
Hours of study per day:	3.62

MOST POPULAR MAJORS BY %

Biology:	11
English:	11
Psychology:	11

% GRADS WHO PURSUE

Law:	9
MBA:	3
Medicine:	8
M.A., etc.:	19

What do students think about Rhodes College?

■ **Academics** Like Tulane University in Louisiana, Rhodes College offers its students the best of many worlds: a highly touted academic program, a beautiful, bucolic campus, and accessibility to a major metropolis. Rhodes students enjoy one benefit their counterparts in New Orleans don't: tremendous intimacy. With 1400 undergraduates, Rhodes is only one fourth Tulane's size (and, unlike Tulane, has no graduate students). Its academic offerings, both in preprofessional and liberal arts fields, are considered "superior." Probably Rhodes' finest asset is its excellent, highly committed faculty. As one satisfied student reported, "Professors are always available and very challenging. Teaching is their main objective, and personal relationships easily develop between profs and students." Another concurred: "Professors keep their doors open while they are in their offices, and encourage students to stop by and discuss reading material, debate current events, or just chat." The administration also won praise for being "open to students' ideas. If you have the initiative, anything can be done." Most respondents agreed that "the school's administration always hears what students need, if not always what they want." The honor code is widely respected: tests are not proctored, yet "cheating incidents are rare," according to students, and those that occur are handled by a student-run honor council. For most students, Rhodes' big attraction is its reputation with graduate schools: the school claims its students' acceptance rate in such programs is over 90 percent.

■ **Life** Most Rhodes students agree that a strong sense of community (a word we saw over and over in our surveys) is integral to life at Rhodes. People here are filled with "Southern hospitality; there is a warm smile on every face you encounter." The campus is "incredibly gorgeous" by all accounts, and students consider the surrounding city of Memphis "a perfect blend between a small-town community and a big metropolis." Greeks dominate the social scene, claiming over half the students as members, but are not the only options. "There are plenty of opportunities to get involved elsewhere." Student life has been dramatically affected by what students perceive as an "overly restrictive" alcohol policy; many contended the new restrictions "have seriously damaged the social scene at Rhodes. Parties are 'closed' and taken off campus…although there is a 'care cab' service, some students fear alcohol policy violations and risk accidents instead of fines."

■ **Students** One Rhodes undergrad summed up: "Rhodes is pretty conservative, but the student body is intelligent and open to new ideas." There isn't a lot of ethnic diversity here—the minority population is a tiny 8 percent—but students asserted that "race relations are good," such as they are. Students come from 36 states and 7 foreign countries, but the predominant feel in the student body is definitely Southern and affluent.

RHODES COLLEGE

Admissions

The admissions office reports that the application process "allows you to show how you use your out-of-class time, what your special interests are, and what you have contributed to your school or community. The essay is particularly important in the selection process…not only does the essay allow you to demonstrate your writing skills, but it also gives you the opportunity to address a topic of personal importance to you." Applicants are expected to complete 16 or more academic units in high school, including four years of English, two years of a foreign language, and three years of math. Two years of a lab science and two years of social studies are "strongly recommended." Math, science, economics, and computer students should have completed a fourth year of math. Students must submit scores for either the SAT or ACT. Rhodes applicants often also apply to Vanderbilt, Emory, Wake Forest, Sewanee, and Duke.

Financial Aid

The financial aid office at Rhodes College requires applicants to submit the FAF, a form generated by the school, and their parents' most recent tax return. Rhodes awards merit-based grants for academic excellence (average value: $6,289) and for talent in the fine arts ($6,581). Grants are also awarded to select children of Presbyterian ministers, Presbyterian students chosen by the Session of their local church, and a limited number of international students. Residents of the state of Tennessee may receive a Tennessee Student Assistance Award (a need-based grant). The deadline in the FA sidebar is a *priority* deadline.

A note from the Rhodes College Admissions Office:

"It's not just one characteristic which makes Rhodes different from other colleges, it's a special blend of features which sets us apart. We are a selective liberal arts college, yet without a cutthroat atmosphere; we are a small community, yet located in a major city; we are in a metropolitan area, yet offer one of the most beautiful and serene campuses in the nation. Our students are serious about learning and yet know how to have fun and are committed to being involved on campus and in community life. They live together in an atmosphere of trust and respect brought about by adherence to the Honor Code. And they know that learning at Rhodes doesn't mean sitting in a lecture hall and memorizing the professor's lecture. It means interaction, discussion, and a process of teacher and student discovering knowledge together. Rhodes is a place that welcomes new people and new ideas. It's a place of energy and light, not of apathy and complacency. Everyone who is a part of the Rhodes Community is striving to be the best at what she/he does."

ADMISSIONS FACTS

Competitiveness Rating:	**83**
% of applicants accepted:	72
% acceptees attending:	28

FRESHMAN PROFILE

Average verbal SAT:	570*
Average math SAT:	620*
Average ACT:	27*
Graduated top 10% of class:	53
Graduated top 25% of class:	80
Graduated top 50% of class:	96

DEADLINES

Early decision/action:	11/15
Early dec./act. notif.:	12/15
Regular admission:	2/1
Regular adm. notif.:	4/1

APPLICANTS ALSO LOOK AT

and often prefer:
Duke U.

and sometimes prefer:
Davidson College
Wake Forest U.
U. Tennessee–Knoxville
Georgetown U.
Emory U.

and rarely prefer:
Vanderbilt U.

ADDRESS

Undergraduate Admissions
2000 North Parkway
Memphis, TN 38112-1690
901-726-3700

FINANCIAL FACTS

In-state tuition ($):	12,800
Out-of-state tuition ($):	12,800
Room & board:	4,516
FA application deadline:	2/1
% frosh receiving FA:	67
PT earnings per yr. ($):	975

TYPE OF AID: % of students ($)

FA of some kind:	69 (NA)
Need-based grants:	NA (6,005)
Merit-based grants:	NA
Loans:	NA (4,049)
Work study:	NA
Student rating of FA:	98

RICE UNIVERSITY

Houston, TX

What do students think about Rice University?

■ **Academics** Rice University lives up to its reputation as the "Ivy of the South" in all but one regard: its tuition and fees. Named the "best college buy in 1991–92" by *Money* magazine, Rice relies on its massive endowment to keep prices down while providing first-rate instruction and facilities. Departments are solid across the board, from the better-known engineering, business, and natural sciences departments to the recently upgraded liberal arts and social sciences programs (such as political science, music, and English). Rice has addressed past criticisms that its graduates are not well rounded by adding new core requirements for liberal arts and science courses. A unique feature of academic life here is an honor code that allows students to take exams unproctored. Students gave their professors high marks. Wrote one, "The faculty is excellent and very concerned with the students' well-being, both in class and out." Students take their academic responsibilities very seriously. An unusual number go out of their way to accumulate more, in fact, by declaring double majors. One of the nicest aspects of life at Rice, however, is that while students pursue their studies vigorously, they don't do so at the expense of a healthy social life. Wrote one student, "This is a wonderful place for people who are passionate about both education and life. When studying for class, we dedicate all energy to that purpose. But when party time comes, watch out!"

■ **Life** Rice offers students a wide variety of extracurricular activities as well as a wide variety of quality academics. Wrote one student, "students are expected to be involved in activities other than classes. Rice offers essentially every activity that an enormous state university does, but since we have a small student body, every student can become actively involved, doing real things instead of grunt work. If you want to act, dance, write for the newspaper, be on the radio, debate, or play sports, go to Rice." The absence of the Greek system notwithstanding, Rice students find both the time and the opportunities to party. The administration takes a *laissez-faire* attitude toward drinking. Reported one student, "I don't know of too many other campuses where you can play beer-golf with tennis balls on the main quad and have faculty and administrators come out and join you, rather than chase you away." Students praised both the beautiful campus and the residential system, which places students in small residential colleges "that help students feel like they are a family." Students also like the city of Houston, which reportedly provides "excellent opportunities for internships junior/senior years."

■ **Students** Rice students characterize themselves as friendly, "very career-oriented, and fairly unconcerned with the world 'outside the hedges'" that surround the campus. Students here are ambitious: nearly half go on to receive graduate degrees after graduation. Men outnumber women three to two, but none of our respondents mentioned that the lopsided balance was a problem.

RICE UNIVERSITY

Admissions

The most recent Rice catalog reports that Admissions Committee decisions are based "not only on high school grades and test scores, but also on such qualities as leadership, participation in extracurricular activities, and personal creativity." Still, admissions are extremely competitive, and the school, true to its claim, does "attempt to seek out and identify those students who have demonstrated exceptional ability and the potential for personal and intellectual growth." Applicants are required to take the SAT and three achievement exams (which three differs depending on the program to which one applies; contact the school for details). Interviews are recommended, but not required. Applicants are expected to have completed a college prep curriculum that includes: four years of English; three years of math; two years each of social studies; a foreign language, and lab science; and, four years of academic electives. Rice has two rounds of early decision admissions: the deadline for the first is November 1; for the second (called "interim decision"), December 1.

Financial Aid

The financial aid office at Rice requires applicants to submit the FAF, a form generated by the school, and copies of their and their parents' most recent tax returns. Rice offers a number of academic scholarships, as well as scholarships for those with special talents in the arts, music, and drama. Rice students borrow money from the Stafford, Perkins, and PLUS/SLS loan programs. School loans are available, but only for short terms and only in emergency situations. Employment opportunities, both on- and off-campus, are available to all students. The school catalog reports that "Rice *attempts* to give the students sufficient aid to meet educational expenses (emphasis added)."

Excerpted from Rice University promotional materials:

"Dedicated to "the advancement of letters, science, and art," Rice is private, independent, nonsectarian, and coeducational. It includes among its academic divisions both undergraduate and graduate studies in the humanities, social sciences, natural sciences, engineering, architecture, administrative sciences, and music.

"Highly talented students with diverse interests are attracted to Rice by the opportunities for creative learning. They find rewarding student-faculty relationships, options for individually tailored programs of study, opportunities for research, cooperative activities with other institutions in the nation's fourth largest city, and the unique experience of residential colleges."

ADMISSIONS FACTS

Competitiveness Rating:	**98**
% of applicants accepted:	25
% acceptees attending:	47

FRESHMAN PROFILE

Average verbal SAT:	632*
Average math SAT:	692*
Average ACT:	NA
Graduated top 10% of class:	86
Graduated top 25% of class:	96
Graduated top 50% of class:	99

DEADLINES

Early decision/action:	11/1
Early dec./act. notif.:	12/1
Regular admission:	1/1
Regular adm. notif.:	4/1

APPLICANTS ALSO LOOK AT

and often prefer:
Harvard/Radcliffe College

and sometimes prefer:
Stanford U.
Princeton U.
U. Virginia

and rarely prefer:
Columbia U.
Haverford College
Emory U.
Duke U.
U. Texas–Austin

ADDRESS

Undergraduate Admissions
P.O. Box 1892
Houston, TX 77251
713-527-4036

FINANCIAL FACTS

In-state tuition ($):	7,700
Out-of-state tuition ($):	7,700
Room & board:	4,900
FA application deadline:	6/1
% frosh receiving FA:	91
PT earnings per yr. ($):	945

TYPE OF AID: % of students ($)

FA of some kind:	76 (NA)
Need-based grants:	NA
Merit-based grants:	NA
Loans:	NA
Work study:	NA
Student rating of FA:	82

UNIVERSITY OF RICHMOND

CAMPUS LIFE

Quality of Life Rating: **90**

Type of school:	private
Affiliation:	Baptist
Environment:	city

STUDENT BODY

FT undergrad enrollment:	2,826
% male/% female:	50/50
% out-of-state:	80
% live on campus:	95
% African-American:	3
% Asian:	1
% Caucasian:	95
% Hispanic:	<1
% foreign:	1
% transfers:	2

WHAT'S HOT

good-looking students

dorm comfort

campus appearance

deans

intramural sports

profs outside class

administration (overall)

town-gown relations

honesty

food

WHAT'S NOT

diversity

dating

gay community visible

ACADEMICS

Academic Rating: **81**

Calendar:	semester
Student/teacher ratio:	14/1
% doctorates:	86
Profs interesting:	85
Profs accessible:	93
Hours of study per day:	3.13

MOST POPULAR MAJORS BY %

Business:	16
English:	10
Political Science:	9

% GRADS WHO PURSUE

Law:	4
MBA:	2
Medicine:	2
M.A., etc.:	14

What do students think about the University of Richmond?

■ **Academics** The undergraduate division of University of Richmond is divided into three schools: Richmond College, the liberal arts school for men; Westhampton College, the liberal arts school for women; and the Robins School of Business, which is co-ed and attended by juniors and seniors who transfer from the liberal arts branches. Wrote one student, "There is a definite contrast between the business school (*excellent*) and the liberal arts (*satisfactory*)." Business and economics are the most popular majors, although history, psychology, and international studies are among the other popular departments. Academics are challenging but not impossible, and for most students, social considerations outweigh academic ones. Whether it's because students are shallow or because the school doesn't push them hard enough is a matter students debate, but most agree that the motivated student will find plenty to keep him busy. Other assets: professors are very helpful ("Most teachers give out their home phone numbers, and all my professors know my name"); and classes are small and rarely taught by TAs.

■ **Life** University of Richmond has a "country club" campus, and it's so beautiful that "most people come here for the beauty of the campus, period!" Smack in the middle is a large man-made lake that separates the men's college from the women's. Said one student, "The lake in the middle of campus does a whole lot more than provide scenery." Indeed: the lake bears imposing physical testimony to what many think is Richmond's greatest shortcoming: the "coordinate system" (the school's name for its separation of undergraduates into single-sex colleges). Although men and women attend classes together, "relationships between men and women are limited. This is obvious in classrooms and the dining hall, where the majority of men and women sit at separate tables." The Greeks play a major role in the school's social life, but be forewarned: they are currently under review by the school's conservative Baptist administration. Also, for a woman to attend a frat party, she must make sure her name has been included on a guest list drawn up in advance. "It's a big hassle," wrote one woman. For non-Greeks, "There are options if you have a car and money to burn." These options include the mountains, the beach, downtown Richmond, and Washington, D.C. There are on-campus options as well. Wrote one student, "There's something to do every night on campus. The university provides a lot of activities for free: movies, concerts, food, etc."

■ **Students** Students readily admit that the UR student body is homogeneous: "It's also known as the University of Rich Kids," wrote one. Said another, "The campus is very rich, very white, very closed-minded, and very conservative." "Those who don't fit the mold," wrote another, "may find it hard to fit in." Despite the school's Southern location, there are "lots of Northerners, especially from New Jersey," explained one Southern student. "But, the school is still polite anyway, thanks to all those good old Southerners who balance it out!" Students are politically conservative and report that there is a healthy interest in religion on campus.

UNIVERSITY OF RICHMOND

Richmond, VA

Admissions

The admissions office reports that "admissions decisions are based on the following: 50 percent of the decision is based on the applicant's high school record, 30 percent on three required achievement tests (English composition, Math I or II, and a third test of your choice), and 20 percent on the SAT. Essays, recommendations, and activities are tie-breakers. These figures are guidelines; no formula is used." Interviews are not offered. University of Richmond does not require any specific high school curriculum "as high schools vary in curriculum offerings," but a standard college preparatory curriculum is your best bet. The school requires either the SAT and three achievements *or* the ACT. Applicants to URichmond are often also applicants to University of Virginia, William and Mary, Wake Forest, Duke, and James Madison.

Financial Aid

The financial aid office at the University of Richmond requires applicants to submit the FAF. UR awards merit scholarships on the basis of athletic talent (7% of the students received one in 1991–92; average value: $9,064) and academic excellence (12%; $4,809). Last year, the FA office recommended Stafford loans for 80% of all students to whom it awarded assistance. The school also recommends PLUS and SLS loans to aid recipients.

A note from the University of Richmond Admissions Office:

"The University of Richmond combines the characteristics of a small college with the range and diversity of a major university. Small class size and close interaction with professors give each student a personal angle in the learning process. At the same time, the University offers a wide range of academic opportunities through internships, study abroad and undergraduate research, in over 44 majors in the Arts and Sciences, Business and Leadership Studies. (The Jepson School of Leadership Studies is the first such program at the undergraduate level in the nation.)

"The university's unique coordinate colleges provide a single-gender residential system within the framework of a fully coeducational academic program. Over 95% of Richmond students live on campus all four years, although they are not required to do so. Over 175 clubs and organizations keep Richmond students active on campus and in their surrounding community.

"The university is located about six miles from the heart of Richmond in a suburban setting. Situated around a 10-acre lake, Richmond is characterized by tall pines, rolling hills, and unique Collegiate Gothic architecture, making it one of the most beautiful campuses in the nation."

UNIVERSITY OF ROCHESTER

Rochester, NY

CAMPUS LIFE

Quality of Life Rating:	**80**

Type of school:	private
Affiliation:	none
Environment:	city

STUDENT BODY

FT undergrad enrollment:	4,823
% male/% female:	55/45
% out-of-state:	52
% live on campus:	89
% African-American:	6
% Asian:	.8
% Caucasian:	78
% Hispanic:	4
% foreign:	4
% transfers:	4

WHAT'S HOT

library
dorm comfort
doing all the reading
cost of living
living on campus
profs lecture a lot
catalog

WHAT'S NOT

in-class discussion
small lectures
suitcase syndrome
caring about politics
marriage
prudism

ACADEMICS

Academic Rating:	**87**

Calendar:	semester
Student/teacher ratio:	6/1
% doctorates:	96
Profs interesting:	73
Profs accessible:	72
Hours of study per day:	3.35

MOST POPULAR MAJORS BY %

Psychology:	14
Political Science:	13
Biology:	9

% GRADS WHO PURSUE

Law:	9
MBA:	2
Medicine:	8
M.A., etc.:	26

What do students think about the University of Rochester?

■ **Academics** The University of Rochester has traditionally been known best for its math and science departments. However, the "home of the Bausch & Lomb scholars, Wilson scholars, and Xerox" has enough diversity in its academic offerings to "dispel the myth that the U of R is solely an engineering/premed breeding ground." Although numerous students in our survey consider the workload "heavy and tough…they don't mess around!," most also believe their rigorous courses are "extremely rewarding." Rochester has several unique opportunities to offer its students: one is the world-renowned Eastman School of Music (the administration encourages interested, qualified students to take courses there). Another is "University Day," which happens every Wednesday: classes end by noon, and students spend the rest of the day attending school-sponsored seminars and other extracurriculars. Also distinct to the U of R is a special program called "Take Five," an attractive option for students who find themselves unable to fit enough courses of interest into a four-year schedule. One student wrote, "As a chemical engineer, I have very little time to take courses outside my major. The U of R has given me the opportunity to stay here for an additional year—tuition free—to pursue my interest in Japanese history and culture." In general, students here are positive and enthusiastic about their academic life; some consider the U of R "better than the Ivies but without the reputation… it's the jewel of upper New York State."

■ **Life** Cold weather is a given in Rochester: "Siberia for eight months of the year" is a popular description among students we surveyed. It is actually possible to avoid a great deal of winter misery because of the convenient sets of indoor tunnels beneath the campus. Nevertheless, the consensus seems to be that one should "come for the education, not the weather." Despite the academic pressures at the U of R (or perhaps because of them), weekends are rife with partying opportunities. Fraternities and sororities figure prominently in the social scene, and Greek activities dominate. One student observed, "Many people claim to be anti-Greek, but they tend to show up at frat parties anyway." There are varying degrees of social contentment here: some students have "too many parties to choose from," some contend that "freshman males lead lives of quiet desperation," and some prefer to socialize electronically in the generally comfy and spacious dorms.

■ **Students** The typical student at the University of Rochester is relatively conservative ("we need more liberals on campus!"), although the majority of students we asked were politically apathetic. A small, private school despite its public-sounding name, the U of R has trouble living up to the diversity described in its brochures. "The minority population is sorely lacking both in presence and diversity, especially in the black and Hispanic sectors. After the quotas are met, the administration doesn't seem to put any real effort into finding interesting minority students—in fact, any minority students at all."

UNIVERSITY OF ROCHESTER

Rochester, NY

Admissions

The admissions office reports that "each application is given careful and individual consideration. We seek students who are well qualified academically and who will also contribute in a meaningful way to the life of the campus community." High school curriculum and GPA are considered the most important components of your application here; next, in order of importance, are extracurricular activities, essays, letters of recommendation, interviews, and standardized test scores. URochester does not require any specific high school curriculum. The school does require either SAT or ACT scores. Applicants to the University of Rochester often are also applicants to Cornell U., Boston U., the SUNY schools, Syracuse U., and Washington U.

Financial Aid

The financial aid office at University of Rochester requires applicants to submit the FAF, their parents' most recent tax return, and a form generated by the school. In addition, some applicants may be asked to supply social security documentation and W-2 forms. In 1991–92, 70 percent of the freshman class received some form of financial aid. The average financial aid package for a freshman that year was made up of grants (average value: $11,800), loans ($3,200), and employment ($1,250). University of Rochester offers loans of up to $4,000 a year to all students, including those ineligible for financial aid, currently at 9.34% interest; these loans must be paid back within ten years of their origination date (repayment begins sixty days after origination).

A note from the University of Rochester Admissions Office:

"The University of Rochester has often been called an 'insider's university.' It has a very high profile among those who teach and work in higher education across the country, but perhaps to a lesser extent among the general public. Rochester prides itself on its personal scale, which we think allows students to make the best use of the professional and liberal arts program. In addition to being an exceptionally good university for undergraduates, Rochester's graduate and professional programs (such as medicine, music, optics, psychology) are of extremely high caliber as well."

ADMISSIONS FACTS

Competitiveness Rating:	**83**
% of applicants accepted:	61
% acceptees attending:	24

FRESHMAN PROFILE

Average verbal SAT:	540*
Average math SAT:	607*
Average ACT:	27*
Graduated top 10% of class:	50
Graduated top 25% of class:	85
Graduated top 50% of class:	96

DEADLINES

Early decision/action:	11/1
Early dec./act. notif.:	12/15
Regular admission:	1/15
Regular adm. notif.:	4/15

APPLICANTS ALSO LOOK AT

and often prefer:
Cornell U.

and sometimes prefer:
Washington U.
Franklin & Marshall College
SUNY Buffalo
U. Vermont
Syracuse U.

and rarely prefer:
Boston U.
SUNY Albany
NYU

ADDRESS

Undergraduate Admissions
Rochester, NY 14627
716-275-3221

FINANCIAL FACTS

In-state tuition ($):	15,150
Out-of-state tuition ($):	15,150
Room & board:	5,750
FA application deadline:	2/15
% frosh receiving FA:	70
PT earnings per yr. ($):	1200

TYPE OF AID: % of students ($)

FA of some kind:	63 (16,318)
Need-based grants:	NA (11,800)
Merit-based grants:	NA
Loans:	NA (3,200)
Work study:	NA (1,250)
Student rating of FA:	82

ROCHESTER INSTITUTE OF TECHNOLOGY

Rochester, NY

What do students think about RIT?

■ **Academics** Looking for a demanding arts and technology school, one that has valuable relationships with major industries, state-of-the-art facilities, and an intense (but not cutthroat) student body? If you can stand cold weather, Rochester Institute of Technology just might be the place. Computer science, electrical engineering, photography, and business and management are among the most popular majors here; the biology and chemistry departments also received students' praise. The photography department is nationally respected and boasts outstanding facilities. Facilities for the hearing impaired are also reportedly among the best in the country. Located in the hometown of Xerox, Kodak, and Bausch and Lomb, RIT provides its career-minded students with plenty of opportunities for internships. The pressure to succeed is great here: wrote one student, "Classes are difficult and require a lot of work. But if you are determined and have the will, you can succeed. The school is very prestigious and graduates are in demand." The pressure is intensified by a quarterly academic schedule, which causes courses to fly by. "It's impossible to get ahead of your work," wrote one student, "the trick is not to fall too far behind." Professors received below average grades from students. A civil engineer reported that "the professors have great knowledge about the subjects but have trouble conveying their ideas to students."

■ **Life** As one undergrad put it, "Come to RIT for the education, not for the social life." Several factors conspire to make social life less than ideal at the school. There's the male-female ratio (seven to three); there's the fact that many students leave campus almost every weekend; there's location (even though the school is located in a small city, students are "very much detached from the mainstream local and downtown social scenes"); and there's the weather. "The weather here is not for wimps!" exclaimed one student; said another, referring to frequently windy conditions, "Art students beware! Your portfolio will magically transform into a kite as you walk across campus." Campus decor can be summed up in one word: brick. "This school looks like one extensive sidewalk to the Wizard of Oz," wrote one student; another offered this insight: "Too many bricks and not enough chicks." Students gave the food above-average marks.

■ **Students** Although almost one fourth of the RIT student body is made up of minorities, each of the minority populations is, in itself, relatively small. Asians make up the largest minority group. Almost two thirds of the students are from New York State, and most of the rest are from neighboring states. They are a serious, studious, apolitical lot. Among the student bodies profiled in this book, they are among the bottom 10 percent in terms of their overall happiness at school.

ROCHESTER INSTITUTE OF TECHNOLOGY

Rochester, NY

Admissions

According to RIT's undergraduate catalog, "Factors in the admission decision include, but are not limited to, past high school and/or college performance—particularly in required academic subjects— admission test scores, competitiveness of high school or previous college, and other educational experiences (military, etc.). An admission interview and recommendations from those familiar with your academic performance are often influential as well. Students applying to RIT choose a specific program. Applicants are encouraged to indicate second and third program choices as well. For the undecided student, RIT offers a number of academic opportunities, including Technical and Liberal Studies, Undeclared Science, Undeclared Engineering, and Undeclared Business options." SAT or ACT scores must be submitted. RIT has a rolling admissions policy. The catalog notes "Because of this policy, and because some RIT programs fill to capacity very early in the year, it is to a student's advantage to apply early."

Financial Aid

Financial aid applicants to Rochester Institute Technology must complete the FAF. Seven percent of all undergrads received an academic scholarship last year; the average award value was $2,065. RIT awards no other merit-based scholarships. The FA office recommended Stafford loans to 90% of all financial aid recipients; Perkins, PLUS, and SLS are among the other loans recommended. Priority is given to applications received by March 1.

Excerpted from RIT promotional materials:

"It's a teaching and learning community. Our students are learning about careers in corporations, government agencies, and laboratories throughout New York State, across the U.S., and around the world. They're learning in modern laboratories with modern equipment and through simulated cases set up in the classroom. They're learning in career planning workshops and through discussions with professionals in the forefront of their fields.

"Our academic programs are challenging with top-notch faculty and excellent facilities. We want these programs to be worth your time and enjoyable because at RIT we take careers and academics seriously. We also offer exciting and worthwhile programs outside of the classroom—campus activities, speakers, independent study, research, and close work with faculty."

ADMISSIONS FACTS

Competitiveness Rating:	**67**
% of applicants accepted:	78
% acceptees attending:	38

FRESHMAN PROFILE

Average verbal SAT:	487*
Average math SAT:	550*
Average ACT:	24
Graduated top 10% of class:	24
Graduated top 25% of class:	51
Graduated top 50% of class:	79

DEADLINES

Early decision/action:	12/1
Early dec./act. notif.:	12/15
Regular admission:	rolling
Regular adm. notif.:	rolling

APPLICANTS ALSO LOOK AT

and often prefer:
Cornell U.

and sometimes prefer:
SUNY Binghamton
Cargenie Mellon U.

and rarely prefer:
SUNY Albany
Drexel U.
Syracuse U.
Boston U.
SUNY Buffalo
Northeastern U.

ADDRESS

Undergraduate Admissions
One Lomb Memorial Drive
Rochester, NY 14623-0887
716-475-2400

FINANCIAL FACTS

In-state tuition ($):	11,823
Out-of-state tuition ($):	11,823
Room & board:	5,034
FA application deadline:	3/15
% frosh receiving FA:	66
PT earnings per yr. ($):	1900

TYPE OF AID: % of students ($)

FA of some kind:	67 (NA)
Need-based grants:	67 (4,100)
Merit-based grants:	NA
Loans:	58 (4,100)
Work study:	30 (1,353)
Student rating of FA:	76

ROSE-HULMAN INSTITUTE OF TECHNOLOGY

Terre Haute, IN

CAMPUS LIFE

Quality of Life Rating: **82**

Type of school:	private
Affiliation:	none
Environment:	city

STUDENT BODY

FT undergrad enrollment:	1,300
% male/% female:	100/0
% out-of-state:	40
% live on campus:	70
% African-American:	2
% Asian:	5
% Caucasian:	93
% Hispanic:	<1
% foreign:	2
% transfers:	2

WHAT'S HOT

studying hard
administration (overall)
dorm safety
small lectures
deans
cost of living
bursar
conservative politics
attending all classes
profs outside class

WHAT'S NOT

gay community visible
diversity
location

ACADEMICS

Academic Rating: **87**

Calendar:	quarters
Student/teacher ratio:	13/1
% doctorates:	93
Profs interesting:	85
Profs accessible:	89
Hours of study per day:	4.12

MOST POPULAR MAJORS BY %

Electrical Engineering:	30
Mechanical Engineering:	25
Chemical Engineering:	15

% GRADS WHO PURSUE

Law:	2
MBA:	5
Medicine:	5
M.A., etc.:	8

What do students think about Rose-Hulman?

■ **Academics** Students and professors at Rose-Hulman have a truly strange relationship. Everybody knows that engineers are supposed to complain that their professors are incomprehensible and/or completely unconcerned with their undergraduate students. At Rose-Hulman, however, students have nothing but nice things to say about their instructors. "Although this college is very intense," wrote one, "the amount of time given to students by the lecturers is first class. Professors are always willing to help." Said another, "The faculty and staff are friendly and really care about their work," and one student even reported that "most faculty accept phone calls at home." Several students complained that professors are quick to try new, unproven methods of teaching this difficult material ("which makes us feel like guinea pigs in a lab," wrote one student), but overall it's hard to imagine a group of engineers being happier with their profs. As for the workload, one student put it this way: "Sleep is for wimps." RH students put in over four hours a day outside the classroom, and many are practically glued to their computers. All engineering majors are reputedly of uniform quality. The school offers a unique program in applied optics.

■ **Life** Rose-Hulman is, for the time being, an all-male school. Students study almost non-stop. The town in which it's located, Terre Haute, is often referred to by students as "Terrible Hole." What is the social scene like here? It's great...NOT! There are two other colleges close by, a women's school (St. Mary's in the Woods) and a large co-ed school (Indiana State University), but, as one student reported, "the other two schools have very little to do with us. And, there's nothing to do in town." Most students claim not to mind the dull social atmosphere, explaining that they would have no time to enjoy themselves even if things were better. When students do leave the computer labs and libraries, they step out onto a campus that is "very nice, a lot like home. I can go out in the woods or go swimming or fishing in the pond." Almost half the students belong to fraternities, and many make time to participate in intramural sports.

■ **Students** The Rose student body is about as uniform as one can get. After all, all students are male, almost all are white (Asian and black populations are well under 100 each), and, of course, they're all engineers. The situation changes somewhat in 1995, when Rose-Hulman goes coed. Most students welcome the change ("It should improve both social conditions and student work ethics"), although a few fear that once it happens, "nobody's going to get any work done." Students are very conservative, and what few gays attend school here keep their preferences well hidden: wrote one student, "If a group of gays ever tried to form an organization, I wouldn't doubt a death or two." Even though the students are hard-working engineers, one insists, "We are not a bunch of zit-popping, paste-eating, mouth-breathing, pencil-neck geeks who sit around discussing this week's episode of *Star Trek*."

ROSE-HULMAN INSTITUTE OF TECHNOLOGY

Terre Haute, IN

Admissions

The admissions office reports that "95 percent of our freshman class ranked in the top fifth of their high school graduating classes." Admissions does not consider anyone who scores below a 1000 combined total on the SAT, or below 22 English, 28 Math on the ACT. Rose-Hulman looks first to the quality of courses you took in high school, then to your GPA in those courses. Standardized test scores are considered next-most important, followed by letters of recommendation, extracurricular activities, interview, and essays. Applicants are required to have completed four years of math and English, as well as chemistry and physics. Achievement tests are not required. Rose-Hulman applicants most often also apply to Purdue, MIT, the service academies, and Carnegie Mellon.

Financial Aid

Applicants for financial aid at Rose-Hulman may submit an FAF or FFS, but the former is preferred. The school gives out academic-performance scholarships: last year, 39% of all undergrads received one, with an average scholarship value of $1,171. Overall, 90% of the class of '95 received some form of financial aid; the average package value was $8,500. Hulman's FA office recommended Perkins loans to 38% of its students (average loan: $964), Stafford loans to 65% ($2,992) and PLUS/SLS loans to 19% ($3,566) last year. The 3/1 deadline for forms is a closing deadline; priority is given to applicants whose materials are received by 12/1/92.

A note from the Rose-Hulman Admissions Office:

"Rose-Hulman is an undergraduate oriented college of engineering and science where all of the teaching is done by professionals—not graduate students. $15 million in new laboratory facilities. A national leader in undergraduate engineering and science education."

RUTGERS UNIVERSITY

New Brunswick, NJ

CAMPUS LIFE

Quality of Life Rating: **68**

Type of school: public
Affiliation: none
Environment: city

STUDENT BODY

FT undergrad enrollment: 21,440
% male/% female: 48/52
% out-of-state: 10
% live on campus: 60
% African-American: 9
% Asian: 10
% Caucasian: 70
% Hispanic: 6
% foreign: 2
% transfers: 6

WHAT'S HOT

caring about politics
diversity
gay community visible
college newspaper
dating

WHAT'S NOT

small classes (overall)
campus easy to get around
administration (overall)
catalog
honest students
campus appearance
profs outside class
profs in class
TAs teach intros

ACADEMICS

Academic Rating: **75**

Calendar: semester
Student/teacher ratio: 15/1
% doctorates: 90
Profs interesting: 66
Profs accessible: 66
Hours of study per day: 3.22

MOST POPULAR MAJORS BY %

Social Sciences: 28
Engineering: 10
Psychology: 9

What do students think about Rutgers University?

■ **Academics** Even Rutgers University's own students are sometimes surprised by the breadth and quality of academic offerings at their school. Wrote one undergrad, "I am constantly amazed by the high caliber of professors and the academic resources available to students. If one wants to, the sky is the limit when it comes to challenging academic educational pursuits." With over 35,000 undergraduates, Rutgers can and does "provide something for almost everybody (and, it's cheap)." The Rutgers University system encompasses six liberal arts colleges (including Douglass, an all-women's college) as well as schools of the arts, business, nursing, pharmacy, and engineering. The school is so huge that it doesn't all fit in one city. Rutgers has separate campuses in New Brunswick (the main campus), as well as in Camden and Newark. The size and spread-out campuses make Rutgers a more difficult school to administer than most large schools, and, unsurprisingly, the students gave RU's administration very low grades. Wrote one student, "This school has more bureaucracy than D.C. itself." Although professors received relatively low grades for accessibility, several students pointed out, "Professors love students who take the initiative, and many undergrads work as research assistants, teaching assistants, and administrative personnel. The opportunities are there, it's just that most students don't use them." Students report that academics are challenging. Wrote one, "Everyone I know is staying for at least an extra semester. Trying to graduate on time is like trying to get from one campus to another in less than 40 minutes: beyond hope."

■ **Life** The residential population at Rutgers (about half the students) participate actively in extracurricular clubs and organizations. Explained one student, "Activities range from the Rutgers Ambulance Service to Model United Nations to one of the best college newspapers in the country." The Greek system serves as a focal point of social life. Because New Brunswick is an "unexciting" location, on-campus parties and drinking make up a big part of students' social activities. Thursday is a big party night, since many students go home for the weekend. Still, one student wrote that "because almost all students are from New Jersey, people go home a lot, but the campus doesn't empty." Intercollegiate sporting events are popular, and for big-time entertainment, New York City is only a commuter train ride away.

■ **Students** Rutgers' student body is made up almost entirely of New Jersey natives. The New Brunswick campus has a 30 percent minority population, leading one student to describe the school as "a melting pot of every religion, ethnicity, and sexual preference, all of which have at least one club or organization." Although the average student is politically in the middle of the road, there is a vocal leftist population on campus. Explained one student, "If you were here for a week, you'd think you were back in the radical protest days of the sixties." The size of the school "guarantees that you can find people you get along with."

RUTGERS UNIVERSITY

Admissions

Rutgers's viewbook states that in the admissions process, primary emphasis is placed on "your past academic performance as indicated by high school grades (particularly in required academic subjects), your class rank, the strength of your academic program (the number of subjects, honors courses, and advanced placement classes you've completed), your standardized test scores on the SAT or ACT, any special talents you may have, and your participation in school or community activities. In general, 16 course units are required for each of Rutgers's undergraduate schools and colleges, including four years of English, and three years of mathematics. Other distributional requirements (and admissions deadlines, for that matter) vary greatly depending on the school or college to which you're applying. All applicants must submit SAT or ACT scores.

Financial Aid

Applicants for financial aid at Rutgers must complete the NJFAF (out-of-state applicants should complete the FAF). Last year, awards ranged from $400 to $8,500, and over half the student body received some form of aid. Merit awards from both the university and the State of New Jersey are available for up to $20,000 over four years for students who show superior academic performance and outstanding achievement on the SAT or ACT (regardless of financial need). New Jersey residents may also qualify for the state's Educational Opportunity Fund, a program which provides aid for residents whose "financial need and scholastic background might otherwise prevent them from attending college." For most of the schools and colleges, priority consideration is given to applications received by March 1.

Excerpted from Rutgers University promotional materials:

"Chartered in 1766 as Queen's College, the eighth institution of higher learning to be founded in the colonies, Rutgers University opened its doors in New Brunswick in 1771 with one instructor, one sophomore, and a handful of freshmen. During this early period the college developed as a classical liberal arts institution. In 1825, the name of the college was changed to Rutgers to honor a former trustee and revolutionary war veteran, Colonel Henry Rutgers.

"Today, Rutgers continues to grow, both in its facilities and in the variety and depth of its educational and research programs. The university's goals for the future include the continued provision of the highest quality undergraduate and graduate education along with increased support for outstanding research to meet the needs of society and fulfill Rutgers' role as the State University of New Jersey."

ADMISSIONS FACTS

Competitiveness Rating:	**81**
% of applicants accepted:	54
% acceptees attending:	23

FRESHMAN PROFILE

Average verbal SAT:	515
Average math SAT:	595
Average ACT:	NA
Graduated top 10% of class:	40
Graduated top 25% of class:	80
Graduated top 50% of class:	95

DEADLINES

Early decision/action:	NA
Early dec./act. notif.:	NA
Regular admission:	1/15
Regular adm. notif.:	4/15

APPLICANTS ALSO LOOK AT

and often prefer:
U. Pennsylvania
Cornell U.
U. Virginia

and sometimes prefer:
Boston College
New Jersey Tech
Penn State U.

and rarely prefer:
Trenton State College
Seton Hall U.
George Washington U.

ADDRESS

Undergraduate Admissions
P.O. Box 2101
New Brunswick, NJ 08903-2101
908-932-3770

FINANCIAL FACTS

In-state tuition ($):	3,114
Out-of-state tuition ($):	6,338
Room & board:	3,940
FA application deadline:	3/1
% frosh receiving FA:	62
PT earnings per yr. ($):	990

TYPE OF AID: % of students ($)

FA of some kind:	50 (NA)
Need-based grants:	NA
Merit-based grants:	NA
Loans:	NA
Work study:	NA
Student rating of FA:	67

ST. BONAVENTURE UNIVERSITY

CAMPUS LIFE

Quality of Life Rating:	**79**
Type of school:	private
Affiliation:	Roman Catholic
Environment:	city

STUDENT BODY

FT undergrad enrollment:	2,199
% male/% female:	49/51
% out-of-state:	25
% live on campus:	79
% African-American:	1
% Asian:	1
% Caucasian:	93
% Hispanic:	1
% foreign:	3
% transfers:	13

WHAT'S HOT

college radio station
dorm comfort
small lectures
living on campus
religion
small labs and seminars
dorm safety
campus appearance
intramural sports

WHAT'S NOT

fraternities/sororities
location
food
diversity

ACADEMICS

Academic Rating:	**69**
Calendar:	semester
Student/teacher ratio:	14/1
% doctorates:	46
Profs interesting:	77
Profs accessible:	85
Hours of study per day:	3.17

MOST POPULAR MAJORS BY %

Accounting:	12
Elementary Education:	11
Mass Communications:	11

% GRADS WHO PURSUE

Law:	NA
MBA:	NA
Medicine:	NA
M.A., etc.:	22

What do students think about St. Bonaventure University?

■ **Academics** St. Bonaventure is a Franciscan school catering to the career-minded student: business and management, communication, and education majors claim well over half the enrollees. That doesn't mean that instruction begins and ends with such mundane studies, however: required courses in theology, liberal arts, math, science, and philosophy account for half the credits needed to graduate. Other notable features of a St. Bonaventure education include its numerous opportunities for internships and the school's Mentor Program, through which students meet one-on-one with professionals in their chosen fields for guidance. Students reported that their classes are small, enabling them "to get personal attention, which makes for an intense learning experience." Several students commented favorably on the professors. Said one, "There is a bond between students and faculty. Most faculty treat students as equals. They're also tremendously willing to help." As a group, however, St. Bonnie's instructors received only average grades for in-class performance (although students gave them good marks for accessibility outside the classroom).

■ **Life** Even though it's a Catholic school, St. Bonnie has more than its fair share of parties. One student complained that "there is too much focus on partying and not enough on studying. Partying on weekends is OK, but seven days a week? Come on. If you study here, you're looked at funny." Drinking is very popular with the students. There are no fraternities or sororities: parties occur in off-campus apartments or, in smaller groups, in the dorms. Dormitories are safe and comfortable. They are also single-sex dorms, and "intervisitation" rules are strictly enforced. The rules prohibit opposite-sex visitors after 1 a.m. during the week, 2 a.m. during the weekend. "It's ridiculous," wrote one student. "What are two people going to do after 1 or 2 that cannot be done earlier? For $15,000, I should be allowed to decide when a friend leaves my room." The campus is very attractive and "small enough to allow you to know everyone." Students complained about the food ("It's terrible") and gave the town of St. Bonaventure low grades. Students reportedly have a "high school spirit" and actively support their sports teams, both good (rugby) and once-but-no-longer-any-good (basketball). Many participate in intramural sports.

■ **Students** Minorities represent a tiny fraction of the student body here. Wrote one black student (not the *only* one, but...), "If you are a black student, Bonaventure may give you extreme culture shock. The student body is less than one percent black! If you're looking to be empowered by a militant black professor, go to Howard." Students are predominantly white, Catholic, and conservative. Several non-Catholics reported that liberal opinions are met with some antagonism, and another reported, "If you do not drink, are a minority, or don't play sports, don't bother to apply."

St. Bonaventure University

Admissions

The Saint Bonaventure Univeristy undergraduate catalog states, "Acceptance is based on potential for successful study." The admissions committee first considers your high school curriculum "related to rigor of program" and your GPA. These are followed (in order of importance) by your standardized test scores (you must take either the SAT or ACT), letters of recommendation, extracurriculars, essays and interviews (the last two are optional, but strongly recommended). Minimum course preparation should include three years each of math, science, history/social studies, language and English. Students who apply to Saint Bonaventure also often apply to Providence College, Villanova, and Ithaca.

Financial Aid

The financial aid office at St. Bonaventure requires applicants to submit the FAF. The school awards merit grants for academic excellence and athletic ability. The school catalog lists the following loan options: Stafford, Perkins, PLUS, SLS, and a university-sponsored loan.

A note from the St. Bonaventure Admissions Office:

"The St. Bonaventure University Family has been imparting the Franciscan tradition to men and women of a rich diversity of backgrounds for more than 130 years. This tradition encourages all who become a part of it to face the world confidently, respect the earthly environment and work for productive change in the world. The charm of our campus and the inspirational beauty of the surrounding hills provide a special place where growth in learning and living is abundantly realized.

"Four years of college will pass quickly and during this time you will want to make the most of your educational experience. St. Bonaventure University provides the opportunity for a challenging, supportive, active and affordable educational experience.

"Academics at St. Bonaventure are challenging. Small classes and personalized attention encourage individual growth and development for students. St. Bonaventure's nationally known Schools of Arts and Sciences, Business Administration and Education offer majors in 31 disciplines. The School of Graduate Studies also offers several programs leading to the Masters degree.

"Affordability will make your experience a reality. St. Bonaventure has been placed on Barrons Annual Three Hundred Best Buys in Higher Education and *Money* magazine has rated St. Bonaventure 81st in its *MONEYGUIDE* to America's Best College Buys. Getting the most for your money is top priority not only for you but also for St. Bonaventure."

ADMISSIONS FACTS

Competitiveness Rating:	**74**
% of applicants accepted:	82
% acceptees attending:	38

FRESHMAN PROFILE

Average verbal SAT:	469
Average math SAT:	524
Average ACT:	22
Graduated top 10% of class:	13
Graduated top 25% of class:	42
Graduated top 50% of class:	81

DEADLINES

Early decision/action:	NA
Early dec./act. notif.:	NA
Regular admission:	4/15
Regular adm. notif.:	rolling

APPLICANTS ALSO LOOK AT

and often prefer:
Villanova U.

and sometimes prefer:
SUNY Geneseo
SUNY Buffalo
Providence College
Ithaca College

and rarely prefer:
Syracuse U.

ADDRESS

Undergraduate Admissions
Rte. 417
St. Bonaventure, NY 14778
716-375-2400

FINANCIAL FACTS

In-state tuition ($):	8,842
Out-of-state tuition ($):	8,842
Room & board:	4,294
FA application deadline:	3/1
% frosh receiving FA:	79
PT earnings per yr. ($):	800

TYPE OF AID: % of students ($)

FA of some kind:	85 (NA)
Need-based grants:	NA
Merit-based grants:	NA
Loans:	NA
Work study:	NA
Student rating of FA:	84

ST. JOHN'S COLLEGE

Annapolis, MD

CAMPUS LIFE

Quality of Life Rating:	**85**
Type of school:	private
Affiliation:	none
Environment:	city

STUDENT BODY

FT undergrad enrollment:	418
% male/% female:	57/43
% out-of-state:	86
% live on campus:	75
% African-American:	3
% Asian:	6
% Caucasian:	88
% Hispanic:	2
% foreign:	3
% transfers:	9

WHAT'S HOT

in-class discussion
deans
honesty
gay community accepted
doing all assigned reading
small lectures
interaction among students
profs outside class
leftist politics

WHAT'S NOT

fraternities/sororities
requirements are easy
diversity
religion

ACADEMICS

Academic Rating:	**82**
Calendar:	semester
Student/teacher ratio:	8/1
% doctorates:	69
Profs interesting:	90
Profs accessible:	97
Hours of study per day:	3.58

MOST POPULAR MAJOR BY %

Liberal Arts:	100

% GRADS WHO PURSUE

Law:	3
MBA:	2
Medicine:	3
M.A., etc.:	15

What do students think about St. John's College?

■ **Academics** St. John's College, often called "the great books school," is what 16th-century utopian thinkers might have come up with had they been asked to devise the "ideal" college education. Here students pursue a curriculum composed entirely of required courses; learn ancient Greek, French, classical mathematics, science, music, literature and philosophy; and attend classes led by "tutors" capable of teaching any of the courses offered at SJC. They are not lectured to, but rather are taught in the discussion-oriented Socratic method (the same method used by law professors and the Princeton Review!). There are no grades; instead, once a semester each student attends a session in which he listens to his tutors discuss the merits and faults of his work. Most students at SJC love it emphatically; they ranked 24th happiest in the country, and gave their school very high marks in almost every academic category. They study very hard—over three and a half hours a day—and actively participate in every class. "Tutors at SJC do not fill our heads with information; rather, they ask questions that will help us examine ourselves and the world," explained one Johnnie. The strength of the system, the intensely participatory classroom atmosphere, is also its chief potential drawback. Several disgruntled students agreed with their classmate who told us that "because same students don't prepare adequately for class, in-class discussions are often weak." Those who don't like it usually bail out very early. Note that SJC accepts no transfer credit: you must complete the entire four-year program here to earn an SJC degree.

■ **Life** The defining characteristic of life here seems to be the tight-knit community of scholars and students. As one student explained, "There is a very warm community feeling; people explore problems (intellectual, personal, college-related) through serious discussion." Students told us a lot about academics, relatively little about life outside the classroom. They did say the food is bad, and one student warned, "be ready for a relatively ascetic lifestyle." Although they're serious, St. John's kids party just like everybody else. Beer is the preferred method of intoxication. The one complaint we heard most often was about the school's size: because of "the tiny size of the student body," said one student, "you can encounter the same people too often."

■ **Students** Johnnies admit that they are a relatively homogeneous group. The typical SJC student is white, very intellectual, leftist politically, liberal on romantic issues, pretty darn serious, and perhaps a little geeky. Said one, "When you first come here, you think everybody's really strange. Over time, though, you realize everybody is, and so are you. No big deal." Are you SJC material? A joke one student told us might be the acid test: "Q: What did the Chorus say to Creon after Oedipus poked out his eyes? A: Now that's a face only a mother could love."

ST. JOHN'S COLLEGE

Admissions

The admissions office reports that "there are no cut-offs; all applications are reviewed individually. We *do not* require any test scores." St. John's considers essays (which is "lengthy and reflective") the most important part of your application; also considered, in decreasing order of importance, are high school curriculum/GPA, letters of recommendation, standardized test scores (which, while not required, "may prove helpful"), and extracurricular activities. Applicants must have completed two years of both a foreign language and science, as well as Algebra I and II, and geometry. Admissions are rewarded on a rolling basis; those who apply late but are accepted may enroll the following year. St. John's applicants most often also apply to Oberlin, Harvard, University of Chicago, Reed, Bard, Brown, and Princeton.

Financial Aid

The financial aid office at St. John's College requires FA applicants to submit the FAF, your parents' most recent tax return, and a form generated by the school. All grants here are awarded on the basis of need. Loans taken by St. John's students include the Stafford loan (80% of the students here took them in 1991–92; the average value: $2700) and Perkins loan (20%; $2250).

A note from the St. John's Admissions Office:

"St. John's offers an interdisciplinary liberal arts and sciences curriculum structured around seminars on major works of literature, philosophy, theology, psychology, political science, economics, and history. These discussions are supported by tutorials in mathematics, language, and music, and by laboratory sessions. There are no separate departments or majors, and there is no artificial separation of the humanities from the sciences. Only original works are read; there are no textbooks. And there are no lectures, because all our classes are small discussion groups.

"Our students represent nearly all 50 states and several foreign countries. They are young men and women from diverse backgrounds who habitually read good books and value serious conversations. Their interest in the life of ideas and their enthusiasm for active participation in their own education are their distinguishing characteristics."

ADMISSIONS FACTS

Competitiveness Rating:	**75**
% of applicants accepted:	83
% acceptees attending:	56

FRESHMAN PROFILE

Average verbal SAT:	597*
Average math SAT:	630*
Average ACT:	NA
Graduated top 10% of class:	33
Graduated top 25% of class:	64
Graduated top 50% of class:	86

DEADLINES

Early decision/action:	NA
Early dec./act. notif.:	NA
Regular admission:	rolling
Regular adm. notif.:	rolling

APPLICANTS ALSO LOOK AT

and often prefer:
Oberlin College
Harvard/Radcliffe College
Princeton U.

and sometimes prefer:
Brown U.
U. Chicago
Reed College

and rarely prefer:
Kenyon College
Grinnell College
Bard College

ADDRESS

Undergraduate Admissions
P.O. Box 1671
Annapolis, MD 21404
301-263-2371

FINANCIAL FACTS

In-state tuition ($):	14,262
Out-of-state tuition ($):	14,262
Room & board:	4,696
FA application deadline:	3/1
% frosh receiving FA:	50
PT earnings per yr. ($):	1700

TYPE OF AID: % of students ($)

FA of some kind:	50 (12,167)
Need-based grants:	50 (7,887)
Merit-based grants:	0
Loans:	NA
Work study:	NA
Student rating of FA:	94

ST. JOSEPH'S UNIVERSITY

Philadelphia, PA

CAMPUS LIFE

Quality of Life Rating: 73

Type of school:	private
Affiliation:	Roman Catholic
Environment:	city

STUDENT BODY

FT undergrad enrollment:	3,972
% male/% female:	47/53
% out-of-state:	40
% live on campus:	55
% African-American:	6
% Asian:	2
% Caucasian:	89
% Hispanic:	2
% foreign:	3
% transfers:	4

WHAT'S HOT

conservative politics
top 40
intramural sports
beer
marriage
suitcase syndrome
religion
hard liquor

WHAT'S NOT

gay community visible
honesty
caring about politics
dorm safety
gay community accepted
campus easy to get around

ACADEMICS

Academic Rating: 77

Calendar:	semester
Student/teacher ratio:	16/1
% doctorates:	89
Profs interesting:	80
Profs accessible:	72
Hours of study per day:	2.96

MOST POPULAR MAJORS BY %

Food Marketing:	10
Marketing:	8
English:	7

% GRADS WHO PURSUE

Law:	6
MBA:	12
Medicine:	5
M.A., etc.:	13

What do students think about St. Joseph's University?

■ **Academics** St. Joseph's University's focuses primarily on preparing students for the business world. Well over half the students major in business-related fields. But because of the school's affiliation with the Catholic church, students also receive a solid grounding in theology and the liberal arts; said one student, St. Joe's "has a unique blend of diverse interests which have been brought into harmony by the Jesuit tradition of education." Other departments garnering students' praise are political science, biology, and chemistry. Wrote one chem major, "In our department, professors and students associate like one big family. The atmosphere of this department is great since the emphasis is placed on learning rather than on grades." As one might expect, SJU students are very career-oriented. Said one, "Students here generally seem interested in their job prospects—particularly food marketing and accounting majors—but liberal arts majors are also numerous." Students gave all aspects of the school's administration low grades; one complained that "St. Joe's has a tendency to over-emphasize the importance of campus appearance and neglect things like the library, class offerings, and the condition of the classrooms. Shrubs and bushes are nice, but I would prefer library books younger than myself and classroom temperatures below 85 degrees."

■ **Life** Although located in Philadelphia, most St. Joe's students pursue their social lives on campus. St. Joe's Division I teams are popular, as are fraternities and sororities, and students actively participate in intramural sports. Intramurals, intercollegiate sports, and fraternities all received substantially higher grades from students than did Philadelphia, probably because the area immediately surrounding the campus is neither a hopping social center nor a cozy, safe suburb. There are some bars in the neighborhood, and according to one student, "During junior and senior years, bars are the common hangout; if your birthday is late in the school year (i.e., you turn 21 during spring semester), you'll get left out of a lot of socializing." Students like the campus "because it's not too big and not too small. Everyone knows or at least knows of everyone else and most people go out of their way to make you feel as though you belong." Social life is hampered by the fact that many students commute, while others leave every weekend. One resident bemoaned the situation, saying, "There is nothing—absolutely nothing—to do on campus. Students either go to other schools or make their own fun off-campus every weekend."

■ **Students** St. Joe's student body is fairly homogeneous. Most students are white, Catholic, and very conservative (but fairly apathetic) politically. Complained one student, "If you are an Asian student interested in meeting other Asians, this is not the place to go." Students are religious, but not terribly so for those enrolled at a religious school.

ST. JOSEPH'S UNIVERSITY

Philadelphia, PA

Admissions

St. Joseph's University looks primarily at your high school curriculum/GPA and standardized test scores; other components of your application are considered only if one or both of these are substandard. In such cases, letters of recommendation, essays, extracurricular activities, and interviews are all considered in the final admissions decision. Applicants are required to have completed four years of English, three years of math, two years each of a foreign language and natural sciences, and one year of history. St. Joe's accepts either the SAT or the ACT; achievement exams are not required (English composition is recommended, however). Applicants to St. Joseph's are often also applicants to Villanova and LaSalle.

Financial Aid

Financial aid applicants to St. Joseph's must complete the Pennsylvania State Grant and Federal Aid Application (it's preferred that out-of state applicants complete this form as well, but they may substitute the FAF), and a form generated by St. Joseph's financial aid office. They must also submit a copy of their parents' most recent tax return. A number of scholarships are available, including awards for academic and athletic merit, community service, departmental concentration, and minority status. Full-tuition Board of Directors Scholarships are available for students in the top 1% of their graduating class with SAT scores of at least 1300, and an "outstanding high school curriculum".

A note from the Saint Joseph's University Admissions Office:

"Saint Joseph's is an internationally recognized Jesuit University that has distinguished itself through its personal size, extraordinary faculty, and comprehensive academic programs. This unique learning climate is strengthened by an ethical framework that enables students to make choices and decisions in their personal and professional lives. Students have an exceptional awareness of their social environment, with approximately 50 percent involved in community service throughout the Philadelphia area, the country, and the world. The university has a decidedly international focus, both in its curriculum and its population. Students are encouraged to participate in one of its many study-abroad and study tour options. Students also have a broad choice of academic programs, including the highly acclaimed food marketing program and the newly developed pharmaceutical marketing program...First and foremost, Saint Joseph's means academic excellence. Says one graduate, "Saint Joseph's is ahead of its time. With its state-of-the-art facilities and incredible professors, Saint Joe's has given me a head start in the working world."

ADMISSIONS FACTS

Competitiveness Rating:	**78**
% of applicants accepted:	74
% acceptees attending:	36

FRESHMAN PROFILE

Average verbal SAT:	500*
Average math SAT:	535*
Average ACT:	NA
Graduated top 10% of class:	45
Graduated top 25% of class:	71
Graduated top 50% of class:	95

DEADLINES

Early decision/action:	1/15
Early dec./act. notif.:	2/15
Regular admission:	3/1
Regular adm. notif.:	3/31

APPLICANTS ALSO LOOK AT

and often prefer:
Syracuse U.

and sometimes prefer:
Penn State U.
Fairfield U.
Temple U.

and rarely prefer:
Villanova U.
Boston College

ADDRESS

Undergraduate Admissions
5600 City Avenue
Philadelphia, PA 19131
215-660-1300

FINANCIAL FACTS

In-state tuition ($):	10,330
Out-of-state tuition ($):	10,330
Room & board ($):	5,000
FA application deadline:	2/15
% frosh receiving FA:	91
PT earnings per yr. ($):	900

TYPE OF AID: % of students ($)

FA of some kind:	80 (NA)
Need-based grants:	NA
Merit-based grants:	NA
Loans:	NA
Work study:	NA
Student rating of FA:	75

ST. LAWRENCE UNIVERSITY

Canton, NY

CAMPUS LIFE

Quality of Life Rating: 86

Type of school:	private
Affiliation:	none
Environment:	suburban

STUDENT BODY

FT undergrad enrollment:	1,928
% male/% female:	51/49
% out-of-state:	51
% live on campus:	99
% African-American:	3
% Asian:	1
% Caucasian:	94
% Hispanic:	1
% foreign:	3
% transfers:	2

WHAT'S HOT

Grateful Dead
food
marijuana
dorm comfort
library
overall happiness
small classes (overall)
profs outside class
hard liquor
fraternities/sororities

WHAT'S NOT

diversity
gay community visible
religion
location

ACADEMICS

Academic Rating: 82

Calendar:	semester
Student/teacher ratio:	11/1
% doctorates:	87
Profs interesting:	85
Profs accessible:	88
Hours of study per day:	3.02

MOST POPULAR MAJORS BY %

Social Sciences:	43
Psychology:	11
Letters/Literature:	7

What do students think about St. Lawrence University?

■ **Academics** St. Lawrence University offers a traditional liberal arts education in the seclusion of frigid upstate New York. By reputation it's a laid-back party school, but many students here are eager to refute that stereotype. One wrote that "the school's undeserved party reputation overshadows the facilities and faculty, which are first-rate. You will get incredible attention and opportunities if you wish to excel. Too many people sell SLU short." Whether or not the school has earned its reputation, students do put in their hours of work here—"More than they're willing to let on," said several respondents. English, economics, history, political science, and government are all popular majors here, and, according to one bio major, "This school has a phenomenal science department, especially biology and chemistry, for a small liberal arts school. The faculty prepares us well to continue our educations, especially in medical or dental school." SLU sponsors a wide variety of semester abroad programs, which many of our respondents recommended enthusiastically. Profs received high marks, as did class size.

■ **Life** The social scene at SLU is "very intense. There is always something going on at night. As such, the social climate of SLU produces two types of students. There are those who, except for attending classes, just hang out all day, every day. They usually do very, very poorly. Then there are those who devote three hours an afternoon or morning to their studies. Both go out every night, but the latter end up with a solid education after four years." Drinking is very popular, "Especially," wrote one student, "on weekends and Wednesdays ('flip night' at two favorite local bars—you call 'heads' or 'tails' and if the bartender's coin matches your call, the beer is *free*!)" The Greeks play a major role here. There are plenty of opportunities for outdoor activities, although a tolerance for bitter cold is a prerequisite for enjoying them. A car is recommended since "the population of Canton frequently matches our winter temperature. Students travel to Burlington, Syracuse, Ottawa, and Montreal." Intercollegiate sports, especially SLU's Division I hockey team, are very popular. "Whether or not you like hockey before you get here, you will by the time you leave," wrote one student.

■ **Students** Most SLU students will agree that their student body is homogeneous and that their classmates are laid-back and friendly. Whether all SLU students are wealthy prepsters, as they are reputed to be, is another question. Said one student: "SLU students truly wear L.L. Bean and Patagonia ensembles, summer on Nantucket or the Vineyard, and desire jobs on Wall Street or in a law office." A minority, but a vocal minority, disagrees. One student wrote that "the stereotype of St. Lawrence as a playground for the children of the rich and famous no longer applies." There is a fair-sized "crunchy granola" contingent, and Deadheads abound. Students are politically conservative and not terribly tolerant of alternative lifestyles.

ST. LAWRENCE UNIVERSITY

Admissions

The most recent St. Lawrence catalog states, "The university is interested in enrolling students who not only give proof of academic curiosity and ability, but also take an interest in the lives and welfare of others and demonstrate a willingness to place themselves in situations that call for personal initiative and leadership." The admissions committee is interested "first and foremost" with your academic transcript, both in the types of courses you've taken and your success in those courses. The school then considers, in descending order of importance: letters of recommendation, standardized test scores, and personal qualities, as indicated in essays and an interview ("encouraged," not required). Applicants must take the SAT and the English Achievement, or the ACT. Applicants are expected to have completed the following high school curriculum: four years of English; three years of social studies, math, science, and a foreign language; and, three units of academic electives. Math and science applicants should have further preparation in their chosen fields.

Financial Aid

The financial aid office at St. Lawrence requires applicants to submit the FAF, a copy of their and their parents' most recent tax return, and a form generated by the school. St. Lawrence does not award merit grants; all assistance is awarded on the basis of need only. St. Lawrence participates in the College Work-Study program.

A note from the St. Lawrence University Admissions Office:

"St. Lawrence is an independent, nondenominational liberal arts and sciences university, and the oldest coeducational institution in New York State.

"The campus is comprised of 30 buildings, two of which are on the National Historic Register, in a country setting at the edge of the village of Canton, N.Y. St. Lawrence's 1,000 acres include a golf course, cross-country ski trails, and jogging trails at the outer edges of campus.

"Canton is a town of 7,00 people who welcome St. Lawrence students into their gift and clothing shops, grocery stores, restaurants, and movie theater. The University is 90 minutes from the capital of Canada, one-half hour from Adirondack Park and the Thousand Islands, and two hours from Montreal, Canada."

ADMISSIONS FACTS

Competitiveness Rating:	**78**
% of applicants accepted:	70
% acceptees attending:	30

FRESHMAN PROFILE

Average verbal SAT:	504
Average math SAT:	559
Average ACT:	NA
Graduated top 10% of class:	NA
Graduated top 25% of class:	NA
Graduated top 50% of class:	NA

DEADLINES

Early decision/action:	12/15
Early dec./act. notif.:	w/in 3 wks.
Regular admission:	2/1
Regular adm. notif.:	rolling

APPLICANTS ALSO LOOK AT

and often prefer:
Middlebury College
Colby College
Colgate U.

and sometimes prefer:
Syracuse U.
Hamilton College
Bates College
Skidmore College

and rarely prefer:
Union College
Denison U.

ADDRESS

Undergraduate Admissions
Canton, NY 13617
315-379-5261

FINANCIAL FACTS

In-state tuition ($):	15,620
Out-of-state tuition ($):	15,620
Room & board:	5,050
FA application deadline:	2/15
% frosh receiving FA:	50
PT earnings per yr. ($):	1000

TYPE OF AID: % of students ($)

FA of some kind:	55 (NA)
Need-based grants:	NA
Merit-based grants:	NA
Loans:	NA
Work study:	NA
Student rating of FA:	88

SAINT LOUIS UNIVERSITY

Saint Louis, MO

What do students think about St. Louis University?

■ **Academics** St. Louis University's slogan is "Excellence is Affordable," and, like other prominent Catholic schools, SLU indeed provides a private school education at a reasonable price. Preprofessional programs are most popular here, especially pre-medicine. Education, international business, and communication all also received good grades from students. Course offerings were touted by students as "challenging," and professors received high ratings for teaching and accessibility. One student wrote, "The teachers are always willing to help; they want you to learn and do well. They seem to take students' doing well as a personal achievement." Another agreed: "the student/teacher ratio is excellent, and the professors are wonderful." All students must complete a core curriculum meant to guarantee a broad-based education. Science, math, humanities, and ethics all figure into the core. The core emphasizes classical literature and philosophy, leading several students to joke that "SLU provides the best 12th-century education money can buy." All in all, though, we found student attitudes toward academics at SLU to be quite positive.

■ **Life** St. Louis University is primarily a commuter school. About half of its students live on campus, and many of them are from the St. Louis area. Accordingly, "the parking lots empty on weekends," and the social scene quiets down after Thursday night. Students agree that "to make the most of SLU, you *have* to get involved in student activities." Participation in community service programs is particularly high: Other activities, though popular, reportedly suffer from a lack of funding. SLU's Jesuit tradition carries on today in the form of nightly student masses and commitment to the Catholic faith for about two thirds of the student population. The campus itself, right in the middle of St. Louis, is not beautiful, but it is constantly improving, as is the surrounding urban area ("Although it could be better," warned one student). The first-rate sports complex garners compliments from students, and SLU boasts an athletic shining star in the form of the highly ranked Billikens soccer team. A new theater complex has also recently been added to the campus.

■ **Students** More than half of SLU's students hail from Missouri, and by their own account, the undergraduate population is not terribly diverse. Students described themselves as "very conservative and Midwestern" as a group. However, the atmosphere here is relatively accepting of everyone, and, although students identify themselves as politically apathetic, they are extremely involved in community service. A lot of students fall into the "non-traditional" category: they are older students returning for degrees while continuing their careers. Among the "traditional" population, there is a strong predisposition toward preprofessionalism ("Sometimes I feel like I'm at a trade school for doctors and lawyers," wrote one student).

SAINT LOUIS UNIVERSITY

Saint Louis, MO

Admissions

The admissions office at St. Louis University reports that, when assessing applicants, it first considers high school performance. It then considers, in descending order of importance, standardized test scores, letters of recommendation, essays, and extracurricular activities. Applicants must submit scores for either the SAT or the ACT, and are recommended to have completed the following high school curriculum: four years of English, three years of math, and two years each of science, social studies, and foreign language. The school's catalog notes, "The student's record must show courses and grades indicating intellectual ability and progress; the pattern of courses should show purpose and continuity and furnish a background for the freshman curriculum offered by the University."

Financial Aid

The financial aid office at St. Louis University requires applicants to submit the FAF, a form generated by the school, and their and their parents' most recent tax returns. Academic scholarships are awarded on the basis of high school record, test scores, and "academic promise." Merit grants are also awarded to those with special skills in music, the arts, drama, and athletics. Still other grants are available to those who demonstrate the spirit of volunteerism and community service and to minority students. The school's most recent catalog recommends only the Stafford and Perkins loans.

A note from the Saint Louis University Admissions Office:

"Saint Louis University, a Catholic, Jesuit University founded in 1818 is the second oldest Jesuit University in the continental United States. It is also the oldest university west of the Mississippi River with one of the largest medical centers under Catholic auspices in the country.

"Our campus in Madrid, Spain, is one of the largest European campuses of an American University. In addition, its Parks College in Cahokia, Illinois, is the nation's foremost aviation educator.

"The University residence halls are nationally known for innovative personalization and community development programs.

"Over the past few years, Saint Louis University has initiated numerous scholarship programs for academic merit, community service, and special scholarships for African-Americans."

ADMISSIONS FACTS

Competitiveness Rating:	**68**
% of applicants accepted:	85
% acceptees attending:	40

FRESHMAN PROFILE

Average verbal SAT:	463*
Average math SAT:	527*
Average ACT:	24*
Graduated top 10% of class:	24
Graduated top 25% of class:	38
Graduated top 50% of class:	96

DEADLINES

Early decision/action:	NA
Early dec./act. notif.:	NA
Regular admission:	rolling
Regular adm. notif.:	rolling

APPLICANTS ALSO LOOK AT

and sometimes prefer:
Marquette U.
U. Illinois
U. Wisconsin–Madison
Washington U.

and rarely prefer:
Creighton U.
Indiana U.
Kansas State U.

ADDRESS

Undergraduate Admissions
221 N. Grand Blvd.
Saint Louis, MO 63103
314-658-2500

FINANCIAL FACTS

In-state tuition ($):	9,160
Out-of-state tuition ($):	9,160
Room & board:	4,230
FA application deadline:	4/1
% frosh receiving FA:	80
PT earnings per yr. ($):	2000

TYPE OF AID: % of students ($)

FA of some kind:	80 (NA)
Need-based grants:	NA
Merit-based grants:	NA
Loans:	NA
Work study:	NA
Student rating of FA:	82

ST. MARY'S COLLEGE OF CALIFORNIA

Moraga, CA

CAMPUS LIFE

Quality of Life Rating: **89**

Type of school:	private
Affiliation:	Roman Catholic
Environment:	city

STUDENT BODY

FT undergrad enrollment:	1,975
% male/% female:	48/52
% out-of-state:	12
% live on campus:	60
% African-American:	4
% Asian:	4
% Caucasian:	79
% Hispanic:	8
% foreign:	4
% transfers:	NA

WHAT'S HOT

small lectures
campus easy to get around
campus appearance
overall happiness
in-class discussion
attending all classes
religion

WHAT'S NOT

fraternities/sororities
gay community visible
ethnic diversity

ACADEMICS

Academic Rating: **80**

Calendar:	4-1-4
Student/teacher ratio:	16/1
% doctorates:	87
Profs interesting:	86
Profs accessible:	86
Hours of study per day:	3.00

MOST POPULAR MAJORS BY %

Business & Management:	51
Health Sciences:	16
Multi-Interdisciplinary Studies:	9

What do students think about St. Mary's College?

■ **Academics** Described by students as "an excellent place to get a personalized education," St. Mary's College of California school provides a solid liberal arts education even to the business-oriented students who make up the majority. Business and management majors claim over half the students here. Other popular majors include pre-medical sciences, communication, and psychology. All students must complete a rigorous core curriculum, the centerpiece of which is the Great Books Seminar Program. This program received student commendations for its provocative, discussion-oriented approach to the classics: "It really makes you think and discuss." All classes, not just seminars, are small and informal. Students agreed that "it's nice to have teachers who know your name"; and the faculty won raves for being "easily accessible, informative, and energetic." Other perks include a January semester, during which students are encouraged to pursue experimental studies, internships, and travel; and the possibility of overseas study with affiliated Catholic institutions in Rome, France, and England. In general, courses here are difficult. However, students feel that the immediate challenge leads to greater rewards, so they study quite hard. The emphasis is on individual achievement rather than head-to-head competition, and this atmosphere makes for a productive, healthy environment. One student summed up: "The Christian Brothers are caring men whose philosophy of teaching is to help the students reach their full potential."

■ **Life** One student wrote that the social life at St. Mary's is "like a country club; it doesn't get any better. If you happen to get bored of the club, there's always the City (San Francisco) or Berkeley." The campus is lovely, the dorms are comfortable and safe, getting around is easy, and the overall happiness level, as reported on our surveys, is extraordinarily high. At this "beautiful school surrounded by lush green hills," the atmosphere is understandably "as relaxed as it can be." Religious commitment is an important part of life here. The social scene includes no fraternity or sorority bashes, but parties are frequent and fun nonetheless. The one complaint we received involved "drunken scamming." Some students lamented the necessity for "both guys and girls to rely on the party scene to find mates."

■ **Students** St. Mary's students, most of whom are Roman Catholic and angling toward business careers, are predictably conservative socially and politically. It should come as no surprise that there is no visible gay presence on campus (in fact, one student was even offended that we asked about it). The school has a 21 percent minority population, and the different ethnic types that are present on campus feel they are well accepted. But, perhaps because of their similar backgrounds and goals, students rated the diversity of their student body as low.

St. Mary's College of California

Moraga, CA

Admissions

From the Saint Mary's viewbook: "The chief qualities sought in a candidate for admission are intellectual aptitude (as evidenced by at least 15 units of college-preparatory courses with a minimum B average), seriousness of purpose, and moral integrity. The secondary school record is considered the most reliable measure of potential college ability. Scores on the SAT or the ACT and extracurricular accomplishments may strengthen an application insofar as they indicate special talents, maturity, and perseverance." Applicants must submit SAT or ACT scores. The recommended high school curriculum includes four years of English, two years each of mathematics and foreign language, and one year each of natural science and social science (lab sciences are recommended as well).

Financial Aid

Financial aid applicants to St. Mary's must complete the FAF (California residents should submit the SAAC instead) and a form generated by the St. Mary's financial aid office. The school's institutional budget for financial aid has increased 25% over last year. Approximately half of the students who applied for financial assistance in '91–'92 received some form of aid. St. Mary's offers its own college scholarships (based on academic ability and financial need) and athletic grants. Tuition allowances (50% off tuition) are available to families with four or more children enrolled at the College. Students are notified of their awards around April 15.

A note from the Saint Mary's of California Admissions Office:

"Today Saint Mary's College continues to offer a value-oriented education by providing a classical liberal arts background second to none. The emphasis here is on teaching an individual how to think independently and responsibly, how to analyze information in all situations, and how to make choices based on logical thinking and rational examination. Such a program develops students' ability to ask the right questions and to formulate meaningful answers, not only within their professional careers, but for the rest of their lives.

"Saint Mary's College is committed to preparing young men and women for the challenge of an ever-changing world, while remaining faithful to an enduring academic and spiritual heritage.

"We believe the purpose of a college experience is to prepare men and women for an unlimited number of opportunities. We believe this is best accomplished by educating the whole person, both intellectually and ethically. And we believe this is reaffirmed in our community of Brothers, in our faculty, and in our personal concern for each student."

ADMISSIONS FACTS

Competitiveness Rating:	81
% of applicants accepted:	63
% acceptees attending:	35

FRESHMAN PROFILE

Average verbal SAT:	494
Average math SAT:	536
Average ACT:	NA
Graduated top 10% of class:	34
Graduated top 25% of class:	78
Graduated top 50% of class:	99

DEADLINES

Early decision/action:	NA
Early dec./act. notif.:	NA
Regular admission:	5/15
Regular adm. notif.:	rolling

APPLICANTS ALSO LOOK AT

and sometimes prefer:
UC Davis

and rarely prefer:
Loyola Marymount U.
Santa Clara U.
UC Santa Barbara
U. Pacific

ADDRESS

Undergraduate Admissions
1928 St. Mary's Road
Moraga, CA 94575
415-631-4224

FINANCIAL FACTS

In-state tuition ($):	10,936
Out-of-state tuition ($):	10,936
Room & board ($):	5,430
FA application deadline:	3/15
% frosh receiving FA:	55
PT earnings per yr. ($):	1,500

TYPE OF AID: % of students ($)

FA of some kind:	55 (NA)
Need-based grants:	NA
Merit-based grants:	NA
Loans:	NA
Work study:	NA
Student rating of FA:	85

ST. MARY'S COLLEGE OF MARYLAND

St. Mary's City, MD

What do students think about St. Mary's College, Maryland?

■ **Academics** Although its name might lead you to think otherwise, St. Mary's is a public school, not a Catholic school. Nor is it a typical public school: in fact, in size, approach to academics, and level of commitment on the part of the faculty, St. Mary's is much more comparable to a small private liberal arts college. Located on a fertile river front, St. Mary's maintains an excellent department in marine biology; economics, psychology, English, and history are other departments that were popular with our respondents. Students report that access to faculty is good, classes are small and personal, and, "Although it is a serious academic school, it is not a tense school." Best of all, St. Mary's is eminently affordable, although some students worry that may not remain the case indefinitely. Wrote one undergrad, "With recent popularity, as indicated by issues of popular news magazines, St. Mary's has become very image conscious, which, combined with tuition increases to decrease institutional dependence on state funds, will probably turn this school, quite rapidly, into another snooty private college."

■ **Life** Wrote one student, "You can't go wrong telling people where we are: We're St. Mary's College at St. Mary's City on the St. Mary's River in St. Mary's County!" The college has a "gorgeous campus" and the river provides a "great waterfront," but the *city* of St. Mary's…well, as one student put it, "The nearest town is only eight miles away! It's historic Saint Mary's City, a popular attraction consisting of two shacks and a dirt path. Come visit and you will find out why we say, 'St. Mary's isn't the edge of the world , but you can see it from here!'" One student favorably noted, "Historic ruins are great for tripping in," but most agreed that "St. Mary's is like a paradise in the middle of a barren desert. The campus is beautiful and fun, but, beyond the campus gates, there is nothing." School-sponsored activities are relatively sparse, and partly as a result, students report that drinking is a very popular pastime. One student complained, "As a student who does not drink, it is pretty hard to find things to do on weekends. The college rarely has anything to do on Friday or Saturday nights, except maybe a movie or a sporting event." While most students agree that campus life is slow, many also added, "The friendships one forms here more than makes up for it." Summed up one student: "Everyone really gets along and parties with each other." Washington, D.C. is only 90 minutes away by car.

■ **Students** The student body here is made up mostly of Maryland natives, although a recent surge in publicity about the school's quality and cost is drawing more out-of-state students. About 100 black students make up most of the minority population; those we spoke with reported a high level of satisfaction with the school. Several students noted that the student body is "generally very close and friendly because it's like one big fraternity."

ST. MARY'S COLLEGE OF MARYLAND

St. Mary's City, MD

Admissions

Saint Mary's College of Maryland's Admissions office writes, "We do not use 'cut-offs.' We attempt to review the applicant as a package with the most important part of this package being course work and a student's willingness to take difficult classes in high school." In addition to the selectivity of your high school course work, the committee considers your GPA (calculated since ninth grade in academic subjects only: English, math, science, social studies, and foreign languages—the average GPA for entering freshmen is a 3.00). These are followed, in order of importance, by your essays, standardized test scores, interview, extracurriculars, and letters of recommendation. All applicants are required to take the SAT. Letters of recommendation are not required, but are recommended, particularly if the committee feels an application needs further support. The interview is also optional, but recommended. Applicants to St. Mary's also often apply to U. of Maryland, James Madison, Loyola College (MD), and Dickinson College.

Financial Aid

Financial aid applicants to St. Mary's must complete the FAF and a form generated by the St. Mary's financial aid office. In '91–92, the average award for an incoming freshman (class of '95) was $4,395. Overall, 35% of the class received some form of aid. Among the scholarship available are Brent-Calvert Fellowships (exceptionally talented students accepted into the college's Honors Program) and Matthias D'Sousa Scholarships (African-Americans who show academic merit); award amounts for both of these may cover complete tuition, room and board; they are open to Maryland residents only, however. Other scholarships are available for academically talented students, physically handicapped students, and students showing artistic talent. Matthias D'Sousa need-based grants are also available; the average value of one is $2,100. The deadline for St. Mary's scholarships is February 1, and for all financial aid forms is March 15.

A note from the St. Mary's College of Maryland Admissions Office:

"St. Mary's College of Maryland...occupies a distinctive niche and represents a real value in American higher education. It is a public college, dedicated to the ideal of affordable, accessible education but committed to quality teaching and excellent programs for undergraduate students. The result is that St. Mary's offers the small college experience of the same high caliber usually found at prestigious private colleges, but at public college prices. Recently designated by the state of Maryland as 'A Public Honors College,' one of only two public colleges in the nation to hold that distinction, St. Mary's has become increasingly attractive to high school students. Admission is very selective, with eight to 10 applicants for each spot in the freshman class..."

ADMISSIONS FACTS

Competitiveness Rating:	**82**
% of applicants accepted:	39
% acceptees attending:	36

FRESHMAN PROFILE

Average verbal SAT:	569
Average math SAT:	593
Average ACT:	NA
Graduated top 10% of class:	37
Graduated top 25% of class:	68
Graduated top 50% of class:	92

DEADLINES

Early decision/action:	1/10
Early dec./act. notif.:	2/15
Regular admission:	1/15
Regular adm. notif.:	4/1

APPLICANTS ALSO LOOK AT

and often prefer:
Bucknell University
Lehigh U.
U. Delaware
Johns Hopkins U.

and sometimes prefer:
Dickinson College
James Madison U.
Loyola College–Maryland

and rarely prefer:
U. Maryland

ADDRESS

Undergraduate Admissions
St. Mary's City, MD 20686
301-862-0292

FINANCIAL FACTS

In-state tuition ($):	2,300
Out-of-state tuition ($):	4,100
Room & board:	4,100
FA application deadline:	3/15
% frosh receiving FA:	NA
PT earnings per yr. ($):	662

TYPE OF AID: % of students ($)

FA of some kind:	50 (4,200)
Need-based grants:	25 (4,300)
Merit-based grants:	32 (3,993)
Loans:	13 (2,639)
Work study:	26 (830)
Student rating of FA:	77

ST. OLAF COLLEGE

Northfield, MN

CAMPUS LIFE

Quality of Life Rating:	**87**
Type of school:	private
Affiliation:	Lutheran
Environment:	suburban

STUDENT BODY

FT undergrad enrollment:	3,008
% male/% female:	47/53
% out-of-state:	42
% live on campus:	85
% African-American:	1
% Asian:	3
% Caucasian:	94
% Hispanic:	1
% foreign:	2
% transfers:	2

WHAT'S HOT

marriage
religion
good-looking students
administration (overall)
town-gown relations
cost of living
profs outside class
deans
campus appearance
overall happiness
profs in class
leftist politics

WHAT'S NOT

fraternities/sororities
diversity

ACADEMICS

Academic Rating:	**79**
Calendar:	4-1-4
Student/teacher ratio:	13/1
% doctorates:	71
Profs interesting:	89
Profs accessible:	89
Hours of study per day:	3.65

MOST POPULAR MAJORS BY %

Social Sciences:	23
Visual & Performing Arts:	13
Letters/Literature:	11

% GRADS WHO PURSUE

Law:	2
MBA:	1
Medicine:	3
M.A., etc.:	20

What do students think about St. Olaf College?

■ **Academics** Regional college counselors unanimously ranked St. Olaf a "superior" school; one went so far as to compare it favorably to Wesleyan, Swarthmore, and nearby Carleton. Relatively unknown outside the Midwest, St. Olaf has earned this regional reputation through its dedication to the liberal arts ("They are called liberal because they help liberate us," the school asserts in its catalog), its strong programs in nursing, music, and the sciences, and its capable faculty. Students here spend nearly half their time fulfilling distribution requirements (including three religion courses: St. Olaf is a Lutheran school) aimed at providing a well-rounded education. An extensive study abroad program, which more than half the students take advantage of, serves the same purpose. As at many other small liberal arts schools, students work hard (studying over three-and-a-half hours a day) and report a high degree of satisfaction with the education they receive. Summed up one student, "The St. Olaf environment is a coherent combination of social and academic alternatives. Students cross a variety of avenues throughout their St. Olaf education, and the majority of our learning here comes through our access to these experiences."

■ **Life** St. Olaf's strong ties with the Lutheran church mandate strict school policies concerning drinking, drug use, and "inter-visitation" between the sexes. One student complained: "St. Olaf's school policies are very unrealistic. Just because of the school's affiliation, the administration denies the legal use of alcohol on campus, while many people *obviously* drink lots on weekends." The school is even strict about cars: students can't have one on campus without permission, which is hard to get. (Commented one student, "The car policy is very restrictive *despite* the semi-rural location of Northfield.") With a restrictive administration, no Greek system, and a home town that has only two bars (and little else), St. Olaf has the potential to rank among the nation's least "party-friendly" schools. Fortunately, the more secular Carleton College is nearby, and frequent Carleton parties help make up for the staid social scene at St. Olaf. In a way, St. Olaf students have the best of both worlds, heading over to Carleton when they want to party, then returning to their own serene, beautiful campus to study. Sports, both intercollegiate and intramural, are popular, and the region offers an ideal setting for cross-country skiing and other outdoors activities. Students actively participate in a wide range of extracurricular clubs, many of which are religiously oriented.

■ **Students** St. Olaf students ranked their student body low on diversity. The school has only a 6 percent minority population, which translates into roughly a hundred Asians, thirty Blacks, and a whole lot of Midwestern, Lutheran whites. Students are politically liberal but are socially conservative because they are more religious than most (although, according to one detractor, "St. Olaf students like to think they are religious, but there is more piety than religion here").

ST. OLAF COLLEGE

Admissions

St. Olaf's admissions office writes that there are no "cut-offs" used in the admissions process. According to the college's catalog, "We seek to fill each class with a diverse and energetic group of students who are eager to undertake the challenges of a liberal education…in considering admission we consider academic achievement, academic aptitude, and personal qualifications as well as leadership and significant involvement in school and community." Weighed most heavily in your application package are your high school record and GPA. These are followed, in order of importance, by your standardized test scores (SAT or ACT), letters of recommendation, essays, extracurriculars, and interview. The recommended program of study for high school includes four years of English, at least three years each of mathematics and social studies, and at least two years each of natural sciences and a foreign language (with one of the foreign language years being senior year). Students who apply here also often apply to Gustavus Adolphus, Carleton, U. of Minnesota, Northwestern, and Macalaster.

Financial Aid

Financial aid applicants to St. Olaf's must complete the FAF or FFS and a form generated by the St. Olaf's financial aid office. Eighty-two percent of those in the class of '95 who applied for financial assistance received some type of aid (60% overall). The average award value was $10,521. Forty-two percent of last year's undergrads took out Stafford loans (average amount: $2,607) and 17% took out Perkins loans (average value: $1,497). St. Olaf's also offers its own institutional loans; in '91–'92, 59% of all undergrads took one out; the average value was $3,047. While St. Olaf's awards no merit-based grants, 1% of all undergrads last year received a National Merit Scholarship, with an average value of $750.

A note from the St. Olaf College of Maryland Admissions Office:

"St. Olaf College provides an education in the liberal arts that is rooted in the Christian Gospel and offered with a global perspective. Fifty to sixty percent of each graduating class will have studied overseas during the four years at St. Olaf. The Paracollege and Great Conversation programs offer alternatives to the traditional curriculum."

ADMISSIONS FACTS

Competitiveness Rating:	**79**
% of applicants accepted:	70
% acceptees attending:	50

FRESHMAN PROFILE

Average verbal SAT:	530
Average math SAT:	580
Average ACT:	26
Graduated top 10% of class:	42
Graduated top 25% of class:	77
Graduated top 50% of class:	94

DEADLINES

Early decision/action:	11/15
Early dec./act. notif.:	12/1
Regular admission:	2/1
Regular adm. notif.:	6/15

APPLICANTS ALSO LOOK AT

and often prefer:
Gustavus Adolphus College
Northwestern U.

and sometimes prefer:
Carleton College

and rarely prefer:
U. Minnesota

ADDRESS

Undergraduate Admissions
1520 St. Olaf Avenue
Northfield, MN 55057-1098
507-663-3025

FINANCIAL FACTS

In-state tuition ($):	12,080
Out-of-state tuition ($):	12,080
Room & board:	3,345
FA application deadline:	3/1
% frosh receiving FA:	57
PT earnings per yr. ($):	1000

TYPE OF AID: % of students ($)

FA of some kind:	56 (9,755)
Need-based grants:	57 (5,217)
Merit-based grants:	1 (750)
Loans:	59 (3,047)
Work study:	61 (1,072)
Student rating of FA:	94

SANTA CLARA UNIVERSITY

Santa Clara, CA

CAMPUS LIFE

Quality of Life Rating: 83

|---|---|
Type of school:	private
Affiliation:	Catholic
Environment:	city

STUDENT BODY

FT undergrad enrollment:	3,717
% male/% female:	52/48
% out-of-state:	39
% live on campus:	50
% African-American:	3
% Asian:	17
% Caucasian:	69
% Hispanic:	10
% foreign:	7
% transfers:	4

WHAT'S HOT

religion
doing all the reading
attending all classes
studying hard
profs teach intros
profs outside class

WHAT'S NOT

dating
library
requirements easy
caring about politics

ACADEMICS

Academic Rating: 80

Calendar:	quarterly
Student/teacher ratio:	14/1
% doctorates:	85
Profs interesting:	84
Profs accessible:	87
Hours of study per day:	3.64

MOST POPULAR MAJORS BY %

Business & Management:	26
Engineering:	13
Social Sciences:	12

% GRADS WHO PURSUE

Law:	3
MBA:	1
Medicine:	2
M.A., etc.:	14

What do students think about Santa Clara University?

■ **Academics** Santa Clara University is a small school with very big ambitions. Originally a school exclusively for Catholics, this increasingly diverse institution continues to funnel its considerable resources into improving itself. By following this strategy, the school has measurably improved its facilities, faculty and reputation in recent years. Classes (especially in SCU's strong engineering program) are small, taught by professors (rarely by TAs), and generally "challenging and excellent." The work ethic is intense; students gave themselves high marks for attending all classes, doing all assigned reading, and studying hard in general. One warned that "if you don't have the motivation to study every day, you'll never make it!" There are isolated complaints that SCU has drifted too far away from its original mission ("to educate, not to train"). One student wrote that "the school claims to be a Jesuit university, but the Jesuit philosophy does not coincide with the curriculum, especially in the Schools of Business and Engineering" (SCU's most popular divisions). Others would point out, however, that the school requires a comprehensive liberal arts core curriculum for all students. Overall, the level of satisfaction here is high. Wrote one typical junior, "The classroom and learning environment here at SCU is amazing! Levels of discussion are mind-numbing, and access to professors is excellent."

■ **Life** Santa Clara's campus is beautiful and quaint. For some students, social life begins and ends there ("The dorms are *very* important socially," wrote one student). Students feel that the "closeness of the small student body" makes for a "comfortable, warm experience" at SCU. Many feel the campus is a little too closely knit, however, claiming that "people here rarely date, and when they do, the masses have them married off after two dates. Who needs it?" Temporary escape from Santa Clara is easy, though. Explained one student, "San Francisco, Napa Valley and Santa Cruz are all short drives away, which makes up for the fact that Santa Clara is located in a relatively unpleasing area." Most students agree that the "city of Santa Clara is pretty boring," and that "in the area of alternative social activities, Santa Clara has a long way to go." But one student who turned down MIT, Williams, and UC Berkeley to attend SCU completely disagreed, writing, "There are so many opportunities here—a wealth of multi-cultural clubs, incredible study abroad programs (my summer in Assisi, Italy was an unforgettable experience), many campus leadership positions, more sports clubs and teams than I'd ever imagined, and popular community service organizations. The small size of SCU definitely does not hinder one's access to diverse outside opportunities."

■ **Students** The once "mostly Catholic, elite white population" of SCU is changing rapidly. It now boasts a minority population of over 30 percent. The administration continues to emphasize its ethnic recruiting program. Students are generally very studious and conservative, both socially and politically.

SANTA CLARA UNIVERSITY

Admissions

From Santa Clara's undergraduate catalog: "The University makes selective decisions regarding applicants for admission based on the following criteria: first, high school record; second, scores on College Entrance Examination Board tests; third, school recommendations; fourth, personal factors such as extracurricular involvement, character and leadership; fifth, relationship to the University. Admission to freshman standing at Santa Clara depends on a continued high level of performance during the remainder of the applicant's senior year in high school and on receipt of a high school diploma. If a significant change occurs in academic work during this year, the Committee will reevaluate the acceptance in light of that change." The recommended high school curriculum includes four years of English, two years of algebra, one year of history, three years of a single foreign language, one year of geometry, and one year of lab science. Business, social science, natural science, mathematics, and engineering majors should take trigonometry and additional science courses as well. All students must submit SAT (preferred) or ACT scores.

Financial Aid

Financial aid applicants to Santa Clara University must complete the FAF (California residents should complete the SAAC). Santa Clara U. offers a "Third-Child Family Grant to any family which has three dependents enrolled in the university concurrently as undergraduates. The grant is a one-half tuition reduction. Scholarships are available for academic and leadership merit, alumni and religious affiliations, and talent in the arts. In addition to Perkins and Stafford loans, the Santa Clara financial aid office recommends SLS, PLUS, and Family Ed loans.

Excerpted from Santa Clara University promotional materials:

"Inspired by the love of God to serve through education, begun by the Franciscans who founded Mission Santa Clara in 1777 and continued by the Jesuits who opened the College in 1851, Santa Clara University declares its purpose to be the education of the human person within the Catholic and Jesuit tradition. The University is thus dedicated to a community of highly qualified scholars, teachers, students, and administrators...; an education that, in its emphasis on undergraduate studies...stresses moral as well as intellectual values...; an integrated curriculum designed not only to provide scientific and humanistic knowledge...but also to fully demonstrate the unity of all forms of knowledge...; and, the encouragement of teaching excellence and scholarly research..."

ADMISSIONS FACTS

Competitiveness Rating:	77
% of applicants accepted:	71
% acceptees attending:	38

FRESHMAN PROFILE

Average verbal SAT:	505
Average math SAT:	581
Average ACT:	NA
Graduated top 10% of class:	36
Graduated top 25% of class:	71
Graduated top 50% of class:	95

DEADLINES

Early decision/action:	NA
Early dec./act. notif.:	NA
Regular admission:	2/1
Regular adm. notif.:	4/1

APPLICANTS ALSO LOOK AT

and often prefer:
UC Los Angeles
Stanford U.

and sometimes prefer:
Pomona College
UC Irvine
UC Santa Cruz
UC Santa Barbara
UC Berkeley

and rarely prefer:
Loyola Marymount U.
UC San Diego

ADDRESS

Undergraduate Admissions
500 El Camino Real
Santa Clara, CA 95053
408-554-4700

FINANCIAL FACTS

In-state tuition ($):	11,271
Out-of-state tuition ($):	11,271
Room & board:	5,292
FA application deadline:	2/1
% frosh receiving FA:	53
PT earnings per yr. ($):	1300

TYPE OF AID: % of students ($)

FA of some kind:	56 (NA)
Need-based grants:	NA
Merit-based grants:	NA
Loans:	NA
Work study:	NA
Student rating of FA:	86

SARAH LAWRENCE COLLEGE

Bronxville, NY

CAMPUS LIFE

Quality of Life Rating: **74**

Type of school:	private
Affiliation:	none
Environment:	suburban

STUDENT BODY

FT undergrad enrollment:	945
% male/% female:	27/73
% out-of-state:	80
% live on campus:	85
% African-American:	9
% Asian:	6
% Caucasian:	76
% Hispanic:	8
% foreign:	8
% transfers:	6

WHAT'S HOT

gay community accepted
in-class discussion
marijuana
leftist politics
small labs and seminars
deans
college theatre
profs outside class
profs in class

WHAT'S NOT

fraternities/sororities
sports
town-gown relations
religion
location

ACADEMICS

Academic Rating: **85**

Calendar:	semester
Student/teacher ratio:	8/1
% doctorates:	90
Profs interesting:	91
Profs accessible:	92
Hours of study per day:	2.97

MOST POPULAR MAJORS BY %

Social Sciences:	20
Letters/Literature:	15
Visual & Performing Arts:	15

% GRADS WHO PURSUE

Law:	10
MBA:	NA
Medicine:	5
M.A., etc.:	23

What do students think about Sarah Lawrence College?

■ **Academics** Sarah Lawrence College stresses the "liberal" in liberal arts. Here, students declare no official majors, receive extensive written evaluations of their work instead of grades (although letter grades are kept on file for graduate schools), and meet regularly with their faculty advisors (called "dons") to fashion curricula suited to their individual interests and abilities. Students are particularly enthusiastic about their close relationships with faculty members: wrote one, "I have stayed through the ups and downs because I believe there is nowhere in the country where I can work so independently yet have constant contact with professors." Popular fields of study include writing, drama, English, art and art history. The pre-medical sciences are strong enough to send 5 percent of SLC graduates on to medical school. While most students feel that "SLC provides self-motivated students with unique educational opportunities," some complain that the program inspires students to be "too individualistic and self-centered." Others find the academic approach here "too liberal for its own good. Political correctness is at times taken to the point where honesty is condemned, and that's not healthy." The mood here is definitely intense: one student described the school as "like being in an asylum for very intelligent, creative people. But, there are many sane people on campus who utilize the wonderful academics and send the students back down to earth. These people will most definitely be the new minds of our generation."

■ **Life** SLC students rated Bronxville "extremely boring." Fortunately, noted one student, "We're near New York City, arguably the greatest city in the world." On campus students enjoy a small academic community they describe as "intense but caring." There is no Greek system and students report that they care little about what few competitive and intramural sports they have on campus: as a result, "Social life is restricted to small parties and small groups hanging out, smoking pot and drinking. No dating goes on: the general social scene sucks." Dating and other social events are hampered by a lopsided one to three male-female ratio. Students gave the dormitories and campus high marks for both beauty and convenience.

■ **Students** Said one student, "SLC is full of freaks, but in an excellent way. It's an intense environment and definitely not for everyone, but if you're right here, it's a perfect fit. There are no boundaries here." Other students, though, complain about the preponderance of "rich kids who were never taught any responsibility, beautiful people, and women who diet excessively." Despite a 25 percent minority population, students described their student body as homogeneous; reported one, "This school does not actively recruit students of varied socio-economic and ethnic backgrounds." Students identified themselves as very far to the left politically, although one detractor summed up the political situation here as "a lot of talk, but not very much action."

SARAH LAWRENCE COLLEGE

Bronxville, NY

Admissions

From Sarah Lawrence's undergraduate catalog: "Recognizing that creativity, motivation, and intellectual promise manifest themselves differently in different individuals, we consider many factors in addition to traditional academic criteria in assessing the applicant's abilities and potential... Because we value strong writing skills and the clear expression of interests, attitudes, and goals, the Committee looks closely at an applicant's response to the essay questions on the application form. The school record and counselor and teacher recommendations are also critical elements of an applicant's credentials. Test scores are used as an added indication of an applicant's academic aptitude and achievement. To round out a candidate's admissions file, a personal interview, preferable on campus, is strongly recommended." Applicants must submit SAT or ACT or three Achievement test scores. Those opting do submit Achievements are advised to take one English Composition (with or without essay), one test in math or science, and one test in languages, literature, or history. Applicants who have made a significant commitment to one or more of the arts are encouraged to submit examples of their work. A second early decision deadline (other than that shown in the sidebar) is available: applicants who apply by January 1 will receive notification by February 15.

Financial Aid

Financial aid applicants to Sarah Lawrence must complete the FAF and a form generated by Sarah Lawrence's financial aid office, and submit a copy of their parents' tax return. Sarah Lawrence College Gift Aid grants are awarded on the basis of financial need and merit. In addition to TAP and Regents Scholarships for New York State residents, various other outside scholarships are available.

A note from the Sarah Lawrence College Admissions Office:

"Founded in 1926 and coeducational since 1968, Sarah Lawrence College has a history of bringing innovations to American higher education. These have included fully integrating the arts into the academic curriculum; requiring Freshman Studies seminars which introduce the sophisticated methods of reasoning on which a college education is founded; establishing the country's first full-scale undergraduate program specifically designed for adults returning to college; and developing the first undergraduate program in women's history. More recently, the College has introduced a new graduate program in the Art of Teaching; courses exploring the implications of nuclear technology; and lecture series which bring experts to the campus to explore with students possible solutions to contemporary social problems."

ADMISSIONS FACTS

Competitiveness Rating:	**76**
% of applicants accepted:	49
% acceptees attending:	39

FRESHMAN PROFILE

Average verbal SAT:	580
Average math SAT:	570
Average ACT:	26
Graduated top 10% of class:	29
Graduated top 25% of class:	58
Graduated top 50% of class:	86

DEADLINES

Early decision/action:	11/15
Early dec./act. notif.:	12/15
Regular admission:	2/1
Regular adm. notif.:	early April

APPLICANTS ALSO LOOK AT

and often prefer:
Barnard College
Bryn Mawr College
Vassar College

and sometimes prefer:
Hampshire College
Bennington College

and rarely prefer:
NYU
Bard College

ADDRESS

Undergraduate Admissions
Bronxville, NY 10708
914-395-2510

FINANCIAL FACTS

In-state tuition ($):	16,400
Out-of-state tuition ($):	16,400
Room & board:	6,400
FA application deadline:	2/1
% frosh receiving FA:	50
PT earnings per yr. ($):	1200

TYPE OF AID: % of students ($)

FA of some kind:	50 (NA)
Need-based grants:	NA
Merit-based grants:	NA
Loans:	NA
Work study:	NA
Student rating of FA:	81

SETON HALL UNIVERSITY

South Orange, NJ

What do students think about Seton Hall University?

■ **Academics** "It may have taken a Big East championship to get us noticed," explained one current Seton Hall University student, "but we're NOT just basketball." Seton Hall is trying to make the same big splash in the academic world that it made in the sports world when, in 1989, it beat out schools five times its size to earn a berth in the NCAA finals. The school still primarily serves those looking for career-specific educations. Nursing, communications, education, and business-related majors are the most popular choices here. However, curriculum requirements incorporate a heavy dose of liberal arts courses into every undergraduate's studies. Like many Catholic universities, SHU is cheap by private school standards, but services for students are top-notch. Said one student, "People working at SHU are very cooperative, helpful and are very easy to associate with." A business student noted the accessibility of SHU professors, writing, "Although recently becoming a more popular school, SHU has maintained a very good student-teacher ratio of 17 to 1. This provides the opportunities for teachers to meet and know the students as people, not as a number." Students did complain that administrative chores sometimes entailed navigating a great deal of red tape, and gave their library very low marks (note, however, that a new one is being built).

■ **Life** SHU students enjoy "a small, closely knit community where everyone knows each other." Unfortunately, social life at Seton Hall is curtailed by the fact that fewer than half the students live on campus (the school has a large commuter population). To make matters worse, "too many people go home over the weekend," and hometown South Orange, while close to New York City, is itself no hotbed of excitement. Explained one student, "Since the surrounding city doesn't offer much socially, I feel like I am trapped. On weekends, there is absolutely nothing to do. I came to college to get away from home, yet I find myself going back home almost every weekend." Said another, "the weekend life at this campus is *so* lame. Thursday, though, is a major drinking night. There are about five or six quality bars and clubs within walking distance, and they're very easy to get into without proof of age." Campus activities are plentiful "but very few take advantage of them," and "fraternities and sororities are very active on campus: over one quarter of all students belong to a Greek organization." Of course, there's Seton Hall basketball, still popular even though the team has failed to match its "mouse that roared" feat of a few years ago. A final note to commuters: "Be sure to get a club and a car alarm. Also, the speed bumps at the front gate are too high!"

■ **Students** Seton Hall has a 17 percent minority population made up predominantly of blacks and Hispanics. Although a few respondents wrote that "racial tensions are high," most told us that relations between groups are about normal. Students are very conservative politically. New Jersey natives make up over three quarters of the student body.

SETON HALL UNIVERSITY

Admissions

The admissions office reports that it uses "no cut-offs or formulas. Every folder is individually reviewed by at least two [admissions] counselors." High school curriculum/GPA and standardized test scores are considered to be of primary importance; extracurricular activities, an interview (required for some, recommended for all others), and essays are also considered. Applicants are required to have completed Algebra I and II, geometry, one year of lab science, two years of a foreign language, and four years of English. Either the SAT or the ACT is required. Applicants to Seton Hall who apply elsewhere most often apply to Rutgers, Villanova, and Montclair State. Note: nearly all wait-listed students were ultimately admitted in 1991.

Financial Aid

The financial aid office at Seton Hall University requires applicants to submit the FAF. The school awards merit scholarships for academic excellence, athletic ability, and artistic skill. Special scholarships are set aside for transfer and minority students. Department-specific grants are also available. Seton Hall's catalog lists the following loan options for students: Stafford, Perkins, PLUS, and Student Nursing. The catalog also states, "Because some funds are limited, applications are considered on a first-come, first-served basis." The deadline listed below is a *priority* deadline.

A note from the Seton Hall Admissions Office:

"Seton Hall is a snapshot of what it will be like in the 21st century, with this many different people getting along in this small a space. And we want our curriculum to reflect that, to be a mirror of who we are. We pay special attention to our freshmen, and have been nationally recognized for excellence in our Freshman Studies program. As a Catholic University, we are committed to life-long learning, communication, and civic values."

ADMISSIONS FACTS

Competitiveness Rating:	**65**
% of applicants accepted:	66
% acceptees attending:	26

FRESHMAN PROFILE

Average verbal SAT:	453
Average math SAT:	507
Average ACT:	NA
Graduated top 10% of class:	19
Graduated top 25% of class:	45
Graduated top 50% of class:	78

DEADLINES

Early decision/action:	NA
Early dec./act. notif.:	NA
Regular admission:	3/1
Regular adm. notif.:	rolling

APPLICANTS ALSO LOOK AT

and sometimes prefer:
Providence College
Villanova U.
Trenton State College
U. Connecticut

and rarely prefer:
St. Bonaventure U.
Fairfield U.
Hofstra U.

ADDRESS

Undergraduate Admissions
South Orange Ave.
South Orange, NJ 07079
201-761-9332

FINANCIAL FACTS

In-state tuition ($):	9,900
Out-of-state tuition ($):	9,900
Room & board:	5,418
FA application deadline:	4/1
% frosh receiving FA:	65
PT earnings per yr. ($):	1300

TYPE OF AID: % of students ($)

FA of some kind:	65 (NA)
Need-based grants:	NA
Merit-based grants:	NA
Loans:	NA
Work study:	NA
Student rating of FA:	67

SIMMONS COLLEGE

Boston, MA

CAMPUS LIFE

Quality of Life Rating:	**84**
Type of school:	private
Affiliation:	none
Environment:	city

STUDENT BODY

FT undergrad enrollment:	1,227
% male/% female:	0/100
% out-of-state:	47
% live on campus:	70
% African-American:	3
% Asian:	3
% Caucasian:	87
% Hispanic:	2
% foreign:	3
% transfers:	5

WHAT'S HOT

location
dorm safety
honesty
doing all the reading
small classes (overall)
deans
profs in class
gay community accepted
studying hard
cost of living

WHAT'S NOT

intramural sports
fraternities/sororities
marijuana
beer

ACADEMICS

Academic Rating:	**80**
Calendar:	semester
Student/teacher ratio:	10/1
% doctorates:	78
Profs interesting:	90
Profs accessible:	85
Hours of study per day:	3.64

MOST POPULAR MAJORS BY %

Business & Management:	23
Social Sciences:	15
Health Sciences:	10

% GRADS WHO PURSUE

Law:	2
MBA:	1
Medicine:	1
M.A., etc.:	6

What do students think about Simmons College?

■ **Academics** Simmons is a women's college with two prominent assets: rock-solid pre-professional and career-oriented programs (especially in the fields of nursing, physical therapy, and business and management); and its location in central Boston. Of course, there's a third characteristic that, to many, is the school's greatest asset: the all-female student body. Explained one student, "People may think that not having guys around is terrible but I think it gives you a chance to look inside yourself. All of my personal goals, decisions, and opinions are changing just because I don't have the 'male influence' every day." Said another, "I love the single-sex atmosphere and find it conducive to a greater solidarity among students." Students here work hard—in terms of study time, they are among the top 15 percent of student bodies profiled in this book. The Simmons curriculum is demanding, requiring all students to complete 40 hours of liberal arts and sciences classes, another 20 to 40 hours of courses in their major fields, and between eight and 16 hours of independent study. The final requirement may be fulfilled by an internship as well as by a research project. The student-teacher ratio here is low, and students reported that professors were both effective in class and very accessible and caring outside the classroom.

■ **Life** At most women's colleges, students complain about how few opportunities they have to socialize with men. Not so at Simmons: the school's location in central Boston affords Simmons women plenty of opportunities to meet college-age men if they so desire. Asked what they liked most about their school, the most students chose its location: "Boston is the #1 college town, no doubt about it," wrote one student. Because the school has a pleasant, self-contained campus, students enjoy "the best of both worlds. When you're in the dorms or on campus, you forget you're in the middle of a big city. Yet, when you're looking for something to do, the options are endless." On campus, students are provided "many opportunities to pursue leadership positions and non-academic interests," according to one undergrad. Students approve of the new sports center, which one described as "awesome."

■ **Students** Thirteen percent of Simmons students are minorities: the minority population of approximately 160 is split evenly among Asians, blacks, and Hispanics. Accordingly, the tone of the student body (as it were) is set by the white, affluent New England women who make up the majority. Several students complained that this majority can be closed-minded when it comes to anything perceived as eccentric: wrote one, "If you don't have the right clothes and money, forget about it! If your daddy is not filthy rich, you are looked down upon (by most). If you are the least bit different (overweight, radical dress, etc.), girls stick their noses up at you." Most students who fit the majority mold, however, would agree with the woman who wrote that "the Simmons community is very supportive, encouraging, and inspiring."

SIMMONS COLLEGE

Admissions

From the Simmons undergraduate catalog: "To retain [Simmons'] diversity...means its policies must be flexible, focusing on each applicant's qualities of scholarship and character...The most important [credential] is the high school record. A careful study of the number and level of courses that a student has taken, her grades, and her school's recommendations give the [Admissions] Committee an indication of the level of work she can be expected to do in college. What the student has to say about herself, in writing her application and during an interview, tells the Committee about her interests and the kind of activities to which she has devoted her time and energy. Finally, the results of the required standardized tests help complete the picture." The recommended high school curriculum includes four years of English, three years each of mathematics, foreign language, and social science, and two years of natural science. Applicants must submit SAT or ACT scores. An interim early decision plan is available: applicants who submit materials by January 1 will receive notification by February 1.

Financial Aid

Financial aid applicants to Simmons must complete the FAF and a form generated by the financial aid office, and submit a copy of their most recent tax return. Simmons's financial aid office writes that it makes "educational opportunities available to as many capable, promising students as possible, and welcomes applications from students who could not meet their expenses at the college without assistance." All merit scholarships received by students at Simmons last year were academic-based; among them were President's Scholarships (3% of undergrads, average value of $3,000), Honors Scholarships (4%; $4,000), Ferebee Scholarships (2%; $4,000) and Boston Scholarships (1%; $13,632). Twenty-two percent of Simmons' students took out Perkins loans in '91–'92 (average value: $1,500), 38% took out Stafford loans (average: $2,900), and 11% took out Simmons' own institutional loans (average: $1,500).

Excerpted from Simmons College promotional materials:

"The Simmons idea is not novel today; indeed, its time has come. Since the early 1900s there have been dramatic changes in society's attitudes toward women and in women's perception of themselves and what they contribute in every field of activity. Simmons College has not only kept pace with these changes, it has helped to shape them in its classrooms and by the example of its graduates in the careers they have undertaken and the leadership they have provided."

ADMISSIONS FACTS

Competitiveness Rating:	**63**
% of applicants accepted:	79
% acceptees attending:	31

FRESHMAN PROFILE

Average verbal SAT:	433*
Average math SAT:	483*
Average ACT:	24*
Graduated top 10% of class:	14
Graduated top 25% of class:	44
Graduated top 50% of class:	81

DEADLINES

Early decision/action:	11/15
Early dec./act. notif.:	12/15
Regular admission:	2/1
Regular adm. notif.:	4/15

APPLICANTS ALSO LOOK AT

and often prefer:

Boston College

U. NC–Chapel Hill

and sometimes prefer:

Wheaton College

Wellesley College

Bryn Mawr College

ADDRESS

Undergraduate Admissions

300 The Fenway

Boston, MA 02115

617-738-2107

FINANCIAL FACTS

In-state tuition ($):	13,632
Out-of-state tuition ($):	13,632
Room & board:	6,000
FA application deadline:	2/1
% frosh receiving FA:	52
PT earnings per yr. ($):	1800

TYPE OF AID: % of students ($)

FA of some kind:	46 (13,200)
Need-based grants:	56 (8,900)
Merit-based grants:	13 (4,000)
Loans:	53 (2,600)
Work study:	37 (1,700)
Student rating of FA:	83

SIMON'S ROCK OF BARD COLLEGE

Great Barrington, MA

CAMPUS LIFE

Quality of Life Rating: **75**

Type of school:	private
Affiliation:	none
Environment:	suburban

STUDENT BODY

FT undergrad enrollment:	273
% male/% female:	45/55
% out-of-state:	77
% live on campus:	98
% African-American:	7
% Asian:	7
% Caucasian:	83
% Hispanic:	2
% foreign:	2
% transfers:	NA

WHAT'S HOT

gay community accepted
in-class discussion
marijuana
interaction among students
leftist politics
small classes (overall)
profs in class
doing all the reading
living on campus
caring about politics
Grateful Dead
profs accessible

WHAT'S NOT

fraternities/sororities
religious clubs

ACADEMICS

Academic Rating: **85**

Calendar:	semester
Student/teacher ratio:	9/1
% doctorates:	76
Profs interesting:	94
Profs accessible:	89
Hours of study per day:	3.31

MOST POPULAR MAJORS

Environmental Science
Language and Literature
Social Sciences

What do students think about Simon's Rock College?

■ **Academics** Simon's Rock of Bard College provides a welcome academic haven for nearly 300 very unique students. What sets them apart is their age (usually between 15 and 18), and the fact that most of them are high school dropouts. Indeed, this innovative college prides itself on rescuing extremely gifted young people who are bored or unhappy in high school. Simon's Rock is "for people who feel that our educational system has them in a choke hold. It is a welcome release and a wonderful opportunity," wrote one student. The academics are considered "astounding" and professors are "vital and exciting." Classes are small and very difficult, and the curriculum veers toward the unconventional: independent studies and creative arts majors are very common. There are "few required courses, no teaching assistants, and as much student-teacher contact as you need." One student said, "In an atmosphere which provides almost unequaled support for learning (intellectual or otherwise), one is limited only by the difficult transition between adolescence and freedom which we go through. Never has there been a greater concentration of unique and intelligent life."

■ **Life** One literature major wrote, "Simon's Rock is the only place where every human being misunderstood socially, politically, emotionally, sexually, and intellectually comes together for a once-in-a-lifetime challenge." It is true that most are here because they do not fit into the mainstream, and this shared history creates "a special bond among students. Most of us are being accepted for the first time in our lives." The social life is varied; some love the fact that "there's no single social norm," while others find it "insane," lamenting the lack of "normal extracurricular activities. Instead, there is a 'Rocky Horror Picture Show' group and a Marquis de Sade Fan Club." The campus is "very liberal, very sexually active, and there is an unmistakable drug presence (mostly pot and acid)." One student explained, "The normal 'experimentation' that happens between ages 15 and 18 is discouraged by parents, but that's not the Resident Director's job. So sex, drugs, etc. are prevalent here. Since classes are very challenging, the weekends are for decompression, which in some cases includes pot and alcohol." The size and intimacy of "the Rock" help early entrants "to make the transition from high school to college, from living at home to living on your own." But most do not stay for four years. As one student told us, "After a while it just gets too small and it becomes time to move on. Usually two years are enough."

■ **Students** Simon's Rock is "not for the fainthearted and/or conservative," according to students. Political opinions, mostly quite liberal ones, are expressed strongly and often; one student wryly called his peers "a bunch of rich kids pretending to be working-class revolutionaries." They actually are a bunch of young, lively, extremely bright students who have forsaken stifling high school experiences in exchange for a great educational head start.

SIMON'S ROCK OF BARD COLLEGE

Great Barrington, MA

Admissions

The Simon's Rock Admissions Department states "We require a personal interview, which usually involves parents as well (as the student). Our application 'essays' are a bit unusual in that we require our applicants to read one of our Freshman Seminar texts (Plato's *Apology*) and reflect upon it. We also ask them to pick an issue of public concern and compose a letter to the local or national authorities. We get a copy of this letter." At Simon's Rock, the admissions committee first looks at your GPA, followed by your interview, essays, letters of recommendation, extracurriculars, and standardized test scores, in descending order of importance. Applicants must have taken the SAT, PSAT, or the ACT, and have completed two years of college preparatory courses. In addition, the committee looks for "maturity, good humor, and a lively intellect."

Financial Aid

Simon's Rock requires financial aid applicants to complete the FAF and submit a copy of their parents' most recent tax return. Last year, 9% of the school's undergrads received academic grants (average value: $1,600). Overall last year, 75% of the freshman class applied for some form of aid, and 70% of those who applied received an award of some kind (average value: $9,700). A quarter of all '91–'92 undergrads took out Perkins loans (average value: $1,000), and 62% took out Stafford loans (average value: $2,500). The financial aid office writes, "Aid for returning students is adjusted by academic performance…Students with GPAs above 3.0 are awarded additional aid and those with GPAs below 2.5 will have aid reduced." There is no hard deadline for financial aid applications at Simon's Rock; notification of awards begins in April.

A note from the Simon's Rock Admissions Office:

"Simon's Rock is, as far as we know, the only four-year college in the U.S. wholly devoted to early admission. Our students typically enroll after completing the 10th or 11th grade, and pursue a full-time course of study in the liberal arts and sciences. The college offers a two-year A.A. degree and a four-year B.A. degree.

"Who goes to college two years early? Very serious students, for the most part. Our freshmen have often had excellent high school records, but found themselves wanting more challenge than even AP or Honors classes could offer. Simon's Rock also believes that 16-year-olds deserve to be taken seriously, which is an idea many students find attractive."

ADMISSIONS FACTS

Competitiveness Rating:	*83*
% of applicants accepted:	62
% acceptees attending:	69

FRESHMAN PROFILE

Average verbal SAT:	587
Average math SAT:	589
Average ACT:	NA
Graduated top 10% of class:	NA
Graduated top 25% of class:	NA
Graduated top 50% of class:	NA

DEADLINES

Early decision/action:	NA
Early dec./act. notif.:	NA
Regular admission:	6/30
Regular adm. notif.:	rolling

APPLICANTS ALSO LOOK AT

and sometimes prefer:
Clarkson University
U. Texas–Denton
Preparatory schools

(see left; *Note from Admissions Office*)

ADDRESS

Undergraduate Admissions
84 Alford Road
Great Barrington, MA 01230
413-528-0771

FINANCIAL FACTS

In-state tuition ($):	14,160
Out-of-state tuition ($):	14,160
Room & board:	5,350
FA application deadline:	6/15
% frosh receiving FA:	71
PT earnings per yr. ($):	1000

TYPE OF AID: % of students ($)

FA of some kind:	67 (9,700)
Need-based grants:	67 (7,900)
Merit-based grants:	9 (1,600)
Loans:	NA
Work study:	33 (1,200)
Student rating of FA:	83

439

SKIDMORE COLLEGE

Saratoga Springs, NY

CAMPUS LIFE

Quality of Life Rating: **88**

Type of school:	private
Affiliation:	none
Environment:	suburban

STUDENT BODY

FT undergrad enrollment:	2,123
% male/% female:	44/56
% out-of-state:	69
% live on campus:	83
% African-American:	4
% Asian:	3
% Caucasian:	88
% Hispanic:	3
% foreign:	3
% transfers:	1

WHAT'S HOT

college theater groups
dorm comfort
dorm safety
college radio station
Grateful Dead
marijuana
small classes
profs accessible
good-looking students

WHAT'S NOT

fraternities/sororities
religion
diversity

ACADEMICS

Academic Rating: **80**

Calendar:	semester
Student/teacher ratio:	11/1
% doctorates:	70
Profs interesting:	89
Profs accessible:	92
Hours of study per day:	3.41

MOST POPULAR MAJORS BY %

Government:	15
English:	14
Business:	13

% GRADS WHO PURSUE

Law:	7
MBA:	3
Medicine:	2
M.A., etc.:	18

What do students think about Skidmore College?

■ **Academics** Major renovations to the campus and administration efforts to attract a more competitive student body led several independent college counsellors to report that Skidmore College "has come a long way and continues to improve." Long a popular choice with Eastern prepsters, Skidmore strengths are in the "liberal arts, fine arts, and performing arts," according to another area counselor. A core curriculum, called Liberal Studies, exposes students to a solid grounding in the "greatest hits" of Western arts and sciences. Said one student, "The Liberal Studies sequence at Skidmore is a valuable supplement to a solid liberal arts education. Liberal Studies I: *The Human Experience* epitomizes Skidmore's vision of the student body as open-minded and appreciative of today's diverse, complex, and often ambiguous global community." Multiculturalism and political correctness are hot issues here, more so with professors and administrators than with students. Students praise their professors and administration ("President Porter is very accessible; there was even a raffle to change places with the president for a day, where a student would perform his duties and he would attend classes," reported one student).

■ **Life** Skidmore students love Saratoga Springs, "a beautiful town with a great history." The town "has excellent work/internship opportunities, great social opportunities, and of course the famous racetrack." Students head into town to hit the bars: a student told us that "for non-drinkers or those without ID, alternative social activities are sometimes tough to find." The area affords outdoorsmen/women opportunities for white-water rafting, skiing, and hiking. Campus clubs and organizations are plentiful, and the college radio station is very popular in the area. Dating is made a little difficult by the disproportionate number of women here—the male-female ratio is about 2:3. Skidmore has the nation's third best dorms! Reported one student, "About half the sophomore class has single rooms. Juniors are pretty much guaranteed a single with a window!"

■ **Students** Skidmore's student body has traditionally included a large share of rich preppies. The administration has made efforts recently to attract a more diverse student body, with mixed results. Reported one senior, "Skidmore is a lot less materialistic than it was three years ago when I got here. In fact, the school now has a Deadhead feel. Diversity is still lacking, but awareness is more prevalent that it used to be." Most students find their classmates superficially open and friendly, but cliquish and difficult to get to know well. While students identified themselves as politically left of center, many wrote to tell us that their classmates were basically apathetic: said one, "The professors are more liberal than the student body, and that division widens yearly."

SKIDMORE COLLEGE

Saratoga Springs, NY

Admissions

The admissions office reports that it "seeks students who demonstrate intellectual curiosity, open-mindedness, an energetic commitment to learning, and a concern for others. The Admissions Committee's primary emphasis is on the strength of the candidate's academic record, personal qualities, accomplishments, interests, and capacity for growth. Although a personal interview is not required, it is strongly recommended." Letters or recommendation are relatively important here. Standardized test scores (either the SAT or ACT) are required, but are reportedly de-emphasized in the admissions process. Applicants must have completed four years of English, and three years each of math, science, social studies, and a foreign language. Skidmore applicants most often apply as well to University of Vermont, Vassar, Wesleyan, UConn, Bates, Union, URochester, and Boston U.

Financial Aid

The financial aid office at Skidmore College requires applicants to submit the FAF, a form generated by the school, and their parents' most recent tax return. The only merit-based grant offered at Skidmore is the Filene Music scholarship: 18 students received one in 1991–92 (average value: $6,000). In 1991–92, approximately one third of entering freshmen received an aid package of some kind.

A note from the Skidmore College Admissions Office:

"Skidmore's Liberal Studies Curriculum is a highly interdisciplinary core curriculum which enriches a student's first two years of study. Students take one course in each of four liberal studies areas, beginning with Liberal Studies I: *The Human Experience*. This is a cornerstone course which is team-taught to all freshmen by 28 professors from virtually every department in the college. It involves lectures, performances, films, and regular small group discussions. Students then take one liberal studies course in each of the three succeeding semesters in the following areas: Cultural Traditions and Social Change, Artistic Forms and Critical Concepts, and Science, Society, and Human Values. The purpose of this constellation of courses is to show the important academic interrelationships across disciplines, across cultures, and across time. The result is that our students learn to look for connections among the disciplines rather than seeing them in isolation. Students also learn to appreciate the breadth of the faculty during their first two years, as well as gain a strong sense of intellectual community with their class. With this interdisciplinary foundation under their belts by the end of the sophomore year, students are better prepared to then select a major (or combination of majors) that matches their interests."

ADMISSIONS FACTS

Competitiveness Rating:	*81*
% of applicants accepted:	50
% acceptees attending:	25

FRESHMAN PROFILE

Average verbal SAT:	540
Average math SAT:	600
Average ACT:	26
Graduated top 10% of class:	35
Graduated top 25% of class:	71
Graduated top 50% of class:	95

DEADLINES

Early decision/action:	12/15
Early dec./act. notif.:	1/15
Regular admission:	2/1
Regular adm. notif.:	4/1

APPLICANTS ALSO LOOK AT

and often prefer:
Trinity College
Middlebury College
Vassar College

and sometimes prefer:
Syracuse U.
American U.
Boston U.

and rarely prefer:
Clark U.

ADDRESS

Undergraduate Admissions
Saratoga Springs, NY 12866
518-587-7569

FINANCIAL FACTS

In-state tuition ($):	15,785
Out-of-state tuition ($):	15,785
Room & board:	5,090
FA application deadline:	2/1
% frosh receiving FA:	34
PT earnings per yr. ($):	1000

TYPE OF AID: % of students ($)

FA of some kind:	47 (11,404)
Need-based grants:	NA (6,000)
Merit-based grants:	NA (2,577)
Loans:	NA
Work study:	25 (810)
Student rating of FA:	89

SMITH COLLEGE

Northampton, MA

CAMPUS LIFE

Quality of Life Rating:	**89**
Type of school:	private
Affiliation:	none
Environment:	suburban

STUDENT BODY

FT undergrad enrollment:	2,561
% male/% female:	0/100
% out-of-state:	83
% live on campus:	88
% African-American:	4
% Asian:	10
% Caucasian:	77
% Hispanic:	3
% foreign:	6
% transfers:	4

WHAT'S HOT

gay community accepted
food
dorm comfort
honesty
studying hard
profs in class
leftist politics
small classes (overall)
deans
profs accessible

WHAT'S NOT

fraternities/sororities
marijuana
beer

ACADEMICS

Academic Rating:	**90**
Calendar:	semester
Student/teacher ratio:	10/1
% doctorates:	90
Profs interesting:	95
Profs accessible:	90
Hours of study per day:	3.97

MOST POPULAR MAJORS BY %

Government:	13
Art:	9
English:	9

% GRADS WHO PURSUE

Law:	7
MBA:	1
Medicine:	3
M.A., etc.:	16

What do students think about Smith College?

■ **Academics** "Behind every great woman is a great women's college," reads a popular Smith College T-shirt. Judging by the comments we received, students here consider "great" an understatement when referring to their school. Academics are "fantastic," "top-notch," "intense" and, some declared, "daunting but very rewarding in the end." This bastion of academic strength earns its kudos. Smith boasts "small classes, open and fascinating professors, a wide selection of courses you are practically guaranteed to get," and generally excellent departments (standouts are art history, English, economics, women's studies, performing/visual arts, government, and the natural sciences). Smith encourages independence with its lack of a core curriculum. Undergraduates design their own courses of study from their first day here. Students appreciated the fact that professors teach every class—"There are no teaching assistants at Smith!"—and felt they "could not ask for a better school. There is plenty of academic freedom and encouragement to explore your interests and talents."

■ **Life** Many students here think that, socially, they have "the best of both worlds: you can go away to meet people at other schools on the weekends, and concentrate on your studies during the week." They love the Five College system (which also includes Amherst, Mount Holyoke, UMass–Amherst, and Hampshire). One student raved, "The Five Colleges provide limitless possibilities. Too good to be true? No way!" All agree that Smithies do have to make some effort ("You give up a social life on a silver platter, but you gain much more in self-confidence and all the other qualities that make you a better/happier person"). The campus is pretty quiet during the week, and imported men abound on the weekends. This issue provoked some sharp responses in our surveys. One student complained, "Men come here expecting to find desperate women—and they do." Clearly, this atmosphere is not for everyone; some who avoid the "meat market" griped that "there is nothing to do, so you are forced to study or vegetate." The housing system (large houses holding small groups of students, each complete with kitchen, fireplace, piano, etc.) received high marks from students, as did the food and the "extremely personable" atmosphere on campus. Many agreed, "Once you get here you realize what a great environment a women's college is, and the huge amount of support you get from the friends you make."

■ **Students** Smithies, in general, tend to be rather liberal politically. So liberal, in fact, that a large number of our respondents described themselves as "leftists." One student observed, "the politically correct atmosphere is so intense that it scares many students into silence or apathy." There is little ethnic diversity, though it is growing from class to class. Some students "frown on the overzealous feminists," but most feel the environment is very accepting of everyone, including the large gay contingent. Smith College is hailed as "a wonderfully affirming atmosphere for women."

SMITH COLLEGE

Admissions

Smith's admissions office considers your high school record (including "strength of courses", etc.) along with your GPA as the most heavily weighed factors in your application. After these, in order of importance, come your letters of recommendation, essays, standardized test scores, extracurriculars and your interview. All applicants must submit either ACT or SAT scores. The "highly recommended" high school course load includes four years of English, three years of math, three years of a foreign language (or two years each of two foreign languages), two years of science, and two years of history. Smith applicants also often apply to Wellesley, Mount Holyoke, Bryn Mawr, Brown, and Vassar.

Financial Aid

The financial aid office at Smith College requires applicants to submit the FAF, their parents' most recent tax return, and a form generated by the school. The financial aid office reports that "Smith College makes every effort to meet fully the documented need, as calculated by the college, of all admitted students. In 1991–92, over 52% of the student body received some form of financial assistance, with an average financial aid package of $15,050." Students here receive a wide variety of loans. Those most commonly taken in 1991–92 were Stafford loans (47% of the students received them; average value: $3,062), PLUS loans (6%; $3,625), and Perkins loans (4%; $1,876).

A note from the Smith College Admissions Office:

"Smith students choose from 1,000 courses in more than 50 areas of study. There are no specific course requirements outside the major; students meet individually with faculty advisers to plan a balanced curriculum.

"Smith programs offer unique opportunities, including the chance to study abroad at another college in the United States and to learn first-hand about the federal government. The Ada Cornstock Scholars Program encourages women beyond the traditional age to return to college and complete their undergraduate studies.

"Smith is located in the scenic Connecticut River valley of western Massachusetts near a number of other outstanding educational institutions. Through the Five College Consortium, Smith, Amherst, Hampshire, and Mount Holyoke colleges and the University of Massachusetts enrich their academic, social, and cultural offerings by means of joint faculty appointments, joint courses, student and faculty exchanges, shared facilities, and other cooperative arrangements."

ADMISSIONS FACTS

Competitiveness Rating:	**89**
% of applicants accepted:	63
% acceptees attending:	44

FRESHMAN PROFILE

Average verbal SAT:	580
Average math SAT:	600
Average ACT:	27
Graduated top 10% of class:	55
Graduated top 25% of class:	91
Graduated top 50% of class:	99

DEADLINES

Early decision/action:	11/15
Early dec./act. notif.:	12/15
Regular admission:	1/15
Regular adm. notif.:	3/30

APPLICANTS ALSO LOOK AT

and often prefer:
Amherst College
Barnard College

and sometimes prefer:
Swarthmore College
Oberlin College
Wellesley College
Wesleyan U.

and rarely prefer:
Mount Holyoke College
Vassar College
Boston College

ADDRESS

Undergraduate Admissions
Northampton, MA 01063
413-585-2500

FINANCIAL FACTS

In-state tuition ($):	15,650
Out-of-state tuition ($):	15,650
Room & board:	6,100
FA application deadline:	2/1
% frosh receiving FA:	55
PT earnings per yr. ($):	660

TYPE OF AID: % of students ($)

FA of some kind:	55 (15,050)
Need-based grants:	52 (9,370)
Merit-based grants:	0
Loans:	NA
Work study:	53 (1,366)
Student rating of FA:	88

CAMPUS LIFE

Quality of Life Rating: **91**

Type of school:	private
Affiliation:	none
Environment:	rural

STUDENT BODY

FT undergrad enrollment:	1,068
% male/% female:	54/46
% out-of-state:	82
% live on campus:	98
% African-American:	1
% Asian:	1
% Caucasian:	97
% Hispanic:	1
% foreign:	2
% transfers:	2

WHAT'S HOT

small lectures
honesty
small classes (overall)
dorm safety
profs accessible
financial aid
profs in class
college radio station
campus appearance
administration (overall)

WHAT'S NOT

rap/hip-hop
diversity
visible gay community
location

ACADEMICS

Academic Rating: **88**

Calendar:	semester
Student/teacher ratio:	10/1
% doctorates:	92
Profs interesting:	97
Profs accessible:	96
Hours of study per day:	3.69

MOST POPULAR MAJORS BY %

English:	18
Political Science:	13
Psychology:	10

% GRADS WHO PURSUE

Law:	9
MBA:	3
Medicine:	8
M.A., etc.:	17

What do students think about Sewanee?

■ **Academics** University of the South receives high grades from its students across the board for academics. "An outstanding liberal arts college" is how one student accurately describes it, but the school is also strong enough in the sciences that 8 percent of its graduates go on to med school. With just over 1000 undergraduates, students get tons of personal attention. "The most incredible thing about Sewanee is its close student-faculty relations" is how one student put it. Said another, "professors often have students over for dinner and are very open to meeting in places outside of the classroom." The administration also receives high grades, reinforcing the feeling that there are very few rifts in the Sewanee community. No wonder students here ranked fourth happiest in the nation! Sewanee students study hard—almost three-and-three-quarter hours a day—and live by a well-enforced honor code. "To cheat, steal, or lie here is like smoking marijuana in a police station—you're bound to be caught," explained one student. "There is a tremendous amount of pressure to be a person of integrity and to perform academically." Top students enter the Order of Gownsmen—a student honor society that helps govern the school. Members are allowed to skip classes without receiving "cut notices" and may dismiss a class if the professor is 15 minutes late. Gownsmen are required to wear gowns to class, a requirement some, but not all, professors enforce.

■ **Life** Simply put, if you love the outdoors, you'll love life at Sewanee. Located in the Tennessee mountains, the place is gorgeous. In the words of one student, "You have to see it to believe it." The setting provides lots of opportunities for kayaking, hiking, and spelunking, and natural science students note that it's like living in a giant lab. The campus is modeled after Oxford, and students fall in love with its staid Gothic architecture. In fact, students ranked their campus the seventh most beautiful in the country. Although "the town of Sewanee is unexciting," said one student, "the campus social life is extremely well-provided for." Sewanee students have a regional reputation as drinkers, and though they hardly deny it, they repeatedly reported that drinking never gets in the way of academics here.

■ **Students** You could pretty much paint a portrait of the students here with just one color: the student body is 97 percent white. Students are predominantly religious, conservative, and Southern, although several reported that a "new hippy movement evolving from Northeast boarding schools is taking over. Grateful Dead stickers on the BMW are in!" As one student said, University of the South "isn't a melting pot, but rather a smelting pot turning out tie-wearing businessmen." Women reported that the men are good-looking, but the men did not return the compliment.

UNIVERSITY OF THE SOUTH

Admissions

The admissions office reports, "We do not have specific cut-off scores or grades. We review the student's high school record. We expect students to challenge themselves with advanced classes—when they are offered. Average unweighted GPA is 3.2 and the middle 50 percent scored between 25–29 (ACT) and 1070–1230 (SAT) in 1991. Every application is reviewed." GPA, curriculum, and standardized test scores are most important; essays, letters of recommendation, and extracurricular activities are also considered. Applicants are required to have completed four years of English, three years of math, and two years each of science, social studies, and a foreign language. Either the SAT or ACT is required. Applicants to University of the South often also apply to Vanderbilt, Rhodes, Washington & Lee, Wake Forest, and University of Virginia.

Financial Aid

The financial aid office at University of the South requires applicants to submit the FAF or the FFS, their parents' most recent tax return, and a form generated by the school. The school reports, "Financial aid funds are allocated to students both of the basis of merit and need in order to provide the maximum number of students with funds to use toward the cost of their Sewanee education. [The school] is committed to the principle that *insofar as possible* no student whose application for admission is accepted will be denied the opportunity to attend because of financial reasons." Sewanee awards merit grants to minority students (2% of the student body; average value: $1,056) and children of the clergy (2%; $1,000); it also awards academic scholarships (6%; $4,789). In addition, students take out Stafford loans (25%; $1,754), Perkins loans (21%; $1,440), and SLS/PLUS loans (6%; $3,588).

A note from the University of the South Admissions Office:

"The University of the South, popularly known as Sewanee, is consistently ranked among the top tier of national liberal arts universities. Sewanee is committed to an academic curriculum which focuses on the liberal arts as the most enlightening and valuable form of undergraduate education. Founded by leaders of the Episcopal Church in 1857, Sewanee continues to be owned by 28 Episcopal dioceses in 12 states. The university is located on a 10,000-acre campus atop Tennessee's Cumberland Plateau between Chattanooga and Nashville. The university has an impressive record of academic achievement—22 Rhodes Scholars and 16 NCAA Postgraduate Scholarship recipients have graduated from Sewanee."

ADMISSIONS FACTS

Competitiveness Rating:	**82**
% of applicants accepted:	69
% acceptees attending:	37

FRESHMAN PROFILE

Average verbal SAT:	558
Average math SAT:	595
Average ACT:	26
Graduated top 10% of class:	44
Graduated top 25% of class:	83
Graduated top 50% of class:	99

DEADLINES

Early decision/action:	11/15
Early dec./act. notif.:	12/15
Regular admission:	2/1
Regular adm. notif.:	4/1

APPLICANTS ALSO LOOK AT

and often prefer:
Washington and Lee U.

and sometimes prefer:
Davidson College
Vanderbilt U.
Wake Forest

and rarely prefer:
Rhodes College
U. Tenessee

ADDRESS

Undergraduate Admissions
University Avenue
Sewanee, TN 37375-4004
615-598-1238

FINANCIAL FACTS

In-state tuition ($):	13,900
Out-of-state tuition ($):	13,900
Room & board:	3,700
FA application deadline:	3/1
% frosh receiving FA:	48
PT earnings per yr. ($):	1000

TYPE OF AID:	% of students ($)
FA of some kind:	41 (12,418)
Need-based grants:	40 (9,800)
Merit-based grants:	10 (2,282)
Loans:	28 (2,261)
Work study:	35 (925)
Student rating of FA:	95

UNIVERSITY OF SOUTH CAROLINA

Columbia, SC

CAMPUS LIFE

Quality of Life Rating:	**75**
Type of school:	public
Affiliation:	none
Environment:	city

STUDENT BODY

FT undergrad enrollment:	13,538
% male/% female:	48/52
% out-of-state:	19
% live on campus:	42
% African-American:	14
% Asian:	2
% Caucasian:	82
% Hispanic:	1
% foreign:	2
% transfers:	20

WHAT'S HOT

dating
diversity
conservative politics
hard liquor

WHAT'S NOT

campus easy to get around
studying hard
profs accessible
doing all the reading
honesty
profs in class
small labs and seminars
small classes (overall)
profs teach intros
overall happiness

ACADEMICS

Academic Rating:	**70**
Calendar:	semester
Student/teacher ratio:	17/1
% doctorates:	79
Profs interesting:	67
Profs accessible:	63
Hours of study per day:	2.52

MOST POPULAR MAJORS

Business
Engineering
Journalism

% GRADS WHO PURSUE

Law:	NA
MBA:	NA
Medicine:	NA
M.A., etc.:	19

What do students think about the U. of South Carolina?

■ **Academics** As one University of South Carolina undergrad wrote, "The most exciting thing about USC is the international programs. People can pay USC tuition and study abroad; it's a great opportunity." International studies (particularly international business), a challenging honors program for qualified students, and an attractive tuition rate are what draw the serious student to USC's Columbia campus. Of course, there are those who come for the good times, but as one student explained, "Everyone thinks this is a party school, and it is, but you can still get some semblance of a college education here." Majors other than international studies receiving the praise of undergrads are those related to business, criminal justice, political science, and history. The English department is very good, and one student reported that the school is taking "big strides toward improving all liberal arts." Math, engineering, and computer science are among the majors that suffer from professors "who just can't teach." As at many inexpensive public institutions, TAs teach more than their fair share of courses, classes can be very large (and important ones difficult to gain admission to), and the bureaucracy can be overwhelming. Hidden beneath all those problems can be a good education, however, at an affordable price. As a transfer from Denison explained, "I'd rather spend that extra tuition money on a new car."

■ **Life** Explained one student, "We may suck on the football field, but we sure know how to tailgate!" USC tailgate parties, which reputedly feature every manner of intoxicant, are notorious throughout the South. Of course, Saturdays mornings in the fall don't account for the entirety of social life here. For the 19 percent of the students who go Greek, there are frequent frat parties; for the rest there's hanging out in dorms, off-campus residences, and the city of Columbia, which students gave average marks. Fewer than half the students live on campus, and some of them pack up and go home every weekend, but with 16,000+ undergraduates there's always plenty of people around at all times. Some would say too many people. Complained one student, "Every year, an even larger number of applicants is accepted, but the university can't accommodate them. Housing, class size, parking, availability of books and other resources (e.g. computers and lab supplies) are a constant and increasing hassle."

■ **Students** Over three quarters of USC's students are native South Carolinians. With African Americans making up 14 percent of this large student body, USC has one of the nation's largest black student bodies. Sadly, race relations could be better: as one black student explained, "In the South, racism is far from over. Not the 'spit in your face,' 'no blacks allowed' kind, but more of a back-stabbing process. Express your ethnicity and you'll receive a lot of negative comments." Students recognize the existence of a considerable gay population, but they too are shunned by the majority. Most students are politically conservative, and a significant portion of the population considers itself religious.

UNIVERSITY OF SOUTH CAROLINA

Columbia, SC

Admissions

At the University of South Carolina, the admissions committee first looks at your GPA and class rank. These are followed (in order of importance) by your standardized test scores, and letters of recommendation. Students must take the SAT (preferred) or the ACT. They must also have completed four units of English, three units of math (including Algebra I & II and Geometry), two units of lab science, three units of social studies and two units of foreign language. Applicants from South Carolina who have performed well during their high school careers but who do not score well on entrance exams should inquire about the "Opportunity Scholars Program," in which some freshmen applicants are selected for a "Provisional Year." Students who apply to U. South Carolina also often apply to Clemson, Furman, UNC and NC State.

Financial Aid

The financial aid office at the University of South Carolina requires applicants to submit an form generated by the school and "any MDE need-analysis form approved by the USDE" (such as the FAF or the FFS). The school awards merit grants on the basis of academic excellence and leadership (13% of the students receive them; average value: $1,309) and athletic skill (4%; $2,638). In 1991–92, 44% of all incoming freshmen received a financial aid award (average value: $3,826). The deadline listed below is a *priority* deadline; FA applications are accepted after the deadline but are given lower priority.

A note from the University of South Carolina Admissions Office:

"Students at the Columbia campus come from various backgrounds, with different career goals and levels of aspiration. The distinctiveness of USC Columbia lies in the conspicuous diversity that nurtures and stimulates students, faculty and constituents. USC Columbia provides equitable access to the full range of its opportunities, resources, and activities.

"USC Columbia seeks to attract curious, energetic people who are committed to learning, who are capable of self-discipline, and who wish to benefit from the variety of experiences provided by a major university with local, national, and international students, faculty and staff. The University strives to educate graduates who are capable of excelling in their chosen fields, who are dedicated to learning throughout their lives, and who are responsible citizens in a complex society requiring difficult ethical and value-related decisions. By offering its students reasonable freedom to select from among the many experiences available, USC Columbia encourages students to seek their full potential."

ADMISSIONS FACTS

Competitiveness Rating:	**71**
% of applicants accepted:	81
% acceptees attending:	43

FRESHMAN PROFILE

Average verbal SAT:	457
Average math SAT:	511
Average ACT:	NA
Graduated top 10% of class:	29
Graduated top 25% of class:	64
Graduated top 50% of class:	93

DEADLINES

Early decision/action:	NA
Early dec./act. notif.:	NA
Regular admission:	rolling
Regular adm. notif.:	rolling

APPLICANTS ALSO LOOK AT

and often prefer:
College of William & Mary
Southern Methodist U.

and sometimes prefer:
Duke U.
Furman University
Clemson U.

and rarely prefer:
Florida State U.
Syracuse U.

ADDRESS

Undergraduate Admissions
Columbia, SC 29208
803-777-7700

FINANCIAL FACTS

In-state tuition ($):	2,560
Out-of-state tuition ($):	6,400
Room & board:	3,000
FA application deadline:	4/15
% frosh receiving FA:	25
PT earnings per yr. ($):	1166

TYPE OF AID: % of students ($)

FA of some kind:	42 (4,411)
Need-based grants:	4 (1,701)
Merit-based grants:	NA
Loans:	39 (3,141)
Work study:	5 (1,658)
Student rating of FA:	72

UNIVERSITY OF SOUTHERN CALIFORNIA

Los Angeles, CA

What do students think about USC?

■ **Academics** "University of Southern California has its pros and cons just like any other college," explained one undergrad, "but our school provides more of everything, campus life, sports, academics, and diversity within the student body and the community." With over 15,000 undergraduate students, USC is in fact large enough to offer "more of everything," although pre-professional and entertainment-oriented education is what it offers best. Business and management majors claim almost one third of the students here and are excellent; also top-flight are departments in film (Steven Spielberg graduated from USC), television, drama, and journalism. Engineering is strong, and in more strictly academic pursuits, the social sciences are considered good, the liberal arts are not. In most every case, professors are unusually accessible for those at a large university. Explained one student, "it is very easy to visit teachers, but students are apathetic and don't take advantage of the opportunity." Highly motivated students may choose to pursue the Thematic Option, a challenging, prestigious honors program that fulfills general education requirements with an interdisciplinary curriculum stressing the interrelations among different academic fields.

■ **Life** USC is located in a section of Los Angeles described by several students as a "high-crime area." Students are quick to add, "Even though we live in the ghetto, our campus is extremely safe," and one student defended the location as "central to everything in Los Angeles." However, most students choose to seek their entertainment on-campus. Fraternities play a huge role in the USC social scene, partly because the surrounding area is perceived as inhospitable, and partly because USC attracts the kind of students that loves fraternity parties. Football is the other central component of life at USC, so popular that it almost single-handedly inspires the school spirit for which the university is famous. When students do leave campus, they usually head for one of the many gorgeous beaches that are within a half-hour's drive of the campus. Students gave the dormitories and campus beauty low grades.

■ **Students** Given the popularity of its arts and business departments, one would expect USC's student body to be an odd mix aesthetes and careerists. USC's arts programs are geared toward Hollywood mainstream entertainment, however, and so 'preprofessional' describes the entire student body fairly accurately. Wealthy students are ubiquitous; one student wrote that "our reputation as the 'University of Spoiled Children' and the 'University of Special Connections' is very fitting." USC has a large minority population: Asians and Hispanics are the best-represented groups, and there is also a sizeable black population. Students reported that relations between ethnic groups are not good. Wrote one student, "The prejudice thing on this campus is really sad—it's a two-way street and it looks like the road is going to be open for a lot longer. Aside from that, our school is the best."

UNIVERSITY OF SOUTHERN CALIFORNIA

Los Angeles, CA

Admissions

According to its undergraduate catalog, the prime factors given consideration for admission to USC are "an applicant's previous academic success and the quality of all materials presented. To assure diversity in the composition of the student body, other considerations may include outstanding talent and abilities, extracurricular activities, and letters of recommendation." The various schools and departments at USC have their own individual requirements for admission, and some have separate deadlines as well. General academic requirements include a high school record comprised of "a minimum of 16 year-long courses in any combination of the following...: 13 year-long courses in English, humanities, mathematics, natural sciences, social sciences, and foreign languages; [and] three additional year-long courses" in the previously mentioned areas, or in the arts, journalism, or computer science. The admissions committee will consider variations from the recommended program, depending on the individual's "promise of academic success and the quality of the total record." All applicants must submit SAT or ACT scores, and are strongly encouraged to take three Achievement tests, one of them being English composition.

Financial Aid

Financial aid applicants to USC must complete the SAAC (either the CSS or the ACT form—out-of-state residents must complete the FAF or FFS) and a form generated by USC's financial aid office. In addition, all applicants must submit copies of their own and their parents' tax returns. Scholarships available include those for merit in performing arts, academics and athletics; minority and alumni scholarships are also offered. To ensure an offer of assistance being sent before May 1, materials should be submitted by February 15.

A note from the University of Southern California Admissions Office:

"USC's faculty have won over 500 national and international awards for research and teaching excellence. But in spite of USC's reputation as a major research institution, USC professors maintain an important balance between research activity and teaching undergraduate students. Full-time professors teach all 250 of the General Education courses offered by the College of Letters Arts and Sciences, and even among USC's distinguished professional schools it would be unusual for a class to be conducted by a teaching assistant. The average class size is 26, and 75% of all the classes have fewer than 30 students. Only 10 classes have more than 250 in the main lectures. Freshman Seminars (limited to 15 students each) , Freshman Honors Research, and USC's Thematic Option provide unusual opportunities for bright, talented and highly motivated students. Extensive opportunities exist for undergraduate students to become involved in research with nationally and internationally acclaimed faculty."

ADMISSIONS FACTS

Competitiveness Rating:	**76**
% of applicants accepted:	70
% acceptees attending:	29

FRESHMAN PROFILE

Average verbal SAT:	513*
Average math SAT:	580*
Average ACT:	NA
Graduated top 10% of class:	40
Graduated top 25% of class:	75
Graduated top 50% of class:	85

DEADLINES

Early decision/action:	NA
Early dec./act. notif.:	NA
Regular admission:	3/1
Regular adm. notif.:	rolling

APPLICANTS ALSO LOOK AT

and often prefer:
UC Los Angeles

and sometimes prefer:
Loyola Marymount U.
Georgetown U.
U. Washington
U. Texas
Emory U.

and rarely prefer:
UC Riverside
U. Arizona

Address

Undergraduate Admissions
University Park
Los Angeles, CA 90089-0911
213-740-6753

FINANCIAL FACTS

In-state tuition ($):	14,112
Out-of-state tuition ($):	14,112
Room & board:	5,500
FA application deadline:	2/15
% frosh receiving FA:	61
PT earnings per yr. ($):	NA

TYPE OF AID: % of students ($)

FA of some kind:	60 (NA)
Need-based grants:	NA
Merit-based grants:	NA
Loans:	NA
Work study:	NA
Student rating of FA:	74

SOUTHERN METHODIST UNIVERSITY

Dallas, TX

What do students think about SMU?

■ **Academics** With just over 5,000 full-time undergrads, SMU offers many of the benefits of a small college as well as the diversity of a university. There is a clear preference among students for pre-professional training—one quarter of the students pursue business and management degrees—but the school is large enough to accommodate excellent liberal arts and fine arts departments also. Many students lauded the Meadows School of the Arts and noted that it is a moving force in the Dallas art community. Yet the school is small enough to give students that personal touch—"Professors and administrators are interested in the students" is how one student put it. You won't have to go it on your own here: as one respondent reported, "The Advising Center does a great job helping you decide upon a major and then aiding in determining class schedules." Still, most students do not perceive SMU as a major academic force. One complained, "The faculty, classes, and many activities open to students make SMU a good institution, but if the academic standards were raised, it could be great!" Most blame the situation on their classmates (see "Students," below).

■ **Life** Even though SMU is located in a major metropolitan area, campus life here is dominated by fraternities and the vast array of extracurricular activities in which students participate. At only seven of the schools we surveyed are frats more popular. As for extracurriculars, one student reported, "We are told as freshmen that if you are not involved in at least one organization, you are basically nonexistent at SMU and you won't grow." Said another, "I recommend that everyone try to be involved in at least one student group. With over 150 to chose from, there is something for everyone." Be prepared to feel alienated here if you don't like group activities like frat parties and student government meetings. When they do venture off-campus, students enjoy the benefits of being in Dallas.

■ **Students** It's no secret that SMU students are stereotypically rich, white, conservative, and elitist. The school has tried to remedy its public relations problem by recruiting more middle-class and minority students, but, as one student explained, "The majority of students who attend SMU come here because of the stereotype." Said another bluntly, "If you're looking for Polo and Laura Ashley country, come to SMU." Still, the university's efforts haven't been entirely in vain, as one black senior noted: "SMU has gotten better over the past few years as far as admitting and recruiting minorities. I was the only black (or minority, for that matter) in over 95 percent of all classes taken at SMU. However, this semester, I have seen and spoken with more minorities than all previous semesters. I felt more comfortable this semester than any before. Better late than never!" Several Easterners, apparently unused to having complete strangers smile and say "hi" to them, noted their surprise at how gracious their classmates were.

SOUTHERN METHODIST UNIVERSITY

Dallas, TX

Admissions

Southern Methodist U. states that all factors in the application are treated equally—"No one item is given precedent over another. The entire application package is considered for acceptance at Southern Methodist University. Though an interview is optional, it is always recommended." The admissions committee requires submission of essays, letters of recommendation, high school transcript and GPA, and either SAT or ACT scores. Applicants to SMU also often apply to Baylor, Emory, Texas Christian University, Tulane, USC, UT Austin, and Vanderbilt.

Financial Aid

The financial aid office at SMU requires applicants to submit the FFS and a form generated by the school. The school reports that "SMU has historically met the demonstrated need of every admitted student through need-based aid, academic scholarships, performance scholarships, and student employment, as well as through traditional loans and grants." In 1991–92, 29% of the students received Stafford loans with an average value of $3,790; SMU also provides a long-term institutional loan; in 1991–92, 15% of the students took one (avg. value: $7,350). The school reports, "The University's Family Assistance Loan Program (FAL) provides help for families that do not meet criteria for state or federal aid. For those who qualify, SMU offers up to $15,000 at 7% interest with eight years to repay payments."

A note from the Southern Methodist University Admissions Office:

"Southern Methodist University is a private, coeducational university five miles north of the heart of Dallas, situated on a park-like campus with tree-lined streets. Founded in 1911 by what today is the United Methodist Church, the University welcomes students of every religion, race, ethnic origin, and economic background and furthermore meets the demonstrated financial need of qualified students.

"SMU's programs are characterized by small classes and a low student/faculty ratio of 14:1. The 5,300 undergraduates are taught by faculty members, not graduate assistants. The opportunities available to undergraduates in four schools—Dedman College, the school of humanities and sciences; the Meadows School of the Arts; the Edwin L. Cox School of Business; and the School of Engineering and Applied Science—are enhanced by the resources, facilities, and faculty of the University's graduate and professional programs (in communication, the arts, engineering, the humanities and sciences, business, theology, and law)."

ADMISSIONS FACTS

Competitiveness Rating:	**79**
% of applicants accepted:	63
% acceptees attending:	34

FRESHMAN PROFILE

Average verbal SAT:	507
Average math SAT:	573
Average ACT:	NA
Graduated top 10% of class:	40
Graduated top 25% of class:	73
Graduated top 50% of class:	95

DEADLINES

Early decision/action:	11/1
Early dec./act. notif.:	NA
Regular admission:	4/1
Regular adm. notif.:	rolling

APPLICANTS ALSO LOOK AT

and often prefer:
Georgetown U.
Northwestern U.

and sometimes prefer:
Rhodes College
U. Texas/Austin
Tulane University
Emory U.

and rarely prefer:
Texas Christian U.
Pepperdine U.
Baylor U.

ADDRESS

Undergraduate Admissions
Dallas, TX 75275
214-692-2058

FINANCIAL FACTS

In-state tuition ($):	9,440
Out-of-state tuition ($):	9,440
Room & board:	4,150
FA application deadline:	3/15
% frosh receiving FA:	60
PT earnings per yr. ($):	NA

TYPE OF AID: % of students ($)

FA of some kind:	53 (11,450)
Need-based grants:	53 (3,169)
Merit-based grants:	30 (2,599)
Loans:	53 (2,436)
Work study:	35 (704)
Student rating of FA:	91

SOUTHWESTERN UNIVERSITY

Georgetown, TX

CAMPUS LIFE

Quality of Life Rating: **81**

Type of school:	private
Affiliation:	Methodist
Environment:	suburban

STUDENT BODY

FT undergrad enrollment:	1,210
% male/% female:	45/55
% out-of-state:	10
% live on campus:	74
% African-American:	3
% Asian:	4
% Caucasian:	84
% Hispanic:	8
% foreign:	2
% transfers:	2

WHAT'S HOT

honesty
profs accessible
profs in class
doing all the reading
caring about politics
cost of living
religious clubs
attending all classes
small classes (overall)
administration (overall)
profs teach intros

WHAT'S NOT

college radio station
marijuana
location

ACADEMICS

Academic Rating: **85**

Calendar:	semester
Student/teacher ratio:	13/1
% doctorates:	91
Profs interesting:	89
Profs accessible:	92
Hours of study per day:	3.45

MOST POPULAR MAJORS BY %

Business:	13
Psychology:	12
Biology:	8

% GRADS WHO PURSUE

Law:	8
MBA:	10
Medicine:	5
M.A., etc.:	22

What do students think about Southwestern University?

■ **Academics** Southwestern students often look over their shoulders at nearby UT Austin. Sniped one, "If you want everything but academics, go to the University of Texas; otherwise, come here." Others who praised SU felt compelled to tell us how much *better* it is than UT. This rivalry must be rooted entirely in geography, because the two schools are comparable in terms of location and little else. UT Austin is a huge, research-oriented public university; Southwestern, conversely, is a small, liberal arts private school where professors make teaching their top priority. Many students pursue career-track majors—business and management claims almost one quarter of the students, and education and engineering are both popular— but a solid core curriculum requires all students to acquire a solid liberal arts background. Students praised the school's "excellent studies abroad pro- grams" (about 30 percent spend time overseas) and the Brown Symposium, a three-day series of seminars during spring semester (during which classes are suspended and scholars from around the world come to deliver lectures and lead discussions). But they saved their greatest praise for the teachers, whom they ranked among the top 15 percent in the nation. One wrote that "SU professors do not fit the general Southern college professor stereotype. They are extremely liberal and open-minded. They love to shock their stu- dents who, for the most part, are much more conservative." Another student reported that "professors often participate on intramural teams and come to parties." The end result is "a very supportive environment."

■ **Life** SU is located in Georgetown, a small town that "closes at 11 p.m. on weekends." Its pace may not be for everyone: complained one student, "Southwestern challenges the student in every possible area, especially when it comes to finding something to do on weekends." However, as one classmate countered, "Georgetown is not 'exciting' but it does have things to look at, and Austin nearby provides anything a student would like to do." Austin is 20 minutes away by car and is a great college town. For some, the location is ideal, "close enough to Austin, yet far enough away that the city isn't a constant distraction." Most students, however, rated Georgetown "no fun." Campus social life centers around frats and sororities, but unlike many campuses at which frats are the "only game in town," excessive drinking is not a big problem here.

■ **Students** SU has a sizeable minority population made up mostly of His- panic students. Black students complained that a scarcity of black class- mates makes social life difficult. "But," said one, "if you can stand having no social life and enjoy spending eight hours a day in the computer lab, then SU is for you. The people are nice enough and many of the professors are easygoing." Students are politically in the middle of the road, which makes them liberal by Texas standards. Most find SU to be a "friendly campus community" although a considerable minority felt their classmates were "cliquish." Said one Houston native, "There is a small-town atmosphere that is almost suffocating for those of us who are from the city."

SOUTHWESTERN UNIVERSITY

Admissions

The admissions office reports that it uses "no cut-offs or formulas. We consider each candidate on his or her own merits. Each student is reviewed by the same process. We are always looking for a 'balanced' class: quality, geographic distribution, ethnicity, male/female, alumni ties and so on; however, NO student will be admitted we do not believe is qualified." Admissions officers here look first at your high school curriculum/GPA and standardized test scores; next, they consider your personal interview, essays, letters of recommendation, and extracurricular activities. A minimum of 16 academic credits are recommended ("Most submit more!") and must include four years of English, three years each of math, science, foreign language, and social studies/history. Applicants to Southwestern most often also apply to UTexas-Austin, Texas A & M, Trinity U., Austin College, SMU, Baylor, TCU, and Rice.

Financial Aid

The financial aid office at Southwestern University requires applicants to submit the FAF. The FA office reports that its "emphasis is on providing need-based assistance," but nearly one third of the students receive merit grants awarded on the basis of academic merit and/or "other competitive" qualities. Athletic scholarships were available until recently but no longer are. In 1990–91, Southwestern students received Stafford loans (36% of the students; average value: $2,551), Perkins loans (12.5%; $1,834), and PLUS loans (4%; $3,254).

A note from the Southwestern University Admissions Office:

"Southwestern University is a selective, undergraduate liberal arts and sciences university affiliated with the United Methodist Church. With an endowment of approximately $150 million and a student body of 1,200, our endowment per student is one of the highest in the nation. Southwestern emphasizes an education to prepare persons for leadership in the global community through many study-abroad options and a university-wide commitment to internationalization of the curriculum."

ADMISSIONS FACTS

Competitiveness Rating:	**83**
% of applicants accepted:	66
% acceptees attending:	42

FRESHMAN PROFILE

Average verbal SAT:	533
Average math SAT:	581
Average ACT:	25
Graduated top 10% of class:	51
Graduated top 25% of class:	85
Graduated top 50% of class:	99

DEADLINES

Early decision/action:	11/1
Early dec./act. notif.:	12/1
Regular admission:	2/15
Regular adm. notif.:	3/31

APPLICANTS ALSO LOOK AT

and often prefer:
U. Texas/Austin
Baylor U.
Rice U.

and sometimes prefer:
Texas Christian U.

and rarely prefer:
Texas A&M U.
Austin College
Trinity University

ADDRESS

Undergraduate Admissions
University at Maple
Georgetown, TX 78626
800-252-3166

FINANCIAL FACTS

In-state tuition ($):	9,400
Out-of-state tuition ($):	9,400
Room & board:	4,081
FA application deadline:	3/15
% frosh receiving FA:	66
PT earnings per yr. ($):	1200

TYPE OF AID: % of students ($)

FA of some kind:	66 (NA)
Need-based grants:	53 (3,169)
Merit-based grants:	30 (2,599)
Loans:	53 (2,436)
Work study:	35 (704)
Student rating of FA:	91

SPELMAN COLLEGE

Atlanta, GA

What do students think about Spelman College?

■ **Academics** Spelman College is one of only two remaining all-female black colleges in the country. It is also, arguably, becoming the nation's pre-eminent black institution: always well regarded, Spelman received a big boost in both its reputation and its ability to serve its students when Bill Cosby donated $20 million to the school several years ago (Spelman, not coincidentally, is the model for Hillman College in the Cosby-produced series *A Different World*). Women who choose Spelman do so for the opportunity to be surrounded by others like themselves: black, bright, and highly motivated. Explained one, "Spelman College is a great school for up-and-coming African-American females. The school gives us the opportunity to relate our life experiences to the outside world. Here, we learn to express ourselves and to stand up for what we believe in." Pre-professional majors—computer science, pre-med, pre-law, and pre-business—are most popular with Spelman women, but all students receive a well-rounded education in communication skills, science, math, social science, fine arts, and literature because of a rigorous core curriculum (which claims about one third of the credits necessary for graduation). Students reported that classes were small and that professors are reasonably accessible outside of class; their main complaint concerned the library, which they consider too small and not up-to-date. Spelman students can, and do, take courses at all-male Morehouse College across the street.

■ **Life** Both because Morehouse is across the street and because of the school's location in a major urban area, Spelman women have little trouble finding active social lives; in fact, Spelman women are among the most active daters in the country. Greek life plays a major part in the Spelman social scene (even though only 15 percent of the students actually pledge a sorority); Greek parties at Spelman and Morehouse are generally big events. Also popular are extracurricular clubs, particularly community service and leadership organizations. Sports are not so popular, despite the fact that several of Spelman's teams (most notably volleyball and tennis) are quite good. Students complain that the athletic facilities are poor, which might explain the lack of interest in intramural sports. Like most students in Atlanta, Spelmanites love their hometown, both for the cultural and social opportunities it provides them. Summed up one woman: "I would recommend Spelman College to any young lady who wants to get the full experience of college life."

■ **Students** The typical Spelman student is black, female, and extremely dedicated to career pursuits. She is also religious (church services are a regular part of most students' lives), socially conservative (drug use and homosexuality are generally frowned upon), and politically liberal. Spelmanites have a nasty reputation for snobbishness, one that was confirmed by one of our respondents: "Spelman takes a while to get used to. The students are very 'cliquish,' and if you don't fit into one of those cliques, you may get lonely."

SPELMAN COLLEGE

Atlanta, GA

Admissions

From Spelman's undergraduate catalog: "Spelman values diversity among its student body and encourages applications from qualified students who come from a wide variety of cultural and social-economic backgrounds. In selecting students for admission, the College considers the following factors: high school records, rank in class, SAT or ACT scores, the student's personal statement (essay), letters of recommendation (especially those from school personnel), and evidence of special talent, leadership, or involvement in areas of social concern. Each application is given careful consideration and the admission decision is never made solely on the basis of a single factor." The preferred high school record includes at least a "C" average, with the applicant having taken four units of English, two units of science (including at least one lab science), two units of mathematics (including at least one algebra), and two other units in foreign language, literature, social science, or science. In addition, all applicants must submit SAT or ACT scores. In special cases, a personal interview may be required.

Financial Aid

Financial aid applicants to Spelman College must complete the FAF and a form generated by Spelman's financial aid office. Merit scholarships at Spelman are awarded based on "character, scholastic record, and seriousness of purpose." Scholarships are also available for artistic talent, academic merit, residency, and religious affiliation. Undergrads who plan to teach in an accredited Georgia public school after graduation may receive awards from the Teacher Training program. Georgia residents may be able to receive aid from the Georgia Tuition Grant Program.

Excerpted from Spelman College promotional materials:

"As an outstanding historically black college for women, Spelman strives for academic excellence in liberal education. This predominantly residential private college provides students with an academic climate conducive to the full development of their intellectual and leadership potential. The College is a member of the Atlanta University Center consortium, and Spelman students enjoy the benefits of a small college while having access to the resources of the other five participating institutions.

"The purpose extends beyond intellectual development and professional career preparation of students. It seeks to develop the total person. The College provides an academic and social environment which strengthens those qualities that enable women to be self-confident as well as culturally and spiritually enriched. This environment attempts to instill in students both an appreciation for the multicultural communities of the world and a sense of responsibility for bringing about positive change in those communities."

ADMISSIONS FACTS

Competitiveness Rating: 84
% of applicants accepted: 34
% acceptees attending: 36

FRESHMAN PROFILE
Average verbal SAT: 480
Average math SAT: 510
Average ACT: 23
Graduated top 10% of class: 49
Graduated top 25% of class: 80
Graduated top 50% of class: 97

DEADLINES
Early decision/action: 11/15
Early dec./act. notif.: 12/15
Regular admission: 2/1
Regular adm. notif.: 3/1

APPLICANTS ALSO LOOK AT
and often prefer:
Georgia Tech
and sometimes prefer:
Clark College
U. Maryland–College Park
Emory U.
U. Georgia
Hampton College
Howard College

ADDRESS
Undergraduate Admissions
350 Spelman Lane S. W.
Atlanta, GA 30314-4399
404-681-3643

FINANCIAL FACTS
In-state tuition ($): 5,800
Out-of-state tuition ($): 5,800
Room & board: 4,720
FA application deadline: 4/1
% frosh receiving FA: NA
PT earnings per yr. ($): NA

TYPE OF AID: % of students ($)
FA of some kind: 83 (NA)
Need-based grants: NA
Merit-based grants: NA
Loans: NA
Work study: NA
Student rating of FA: NA

STANFORD UNIVERSITY

CAMPUS LIFE

Quality of Life Rating:	**88**
Type of school:	private
Affiliation:	none
Environment:	city

STUDENT BODY

FT undergrad enrollment:	6,555
% male/% female:	55/45
% out-of-state:	63
% live on campus:	91
% African-American:	8
% Asian:	16
% Caucasian:	59
% Hispanic:	10
% foreign:	3
% transfers:	NA

WHAT'S HOT

interaction among students
registration
diversity
gay community accepted
honest students
overall happiness
intercollegiate sports
college theater
town-gown relations
library
campus appearance
intramural sports

WHAT'S NOT

dating
marijuana

ACADEMICS

Academic Rating:	**92**
Calendar:	quarters
Student/teacher ratio:	9/1
% doctorates:	99
Profs interesting:	78
Profs accessible:	79
Hours of study per day:	3.51

MOST POPULAR MAJORS BY %

Letters/Literature:	35
Social Sciences:	21
Life Sciences:	18

% GRADS WHO PURSUE

Law:	7
MBA:	2
Medicine:	10
M.A., etc.:	23

What do students think about Stanford University?

■ **Academics** Stanford University combines top-flight academics with things no Ivy League school has yet attained: an "almost carefree" atmosphere, nationally ranked athletics, and nearly constant California sunshine. One of the finest schools in the nation—wrote one area counselor, "Few get in: those who do work hard and love it"—Stanford boasts "exceptionally strong academic programs across the board. Engineering and all the physical sciences are nationally renowned; the liberal arts are most popular, however, and are also excellent. All students must complete a wide variety of distribution requirements, but these and all courses pass by quickly because of the quarterly academic schedule. Students report that they feel little of the academic pressure noted by students at most other top-notch schools. As one student explained, the large number of pass/no-credit options and the predominantly laid-back attitudes of the student body encourages students "to be self-motivated. Competitiveness is not apparent." One negative: as at many prestigious universities, a considerable number of undergrads are disappointed to discover that other concerns—graduate students, research, publishing—interest some professors more than do undergraduate students.

■ **Life** One student called Stanford "the undiscovered utopia," and most of her classmates would concur. Students reported themselves very happy with the school. The sprawling, beautiful campus received high ratings; its one drawback may be that it is too large to negotiate on foot. ("Don't come here if you don't like to bike!") Those from out of state especially raved about the weather: "It's nice that the entire state seems to be set at room temperature all winter," wrote one. Students have many options as far as housing; dorms, "theme houses," (where students sharing majors, ethnic backgrounds, etc. reside together), and off-campus housing are all popular. Socially, there is some cliquishness, perhaps due to Stanford's residential sprawl. Students complained, "People here meet about as freely as prisoners. All you do is spend time with the people in your dorm, which is fun but gets old." Dating is very uncommon on campus. One student griped, "There is no explanation for this, and everybody wants it to change, but there is no scamming, dating, hooking up or sex at Stanford." Another remarked, "There's more sexual activity in a monastery." Sports, both intercollegiate and intramural, are popular diversions, as are the many extracurricular opportunities.

■ **Students** With a 41 percent minority population, Stanford attracts a truly diverse student body. Students report that interaction between groups is friendly and frequent, and that there is little pressure to conform to a norm. One student summed up: "When I came to Stanford, I was a bit disappointed. The professors are not *the* best. The classes are not *the* best. What is best are the students, intellectual and caring, who truly want the most out of their lives."

STANFORD UNIVERSITY

Admissions

Stanford's guidelines for admission state, "The primary criterion for admission is academic excellence: a compound of exceptional capacity, scholastic performance in relation to available opportunities, and promise of intellectual growth...a secondary criterion is personal achievement outside the classroom in a range of pursuits including academic activities, the creative and performing arts, community service and leadership, athletics and other extracurricular areas." Stanford considers (in rough order of importance) your scholastic performance (both GPA and course selection), standardized tests, extracurriculars, personal statement, and letters of recommendation. "A solid secondary school program is recommended, including the strongest possible training in English, mathematics, one foreign language, and courses in science and social studies." Since applicants come from varied backgrounds, particular attention is paid to "how well students have used available resources." SAT or ACT scores are required; three Achievements are strongly recommended.

Financial Aid

The financial aid office at Stanford University requires applicants to submit the FAF and a form generated by the school. The school reports, "Stanford is committed to meeting the computed financial need of its undergraduate students. The decision to admit a student, except in the case of foreign students, is made without regard to whether the student may require financial aid." The school also writes: "To qualify for scholarship aid, undergraduate students are expected to accept up to approximately 25% of their cost of attendance in self-help (long-term loan and term-time job)."

A note from the Stanford University Admissions Office:

"The Leland Stanford Jr. University was founded in 1885 by Senator and Mrs. Leland Stanford, who established the institution in memory of their only child, Leland Jr., who died at an age when many young people are planning a college education. The Stanfords designed the University to incorporate the goals of humanism, practicality, and excellence. They patterned the institution after the great European universities rather than the colleges of the eastern United States of the time. They intended that students receive a broad liberal education that would be useful—a concept maintained at Stanford today.

"Stanford is adjacent to Palo Alto and 30 miles south of San Francisco. The Pacific Ocean is 20 miles to the west; the Monterey peninsula is 75 miles to the south. The Sierra Nevada Mountains, 160 miles away and the site of several national parks, are a popular resort area for camping, hiking, and skiing."

ADMISSIONS FACTS

Competitiveness Rating:	**100**
% of applicants accepted:	22
% acceptees attending:	56

FRESHMAN PROFILE

Average verbal SAT:	657*
Average math SAT:	710*
Average ACT:	31*
Graduated top 10% of class:	90
Graduated top 25% of class:	98
Graduated top 50% of class:	100

DEADLINES

Early decision/action:	NA
Early dec./act. notif.:	NA
Regular admission:	12/15
Regular adm. notif.:	4/1

APPLICANTS ALSO LOOK AT

and sometimes prefer:
Harvard/Radcliffe College
MIT
Caltech

and rarely prefer:
Duke U.
U. Virginia
Northwestern U.
U. Southern Calif.

ADDRESS

Undergraduate Admissions
Stanford, CA 94305-3005
415-723-2091

FINANCIAL FACTS

In-state tuition ($):	15,102
Out-of-state tuition ($):	15,102
Room & board:	6,160
FA application deadline:	2/1
% frosh receiving FA:	61
PT earnings per yr. ($):	1940

TYPE OF AID: % of students ($)

FA of some kind:	62 (11,000)
Need-based grants:	44 (NA)
Merit-based grants:	NA
Loans:	46 (2,444)
Work study:	NA
Student rating of FA:	77

STEVENS INSTITUTE OF TECHNOLOGY

Hoboken, NJ

What do students think about the Stevens Institute?

■ **Academics** How often do you hear a technological institute described as "caring"? Not one, but two area college counselors used that word to describe the Stevens Institute of Technology. That's because the school has initiated programs intended to relieve the stress common to students at all engineering schools. Extensive tutoring is available to students who fall below the class average, and smaller review sessions are part of all large lecture courses. All courses taken by freshmen and sophomores are mandatory, taking the pressure out of schedule-making. Finally, students who feel the workload is too great to complete in four years may continue to take courses toward their degrees for a fifth year, at no additional cost. The quality of academics at Stevens are, according to another area counselor, "solid, nearly as good as those at Rensselaer." Students agree that "you are not allowed to sleep or have fun, but the education is the best!" Electrical, computer, mechanical and civil engineering are both excellent and popular with the students; physics and management are among the other popular majors. Students gave their professors low marks as teachers, mainly because "most don't speak English too well," but the overwhelming majority felt that they were getting a good education nonetheless. Many students did feel that the administration could stand improvement, however, complaining that it was large and obtrusive ("There's an entire floor of the administration building for every hundred students"), yet also ineffective (the registrar, bursar, and library system all received extremely low grades). All these complaints, however, pale beside Stevens's ability to serve the student body's chief goals, summed up by the student who wrote, "this school is hard, but when I graduate I will be set."

■ **Life** Explained one student: "The bottom line is this: if you come here for the education, you made the right choice. If you come here for social life, athletics, or extracurricular activities, I have a bridge I'd like to sell you." Students complain that the workload and the extremely unfavorable male-female ratio (three to one—"Stevens needs a LOT more females," wrote one man) kill any chances students here might have for a normal social life. For those who can make leisure time, New York City is a short commuter train ride away. Hoboken has some nice restaurants and clubs, but students go to New York when they really want to blow off steam. The campus is pleasant, "aesthetically pleasing as well as conveniently situated alongside the Hudson, and, we have the *best* view of New York."

■ **Students** Only three fifths of Stevens's student body is white. Asians make up a sizeable part of the minority population, and Hispanics are also well represented. One student wrote that "the vast diversity among the students provides for interesting interactions." Students are extremely goal-oriented and single-minded in pursuit of their degrees.

STEVENS INSTITUTE OF TECHNOLOGY

Hoboken, NJ

Admissions

All applicants to Stevens Institute of Technology must take the SAT or ACT. Accelerated Pre-Med or Pre-Dentistry students must take the SAT and three Achievements: English, Math I or II, and either Biology or Chemistry. The recommended high school curriculum varies for each area of study. In general, four years of English, three years of mathematics, and one year of science are required. Computer Science and engineering prospects should have an additional year of math, and two sciences (1 chemistry, 1 physics). Science and Mathematics applicants, and accelerated Pre-Med or Dentistry applicants should have three years of science (biology, chemistry, physics) and an additional year of mathematics. Interview required for most applicants. Additional plusses are AP courses, and knowledge of computer language for Computer Science applicants.

Financial Aid

Financial aid applicants to the Stevens Institute of Technology must complete the FAF. The Institute awards fellowships with values ranging from $3,000 to $10,000. In '91–'92, 6% of all undergrads received one (the average value was $5,000). SIT awards scholarships for academic merit and leadership. In addition to Stafford loans (recommended to 60% of FA applicants), SIT recommends PLUS, PLATO, and ECC Credit Line loans. Priority date for consideration is February 1.

Excerpted from Stevens Institute of Technology promotional materials:

"To be able to dream, design, and discover, you must find a college with an outstanding reputation that is open to new ideas and your unique vision. You must think about issues in choosing your school that some of your friends will not even consider.

"Take a close look at Stevens Institute of Technology. We have an exceptional tradition of educating life long creators and inventors, who devote their careers to making the potential possible. Maybe you're one of us."

ADMISSIONS FACTS

Competitiveness Rating:	**85**
% of applicants accepted:	75
% acceptees attending:	30

FRESHMAN PROFILE

Average verbal SAT:	540
Average math SAT:	665
Average ACT:	NA
Graduated top 10% of class:	50
Graduated top 25% of class:	95
Graduated top 50% of class:	100

DEADLINES

Early decision/action:	NA
Early dec./act. notif.:	NA
Regular admission:	3/1
Regular adm. notif.:	rolling

APPLICANTS ALSO LOOK AT

and often prefer:
RPI

and sometimes prefer:
Carnegie Mellon U.

and rarely prefer:
Rutgers U./Rutgers College
New Jersey Tech

ADDRESS

Undergraduate Admissions
Castle Point on the Hudson
Hoboken, NJ 07030
201-420-5194

FINANCIAL FACTS

In-state tuition ($):	14,800
Out-of-state tuition ($):	14,800
Room & board:	4,900
FA application deadline:	3/1
% frosh receiving FA:	72
PT earnings per yr. ($):	2000

TYPE OF AID: % of students ($)

FA of some kind:	75 (NA)
Need-based grants:	77 (6,250)
Merit-based grants:	NA
Loans:	72 (4,200)
Work study:	13 (1,080)
Student rating of FA:	76

STATE UNIVERSITY OF NEW YORK AT ALBANY

Albany, NY

CAMPUS LIFE

Quality of Life Rating:	**65**
Type of school:	public
Affiliation:	none
Environment:	city

STUDENT BODY

FT undergrad enrollment:	10,898
% male/% female:	51/49
% out-of-state:	4
% live on campus:	60
% African-American:	8
% Asian:	4
% Caucasian:	65
% Hispanic:	5
% foreign:	1
% transfers:	10

WHAT'S HOT

marijuana
rap/hip-hop
hard liquor
Grateful Dead

WHAT'S NOT

campus appearance
small lectures
small labs and seminars
small classes (overall)
registration
food
financial aid
intercollegiate sports
administration (overall)

ACADEMICS

Academic Rating:	**74**
Calendar:	semester
Student/teacher ratio:	18/1
% doctorates:	98
Profs interesting:	69
Profs accessible:	67
Hours of study per day:	2.65

MOST POPULAR MAJORS BY %

Social Sciences:	27
Business & Management:	16
Letters/Literature:	16

% GRADS WHO PURSUE

Law:	NA
MBA:	NA
Medicine:	NA
M.A., etc.:	45

What do students think about SUNY Albany?

■ **Academics** For years SUNY Albany has been a rising star in the SUNY system. The school unquestionably has a strong business department, while the psychology and English departments continue to attract students from all over the state. Government and political science students benefit from the school's location in the state capital. And, students in some of the less-popular majors (such as women's studies and philosophy) noted that they get much more individual attention than they ever expected at this big school. Unfortunately, a state budget crisis threatens to turn back, or at least halt, the progress SUNY Albany has made in recent years. Wrote one student, "the state budget crisis has caused tuition increases and cutbacks in services. I have specifically felt these cuts because my computer course for my social sciences minor has been cancelled and there have been reductions in my major department, geography, and planning." Complaints that classes are over-enrolled or unavailable are common, and drop/add procedures and registration are reportedly nightmarish. Wrote one student, "When it comes time to get on line to register, I feel like a Soviet citizen waiting for toilet paper."

■ **Life** SUNY Albany undergrads complain that their classmates lack school spirit. One lamented that "it's a school of 16,000+, but on a good day there might be 2,000 people at a football game." Not surprisingly, students reported that events organized on campus are sparsely attended: "Most socializing at Albany takes place off-campus," wrote one. Most students fall into the "party away your free time" rut, leading one to suggest that "if you don't drink or do drugs, you might find Albany pretty boring." Fraternities and sororities are very popular, and there are plenty of campus clubs and organizations in existence, even if few students take advantage of them. The campus itself is the fifth least attractive of those we canvassed. "It looks like a prison," wrote one student; another tried to put a positive spin on the issue, cheerfully proclaiming that "there is more concrete per capita on campus than there is at any other institution of higher learning anywhere in the world!" Commuters, beware: parking is extremely difficult. Students gave the town of Albany average grades. One positive aspect of the location is that "the school's proximity to the city and the mountains allows for frequent trips in different directions."

■ **Students** SUNY Albany has done a good job of attracting minority students; only two thirds of the student body is made up of white students. One undergrad speculated that "no other college enrolls a more wide-ranging ethnic/racial student body. This provides an opportunity for minorities as well as majorities to contribute." Unfortunately, race relations could be better: many whites come from sheltered Long Island and upstate areas and are extremely conservative. One student wrote, "Affirmative action and multiculturalism are killing this school": sadly, minority students should prepare themselves to encounter such attitudes here. Practically all the students are from New York state.

STATE UNIVERSITY OF NEW YORK AT ALBANY

Albany, NY

Admissions

SUNY Albany's most recent catalog states, "Since academic record is considered to be the best predictor of academic success here, the high school record [of an applicant is] examined in light of one's overall GPA, courses taken, end-of-course Regents examinations and grades (for New York students only), and rank in class." The admissions office also takes standardized test scores (either the SAT or ACT are accepted) and letters of recommendation into consideration. Applicants are required to have completed 18 units of high school academic course work; the school recommends that this curriculum include two to three units of mathematics, at least two units of lab science, and "concentrated study" in a foreign language.

Financial Aid

The financial aid office at SUNY Albany requires applicants to submit the FAF. Last year, SUNY Albany students received over 3,000 state-sponsored academic scholarships (recipients must be New York State residents; values vary from a few hundred to a few thousand dollars); the school also awarded a limited number of partial academic scholarships from its own endowment. Last year, SUNY Albany students borrowed the following average amounts from major student loan programs: Stafford (25% of the students to a Stafford loan; average value: $2,600), Perkins (10%; $1,526), PLUS (3%; $3,386), and SLS (1%; 1,408).

Excerpt from SUNY Albany promotional materials:

"State University of Albany is the senior campus of the SUNY system, the largest system of public higher education in the nation. As one of four university centers in that system, Albany offers undergraduate and graduate education in a broad range of academic fields at the bachelor's, master's, and doctoral degree levels. Instructional excellence is assured through the quality of the faculty and the fact that the University has designed its academic programs to allow students to achieve maximum intellectual growth, as well as through training to help meet career objectives. Students are encouraged to challenge themselves, to explore freely the world about them, and then to accept the responsibility that comes with challenge and freedom."

ADMISSIONS FACTS

Competitiveness Rating:	87
% of applicants accepted:	60
% acceptees attending:	25

FRESHMAN PROFILE

Average verbal SAT:	518
Average math SAT:	607
Average ACT:	NA
Graduated top 10% of class:	33
Graduated top 25% of class:	87
Graduated top 50% of class:	99

DEADLINES

Early decision/action:	rolling
Early dec./act. notif.:	rolling
Regular admission:	3/1
Regular adm. notif.:	rolling

APPLICANTS ALSO LOOK AT

and often prefer:
Cornell U.

and sometimes prefer:
SUNY Binghamton
U. Rochester
Fordham U.
Syracuse U.

and rarely prefer:
U. Mass.–Amherst
Hofstra U.

ADDRESS

Undergraduate Admissions
1400 Washington Avenue
Albany, NY 12222
518-442-5435

FINANCIAL FACTS

In-state tuition ($):	2,150
Out-of-state tuition ($):	5,750
Room & board:	3,666
FA application deadline:	2/15
% frosh receiving FA:	73
PT earnings per yr. ($):	NA

TYPE OF AID: % of students ($)

FA of some kind:	70 (NA)
Need-based grants:	NA
Merit-based grants:	NA
Loans:	NA
Work study:	NA
Student rating of FA:	58

STATE UNIVERSITY OF NEW YORK AT BINGHAMTON

Binghamton, NY

What do students think about SUNY Binghamton?

■ **Academics** Why would a student accepted at Harvard and Yale opt for SUNY Binghamton instead? Maybe it's because Binghamton's tuition is approximately *one seventh* the tuition at an Ivy League school. Still, why Binghamton and not some other state school? Because few other public institutions in the nation offer so much in the way of academics and economy. One independent counselor called it a "good alternative to private colleges"; said another, Binghamton is "superior: it has excellent programs and facilities." Pre-professional majors such as accounting, nursing, and pre-med are top-notch. Psychology and English are also popular majors here. Students don't work terribly hard—our survey showed they put in just two and a half hours of study a day—but quite a few respondents noted that their classmates "care a lot about academics and all have really, really high aspirations." Summed up one student, "SUNY Binghamton is a bargain at twice the price." Given New York State's current financial woes, that student may get a chance to prove his claim; as this book was going to press, the state legislature was considering substantial tuition increases at all SUNY schools.

■ **Life** "School spirit—what's that?" asked one typical Binghamton student. The biggest complaint of students here was that their school lacked a sense of community. Some thought that the addition of a football team would help; others felt that a lot more is needed, and blamed the nonchalance of their classmates for the problems. Social life centers around dorm and frat parties and the occasional trip into the town of Binghamton. Said one student, "Good times do not come to you here, you have to look for them. Joining a frat or sorority or some other such organization helps. Actually, so long as you have good friends, it doesn't matter where you are." The campus is huge and wooded, and dorms are serviceable but institutional. It rains a lot; as one student explained, "Binghamton is always gray. The two days a week we have sun, it's beautiful, but otherwise, sunglasses are not a must unless you're artsy-fartsy." Warning: "If you have allergies or sinus problems, attending SUNY Binghamton is an act of masochism."

■ **Students** Most of Binghamton's students come from New York, and a large portion of them are from down-state. Said a student from Queens, "It seems as if the young adult population of New York City and Long Island has been transplanted here to Binghamton." According to one student, Binghamton is "a very politically active school. What the activists' objectives are—I don't know. But for anyone interested in protesting something, SUNY Binghamton is the right school for you." Although the school has a sizeable minority population, students gave themselves low marks for interaction. "The boast of diversity here is accurate, although groups tend to stick to themselves once they get here," explained one student. Another said his school was "the melting pot of middle New York State, but the heat is turned on fairly low."

STATE UNIVERSITY OF NEW YORK AT BINGHAMTON

Binghamton, NY

Admissions

According to SUNY Binghamton's brochure, "Each application is evaluated for overall grade average, class ranking, courses selected, SAT or ACT scores, activities, and special talents." The recommended high school curriculum includes four units of English, two to three units of mathematics, two units each of natural science and social science, and three units of foreign language. All applicants must submit SAT (preferred) or ACT scores. Priority consideration is given to applications received by March 15.

Financial Aid

The financial aid office at SUNY Binghamton requires applicants to submit the FAF. New York State residents are eligible for a number of state-sponsored Regents scholarships, which are awarded for academic excellence; the school also awards a small number of academic scholarships, as well as merit grants for athletes and those with special talents in the arts. Eligible students are encouraged to borrow from the Stafford, Perkins, and Nursing loan programs.

Excerpted from SUNY Binghamton promotional materials:

"The State University of New York at Binghamton, one of this country's most distinguished public universities, is remarkable for the richness and diversity of its educational programs. One of four University Centers of the State University of New York, SUNY Binghamton offers programs leading to the bachelor's, master's, and doctor of philosophy degrees. A vital blend of outstanding undergraduate programs in the arts and sciences, superior professional schools of moderate size, selected interdisciplinary and career-oriented programs, nationally recognized doctoral programs, and several organized research centers represent an intellectual environment of the first order.

"SUNY Binghamton challenges academically motivated students to work to their intellectual capacities. In all its programs, the University seeks to enhance the self-development of students so that they may become informed and effective participants in public affairs and in their subsequent educational and vocational pursuits."

ADMISSIONS FACTS

Competitiveness Rating:	**90**
% of applicants accepted:	43
% acceptees attending:	29

FRESHMAN PROFILE

Average verbal SAT:	527
Average math SAT:	615
Average ACT:	53*
Graduated top 10% of class:	71
Graduated top 25% of class:	97
Graduated top 50% of class:	98

DEADLINES

Early decision/action:	rolling
Early dec./act. notif.:	rolling
Regular admission:	rolling
Regular adm. notif.:	rolling

APPLICANTS ALSO LOOK AT

and often prefer:
Columbia U.

and sometimes prefer:
RPI
Vassar College
SUNY Albany

and rarely prefer:
CUNY–Queens College
U. Vermont
Fordham U.
Haverford College
SUNY–Buffalo

ADDRESS

Undergraduate Admissions
Vestal Parkway, East
Binghamton, NY 13902-6000
607-777-2171

FINANCIAL FACTS

In-state tuition ($):	2,150
Out-of-state tuition ($):	5,750
Room & board:	4,388
FA application deadline:	2/15
% frosh receiving FA:	65
PT earnings per yr. ($):	950

TYPE OF AID: % of students ($)

FA of some kind:	56 (NA)
Need-based grants:	NA
Merit-based grants:	NA
Loans:	NA
Work study:	NA
Student rating of FA:	57

STATE UNIVERSITY OF NEW YORK AT BUFFALO

Buffalo, NY

What do students think about SUNY Buffalo?

■ **Academics** With almost 19,000 undergraduate students, SUNY Buffalo (referred to as UB—University of Buffalo—by its students) is by far the largest school in the SUNY system. The Amherst campus, where undergraduates study, covers a vast expanse of territory, so the school's size can at first be overwhelming. But as one student explained, "some students are intimidated by a large school, but you get lost only if you let yourself." Engineering, business, and premed are the school's main drawing cards, although the liberal arts and several other career-oriented programs (physical and occupational therapy, architecture) are reportedly very good. Introductory classes are huge and are frequently taught by graduate students, but a physical therapy major wrote, "Once you advance in your major, classes are smaller (20-40 students) and most are taught by professors." Students gave the library excellent marks but felt that, on the whole, the school is poorly administered. Class registration is a real time-eater, and it's not always easy to get into mandatory classes. Said one student of the amount of effort she put into registration, "If I actually got into my classes, life would become very boring." All in all, though, the school is no better or worse run than other comparably sized universities.

■ **Life** One student reported that UB, like many large universities, "offers something for everyone. The number and variety of athletic, academic, and social organizations to choose from are great. People might think that by coming to such a large school they sacrifice their identity and become 'just a number.' But if a person is willing to make some effort and interact with the staff here, he doesn't necessarily lose his identity. I'll probably pursue my master's degree here, too." Students like the city of Buffalo a lot. Unfortunately, as a student who lives off-campus told us, "the campus is completely isolated from the city. I can't imagine how dorm life is bearable." In fact, undergrads did give all aspects of dorm life low grades; the food received similarly poor marks. The campus is institutional and a little difficult to get around—"We need a transportation system between the campus and dormitories," complained one student. Students enjoy an active dating scene despite a lopsided male-female ratio. Winters are long and cold.

■ **Students** Practically all UB students are from New York State. Locals make up the majority of the student body, but the school is good enough to draw from all over the state, and many students are from New York City and Long Island. One quarter of the students are minorities. Most students identified themselves as politically apathetic. Explained one, "With all the diversity this school offers (ethnic, communal, language, cultural, racial, economic), it is a great place to be. What it needs, however, is more sociopolitical consciousness and comfort from sub-zero temperatures."

STATE UNIVERSITY OF NEW YORK AT BUFFALO

Buffalo, NY

Admissions

From SUNY Buffalo's undergraduate catalog: "Competition for available places is keen. Mean combined SAT scores for accepted students are typically above 1100 and mean high school averages are above 90. Selection of the freshman class is based upon an examination of three scholastic measures: a cumulative high school average through the junior year; a three-year percentile rank-in-class; and standardized test scores....While not required, letters of recommendation and personal statements from students are reviewed by the admissions committee. These documents are often invaluable in explaining and amplifying the quantitative measures considered....A limited number of freshmen may be offered admission to the University based upon documented evidence of special talents or special circumstances. Exceptional creative talent in art, music, theatre, writing, special academic achievement, demonstrated leadership, outstanding athletic ability, and community service are examples of such talents reviewed by the admissions committee in recent years." All applicants must submit SAT or ACT scores. A standard college prep program in high school is recommended, including four years of English, at least three years each of foreign language, social science and mathematics, and at least two years of natural science.

Financial Aid

The financial aid office at SUNY Buffalo requires applicants to submit the FAF. New York State residents are eligible for a number of state-sponsored Regents scholarships, which are awarded for academic excellence; the school also awards a small number of academic scholarships, as well as merit grants for athletes and those with special talents in the arts. Eligible students are encouraged to borrow from the Stafford, Perkins, and Nursing loan programs.

Excerpted from SUNY Buffalo promotional materials:

"At State University of New York at Buffalo, a new undergraduate college with a curriculum for the 21st century is being developed as a means of emphasizing and enriching an undergraduate education program that already awards the largest number of bachelor's degrees in the State each year.

"Steeped in tradition, modern in focus, large in concept, and personal in form, UB is a university in the richest sense. Important in graduate and professional education, it displays also remarkable breadth, diversity, and quality in undergraduate programs in the humanities, natural sciences, social sciences, and fine arts. In short, New York State's major public university provides unparalleled opportunities for learning, for career preparation, for developing a rewarding way of life."

STATE UNIVERSITY OF NEW YORK AT STONY BROOK

Stony Brook, NY

What do students think about SUNY Stony Brook?

■ **Academics** SUNY Stony Brook is a big university with a staff devoted primarily to research. Accordingly, students get the opportunity to study with some brilliant scholars, particularly in the hard sciences, engineering, and the psychology department. The downside is that some professors are more dedicated to their research than to their undergraduates and, not surprisingly, professors here received low grades for in-class and out-of-class performance. Be prepared to fend for yourself: students told us that a good education is available here, but you'll have to find it on your own. "Large" and "impersonal" were words commonly used to describe the administration, whom students gave uniformly poor grades. State budget cuts have hurt the school, and several students complained of over-crowded or cancelled courses. Still, the school is academically strong and students are very competitive. Perhaps too competitive: respondents told us that there is "excessive cheating during final exams." Most students agree that they're getting a good deal: said one, "Stony Brook is a large public university and functions well within those parameters," while another described his school as "a very good deal for the money, very academically oriented, and very thorough."

■ **Life** Stony Brook is considered a commuter school, but, with almost half its 9000 undergraduates living on campus, there is still a sizeable resident community. Living conditions, unfortunately, are less than optimal: students graded the dorms, campus, and food "uncomfortable," "ugly," and "awful," respectively. The school has a reputation as a party school, and our survey showed drug use to be above the national average, but drinking, while popular, is less so than at most other schools. Still, some students concurred with the one who told us that "the bars in Stony Brook are located within a one-mile radius of campus and are jammed with students." Long Island's South Shore is only a half-hour's drive (or bus ride) away and provides excellent distraction in the early fall and late spring. New York City is about an hour away via the Long Island Railroad.

■ **Students** Many SUNY Stony Brook students are from the area: the school won't provide housing for those whose parents' homes are within a 10-mile radius of the school, and that restriction affects a lot of students. The science and engineering programs attract some students from outside the area and even a few hundred foreign nationals. Said one student in reference to the school's 48 percent minority population, "Stony Brook *is* cultural diversity." However, because of the school's size and the large commuter population, there is little sense of community among the students, and interaction among different groups is minimal, but not impossible.

STATE UNIVERSITY OF NEW YORK AT STONY BROOK

Stony Brook, NY

Admissions

The admissions office reports that "one of our goals is to attract students who meet our rigorous academic standards and will be able to contribute to the enrichment of campus life. We seek students with a minimum of an 85 high school average and a combined SAT score above 1000 (ACT composite: 25). Acceptance into the university does not guarantee admission into select programs...such as engineering, business, computer science, applied mathematics and statistics, and health sciences. Professional counselors who are sensitive to individual backgrounds and high school experiences review applications for admission....Students who demonstrate potential in other ways—through leadership in school projects, athletics, or the arts, for example—receive special consideration." SUNY Stony Brook applicants most often also apply to other SUNY campuses (Binghamton and Albany), Cornell U., Hofstra, and NYU.

Financial Aid

The financial aid office at SUNY Stonybrook requires applicants to submit the FAF and a form generated by the school. The school's application brochure states, "The university awards both full and partial tuition scholarships to selected students based on their merit and/or need." Students with a high school average of 92 and a combined SAT score of 1200 are eligible for the Provost's Honors College Scholarship. Campus-based loans include the Perkins and Stafford loans.

A note from the SUNY Stony Brook Admissions Office:

"New York State's only public university to be classified by the Carnegie Foundation as one of the nation's 70 leading research institutions, Stony Brook has exceptional strength in the sciences, mathematics, humanities, fine arts, social sciences, engineering and health professions. Stony Brook's undergraduate degree programs are augmented by a number of special academic opportunities. Among them are: living/learning centers that integrate academic pursuits with residential life; the Honors College for outstanding students offers a four-year sequence of interdisciplinary seminars taught by some of Stony Brook's most respected faculty; federated learning communities, a nationally acclaimed "experiment" in interdisciplinary education that brings a small group of students together with a faculty "Master Learner" in six courses centered on a common theme; the Undergraduate Research and Creative Activities (URECA) program that enables students and faculty to work as partners on joint research projects; and the Scholars for Medicine program that enables up to 10 sophomores annually to secure guaranteed admission to Stony Brook's School of Medicine."

ADMISSIONS FACTS

Competitiveness Rating:	**74**
% of applicants accepted:	59
% acceptees attending:	24

FRESHMAN PROFILE

Average verbal SAT:	435
Average math SAT:	545
Average ACT:	NA
Graduated top 10% of class:	25
Graduated top 25% of class:	67
Graduated top 50% of class:	94

DEADLINES

Early decision/action:	rolling
Early dec./act. notif.:	rolling
Regular admission:	7/31
Regular adm. notif.:	rolling

APPLICANTS ALSO LOOK AT

and often prefer:
SUNY Binghamton
NYU

and sometimes prefer:
SUNY Buffalo
SUNY Albany
CUNY–Queens College
CUNY–Hunter College
Hofstra U.

and rarely prefer:
Boston U.
Syracuse U.

ADDRESS

Undergraduate Admissions
Stony Brook, NY 11794
516-632-6868

FINANCIAL FACTS

In-state tuition ($):	2,150
Out-of-state tuition ($):	5,750
Room & board:	4,155
FA application deadline:	2/15
% frosh receiving FA:	40
PT earnings per yr. ($):	1000

TYPE OF AID: % of students ($)

FA of some kind:	35 (NA)
Need-based grants:	NA
Merit-based grants:	NA
Loans:	NA
Work study:	NA
Student rating of FA:	65

SWARTHMORE COLLEGE

Swarthmore, PA

CAMPUS LIFE

Quality of Life Rating:	**90**
Type of School:	private
Affiliation:	none
Environment:	city

STUDENT BODY

FT undergrad enrollment:	1,320
% male/% female:	52/48
% out-of-state:	10
% live on campus:	93
% African-American:	8
% Asian:	8
% Caucasian:	80
% Hispanic:	2
% foreign:	8
% transfers:	11

WHAT'S HOT

gay community accepted
deans
studying hard
honesty
leftist politics
cost of living
small classes (overall)
administration (overall)
profs outside class
dorm comfort
campus appearance
profs in class

WHAT'S NOT

fraternities/sororities
dating

ACADEMICS

Academic Rating:	**88**
Calendar:	semester
Student/teacher ratio:	10/1
% doctorates:	93
Profs interesting:	92
Profs accessible:	94
Hours of study per day:	4.1

MOST POPULAR MAJORS BY %

Letters/Literature:	35
Social Sciences:	30
Physical Sciences:	25

% GRADS WHO PURSUE

Law:	10
MBA:	4
Medicine:	12
M.A., etc.:	16

What do students think about Swarthmore College?

■ **Academics** As a popular T-shirt at Swarthmore College reads, "Anywhere else it would have been an A…really!" Swarthmore is said to be one of the most academically intense schools in the country. "Compared to Swarthmore, an operating room is relaxed," is how one student put it. Our survey results confirmed that reputation. "Swatties" rated among the top 5 percent in the nation in terms of workload and commitment to their studies. Most report spending many hours daily on course work, and one characteristically explained, "Even if you do your work it's a struggle to do well." The liberal arts and pre-medical sciences are the most popular fields here; nearly half the students go on to graduate school. Students had little but praise for their professors. Wrote one student, "The best thing about Swat is having the privilege to study with amazing profs who not only know their fields, but WANT to be teaching them to undergrads. Second best is having the privilege to study with bright, interested students who want to make a difference." Classes are uniformly small enough to include lots of individual attention, and are all taught personally by professors (no TAs allowed). Students rave about the high level of intellectual curiosity on campus— "Every tree is labeled" for the edification of the interested—and report an exceptionally low incidence of cheating. About their only complaint concerned the stress level, which most agreed was at an unhealthy level.

■ **Life** Most members of the generally happy Swarthmore family concede that they "could use more frolicking." The intense academic emphasis prompts many to make even Friday night "a study night." Some students entirely "refuse to date, because it may distract them from their work." Not all subscribe to this Spartan ethic, however. One student commented, "If Swarthmore isn't a party school on the weekends, I'd hate to see what a party school is." Students rate the beauty and comfort of their surroundings very highly, and most love living on campus. Casual dating is not a popular option; people tend to go for "*serious* long-term relationships." The small size of the school (about 1,300) makes for an intimate, homey community, although some consider it a little too small. Everyone definitely "knows everyone else's business." Nearby Philadelphia is accessible via an on-campus train, should escape to urban anonymity become necessary.

■ **Students** The student body here is "diverse and very opinionated." A left-leaning community overall, Swarthmore has an unusually visible and well-accepted gay minority. According to one student, most people are "generally well-informed and sensitized to political events. This stimulates compelling discussion and debate at the dinner table and in the dorm room. I have learned as much from my friends as from my professors." Minority students make up 20 percent of the student body, with blacks and Asians accounting for the largest minority populations.

SWARTHMORE COLLEGE

Admissions

Selection at Swarthmore is based on: 1) record in secondary school; 2) recommendations from school personnel; 3) standardized test scores (SAT and three Achievements required; one Achievement must be English Composition; engineering applicants must take a Math Achievement); 4) a brief essay (subject is specified); 5) "Reading and experience, both in school and out." Other factors include "Strength of character, promise of growth, initiative, seriousness of purpose, distinction in personal and extracurricular interests, and a sense of social responsibility." No specific high school curriculum is required, but preparation should include "accurate use of the English language in reading, writing and speaking, comprehension and application of the principles of mathematics, the strongest possible command of one or two foreign languages…[and] substantial course work in (a) history and social studies, (b) literature, art, and music, and (c) the sciences. Engineering majors should present work in chemistry, physics, and four years of mathematics, including algebra, geometry, and trigonometry. A "Winter Early Decision is available (in addition to the fall plan mentioned in the sidebar); the application deadline is January 1. Candidates are notified by February 1.

Financial Aid

Financial aid applicants to Swarthmore must complete the FAF. Applicants are expected to meet the a portion of their need (between $800 and $2,600) through Stafford, Perkins, and Swarthmore College loans. PLUS and PHEAA loans are also recommended by Swarthmore. Included among the many academic and merit scholarships available are the Swarthmore College National Scholarships, which are awarded "on occasion" to outstanding men and women in the freshman class. The scholarships last for four years, and are awarded based on "scholarship, leadership, character, and responsibility." The amount varies from $3,000 to the full cost of all expenses, depending on financial need of the recipient.

Excerpted from Swarthmore College promotional materials:

"The purpose of Swarthmore College is to make its students more valuable human beings and more useful members of society. While it shares this purpose with other educational institutions, each school, college, and university seeks to realize that purpose in its own way. Each must select those tasks it can do best. By such selection it contributes to the diversity and richness of educational opportunity which is part of the American heritage.

"Swarthmore seeks to help its students realize their fullest intellectual and personal potential combined with a deep sense of ethical and social concern."

ADMISSIONS FACTS

Competitiveness Rating:	**96**
% of applicants accepted:	32
% acceptees attending:	34

FRESHMAN PROFILE

Average verbal SAT:	639
Average math SAT:	673
Average ACT:	NA
Graduated top 10% of class:	80
Graduated top 25% of class:	95
Graduated top 50% of class:	145

DEADLINES

Early decision/action:	11/15
Early dec./act. notif.:	12/15
Regular admission:	2/1
Regular adm. notif.:	4/15

APPLICANTS ALSO LOOK AT

and sometimes prefer:

U. Pennsylvania
Columbia U.
Yale U.
Williams College
Brown U.
Wesleyan U.

and rarely prefer:

Vassar College
Haverford College
U. Chicago

ADDRESS

Undergraduate Admissions
Swarthmore, PA 19081
215-328-8300

FINANCIAL FACTS

In-state tuition ($):	16,465
Out-of-state tuition ($):	16,465
Room & board:	5,520
FA application deadline:	2/1
% frosh receiving FA:	55
PT earnings per yr. ($):	1500

TYPE OF AID % of students ($)

FA of some kind:	60 (NA)
Need-based grants:	NA
Merit-based grants:	NA
Loans:	NA
Work study:	NA
Student rating of FA:	87

SWEET BRIAR COLLEGE

Sweet Briar, VA

What do students think about Sweet Briar College?

■ **Academics** "There is a false view that Sweet Briar is a finishing school and a stepping stone toward marriage," explained one Sweet Briar College student. "The women who are here are serious about their studies and their future careers, and they are *falsely* categorized as MRS. degree candidates who attend an easy college." Our survey results back up this assertion: the women of Sweet Briar take their academics seriously, attending all classes (a must: the school is so small that any absences are obvious) and then studying an additional three-and-a-half hours a day. A traditional liberal arts college, Sweet Briar requires all students to complete a wide range of distribution requirements. Many students pursue double majors. English, government, economics, psychology, and international affairs are among the popular departments. Most Sweet Briar women are very happy with the school they chose. Wrote one, "At Sweet Briar, a student's opportunities are endless, ranging from one-on-one attention she receives from professors, to the small classes (average size: eight to 12), to going abroad to study for a semester or year, to doing an internship in your field of study." Students praised their teachers (who "take both a professional and a personal interest in the students," and who "concentrate on teaching, not on publishing their own work, during the semester"), administrators, classmates, and surroundings. And, they appreciate the benefits of attending a small school. Summed up one, "Because the school is so small women are able to develop their strengths, improve on their weaknesses, and really focus on themselves."

■ **Life** Sweet Briar's large wooded campus is gorgeous. As one woman put it, "My college counselor told me Sweet Briar is the most beautiful college campus, and I believe he was right. That's what initially attracted me to the school. When I toured the school, though, I realized that the beauty of the school was deeper than the 3,300 acres; it's in the administration, faculty, staff, and the students. Sweet Briar is a family-oriented community." Other facilities—dorms, cafeteria, library—are also first-rate. Sports, outdoor activities, and extracurricular clubs are all popular. Because nearby schools—UVa, Hampden-Sydney, Washington and Lee—provide plenty of opportunities to meet men, Sweet Briar students don't complain about a lack of male companionship, as many other women's school students do. Explained one student, "Socially, you can't go wrong at Sweet Briar, whether it's packing your bags to go to neighboring colleges or just hanging out with your Sweet Briar buddies."

■ **Students** Sweet Briar students are a fairly homogeneous group. Most are white, conservative, Southern, and from fairly affluent families. The students report that their classmates are generally warm, friendly, and outgoing, but that alternative lifestyles and progressive politics are not entirely welcome on their campus.

SWEET BRIAR COLLEGE

Admissions

The Sweet Briar admissions committee told us, "Faculty are highly involved in our admissions process. We encourage prospective students to work closely with their SBC Admissions Counselor, particularly if there are extenuating circumstances in regard to the academic record. On-campus interviews are highly recommended, although not required." Most important in your application to Sweet Briar are your GPA, the difficulty of your high school courses, and the quality of your high school. These are followed (in order of importance) by letters of recommendation, standardized test scores, essays, extracurriculars, and your interview. If you take the SAT, you must also take three Achievement tests, one of which must be English. The Test of English as a Foreign Language (TOEFL) is required of all foreign students. Students should have completed four years of English, three of math (two algebra, one geometry), two sequential years of a foreign language, three years of social studies (including two of history, one of which must be U.S. History) and two years of lab science. Sweet Briar applicants also often apply to Hollins, Mount Holyoke, Randolph-Macon Woman's College, Smith and Vanderbilt.

Financial Aid

The financial aid office at Sweet Briar College requires applicants to submit the FAF and their parents' most recent tax return. Sweet Briar reports that it meets "100% of demonstrated need, based on tuition, room and board. Need-based financial aid awards typically are composed of at least 65% grant money. The college offers an early estimator service upon request for families interested in need-based assistance. Academic scholarships offered to freshmen range from $3,500 to $12,500 per year and are renewable based on minimum cumulative GPA." The deadline listed below is a *priority* deadline; FA applications received between March 2 and April 1 are accepted but are given lower priority.

A note from the Sweet Briar Admissions Office:

"The young woman who applies to Sweet Briar is mature and far-sighted enough to know what she wants from her college experience. She realizes that the college she chooses must be right for her own personal growth and intellectual development. Sweet Briar attracts the ambitious student who enjoys being immersed not only in a first-rate academic program, but in a variety of meaningful activities outside the classroom. Our students take charge and revel in their accomplishments. This attitude follows graduates, enabling them to compete confidently in the corporate world and in graduate school."

ADMISSIONS FACTS

Competitiveness Rating:	**66**
% of applicants accepted:	82
% acceptees attending:	41

FRESHMAN PROFILE

Average verbal SAT:	467*
Average math SAT:	503*
Average ACT:	NA
Graduated top 10% of class:	35
Graduated top 25% of class:	51
Graduated top 50% of class:	79

DEADLINES

Early decision/action:	11/15
Early dec./act. notif.:	12/15
Regular admission:	2/15
Regular adm. notif.:	3/15

APPLICANTS ALSO LOOK AT

and often prefer:
Smith College
Mt. Holyoke College
Randolph-Macon College

and sometimes prefer:
U. Richmond

and rarely prefer:
Mount Vernon College

ADDRESS

Undergraduate Admissions
Box B
Sweet Briar, VA 24595-9999
804-381-6142

FINANCIAL FACTS

In-state tuition ($):	12,005
Out-of-state tuition ($):	12,005
Room & board:	4,850
FA application deadline:	3/1
% frosh receiving FA:	66
PT earnings per yr. ($):	750

TYPE OF AID % of students ($)

FA of some kind:	58 (12,903)
Need-based grants:	39 (5,991)
Merit-based grants:	18 (2,903)
Loans:	62 (2,799)
Work study:	34 (845)
Student rating of FA:	100

SYRACUSE UNIVERSITY

CAMPUS LIFE

Quality of Life Rating: **77**

Type of School:	private
Affiliation:	none
Environment:	city

STUDENT BODY

FT undergrad enrollment:	12,119
% male/% female:	49/51
% out-of-state:	65
% live on campus:	75
% African-American:	9
% Asian:	3
% Caucasian:	84
% Hispanic:	3
% foreign:	2
% transfers:	3

WHAT'S HOT

college radio station
intercollegiate sports
marijuana
rap/hip-hop
college newspaper

WHAT'S NOT

small lectures
honesty
financial aid
interaction among students
town-gown relations
bursar
small labs and seminars

ACADEMICS

Academic Rating: **75**

Calendar:	semester
Student/teacher ratio:	11/1
% doctorates:	75
Profs interesting:	70
Profs accessible:	71
Hours of study per day:	2.88

MOST POPULAR MAJORS BY %

Business & Management:	19
Social Sciences:	19
Communications:	13

% GRADS WHO PURSUE

Law:	6
MBA:	10
Medicine:	5
M.A., etc.:	10

What do students think about Syracuse University?

■ **Academics** Syracuse is a large private university best known for its excellent communications department, which continues to offer one of the nation's top programs for journalists and telecasters. The engineering, pre-business, public affairs, and natural sciences departments are also strong, however, and very popular with undergraduates. Size is one of the chief benefits of SU, whose undergraduate programs are so extensive that they are subdivided into 21 "academic units"—said one student, "I came here because I wanted a wide variety of academic and social opportunities in a non-urban setting." It's also one of the chief drawbacks: as one student explained, "You can find a lot of rewarding, challenging activities and classes, but you can also get a state college education at private school prices." Networking skills and personal initiative are necessary to navigate the bureaucracy here, but even students with these traits aren't guaranteed smooth sailing. Several students complained, "There are a lot of great courses offered (which is why I came here) but most are impossible to get into if you aren't in that department or not a senior." Class size and administrators received low marks, especially considering the fact that this is a private school. Students also complained that too many introductory courses are taught by teaching assistants.

■ **Life** Students gave the city of Syracuse low grades, and ranked their relations with their neighbors particularly bad. Reported one, "There is a very poor relationship between the community and the university. It's very upsetting as a student to live in a community which, for the most part, resents your entire existence." The city's inhospitable winter climate further discourages students from venturing into the city during much of the school year. Sports are the main rallying point for students—"the only time there is unity among a majority of students is during a Dome football or basketball game," said one student. The lacrosse team is among the best in the country and is also extremely popular with students. Fraternities and sororities play a major role in the social scene here (one student told us, "If you're not in one, you're a social outcast"). As students have few other social outlets, it comes as no surprise that partying, either with the Greeks or in the neighborhood bars, is a popular way to break the tedium.

■ **Students** Syracuse attracts a relatively well-diversified student body—nearly one in 10 students is African-American—but students uniformly agree interaction between groups is minimal. The student body leans to the left politically, and liberal students are more vocal about their opinions than are their conservative classmates. Even though they complain quite a bit, students gave themselves a solid "B," just below the national average, when grading their own happiness.

SYRACUSE UNIVERSITY

Admissions

The Syracuse admissions application notes, "Every candidate is evaluated individually by the admissions committee. We encourage you to keep in touch with us. If you have questions during the admissions process, or would like to offer additional information for the committee's consideration, call or write us. We will be glad to hear from you." Syracuse uses no specific cut-offs or formulas. The admissions committee first looks at our high school curriculum and GPA. These are followed, in order of importance, by your standardized test scores, letters of recommendation, interview, essays, and extracurriculars. Applicants must take the SAT or ACT, but are not required to take Achievements. They should also have completed four years of English, three years of mathematics, three years of science, three years of social studies, and two years of a foreign language. Students who apply to Syracuse most often also apply to Boston U., Penn State, and Cornell.

Financial Aid

The financial aid office at Syracuse University requires applicants to submit the FAF. The school awards merit scholarships on the basis of athletic ability and/or skill in the creative and performing arts. Last year, Syracuse students took out Stafford loans (43% of the students; average value: $3,000), Perkins loans (20%; $1,465), PLUS loans (8%; $3,750), and a Federal loan for nursing students (1%; $2,000). In 1991–92, the average financial aid award to freshmen was $11,400, considerably more than the average award to sophomores and upperclassmen.

A note from the Syracuse University Admissions Office:

"Syracuse is a university that reflects a multidimensional focus, where different points of view not only coexist but blend to reinforce one another. This is especially important for students to consider when deciding what college to attend. One of the first questions students have is size. Students may hear good reasons for choosing a small college offering personal attention, and reasons for choosing a large university with more diversity and specialized facilities.

"At Syracuse we don't think of 'large' and 'small' as opposites; we see them as two different opportunities that exist side by side. Our students are enrolled in one of 12 undergraduate colleges, providing an immediate identification and 'home' for freshman. Together, they make up a total undergraduate enrollment of 12,000 students— which means the University is large enough to offer hundreds of academic programs, over 1,000 faculty members, state-of-the-art laboratories, a library with 2.3 million volumes, and computer facilities only a major university can provide."

ADMISSIONS FACTS

Competitiveness Rating:	76
% of applicants accepted:	64
% acceptees attending:	32

FRESHMAN PROFILE

Average verbal SAT:	517*
Average math SAT:	573*
Average ACT:	NA
Graduated top 10% of class:	28
Graduated top 25% of class:	67
Graduated top 50% of class:	92

DEADLINES

Early decision/action:	12/1
Early dec./act. notif.:	1/15
Regular admission:	2/1
Regular adm. notif.:	3/15

APPLICANTS ALSO LOOK AT

and often prefer:
Union College
Lehigh U.

and sometimes prefer:
Bucknell U.
Lafayette College
Hobart/William Smith College
Boston U.

and rarely prefer:
SUNY Geneseo
Northeastern U.

ADDRESS

Undergraduate Admissions
201 Administration Bldg.
Syracuse, NY 13244-1120
315-443-3611

FINANCIAL FACTS

In-state tuition ($):	12,640
Out-of-state tuition ($):	12,640
Room & board:	5,860
FA application deadline:	1/31
% frosh receiving FA:	58
PT earnings per yr. ($):	1400

TYPE OF AID % of students ($)

FA of some kind:	60 (9,600)
Need-based grants:	35 (4,550)
Merit-based grants:	40 (6,130)
Loans:	46 (4,100)
Work study:	25 (1,700)
Student rating of FA:	64

TEMPLE UNIVERSITY

Philadelphia, PA

CAMPUS LIFE

Quality of Life Rating:	**65**
Type of School:	public
Affiliation:	none
Environment:	city

STUDENT BODY

FT undergrad enrollment:	14,862
% male/% female:	48/52
% out-of-state:	25
% live on campus:	14
% African-American:	16
% Asian:	7
% Caucasian:	72
% Hispanic:	3
% foreign:	8
% transfers:	NA

WHAT'S HOT

suitcase syndrome
rap/hip-hop
working a job
requirements are easy
food

WHAT'S NOT

campus appearance
dorm safety
bursar
TAs teach upper level courses
overall happiness
town-gown relations
administration (overall)
cost of living

ACADEMICS

Academic Rating:	**73**
Calendar:	semester
Student/teacher ratio:	12/1
% doctorates:	65
Profs interesting:	63
Profs accessible:	64
Hours of study per day:	2.63

MOST POPULAR MAJORS BY %

Business Administration:	7
Radio/TV/Film:	6
Accounting:	5

What do students think about Temple University?

■ **Academics** Like DePaul University in Chicago, Temple has traditionally provided an excellent pre-professional education to a largely working-class student body. Most Temple students cite cost as their chief reason for choosing the school; as one student explained, Temple undergrads receive "a down-and-dirty, no-frills inexpensive institution that gives you what you need." With over 20,000 full- and part-time students, Temple is large enough to offer something for everybody. Communications is the hottest field: one student accurately indicated that "Temple's RTF (radio, television, and film) program is nationally renowned." Business and education majors are also popular. Unfortunately, like many schools dependent on the government for funding, Temple seems currently to be weathering a pretty rough period. "The school cuts too many corners at too great a cost to the student body," said one of the many students who complained about inadequate resources. Students also find all administrative tasks extremely frustrating—"After you register, confirm your financial aid package, and pay your bill, everything else is a breeze"—and one can't help but suspect that a shortage of funds contributes heavily to these problems. Add large classes and mediocre marks for professors and you'll see why Temple students are less happy than most. Still, a large portion of the student body loves the school; one explained that it's because "Temple gives anybody a chance to succeed no matter what his background. If I had to do it all over I'd go to Temple not once but twice."

■ **Life** One campus resident reported, "There is a wide variety of activities available because we are in the city and your fellow students won't let you get bored. You stay active whether you want to or not." Philadelphia does indeed offer students a wide variety of museums, stores, night spots, and sporting events. Life in the city is not without its drawbacks, however: students ranked their relationship with members of the local community thirteenth lowest of the schools we surveyed, mostly because the area is poor and not entirely safe. Students reported that on-campus social life centers around an active dating scene and the school's athletic teams, which are very popular (particularly the men's basketball team). Still, the vast majority of students are commuters, and as a result the campus at times is pretty dead, particularly from Friday through Sunday.

■ **Students** Many students here have major responsibilities other than school, such as families and jobs. Most are commuters; the typical student is rarely on campus except to attend classes and study. Outside of those that serve blacks almost exclusively, very few schools have as proportionally large an African-American population as Temple does. Students disagreed on whether or not interaction between groups was "frequent and easy." Whites and Asians said it was, blacks said it was not.

TEMPLE UNIVERSITY

Philadelphia, PA

Admissions

Temple's admissions committee looks first and foremost at your high school GPA (which must be a minimum of 2.0). This is followed, in order of importance, by standardized test scores, your interview, extracurriculars, essays, and letters of recommendation. To qualify for admission, you must take either the SAT or the ACT (foreign students may take the TOEFL). You should also have completed four years of English, two years of mathematics, two years of a foreign language, one year of history, and one year of a lab science. Students who are planning to major in Dance, the Esther Boyer College of Music, or the Tyler School of Art must either audition or submit a portfolio (whichever is appropriate). Students who apply to Temple also often apply to Penn State.

Financial Aid

Temple requires a FAF, its own financial aid form, and a PHEAA (Pennsylvania Higher Education Assistance Agency) form of its financial aid applicants. Last year, Temple awarded academic scholarships to 10% of all undergrads (average value: $2,300), and athletic scholarships to 2% ($7,200). The FA office also recommended Stafford loans to 59% of undergrads ($2,200 average) and Perkins loans to 3% ($900). Overall, 70% of the class of '95 received some form of aid, with an average award value of $4,850, numbers which diminished only slightly for sophs and upperclassmen (see sidebar). The 5/1 deadline is an in-office deadline.

A note from the Temple Admissions Office:

"Temple University was founded in 1884 by Russell H. Conwell. Rev. Conwell's most famous speech instructed listeners to recognize the potential that existed in their own back yard, rather than searching for riches in distant lands. Called 'Acres of Diamonds,' the speech embodies Rev. Conwell's most fundamental philosophy, that no one who is willing to develop his or her own talents, should be denied the opportunity to do so. This belief became the foundation for Temple University. Our students never stop seeking the best in themselves."

ADMISSIONS FACTS

Competitiveness Rating:	65
% of applicants accepted:	65
% acceptees attending:	47

FRESHMAN PROFILE

Average verbal SAT:	466
Average math SAT:	509
Average ACT:	NA
Graduated top 10% of class:	17
Graduated top 25% of class:	45
Graduated top 50% of class:	79

DEADLINES

Early decision/action:	NA
Early dec./act. notif.:	NA
Regular admission:	6/15
Regular adm. notif.:	rolling

APPLICANTS ALSO LOOK AT

and often prefer:
U. Pittsburgh
Penn State U.–U. Park

and sometimes prefer:
Villanova U.
Drexel U.
Gettysburg College
Lehigh U.
Penn State U.–Westchester

and rarely prefer:
NYU
St. Joseph's U.

ADDRESS

Undergraduate Admissions
Philadelphia, PA 19122-1803
215-787-7200

FINANCIAL FACTS

In-state tuition ($):	4,636
Out-of-state tuition ($):	8,596
Room & board:	4,398
FA application deadline:	5/1
% frosh receiving FA:	NA
PT earnings per yr. ($):	NA

TYPE OF AID % of students ($)

FA of some kind:	63 (4,975)
Need-based grants:	68 (1,800)
Merit-based grants:	NA
Loans:	NA
Work study:	NA
Student rating of FA:	64

UNIVERSITY OF TENNESSEE AT KNOXVILLE

Knoxville, TN

What do students think about University of Tennessee?

■ **Academics** If you are a Tennessean looking for the most demanding academic program in your state, UTK is not where you come looking first (not with Vanderbilt, Sewanee, Fisk, and Rhodes around). As one student explained, "A student here will not be immediately inundated with intellectual fervor—not by a long shot! However, there are enough innovative, intelligent, and inspiring instructors on the faculty that a student who wishes to make the most of his or her college experience can certainly do so." The key here is that UTK's enormity provides a lot of academic opportunities, provided you know where to look. "Hard sciences are strong, and so is engineering," said one student. Said another, "Programs which generate money are better supported by the administration; therefore, humanities programs such as art history and music are not funded as well as those in engineering, sciences, business, etc." Although a sense of "businesslike impersonality" at times prevails here, professors are remarkably accessible after class, compared with those at other public universities.

■ **Life** If you don't know who the Volunteers are, you probably don't belong at UTK. As one student put it, "This is a *huge* sports school." Some students complain that too much attention is paid to sports, particularly football and basketball, but the fact is these complaints will almost certainly go unheeded: the alumni are aggressive Big Orange supporters. Frats and sororities claim about 10 percent of the population and form a social universe of their own. For the rest of the student body there is the Knoxville bar scene—"You only need to be 18 to get in a bar and a baby could probably buy a beer" is how one student explained it—and each other ("If you can't find girls here, you're not looking," enthused one man). This is not a suitcase college and the campus is jumping with parties on weekends. Because of its size, UTK's campus can be a little difficult to get around.

■ **Students** Eighty-six percent of UTK students are from Tennessee. Cost, convenience, and a love of big-time are what bring them here. They are a politically conservative bunch, very much the typical Southern college students. They're not so concerned with appearing tolerant of difference as their Northern counterparts, and they certainly do not care about being "p.c." Typical of men's attitudes towards women here was the student who told us "Southern girls (oo la la) are the best." A gay student told us that his straight classmates' attitude towards him was either to ignore him or to treat him with outright hostility, an assertion borne out by his classmates' answers to questions relating to tolerance of gays on campus. In short, if you're a jock, or comfortable around jocks, you'll fit right in here; otherwise, you'll have to look around to find your niche.

UNIVERSITY OF TENNESSEE AT KNOXVILLE

Knoxville, TN

Admissions

The admissions office at University of Tennessee at Knoxville states that a "minimum 2.0 (GPA) is required to be considered for admission. For 1991 entering freshmen, the average high school GPA was 3.1 and the average ACT was 23.3." UTK first looks at your GPA and then your standardized test scores. These are followed in order of importance by your essays, letters of recommendation, extracurriculars, and interview. All students are required to take either the SAT or ACT, and in general should have completed four units of English, two units of algebra, two units of natural science (including at least one year of biology, chemistry, or physics), two units of a single foreign language, and one unit each of Visual/Performing Arts, American history, another math (geometry, trigonometry, advanced math, or calculus) and European history. Students who apply to UTK also often apply to East Tennessee State, Memphis State, and UT Chattanooga.

Financial Aid

The financial aid office at the University of Tennessee, Knoxville requires applicants to submit the FAF or the FFS and a form generated by the school. All students awarded financial aid must also submit their parents' tax return for verification purposes. The school awards merit scholarships on the basis of athletic skill only; in 1991–92, 276 students received such an award (average value: $5,932). The FA office reports that it recommends the following loan programs: Perkins, SLS, LAW Access, HEAL, and a university-sponsored loan.

A note from the University of Tennessee, Knoxville Admissions Office:

"The largest and most comprehensive campus in Tennessee, UT Knoxville has an enrollment of 25,000 students. More than 300 undergraduate, graduate, and professional degree programs are offered at UTK. The campus of choice for many of the state's top high school graduates including over 100 National Merit Scholars; other good students also succeed here. 'Students come first' is the motto as the campus carries out a three-fold mission of teaching, research, and public service. Located on the Tennessee River in East Tennessee, the campus is within sight of the Great Smokey Mountains."

ADMISSIONS FACTS

Competitiveness Rating:	**71**
% of applicants accepted:	77
% acceptees attending:	57

FRESHMAN PROFILE

Average verbal SAT:	470
Average math SAT:	526
Average ACT:	23
Graduated top 10% of class:	28
Graduated top 25% of class:	55
Graduated top 50% of class:	84

DEADLINES

Early decision/action:	NA
Early dec./act. notif.:	NA
Regular admission:	7/1
Regular adm. notif.:	rolling

APPLICANTS ALSO LOOK AT

and sometimes prefer:
U. Florida
Emory U.
U. Washington
Vanderbilt U.

and rarely prefer:
U. Virginia
U. Kentucky
Auburn U.
Clemson U.
U. South

ADDRESS

Undergraduate Admissions
320 Student Service Building
Circle Park Drive
Knoxville, TN 37996-0230
615-974-2184

FINANCIAL FACTS

In-state tuition ($):	1,798
Out-of-state tuition ($):	5,162
Room & board:	3,166
FA application deadline:	2/1
% frosh receiving FA:	50
PT earnings per yr. ($):	1100

TYPE OF AID % of students ($)

FA of some kind:	50 (NA)
Need-based grants:	NA
Merit-based grants:	2 (5,932)
Loans:	49 (2,234)
Work study:	4 (NA)
Student rating of FA:	80

UNIVERSITY OF TEXAS AT AUSTIN

Austin, TX

What do students think about University of Texas, Austin?

■ **Academics** UT Austin is *more* than affordable; it is, in the words of one undergraduate, "damn cheap!" Tuition is so low that some out-of-state students pay less than they would to go to public institutions in their own home states. But UT Austin has more than just price going for it. It also boasts excellent, varied academic programs and is located in what is arguably America's hippest small city. The school's huge endowment allows it to recruit scholars aggressively, and in recent years the school has attracted top professors in many fields. Business-related majors claim over one fifth the students here; engineering is also popular. Ten percent of the students study communications, and the film school is "up-and-coming." The only drawback is that UT Austin is huge. No, it's damn huge! Over 37,000 undergraduates (and another 12,000 graduate students) crowd the 300-acre campus. Accordingly, students usually have to assert themselves to get to know their professors (although top students qualify for an honors program with smaller classes). Also as you might expect, administering such a large institution is difficult, and the red-tape can be a little daunting, particularly for new students: said one, "The bureaucracy is the worst part of UT. Nobody knows what you want to know." Still, considering UT Austin's size, most administration categories received good marks: only the deans' offices received unusually low scores. Most students know what they're getting into before they arrive, and they feel that UT Austin is a "great school with great diversity, even though it has all the bureaucracy associated with large schools." Facilities are excellent and modern: students gave the library particularly high marks.

■ **Life** Students ranked Austin the tenth best college location in the country. "All Austin needs is a beach," said one student. It *does* have almost everything else, including one of America's most vibrant bar/live-music scenes. Students blend right in to the Austin community: relations between students and locals ranked in the top ten percent in our survey. For those who stay on campus, there are hundreds of clubs and organizations to get involved in. Fraternities and sororities are popular, but the school is large enough and offers enough in the way of activities that a student could have a full social life without ever attending a frat event. Longhorn football is huge, and other intercollegiate sporting events are also very popular.

■ **Students** It's a cliche, but at a school of 37,000, you're going to find someone who fits just about any description. The vast majority of students, nine out of ten, are Texans. Although Texas is a conservative state, UT Austin seems to attract more than it's fair share of "alternative" types. Liberal political ideas scored surprisingly high, as did such "p.c." attitudes as acceptance of the gay community. There are sizeable Hispanic and Asian populations; the African-American population is relatively small.

UNIVERSITY OF TEXAS AT AUSTIN

Austin, TX

Admissions

University of Texas, Austin, determines "regular admissions" on the basis of a formula that favors state residents. Any Texan in the top 10 percent of his/her high school graduating class is admitted, provided s/he has completed a high school curriculum including four years of English, three years each of social studies and math at the level of Algebra I and above, and two years each of lab science and foreign language. No non-resident, on the other hand, is ever guaranteed admissions. A chart outlining the formula is available from the admissions office. Applicants for the honors program (called "plan II") must complete applications including essays, letters of recommendation, and an interview. Plan II artists must submit a portfolio; musicians must audition. UT-Austin applicants are often also applicants to Texas A & M and University of Houston.

Financial Aid

University of Texas-Austin will accept the FAF or FFS, but prefers submission of the USAF (United Student Aid Funds) SingleFile application. In '90–'91, the FA office awarded merit-based grants to 25% of all undergrads, with an average award value of $1,625. The office writes that it "attempts to meet the full need of applicants with documented need to the extent that funds are available. Applicants are encouraged to apply early to receive maximum consideration for funds." Overall in '90–'91, 35% of all freshmen received aid of some kind (44% applied). The average freshmen award was $2,900. UT-Austin has no absolute FA application deadline; the deadline shown (see sidebar) is for priority consideration.

A note from the University of Texas Admissions Office:

"The University of Texas at Austin is a public institution, offering over 100 majors in Business Administration, Communication, Education, Engineering, Fine Arts, Liberal Arts, Natural Sciences, and Pharmacy."

ADMISSIONS FACTS

Competitiveness Rating:	**82**
% of applicants accepted:	67
% acceptees attending:	56

FRESHMAN PROFILE

Average verbal SAT:	511
Average math SAT:	584
Average ACT:	24
Graduated top 10% of class:	49
Graduated top 25% of class:	84
Graduated top 50% of class:	99

DEADLINES

Early decision/action:	NA
Early dec./act. notif.:	NA
Regular admission:	3/1
Regular adm. notif.:	rolling

APPLICANTS ALSO LOOK AT

and often prefer:
Baylor U.
Rice U.
U. Notre Dame

and rarely prefer:
Clemson U.
U. Houston–U. Park

ADDRESS

Undergraduate Admissions
Austin, TX 78712-1157
512-471-7601

FINANCIAL FACTS

In-state tuition ($):	916
Out-of-state tuition ($):	3,620
Room & board:	3,330
FA application deadline:	3/15
% frosh receiving FA:	33
PT earnings per yr. ($):	NA

TYPE OF AID % of students ($)

FA of some kind:	48 (3,200)
Need-based grants:	22 (1,825)
Merit-based grants:	25 (1,625)
Loans:	24 (2,700)
Work study:	5 (1,250)
Student rating of FA:	75

TEXAS CHRISTIAN UNIVERSITY

Fort Worth, TX

What do students think about Texas Christian University?

■ **Academics** TCU students are enthusiastic about their professors, whom they find to be personable and approachable. Comments such as "The majority of the teachers at TCU work very closely with the students" and "The teaching staff here is incredible and there are few 'weed out' classes; I have yet to take a class that was not exhilarating in some way" were common on our surveys. Pre-business is big here: nearly one in 10 graduates enters an MBA program within a year of graduation. So too are most other career-track majors: education, communications, the health sciences, and computer science are all strong and popular departments. Despite the pre-professional disposition of the student body, the traditional arts and sciences are hardly neglected at TCU: all students here must complete, by the end of sophomore year, a broad range of distribution requirements in the humanities, sciences, fine arts, and religion. A frequent complaint among those we surveyed was that the administration is secretive and unresponsive to student input: these complaints are particularly surprising in light of the apolitical nature of TCU students. If you have trouble dealing with powerful and occasionally arbitrary authorities, you might want to think twice before applying here.

■ **Life** TCU students are, overall, a happy group. They don't work too hard, love their surroundings (Fort Worth and nearby Dallas), and find each other extraordinarily attractive. "This school has had the best-looking women in Texas four years running!" enthused one senior. The lopsided male: female ratio can be problematic, as one woman pointed out: "If you're a girl looking for lots of dates, just remember that the 'girl to guy' ratio is 3 to 2 and getting asked out is a feat in itself!" Conservative politically and socially, students rate marriage very high among their goals. Greek life is very important here: second only to football in the hearts of most students.

■ **Students** "If diversity at college is what you're looking for—don't look here!" reported one TCU student, expressing a sentiment echoed by many of her classmates. Not everyone matches the description "white, affluent, and conservative," but many do. Add "attractive" and "fraternity/sorority member" to the description and you won't eliminate many students. The lack of diversity and the domination of social life by the Greeks are about the only complaints students seem to have about their classmates, however. As one student put it, "I expect I'll never find another body of individuals so kind or friendly again." For those few students who don't fit into the mainstream here, however, things can be a bit more difficult. As one Hispanic student told us, "Racism here is not usually blatant, but is subtle and therefore harder to combat. I don't see a great deal of school-based support and students who aren't members of a minority tend to be apathetic. I've pretty much been left to my own devices, but I'm doing fine anyway."

TEXAS CHRISTIAN UNIVERSITY

Fort Worth, TX

Admissions

Texas Christian's application for admission notes, "TCU's selection process takes into account the application, essay, high school or college transcript, counselor and teacher evaluations, and standardized test scores when appropriate. The quality and quantity of coursework taken are extremely important." Applicants are required to take the SAT or ACT, and are strongly urged to test twice before the second semester of senior year. Achievement tests are not required. The recommended high school curriculum includes four years of English, three years each of mathematics and social sciences, two years each of foreign language and physical science, and one year of biology. Students who wish to be considered for academic scholarship awards and students who would like to be evaluated on their transcript through junior year only should apply by January 15.

Financial Aid

Financial aid applicants to Texas Christian University must complete the FAF and a form generated by TCU's financial aid office, and must submit a copy of their parent' most recent tax return. TCU offers scholarships for athletic merit; in '91–'92, 5% of all undergrads received one (average value: $11,209). Scholarships are also awarded for talent in the fine arts; 3% of '91–'92 undergrads received one of these (average value: $2,500). Students in the top 15% of their high school class who present an SAT score of at least 1100 (or ACT of 27) and whose applications for admissions are postmarked by January 15 are automatically considered for a TCU academic scholarship; other academic scholarships (including the Chancellor Scholarship, which covers four years of tuition) and non-academic scholarships (orchestra, religious affiliation, etc.) are available as well.

Excerpted from Texas Christian University promotional materials:

"Our objective is to provide undergraduate and graduate instruction informed by research, to offer such undergraduate and graduate studies as will enable students to enter fruitful careers, to promote a mental, spiritual, and physical well-being of our students, to encourage continuous self-education, and to maintain a vital and inviting setting for learning and living in which the resources of the University are available while the atmosphere of a residential college is preserved.

"We intend to maintain and establish only undergraduate and graduate programs that are aimed toward excellence and contribute to the wholeness of the University. We are convinced that there must be a general compatibility among the values and daily practices of the University and its several units. We hope to perpetuate diversity in our programs and people, for we believe that no single vision will suffice for direction in a complex enterprise."

ADMISSIONS FACTS

Competitiveness Rating:	**67**
% of applicants accepted:	80
% acceptees attending:	38

FRESHMAN PROFILE

Average verbal SAT:	473*
Average math SAT:	530*
Average ACT:	23*
Graduated top 10% of class:	25
Graduated top 25% of class:	55
Graduated top 50% of class:	82

DEADLINES

Early decision/action:	11/15
Early dec./act. notif.:	1/1
Regular admission:	2/15
Regular adm. notif.:	4/1

APPLICANTS ALSO LOOK AT

and sometimes prefer:
Southern Methodist U.
Trinity U.
Baylor U.

and rarely prefer:
Southwestern U.
U. Texas–Austin
Rice U.
Texas A & M U.

ADDRESS

Undergraduate Admissions
2800 South University Drive
Fort Worth, TX 76129
817-921-7490

FINANCIAL FACTS

In-state tuition ($):	7,320
Out-of-state tuition ($):	7,320
Room & board:	3,058
FA application deadline:	5/1
% frosh receiving FA:	53
PT earnings per yr. ($):	3000

TYPE OF AID % of students ($)

FA of some kind:	58 (NA)
Need-based grants:	32 (3,300)
Merit-based grants:	NA
Loans:	20 (2,500)
Work study:	9 (1,224)
Student rating of FA:	89

TRENTON STATE COLLEGE

Trenton, NJ

CAMPUS LIFE

Quality of Life Rating:	**73**
Type of School:	public
Affiliation:	none
Environment:	city

STUDENT BODY

FT undergrad enrollment:	5,106
% male/% female:	38/62
% out-of-state:	8
% live on campus:	50
% African-American:	9
% Asian:	2
% Caucasian:	85
% Hispanic:	4
% foreign:	2
% transfers:	7

WHAT'S HOT

suitcase syndrome
Top 40
dating

WHAT'S NOT

dean
registration
studying hard
catalog
doing all the reading
administration (overall)
caring about politics
overall happiness

ACADEMICS

Academic Rating:	**75**
Calendar:	semester
Student/teacher ratio:	15/1
% doctorates:	72
Profs interesting:	75
Profs accessible:	73
Hours of study per day:	2.71

MOST POPULAR MAJORS BY %

Visual & Performing Arts:	13
Engineering Technologies:	7
Psychology:	7

% GRADS WHO PURSUE

Law:	2
MBA:	5
Medicine:	1
M.A., etc.:	16

What do students think about Trenton State College?

■ **Academics** Which Trenton State College is the *real* TSC: the one highly touted by *U.S. News & World Report* and *Money* magazine (the latter called the school "the third-best college buy in America"), or the one about which students in our survey complained with such surprising frequency? The truth is somewhere in the middle. TSC has earned a good reputation, but perhaps not one as good as the one it now has, which explains why so many students at this fine school expressed disappointment. TSC has earned accolades for its affordability, competitive student body, uniformly good academic departments, and top-notch science facilities, as well as for the fact that full professors teach all courses here. The school's honors program also allows superior students a great degree of autonomy in fashioning their studies. Business administration, education, and pre-medical sciences are among the most popular and highly touted departments here. All students complete a wide assortment of math, science, and liberal arts courses, regardless of major. Despite the school's assets, however, most students we surveyed expressed serious reservations about some aspect of life at TSC. The administration was the favorite target of most students. Many voiced the opinion that the school showed more concern for presenting "a good front" and attracting future students than for providing for currently enrolled students. Students complained that "advisement and guidance overall are below substandard," that "the faculty is understaffed," and that "administrators and staff are rude and not helpful." Furthermore, students gave below average grades to the faculty, purported to be one of TSC's great strengths.

■ **Life** TSC students gave the city of Trenton very low grades. Wrote one student, "There's nothing within walking distance. There are few clubs and bars and no coffee houses." Social life revolves almost entirely around drinking ("There is a very minimal amount of social activity offered on and around this campus"), leading one student to explain that "the biggest downfall of this place is the lack of things for students under 21 to do on weekends." There is a fairly popular Greek system, but all the frat houses are located off-campus, "which is stupid because it promotes drinking and driving." The campus itself is "scenic" and the dorms are "comfortable, once you get used to group showers." One student summed up: "If you're looking for a good, challenging education, then TSC is for you. But if you want an all-around college experience, I'd suggest other schools."

■ **Students** The vast majority of TSC students are from New Jersey. A 15 percent minority population is made up mostly of blacks. Because TSC is one of the most competitive public institutions in the country, students are very bright. Students are conservative, both politically and socially. By one student's measure they are also "very closed-minded. I'd be very afraid to be gay here."

TRENTON STATE COLLEGE

Trenton, NJ

Admissions

From Trenton State's undergraduate catalog: "Most students not only apply for admission into the college, but also for acceptance into the major of their choice, although new freshmen who wish to explore various academic opportunities may apply for 'open option' status and select a major by the end of their freshman year. Because of the demand and differences in program size, the number of spaces available for freshman varies from major to major." Applicants are judged primarily on their high school academic and extracurricular records and their standardized test scores. A minimum of sixteen high school units is required, including four units of English, two each of social studies, mathematics and laboratory sciences, and six units of college-prep level electives. All applicants must submit SAT or ACT scores; those applying to the Electronics Engineering Technology Department must also submit scores from the Math I or II Achievement Test.

Financial Aid

Trenton State requires financial aid applicants to complete the FAF and a form from its own financial aid office. The school awards various grants for academic merit. Overall last year, 68% of the freshman class applied for some form of aid, and 60% of those who applied (40% overall) received an award of some kind (average value: $3,250). Among the loans available are those from the Governor's Teaching Scholars Program, which provides scholarship loans of up to $7,500 per year to "academically talented New Jersey high school seniors." The complete amount borrowed (up to $30,000) is redeemable based upon "successful teaching service in New Jersey public schools."

Excerpted from Trenton State College promotional materials:

"Trenton State is a highly selective institution which provides students with an opportunity to participate in a unique community of learners. This community calls upon its members to recognize and strive for excellence, and to develop the objectivity and capacity for change which are marks of educated persons. It also calls upon them to participate in service to others and to exhibit a respect for and appreciation of diversity.

"In a learning partnership with faculty, students will enhance their skills, expand their knowledge, and formulate the values and attitudes necessary to assume the responsibilities of an increasingly complex society. They will be expected to develop the ability to express themselves effectively, independently, and creatively. They will be expected to learn and live within an ethical perspective and to demonstrate habits of reasoned judgment and responsible action."

TRINITY COLLEGE

CAMPUS LIFE

Quality of Life Rating:	**82**
Type of School:	private
Affiliation:	none
Environment:	city

STUDENT BODY

FT undergrad enrollment:	1,739
% male/% female:	53/47
% out-of-state:	76
% live on campus:	92
% African-American:	6
% Asian:	6
% Caucasian:	84
% Hispanic:	3
% foreign:	2
% transfers:	2

WHAT'S HOT

good-looking students
Grateful Dead
financial aid
small classes (overall)
deans
living on campus
catalog

WHAT'S NOT

town-gown relations
gay community visible
marriage
alternative rock

ACADEMICS

Academic Rating:	**83**
Calendar:	semester
Student/teacher ratio:	11/1
% doctorates:	87
Profs interesting:	83
Profs accessible:	83
Hours of study per day:	3.19

MOST POPULAR MAJORS BY %

Social Sciences:	42
Letters/Literature:	15
Psychology:	9

What do students think of Trinity College (Connecticut)?

■ **Academics** Trinity College, traditionally known as Connecticut's safety school for Ivy League aspirants, is becoming the first choice of more and more top students. Its "small classes, excellent professors, and very competitive academic structure" garnered rave reviews from current undergrads. Standout departments include most liberal arts offerings (especially history and philosophy), economics, psychology and the interdisciplinary, by-invitation-only Guided Studies programs. The amount of academic pressure depends largely on the individual. As one put it, "if you want to excel there's plenty of room, and if you want to slide there's plenty of beer—it's up to you." Requirements here are demanding: students must complete distribution requirements (five courses) *and* an interdisciplinary minor (six courses) as well as a major. Trinity offers a vast array of internships: 65 percent of students take advantage of the opportunity to work at local insurance companies or in state government. Study abroad is also encouraged: Trinity has a campus in Rome and is part of a consortium in Spain. Approximately one third of Trinity's students spend at least one semester abroad. Students reported a high degree of success in dealing with the administration. Deans received very high marks, as did the financial aid office.

■ **Life** As one undergrad wrote, "A Trinity education means more than academics; it provides experience through community activities, clubs, sports, and so much more." Chances to get involved are plentiful here, and many students participate in more than one extracurricular activity. As at most Catholic schools, community service is quite popular. The Division III intercollegiate sports, particularly basketball and hockey, are extremely popular. Social life is lively almost every night of the week ("It's a huge party school! Ask around!")—it's so lively, in fact, that the administration recently limited weeknight parties to groups of 100 or fewer. Fraternities are alive and well ("Greeks rule!"), but there is little peer pressure to rush. Almost everyone lives on campus, with few complaints except that the Department of Residential Life can be "unbearable" to deal with. "Camp Trin-Trin" is indeed a lovely place to live, and the serenity of the campus combines with a prevalent fun-loving attitude here to create a "comfortable and happy" atmosphere.

■ **Students** Despite efforts by the administration to increase diversity on campus, Trinity remains in essence a white, preppie enclave. The political climate is basically conservative, but not actively so. The contentedness that pervades the campus translates into apathy toward outside issues. There is no visible gay community at Trinity, nor is there evidence of alternative-lifestyle consciousness in general. Students at Trinity College are primarily interested in getting a high-quality education while having fun, and most agree that Trinity provides them with ample amounts of both.

TRINITY COLLEGE

Admissions

Trinity College's bulletin notes that students don't always realize the significance of personal qualities in the admissions process: "Colleges are interested in more than prospective students' achievements or skills. We are keenly interested in attracting and admitting candidates who not only give ample proof of academic prowess, but also show evidence of such personal qualities as honesty, fairness, compassion, altruism, leadership, and initiative in their high school years." Trinity employs no cut-offs, minimums, or formulas; in order of importance, the admissions committee considers an applicant's high school curriculum and overall record (including GPA), standardized test scores, letters of recommendation, essays, extracurriculars, and interview. ACT or SAT scores are required, and applicants are strongly urged to take the English Composition with essay Achievement Test. All applicants should also have completed at least 16 academic units in high school, including four years of English, two years each of foreign language and algebra, and one year each of geometry, history, and lab science. Children of alumni are given preference over other applicants of similar qualifications. Students who apply to Trinity College most often also apply to Middlebury, Tufts, Connecticut College, Colgate, and Wesleyan.

Financial Aid

The financial aid office at Trinity College requires applicants to submit the FAF, a form generated by the school, and their parents' most recent tax return. Trinity does not award merit-based grants; however, it does offer scholarships to those preparing for the ministry. Students most frequently borrow from the Stafford and Perkins loan programs; Trinity also has a number of endowed loans that it administers through its financial aid office.

A note from the Trinity College Admissions Office:

"Trinity's location in a major metropolitan area offers its students opportunities not as readily available at other selective New England liberal arts colleges in more rural settings. Well over one half of Trinity's students take advantage of internships in business, the arts, government, law, education, medicine, etc., in the Hartford area. Additionally, several hundred students are engaged in volunteer activities in the broader community through the Community Outreach program. However, Trinity's beautiful campus means that students need not give up a classical collegiate atmosphere in order to take advantage of the opportunities made possible by the College's city setting."

ADMISSIONS FACTS

Competitiveness Rating:	**85**
% of applicants accepted:	50
% acceptees attending:	29

FRESHMAN PROFILE

Average verbal SAT:	560
Average math SAT:	620
Average ACT:	27
Graduated top 10% of class:	41
Graduated top 25% of class:	83
Graduated top 50% of class:	98

DEADLINES

Early decision/action:	12/1
Early dec./act. notif.:	12/31
Regular admission:	1/15
Regular adm. notif.:	4/10

APPLICANTS ALSO LOOK AT

and often prefer:
Amherst College
Yale U.
Harvard/Radcliffe College
U. Pennsylvania
Tufts U.

and sometimes prefer:
Boston College
Georgetown U.

and rarely prefer:
Connecticut College
Fairfield U.

ADDRESS

Undergraduate Admissions
300 Summit Street
Hartford, CT 06106
203-297-2180

FINANCIAL FACTS

In-state tuition ($):	16,220
Out-of-state tuition ($):	16,220
Room & board:	4,820
FA application deadline:	2/15
% frosh receiving FA:	40
PT earnings per yr. ($):	1400

TYPE OF AID % of students ($)

FA of some kind:	42 (NA)
Need-based grants:	NA (12,000)
Merit-based grants:	0
Loans:	NA (3,000)
Work study:	40 (1,030)
Student rating of FA:	90

TRINITY UNIVERSITY

San Antonio, TX

CAMPUS LIFE

Quality of Life Rating: **83**

Type of School:	private
Affiliation:	Presbyterian
Environment:	city

STUDENT BODY

FT undergrad enrollment:	2,223
% male/% female:	48/52
% out-of-state:	43
% live on campus:	71
% African-American:	2
% Asian:	5
% Caucasian:	83
% Hispanic:	9
% foreign:	3
% transfers:	1

WHAT'S HOT

food
dorm comfort
intramural sports
library
small lectures
profs outside class

WHAT'S NOT

dating
dorm safety
diversity
rap/hip-hop
college newspaper

ACADEMICS

Academic Rating: **87**

Calendar:	semester
Student/teacher ratio:	11/1
% doctorates:	94
Profs interesting:	88
Profs accessible:	89
Hours of study per day:	2.87

MOST POPULAR MAJORS BY %

Business & Management:	24
Social Sciences:	15
Physical Sciences:	10

% GRADS WHO PURSUE

Law:	12
MBA:	2
Medicine:	8
M.A., etc.:	56

What do students think about Trinity University?

■ **Academics** Even in recessionary 1991, Trinity University continued to spend money to build its ever-burgeoning reputation, doling out for both outstanding professors and top-rung students. "Many students come here simply because Trinity gave them the most money," explained one undergrad. Once here, students have access to an excellent, well-rounded education in an intimate environment ("Profs are very accessible and classes are small," reported a typical respondent). All students complete a rigorous set of general education requirements that accounts for over one quarter of the credits toward graduation: these courses include both Western and non-Western liberal arts studies, math, science, and ethics. Business and management majors claim nearly 25 percent of the students. Communications, pre-medical sciences, English, and history are among the other popular majors. Most respondents to our survey had something to say about the school's activist administration, much of it negative. Wrote one, "We have a definite 'Big Brother' atmosphere. The administration is clinging to a set of morals held over from the 1950s." Another student countered, "A couple of years ago, the administration changed this school from a 'country club for rich kids' into a well-known academic institution. Now they're working on sports and ethnic diversity. While occasionally repressive, the administration has done well and I have faith that it will continue to do so."

■ **Life** Trinity's administration has tried to curtail its students' partying habits, but the party continues nonetheless. There are more Trinity students than ever, however, who find the excessive drinking and debauchery distasteful. "This is basically a huge day-care center for middle-class and upper-middle-class families," wrote one of the new breed of Trinity undergrads. Students report a surprising diversity of extracurricular and social activities for a small school. Wrote one, "Most students are able to find a social group with which to bond. Whether it be a sorority, fraternity, an athletic team, drama, volunteer action, or church groups, it seems everyone finds a niche in which to settle to be happy." Opportunities to date other Trinity students, however, are rare. As one student explained, "Trinity's size lends itself to an incestuous environment which makes dating a real drag! Otherwise, this place kicks butt!" The campus is beautiful and meticulously maintained ("The gardener to student ratio is the best in the nation"). Students gave San Antonio (home of the Alamo and great Tex-Mex food and music) good marks.

■ **Students** Students reported that there is practically no ethnic diversity at Trinity, a considerable Hispanic population notwithstanding. "The students here are too much alike," complained one student. Another described the student body as "an inebriated upper-crust white bread group with an extremely limited interest in anything that happens in the outside world." Trinity's aggressive recruitment of top students has brought a nearly 50 percent out-of-state population to the school.

TRINITY UNIVERSITY

San Antonio, TX

Admissions

The admissions office at Trinity University requires applicants to have completed the following high school curriculum: "four years of English, three years of college-preparatory mathematics, including either trigonometry or pre-calculus, two years of laboratory science, two years of social studies, and two years of a foreign language." Applicants are also required to submit results for either the SAT or the ACT; achievement exams are recommended but not required (as is an on-campus interview).

Financial Aid

Financial aid applicants to Trinity University must complete the FAF. In '91–'92, 23 percent of all undergrads at Trinity received an academic scholarship. The average value was $3,134. Scholarships are available for leadership, residency, religious affiliation, and minorities.

Excerpted from Trinity University promotional materials:

"We believe that an education of enduring substance is one delivered by internationally recognized, active scholars working with small classes. The Trinity faculty, 94 percent of whom hold doctoral degrees, is committed both to undergraduate teaching and to research. All levels of students, freshmen and sophomores included, are encouraged to participate in significant research projects.

"In addition, Trinity's nineteen endowed distinguished professorships attract renowned scholars who greatly enrich our students' experiences.

"The student/faculty ratio at Trinity is 11:1, and no classes are taught by graduate students or teachings assistants. The close association between students and professors intensifies the learning experience, as research, lectures, writings, and artistic projects are undertaken."

ADMISSIONS FACTS

Competitiveness Rating:	87
% of applicants accepted:	75
% acceptees attending:	36

FRESHMAN PROFILE

Average verbal SAT:	576
Average math SAT:	626
Average ACT:	27
Graduated top 10% of class:	66
Graduated top 25% of class:	93
Graduated top 50% of class:	100

DEADLINES

Early decision/action:	11/15
Early dec./act. notif.:	12/15
Regular admission:	2/1
Regular adm. notif.:	3/31

APPLICANTS ALSO LOOK AT

and often prefer:
Rice U.
Duke U.
U. Texas–Austin

and sometimes prefer:
Texas Christian U.
Tulane U.
Vanderbilt U.
Texas A & M U.

ADDRESS

Undergraduate Admissions
715 Stadium Drive
San Antonio, TX 78212
512-736-7207

FINANCIAL FACTS

In-state tuition ($):	10,200
Out-of-state tuition ($):	10,200
Room & board:	4,800
FA application deadline:	2/1
% frosh receiving FA:	78
PT earnings per yr. ($):	1000

TYPE OF AID % of students ($)

FA of some kind:	70 (NA)
Need-based grants:	41 (9,888)
Merit-based grants:	NA
Loans:	NA
Work study:	NA (1,044)
Student rating of FA:	84

TUFTS UNIVERSITY

Medford, MA

What do students think about Tufts University?

■ **Academics** Tufts University has a reputation as the "Ivy League dumping ground"—the "safety" choice of Easterners applying to the Ivies. As one student explained, "Many here apply to an Ivy as their reach, but have Tufts as their first real choice. The result is really smart, hard workers who weren't quite genius-geeky enough for their first-choice schools." Once here, students settle into a demanding academic environment notable for several features. First are the professors, whom students found accessible and friendly. Second are "the nation's best orientation program, especially the Exploration Program from the Experimental College," which has students and professors co-teach introductory courses in fields of common interest and expertise. There's also a sophomore year abroad, taken advantage of by almost one quarter of the class. Students rave about the size of the student body, large enough to support a wide range of academic fields but small enough to feel like a community—"Walking around you always see people you know, but you also see people you don't." The biggest negative here: "The library sucks."

■ **Life** Tufts offers students an attractive, hilly, suburban campus less than a half-hour's commute from Boston. No wonder many students call the location "perfect." Said one enthusiast, "Tufts has just about everything a college student would want, from hills to flatlands, parties to quiet nights, a city and a suburb, as well as all kinds of people. There's nowhere else I'd rather be at this time in my life." Another student warned that "people who don't like walking up and down hills may not be particularly happy here at Tufts." School spirit is low—"Nobody goes to the games or pep rallies"—and on-campus activities that don't serve alcohol are poorly attended. Also, dating just doesn't happen very often, as one student explained: "The dating scene stinks—everyone already has someone at home, someone here, or is just looking for sex." The food is great.

■ **Students** Our respondents had a lot to say about the diversity of the student body here, mostly negative. The comment, "For all the hype about diversity, I have not found Tufts to be a particularly diverse university," was typical. Students felt that administrators were more interested in the perception of diversity than in diversity itself, and characterized their classmates as friendly but cliquish. There is a sizeable leftist population here, and gay students are active, but there is also a large group of students who resent their "p.c." classmates. One went so far as to say that "there is an atmosphere of barely checked violence at Tufts." Still, students ranked themselves "very happy" overall, so these complaints are not major, regardless of how strenuously students voiced them. Students don't work terribly hard yet express overall satisfaction with their education: they are bright but not driven in the way many of their Ivy League peers are.

TUFTS UNIVERSITY

Medford, MA

Admissions

Tufts' undergraduate catalog states that admission "is not based solely on numerical signs of success or common patterns of achievement. The Committee on Admissions feels a responsibility to reflect in its decisions the diversity and excitement of the University itself. The Committee on Admissions is concerned with the quality of the applicant's program, performance in that program, results on standardized tests, personal recommendations, special talents, and finally evidence of enthusiasm for scholarly work, genuine intellectual curiosity, creativity, independence and resolution....The best preparation is a sound foundation in English, both in literature and in writing, plus mathematics, foreign languages, social studies, and laboratory science....Applicants of high ability and promise, however, are considered regardless of their preparation." All applicants must submit SAT or ACT scores, and three Achievement scores, one of which must be English Composition. Engineering prospects' other two Achievements must be Math (I or II) and either Physics or Chemistry. Early Decision applications received before November 1 will be "acted on" by December 15. Applicants may apply Early Decision up until the regular admissions deadline, simply by stating that request in writing.

Financial Aid

Financial aid applicants to Tufts must complete the FAF and a form generated by Tufts' financial aid office. In '89–90, 40% of all full-time undergraduates received over $29 million in grants, loans, and employment. The average aid package was $10,720, which was 77% of the tuition at the time. Thirty-six percent of the entering class of freshmen received aid; the average grant was $9,200, and the average aid package was $11,800.

A note from the Tufts University Admissions Office:

"Tufts University, on the boundary between Medford and Somerville, sits on a hill overlooking Boston, five miles northwest of the city. The campus is a tranquil New England setting within easy access by subway and bus to the cultural, social, and entertainment resources of Boston and Cambridge.

"Since its founding in 1852 by members of the Universalist church, Tufts has grown from a small liberal arts college into a nonsectarian university of over 7,000 students. By 1900 the college had added a medical school, a dental school, and graduate studies. The university now also includes the Fletcher School of Law and Diplomacy, the Graduate School of Arts and Sciences, the School of Veterinary Medicine, the School of Nutrition, and the Sackler School of Graduate Biomedical Sciences."

ADMISSIONS FACTS

Competitiveness Rating:	**93**
% of applicants accepted:	46
% acceptees attending:	34

FRESHMAN PROFILE

Average verbal SAT:	614
Average math SAT:	673
Average ACT:	28
Graduated top 10% of class:	74
Graduated top 25% of class:	93
Graduated top 50% of class:	99

DEADLINES

Early decision/action:	11/15, 1/1
Early dec./act. notif.:	2/1
Regular admission:	1/1
Regular adm. notif.:	4/15

APPLICANTS ALSO LOOK AT

and often prefer:
Harvard/Radcliffe College
Duke U.
Brown U.
Dartmouth College
U. Pennsylvania

and sometimes prefer:
Northwestern U.
U. Mass–Amherst

and rarely prefer:
Boston College
Brandeis U.

ADDRESS

Undergraduate Admissions
Medford, MA 02155
617-381-3170

FINANCIAL FACTS

In-state tuition ($):	16,755
Out-of-state tuition ($):	16,755
Room & board:	5,300
FA application deadline:	2/1
% frosh receiving FA:	36
PT earnings per yr. ($):	1400

TYPE OF AID % of students ($)

FA of some kind:	44 (NA)
Need-based grants:	NA
Merit-based grants:	NA
Loans:	NA
Work study:	NA
Student rating of FA:	71

TULANE UNIVERSITY

CAMPUS LIFE

Quality of Life Rating:	*86*
Type of School:	private
Affiliation:	none
Environment:	city

STUDENT BODY

FT undergrad enrollment:	5,560
% male/% female:	53/47
% out-of-state:	79
% live on campus:	50
% African-American:	9
% Asian:	3
% Caucasian:	83
% Hispanic:	4
% foreign:	3
% transfers:	2

WHAT'S HOT

location
financial aid
registration
hard liquor
marijuana
overall happiness
beer

WHAT'S NOT

rap/hip-hop
library
cost of living

ACADEMICS

Academic Rating:	*80*
Calendar:	semester
Student/teacher ratio:	14/1
% doctorates:	98
Profs interesting:	75
Profs accessible:	81
Hours of study per day:	2.85

MOST POPULAR MAJORS BY %

Social Sciences:	31
Business & Management:	14
Engineering:	10

% GRADS WHO PURSUE

Law:	10
MBA:	6
Medicine:	9
M.A., etc.:	55

What do students think about Tulane University?

■ **Academics** Always counted among the top undergraduate schools in the South, Tulane University has in the past few years made some major changes in an effort to upgrade further its already excellent facilities and programs. A recently completed computer center, a new home (and expanded faculty) for the Freeman School of Business, and a new student athletic center are among the additions that led one student to speculate that "the administration is working very hard to get Tulane up there with the big boys. I think I am leaving a better school than I came into." Besides business, Latin American studies (and international studies in general), architecture, engineering, and English are said to be the top programs of study here. All liberal arts students (everyone except engineers, architects, and business students) must complete a demanding core curriculum with a strong emphasis on natural sciences and the liberal arts; other students fulfill some, but not all, such requirements. One student described Tulane as "a comfortably sized school in a good-sized city with personable teachers and plenty of help programs for students." Indeed, while students enjoy only moderate access to their professors outside the classroom, numerous counseling and tutoring options help prevent students from becoming just another number on an attendance sheet. The demands academics make on students' time here varies from program to program, but most students describe the school as "low-pressure."

■ **Life** Tulane University is "a miniature New Orleans in the middle of New Orleans, a true party-like atmosphere," which is what led one area college counselor to describe Tulane as "outstanding in spite of, or because of, its location." Overall students love New Orleans ("It's Mardi Gras all year round," exclaimed one student), although a few find the city too distracting. "New Orleans is too much fun and the city revolves around alcohol," said one student. "It makes it hard to concentrate on academics." New Orleans has a very active night life that centers around its homegrown Zydeco and Cajun cultures, and spending a night out on the town drinking is a very popular diversion among students. One student summed up New Orleans this way: "The bars never close, the music scene is intense, and the weather has it all." The campus is beautiful and conveniently located for those who want to take advantage of the city. The Greek system is surprisingly popular considering the school's urban location. Students report that "athletics are up and coming, especially basketball." On-campus food is not so good, but access to Louisiana *haute cuisine*—gumbo and crawfish po' boys—is within walking distance.

■ **Students** Tulane attracts a 17 percent minority population, over half of which is made up of African-Americans. Students rated the student body diverse but reported that cliquishness prevails here; students with similar backgrounds and goals tend to stick together. The school draws students from nearly every state and 19 foreign countries, but the majority of students are Southerners.

TULANE UNIVERSITY

Admissions

Tulane's undergraduate bulletin states, "We look closely for intelligence, motivation, achievement, and character. Academic potential is essential. At the same time, we are concerned that our students exhibit energy and an ability to contribute constructively to campus life outside the classroom. Beyond this, we seek students from varied backgrounds and lifestyles, for we believe that student diversity enhances education." Tulane's admissions office first considers an applicant's high school GPA and curriculum, along with his or her extracurriculars. These are followed, in order of importance, by standardized test scores, the application essay, and letters of recommendation. While no cut-offs are used, "The majority of those students considered competitive for admission will be 'B' average or better students typically ranking in the top one third of their class." SAT or ACT scores must be submitted, and applicants should have completed at least four years of English, three years of mathematics (four years for those planning to major in scientific fields), and two years each of foreign language, lab science, and social studies. Students who apply to Tulane most often also apply to Vanderbilt, Emory, Washington U., Boston U., and U. of Pennsylvania.

Financial Aid

Tulane requires a FAF and a copy of the parents' most recent tax return of its financial aid applicants. Last year, Tulane awarded academic merit grants to 14% of all undergrads (average value: $11,400), and athletic merit grants to 12% ($5,640). Overall last year, 53% of all freshmen received some form of financial aid, with an average award value of $17,900. Tulane recommended Perkins loans to 33% of its undergrads in '91–'92 (average loan: $1,100), Stafford loans to 41% ($2,300), and PLUS loans to 10% ($2,940). Tulane's 3/1 deadline is an in-office deadline.

A note from the Tulane University Admissions Office:

"Tulane University has seized the challenges of the 1990s with the recently completed A.B. Freeman School of Business; a Performing Arts Center; a multi-million-dollar renovation of all residence halls and the University Center; modern facilities for varsity athletics; the $12-million Center for Energy and Biotechnology; the $14-million Student Recreation Center; a coordinated Research Instrumentation Facility housing state-of-the-art scientific equipment; and the latest computing facilities afforded by a $15-million, five-year campus-wide computing plan. Founded in 1834 and reorganized as Tulane University in 1884. Tulane is one of the major private research universities in the South. The Tulane campus offers a traditional collegiate setting in an attractive residential neighborhood."

ADMISSIONS FACTS

Competitiveness Rating:	**78**
% of applicants accepted:	72
% acceptees attending:	27

FRESHMAN PROFILE

Average verbal SAT:	558
Average math SAT:	597
Average ACT:	NA
Graduated top 10% of class:	36
Graduated top 25% of class:	66
Graduated top 50% of class:	94

DEADLINES

Early decision/action:	11/1
Early dec./act. notif.	12/15
Regular admission:	1/15
Regular adm. notif.:	4/15

APPLICANTS ALSO LOOK AT

and sometimes prefer:
U. Texas–Austin
Northwestern U.
Florida State U.
Washington U.

and rarely prefer:
Skidmore College
Southern Methodist U.
U. Richmond

ADDRESS

Undergraduate Admissions
6823 St Charles Ave
New Orleans, LA 70118
504-865-5731

FINANCIAL FACTS

In-state tuition ($):	16,750
Out-of-state tuition ($):	16,750
Room & board:	5,505
FA application deadline:	3/1
% frosh receiving FA:	60
PT earnings per yr. ($):	1450

TYPE OF AID % of students ($)

FA of some kind:	60 (16,975)
Need-based grants:	41 (11,700)
Merit-based grants:	NA
Loans:	NA
Work study:	24 (1,300)
Student rating of FA:	93

UNION COLLEGE

CAMPUS LIFE

Quality of Life Rating: **79**

Type of School:	private
Affiliation:	none
Environment:	city

STUDENT BODY

FT undergrad enrollment:	1,987
% male/% female:	56/44
% out-of-state:	45
% live on campus:	76
% African-American:	3
% Asian:	5
% Caucasian:	87
% Hispanic:	3
% foreign:	2
% transfers:	1

WHAT'S HOT

college radio station
small lectures
dorm comfort
profs outside class
fraternities/sororities
cost of living
living on campus

WHAT'S NOT

location
gay community visible
town-gown relations
diversity
library
working a job

ACADEMICS

Academic Rating: **84**

Calendar:	trimester
Student/teacher ratio:	12/1
% doctorates:	93
Profs interesting:	83
Profs accessible:	90
Hours of study per day:	3.16

MOST POPULAR MAJORS BY %

Biology:	12
Political Science:	10
Psychology:	8

% GRADS WHO PURSUE

Law:	9
MBA:	1
Medicine:	9
M.A., etc.:	16

What do students think about Union College?

■ **Academics** One Union College undergraduate reported that "this school offers just about everything a large school does, without all of the people." Indeed, two of Union's great assets are its comfortable size and diversity of fine programs: the school's 2,000 undergrads pursue a wide variety of career-oriented and liberal arts studies. Engineering is popular and excellent, as are the pre-medical majors. Political science, history, economics, and English are among the favorite liberal arts departments. The school recently instituted a core curriculum that requires all students to acquire a comprehensive education in Western culture, as well as a grounding in math and the sciences. Classes are small and, best of all, the professors are extremely accessible. "When professors offer their home phone numbers so you can get help over the weekend, you know you're getting your money's worth," reported one student. Several students remarked on the Term Abroad program, which almost half of Union's students take advantage of. Said one, "I spent my Junior fall semester in Bath, England. It was a fabulous experience. I can't imagine another school offering a better program." Students gave the library low marks. One explained: "The library and theatre (a national historic landmark) are both in need of extensive repair and renovation, a condition brought about partly by negligence." The school's trimester schedule means that the school year does not end until June.

■ **Life** Social life at UC pretty much fits the stereotype for a small school in an unexciting town. Social opportunities are limited, with fraternities providing the setting for most of the socializing. Said one student, "If you don't like fraternity parties, don't come here." The development of a healthy dating scene is hindered by the lopsided male:female ratio, as men outnumber women almost three to two. Drinking is a very popular way to spend free time, as are occasional roadtrips to Saratoga Springs. Schenectady is not popular with students, who ranked it the seventh worst college town in the nation. The campus is "absolutely breathtaking," and the dorms are comfortable, although the lack of kitchen facilities drives many students to off-campus housing. Students sharing common interests take houses together. Explained one student, "The best feature is the houses. As a member of the computer science house, I have learned first-hand what they have to offer: friendship, support and a very strong environment. Our motto is: "We do more after midnight than most people do all day.""

■ **Students** As one Union student put it, "The student body is overly homogeneous but students are very friendly and down-to-earth." There is a 13 percent minority population, but, "For the most part, students of different cultures stick closely together. We say we want to teach each other about our different cultures but it is mostly talk...how sad." The school's pricey tuition guarantees that a lot of undergrads are from very affluent families.

UNION COLLEGE

Admissions

The admissions office reports that "The goal of the admissions process is to bring together on our campus a mix of students who will have a general educational impact on each other, in and out of class. While we use no formulas in admissions, a strong academic track record is certainly necessary and we have designed our application process to allow students to highlight their candidacies as 'whole people.' At Union we encourage prospective applicants to approach the admissions process in this creative spirit." Primarily, Union looks at your GPA and the quality of your high school program, along with your class rank. After these, in descending importance, they consider letters of recommendation, essays, extracurriculars, your interview and standardized test scores. They require that you take either the ACT or 3 Achievements (including English Composition), and that you have completed four years of English, two years of a foreign language, and two-and-one-half years of mathematics. Students who apply to Union most often also apply to Cornell, Colgate, Tufts, Hamilton, and Trinity College(CT).

Financial Aid

Union College's financial aid office requires its own form, an FAF, a copy of your parents' most recent tax return and, if applicable, a divorced/separated statement and/or business supplement. The school does not award any merit-based grants. Last year, the FA office recommended Perkins loans to 7% of all undergrads (average value: $1,667), Stafford loans to 35% ($2,723), its own institutional loans to 3% ($2,660), and PLUS loans to 2% ($3,750). Overall, 53% of the class of '95 applied for some form of financial aid; of those who applied, 84% received an award of some kind, with an average value of $14,300.

A note from the Union College Admissions Office:

"Union College is an independent, primarily undergraduate, residential college for men and women of high academic promise and strong personal motivation. Throughout its history Union has been distinguished by its commitment to the idea that both experience and reflection are necessary to a proper education. In the past, that commitment was evidenced when Union became the first liberal arts college to offer engineering. Today, that commitment is reflected in our nationally recognized General Education Curriculum, which combines elements of choice within a structure of requirements and incentives; our extensive Terms Abroad program, which attracts more than 40 percent of our students; and our vigorous encouragement of undergraduate research."

ADMISSIONS FACTS

Competitiveness Rating:	**85**
% of applicants accepted:	52
% acceptees attending:	31

FRESHMAN PROFILE

Average verbal SAT:	NA
Average math SAT:	NA
Average ACT:	27
Graduated top 10% of class:	45
Graduated top 25% of class:	84
Graduated top 50% of class:	98

DEADLINES

Early decision/action:	2/1
Early dec./act. notif.:	rolling
Regular admission:	2/1
Regular adm. notif.:	4/15

APPLICANTS ALSO LOOK AT

and often prefer:
Brown U.
Hamilton College

and sometimes prefer:
Tufts U.
SUNY Buffalo
Cornell U.
St. Lawrence U.
Franklin & Marshall College

and rarely prefer:
Connecticut College
Lehigh U.

ADDRESS

Undergraduate Admissions
Schenectady, NY 12308
518-370-6112

FINANCIAL FACTS

In-state tuition ($):	15,420
Out-of-state tuition ($):	15,420
Room & board:	5,395
FA application deadline:	2/1
% frosh receiving FA:	53
PT earnings per yr. ($):	1100

TYPE OF AID % of students ($)

FA of some kind:	57 (14,200)
Need-based grants:	38 (9,200)
Merit-based grants:	NA
Loans:	NA (2,600)
Work study:	32 (1,100)
Student rating of FA:	83

VANDERBILT UNIVERSITY

Nashville, TN

CAMPUS LIFE

Quality of Life Rating: **89**

Type of School:	private
Affiliation:	none
Environment:	city

STUDENT BODY

FT undergrad enrollment:	5,216
% male/% female:	51/49
% out-of-state:	84
% live on campus:	90
% African-American:	4
% Asian:	4
% Caucasian:	88
% Hispanic:	1
% foreign:	2
% transfers:	1

WHAT'S HOT

good-looking students
registration
cost of living
marriage
administration (overall)
food
hard liquor
conservative politics
campus appearance
location

WHAT'S NOT

diversity
interaction among students
in-class discussion
requirements easy

ACADEMICS

Academic Rating: **86**

Calendar:	semester
Student/teacher ratio:	8/1
% doctorates:	92
Profs interesting:	81
Profs accessible:	81
Hours of study per day:	3.23

MOST POPULAR MAJORS BY %

Human Development:	14
Economics:	9
English:	6

% GRADS WHO PURSUE

Law:	12
MBA:	8
Medicine:	8
M.A., etc.:	12

What do students think about Vanderbilt University?

■ **Academics** Students at Vanderbilt University claim the best of both worlds: top-notch academics (evidenced by the fact that nearly half the school's graduates proceed to graduate school) and a friendly, laid-back Southern atmosphere. "There is a sense of academic excellence here," wrote one undergraduate, "but without cutthroat competition." It's the kind of place where students can admit to studying over three hours a day, then turn around and report that "academic pressure is virtually nonexistent, unless one places it on one's self." A smooth-running administration nurtures this atmosphere, as do approachable, caring professors "Dedicated" is a word several respondents used to describe the faculty. Wrote one student, "Professors are so accessible, many of them welcome students to their homes." Students favor pre-professional studies, but a broad-ranging core curriculum guarantees that all learn the rudiments of writing, humanities, mathematics, and natural and social sciences. Pre-business majors, such as economics, are both popular and strong, as are the pre-medical sciences, engineering, English, and psychology.

■ **Life** As one student put it, "Vanderbilt University can be the ideal situation for college or your worst nightmare. When you arrive as a freshman, you pretty much deduce within weeks if you love it or hate it." To love it, you have to either love or be able to ignore a very active Greek scene, one that defines many students' social lives. One student explained that "this campus is segregated into a Greek and non-Greek faction, and there is unfortunately little social activity outside the Greek system for students under 21." The Greeks have been so dominant a force that Vandy's administration has recently tried to curb their influence. Reported one student, "The party scene and the Greek scene have been actively toned down by the administration, and a happy result of this is that more of us are exploring Nashville (the 'hip' Nashville, not the 'country' Nashville)." Drinking is a popular pastime for all students. Wrote one, "While this school is tough academically, it's also very social. Parties start on Tuesdays, except during test weeks." Students praised the Student Recreation Center ("It's incredible—the majority of students work out all the time!") and the campus. The most often cited negative: the Nashville weather. Advised one undergrad, "Bring your umbrella."

■ **Students** One Vandy student described her classmates as "a microcosm of the country club set, a cult of Southern gentility and graciousness cut off from the 'real world.'" The generalization is fairly accurate but is becoming less so every year because of efforts to recruit a more diverse student body. Several students reported that the school seems to becoming "much less conservative and more homogeneous." Still, Vandy has one of the nation's most politically and socially conservative student bodies, and more than a few expressed their desire that the school remain that way. Minority representation is scant.

VANDERBILT UNIVERSITY

Nashville, TN

Admissions

The Vanderbilt admissions office reports, "There are no 'cut-offs.' We use predicted grade point average formulas for some applicants." Primarily, Vanderbilt looks at your GPA and your standardized test scores. After these, they consider (in order of importance) your letters of recommendation, extracurricular activities, and essays. They require that you take either the ACT or SAT (the latter is preferred), and three Achievement tests (one must be Math 1, 2 or 2C, one must be English Composition; the third is up to you). You must also have completed four years of English, two years of a foreign language, and three years of Mathematics. It is recommended that engineering applicants complete an additional year of Math and two years of Science. For students who apply to the Blair School of Music an audition is the primary factor in the application. Students who apply to Vanderbilt most often also apply to Emory and Duke.

Financial Aid

Vanderbilt's financial aid office requires applicants to complete its own form and a FAF, and to submit a copy of the parents' most recent tax return. The school awarded athletic grants to 3% of all undergrads last year (average value: $18,752) and academic scholarships to 6% ($10,732). In the same year, the FA office recommended Perkins loans to 12% of the student body (average loan: $1,378), its own institutional loans to 9% ($1,239), PLUS loans to 4% ($3,594), and Stafford loans to 21% ($3,200). The average award for a member of the class of '95 was $16,223; about 38% received an award of some kind. The deadline of 2/15 (see sidebar) is a priority date, not a closing date.

A note from the Vanderbilt University Admissions Office:

"Exceptional accomplishment and high promise in some field of intellectual endeavor are essential. The student's total academic and non-academic record is reviewed in conjunction with recommendations and personal essays. For students at Blair School of Music, the audition is a prime consideration."

ADMISSIONS FACTS

Competitiveness Rating:	**86**
% of applicants accepted:	59
% acceptees attending:	34

FRESHMAN PROFILE

Average verbal SAT:	562
Average math SAT:	628
Average ACT:	27
Graduated top 10% of class:	55
Graduated top 25% of class:	84
Graduated top 50% of class:	99

DEADLINES

Early decision/action:	11/1
Early dec./act. notif.:	12/15
Regular admission:	1/15
Regular adm. notif.:	4/1

APPLICANTS ALSO LOOK AT

and sometimes prefer:
Washington and Lee U.
U. Virginia
Northwestern U.
Clemson U.
Washington U.

and rarely prefer:
Auburn U.
U. Richmond
U. Kentucky

ADDRESS

Undergraduate Admissions
West End Avenue
Nashville, TN 37240
615-322-2561

FINANCIAL FACTS

In-state tuition ($):	14,975
Out-of-state tuition ($):	14,975
Room & board:	5,420
FA application deadline:	2/15
% frosh receiving FA:	38
PT earnings per yr. ($):	1500

TYPE OF AID % of students ($)

FA of some kind:	36 (14,728)
Need-based grants:	29 (9,455)
Merit-based grants:	10 (13,542)
Loans:	23 (3,200)
Work study:	12 (1,600)
Student rating of FA:	87

VASSAR COLLEGE

Poughkeepsie, NY

What do students think about Vassar College?

■ **Academics** According to one area counselor, Vassar College is a school which "the students adore." And why not? Its academics are first-rate and geared toward the preferences of students: enthused one, "The lack of a core curriculum enables me to major in sociology with a molecular biology correlate, and still go premed." Many students design their own majors and are given free rein to explore and grow academically ("the top flight teaching staff has given me a passion for study I never knew was there," wrote one student). Professors are extremely accessible; most, in fact, live on campus. Said one student, "I like the fact that two professors live in each dorm. They are often seen at ACDC (All-Campus Dining Center), where sharing meals with students is commonplace." Courses are generally small, and liberal arts departments are still the best here, especially English and art history. The visual and performing arts are also popular, particularly in drama. The library wins raves for its aesthetic appeal and conduciveness to study.

■ **Life** Vassar is close to New York City, in both geography and spirit. The college is quite cosmopolitan, and there is some tension between Vassar and the neighboring industrial town of Poughkeepsie. One student reported that "the people at Vassar are trying to move the city-sophisticate attitude from New York City into a very economically depressed community. Maybe that's why there isn't much communication between the city and the college." The campus itself is "incredible," and students enjoy the social life available there. The mood is "generally cheery" and students like the fact that people "support everything you do, from experimenting with drugs to not drinking at a keg party." The male-female ratio is still nearly two to three even after years of co-education (Vassar was once an all-women's school), but the neurotic dating scene on campus still draws criticism. One student asserted that dating at Vassar is "typified by those who seem married and those who sleep around, leaving little room for the more casual, yet less promiscuous approach." Several respondents pointed out that there are many social options and activities on campus, including "a wide range of clubs, lectures, and movies when one needs to get closer to or further away from the people here." And, of course, there's always New York City.

■ **Students** "If the college would pay as much attention to diversity of students as they do to the landscape, we would be very multicultural," wrote one Vassar student. The truth is, it does and they are. Vassar has an almost 25 percent minority population, and students are proud of their "microcosm of America." There are strong, visible gay and alternative communities (some even believe "it is becoming 'in' to be bisexual at Vassar"), and "issues like homosexuality and race relations are full-blown." Said one student, "Vassar offers a little bit of everything: Democrats, hippies, gays, feminists, conservatives, fascists, communists, activists, and people with no opinion are *all* rampant here."

VASSAR COLLEGE

Poughkeepsie, NY

Admissions

From the Vassar undergraduate catalog: "There are no rigid requirements as to secondary school programs, and patterns vary, but Vassar expects candidates to have elected the most demanding courses available. Ordinarily, the candidate should have had four years of English, *including both literature and continuous practice in writing;* at least three years of mathematics; at least two years of laboratory science; three years of social science with a minimum of one year of history; and three years of one ancient or modern foreign language or two years of one language and two of a second. Additional work should be elected in fully credited academic subjects in the humanities, the natural and social sciences, and the arts. Students should take some portion of their work in enriched or honors courses or in the CEEB Advanced Placement Program where they are available. Special attention is given to the academic content of the program candidates select in the senior year." All applicants must submit scores from the SAT and any three Achievements, or the ACT. A second Early Decision deadline is available other than that shown in the sidebar); the application deadline is January 15; notification letters are mailed February 1.

Financial Aid

Financial aid applicants to Vassar must complete the FAF and a form generated by Vassar's financial aid office. All New York residents are also required to apply for New York State's Tuition Assistance Plan (TAP). In '89–'90, over 58 percent of all undergrads received financial aid from Vassar and outside sources; total aid exceeded $11.5 million. One of the more unusual loan plans available at Vassar is the Hager Scholar Program; it provides interest-free loans of $4,000 per academic year to a small number of juniors and seniors who are selected "on the basis of academic excellence, service to the college community, and financial need." Recipients accept an unwritten moral obligation to repay the loan at some future time.

ADMISSIONS FACTS

Competitiveness Rating:	**92**
% of applicants accepted:	43
% acceptees attending:	34

FRESHMAN PROFILE

Average verbal SAT:	634
Average math SAT:	649
Average ACT:	NA
Graduated top 10% of class:	57
Graduated top 25% of class:	97
Graduated top 50% of class:	100

DEADLINES

Early decision/action:	12/1
Early dec./act. notif.:	12/15
Regular admission:	1/15
Regular adm. notif.:	mid-April

APPLICANTS ALSO LOOK AT

and often prefer:
Wesleyan U.
Brown U.
SUNY Binghamton

and sometimes prefer:
Barnard College
Northwestern U.
Middlebury College

and rarely prefer:
Skidmore College
Union College

ADDRESS

Undergraduate Admissions
Poughkeepsie, NY 12601
914-437-7300

FINANCIAL FACTS

In-state tuition ($):	16,250
Out-of-state tuition ($):	16,250
Room & board:	5,260
FA application deadline:	2/15
% frosh receiving FA:	43
PT earnings per yr. ($):	1100

TYPE OF AID % of students ($)

FA of some kind:	53 (NA)
Need-based grants:	NA
Merit-based grants:	NA
Loans:	NA
Work study:	NA
Student rating of FA:	88

CAMPUS LIFE

Quality of Life Rating:	**83**
Type of School:	public
Affiliation:	none
Environment:	city

STUDENT BODY

FT undergrad enrollment:	7,583
% male/% female:	46/54
% out-of-state:	49
% live on campus:	46
% African-American:	1
% Asian:	3
% Caucasian:	94
% Hispanic:	1
% foreign:	1
% transfers:	NA

WHAT'S HOT

marijuana
Grateful Dead
location
hard liquor
good-looking students
overall happiness
beer
attending all classes

WHAT'S NOT

diversity
religious clubs
administration (overall)
small classes (overall)
in-class discussion
caring about politics

ACADEMICS

Academic Rating:	**75**
Calendar:	semester
Student/teacher ratio:	16/1
% doctorates:	82
Profs interesting:	77
Profs accessible:	79
Hours of study per day:	3.32

MOST POPULAR MAJORS

Business Administration
English
Political Science

% GRADS WHO PURSUE

Law:	4
MBA:	2
Medicine:	2
M.A., etc.:	11

What do students think about the University of Vermont?

■ **Academics** The University of Vermont toes the precarious line between good academics and good parties—and for the most part, manages to succeed at both. Students here study more than the average, and attend classes more regularly than is usual at large state schools. Students gave their professors relatively high grades for in-class teaching skills and out-of-class accessibility (again, no small feat at a large university). UVM is particularly strong in health- and environment-related areas. "The Environmental Studies program is fantastic!" reported one major. Business and management majors are also popular, as are psychology and political science. As at most state universities, many courses are overcrowded, and registration is annoying at best ("Classes are *always* full, especially English," wrote one undergrad); students find the school poorly run and the administration "a source of dismay." One student contended, "Intro classes have the consistency of Cheez Whiz—they go down easy, they taste horrible, and they are not good for you." However, UVM's overall academic reputation is quite good, and deservedly so. Its strong record has attracted many non-Vermont residents ("flatlanders"), despite a hefty out-of-state fee.

■ **Life** Burlington, Vermont has been described as the ideal college town. Students here are in love with this clean and picturesque city, and ranked it among the top 15 percent of college sites covered by our survey. No wonder so many students flock here from neighboring Massachusetts and Connecticut; Burlington is "a small city with big city opportunities (concerts, malls, people) and small-town hospitality, safety and fun." Nearby are all the benefits of rural Vermont: skiing, mountain biking, hiking, climbing and other outdoor pastimes are very accessible and popular among students; explained one, "If you can't find students in the library on a Saturday or Sunday, then they're probably on the slopes." UVM's campus is quite beautiful as well, and most are happy living there; dorms are within easy walking distance of both classes and downtown. Sports are, predictably, very popular. Greek life, while popular, is not a dominant force on campus. As successful as it is academically, UVM is also a big party school. Drinking is a very popular pastime, and a large "pseudo-hippie" contingent guarantees the availability of pot and countless Grateful Dead bootlegs. However, balance is the key: "If you want to party, ski and have fun, go to UVM. But if you want to stay, you've got to work HARD!!!"

■ **Students** Diversity is not one of UVM's assets: all but a handful of students are white. Politically, students are conservative and basically uninvolved. Although there is a fairly visible gay presence on campus, tolerance of gay students is quite low. One student further complained that UVM "is still extremely sexist. It needs *more* women faculty in all departments and more attention paid to women's issues and sexual crimes on campus." Many students encounter no such problems, however, and describe their classmates as "laid-back and extremely friendly."

UNIVERSITY OF VERMONT

Admissions

In assessing your application to the University of Vermont, the admissions office looks primarily at your high school curriculum and GPA, as well as your standardized test scores. The school also considers, in order of descending importance, essays, letters of recommendation, extracurricular activities, and an optional interview. Applicants are required to have completed four years of English, three years each of social studies and math (two years of algebra, one of geometry), and two years each of a single foreign language and science (including at least one lab science). University of Vermont requires either the SAT or the ACT, but prefers the SAT. Applicants to University of Vermont most often also apply to Boston College, Middlebury, Cornell U., University of Massachusetts-Amherst, and University of New Hampshire.

Financial Aid

The financial aid office at University of Vermont requires applicants to submit the FAF. UVM awards merit scholarships on the basis of athletic ability (1% of all students received one in 1991–92; average amount: $9,862) and scholarship (for Vermont residents; last year, fewer than 1% of the students received this award; average value: $4,270). Last year, the FA office recommended Stafford loans for 80% of all financial aid recipients; the school also recommends PLUS and SLS loans and provides university-sponsored loans to some FA recipients. The deadline listed in the FA sidebar is a *priority* deadline.

A note from the University of Vermont Admissions Office:

"The University of Vermont was founded in the classic tradition: with a primary emphasis on liberal arts and undergraduate education. UVM has since expanded to include eight colleges and schools: Arts & Sciences, Agriculture & Life Sciences, Allied Health, Business, Education & Social Services, Engineering & Math, Natural Resources, Nursing, as well as a highly respected Medical School and Graduate College. Each of our professional programs combines a broad educational background with specialized training for its students. As a medium-sized public university (8,000 undergraduates, 1,200 graduates and medical students) UVM offers students the best of a large, comprehensive university environment, and a small, approachable college atmosphere."

ADMISSIONS FACTS

Competitiveness Rating:	**75**
% of applicants accepted:	73
% acceptees attending:	34

FRESHMAN PROFILE

Average verbal SAT:	498
Average math SAT:	569
Average ACT:	NA
Graduated top 10% of class:	26
Graduated top 25% of class:	68
Graduated top 50% of class:	96

DEADLINES

Early decision/action:	11/1
Early dec./act. notif.:	12/15
Regular admission:	2/1
Regular adm. notif.:	3/15

APPLICANTS ALSO LOOK AT

and often prefer:
U. Colorado at Boulder
Dartmouth College

and sometimes prefer:
SUNY Binghamton
Middlebury College
Washington U.

and rarely prefer:
Bates College
U. Rochester
Skidmore College
U. Connecticut

ADDRESS

Undergraduate Admissions
South Prospect Street
Burlington, VT 05401-0160
802-656-3370

FINANCIAL FACTS

In-state tuition ($):	4,900
Out-of-state tuition ($):	13,500
Room & board:	4,358
FA application deadline:	3/1
% frosh receiving FA:	43
PT earnings per yr. ($):	NA

TYPE OF AID % of students ($)

FA of some kind:	40 (NA)
Need-based grants:	NA
Merit-based grants:	2 (7,756)
Loans:	36 (3,522)
Work study:	18 (1,200)
Student rating of FA:	69

VILLANOVA UNIVERSITY

CAMPUS LIFE

Quality of Life Rating: **76**

Type of School:	private
Affiliation:	Roman Catholic
Environment:	suburban

STUDENT BODY

FT undergrad enrollment:	6,510
% male/% female:	53/47
% out-of-state:	70
% live on campus:	51
% African-American:	3
% Asian:	3
% Caucasian:	91
% Hispanic:	2
% foreign:	1
% transfers:	2

WHAT'S HOT

religion
intercollegiate sports
good-looking students
catalog
living on campus
dorm safety
small lectures
beer
conservative politics

WHAT'S NOT

diversity
gay community visible
town-gown relations
working a job

ACADEMICS

Academic Rating: **78**

Calendar:	semester
Student/teacher ratio:	14/1
% doctorates:	85
Profs interesting:	77
Profs accessible:	81
Hours of study per day:	3.01

MOST POPULAR MAJORS

Political Science
Communication
Business

% GRADS WHO PURSUE

Law:	7
MBA:	2
Medicine:	3
M.A., etc.:	12

What do students think about Villanova University?

■ **Academics** The students at the Roman Catholic-affiliated Villanova University report that their school "places a definite emphasis on spiritual and personal growth." Although non-Catholics also attend VU, the influence of the Augustinian fathers who govern the school is felt everywhere, from the well-attended daily masses to the single-sex dorms, where much-resented visitation rules are enthusiastically enforced (note: the school has one co-ed dormitory). VU's business subdivision, the College of Commerce and Finance, is the school's best, although, as one student reported, "The nursing program is one of the best in the state," and the engineering school is also winning a good reputation. Students gave below-average marks to professors and class size, and several complained about the lack of direction given. Wrote one, "There are few opportunities for guidance in finding a major or a career here."

■ **Life** The quality of life at VU is less than optimal, to say the least. The school is located in an affluent suburb of Philadelphia, and many students complained that "local residents despise Villanova students. The local police have nothing else to keep them busy so they search out off-campus parties with a vengeance." To make things worse, on-campus housing is in short supply, and off-campus residences welcoming students are scarce. It's a problem partly created by the school's strict dorm policies: visitation rules and drinking regulations force all partying to off-campus residences. VU students party pretty hard, so it's no wonder local landlords don't actively seek them as tenants. The social scene centers on drinking and can get pretty monotonous. Wrote one student, "Social life is lacking for anyone who doesn't dig the cliquish sorority/fraternity scene. For a person like me, getting to Philadelphia is virtually my only hope of salvation from this pit of boredom." And yet, when we asked students how happy they were here, they graded themselves only slightly below the national average. Are they masochists? Do they just enjoy complaining? Did they understand our question? Students did note some positive aspects about VU: chiefly, the proximity of Philadelphia, and the ardent school spirit nurtured by the school's fanatically supported athletic teams. During basketball season, at least, VU students wouldn't want to be anywhere else.

■ **Students** Villanova students ranked themselves third least diverse among the student bodies profiled in this book. Said one, "they don't call it Vanillanova for nothing. There are about 10 minority students on campus and they're all on the basketball team." In fact, there are about 500 minority students: among them, blacks, Hispanics, and Asians are represented about equally. Students are conservative politically, but mostly they just don't care: VU students ranked among the nation's least interested in politics. The atmosphere here, explained one student, is "very uptight; also, everyone has a tendency to be rather clone-like J. Crew wanna-bes." Over three quarters of the students are Catholic.

VILLANOVA UNIVERSITY

Admissions

Villanova's admissions office states that there are cut-offs "Only for Early Action—students must be in the top 10 percent of their high school class with minimum combined SAT scores of 1200. There are no cut-offs for Regular Decision applicants." The admissions committee first looks at your high school GPA. This is followed (in order of importance) by your standardized test scores, extracurriculars, essays, letters of recommendation, and interview. Students must take the SAT or ACT, and those applying to the College of Liberal Arts and Sciences must take Achievements as well. Applicants should also have completed four years of English, at least three years of mathematics, at least one year of science, and two years of foreign language (certain majors). Villanova applicants also often apply to Boston College, Notre Dame, Rutgers, Fairfield, and Penn State.

Financial Aid

The financial aid office at Villanova University requires applicants to submit the FAF, a form generated by the school, and their parents' most recent tax return. Returning students must also file a PHEAA form. Merit-based grants are awarded for athletic ability (in 1991–92, 4% of all undergrads received one; average value: $11,460) and academic skill (3%; $7,175). Ninety percent of all financial aid recipients last year were recommended for Stafford loans; other loans recommended by Villanova include the PLUS loan, the PHEAA alternative loan, and the TERI loan.

A note from the Villanova University Admissions Office:

"It is sometimes difficult to find a college or university that is absolutely right for you. Maybe you're looking for a school that offers a wide choice of academic programs and has a reputation for solid academic quality. You probably want a friendly, small-campus atmosphere with a faculty that gives personal attention to every student, preferably with the cultural attractions of a big campus and close to a major city. A high quality student body is also important… You will want to make recreation and fun an important part of your college experience too.

"Finding all this at one campus can be tough; but it's all here at Villanova, along with the unique heritage of the priests and brothers of the Order of St. Augustine, who founded the University in 1842. The Augustinian tradition continues today…a tradition of education dedicated to the pursuit of wisdom and charity—values that are inherent in the Judeo-Christian ethic. Our goal at Villanova is to help each student realize his and her full potential development, with the added hope that each one also grows in staunch independence of mind and in generous commitment to the service of God, society and our fellow humans."

ADMISSIONS FACTS

Competitiveness Rating:	**80**
% of applicants accepted:	65
% acceptees attending:	31

FRESHMAN PROFILE

Average verbal SAT:	516
Average math SAT:	592
Average ACT:	26
Graduated top 10% of class:	36
Graduated top 25% of class:	74
Graduated top 50% of class:	98

DEADLINES

Early decision/action:	12/15
Early dec./act. notif.:	1/15
Regular admission:	1/15
Regular adm. notif.:	4/1

APPLICANTS ALSO LOOK AT

and often prefer:
Georgetown U.

and sometimes prefer:
St. Joseph's U.
College of the Holy Cross
Fordham U.
Boston College

and rarely prefer:
Seton Hall U.
U. Rhode Island
Trenton State College
Gettysburg College

ADDRESS

Undergraduate Admissions
Villanova, PA 19085-1672
215-645-4000

FINANCIAL FACTS

In-state tuition ($):	12,100
Out-of-state tuition ($):	12,100
Room & board:	5,220
FA application deadline:	3/15
% frosh receiving FA:	50
PT earnings per yr. ($):	2000

TYPE OF AID % of students ($)

FA of some kind:	48 (NA)
Need-based grants:	27 (5,500)
Merit-based grants:	7 (9,500)
Loans:	35 (3,300)
Work study:	6 (1,200)
Student rating of FA:	67

UNIVERSITY OF VIRGINIA

Charlottesville, VA

What do students think about the University of Virginia?

■ **Academics** University of Virginia, the school founded by Thomas Jefferson, is a state-affiliated university with a reputation most private schools would envy. *U.S. News & World Report* ranked it among the nation's 25 best: among state schools, only UC Berkeley ranked higher. Most state universities accept over two thirds of their applicants; UVA *rejects* over two thirds. The reason is not just that UVA offers a tremendously diverse array of programs but that so many of those programs are among the best in the country. English, religious studies, engineering, history, and government are the best known, but academics are uniformly excellent. Furthermore, students receive more personal attention from their professors than do others at large universities. One environmental science major reported, "I just transferred from a small, private liberal arts college, and the amount of attention I've received from professors here exceeds what I got there tenfold. I can't imagine the professors anywhere being more dedicated to the success of their students." While most state-funded schools are, at best, adequately run, at this one students actually like their deans and administrators, and the library is also excellent. About the only real complaint we heard concerning academics is that lecture classes tend to be large.

■ **Life** Movies set at idealized universities might very well model their settings after UVA. The grounds are beautiful, the dorms are livable, and the students are well dressed, clean-scrubbed, and good looking. In fact, UVA is so meticulous about its campus that one student, bemoaning state budget cuts, complained: ("They'll slash our budget and reduce the number of courses available to an ever-growing number of students, but you'd better believe all the leaves will be raked up." An Honor and Judicial system "that works") deals with the problem of cheating: students caught can either withdraw from school or go before a jury of their peers. School spirit is very big here: students refer to themselves as Cavaliers (after the sports teams) or 'hoos' (short for 'wahoos') and wear dress clothes to go to sporting events, which are extremely popular. UVA has long had a reputation as a party school, and its students continue to maintain that tradition. Fraternities and sororities play a major role in social life, as does alcohol.

■ **Students** There is a 21% minority population here, but the students are the first to admit that the student body is segregated. Preppy attire is *de rigueur*, and a social, if not political, conservatism is pervasive. Still, students of every demographic group are measurably happier here than their average counterparts elsewhere. Explained one, "Although the student body itself isn't very well integrated, something about being a student here does tie us all together. I know it sounds corny to non-Cavaliers, but something pervasive and contagious is alive and well in Hoo-ville. I won't call it Mr. Jefferson's spirit, but it is something that settles into your heart first year and never leaves. At worst, it'll make you wear orange pants (*one of the school's colors*). At best, it'll hum in the back of your thoughts for the rest of your life."

UNIVERSITY OF VIRGINIA

Admissions

Applicants to the University of Virginia apply to one of four schools: The College of Arts and Sciences, the School of Engineering and Applied Science, the School of Architecture, or the School of Nursing. The primary criterion for admission to the freshman class is "demonstrated academic achievement in a challenging secondary school program." This record is established by "outstanding grades, high rank in class, good performance in Advanced Placement and honors courses, and superior scores on College Board Achievement Tests…" The secondary school program should include four units of English, four units of mathematics, two units of foreign language, two units of science (choosing from biology, chemistry, and physics) and one unit of social studies. The admissions committee also examines the application form "for what it reveals about extracurricular successes, special talents and interests, goals, background, and the applicant's ability to write correct, concise English prose. A letter of recommendation from the secondary school is also required." All applicants must submit scores from the SAT and three Achievement tests, including English Composition (with or without essay), Mathematics I or II, and either a Science, a Foreign Language or History for the third test. A final note: about 20 % of the freshman class is admitted through Early Decision each year.

Financial Aid

Financial aid applicants to the University of Virginia must complete the FAF and, upon receipt of an award, submit a copy of their parents' most recent tax return. Thirty-three percent of the class of '95 received some type of aid upon entry to the University; the average value was $5,600. In '90–'91, 4% of all undergrads received athletic grants (average value: $7,594), and 3% received academic grants (average: $4,050). Nine percent of all undergrads took out Perkins loans (average loan value: $1,700), and 9% took out Stafford loans (average: $2,720).

Excerpted from University of Virginia promotional materials:

"The central purpose of the University of Virginia is to enrich the mind by stimulating and sustaining a spirit of free inquiry directed to understanding the nature of the universe and the role of mankind in it. Activities designed to quicken, discipline, and enlarge the intellectual and creative capacities, as well as the aesthetic and ethical awareness, of the members of the University, and to record, preserve, and disseminate the results of intellectual discovery and creative endeavor serve this purpose. In fulfilling it, the University places the highest priority on achieving eminence as a center of higher learning."

ADMISSIONS FACTS

Competitiveness Rating:	**93**
% of applicants accepted:	32
% acceptees attending:	52

FRESHMAN PROFILE

Average verbal SAT:	569
Average math SAT:	639
Average ACT:	NA
Graduated top 10% of class:	72
Graduated top 25% of class:	96
Graduated top 50% of class:	100

DEADLINES

Early decision/action:	11/1
Early dec./act. notif.:	12/1
Regular admission:	1/2
Regular adm. notif.:	4/1

APPLICANTS ALSO LOOK AT

and often prefer:
Duke U.

and sometimes prefer:
U. Notre Dame
U. NC–Chapel Hill

and rarely prefer:
College of William & Mary
Virginia Polytech
George Washington U.
Bucknell U.
Boston U.

ADDRESS

Undergraduate Admissions
Charlottesville, VA 22906
804-924-7751

FINANCIAL FACTS

In-state tuition ($):	2,740
Out-of-state tuition ($):	8,950
Room & board:	3,312
FA application deadline:	3/1
% frosh receiving FA:	35
PT earnings per yr. ($):	NA

TYPE OF AID:	% of students ($)
FA of some kind:	28 (5,740)
Need-based grants:	21 (4,428)
Merit-based grants:	NA
Loans:	15 (2,550)
Work study:	3 (1,380)
Student rating of FA:	73

VIRGINIA POLYTECHNIC INSTITUTE & STATE U.

Blacksburg, VA

CAMPUS LIFE

Quality of Life Rating: **82**

Type of school:	public
Affiliation:	none
Environment:	suburban

STUDENT BODY

FT Undergrad Enrollment:	18,266
% male/% female:	59/41
% out-of-state:	25
% live on campus:	45
% African-American:	5
% Asian:	6
% Caucasian:	87
% Hispanic:	1
% foreign:	6
% transfers:	20

WHAT'S HOT
profs lecture a lot
library
dating
attending all classes
conservative politics
college newspaper
overall happiness
town-gown relations
diversity
beer

WHAT'S NOT
small classes (overall)
in-class discussion
living on campus
profs outside class

ACADEMICS

Academic Rating: **75**

Calendar:	semester
Student/teacher ratio:	17/1
% doctorates:	87
Profs interesting:	72
Profs accessible:	69
Hours of study per day:	3.49

MOST POPULAR MAJORS BY %
Biology:	5
Accounting:	4
Architecture:	4

% GRADS WHO PURSUE
Law:	NA
MBA:	NA
Medicine:	NA
M.A., etc.:	15

What do students think about VPI?

■ **Academics** VPI is not just a technical school. In fact, according to one undergrad, "When it comes to variety of majors, classes, people, activities, almost anything, VPI is the best school in the state. You name it, Tech has it!" Other students were a little less brash, deferring to the University of Virginia by calling their school "Virginia's other great university." With over 18,000 undergraduates, VPI has the resources to offer undergraduates programs in just about any field of study. Technical and pre-professional programs are the most popular: almost one quarter of the students pursue engineering degrees. Students here work hard (said one, "My advice is to hit the books hard from the beginning"), but they must not mind that much, because they ranked high in overall happiness. VPI does have its share of problems. Professors received sub-par grades for both in-class performance and accessibility. One student explained: "Virginia Tech is a research-oriented school. That fact unfortunately shows up in the quality of the teaching. There is a lot of knowledge here, and resources are available, but they are not complemented with communication between professors and students." Upperclassmen remarked that professors are more attentive to their needs than they were when they were sophomores and freshmen. Students gave the library very high marks, and gave the administration average grades (which is good: administrators at large schools almost invariably receive poor grades).

■ **Life** VPI is situated on a huge, beautiful campus. One student reported that she had "fallen in love with Tech's campus. It's set near Jefferson National Park and the Appalachian Mountains. Our Hokie stone buildings give an appearance of an Ivy League college, but we also have the quiet country atmosphere." Said another, "The campus seems very big at first, but the longer you are here and the more people you meet, the smaller it gets." City slickers may feel out of place here, but for the outdoorsy types, "There are tons of things to do nearby: the New River (tubing), the Cascades, Mountain Lake (*Dirty Dancing* was filmed there), good campsites, hiking trails, snow skiing, the list is endless." Students told us they got along well with the people of Blacksburg and gave the town slightly better than average grades. Fraternities and sororities are popular, and students aren't adverse to throwing back a drink every now and then. Intramural and intercollegiate sports are also enjoyed by many. A small number of students are enrolled in the Corps of Cadets, a military outfit.

■ **Students** Three quarters of VPI's students come from Virginia, and most of the rest come from nearby states (although 6 percent of the students are from foreign countries). Most students are white, but there are also decent-sized Asian and African-American populations. Students are conservative and very dedicated to their studies. Said one about his classmates, "people here are generally very nice and very down-to-earth."

VIRGINIA POLYTECHNIC INSTITUTE & STATE U.

Blacksburg, VA

Admissions

The admissions office writes, "Admission to Virginia Tech is selective. We look for a strong 'B' to 'B+' average in college preparatory courses, including English, advanced math, and lab sciences. Students who have challenged themselves in high school are much more likely to receive an offer of admission and to succeed at Virginia Tech." Virginia Tech first looks at your high school curriculum and course selection, followed by your GPA, standardized test scores, and extracurriculars. Interviews, essays, and letters of recommendation are not required, but Tech notes that they will consider anything an applicant submits. In addition to the high school courses noted above, students must take the SAT or ACT for admission, and Math and English Achievements for placement. Students who apply here most often also apply to the University of Virginia, James Madison, Radford, and Penn State.

Financial Aid

The financial aid office at Virginia Tech requires applicants to submit the FAF. Merit based grants are awarded for athletic ability (2% of all students received one in 1991–92; average value: $6,118) and academic excellence (14%; $1,500). Virginia residents are eligible for several state-sponsored grants. VPI recommended Stafford loans for 65% of last year's aid recipients; the school also recommends PLUS/SLS loans and privately funded loan programs.

A note from the Virginia Tech Admissions Office:

"At Virginia Tech, more than 19,000 undergraduate students choose from 76 majors in seven colleges: Agriculture & Life Sciences, Architecture & Urban Studies, Arts & Sciences (the largest), Business, Education, Engineering, and Human Resources. More than 400 student organizations—including academic, social, and religious clubs; student government and media; and special interest groups—thrive on campus. At Virginia's largest university, students have unlimited opportunities. But they also benefit from a low student/teacher ratio (17:1) and a variety of academic programs such as Honors and CO-OP. Virginia Tech offers the best of both worlds in an ideal environment—southwest Virginia's Blue Ridge Mountains."

ADMISSIONS FACTS

Competitiveness Rating:	**78**
% of applicants accepted:	68
% acceptees attending:	41

FRESHMAN PROFILE

Average verbal SAT:	513*
Average math SAT:	583*
Average ACT:	NA
Graduated top 10% of class:	34
Graduated top 25% of class:	69
Graduated top 50% of class:	96

DEADLINES

Early decision/action:	11/1
Early dec./act. notif.:	12/15
Regular admission:	2/1
Regular adm. notif.:	4/15

APPLICANTS ALSO LOOK AT

and often prefer:
Georgia Tech
U. Virginia

and sometimes prefer:
James Madison U.
George Mason U.
College of William & Mary

and rarely prefer:
Clemson U.
Penn State U.
U. Tennessee–Knoxville

ADDRESS

Undergraduate Admissions
Blacksburg, VA 24061-0202
703-231-6267

FINANCIAL FACTS

In-state tuition ($):	2,304
Out-of-state tuition ($):	8,152
Room & board:	2,654
FA application deadline:	3/15
% frosh receiving FA:	41
PT earnings per yr. ($):	900

TYPE OF AID: % of students ($)

FA of some kind:	42 (NA)
Need-based grants:	29 (2,800)
Merit-based grants:	16 (1,986)
Loans:	23 (2,900)
Work study:	4 (1,400)
Student rating of FA:	76

WABASH COLLEGE

CAMPUS LIFE

Quality of Life Rating: **77**

Type of school:	private
Affiliation:	none
Environment:	suburban

STUDENT BODY

FT Undergrad Enrollment:	849
% male/% female:	100/0
% out-of-state:	23
% live on campus:	90
% African-American:	5
% Asian:	4
% Caucasian:	89
% Hispanic:	1
% foreign:	4
% transfers:	1

WHAT'S HOT

financial aid
intramural sports
small classes (overall)
profs in class
profs outside class
studying hard
gay community visible
fraternities/sororities
administration (overall)
conservative politics
attending all classes

WHAT'S NOT

location
marijuana
town-gown relations

ACADEMICS

Academic Rating: **86**

Calendar:	semester
Student/teacher ratio:	11/1
% doctorates:	90
Profs interesting:	95
Profs accessible:	95
Hours of study per day:	3.83

MOST POPULAR MAJORS

English
History
Psychology

% GRADS WHO PURSUE

Law:	7
MBA:	3
Medicine:	10
M.A., etc.:	17

What do students think about Wabash College?

■ **Academics** As one student put it, "Wabash College has everything a student could ask for, except women." Indeed, this tiny all-male school in rural Indiana offers the highly motivated student a challenging, fulfilling college experience. "Wabash is a rigorous, intense, focused school," reported one undergrad, "one that rewards graduates with a true sense of accomplishment and good connections in the business, professional, or graduate school world." Students praise their professors, who teach all classes (no TAs) and whose attentiveness and caring help offset the heavy academic demands. One undergrad wrote that Wabash is "a very tough school—sometimes it feels like we're in a four-year doctoral program for undergrads. But that is countered by the fact that the profs are very accessible—they always make time for you. We never have multiple-guess exams, it's always essays in blue book after blue book after blue book." Students here mostly pursue liberal arts and sciences majors supplemented by a broad set of humanities, science, and language requirements. Classes are "small and centered on discussion, so thorough preparation is necessary." One common complaint among students is that faculty and administrators are much more liberal-minded than the students are. One student wrote that "a generally conservative student body sometimes clashes with a liberal, diversity-seeking faculty and administration. Some students fear that exposing their own, conservative views to professors is academic suicide." In general, however, students are very pleased with the instruction they receive at "the school that takes naive, immature boys and turns them into alert, mature men ready to face the world."

■ **Life** Wabash's single-sex status and remote location combine to create an austere social scene. Wrote one student, "If you're the type to lock yourself in a room and study all the time, this is the place for you. If, on the other hand, you like having a life outside of college, Wabash is not for you." Greek life and frat parties are very popular ("there is a BIG frat influence on everything"), since neither school events nor the town offer much in the way of entertainment. Sports and drinking are the most popular on-campus diversions. Wabash students ranked Crawfordsville, Indiana the second worst college town in the country. "Crawfordsville is disgusting," reported one student, "and the townies hate the students." As a result, students often leave campus for the weekend, either to go home or to visit nearby coed campuses. Several students mentioned talk of Wabash going coed in the near future, but most agreed, "It probably won't happen: there's too much tradition for us even to want to change."

■ **Students** Over three quarters of the men at Wabash are natives of Indiana. The total minority population is less than 10 percent, made up of approximately 50 blacks and 40 Asians. One student noted that "students here tend to be politically conservative," and in fact our survey showed that only ten other competitive schools have student bodies that are more conservative.

WABASH COLLEGE

Admissions

Wabash's admissions office writes, "When reading and assessing potential Wabash applicants for admission, the selection committee primarily focuses on the four-year academic record. Positive consideration is given to applicants who have sought academic challenge through high school by enrolling in the most advanced level classes over a student who has opted for lower level courses." Wabash first looks at your high school course selection and GPA, followed by standardized test scores, letters of recommendation, your interview, essays, and extracurriculars, in that order. Students must submit SAT or ACT scores, and have completed four years of English, three years of math, two years of a foreign language, two years of lab science, and two years of social science (all at the college prep level). Applicants to Wabash often apply to Indiana, Purdue, DePauw, and Notre Dame as well.

Financial Aid

Wabash requires its financial aid applicants to submit a copy of their parents' most recent tax return, and a FAF. Last year, the school awarded academic scholarships to 45% of its students (average scholarship value: $6,670) and talent (fine arts) scholarships to 1% ($8,390). The FA office recommended Stafford loans to 34% of all undergrads (average loan: $2,154) and PLUS loans to 12% ($2,939). The 3/15 deadline shown (see sidebar) is a priority date for materials only (there is no closing date).

A note from the Wabash College Admission Office:

"Wabash College is different—and distinctive—from other liberal arts colleges. Different in that Wabash is an outstanding college for men only. Distinctive in the quality and character of the faculty, in the demanding nature of the academic program, in the farsightedness and maturity of the men who enroll, and in the richness of the traditions that have evolved throughout its 160-year history.

"Wabash is, preeminently, a teaching institution, and fundamental to the learning experience is the way faculty and students talk to each other: with mutual respect for the expression of informed opinion. For example, students who collaborate with faculty on research projects are considered their peers in the research—an esteem not usually extended to undergraduates. The College takes pride in the sense of community that such a learning environment fosters.

"But perhaps the single most striking aspect of student life at Wabash is personal freedom. The College has only one rule: 'The student is expected to conduct himself at all times, both on and off the campus, as a gentleman and a responsible citizen. Wabash College treats students as adults, and such treatment attracts responsible freshmen and fosters their independence and maturity.'"

ADMISSIONS FACTS

Competitiveness Rating:	77
% of applicants accepted:	82
% acceptees attending:	44

FRESHMAN PROFILE

Average verbal SAT:	517*
Average math SAT:	587*
Average ACT:	NA
Graduated top 10% of class:	42
Graduated top 25% of class:	74
Graduated top 50% of class:	94

DEADLINES

Early decision/action:	NA
Early dec./act. notif.:	NA
Regular admission:	3/19
Regular adm. notif.:	rolling

APPLICANTS ALSO LOOK AT

and often prefer:
Indiana U.
U. Notre Dame

and sometimes prefer
DePaul
Valparaiso U.

and rarely prefer:
Purdue U.

ADDRESS

Undergraduate Admissions
P.O. Box 352
Crawfordsville, IN 47933-0352
317-364-4225

FINANCIAL FACTS

In-state tuition ($):	10,500
Out-of-state tuition ($):	10,500
Room & board:	3,665
FA application deadline:	3/15
% frosh receiving FA:	90
PT earnings per yr. ($):	650

TYPE OF AID: % of students ($)

FA of some kind:	87 (NA)
Need-based grants:	28 (2,873)
Merit-based grants:	46 (6,702)
Loans:	46 (2,356)
Work study:	0
Student rating of FA:	100

WAKE FOREST UNIVERSITY

Winston-Salem, NC

What do students think about Wake Forest University?

■ **Academics** Students at Wake Forest University are impressed with their school's growing national reputation, but also wary of what changes this new-found prestige might bring. Said one, "In seeking to gain the national recognition it deserves, Wake must be vigilant not to lose its small-school, friendly character." Another reported that "as the administration ponders the question of which direction to move in, professors wait impatiently for 'national' university status. This can be a frustrating time to be at Wake, yet also exciting, since students are involved in the shaping of its future." Students here work hard, and are rewarded with excellent, accessible professors and facilities that are "fantastic." One freshman said: "I'm a freshman taking introductory classes with the most widely sought-after and professionally esteemed professors on campus. It's as if they wanted students with fresh minds, as if the departments were competing to win over potential majors. Great!" Students also gave administrators high marks. A solid, broad-based core curriculum requires all students to pursue a well-rounded academic program. Students live by an honor code; one told us it is "very strictly adhered to; I am unaware of any infractions in my semesters here," and all students reported that incidents of cheating were very rare.

■ **Life** Most Wake Forest students "are active about campus, whether in Greek life, musical groups, theater, sports, religious groups, or university programs (radio, newspaper, etc.)." Such activities are essential to students' social lives. One student wrote, "If you find your niche here, then you're set: parties, friends, road trips, etc. If you somehow miss out, then there is very little to do except watch everybody else go by. The sure-fire bet is to take a semester at the Wake Forest House in London or Venice. It's almost like 'insta-family' with bonds that last all through college." Students agreed that fraternities and sororities are the "most important factor in the school's social and political spheres." Drinking is popular, drugs are not. Students report, "Beer is like mother's milk to Wake students. We all work so hard during the week that by the time the weekend rolls around many of us stay inebriated for two days straight." Students are conservative about sex; said one, "This place would be a monastery if it weren't for beer and frat parties!" The campus is beautiful (several students wrote that "Wake Forest is like a country club"), the dorms are comfortable and the food is not that bad. The city of Winston-Salem, wrote one student, "is accessible by car, but the campus is self-supporting and self-contained."

■ **Students** Wake Forest draws a large proportion of out-of-state students, but the predominant feel of the student body remains Southern and wealthy. A 9 percent minority population is made up mostly of African-Americans. Students are politically conservative but largely apathetic, and they are fairly religious. They ranked in the top 15 percent of the nation's happiest students.

WAKE FOREST UNIVERSITY

Admissions

The admissions committee at Wake Forest judges your high school course selection, class rank, and SAT scores, which are required. Following these are essays, extracurriculars, and letters of recommendation, all at roughly the same level of importance. While Achievement tests are not required, students who want to qualify for merit-based scholarships should submit three Achievement scores. In addition, students should have completed four units of English, three units of mathematics, two units of history, and social studies, two in a single foreign language, and one unit in the natural sciences. Students who apply to Wake Forest also often apply to UNC–Chapel Hill, Duke, William & Mary, University of Virginia, Vanderbilt and University of Richmond.

Financial Aid

The financial aid office at Wake Forest requires applicants to submit the FAF, a form generated by the school, and their parents' most recent tax return. Merit grants are awarded for athletic skill (7% of the students received one in 1991–92; average value: $11,086), academic ability (6%; $8,000), and for "talent and leadership" (2%; $3,344). Residents of the state of North Carolina are eligible for the North Carolina Legislative Tuition Grant. Loan programs in which Wake Forest students participated last year include: the Stafford loan program, the PLUS loan program, and "a variety of private loans." The school lists no FA application deadline, but notes that applications should be submitted "as soon as possible after January 1...Almost all freshman aid awards are made by May 1 at the latest."

A note from the Wake Forest University Admissions Office:

"The hallmarks of Wake Forest are rooted in our private, coeducational, residential community and kinship shared among our students, faculty, staff, and alumni. As we pursue excellence in the liberal arts and in graduate and professional education, we offer our undergraduates the best of both worlds—the intimacy of a smaller college (3,500 students in Wake Forest College and the School of Business and Accountancy where small classes are taught only by our faculty members) and, at the same time, the complete resources, facilities, and faculty of a teaching and research university having four graduate and professional schools.

"Student life is rich, with activities encompassing a full range of intercollegiate, intramural and club athletics, theme houses, Greek organizations, topical symposia and forums, fine arts and film series, student government, as well as numerous clubs and literary, religious, and journalism opportunities."

ADMISSIONS FACTS

Competitiveness Rating:	**92**
% of applicants accepted:	37
% acceptees attending:	43

FRESHMAN PROFILE

Average verbal SAT:	600*
Average math SAT:	650*
Average ACT:	NA
Graduated top 10% of class:	70
Graduated top 25% of class:	91
Graduated top 50% of class:	98

DEADLINES

Early decision/action:	11/15
Early dec./act. notif.:	w/in 3 weeks
Regular admission:	1/15
Regular adm. notif.:	4/15

APPLICANTS ALSO LOOK AT

and often prefer:
Duke U.
U. NC–Chapel Hill

and sometimes prefer:
Washington and Lee U.
Vanderbilt U.
College of William & Mary
Davidson College

and rarely prefer:
Furman U.
U. Richmond
North Carolina State U.

ADDRESS

Undergraduate Admissions
Box 7305, Reynolda Station
Winston-Salem, NC 27109
919-759-5201

FINANCIAL FACTS

In-state tuition ($):	10,800
Out-of-state tuition ($):	10,800
Room & board:	3,900
FA application deadline:	3/1
% frosh receiving FA:	67
PT earnings per yr. ($):	1250

TYPE OF AID: % of students ($)

FA of some kind:	62 (NA)
Need-based grants:	25 (5,938)
Merit-based grants:	14 (8,829)
Loans:	21 (3,405)
Work study:	8 (1,040)
Student rating of FA:	80

WASHINGTON UNIVERSITY

Saint Louis, MO

CAMPUS LIFE

Quality of Life Rating:	**84**
Type of school:	private
Affiliation:	none
Environment:	city

STUDENT BODY

FT Undergrad Enrollment:	5,027
% male/% female:	52/48
% out-of-state:	81
% live on campus:	60
% African-American:	6
% Asian:	9
% Caucasian:	80
% Hispanic:	2
% foreign:	3
% transfers:	3

WHAT'S HOT

registration
deans
campus appearance
intramural sports
administration (overall)

WHAT'S NOT

intercollegiate sports
working a job
attending all classes
caring about politics

ACADEMICS

Academic Rating:	**84**
Calendar:	semester
Student/teacher ratio:	12/1
% doctorates:	88
Profs interesting:	77
Profs accessible:	80
Hours of study per day:	3.23

MOST POPULAR MAJORS

Biology
Psychology
Engineering

% GRADS WHO PURSUE

Law:	14
MBA:	15
Medicine:	15
M.A., etc.:	17

What is life like at Washington University?

■ **Academics** Washington University is a paradox, a school best known for being underrated. Many comments from students began, "Although WU isn't that well known…," and then went on to explain something great about the school. WU had great successes in sending students to graduate programs (61% of all graduates), particularly to medical school (15% of all graduates), and *U.S. News & World Report* ranked it the 18th best university in the country. Students think highly of most of their professors, although quite a few complained that the school emphasizes research and publishing in its tenure process, with the result being the occasional brilliant-but-entirely-incomprehensible professor. And, as one student told us, "It's not as difficult as its reputation would lead you to believe," an assertion borne out by student response to the question, "How many hours a day do you study?" Their answer, three-and-a-quarter hours, is just about the national average. The pre-professional programs are excellent, as are the economics and science departments. WU recently dissolved its sociology department.

■ **Life** Washington students told us that their campus was quite beautiful, no mean feat for a school located in a major city (actually, the school is in a suburban setting, although it is within the St. Louis borders). Sadly, the city itself, St. Louis, leaves something to be desired: as one student put it, "Don't look to St. Louis to fulfill your wildest dreams of the big city." On campus social life revolves around "The Row," a stretch of fraternity houses. Said one student, "Aside from frat parties, there are few opportunities for all the students to get together. School spirit is absent and sporting events are sparsely attended." As for romantic life, "Students don't date here—they scam on each other and don't go out until they've been seeing each other for months." And although "Washington U. is not a party school—studying is a big weekend activity," drinking and drugs are more popular here than at the average school in this book, probably because so many students find the rest of their social lives boring.

■ **Students** WU is "not the rich kids' college everyone thinks it is…many students receive financial aid." The school received its reputation because (1) its tuition fees are very high, and (2) it draws a lot of well-to-do students from the East Coast. Said one, "I thought I was being unique by going to school in St. Louis and being a New Yorker, but I don't have one friend who is not from the East Coast." Although the students believe they have a well-diversified student body, they gave themselves low marks for interaction. Still, every demographic group ranked higher than the national average for overall happiness.

WASHINGTON UNIVERSITY

Saint Louis, MO

Admissions

From the Washington University undergraduate catalog: "The Committees on Admission study each application, seeking to identify those students of aptitude and character who will not only benefit from the demands of a strong academic program, but also contribute to the Washington University community. The most important factors in their selection include the quality of high school courses, grades, and class rank, and standardized test scores." The recommended high school curriculum for Washington U. includes four years of English, three to four years each of mathematics, history and social sciences, and lab sciences, and two years of a foreign language. "To be competitive, applicants are expected to have challenged themselves as much as possible within their high school curriculum. This includes taking honors, advanced placement, and international baccalaureate courses, if offered." Applicants are required to submit SAT or ACT scores. Achievement Tests are encouraged, but not required.

Financial Aid

Financial aid applicants to Washington University must complete the FAF and submit a copy of their parents' most recent tax return. Early Decision applicants must also complete a form generated by the Washington U. financial aid office. In '90–'91, 18% of all undergrads received academic grants; the average value was $6,089. Scholarships are also awarded for artistic talent, residency and minorities.

Excerpted from Washington University promotional materials:

"Washington University was founded in 1853 by William Greenleaf Eliot to educate the youth of St. Louis. Eliot envisioned a great center of learning west of the Mississippi, "an American University from whose walls the bitterness of party spirit shall forever be excluded…in whose instructions the narrowness of sectarianism can have no place, but the principles of morality and reverential regard for truth…shall be the axioms held above all dispute." His ideal has remained an essential force as Washington has grown into a university of national reputation. In the past academic year, all 50 states and more than 70 nations were represented in Washington's undergraduate student body of 5,080.

"Today, the University continues its pursuit of excellence under Chancellor William H. Danforth. As Eliot intended, Washington offers its students, scholars, and scientists an institution "so strong in its faculty of instruction, so generous in its ideas, so thoroughly provided with all facilities of education, so hospitable to all comers and so rich in its benefactions conferred, that it should gather round itself a constituency of learning and science."

ADMISSIONS FACTS

Competitiveness Rating:	**88**
% of applicants accepted:	59
% acceptees attending:	26

FRESHMAN PROFILE

Average verbal SAT:	559
Average math SAT:	643
Average ACT:	28
Graduated top 10% of class:	62
Graduated top 25% of class:	91
Graduated top 50% of class:	98

DEADLINES

Early decision/action:	12/1
Early dec./act. notif.:	1/1
Regular admission:	1/15
Regular adm. notif.:	4/1

APPLICANTS ALSO LOOK AT

and often prefer:
Tufts U.

and sometimes prefer:
St. Louis U.
Cornell U.

and rarely prefer:
American U.
U. Illinois
Brandeis U.
U. Wisconsin–Madison
Lafayette College

ADDRESS

Undergraduate Admissions
One Brookings Drive
Campus Box 1089
Saint Louis, MO 63130-4899
314-935-6000

FINANCIAL FACTS

In-state tuition ($):	15,950
Out-of-state tuition ($):	15,950
Room & board:	5,127
FA application deadline:	2/15
% frosh receiving FA:	58
PT earnings per yr. ($):	1500

TYPE OF AID: % of students ($)

FA of some kind:	56 (NA)
Need-based grants:	72 (8,946)
Merit-based grants:	NA
Loans:	41 (3,600)
Work study:	25 (1,320)
Student rating of FA:	81

WASHINGTON AND LEE UNIVERSITY

CAMPUS LIFE

Quality of Life Rating: **90**

Type of school:	private
Affiliation:	none
Environment:	suburban

STUDENT BODY

FT Undergrad Enrollment:	1,622
% male/% female:	65/35
% out-of-state:	85
% live on campus:	45
% African-American:	4
% Asian:	1
% Caucasian:	94
% Hispanic:	1
% foreign:	1
% transfers:	1

WHAT'S HOT

honesty
deans
small classes (overall)
administration (overall)
small lectures
library
good-looking students
profs outside class
campus easy to get around
fraternities/sororities
profs in class

WHAT'S NOT

gay community visible
diversity

ACADEMICS

Academic Rating: **85**

Calendar:	4-4-2
Student/teacher ratio:	13/1
% doctorates:	85
Profs interesting:	94
Profs accessible:	94
Hours of study per day:	3.3

MOST POPULAR MAJORS BY %

History:	18
Economics:	11
English:	8

% GRADS WHO PURSUE

Law:	10
MBA:	2
Medicine:	4
M.A., etc.:	8

What do students think about Washington and Lee?

■ **Academics** Washington and Lee University provides its students with the classic "small liberal arts school" experience for a moderate private school price. Students at this traditional Southern school—Robert E. Lee was once college president—enjoy small classes with personable, accessible professors, and a "strong sense of community among the students, faculty, and administration. When students graduate, they feel like they're leaving part of their family behind." An honor code helps nourish that sense of community: students here schedule their own unproctored exams and leave their dorm rooms unlocked, confident that nothing will get stolen. Students also love the unusual academic schedule, which features two full-length terms (fall and winter) and a mandatory six-week term in the spring, during which students participate in seminars and internships or travel abroad. Professors often use the spring term to develop new course ideas and teaching methods. Ten percent of all graduates go on to law school within a year. History, economics, and English are among the most popular majors.

■ **Life** Washington and Lee is a *big* Greek school. One student explained: "Eighty percent of our students pledge to frats and sororities. With 16 frats and 4 sororities, we work hard and play hard here." Greeks dominate the social agenda; wrote one student, "The student body (which, at W & L, means the Greeks) runs the school's activities." Frat parties are frequent, and beer and alcohol, not surprisingly, are practically staples. "If you want to sleep before 2 a.m.," reported one undergrad, "forget it—there are so many drunk people coming in from parties that you could call an AA convention in the hallway." When students stumble home late at night, they do so across a beautiful campus, which one student described this way: "When you think about the classic example of college on a postcard, the image you call up would be W & L. Ivy on the walls, lush green setting, and excellent academics." The housing situation is reportedly excellent; said one student, "Everyone, including freshmen, can get single rooms if he or she wants them. Upperclassmen can (and often do) live off-campus, or in on-campus apartments with kitchens." With its verdant surroundings, comfortable housing, good food, and upwardly mobile Southern student body, it's no wonder many people liken W & L to a country club.

■ **Students** Washington and Lee has fewer than 100 minority students, most of whom are black. Students reported a pervasive conformity among the majority of students. "People here don't like change," warned one; another elaborated, "Make sure you know who you are before you get here. Confidence in who you are will make or break you at W & L. Being an individual is hard but worth it; the price of conformity is too high." The stereotypical W & L student is "Southern gentility who drives a BMW and refers to his or her father as Daddy," a stereotype repeated by enough students that it must have some bearing in truth. Still, those who fit in are extremely satisfied with W & L.

WASHINGTON AND LEE UNIVERSITY

Lexington, VA

Admissions

Washington and Lee considers your high school program of study and the strength of your high school curriculum as the two most important factors in your application. After these, in order of importance, come your GPA and standardized test scores, followed by your letters of recommendation, essays, extracurriculars, and interview. You are required to either take the ACT, or take the SAT plus three Achievements (one of which must be English Composition). You should also have completed at least 16 units of college prep courses, including four years of English, three years of math, two years of a foreign language, and one year of natural science. Students who apply to Wabash most often also apply to the University of Virginia, the College of William and Mary, University of North Carolina–Chapel Hill, Duke, and Wake Forest.

Financial Aid

The financial aid office at Washington and Lee University requires applicants to submit the FAF and a copy of their parents' most recent tax return. All merit-based grants awarded by the school are academic scholarships. The school reports that, although there is no absolute deadline for financial aid application submissions, February 1 is the *priority* deadline; all applications received after that date receive lower priority from the FA office. The affluence of W & L's student body is evidenced by the fact that, despite the school's hefty tuition fee, only 38 percent of freshmen enrolled for the 1991–92 academic year applied for financial aid (26% received some form of assistance).

A note from the Washington and Lee University Admissions Office:

"The most enduring influence on the lives of Washington and Lee students is an Honor System that is administered entirely by the students. Evidence of the Honor System's effectiveness abounds. For instance, students can schedule their own final exams, most of which are unproctored, and almost all of the university's buildings, including the library, are open 24 hours a day."

ADMISSIONS FACTS

Competitiveness Rating:	**92**
% of applicants accepted:	31
% acceptees attending:	41

FRESHMAN PROFILE

Average verbal SAT:	607*
Average math SAT:	649*
Average ACT:	NA
Graduated top 10% of class:	60
Graduated top 25% of class:	90
Graduated top 50% of class:	100

DEADLINES

Early decision/action:	12/1
Early dec./act. notif.:	12/15
Regular admission:	1/15
Regular adm. notif.:	4/1

APPLICANTS ALSO LOOK AT

and often prefer:
U. Virginia

and sometimes prefer:
Davidson College

and rarely prefer:
Wake Forest U.
Rhodes College
Southern Methodist U.
Franklin & Marshall College
James Madison U.
Tulane U.

ADDRESS

Undergraduate Admissions
Lexington, VA 24450
703-463-8710

FINANCIAL FACTS

In-state tuition ($):	11,575
Out-of-state tuition ($):	11,575
Room & board:	4,068
FA application deadline:	11/1
% frosh receiving FA:	28
PT earnings per yr. ($):	875

TYPE OF AID: % of students ($)

FA of some kind:	27 (9,700)
Need-based grants:	20 (7,181)
Merit-based grants:	8 (4,714)
Loans:	22 (4,012)
Work study:	16 (1,100)
Student rating of FA:	84

WELLESLEY COLLEGE

CAMPUS LIFE

Quality of Life Rating:	*88*
Type of school:	private
Affiliation:	none
Environment:	town

STUDENT BODY

FT Undergrad Enrollment:	2,109
% male/% female:	0/100
% out-of-state:	82
% live on campus:	98
% African-American:	7
% Asian:	17
% Caucasian:	72
% Hispanic:	4
% foreign:	6
% transfers:	1

WHAT'S HOT

gay community accepted
honesty
campus appearance
administration (overall)
profs outside class
profs in class
food
dorm comfort
small classes (overall)
leftist politics

WHAT'S NOT

beer
fraternities/sororities
marijuana
diversity

ACADEMICS

Academic Rating:	*91*
Calendar:	semester
Student/teacher ratio:	10/1
% doctorates:	95
Profs interesting:	94
Profs accessible:	93
Hours of study per day:	3.42

MOST POPULAR MAJORS BY %

Social Sciences:	32
Foreign Languages:	15
Psychology:	9

% GRADS WHO PURSUE

Law:	8
MBA:	1
Medicine:	6
M.A., etc.:	30

What do students think about Wellesley College?

■ **Academics** Because of its unique situation as a competitive, all-women's school, Wellesley College inspires great enthusiasm in its students. "Wellesley is a small liberal arts women's college dedicated to developing able, confident, and ambitious women to lead in the forefronts of all fields," wrote one senior. Although we also heard from detractors, most of our respondents were very happy with their choice: as one pointed out, Wellesley's student body is "self-selecting," so most know what they're getting into before they get here, and few leave disappointed. Academics are "quite difficult but invariably interesting"—even those who hate the social scene conceded this—professors are "excellent and caring," and classes are small. Junior year in Aix-en-Provence is highly recommended, both as a mind-broadening experience and as a means to escape the sometimes stifling Wellesley community. Art history, English, and political science are among the most popular majors here, and area counsellors reported that the science departments are strong. Students are torn over the issues of multiculturalism and "political correctness," both of which have taken root here. As students at a women's school they are atypically sensitive to race and gender issues: they just don't agree on the best way to address those issues.

■ **Life** The typical student's attitude here is summed up by this response: "I may not enjoy the social life at Wellesley at all, but the academics are well worth the sacrifice." "You have to make an effort to have a social life" was another comment we heard frequently. Pursuing a social life means taking a 30-minute ride to Cambridge for parties at Harvard and MIT. There are those who find this situation ideal; said one, "I have a great social life, find the academics challenging, and I can balance the two—academics during the week, social life on weekends." The neighboring town is "not much more than a country club gift shop," but Boston makes up for it. So too does the campus, which students ranked among the nation's most beautiful. Sprawling, bucolic, and full of Oxford-style Gothic architecture, it was just edged out by Rhodes and College of the Atlantic in our survey. Life at Wellesley takes a little getting used to—"many first-years consider transferring, but by winter break they love it here!"

■ **Students** Wellesley attracts a good cross-section of bright women, including a sizeable number of foreign nationals. Students here are, on average, considerably left-of-center politically, but there's enough of everybody for students to find their peers. There is a sizeable and visible lesbian population, but, as one student put it, the "perception that this school is only for staunch feminists and homosexuals is totally false." Conservatives, radicals, lesbians, fringe-type rebels all complain that there's too much of everyone else and not enough of them, indicating that Wellesley may have gotten the mix just about right. And remember: "Wellesley is not a girls' school without men but rather a women's college without boys."

WELLESLEY COLLEGE

Wellesley, MA

Admissions

From Wellesley's undergraduate brochure: "Wellesley students have in common the intellectual ability and skill to meet the high academic standards set by the College. In other respects, Wellesley students vary greatly in their interests. The process by which Wellesley selects students is designed to maintain two characteristics: high academic ability and a richly diverse population." The Board of Admission "reviews a range of materials" for each candidate, including secondary school record, rank in class, letters of recommendation form school personnel, the student's essay, scores on aptitude and achievement tests, and, if available, an interview report. While no specific high school curriculum is required, "nearly all accepted students" will have had four years of college preparatory study, including four years of foreign language, four years of mathematics, two years of lab science, and "ample work in writing, literature and history." Candidates are welcome to submit tapes, portfolios, or other evidence of their creative abilities and talents. All applicants must take the SAT and three Achievements (one of which must be English Composition, with or without essay). An on-campus or local alumna interview, while optional, is strongly recommended. An early "evaluation" is available for candidates who wish to know their chances of admission (without the actual decision being made). Applicants must submit materials by January 1; the evaluation is sent by the end of February.

Financial Aid

Financial aid applicants to Wellesley must complete the FAF and a form generated by Wellesley's financial aid office, and submit their own and their parents' most recent tax returns. All awards are need-based only. Fifty-two percent of the class of '95 received some type of aid upon entry to the College; the average value was $14,408. In '90–'91, 8% of all undergrads took out Perkins loans (average loan value: $2,313), 13% took out Wellesley's own institutional loans (average: $2,192), and 38% took out Stafford loans (average: $3,135). In addition to grants and loans, Wellesley offers several payment plans.

Excerpted from Wellesley College promotional materials:

"A student's years at Wellesley are the beginning—not the end—of an education. A Wellesley College degree signifies not that the graduate has memorized certain blocks of material, but that she has acquired the curiosity, the desire, and the ability to seek and assimilate new information. Four years at Wellesley can provide the foundation for the widest possible range of ambitions, and the necessary self-confidence to fulfill them. At Wellesley, a student has *every* educational opportunity. Above all, it is Wellesley's purpose to teach students to apply knowledge wisely, and to use the advantages of talent and education to seek new ways to serve the wider community."

ADMISSIONS FACTS

Competitiveness Rating:	92
% of applicants accepted:	49
% acceptees attending:	46

FRESHMAN PROFILE

Average verbal SAT:	600
Average math SAT:	640
Average ACT:	NA
Graduated top 10% of class:	75
Graduated top 25% of class:	96
Graduated top 50% of class:	100

DEADLINES

Early decision/action:	11/1
Early dec./act. notif.:	12/15
Regular admission:	2/1
Regular adm. notif.:	April

APPLICANTS ALSO LOOK AT

and often prefer:
Brown U.

and sometimes prefer:
Swarthmore College
Boston College
Vassar College
Cornell U.
Johns Hopkins U.
Barnard College
Smith College

and rarely prefer:
Mount Holyoke College

ADDRESS

Undergraduate Admissions
Wellesley, MA 02181
617-235-0320

FINANCIAL FACTS

In-state tuition ($):	15,966
Out-of-state tuition ($):	15,966
Room & board:	5,657
FA application deadline:	2/1
% frosh receiving FA:	44
PT earnings per yr. ($):	1400

TYPE OF AID: % of students ($)

FA of some kind:	49 (13,110)
Need-based grants:	47 (10,343)
Merit-based grants:	NA
Loans:	52 (3,255)
Work study:	41 (1,500)
Student rating of FA:	84

WESLEYAN UNIVERSITY

CAMPUS LIFE

Quality of Life Rating:	***79***
Type of school:	private
Affiliation:	none
Environment:	city

STUDENT BODY

FT Undergrad Enrollment:	2,672
% male/% female:	52/48
% out-of-state:	90
% live on campus:	95
% African-American:	9
% Asian:	7
% Caucasian:	75
% Hispanic:	3
% foreign:	2
% transfers:	8

WHAT'S HOT

gay community accepted
gay community visible
leftist politics
library
honesty
alternative rock
caring about politics
diversity
marijuana
profs in class

WHAT'S NOT

location
dating
fraternities/sororities

ACADEMICS

Academic Rating:	***88***
Calendar:	semester
Student/teacher ratio:	8/1
% doctorates:	82
Profs interesting:	89
Profs accessible:	87
Hours of study per day:	3.5

MOST POPULAR MAJORS BY %

Social Sciences:	34
Letters/Literature:	29
Life Sciences:	9

% GRADS WHO PURSUE

Law:	5
MBA:	3
Medicine:	5
M.A., etc.:	9

What do students think about Wesleyan University?

■ **Academics** Wesleyan University is in many ways the paragon of liberal arts institutions. Despite its university standing, Wesleyan is a small school, with fewer than 2,700 undergraduates and only about 150 graduate students. Over half its students major in liberal arts, and although relatively few students proceed from here directly to graduate programs (only 22 percent), they still attack their studies with vigor (over three and a half hours of study a day). In other words, the "education for education's sake" ethic is alive and well at Wesleyan. Professors here are excellent, "wonderful and really accessible"; they teach all the courses, despite the presence of graduate students to serve as TAs. Students are allowed a lot of flexibility in determining their curricula; independent studies in fields of the students' choosing are not at all uncommon. As one student explained, "Wesleyan demands student responsibility in all forms. We are treated with respect as competent adults and are expected to carry ourselves as such." Students reported that the liberal arts and natural and social science departments are uniformly strong, but noted that the performing and fine arts are not as well supported by the school (with the exception of the film department).

■ **Life** Wesleyan is known as the 'diversity university,' not only for its diverse student body but also for the wide range of academic and social options available to students. As one undergrad reported, organized clubs and activities "are *so* easy to get involved in; I'm only in my second semester and I'm already executive producer of Talk Radio, sports editor of the *Argus,* and membership director of Wesleyan Democrats." Another put it this way: "There are many different activities here, with an emphasis on political groups. Students here are liberal/radical" (see "Students," below). Social situations "run from super-raging to ultra-mellow. You're likely to go to a wild frat party and hang out in a dorm discussing politics and philosophy, all in the same night." There's even a coed fraternity that doubles as a literary club. On-campus housing is pleasant: many dorms are apartment-style and have full kitchens. Pot smoking and "hip" music (alternative and rap) are in with the students. Students ranked Middletown the fifth worst college town in the nation.

■ **Students** "Political correctness" is a hot issue on many campuses today, but only at a few is it more so than at Wesleyan, which has the ninth most left-leaning student body in the nation. Explained one student, "People complain that Wes is too p.c. and closed-mindedly liberal, but I don't know of that many other schools where people think, discuss, argue, and criticize (thoughtfully and intelligently) as much as we do." Still, others felt that many of their classmates had "a tendency to put down anyone who has a viewpoint not deemed politically correct." With a 25% minority population (including 9% African-Americans), WU earns its reputation for diversity. Students are proud of this diversity and report that interaction between groups is relatively frequent and easy.

WESLEYAN UNIVERSITY

Admissions

Students seeking admission to Wesleyan University must submit an application that includes the following: high school transcript, an essay, letters of recommendation, and an evaluation of their abilities by their English teacher. An interview, while not required, is "strongly recommended." All applicants must provide scores for either the SAT or the ACT, as well as three achievements (of which English Composition must be one). The admissions office recommends a college-prep high school curriculum including four years each of English, social studies, science, math, and a foreign language. Applicants to Wesleyan most often also apply to Williams, Haverford, Brandeis, Cornell University, Brown, and Harvard.

Financial Aid

Financial aid applicants to Wesleyan University must complete the FAF and a form generated by Wesleyan's financial aid office, and submit a copy of their parents' most recent tax return. All aid is based on need only. In addition to Stafford loans (recommended to 80 percent of financial aid recipients), Wesleyan recommends PLUS, FELP (Family Education Loan Plan) and SHARE loans.

Excerpted from Wesleyan University promotional materials:

"Wesleyan offers only one undergraduate degree, the Bachelor of Arts. Students may choose from about 950 courses each year and may be counted upon to devise, with the faculty, some 1,500 individual tutorials and lessons.

"True to its name, the University also offers master's degrees in 11 fields of study and doctoral degrees in six. Instruction in 40 major fields of study is given through thirty departments, eight programs, and two centers; through twelve programs abroad; and through other selective New England colleges in the Twelve College Exchange Program.

"Outstanding facilities permit Wesleyan's faculty and students to teach, learn, and live in a very attractive environment. Sophisticated laboratories and an observatory housing Connecticut's largest reflecting telescope serve introductory courses and advanced research alike. More than half of the student body participates in intramural athletics; men and women form twenty-nine teams in intercollegiate competition."

Competitiveness Rating:	**93**
% of applicants accepted:	40
% acceptees attending:	35

FRESHMAN PROFILE

Average verbal SAT:	616
Average math SAT:	668
Average ACT:	NA
Graduated top 10% of class:	65
Graduated top 25% of class:	100
Graduated top 50% of class:	100

DEADLINES

Early decision/action:	11/15
Early dec./act. notif.:	12/15
Regular admission:	1/15
Regular adm. notif.:	4/15

APPLICANTS ALSO LOOK AT

and sometimes prefer:
Amherst College
Princeton U.
Columbia U.
Harvard/Radcliffe College
Swarthmore College

and rarely prefer:
Oberlin College
Brandeis U.
Vassar College
Middlebury College

ADDRESS

Undergraduate Admissions
High Street & Wyllis Avenue
Middletown, CT 06457
203-344-7900

FINANCIAL FACTS

In-state tuition ($):	16,250
Out-of-state tuition ($):	16,250
Room & board:	5,219
FA application deadline:	1/15
% frosh receiving FA:	47
PT earnings per yr. ($):	1300

TYPE OF AID: % of students ($)	
FA of some kind:	46 (NA)
Need-based grants:	39 (10,773)
Merit-based grants:	NA
Loans:	NA (2,850)
Work study:	39 (1,242)
Student rating of FA:	79

WEST VIRGINIA UNIVERSITY

CAMPUS LIFE

Quality of Life Rating: **70**

Type of school:	public
Affiliation:	none
Environment:	suburban

STUDENT BODY

FT Undergrad Enrollment:	14,566
% male/% female:	55/45
% out-of-state:	49
% live on campus:	24
% African-American:	3
% Asian:	1
% Caucasian:	92
% Hispanic:	1
% foreign:	2
% transfers:	3

WHAT'S HOT

marijuana
college newspaper
intercollegiate sports
dating
rap/hip-hop
hard liquor
Top 40

WHAT'S NOT

registration
campus easy to get around
living on campus
TAs teach intros
profs outside class
financial aid
administration (overall)

ACADEMICS

Academic Rating: **72**

Calendar:	semester
Student/teacher ratio:	14/1
% doctorates:	82
Profs interesting:	66
Profs accessible:	63
Hours of study per day:	2.9

MOST POPULAR MAJORS BY %

Business & Management:	17
Engineering:	11
Health Sciences:	10

% GRADS WHO PURSUE

Law:	NA
MBA:	NA
Medicine:	NA
M.A., etc.:	33

What do students think about West Virginia University?

■ **Academics** "West Virginia University is known for its party atmosphere, so many overlook the true value of the education available here," explained one student. "The school has its weaker courses, it's true, but overall the education provided here is strong." Another concurred: "I've noticed that those who come to learn do indeed succeed, and those who come to party are gone within a year." Our survey showed that WVU students attend nearly all classes and put in close to three hours of studying a day afterward, so the days of 'all party, no study' truly are in WVU's past. Business and management, engineering, and health sciences are the most popular fields of study, and all students are obliged to pursue a well-rounded education by the challenging distribution requirements: four courses each in the humanities, natural sciences/mathematics, and social sciences are necessary for graduation. As at most large universities, classes are often huge, professors are often inaccessible, and the bureaucracy can reach nightmarish proportions. Still, those who stick around for all four years feel that, in the end, a WVU education is worth the trouble (particularly considering its bargain-basement price). Said one senior, "Course registration, core curriculum classes, and financial aid can be so frustrating and intense that you feel like you're dealing with the federal government. However, once you are far into your major, the school can begin to shine. Classes delve more deeply into the subjects and the professors give you more attention. I can't say enough good about my program (journalism)." An honors program provides approximately 600 undergrads with smaller classes and more rigorous academics.

■ **Life** Most WVU students would concur with the one who wrote "the social life here is great!" WVU students find ample time to supplement their educations with socializing. Despite a lopsided male-female ratio, students expressed satisfaction with the romantic scene. Fraternity and sorority parties provide the setting for most parties and sponsor several major campuswide festivals (complained one student, "Fraternities and sororities basically control all student activities"). Still, the nucleus of the WVU social universe is intercollegiate sports. Students are ardent supporters of Mountaineer football and basketball. Students gave Morgantown average grades, but noted that relations with local residents could be better. Explained one student, "It's the only town in the U.S. where the students are blamed for every wrongdoing that goes on in town."

■ **Students** A little more than half of WVU's students come from in-state. Many others are from neighboring states, but the school does draw students from all across the country and approximately 300 students from overseas. Over 90 percent of the students are white.

WEST VIRGINIA UNIVERSITY

Admissions

From West Virginia University's undergraduate catalog: "As a land-grant university, West Virginia University has as its primary obligation the people of its own state. Therefore, if you live in West Virginia, you are given preference for admission to the University or to the program of study that you have chosen. If you live elsewhere, a superior record from high school or from a previous college experience earns you similar consideration." Required units of high school study include four years of English, three units of social studies (including U.S. history), two units of mathematics (algebra I and higher) and two units of laboratory science. Two units of a foreign language are strongly recommended, as is an additional unit of mathematics (geometry). Certain colleges and programs (engineering, mineral and energy resources, etc.) have requirements in addition to those listed above. All applicants must submit ACT or SAT scores. West Virginia residents are eligible for admission with a 2.0 GPA and ACT of 19 (combined SAT of 720). Out-of-state applicants are eligible with a 2.25 GPA and an ACT score of 20 (combined SAT of 800). Normally, fulfilling these requirements results in an offer of admission; however, "As space becomes limited, the better-qualified applicants receive first consideration." It is therefore to your advantage to apply early. The priority date for consideration is March 1.

Financial Aid

Financial aid applicants to West Virginia University must complete the FAF and a form generated by WVU's financial aid office. In '90–'91, 12 percent of all undergrads took out Perkins loans (average value was $1,358), and 14 percent participated in the College Work Study Program (average award was $761). Several scholarships are available for West Virginia residents; scholarships are also available for academic merit, performance (performing arts, dance and animal judging), leadership, departmental interest, and minorities. The deadline for consideration for entering freshman scholarships is January 15.

Excerpted from West Virginia University promotional materials:

"West Virginia University combines many of the advantages of a large institution with those of a small one. It is both a comprehensive university offering 176 degree programs from the bachelor's through the doctoral level and a decentralized group of 15 colleges and schools on two campuses in Morgantown, an arrangement which helps maintain the friendly, informal atmosphere of smaller institutions....With 19,997 students in the fall semester of 1989, 1,826 full-time faculty and 2,419 administrative staff. WVU is large enough to support academic diversity....Over the years, 23 students from the University have received Rhodes Scholarships to continue their studies at Oxford University."

ADMISSIONS FACTS

Competitiveness Rating:	**69**
% of applicants accepted:	71
% acceptees attending:	39

FRESHMAN PROFILE

Average verbal SAT:	444
Average math SAT:	507
Average ACT:	22
Graduated top 10% of class:	NA
Graduated top 25% of class:	NA
Graduated top 50% of class:	NA

DEADLINES

Early decision/action:	NA
Early dec./act. notif.:	NA
Regular admission:	rolling
Regular adm. notif.:	rolling

APPLICANTS ALSO LOOK AT

and often prefer:
Miami U.
Marquette U.
Washington U.
James Madison U.

and sometimes prefer:
U. Pittsburgh

and rarely prefer:
Ohio State U.
Penn State U.

ADDRESS

Undergraduate Admissions
P.O. Box 6001
Morgantown, WV 26506-6001
304-293-0111

FINANCIAL FACTS

In-state tuition ($):	1,850
Out-of-state tuition ($):	5,018
Room & board:	3,846
FA application deadline:	3/1
% frosh receiving FA:	44
PT earnings per yr. ($):	1000

TYPE OF AID: % of students ($)

FA of some kind:	54 (NA)
Need-based grants:	NA
Merit-based grants:	NA
Loans:	NA
Work study:	NA
Student rating of FA:	64

CAMPUS LIFE

Quality of Life Rating:	**83**
Type of school:	private
Affiliation:	none
Environment:	suburban

STUDENT BODY

FT Undergrad Enrollment:	1,223
% male/% female:	23/77
% out-of-state:	54
% live on campus:	95
% African-American:	3
% Asian:	4
% Caucasian:	88
% Hispanic:	2
% foreign:	6
% transfers:	2

WHAT'S HOT

bursar
registration
campus easy to get around
caring about politics
living on campus
deans
profs in class
profs outside class
profs teach intro courses

WHAT'S NOT

fraternities/sororities
location
religious clubs
town-gown relations
cost of living

ACADEMICS

Academic Rating:	**82**
Calendar:	semester
Student/teacher ratio:	12/1
% doctorates:	93
Profs interesting:	89
Profs accessible:	88
Hours of study per day:	3.56

MOST POPULAR MAJORS BY %

English:	18
Psychology:	13
Economics:	10

% GRADS WHO PURSUE

Law:	2
MBA:	1
Medicine:	4
M.A., etc.:	3

What do students think about Wheaton College?

■ **Academics** Students reported that things have been "changing rapidly" at Wheaton College since the school went coeducational in 1988, but its commitment to a rigorous liberal arts education provided by "very knowledgeable and extraordinarily accessible" professors has remained steadfast. Our respondents had nothing but praise for their professors (TAs do not teach courses here): wrote one, "Close relationships with instructors and students is of vital importance to Wheaton students. Wheaton offers that personal touch that every young adult needs and wants." Said another, "Most of my profs have great senses of humor. They help make Wheaton what it is: a fun, enthusiastic, competitive college. They really want to see you do your best." Wheaton demands a lot of its students, who must complete a broad range of general education requirements and who study, on average, over three-and-a-half hours a day. History, political science, women's studies, economics, and psychology are among the popular and excellent majors here. Students also praised the administration ("although sometimes they're a *little* uptight and self-righteous," offered one student), and particularly appreciated the active career services office. "The Filene Center for Work and Learning has been very helpful in providing info regarding internships and jobs," wrote one student. "It also helps students write resumes and cover letters."

■ **Life** Wheaton's hometown of Norton is "boring, but located between Boston and Providence, so it's OK." Students warned, however, that "access to a car is a must to reach entertainment." On campus, "Students are encouraged to get involved in extracurricular activities, and do!" There is no Greek system here, but that does not curtail drinking; reported one student, "Like many rural campuses, Wheaton has a strong alcohol presence, but it is kept under control." The most important quality-of-life issue on campus remains the lopsided male:female ratio—women currently outnumber men by more than two to one. One man wrote that this "is a big plus for many guys on campus, who, shall we say, try to take advantage of the situation." Conversely, women report, "There is a misconception that women here are looking to get married or laid, especially by Brown frat boys. They call us 'Wheaties,' as in 'Have you had your Wheaties tonight?' It's very demeaning, and not true!" One other important quality-of-life issue is the small student body: "Be careful what you say here," wrote one student, "because it *will* get around."

■ **Students** Wheaton's student body is not a terribly diverse one. One student described the campus climate as "many WASPs, many Saabs, and a lot of money." Within those parameters, however, students enjoy a "family atmosphere" (although a few detractors felt their classmates were "too cliquish"). Wrote one student, "People on campus are very friendly and are always ready to say "hi" to a stranger. Although there have been times when I disagreed with a policy at this school, I have never regretted my decision to come here and will be sad to leave."

WHEATON COLLEGE

Admissions

Wheaton writes that they use no cutoffs, and that "Beginning with students applying for entrance in 1992, the submission of all standardized test scores is optional for the purposes of admission. Applicants who wish their scores to be considered should arrange for official score reports to be sent from the appropriate testing agency directly to the Wheaton office of Admission....Unofficial test scores (i.e., those reported on high school transcripts) will not be considered." Once you are admitted, to assist Wheaton with your placement in English courses, you must "submit results of either the English Composition Achievement Test (with or without essay) or the ACT upon enrollment..." In order of importance, Wheaton considers your high school GPA, essays, extracurriculars, letters of recommendation, interview, and "demonstrated proficiencies." You must have completed at least four units of English, three to four of math, two to three of science (two lab) and three to four of a foreign language.

Financial Aid

The financial aid office at Wheaton College requires applicants to submit the FAF, a form generated by the school, and their parents' most recent tax return. All grants at Wheaton are awarded on the basis of need only. The school's most recent catalog mentions only the Stafford and Perkins loan programs as options for aid recipients. Limited financial aid is available for Wheaton students who wish to pursue study abroad.

A note from the Wheaton College Admissions Office:

"When an applicant fills out an application for admission to Wheaton, he or she is asked to focus on post-college career, family, and public-service goals (and their interplay) and encouraged to submit a portfolio and disclose characteristics, talents, and concerns hard to express in a traditional application. Identifying individual student aspirations and talents and developing them is central to our educational approach. We teach critical thinking and effective communication in writing intensive courses across the curriculum, and are sensitive to differences in the way individuals learn and express themselves. Our Filene Center for Work and Learning offers internships, community service, and other experiential-learning opportunities and helps forge a link between the liberal arts classroom and the world of work."

ADMISSIONS FACTS

Competitiveness Rating:	**70**
% of applicants accepted:	78
% acceptees attending:	29

FRESHMAN PROFILE

Average verbal SAT:	500
Average math SAT:	540
Average ACT:	22
Graduated top 10% of class:	24
Graduated top 25% of class:	60
Graduated top 50% of class:	85

DEADLINES

Early decision/action:	11/15
Early dec./act. notif.:	1/1
Regular admission:	2/1
Regular adm. notif.:	4/1

APPLICANTS ALSO LOOK AT

and often prefer:
Connecticut College

and sometimes prefer:
Skidmore College
Clark U.
U. Rhode Island

and rarely prefer:
Providence College
U. Mass–Amherst

ADDRESS

Undergraduate Admissions
Norton, MA 02766
508-285-7722

FINANCIAL FACTS

In-state tuition ($):	15,650
Out-of-state tuition ($):	15,650
Room & board:	5,480
FA application deadline:	2/1
% frosh receiving FA:	52
PT earnings per yr. ($):	1300

TYPE OF AID: % of students ($)

FA of some kind:	56 (NA)
Need-based grants:	56 (8,654)
Merit-based grants:	NA
Loans:	60 (4,003)
Work study:	53 (930)
Student rating of FA:	85

WILLAMETTE UNIVERSITY

Salem, OR

CAMPUS LIFE

Quality of Life Rating:	***83***

Type of school:	private
Affiliation:	Methodist
Environment:	city

STUDENT BODY

FT Undergrad Enrollment:	1,537
% male/% female:	48/52
% out-of-state:	50
% live on campus:	70
% African-American:	1
% Asian:	5
% Caucasian:	88
% Hispanic:	3
% foreign:	2
% transfers:	5

WHAT'S HOT

profs outside class
financial aid
administration (overall)
small classes (overall)
bursar
profs teach intros
cost of living
profs in class

WHAT'S NOT

college newspaper
college radio station
diversity
food
location

ACADEMICS

Academic Rating:	***81***

Calendar:	semester
Student/teacher ratio:	15/1
% doctorates:	NA
Profs interesting:	86
Profs accessible:	89
Hours of study per day:	3.3

MOST POPULAR MAJORS BY %

Economics:	20
Political Science:	15
Psychology:	15

% GRADS WHO PURSUE

Law:	20
MBA:	5
Medicine:	10
M.A., etc.:	15

What do students think about Willamette University?

■ **Academics** According to one student at Willamette University, his school is "overall, the best small liberal arts school in the Northwest." Lots of his classmates would agree: our survey showed that students here enjoy small classes, excellent professors, and, despite the fact that they study hard, are among the nation's happier student bodies. Said one environmental science major, "The students are very smart and the competition is stiff." The pre-med departments are top-notch (as are, in fact, most of the natural science departments), sending one in ten graduates on to medical school. The political science program benefits from the school's location, right across the street from the state capitol; an internship program in Washington, D.C., run in conjunction with American University, is also available to poli-sci majors. Music and pre-professional programs are also said to be strong. Distribution requirements guarantee that WU undergrads are exposed to some math, literature, social sciences, natural sciences, and fine arts, whether they want to be or not. All students must also complete a senior project, which, the school's catalog notes, "may be satisfied by completion of a major scientific research project, a senior thesis, or by a professional internship."

■ **Life** This is *Twin Peaks* country, and, not surprisingly, the Willamette campus is replete with natural beauty: said one student, "I love WU, especially the stream with the ducks!" "Size and atmosphere," said another, "is what makes the school a wonderful place to spend your college years." Because the academic atmosphere here is intense, most socializing and partying is confined to the weekends. A third of the students go Greek, and while frats and sororities play a sizeable role in the school's social life, animosity between Greeks and independents is minimal, "especially after second semester rush." One complaint students had was that the school "has no substantial structure for student interaction. There is no student union and the only cafe is *très chic*." When students get a hankering for city life, they trek over to Portland, about an hour's drive.

■ **Students** As one student put it, "The student body is fairly monochromatic and moderate politically, but gradually this is improving. I've seen a lot of progress on this campus, and there is momentum growing in the liberal direction." Said another, "WU is making a concerted effort to recruit a more diverse student body." They are a bright group of people, half of whom will go directly on to graduate school upon graduation. Although one West Coast student found his classmates "rich and stuck up," they're not by East Coast standards: said one transfer from Williams College in Massachusetts, "Students here are a lot less pretentious and snooty than they were at Williams."

WILLAMETTE UNIVERSITY

Admissions

The admissions office at Willamette writes, "Admission to Willamette is selective. A student body demonstrating a diversity of talents, backgrounds, and interests is sought. Willamette actively seeks applicants from a a variety of ethnic, geographic, and socioeconomic backgrounds. Although we have no formal 'cut-offs,' the median GPA in solid subjects for our freshman is 3.55, the median SAT score is between 1100 and 1200, and the median ACT score is 26." Willamette considers your high school GPA as the most important admissions factor, followed (in order) by standardized test scores, letters of recommendation, extracurriculars, and your interview. You must take either the SAT or ACT, and it is recommended that you have completed at least four years of English, and three or more years each of lab science, math, foreign language, and social studies/history. Students who apply here also often apply to Lewis and Clark, U. of Puget Sound, U. of Oregon, Stanford, and Whitman.

Financial Aid

The financial aid office at Willamette University requires applicants to submit the FAF and their parents' most recent tax return. Willamette offers merit grants on the basis of a wide variety of skills, among which are academic excellence, athletic ability, and talent in the creative arts. Eighty-two percent of freshmen enrolled for the 1991–92 academic year applied for financial aid; 78 percent of that freshman class received an aid package (average value: $11,300).

A note from the Willamette University Admissions Office:

"Willamette University, founded in 1842, is the oldest school west of the Missouri River. It is a coeducational, liberal arts and sciences, residential, independent, small (2,400), and selective college. We are located one hour from the Pacific Ocean, the Cascade Mountains, and the City of Portland. Our campus is in the heart of Salem, Oregon's capital, and directly across the street from both the state capitol and the U.S. campus of Tokyo International University. Willamette has long been known for its intellectual vitality, supportive academic community, and close relationships between students and faculty. Some of the words that best describe Willamette include: academic, challenging, personal, friendly, well-located, beautiful, balanced, and historic."

ADMISSIONS FACTS

Competitiveness Rating:	**77**
% of applicants accepted:	82
% acceptees attending:	35

FRESHMAN PROFILE

Average verbal SAT:	530
Average math SAT:	570
Average ACT:	25
Graduated top 10% of class:	41
Graduated top 25% of class:	73
Graduated top 50% of class:	94

DEADLINES

Early decision/action:	12/15
Early dec./act. notif.:	1/15
Regular admission:	2/15
Regular adm. notif.:	4/1

APPLICANTS ALSO LOOK AT

and often prefer
Stanford U.

and sometimes prefer:
Lewis and Clark College
U. Oregon
Oregon State U.
Whitman College

and rarely prefer:
U. Puget Sound
Portland State U.

ADDRESS

Undergraduate Admissions
900 State Street
Salem, OR 97301
503-370-6303

FINANCIAL FACTS

In-state tuition ($):	12,400
Out-of-state tuition ($):	12,400
Room & board:	3,950
FA application deadline:	2/1
% frosh receiving FA:	75
PT earnings per yr. ($):	1000

TYPE OF AID: % of students ($)

FA of some kind:	75 (11,500)
Need-based grants:	NA
Merit-based grants:	NA
Loans:	NA
Work study:	NA
Student rating of FA:	89

COLLEGE OF WILLIAM AND MARY

Williamsburg, VA

CAMPUS LIFE

Quality of Life Rating: **82**

Type of school:	public
Affiliation:	none
Environment:	suburban

STUDENT BODY

FT Undergrad Enrollment:	5,237
% male/% female:	45/55
% out-of-state:	32
% live on campus:	83
% African-American:	6
% Asian:	4
% Caucasian:	84
% Hispanic:	1
% foreign:	3
% transfers:	3

WHAT'S HOT
religious clubs
religion
honesty
cost of living
campus appearance
doing all the reading
profs teach intros
profs teach upper levels

WHAT'S NOT
working a job
marijuana
alternative rock
registration
dating

ACADEMICS

Academic Rating: **85**

Calendar:	semester
Student/teacher ratio:	14/1
% doctorates:	94
Profs interesting:	83
Profs accessible:	82
Hours of study per day:	3.1

MOST POPULAR MAJORS
Business
English
History

% GRADS WHO PURSUE

Law:	7
MBA:	2
Medicine:	7
M.A., etc.:	25

What do students think about William and Mary?

■ **Academics** The College of William and Mary is among the most competitive public schools in the nation. Students are subjected to a formidable battery of core requirements: three courses each in the humanities, social sciences, and physical sciences, plus two upper-level courses in fields outside their majors. Professors are generally good teachers and are very accessible for those at a public institution. One student told us, "Professors here are readily available—I got to know my Russian professor well enough that he spent an afternoon with our family over Christmas break. Most profs don't go quite that far, but it is not uncommon to have lunch with a professor." Another outstanding features is the honor code, which students claim is the oldest in the nation: it allows students to take exams in an unproctored setting. This venerable institution, however, has recently felt the pressure of Virginia's fiscal crisis. Wrote one student, "The school is in the midst of serious budget problems, which are exacerbated by the fact that the administration concentrates on expansion and graduate work rather than maintaining its reputation as an excellent undergraduate liberal arts school." Course selection is among the victims of the budget axe; so far other assets remain intact, but many students voiced concerns that, without more state support, big changes may be in the offing for the school.

■ **Life** William and Mary abuts a major tourist attraction, Colonial Williamsburg. One student commented on the surroundings, "Probably the most unusual thing about William and Mary is its location, next door to 'Colonial Williamsburg.' Williamsburg itself is very touristy and artificial in lots of ways (students equal or outnumber locals, with whom there is no contact). On the flip side, there are many interesting historic things around and the town is damn picturesque, tourists not withstanding." The town does provide some job opportunities for students, but most socializing is done on or immediately around campus, either at frat parties or at local delicatessens. Greek life is very important; said one student, "The main thing to do on weekends is go to fraternity parties and sorority formals—for which it is a huge effort to get a date." But, students claimed that other social outlets exist, and noted that extracurricular clubs and organizations are popular. The campus itself is beautiful; wrote one student, "W & M is a beautiful place to spend your college years. Unfortunately, sometimes it seems that the school pays more attention to the landscaping than it does to the students."

■ **Students** The William and Mary student body is predominantly white; about 300 Blacks constitute the largest minority population. Students are socially conservative: said one, "Those who choose not to dress and act like the majority have to form their own groups outside the mainstream." Most students believe there is a sizeable gay community on campus, but one gay student wrote: "It is rumored that this is a gay campus, but let me tell you, I'm gay and it's been hard to find too many others." Students are the fourth most religious among those at a non-affiliated university.

COLLEGE OF WILLIAM AND MARY

Williamsburg, VA

Admissions

William and Mary told us they use no formulas or cut-offs; they look for a "broad and strong curriculum in high school…In-state residency (is) a major factor." Depth is as important as breadth in your extracurriculars. Most important at William and Mary is your program of study, followed by your high school GPA, standardized test scores, extracurriculars, essays, letters of recommendation, and interview, in that order. You must take either the SAT or ACT, and "to be competitive," you should have completed at least three years of a foreign language, three years of lab sciences, have taken math through Algebra 3/Trigonometry, and have a strong record in English and Social Studies. Applicants to William and Mary often also apply to University of Virginia, Duke, James Madison, University of Richmond, and the Ivy League Schools.

Financial Aid

The financial aid office at the College of William and Mary requires applicants to submit the FAF. The school's 1991–92 catalog states, "In most cases Virginia undergraduates may expect sufficient support to enable them to attend the College for four years, while out-of-state undergraduates may in some cases expect partial support, with the level depending upon the availability of funds." National Merit Scholars and minority students *may* qualify for a limited number of grants; many other grants are available to Virginia residents. William and Mary participates in the Perkins and Stafford loan programs, and encourages needy students to apply for PLUS loans from local bankers.

A note from the College of William and Mary Admissions Office:

"The College of William and Mary is a multifaceted university dedicated to intellectual inquiry, discovery, and dissemination of knowledge. For almost three hundred years, the College's commitment to 'the good arts and sciences' has attracted students of talent and achievement from Virginia and beyond.

"As we embark on our fourth century in 1993, we continue to honor and build upon our traditional strengths, which are at the center of a liberal education, while responding with energy to the emerging needs of the future. We are excited about the breadth of our curriculum: the richness of our offerings and the opportunities we provide for students to gain a global perspective.

"The distinction of its scholar-teachers, the timeless and historic beauty of its campus, the celebration of learning and working together that invigorates its students make William and Mary a community unlike any other, a place of learning that serves as a beacon as well as an anchor."

ADMISSIONS FACTS

Competitiveness Rating:	**93**
% of applicants accepted:	36
% acceptees attending:	44

FRESHMAN PROFILE

Average verbal SAT:	581
Average math SAT:	640
Average ACT:	NA
Graduated top 10% of class:	72
Graduated top 25% of class:	93
Graduated top 50% of class:	100

DEADLINES

Early decision/action:	11/1
Early dec./act. notif.:	12/1
Regular admission:	1/15
Regular adm. notif.:	4/1

APPLICANTS ALSO LOOK AT

and often prefer:

U. Virginia
Georgetown U.
Williams College
Duke U.
Washington and Lee U.

and sometimes prefer:

Wake Forest U.

and rarely prefer:

James Madison U.
U. Richmond
George Mason U.

ADDRESS

Undergraduate Admissions
Williamsburg, VA 23185
804-221-4223

FINANCIAL FACTS

In-state tuition ($):	2,240
Out-of-state tuition ($):	8,960
Room & board:	3,746
FA application deadline:	2/15
% frosh receiving FA:	44
PT earnings per yr. ($):	1300

TYPE OF AID: % of students ($)

FA of some kind:	46 (NA)
Need-based grants:	NA
Merit-based grants:	NA
Loans:	NA
Work study:	NA
Student rating of FA:	75

WILLIAMS COLLEGE

CAMPUS LIFE

Quality of Life Rating: **89**

Type of school:	private
Affiliation:	none
Environment:	suburban

STUDENT BODY

FT Undergrad Enrollment:	2,003
% male/% female:	54/46
% out-of-state:	85
% live on campus:	96
% African-American:	8
% Asian:	9
% Caucasian:	74
% Hispanic:	4
% foreign:	3
% transfers:	1

WHAT'S HOT

administration (overall)
intercollegiate sports
food
honesty
profs in class
intramural sports
campus appearance
profs outside class
doing all the reading
campus easy to get around
attending all classes
gay community accepted

WHAT'S NOT

fraternities/sororities
dating

ACADEMICS

Academic Rating: **91**

Calendar:	4-1-4
Student/teacher ratio:	11/1
% doctorates:	91
Profs interesting:	94
Profs accessible:	91
Hours of study per day:	3.61

MOST POPULAR MAJORS BY %

History:	17
English:	12
Political Science:	9

% GRADS WHO PURSUE

Law:	4
MBA:	1
Medicine:	4
M.A., etc.:	11

What do students think about Williams College?

■ **Academics** Williams College is an excellent, traditional liberal arts school whose traditions date back a long way: the school will celebrate its bicentennial in 1993. That same year, coincidentally, will mark the instatement of new curriculum requirements in non-Western culture, further broadening the already far-reaching studies of Williams students. General education requirements currently demand that students take three courses each in humanities, social sciences, and hard sciences. Another unique feature of the curriculum is the mandatory winter semester, a month-long term during which students pursue studies in less traditional academic subjects. Students commonly spend part or all of their junior year abroad. English, economics, history, political science, and psychology are among the popular majors; pre-medical sciences, such as biology and chemistry, while attracting fewer enrollees, are also reputedly excellent. All students report that their studies are demanding—the average student spends over three-and-a-half hours a day poring over books and lecture notes—and that professors are energetic, helpful, and extremely accessible.

■ **Life** Williamstown, Massachusetts is no bustling metropolis; as one student explained, "The town is really lame, but the surroundings are really beautiful." The campus and surroundings are hospitable to outdoors activities and athletics, both of which are extremely popular. "Sports permeate everything," wrote one student. "Everyone plays something and many people feel more guilty about not putting in weight room and Stairmaster time than they do about not reading the assignment for their next class." Living conditions are nearly ideal: "Our dormitory arrangements—suites with a common room—are very comfortable and particularly conducive to forming close groups of friends," noted one student. There is no Greek scene, but there are plenty of frat-style parties at which kegs of beer are definitely the center of attention. Williams tied one other school in our survey (Colgate) for most beer drunk per capita, rating "beer popularity" a 3.98 on a scale of 0–4. A wide variety of extracurricular activities are available for those so inclined; the campus newspaper, radio station, and theater groups are among the many creative endeavors Williams students undertake in their spare time. Don't come here looking for romance, though: wrote one student, "I'm filling out this survey on Valentine's Day, which we refer to here as 'Black Friday.'" Summed up one student: "Work is our God and athletics and kegs are our opiates."

■ **Students** Students here reported that they enjoy the friendly atmosphere of their small community: wrote one, "At Williams, I made many friends *very* quickly, and strangers even smile and say 'hi' as I walk around campus. Williams is a real community, and I feel very much at home here." The school does a good job of attracting minority students; over one fourth of the student body is made up of minorities. Although there are a lot of jock-scholars at Williams, there are also, according to several of our respondents, "Lots of 'nerds in high school' people here."

WILLIAMS COLLEGE

Admissions

Williams states that "(the) admissions process is attuned to the students it seeks: creative, motivated, independent individuals who value a personal learning environment…Individual admission decisions are based on several factors: academic achievement and promise, personal accomplishments, community involvement and service, and demonstrated extracurricular and artistic talent." The admissions committee first judges your high school GPA, followed, in order of importance, by letters of recommendation, standardized test scores, essays and extracurriculars. Students are required to submit either an SAT or ACT score, and three Achievement test scores, one of which must be English Composition. Also required are a "peer reference," one teacher reference and one guidance counselor letter. Finally, students should have completed four years of English and math, three to four years of a foreign language, and two or more years in social sciences and lab science. Students who apply to Williams also often apply to Princeton, Harvard/Radcliffe, Yale, Amherst, Stanford and Brown.

Financial Aid

The financial aid office at Williams College requires applicants to submit the FAF, a form generated by the school, and copies of their and their parents' tax returns and W-2 statements. The school awards a limited number of academic and minority scholarships; a small number of grants are available to international students. All other grants are awarded on the basis of need. The Williams application brochure lists the following loan options: Stafford, Perkins, PLUS, FEL, and Nellie Mae. Williams allows needy students to pay tuition, interest-free, on an installment plan; this plan requires a $35 administrative fee.

A note from the Williams Admissions Office:

"Williams is proud to offer Oxford-style tutorials, encouraging research and scholarly debate as a course option for all students. Learning to develop and defend an argument, and to respond on the spot to questions, criticisms, and suggestions from a peer and a faculty tutor, are the focal tasks of weekly tutorial meetings. Annually, 30 Williams students devote a full year to the tutorial method of study at Oxford. A quarter of Williams students pursue their education overseas in all corners of the world. Four weeks of Winter Study each year provide time for individualized projects, research, and novel fields of study. For 2,000 undergraduates, a Williams education means over $1,000,000 annually in national grants for science research, and 2,200 forest acres, complete with a treetop canopy walkway—for environmental research."

ADMISSIONS FACTS

Competitiveness Rating:	**96**
% of applicants accepted:	28
% acceptees attending:	41

FRESHMAN PROFILE

Average verbal SAT:	641
Average math SAT:	676
Average ACT:	30
Graduated top 10% of class:	79
Graduated top 25% of class:	93
Graduated top 50% of class:	98

DEADLINES

Early decision/action:	11/15
Early dec./act. notif.:	12/15
Regular admission:	1/1
Regular adm. notif.:	4/1

APPLICANTS ALSO LOOK AT

and often prefer:
Amherst College
Brown U.

and sometimes prefer:
Dartmouth College
Bowdoin College
Cornell U.
Wesleyan U.

and rarely prefer:
Hamilton College
Middlebury College
U. Vermont

ADDRESS

Undergraduate Admissions
P.O. Box 487
Williamstown, MA 01267
413-597-2211

FINANCIAL FACTS

In-state tuition ($):	16,635
Out-of-state tuition ($):	16,635
Room & board:	5,210
FA application deadline:	2/1
% frosh receiving FA:	35
PT earnings per yr. ($):	1225

TYPE OF AID: % of students ($)

FA of some kind:	37 (15,400)
Need-based grants:	37 (NA)
Merit-based grants:	NA
Loans:	NA
Work study:	NA
Student rating of FA:	80

UNIVERSITY OF WISCONSIN–MADISON

Madison, WI

What do students think about the University of Wisconsin?

■ **Academics** As one area college counselor explained, "It takes a self-reliant student to get through the administrative red tape and graduate from University of Wisconsin in four years (many take five, or more), but for those who can handle it, there is something here for everyone." Each year, 30,000 undergraduates (and another 14,000 graduate students) reap the diverse benefits of this reasonably priced, nationally esteemed institution. The engineering and business schools are world class, but career-track majors—journalism, education, the pre-medical sciences—and the social sciences are all well regarded. Everyone here must complete distribution requirements, although the exact requirements vary from division to division; students noted that these requirements, which universally include liberal arts and sciences courses, are "very difficult." Students also reported that, although assistance from professors, TAs, and administrators is difficult to come by, the excellent facilities—especially the libraries and research labs—make their forced independence a little easier to tolerate.

■ **Life** With one of the largest undergraduate populations in the country, Wisconsin can and does support a "vast and extraordinary" array of extracurricular activities. Students who want leadership roles in clubs and other campus organizations must pursue them aggressively—the competition is fierce—but for the timid there is a wide range of movies, concerts, and theatrical productions to attend. Partying, either at the popular fraternities and sororities or at students' residences, is the single most popular activity, however; it's so popular, in fact, that it moved one disgusted student to tell us that, "I thought that, at this university, I'd meet well-rounded, curious, interesting students. However, it seems that parties are more of a social focus than plays, movies, lectures, or any other type of social function that involves intellectually stimulating conversation." Sporting events are also popular, particularly ice hockey, and students report that the intramural sports program enjoys widespread participation. Unusually popular is the school's marching band, called the Fifth Quarter. Two major sources of dissatisfaction here: the dearth of housing and the "unbelievably cold winters."

■ **Students** University of Wisconsin–Madison, is a predominantly white school, but because of the magnitude of the student body, there are decent-sized minority populations: approximately 1000 Asian students, 600 black students, and 600 Hispanic students. Students report that these groups are unfortunately polarized from the mainstream; black students in particular complained, "People here are not very accepting of 'liberal' ideas or people of different backgrounds." Another elaborated, "The actuality is that there are so many different types of people here that everyone can find a group in which they feel comfortable. But *none* of these groups get along with each other. Instead of appreciating differences, people want everyone to accept their own view and be just like them."

UNIVERSITY OF WISCONSIN–MADISON

Madison, WI

Admissions

According to the University of Wisconsin–Madison undergraduate catalog, the following are the minimum requirements for applicants' high school records: four units of English, three units of math (including algebra and geometry), two units of natural science, three units of social studies/history, and two units of a single foreign language. An additional two units of electives should be taken from the areas of fine arts, communication arts, computer science, or statistics, for a total of sixteen units of college preparatory work. Applicants must also rank in the upper half of their high school graduating class. The catalog notes, "Most of our students present credentials exceeding the minimum, resulting in a stimulating and exciting academic environment." Wisconsin state residents must submit ACT scores; out-of-state applicants may submit either SAT or ACT scores.

Financial Aid

Financial aid applicants to the University of Wisconsin–Madison must complete the FAF or FFS and a form generated by U. of Wisconsin's financial aid office, and must submit copies of their parents' tax forms. A large variety of scholarships are available including academic, leadership, artistic talent, athletic ability, minority, and residency. Priority consideration is given to applications received by March 1.

Excerpted from University of Wisconsin–Madison promotional materials:

"The University of Wisconsin-Madison is recognized throughout the world as one of this nation's great universities. You will find a complete spectrum of liberal arts studies and professional programs on one campus. UW-Madison has ranked consistently high in study after study of individual departments and the University as a whole. In countless surveys and analyses from 1900 to the present, the University of Wisconsin-Madison has ranked among the top 10 educational institutions in the country: for academic quality, for excellence of faculty, and for overall undergraduate environment.

"This broad academic strength is an educational gold mine for you. Though the demanding course work and rigorous requirements often mean long hours of study, UW-Madison students seem to thrive on it. You'll find that responsibility for your academic progress lies first and foremost with yourself. You'll also find faculty and staff who are eager to assist you."

ADMISSIONS FACTS

Competitiveness Rating:	**78**
% of applicants accepted:	72
% acceptees attending:	46

FRESHMAN PROFILE

Average verbal SAT:	501
Average math SAT:	589
Average ACT:	26*
Graduated top 10% of class:	33
Graduated top 25% of class:	73
Graduated top 50% of class:	99

DEADLINES

Early decision/action:	NA
Early dec./act. notif.:	NA
Regular admission:	2/1
Regular adm. notif.:	rolling

APPLICANTS ALSO LOOK AT

and often prefer:
Miami U.
UC Berkeley
U. Texas–Austin

and sometimes prefer:
U. Michigan
U. Minnesota

and rarely prefer:
Marquette U.
U. Missouri–Rolla

ADDRESS

Undergraduate Admissions
A.W. Peterson Ofc Bldg
750 University Ave
Madison, WI 53706
608-262-3961

FINANCIAL FACTS

In-state tuition ($):	2,276
Out-of-state tuition ($):	7,377
Room & board:	3,721
FA application deadline:	3/1
% frosh receiving FA:	41
PT earnings per yr. ($):	1600

TYPE OF AID: % of students ($)

FA of some kind:	32 (NA)
Need-based grants:	NA
Merit-based grants:	NA
Loans:	NA
Work study:	NA
Student rating of FA:	NA

CAMPUS LIFE

Quality of Life Rating:	**77**
Type of school:	private
Affiliation:	Lutheran
Environment:	city

STUDENT BODY

FT Undergrad Enrollment:	2,335
% male/% female:	44/56
% out-of-state:	52
% live on campus:	98
% African-American:	5
% Asian:	3
% Caucasian:	90
% Hispanic:	1
% foreign:	5
% transfers:	5

WHAT'S HOT

small lectures
college radio station
Grateful Dead
financial aid
food
profs outside class

WHAT'S NOT

location
gay community visible
town-gown relations
Top 40

ACADEMICS

Academic Rating:	**78**
Calendar:	trimester
Student/teacher ratio:	14/1
% doctorates:	80
Profs interesting:	81
Profs accessible:	87
Hours of study per day:	3.1

MOST POPULAR MAJORS BY %

Business:	16
English:	10
Biology:	8

% GRADS WHO PURSUE

Law:	6
MBA:	8
Medicine:	4
M.A., etc.:	6

What do students think about Wittenberg University?

■ **Academics** Wittenberg University is a fine small liberal arts school. If you haven't heard of it before, that probably has more to do with its location that with the quality of its programs. Students here enjoy the benefits of small classes with interesting, accessible professors and a helpful, caring administration. Students work hard ("Classes are often harder than hell!" claimed one student); the trimester schedule makes terms go by pretty quickly but allows students to concentrate on fewer subjects per term. Several students told us that there is serious talk of switching to a semester schedule. Business and management is the most popular major: one out of every twelve undergrads goes on to get an MBA.

■ **Life** Students at Wittenberg have little reason to leave campus. They ranked Springfield the thirteenth worst college town in the country. Quality of life on campus, however, is excellent. Dorms are comfortable and safe, the campus is beautiful and easy to get around, and even the food is pretty good. Fraternities and sororities play a prominent social role, and, as one student put it, "There are a great number of opportunities for campus-leader types to drown themselves in extracurriculars." Unfortunately, there's not much else. As one student put it, "It is very hard to fit in here if you do not get into some society or frat. I guess you fit in most when you drink excessively and are part of a social group. But Wittenberg provides excellent educational opportunities and that's why I haven't left." Although the school has tried to curtail the heavy partying for which the students are locally known, Wittenberg is still a hard-drinking school, so much so that several students complained, "Everybody here drinks too much." Columbus and Dayton are within an hour's drive, and Cincinnati is about two hours away.

■ **Students** One student described her classmates as "a mixed but moneyed student body, 40% sorority/fraternity pre-professional wanna-bes; 40% Granola–Grateful Dead–Birkenstock world-savers; 20% the rest of us." Ethnically, the school is overwhelmingly white; largely absent is the spirit of "political correctness" and multiculturalism so prevalent at East Coast liberal arts schools. Explained one student, "While there are blacks, gays, international students, etc., they are not totally accepted. Enough people accept them that they can find good friends without too much trouble, but I've been in plenty of situations where others I'm with don't want to sit with 'those people' or go to 'their' kind of parties. I wish those folks would stop wearing their J. Crew-from-off-the-floor and grow up." Said another more succinctly: "Wittenberg is the conservative version of Swarthmore College. If you are a WASP Republican, don't hesitate in applying." On the surface, at least, students are friendly; noted one Philadelphian with surprise, "Everybody here says 'hi' and looks you in the eye, which is a little eerie at first, but easy to get used to."

WITTENBERG UNIVERSITY

Admissions

Wittenberg told us, "The Admissions Committee evaluates each applicant on individual merit and accomplishment as well as potential for growth. Acceptance to Wittenberg is not based solely on GPA, class rank, or testing data. We want individuals who will contribute to all aspects of the community." Wittenberg first considers your GPA, along with the secondary school you attended and your course selection. These are followed (in order of importance) by your interview, letters of recommendation, standardized test scores, extracurricular activities and essays. They require that you take the SAT or ACT; you must also complete four years of English, and at least three years each of mathematics, foreign language, social studies, and science. Students who apply to Wittenberg most often also apply to Miami U. (Ohio), Denison, College of Wooster, Ohio Wesleyan, DePauw, Gettysburg, and Kenyon.

Financial Aid

The financial aid office at Wittenberg University requires applicants to submit the FAF and their parents' most recent tax return. The school awards merit grants on the basis of academic excellence and/or artistic talent (9% of the students received one in 1991–92; average value: $4,330). Special scholarships are available for Lutherans and class valedictorians. In 1991–92, Wittenberg recommended Stafford loans for 90% of its financial aid recipients; students also participated in the Perkins and PLUS loan programs.

A note from the Wittenberg University Admissions Office:

"At Wittenberg, we believe that helping you to achieve symmetry demands a special environment, a setting where you can refine your definition of self yet gain exposure to the varied kinds of knowledge, people, views, activities, options, and ideas that add richness to our lives.

"Neither a huge university where students are usually mass produced, nor a very small college with few options can provide for the intellectual and personal growth required to achieve balance.

"Campus life is as diverse as the interests of our students. Wittenberg attracts students from all over the United States and from many other countries. Historically, the university has been committed to geographical, educational, cultural, and religious diversity.

"With their diverse backgrounds and interests, Wittenberg students have helped initiate many of the more than 100 student organizations that are active on campus. The students will be the first to tell you there's never a lack of things to do on or near the campus any day of the week, if you're willing to get involved."

ADMISSIONS FACTS

Competitiveness Rating:	**75**
% of applicants accepted:	75
% acceptees attending:	33

FRESHMAN PROFILE

Average verbal SAT:	518
Average math SAT:	561
Average ACT:	25
Graduated top 10% of class:	34
Graduated top 25% of class:	64
Graduated top 50% of class:	92

DEADLINES

Early decision/action:	12/15
Early dec./act. notif.:	1/15
Regular admission:	3/15
Regular adm. notif.:	4/1

APPLICANTS ALSO LOOK AT

and often prefer:
DePauw U.
Denison U.
Miami U.

and sometimes prefer:
Ohio Wesleyan U.
Ohio State U.

ADDRESS

Undergraduate Admissions
P. O. Box 720
Springfield, OH 45501
513-327-6314

FINANCIAL FACTS

In-state tuition ($):	12,792
Out-of-state tuition ($):	12,792
Room & board:	4,044
FA application deadline:	3/15
% frosh receiving FA:	55
PT earnings per yr. ($):	1100

TYPE OF AID: % of students ($)

FA of some kind:	57 (NA)
Need-based grants:	47 (7,252)
Merit-based grants:	9 (4,330)
Loans:	36 (3,000)
Work study:	12 (1,000)
Student rating of FA:	89

WOFFORD COLLEGE

CAMPUS LIFE

Quality of Life Rating:	84
Type of school:	private
Affiliation:	Methodist
Environment:	city

STUDENT BODY

FT Undergrad Enrollment:	1,042
% male/% female:	62/38
% out-of-state:	28
% live on campus:	85
% African-American:	8
% Asian:	1
% Caucasian:	89
% Hispanic:	<1
% foreign:	1
% transfers:	3

WHAT'S HOT

small lectures
financial aid
town-gown relations
bursar
living on campus
campus easy to get around
deans
administration (overall)
honesty
overall happiness

WHAT'S NOT

gay community visible
college radio station
college newspaper
diversity

ACADEMICS

Academic Rating:	80
Calendar:	4-1-4
Student/teacher ratio:	15/1
% doctorates:	87
Profs interesting:	85
Profs accessible:	88
Hours of study per day:	3.14

MOST POPULAR MAJORS BY %

English:	14
Biology:	10
Economics:	10

% GRADS WHO PURSUE

Law:	8
MBA:	3
Medicine:	8
M.A., etc.:	15

What do students think about Wofford College?

■ **Academics** Students at Wofford College cherish the school's traditional approach to academics and college life. Wrote one student, "Wofford has a style all its own. We say there's a right way, a wrong way, and a Wofford way, which is to always do things in a classic and traditional manner." The school caters to a pre-professional crowd—one in five graduates goes on to business, medical, or law school—and most students choose majors such as business, economics, and biology to facilitate their goals. The liberal arts, while represented, definitely take a back seat here, although the English department is reportedly as strong as the more popular departments. Small classes, professors "who are very friendly and willing to help with any problems," and a caring administration are among the school's chief assets. Students are hard-working and goal-oriented but not intellectual. Wrote one student, "Wofford does have something to offer those aspiring young intellectuals who are grasping for more than a second run at high school, but most students are just going for that second run."

■ **Life** One student offered that "the school tries to provide a variety of social activities for the students to get them involved and give them something to do on campus." According to the majority of respondents, however, there is only one social activity that matters at Wofford, and that's attending fraternity parties. Almost half the students go Greek. Not surprisingly, some students, particularly independents, complain that the social scene is monotonous. "At frat parties," explained one student, "we just stand around and ask everyone else what they're drinking. Independents go elsewhere for fun and the frats haven't really figured out that they aren't any fun." Drinking in town is curtailed by rigorous local enforcement of drinking-age laws, but students report that drinking is popular and alcohol accessible nonetheless. Safety concerns also discourage students from leaving campus. Explained one student, "There's a bad section of town right across the street from us. But the dorms *are* safe." Sports are quite popular, and although "the athlete is a student first here," tiny Wofford has put together an impressive enough program to gain entry into Division II athletics. Of the school's size, one student remarked: "There's only 1,100 students here; you may not know everyone by name, but you know everybody's face and can tell if somebody is new here."

■ **Students** Most of Wofford's 11 percent minority population is black. Most of the rest fit what one student called "the Wofford mold," defining such students "conservative, upper-middle-class Caucasians who loves fraternities." Another student added, "If you fit the general mold that most Wofford students fit, you'll have a great time, but if you don't, you'll be left out of most of the social life." The majority of students are extremely happy here, however, and explain, "We all get to know one another and feel like a family." As at many Southern schools, students here are relatively religious.

WOFFORD COLLEGE

Admissions

Wofford writes, "In evaluating our applications, our admissions committee uses a formula which predicts GPA. The most heavily weighted item is the applicant's high school curriculum, including Advanced Placement courses and scores. Students who are accepted should project at least a 2.0 GPA based on this formula." For further information, they request that you contact Mr. Charles Gray, who is the director of admissions. In order of importance, the committee considers your GPA, followed by standardized test scores, essays, extracurriculars, your interview, letters of recommendation, and "minority and geographic distribution in the class." You must take the SAT or ACT, and have completed four years of English, four years of mathematics, three years of lab science, and two years each of a foreign language and social science. Applicants to Wittenberg often also apply to Furman, Presbyterian, and Wake Forest.

Financial Aid

The financial aid office at Wofford College requires applicants to submit the FAF. Wofford awards merit grants on the basis of academic excellence (32% of Wofford undergraduates receive them; average value: $4,325) and athletic excellence (15%; $5,147). Loans most frequently drawn by Wofford students include the Stafford loan (31%; $2,944), Perkins loan (8%; $2,169), and the PLUS loan (6%; $3,711).

A note from the Wofford College Admissions Office:

"With the opening of the $5.5 million Franklin W. Olin Building, 1992 promises to be a significant year in Wofford's 138-year history. Offering unique opportunities for using technology in teaching, the building will house the departments of computer science, mathematics, foreign languages, and education. Other recent excitement involves the opening of the new tennis complex and women's residence hall, the celebration of the 50th anniversary of *Phi Beta Kappa* at Wofford; and preparation to be the host for the 1992 NCAA Division II national golf championship."

ADMISSIONS FACTS

Competitiveness Rating:	**81**
% of applicants accepted:	62
% acceptees attending:	37

FRESHMAN PROFILE

Average verbal SAT:	525
Average math SAT:	576
Average ACT:	26
Graduated top 10% of class:	45
Graduated top 25% of class:	78
Graduated top 50% of class:	96

DEADLINES

Early decision/action:	12/1
Early dec./act. notif.:	12/15
Regular admission:	2/1
Regular adm. notif.:	3/1

APPLICANTS ALSO LOOK AT

and often prefer
Wake Forest U.

and sometimes prefer:
U. South Carolina
Furman U.

and rarely prefer:
Clemson U.

ADDRESS

Undergraduate Admissions
429 North Church Street
Spartanburg, SC 29303-3663
803-585-4821

FINANCIAL FACTS

In-state tuition ($):	9,790
Out-of-state tuition ($):	9,790
Room & board:	4,150
FA application deadline:	3/15
% frosh receiving FA:	70
PT earnings per yr. ($):	750

TYPE OF AID: % of students ($)

FA of some kind:	75 (8,857)
Need-based grants:	28 (2,558)
Merit-based grants:	NA
Loans:	NA
Work study:	16 (1,133)
Student rating of FA:	94

CAMPUS LIFE

Quality of Life Rating:	**78**
Type of school:	private
Affiliation:	none
Environment:	city

STUDENT BODY

FT Undergrad Enrollment:	2,593
% male/% female:	82/18
% out-of-state:	50
% live on campus:	48
% African-American:	2
% Asian:	5
% Caucasian:	90
% Hispanic:	1
% foreign:	6
% transfers:	1

WHAT'S HOT

financial aid
studying hard
profs lecture a lot
dorm safety
dorm comfort
cost of living

WHAT'S NOT

college radio station
food
college newspaper
caring about politics
alternative rock
in-class discussion

ACADEMICS

Academic Rating:	**83**
Calendar:	quarters
Student/teacher ratio:	11/1
% doctorates:	85
Profs interesting:	78
Profs accessible:	81
Hours of study per day:	3.64

MOST POPULAR MAJORS BY %

Mechanical Engineering:	32
Electrical Engineering:	19
Civil Engineering:	11

% GRADS WHO PURSUE

Law:	1
MBA:	1
Medicine:	1
M.A., etc.:	15

What do students think about Worcester Polytechnic Institute?

■ **Academics** With the East Coast's most famous technical school only 40 miles away, it's understandable that WPI is sometimes overlooked. However, for the student looking for an excellent engineering education that requires one to broaden his horizons (with a minimum of five humanities courses) and pursue independent research (through the Major Qualifying Project program), WPI may just be the place. In certain respects, WPI students have it all over their counterparts at MIT. WPI students find their professors better in-class and out; like their financial aid packages much more and spend less because they live in Worcester; and don't study nearly as hard while still pursuing a rigorous engineering program. WPI offerings in subjects not related to engineering can be weak, and although the school belongs to the Worcester consortium (a group of ten area schools that allows students at any one to take courses at the others), WPI's quarterly schedule makes participation in the consortium difficult. Still, some students praise the quarter system, which allows students to concentrate on fewer courses at a time.

■ **Life** There is a four-to-one male-female ratio at WPI, and, as you might imagine, this is a problem for a lot of students. Said one man, "There are no women here, and the few that do come here learn basic economics in a hurry: low supply, high demand, high price! Plus, Worcester is a social armpit." Several WPI women expressed pleasure with the imbalance, but the situation isn't really healthy for anyone: very few things in this world are as unpleasant as a rutting engineer. As for the party scene, one student typically recounted, "The life of the school is the Greek system. With so many local students, if it was not for fraternities and sororities, everyone would go home on weekends." Many students go Greek, and, as frat parties are closed, the Greek and independent populations are separate: "It's a miracle there's not open warfare between the Greeks and the GDIs (god-damned independents)," said one student. The school has no student center, a real sticking point for some. As for the town of Worcester, "It sucks!" is the consensus. "Fortunately," said one student, there is no reason to go into town, except the Centrum (an arena that sometimes features the Bruins, Celtics, and national rock tours)." The campus is "very homey and comfortable, an excellent offset to the technically based curriculum."

■ **Students** Unlike MIT, WPI does not have a diverse student body. Ninety percent of the students are white, and half are from Massachusetts. They are intense and studious, but they are *not* nerds (at least not by their own account)! As one student explained, "I think that students from other schools assumed that every student at WPI is a total dork, but they'd be surprised how many different kinds of people there really are here."

WORCESTER POLYTECHNIC INSTITUTE

Worcester, MA

Admissions

At Worcester Polytech, the admissions committee first looks at your GPA and class rank. These are followed, in order of importance, by Achievement scores, SAT or ACT scores, letters of recommendation, your interview, extracurriculars, and essay. To qualify for admissions, you must take three Achievements (one Math, one English, and one science of your choice), and either the SAT or ACT. You should also have completed four years of English, four years of mathematics (including trigonometry and pre-calculus), at least two years of lab science (including chemistry and physics), and one year of US history. Students who apply to WPI also frequently apply to Rensselaer Polytechnic Institute, Massachusetts Institute of Technology, U. Massachusetts—Amherst, Boston U., and Northeastern.

Financial Aid

Worcester Polytech requires its financial aid applicants to submit a copy of their parents' most recent tax return (and W-2's), and a FAF. Returning students must also fill out a form generated by the Worcester FA office. WPI awards no merit-based scholarships, although 2% of its students in '91–'92 received an outside merit scholarship. Last year, the FA office recommended Stafford loans to 68% of all undergrads (average value: $3,070), Perkins loans to 40% ($1,639), and PLUS loans to 10% ($3,530). The average freshman aid award for the class of '95 was $12,298.

A note from the Worcester Polytechnic Institute Admissions Office:

"What makes WPI special is that we offer an academic curriculum that is project based. Known as the 'WPI Plan,' this consists of three research projects that are designed to increase a student's knowledge in a distinct yet interrelated area. The major qualifying project (MQP) is the major research project in your field of study. The Interactive Qualifying Project (IQP) looks at science and technology and how it affects society, and the humanities sufficiency asks you to acquire a depth of knowledge in an area of the humanities and demonstrate that knowledge through a specific project."

ADMISSIONS FACTS

Competitiveness Rating:	**85**
% of applicants accepted:	79
% acceptees attending:	33

FRESHMAN PROFILE

Average verbal SAT:	570*
Average math SAT:	637*
Average ACT:	29
Graduated top 10% of class:	57
Graduated top 25% of class:	91
Graduated top 50% of class:	99

DEADLINES

Early decision/action:	12/1
Early dec./act. notif.:	1/10
Regular admission:	2/15
Regular adm. notif.:	4/1

APPLICANTS ALSO LOOK AT

and sometimes prefer:

MIT
Tufts U.
U. Rhode Island
U. Mass–Amherst

and rarely prefer:

Boston U.
U. New Hampshire
U. Connecticut
Clarkson U.
RPI

ADDRESS

Undergraduate Admissions
100 Institute Road
Worcester, MA 01609
508-831-5286

FINANCIAL FACTS

In-state tuition ($):	13,985
Out-of-state tuition ($):	13,985
Room & board:	4,595
FA application deadline:	3/15
% frosh receiving FA:	70
PT earnings per yr. ($):	800

TYPE OF AID: % of students ($)

FA of some kind:	72 (10,734)
Need-based grants:	70 (6,433)
Merit-based grants:	NA
Loans:	68 (4,527)
Work study:	23 (830)
Student rating of FA:	88

YALE UNIVERSITY

New Haven, CT

CAMPUS LIFE

Quality of Life Rating:	**82**
Type of school:	private
Affiliation:	none
Environment:	city

STUDENT BODY

FT Undergrad Enrollment:	5,179
% male/% female:	57/43
% out-of-state:	87
% live on campus:	90
% African-American:	8
% Asian:	13
% Caucasian:	74
% Hispanic:	5
% foreign:	3
% transfers:	<1

WHAT'S HOT

catalog
deans
classical music
registration
gay community accepted
cost of living
food
living on campus
studying hard
honest students

WHAT'S NOT

dating
fraternities/sororities
dorm comfort
location

ACADEMICS

Academic Rating:	**95**
Calendar:	semester
Student/teacher ratio:	6/1
% doctorates:	96
Profs interesting:	82
Profs accessible:	84
Hours of study per day:	3.46

MOST POPULAR MAJORS BY %

Social Sciences:	30
Letters/Literature:	15
Area & Ethnic Studies:	10

% GRADS WHO PURSUE

Law:	6
MBA:	1
Medicine:	6
M.A., etc.:	15

What do students think about Yale University?

■ **Academics** Yale University "is truly one of America's great schools," wrote one area college counselor. It's an assertion that's hard to debate. As a major national research center, Yale attracts many of the world's great scholars. But unlike other research institutes, Yale devotes a lot of attention to undergraduates. Reported one student, "There is a genuine focus on undergraduates here, the professors seem genuinely to enjoy teaching, and you really do learn a lot in classes." Academic departments are "uniformly excellent" here: among the school's many fine departments, standouts include drama, English, history, and the pre-med program. Yale has no core curriculum, instead requiring students to complete a broad range of general education requirements. Students told us they like the "shopping period" registration system: they don't formally register for classes until two weeks into the semester, so the likelihood of getting stuck with a lousy class or TA is greatly minimized. What they don't like is the administrators who run the university. Among the schools we surveyed, Yale's administration ranked lowest. "Our administration does its absolute best to squelch student input," is how one student summed it up.

■ **Life** It would be foolish to pass up a chance to attend Yale for just about any reason. But if you're unsure of whether you could be happy living and studying for four years in a cold, unfriendly, dangerous city, you owe it to yourself to visit New Haven before deciding that Yale is *the* school for you. Yale students have survived there for centuries, but they're not happy about it. Yalies gave New Haven extremely low marks. One had this to say about his new hometown: "Yale's worst problem is New Haven. It is dangerous and unreceptive to students. Life on and immediately around campus is great, but otherwise it's a real problem." Said another, "New Haven is pretty gross—very dangerous. It's a great eye-opener to the 'real world,' though." As for the on-campus social scene, dating and romance are not popular here. "The dating scene here is as much fun as a root canal" is the way one student put it. Also unpopular are drugs, fraternities (although reportedly Greek life is growing more popular), and, of course, New Haven. Social life at Yale, then, consists of hanging around with other Elis and getting to know their eccentricities pretty well. "Everyone here has quirks," said one student euphemistically. "Yalies are fascinating people, very self-absorbed, but terrific when they decide to think about others."

■ **Students** Yale is famous enough to attract, and wealthy enough to finance, students from all backgrounds, and the result is a bright, diverse academic atmosphere. Be prepared to enter a fast-paced, very competitive community here: as one student put it, "'Intense' is definitely the word for Yalies—we get very involved whatever we do here, be it classes, drama, sports or what have you."

YALE UNIVERSITY

Admissions

From Yale's introductory bulletin: "[While] a very strong performance in a demanding college preparatory program may compensate for modest standardized test scores, it is unlikely that high test scores will persuade the Admissions Committee to disregard an undistinguished secondary school record…No prescribed high school program is necessary to apply to Yale, but students should take the richest possible mix of academic offerings available. Preparation for Yale should combine breadth with rigor…The most important questions the Admissions Committee must resolve are 'Who is likely to make the most of Yale's resources?' and 'Who will contribute significantly to the Yale community?'…In sum, qualifications include not only the reasonably well-defined areas of academic achievement and special skills in nonacademic areas, but also the less tangible qualities of capacity for involvement, commitment and personal growth." All applicants must submit scores for the ACT or SAT plus three Achievements.

Financial Aid

Financial aid applicants to Yale must submit the FAF (California residents may submit the SAAC instead), a form generated by Yale's financial aid office, and a copy of their parents' tax return. All financial aid is based on demonstrated need. The average amount of self-help for freshmen is $4,200, and is usually met via term-time employment and educational loans (the self-help level increases to $5,700 junior year). All students are encouraged to apply for outside scholarships and grants. The first $500 of outside scholarships plus one half of any amount in excess of $500 may be used to reduce a student's self-help level (to a minimum of $1,200). Remaining balances are used to reduce gift aid awarded by Yale.

A note from the Yale University Admissions Office:

"Strong traditions give Yale College its distinctive character. The principles and values of liberal education are powerful here. Knowledge is sought as a good in itself as well as a matter of the greatest utility. The College reflects a careful balance between the complex and the simple, the advanced and the basic, specialization and breadth. Teaching and research are inseparable commitments of our academic mission.

"In addition to its curricular concerns, Yale encourages student interests that make the College a spirited center for arts and athletics, music and drama, religion, politics, community service, and a host of other commitments. At Yale, academic life merges with countless other interests, and the result is a community where young men and women come to know and respect one another as colleagues and friends."

ADMISSIONS FACTS

Competitiveness Rating:	**100**
% of applicants accepted:	20
% acceptees attending:	58

FRESHMAN PROFILE

Average verbal SAT:	660*
Average math SAT:	707*
Average ACT:	NA
Graduated top 10% of class:	95
Graduated top 25% of class:	99
Graduated top 50% of class:	100

DEADLINES

Early decision/action:	11/1
Early dec./act. notif.:	mid-Dec.
Regular admission:	12/31
Regular adm. notif.:	4/1

APPLICANTS ALSO LOOK AT

and sometimes prefer:
Harvard/Radcliffe College
Princeton U.
Swarthmore College
MIT

and rarely prefer:
Amherst College
Northwestern U.
Williams College
Wesleyan U.
U. Pennsylvania

ADDRESS

Undergraduate Admissions
New Haven, CT 06520
203-432-1900

FINANCIAL FACTS

In-state tuition ($):	16,300
Out-of-state tuition ($):	16,300
Room & board:	5,900
FA application deadline:	1/15
% frosh receiving FA:	41
PT earnings per yr. ($):	1900

TYPE OF AID: % of students ($)

FA of some kind:	38 (NA)
Need-based grants:	NA
Merit-based grants:	NA
Loans:	NA
Work study:	NA
Student rating of FA:	78

PART THREE

COLLEGE KIDS SAY THE DARNDEST THINGS

The questionnaire we distributed to college students closed with a free-form "essay question." We told students that we didn't care *what* they wrote: if it was "witty, informative, or accurate," we'd try to get it into this book. We used all the informative and accurate essays to write the student view boxes; below are excerpts from the wittiest, pithiest, and most outrageous essays.

■ *Literary Allusions...*

"To study at this school is to have infinite control over your destiny: you can crouch in your room like Gregor Samsa transformed into a dung beetle, or you can plunge into the infinite sea of faces that each year flood OSU like a tidal wave."

— A.W., Ohio State University

"'Prosperity unbruised cannot endure a single blow, but a man who has been at constant feud with misfortunes develops a skin calloused by time...and even if he falls he can carry the fight upon one knee.' — Seneca on Providence."

— Matthew D., U. of Connecticut

Two jokes about St. John's College students:

1. Q: How many Johnnies does it take to change a light bulb?

   A: Let's define "change" before we go any further.

2. Q: What did the Chorus say to Creon after Oedipus poked out his eyes?

   A: Now that's a face only a mother could love.

— April W., St. John's College

"Very definitely a love/hate relationship here. This is the level of hell that Dante missed."

—Amy P., Caltech

■ *Food...*

"It is a shame that my family pays $12,000 annually for me to eat a different casserole every day."

— S.W., Southwestern University

"The food here is really bad; it's either bland or sickening. You're lucky if they don't screw up the bread."

— Scott P., Bentley College

"When students first arrive, they call the Observatory Hill Dining Facility 'O-Hill.' They soon learn to call it 'O-Hell,' because the food here is beyond revolting."

— Greg F., U. of Virginia

"If I had known that I'd be rooming with roaches and poisoned by the cafeteria staff I would have gone to Wayne State. I really can't complain, though, because I have met my husband here, like my mom did 20 years before."

— M.L.P., Fisk University

"The food here has particularly fancy names, and it seems as though they spend more time thinking of these names than they spend on making decent food."

— Andrew Z., Wheaton College

"If you're looking for gray skies, a gray campus, and gray food, then Albany is the place to be!"

— Michele G., SUNY Albany

"The food isn't that bad, if you don't mind varying shades of brown. On a good day the food on your tray will remind you of the brown paint sampler at your local Sherwin-Williams dealer."

— Rob P., College of the Holy Cross

"You should mention Lil, the lady who has worked in the dining hall for 50 years and who everyone loves. She plays the spoons all the time and runs around."

— Aaron R., Tufts University

"You should mention Lil, who works in the dining hall. She's loony and she knows everyone."

— Mitchell D., Tufts University

■ Home Town...

"People ask me, 'Mike Z., why did you come to NYU?' I tell them, 'I didn't come to NYU, I came to New York City.'"

— Mike Z., NYU

"Change the name of UC Irvine to UC Newport Beach and we would have more girls."

— Pat M., UC Irvine

"As this school is located in a tiny Texas town, a favorite activity is called 'rolling.' Rolling entails piling into a car with many drinks and driving the back country roads. Very slowly."

— Anonymous, Southwestern University

"Worcester—the fart of the Commonwealth."

— David R., Clark University

"Connecticut is a cute state. It's a great place to go to school, but I wouldn't want to live here."

— Claire S., NJ native, Fairfield University

"Binghamton is always gray. The two days a week we have sun, it's beautiful, but otherwise, sunglasses are not a must unless you're an artsy-fartsy pseudo-chic literature and rhetoric/philosophy major."

— Deborah C., SUNY Binghamton

"Socially, the surrounding area is so dead that the Denny's closes at night."

— Thomas R., UC Riverside

"The local liquor stores and towing companies make a lot of money."

— Katherine R., U. of Rhode Island

"Last week's major crime was that my left headlight was out, for which the busy Hanover police pulled me over three times."

— Jon K., Dartmouth College

"It is definitely important to have a car, as the population of Canton frequently matches our winter temperature. 'Canton gray,' our perennial sky color, is one Crayola missed."

— Daniel R., St. Lawrence University

"I'm from L.A. and in my opinion Boston sucks. If you're into the frat/Spuds McKenzie crowd, Boston's the place to be. If you ain't, it's a lame social scene."

— Josh M., Emerson College

"Bloomington, Illinois, was recently voted the sixth most normal location in the U.S. Unfortunately, this translates into one of the most boring places. I liken it to New Haven on an overdose of valium."

— Matthew G., Illinois Wesleyan University

"Contrary to popular belief, cow tipping is definitely passé here."

— Anonymous, U. of Connecticut, Storrs

"Life in New Orleans—'And the people sat down to eat and to drink, and rose up to play.'—Exodus 32:6."

— Theresa W., Tulane University

■   ■   ■

■ Security...

"Campus security is made up of a bunch of midget high school dropouts with Napoleonic complexes who can spot a beer can from a mile away."

— Anonymous, UC San Diego

"I would not recommend walking alone at night because security is not well staffed, and also not armed. What if someone has a gun, what are those rent-a-cops going to do? Say, 'I'll hit you with this club if you don't drop the gun?' Come on!"

— Anonymous, St. Joseph's University

"Public safety here is a joke. The Public Safety officers are like the Keystone Kops on Thorazine."

— Anonymous, Bryn Mawr College

"Our alcohol policy sucks. All of our campus police now think they're T. J. Hooker."

— Anonymous, Dartmouth College

■   ■   ■

■ Classmates...

"Sure, our campus is diverse if you call diverse a campus full of white kids looking to make 30 to 50 grand after graduation."

— Joseph M. C., Davidson College

"Yes, we shave our legs and underarms."

— Dawn P., Wellesley College

"If you're thinking of applying to M.I.T., go ahead. Because, believe it or not, most people here are at least as stupid as you are."

— Patrick L., M.I.T.

"People who go to school here are all pretty good looking, especially the women. It should be renamed UKB, the University of Ken and Barbie."

— Tony H., Arizona State University

"Wesleyan is not only the 'diversity university,' but also the 'controversy university,' the 'fight adversity university,' and the 'if we keep trying we might have some unity' university. We satisfy all types."

— John P., Wesleyan University

"Everyone walks too fast around here. You try to say 'hi' to someone, you've got to time it just right 'cause they aren't going to stop to talk to you. Plus, everyone wears the same clothes!"

— Terry B., Wittenberg University

"Girls over 5'8", watch out—for some reason, guys here have munchkin blood in them or something."

— Robyn A., Tufts University

"A school can be defined by its graffiti and its level of cleverness. Three quarters of our school graffiti is pro- or anti- a specific fraternity, with the other one quarter devoted to homophobic or misogynist theories."

— Matthew E., College of William and Mary

"This is a great university if you're not studying sciences involving animal research, politics, teacher education (certification), or anything that offends any long-haired leftist who's a vegetarian."

— Brock M., U. of Oregon

"This school is filled with wealthy, well-dressed egomaniacs who are about as socially conscious as Marie Antoinette."

— Anonymous, Hofstra University

"When you first come here, you think everybody's really strange. Over time, though, you realize everybody is, and so are you. No big deal."

— Josh B., St. John's College

"University of Chicago's reputation is not entirely deserved. It's not true the place is completely full of nerds. It's only partially completely full of nerds."

— David G., U. of Chicago

"Everyone seems to know someone who invented something like Velcro or whose father is a CEO of a corporation."

— William K., Denison University

"The average F&M student is apathetic, homophobic, emotionally distraught, and living under a false sense of reality. Granted this is a rather harsh statement, and there are exceptions to every rule. But on the whole, a deep, emotionally sound individual is not an example of an average F&M student."

— Anonymous, Franklin and Marshall College

"Don't let anyone try to tell you that this is a diverse but close-knit atmosphere. The people here are about as diverse as a box of nails."

— Cari L., College of the Holy Cross

"UNH is about as diverse as the NHL."

— Curtis E., U. of New Hampshire

"The ethnic diversity on this campus has the consistency of Wonder Bread."

— Marwan K., Colgate University

"Denison has attempted to lose the 'rich kid party school' image and expand the diversity of the student body, but now it is becoming the 'I wish this were still a rich kid party school.' There is an awful lot available here, but students seem unmotivated and lazy."

— Anonymous, Denison University

"They say that Harvard students are arrogant, but where else can you find world-class professors and guest lecturers, world-class students, and world-class attitudes?"

— Edward S., Harvard University

"Although it may not seem like it, RISD is a very religious school. Everyone thinks they're God."

— Neil M., Rhode Island School of Design

"Sometimes people complain about the lack of student involvement. I think someone should really do something about the apathy at St. Lawrence."

— Bill P., St. Lawrence University

"Bates is so diverse! Yesterday I met somebody from Connecticut!"

— Ellen H., Bates College

"If it weren't for me, this university would suck. People were sitting around with their thumbs up their butts until I came here. Now everyone is happier and has more fun. In fact, I bet this survey sucked until I gave you my almighty wisdom."

— Patrick W., U. of Illinois, Urbana

"Rose-Hulman is one of the few places where it's safer to leave a $20 bill on your desk than it is to forget to log out of the computer network."

— Zac C., Rose-Hulman Institute of Technology

■ Administration...

"The only thing the administration does well is tasks involving what Kenneth Boulding would call 'sub-optimization.' Give them something that really doesn't need doing and it will be accomplished efficiently."

— Dana T., U. of Minnesota, Twin Cities

"Our business office may be the smoothest running machine since the Pinto!"

— Robert C., University of Dallas

"Despite the best efforts of the administration to provide TSC students with an inefficient, cold-hearted, red-tape infested, SNAFU-riddled Soviet-style administrative bureaucracy, Trenton State College is a pretty decent place to go for a fairly reasonable amount of money."

— Anonymous, Trenton State College

"The admissions office tries to make you apply based on, 'Well, we're very old and...and...well, we look nice. We'll do whatever it takes to make you happy! Really! I mean it. See my honest smile?' If you visit the school, ditch the tour and the gimmicks and talk to the professors."

— Anonymous, Southwestern University

"Going to a school as small as Emerson means that instead of saying 'screw you, Mr. 90803,' the administration will say, 'screw you, Joe.'"

— "Joe Bloggs," Emerson College

"The dean of students here makes Cruella de Ville look like Cinderella."

— Anonymous, Goucher College

"Our president shakes hands like a girlie man."

— Anonymous, Hamilton College

"Illinois Wesleyan University is unique in that our president also greatly resembles Phil Hartman, the Saturday Night Live cast member."

— Kyle C. H., Illinois Wesleyan University

■ *Similes and Metaphors...*

"Columbia is like a fruit truck. It picks up varied and exotic fruits and deposits them rotten at their destination."

— Paul L., Columbia University

"The U. of Minnesota is a huge black hole of knowledge. It sucks things into it from far and wide, compressing to the essence. Unfortunately, it is very hard to get anything out of a black hole. What I have managed to eke out has been both rewarding and depressing."

— James McDonald, U. of Minnesota

"BU reminds me of a warm summer day: sweaty, sticky, and smelly."

— Douglas G. H., Boston University

"Boulder is the world in a nutshell, served with alfalfa sprouts."

— Glenn H., U. of Colorado, Boulder

"Going to Northwestern is like having a beautiful girlfriend who treats you like crap."

— Jonathan J. G., Northwestern University

"Unless you are totally committed to science, do not come. Caltech has as much breadth as a Russian grocery store."

— Daniel S., Caltech

"Being at Marlboro is like having a recurring bizarre dream. You're not quite sure what it all means, but it happens a lot. If it stopped you'd probably wonder why, but then you'd just eat breakfast."

— Mark L., Marlboro College

"Vassar is like a sexual disease: once you've accepted it it's great, but when you realize you've got another three years to put up with it you go see a medical advisor immediately."

— Henry R., Vassar College

"Vassar is like a big walrus butt: lots of hair but also very moist."

— Calder M., Vassar College

"Attending UC Riverside is like having your wisdom teeth pulled—not very enjoyable, but necessary."

— David E. Y., UC Riverside

"Getting an education from M.I.T. is like getting a drink from a firehose."

— Juan G., M.I.T.

"If Bates was a bakery, many goods would be fresh and rats would be under the counter."

— Anne W., Bates College

"The University of Iowa is the iceberg in the Hell which the state of Iowa has become."

— Robin A., U. of Iowa

"This school is like a tight anus: there's tremendous pressure to come out straight and conformed."

— Stephen J., Washington and Lee University

"Pomona College is a swirling, sucking eddy of despair, filled with small moments of false hope, in an ever-blackening universe."

— Anonymous, Pomona College

"Intro classes have the consistency of Cheez Whiz: they go down easy, they taste horrible, and they are not good for you."

— Pat T., U. of Vermont

"My life here is as the torrential rains of Dhamer upon the Yaktong Valley. I bleat like a llama shedding out of season."

— Ronald M., James Madison University

■   ■   ■

■ Mascots...

"The only thing keeping Tufts from the pinnacle of higher education is its library and failure to replace its mascot, Jumbo the 17-foot-high stuffed elephant."

— Scott T., Tufts University

"TCU is small, friendly, and has a horny toad as its mascot—now beat that!"

— Michael V., Texas Christian University

■ *Sex, Drugs, Rock & Roll...*

"This school is no good for people who like art, music, and Sonic Youth. 'Society is a hole.' There's a quote by Sonic Youth."

— Meghan S., Lake Forest College

"I hate the Grateful Dead! Blech! Why can't my generation listen to their own damn music! AAAARRRGH."

— Anonymous, College of William and Mary

"I am the Lizard King, I can do anything."

— Michael M., U. of Connecticut

"Beam, Bud, beer, babes—the four essential B's."

— "Jim Beam," Wittenberg University

"William and Mary: where you can drink beer and have sex in the same place your forefathers did."

— Adam L., College of William and Mary

"If you know what it's like to sit in organic chemistry at nine a.m. with a hangover, you know what it's like to be at Dartmouth."

— Daryl S., Dartmouth College

"At Harvard, beauty is in the eyes of the beer holder!!"

— Craig V., Harvard University

"Yeah, there aren't any guys, but who doesn't like doing homework on a Saturday night?"

— Nicole C., Wellesley College

"When I visited schools I went to Brown and Northwestern on the same trip. I went to N.U. on a Wednesday and Thursday night. I partied like a champ. At Brown on Friday I was invited to two parties (I should be psyched) but they were both for NUDE people. AUGH YUCK!"

— Silvy N., Northwestern University

"A Denison student might be quoted as saying, 'life is a waste of time, and time is a waste of life; so get wasted all the time, and have the time of your life.'"

— Katherine H., Denison University

"Beer is more abundant than water. The shortage of water is a terrible problem but we find other things to drink."

— J. M., UC Santa Barbara

"UCSB is the only place where U Can Study Buzzed and still ace an exam the next day."

— Tracy B., UC Santa Barbara

"How widely used is beer? Let's just say we have a pipeline directly to the brewery. How many other schools with 4600 students can support three distributors?"

— April M., U. of Missouri, Rolla

"It may take an 'ee' to spell 'geek,' but it also takes an 'ee' to spell 'beer.'"

— H. B., U. of Missouri, Rolla

"Beer, beer, beer, sex, beer, sex, sex, sex, and beer, hangovers, and education. It be fun, mother!"

— Sean S., U. of Illinois, Urbana

"This campus is an extremely great place to spend four college years, but it is still plagued, as all other campuses are, including Christian colleges, with sin. Therefore this campus needs to come under submission to Jesus Christ."

— Laura D., James Madison University

■ Neanderthals...

"If U R looking to settle down with an unattractive big woman, Hofstra is the place."

— Anonymous, Hofstra University

"One thing about Sewanee women is that beauty is only a light switch away. So basically we need some better looking girls."

— Will B., University of the South, Sewanee

"Girls at BYU are like parking spaces: the good ones are taken, the close ones are handicapped or reserved, and the rest are too far out!"

— Todd P., Brigham Young University

"In Rolla, we have tons of women, but not many of them!"

— Todd O., U. of Missouri, Rolla

"The faculty is great, academics are challenging, but the women are liberated and become difficult to live with. To sum it all up, Hendrix is so cool."

— Mike S., Hendrix College

"All the girls are nasty. But I drink and sometimes fool around with them anyway."

— Dan F., Swarthmore College

"UCSD rages—NOT! If you like the ocean and the library and have a fear of parties and girls without facial hair, you've hit the jackpot!!!"

— Spencer M., UC San Diego

"There's a saying I've heard around: nine out of ten girls in California look good, the tenth goes to UCSD."

— Michael K., UC San Diego

"U of C is OK if all you want to do is work, but if you are looking for a good social scene or a hot stinkin' babe, go to California, young man!"

Benjamin D., University of Chicago

"Stay away from 'big haired' babes!"

— Skip S., Clemson University

"Beer, football and boobies are what Clemson is all about!"

— Paul S., Clemson University

"Chicks dig me 'cause I rarely wear underwear, and when I do it's usually something unusual."

— John T., Hamilton College, with thanks to Bill Murray, *Stripes,* the movie

"The men here often complain that there are too few women here; if they took a look in the mirror, maybe they'd realize why girls don't come here!"

— Tara L., Stevens Institute of Technology

■   ■   ■

■ *School Vs. The 'Real World'...*

"College is the best time of your life. Never again will you be surrounded by people the same age as you, free from grown-ups and the threat of working in the real world. Your parents give you money when you ask for it and all you have to do is learn!"

— Jennifer F., Syracuse University

"Real life experience in such concepts— alienation, depression, suppression, isolationism, edge of racial tension, apathy, etc.—before the 'Real World.'"

— Anonymous, NYU

"When we lose a football game to a college with lower academic standards, we console ourselves by saying that one day they will work for us and then we'll get even!"

— Michael J., University of the South, Sewanee

"If you were born with a spoon in your mouth, Fisk University will take it out and instill in you a way to reinstall it yourself."

— Angela F., Fisk University

"University of Chicago sucks! One thing, if you survive this school and graduate sane, then the world can be in social, environmental, political, and economic turmoil, but to you it'll be a weekend in Lake Tahoe."

— Anonymous, U. of Chicago

■　　　　■　　　　■

■ *Schools Vs. "Cats"...*

"Irvine is a charming place to live, work, and shop. It's better than 'Cats,' and it makes me laugh when the ink goes up the wrong pipe."

— Peter T., UC Irvine

"It's better than 'Cats!'"

— Erica F., Sarah Lawrence College

"This is the best college in the country. I loved it. It was better than 'Cats.' I laughed, I cried, I'd go again and again."

— Bob D., Dartmouth College

"I love it! It's much better than 'Cats!' I'll go here again and again!"

— Nicolas A., Carnegie Mellon University

"I laughed, I cried, but it was NOT better than 'Cats!'"

— R. W., Carnegie Mellon University

"I laughed, I cried, it was better than 'Cats!'"

— Richard W., Bates College

"I laugh, I cry, it's better than 'Cats.' I'll do it again and again!"

— Jeff V., Wofford College

"I love it! It's much better than 'Cats!' I want to live here again and again!"

— Shannon C., Eastman School of Music

■ In Case You Were Wondering...

"Columbia College offers broccoli and I like it!"

— John K., Columbia University

"The fishing is great at Campus Lake!"

— Chad A. L., Davidson College

"You forgot to ask the most pertinent question, which is: "Have you ever seen Elvis teach your 100 level courses?"

— Adam L., Alfred University

"I was smart once. I used to sleep. Then I majored in chemical engineering."

— C. C. Smith, Clemson University

"Many professors here believe, contrary to the findings of Galileo, that the universe revolves around them."

— Anonymous, Clarkson University

"My floor rots. I could live at the zoo for the same experience and a lot less money."

— Dennis B., American University

"I'm black, poor and confused; I like the New Kids, and I think Vanilla Ice has been unfairly treated."

— Kimberly B., Hendrix College

"People say the most difficult thing about Harvard is getting in...shyeah, right!"

— Spencer L. Harvard University

"We've got it all—if that's what you want."

— Khoi L., Harvard University

"Moon men landed in the middle quad last week while my peers and I sipped ice milk and listened to passing jets (this happens quite frequently). However, nine people saw my mother on a Tuesday wearing nothing but clothes and a plain tarpaulin, moistened with lemming poop."

— Glenn S., Rhode Island School of Design

"Space cows are all our friends!"

— John L., Rhode Island School of Design

"My school is a melting pot of genius. Whether it is apparent or not, still, as far as all of us being adopted by outer space brothers and made kings and queens of our vast universe, I'd say we'd have the greatest chance of contact with the master outer space race."

— Steve G., Rhode Island School of Design

"Those who oppose the Dark Lord will be crushed, but those who are its friend will receive rewards beyond the dreams of avarice."

— Anonymous, Sarah Lawrence College

"Do I get to keep the pencil?"

— Laura W., University of the South, Sewanee

"Safe sex, #2 pencils, and long lines are the cornerstones of this great institution."

— "Franz Kafka," SUNY Albany

"There is a real problem with moles on this campus; no one is willing to talk about them."

— Alexander D., Bates College

"I can no longer lick the bottoms of my feet. They are dirty. I should wash them. The people I see are very much into proctology. The bus gives you a hard-on with books in your lap. Goodbye."

— Michael A., U. of Rochester

"I don't think I need to be informative, witty, or otherwise about Conn. I love it here, most people I know love it here. It's a good school. I dare you to print that."

— Aaron M., Connecticut College

"Bates College is a phallocentric, logocentric, Greco-Roman, linear-rational, ethnocentric, homophobic, patriarchal institution. How's that for a list of catchwords?"

— Stephen H., Bates College

"I think if our generation's parents knew how consumptive, ill-informed, and drug-addicted their children were, they'd suffer a collective nervous breakdown."

— Anonymous, U. of Denver

"Our school is the school of the future and always will be."

— Chuck C., Rhodes College

"Sarah Lawrence is a haven of unity and acceptance. Every morning at sunrise the entire campus gathers around the flagpole, holds hands and sings "We Are The World." If you're really lucky you get to be Dionne Warwick or Willie Nelson. If you show up late you have to be Bob Dylan. But everyone gets free doughnuts and it's the happiest time of the day for most students. One morning I went hung over and threw up in the middle of the circle. I was so ashamed but then I looked around at the diverse group of smiling faces from all over the country and the world and suddenly I felt better. I went home and threw up some more, thankful to live in the world of love that is Sarah Lawrence."

— Matt F., Sarah Lawrence College
(winner of *The Student Access Essay Contest*—ed.)

"Bentley College has fulfilled all and more of my expectations than I ever imagined."

— Dawn T., Bentley College
(a neat trick —ed.)

PART FOUR

INDEXES

Index of College Counselors

*The authors relied heavily on the following
independent counselors for their assistance:*

■ California

Barbara Barnett
9336 Hidden Valley Drive
Villa Park, CA 92667
(714) 998-5533

College and Career Consultants
250 E. 17 Street, Suite N
Costa Mesa, CA 92627
(714) 646-0156

Arlene Corsello
P.O. Box 5629
Napa, CA 94581
(707) 255-8276

Carol E. DeLucca
3021 White Alder Street
Sonoma, CA 95476
(707) 935-3811
FAX: (707) 935-7611

Elizabeth Hayward
4425 Jamboree Road
Newport Beach, CA 92660
(714) 955-0581

Anne Kogen, Director
American College Placement Service
15928 Ventura Blvd., Suite 227
Encino, CA 91436
(818) 784-6206

■ Colorado

Dr. Steven R. Antonoff
Antonoff Associates, Inc.
425 S. Cherry Street, Suite 215
Denver, CO 80222
(303) 394-2929

Estelle R. Meskin
Educational Consultant
1430 E. Cornell Avenue
Englewood, CO 80110
(303) 781-4145

■ Connecticut

Margery Andrews
Director, College Guidance Service
1471 Ridge Road
North Haven, CT 06473
(203) 281-3746

Geraldine C. Fryer
4725 MacArthur Blvd.
Washington, DC 20007
(202) 333-3230

William M. Morse M.A., Ph.D.
260 Riverside Avenue
Westport, CT 06880
(203) 222-1066

Cornelia Nicholson
Independent Educational Consultant
123 North Street
Watertown, CT 06795
(203) 274-1238

C. Hugh P. Silk
56 Ferry Bridge Road
Washington, CT 06793
(203) 868-7889

Phyllis Steinbrecher
225 Main Street
Westport, CT 06880
(203) 227-3190

■ Florida

Melvin F. Droszcz
10100 W. Sample Road
Coral Springs, FL 33065
(305) 731-1848, (305) 344-7888

■ Illinois

Dennis Beemer, M.Ed.
1071 Creekside Drive
Wheaton, IL 60187
(708) 665-1353

Susan Jeanette Bigg,
M.P.H., Educational Consultant
Chicago, IL 60614
(312) 404-1699

Nancy Gore Marcus
560 Green Bay Road
Winnetka, IL 60093
(708) 446-7557

Robert J. Simmons
College Counseling Network
3026 North Dryden Place
Arlington Heights, IL 60004
(708) 398-7214

Jeanette B. Spires
111 Fallstone Ct.
Lake Forest, IL 60045
(708) 234-7211

■ Indiana

Cynthia Kleit, M.S.
Educational Consultant
9016 Buckthorne Court
Indianapolis, IN 46260
(317) 872-0829

■ Maryland

Zola Dincin Schneider
The College Advisory Service
5812 Warwick Place
Chevy Chase, MD 20815
(301) 654-5889

■ Massachusetts

College Admissions Consultants
94 Station Street
Hingham, MA 02043
(617) 749-2970

■ Missouri

Patricia Adkins Rochette
1001-B West 101 Terrace
Kansas City, MO 64114
(816) 942-0727

■ Nevada

Andrew T.C. Stifler
Educational Consulting Services
2393 Potosi Street
Las Vegas, NV 89102
(702) 253-6464, (702) 877-3589

■ New Jersey

David Mason
1398 Axel Avenue
North Brunswick, NJ 08902
(908) 247-1543

Ronna Morrison
11 Maple Avenue
Demarest, NJ 07627
(201) 768-8250

■ New Mexico

Rusty Haynes
4165 Montgomery NE
Albuquerque, NM 87109
(505) 884-1798

■ New York

Carol Gill
369 Ashford Avee
Dobbs Ferry, NY 10522
(914) 693-8200

Gladys Kleiman
164 Guyon Avenue
Staten Island, NY 10306
(718) 351-7232
 Also:
C.A.P.S.
10 Village Plaza
South Orange, NJ 07079

M and M College Advisors
3 Birch Grove Drive
Armonk, NY 10504
(914) 273-9618

Amie RH Taney
125 Sutton Manor
New Rochelle, NY 10805
(914) 235-8872

Allan W. McLeod
51 East 73rd Street
New York, NY 10021
(212) 535-5824

Frank C. Leana, Ph.D.
Howard Greene & Associates
176A E. 75th Street.
New York, NY 10021
(212) 737-8866

Pearl Glassman Counseling
RRI, BX 350
Pound Ridge, NY 10576
(914) 764-5153

Joan Tager
34 Emerson Avenue
Staten Island, NY 10301
(718) 727-1914
 Also:
10 Village Plaza
South Orange, NJ 07079
(201) 467-1773

Judy Wacht
15 Tulip Lane
New Rochelle, NY 10804
(914) 633-3636

■ North Carolina

Judith Goetzl, M.A.
College Bound Consultants
3325 Chapel Hill Boulevard
Suite #184
Durham, NC 27707
(919) 493-7788

Eric B. Moore
1208 Providence Road
Charlotte, NC 28207
(704) 334-1482

■ Oregon

Nancy Knocke—College Search
2830 SW Vista Drive
Portland, OR 97225
(503) 292-8666

■ Pennsylvania

Lynne H. Martin
105 Bala Ave
Bala Cynwyd, PA 19004
(215) 399-6787

Barbara B. Snyderman, Ph.D.
401 Shady Avenue, Suite C107
Pittsburgh, PA 15206
(412) 361-8887

Suzaane F. Scott, Ed.M.
1538 Woodland Rd
Rydal, PA 19046
(215) 884-0656

Elizabeth Lohmann, EPL Inc.
224 S. Wayne Ave
Wayne, PA 19087
(215) 687-3385

Edith W. Barnes
Academic Directions
1476 Morstein Rd
Westchester, PA 19580
(215) 647-2862

■ Vermont

James Ten Broeck, Ben Mason
Mason & Associates
100 Dorset Street
South Burlington, VT 05403
(802) 658-9622

■ Washington

Pauline B. Reiter, Ph.D.
College Placement Consultants
40 Lake Bellevue #100
Bellevue, WA 98005
(206) 453-1730

Index of Schools